Build Your Own 2D Game Engine and Create Great Web Games

Using HTML5, JavaScript, and WebGL2

Second Edition

Kelvin Sung
Jebediah Pavleas
Matthew Munson
Jason Pace

With
Original Dye character designs by Nathan Evers
Other game character and art design by Kasey Quevedo
Figures and illustrations by Clover Wai

Apress®

Build Your Own 2D Game Engine and Create Great Web Games: Using HTML5, JavaScript, and WebGL2

Kelvin Sung
Bothell, WA, USA

Jebediah Pavleas
Kenmore, WA, USA

Matthew Munson
Lake Forest Park, WA, USA

Jason Pace
Portland, OR, USA

ISBN-13 (pbk): 978-1-4842-7376-0
https://doi.org/10.1007/978-1-4842-7377-7

ISBN-13 (electronic): 978-1-4842-7377-7

Managing Director, Apress Media LLC: Welmoed Spahr
Acquisitions Editor: Spandana Chatterjee
Development Editor: Laura Berendson
Coordinating Editors: Shrikant Vishwakarma

Cover designed by eStudioCalamar

Cover image designed by Freepik (www.freepik.com)

Distributed to the book trade worldwide by Apress Media, LLC, 1 New York Plaza, New York, NY 10004, U.S.A. Phone 1-800-SPRINGER, fax (201) 348-4505, e-mail orders-ny@springer-sbm.com, or visit www.springeronline.com. Apress Media, LLC is a California LLC and the sole member (owner) is Springer Science + Business Media Finance Inc (SSBM Finance Inc). SSBM Finance Inc is a **Delaware** corporation.

For information on translations, please e-mail booktranslations@springernature.com; for reprint, paperback, or audio rights, please e-mail bookpermissions@springernature.com.

Apress titles may be purchased in bulk for academic, corporate, or promotional use. eBook versions and licenses are also available for most titles. For more information, reference our Print and eBook Bulk Sales web page at http://www.apress.com/bulk-sales.

Any source code or other supplementary material referenced by the author in this book is available to readers on GitHub via the book's product page, located at www.apress.com/9781484273760. For more detailed information, please visit http://www.apress.com/source-code.

Printed on acid-free paper

To my wife, Clover, and our girls, Jean and Ruth, for completing my life.
—Kelvin Sung

To my family, for their eternal support throughout my life.
—Jebediah Pavleas

To my mom, Linda, for showing me the value of having fun at work.
—Jason Pace

Table of Contents

About the Authors

Kelvin Sung is a Professor with the Computing and Software Systems Division at the University of Washington Bothell (UWB). He received his Ph.D. in Computer Science from the University of Illinois at Urbana-Champaign. Kelvin's background is in computer graphics, hardware, and machine architecture. He came to UWB from Alias|Wavefront (now part of Autodesk), where he played a key role in designing and implementing the Maya Renderer, an Academy Award–winning image generation system. At UWB, funded by Microsoft Research and the National Science Foundation, Kelvin's work focuses on the intersection of video game mechanics, solutions to real-world problems, and supports for remote collaboration. Together with his students and colleagues, Kelvin has co-authored five books: one on computer graphics (*Essentials of Interactive Computer Graphics: Concepts and Implementation*, A.K. Peters, 2008) and the others on 2D game engines (*Learn 2D Game Development with C#*, Apress, 2013; *Build Your Own 2D Game Engine and Create Great Web Games*, Apress, October 2015; *Building a 2D Game Physics Engine*, Apress, 2016; and *Basic Math for Game Development with Unity 3D*, Apress, 2019).

Jebediah Pavleas received his Master of Science Degree in Computer Science and Software Engineering from the University of Washington Bothell (UWB) in 2016. He also received a Bachelor of Science Degree from UWB in 2012 and was the recipient of the Chancellor's Medal for his class. During his graduate program, Jebediah interned for Microsoft Research's Enable team where he contributed to their Eye-Gaze Wheelchair project (a wheelchair driven with only your eyes for those with ALS). He has co-authored three books on 2D games and game engines (*Learn 2D Game Development with C#*, Apress, 2013; *Build Your Own 2D Game Engine and Create Great Web Games*, Apress, October 2015; *Building a 2D Game Physics Engine*, Apress, 2016). During his time at UWB, his projects included an interactive math application that utilizes Microsoft's Kinect sensor to teach algebra called Kinect Math. Relating to this and other projects, he co-authored publications in *IEEE Computer* and *The Journal of Computing Sciences in Colleges* (CCSC). Jebediah enjoys designing, building, and playing games of all kinds as well as adapting technology for improved accessibility for himself and others.

Matthew Munson is a graduate student in the Computer Science and Software Engineering program at the University of Washington Bothell. He received undergraduate degrees in Computer Science and Software Engineering and Mechanical Engineering at the University of Washington Bothell in 2020. Matthew is interested in operating system development, networking, and embedded systems. As a research assistant, Matthew used cloud computing to analyze years of audio data recorded by hydrophones off the Oregon coast. This data was used to study the effects of climate change and shipping noise on marine mammals. Currently, Matthew is working on a networked augmented reality library that focuses on allowing users to view the same virtual scene from different perspectives.

Jason Pace contributed to a wide range of games as a producer, designer, and creative director over 15 years in the interactive entertainment industry, from ultra-casual puzzlers on mobile to Halo on Xbox. As a designer, Jason builds game mechanics and systems that start from a simple palette of thoughtful interactions (known as the core gameplay loop), progressively introducing variety and complexity to create interactive experiences that engage and delight players while maintaining focus on what makes each e-game uniquely fun.

About the Technical Reviewers

Yusuf Pisan is an Associate Teaching Professor in the School of Computing & Software Systems Division at the University of Washington Bothell. Previously, he has worked at the University of Technology, Sydney, and has been a visiting professor at Harvey Mudd College, University of Southern California, Worcester Polytechnic Institute (WPI), and IT University of Copenhagen (ITU).

His research interests include enabling technologies for computer games, the design of virtual environments that support collaborative work, and computer science education. He founded the Australasian Conference on Interactive Entertainment conference series and helped foster the Australian games community. His list of publications can be found at Google Scholar.

Yusuf has a Ph.D. in Artificial Intelligence from Northwestern University. Before moving to Seattle in 2017, Yusuf lived in the Chicago area for 10 years and Sydney for 20 years.

For more information, see `https://pisanorg.github.io/yusuf/`.

Yogendra Sharma is a developer with experience in the architecture, design, and development of scalable and distributed applications, with a core interest in Microservices and Spring. He currently works as an IoT and Cloud Architect at Intelizign Engineering Services Pvt. Ltd., Pune.

He also has hands-on experience in technologies such as AWS, IoT, Python, J2SE, J2EE, NodeJS, VueJs, Angular, MongoDB, and Docker.

He constantly explores technical novelties, and he is open-minded and eager to learn about new technologies and frameworks. He has reviewed several books and video courses published by Packt.

Acknowledgments

This book project was a direct result of the authors learning from building games for the Game-Themed CS1/2: Empowering the Faculty project, funded by the Transforming Undergraduate Education in Science, Technology, Engineering, and Mathematics (TUES) Program, National Science Foundation (NSF) (award number DUE-1140410). We would like to thank NSF officers Suzanne Westbrook for believing in our project and Jane Prey, Valerie Bar, and Paul Tymann for their encouragements.

This second edition is encouraged by many students and collaborators. In particular, students from CSS452: Game Engine Development (see `https://myuwbclasses.github.io/CSS452/`) at the University of Washington Bothell have been the most critical, demanding, and yet supportive. Through the many games and API extension projects (see `https://html5gameenginegroup.github.io/GTCS-Engine-Student-Projects/`), it became clear that updates are required of the JavaScript and WebGL (Web Graphics Library) versions, the bottom-line synchronization mechanism, and, most significantly, the coverage of the physics engine. Fernando Arnez, our co-author from the first edition, taught us JavaScript. Yaniv Schwartz pointed us toward JavaScript async/await and promise. The discussions and collaborations with Huaming Chen and Michael Tanaya contributed directly to the chapter on game engine physics. Akilas Mebrahtom and Donald Hawkins constructed the extra example at the end of Chapter 9 illustrating potential presets for commonly encountered physical materials. The audio volume control was first investigated and integrated by Kyla NeSmith. Nicholas Carpenetti and Kyla NeSmith developed a user interface API for the initial game engine, which unfortunately did not make it into this edition. These and countless other feedbacks have contributed to the quality and improvements of the book's content.

The hero character Dye and many of the visual and audio assets used throughout the example projects of the book are based on the Dye Hard game, designed for teaching concepts of objects and object-oriented hierarchy. The original Dye Hard development team members included Matthew Kipps, Rodelle Ladia, Chuan Wang, Brian Hecox, Charles Chiou, John Louie, Emmett Scout, Daniel Ly, Elliott White, Christina Jugovic, Rachel Harris, Nathan Evers, Kasey Quevedo, Kaylin Norman-Slack, David Madden, Kyle Kraus, Suzi Zuber, Aina Braxton, Kelvin Sung, Jason Pace, and Rob Nash. Kyle Kraus composed the background music used in the Audio Support project from Chapter 4, originally for the Linx game, which was designed to teach loops. The background audio for the game in Chapter 12 was composed by David Madden and arranged by Aina Braxton. Thanks to Clover Wai for the figures and illustrations.

We also want to thank Spandana Chatterjee for believing in our ideas, her patience, and continual efficient and effective support. A heartfelt thank-you to Mark Powers, for his diligence and lightning-fast email responses. Mark should learn about and consider the option of sleeping some of the time. Nirmal Selvaraj organized everything and ensured proper progress was ongoing.

Finally, we would like to thank Yusuf Pisan for his insightful, effective, and, above all, quick turnaround for the technical review.

All opinions, findings, conclusions, and recommendations in this work are those of the authors and do not necessarily reflect the views of the sponsors.

Introduction

Welcome to *Build Your Own 2D Game Engine and Create Great Web Games*. Because you have picked up this book, you are likely interested in the details of a game engine and the creation of your own games to be played over the Internet. This book teaches you how to build a 2D game engine by covering the involved technical concepts, demonstrating sample implementations, and showing you how to organize the large number of source code and asset files to support game development. This book also discusses how each covered technical topic area relates to elements of game design so that you can build, play, analyze, and learn about the development of 2D game engines and games. The sample implementations in this book are based on HTML5, JavaScript, and WebGL2, which are technologies that are freely available and supported by virtually all web browsers. After reading this book, the game engine you develop and the associated games will be playable through a web browser from anywhere on the Internet.

This book presents relevant concepts from software engineering, computer graphics, mathematics, physics, game development, and game design—all in the context of building a 2D game engine. The presentations are tightly integrated with the analysis and development of source code; you'll spend much of the book building game-like concept projects that demonstrate the functionality of game engine components. By building on source code introduced early on, the book leads you on a journey through which you will master the basic concepts behind a 2D game engine while simultaneously gaining hands-on experience developing simple but working 2D games. Beginning from Chapter 4, a "Design Considerations" section is included at the end of each chapter to relate the covered technical concepts to elements of game design. By the end of the book, you will be familiar with the concepts and technical details of 2D game engines, feel competent in implementing functionality in a 2D game engine to support commonly encountered 2D game requirements, and capable of considering game engine technical topics in the context of game design elements in building fun and engaging games.

New in the Second Edition

The key additions to the second edition include JavaScript language and WebGL API update and dedicated chapters with substantial details on physics and particle systems components.

All examples throughout the entire book are refined for the latest features of the JavaScript language. While some updates are mundane, for example, prototype chain syntax replacements, the latest syntax allows significant improvements in overall presentation and code readability. The new and much cleaner asynchronous support facilitated a completely new resource loading architecture with a single synchronization point for the entire engine (Chapter 4). The WebGL context is updated to connect to WebGL 2.0. The dedicated chapters allow more elaborate and gradual introduction to the complex physics and particle systems components. Detailed mathematical derivations are included where appropriate.

Who Should Read This Book

This book is targeted toward programmers who are familiar with basic object-oriented programming concepts and have a basic to intermediate knowledge of an object-oriented programming language such as Java or C#. For example, if you are a student who has taken a few introductory programming courses, an experienced developer who is new to games and graphics programming, or a self-taught programming enthusiast, you will be able to follow the concepts and code presented in this book with little trouble. If you're new to programming in general, it is suggested that you first become comfortable with the JavaScript programming language and concepts in object-oriented programming before tackling the content provided in this book.

Assumptions

You should be experienced with programming in an object-oriented programming language, such as Java or C#. Knowledge and expertise in JavaScript would be a plus but are not necessary. The examples in this book were created with the assumption that you understand data encapsulation and inheritance. In addition, you should be familiar with basic data structures such as linked lists and dictionaries and be comfortable working with the fundamentals of algebra and geometry, particularly linear equations and coordinate systems.

Who Should Not Read This Book

This book is not designed to teach readers how to program, nor does it attempt to explain the intricate details of HTML5, JavaScript, or WebGL2. If you have no prior experience developing software with an object-oriented programming language, you will probably find the examples in this book difficult to follow.

On the other hand, if you have an extensive background in game engine development based on other platforms, the content in this book will be too basic; this is a book intended for developers without 2D game engine development experience. However, you might still pick up a few useful tips about 2D game engine and 2D game development for the platforms covered in this book.

Organization of This Book

This book teaches how to develop a game engine by describing the foundational infrastructure, graphics system, game object behaviors, camera manipulations, and a sample game creation based on the engine.

Chapters 2–4 construct the foundational infrastructure of the game engine. Chapter 2 establishes the initial infrastructure by separating the source code system into folders and files that contain the following: JavaScript-specific core engine logics, WebGL2 GLSL–specific shader programs, and HTML5-specific web page contents. This organization allows ongoing engine functionality expansion while maintaining localized source code system changes. For example, only JavaScript source code files need to be modified when introducing enhancements to game object behaviors. Chapter 3 builds the drawing framework to encapsulate and hide the WebGL2 drawing specifics from the rest of the engine. This drawing framework allows the development of game object behaviors without being distracted by how they are drawn. Chapter 4 introduces and integrates core game engine functional components including game loop, keyboard input, efficient resource and game-level loading, and audio support.

Chapters 5–7 present the basic functionality of a game engine: drawing system, behavior and interactions, and camera manipulation. Chapter 5 focuses on working with texture mapping, including sprite sheets, animation with sprite sheets, and the drawing of bitmap fonts. Chapter 6 puts forward abstractions for game objects and their behaviors including per-pixel-accurate collision detection. Chapter 7 details the manipulation and interactions with the camera including programming with multiple cameras and supporting mouse input.

Chapters 8–11 elevate the introduced functionality to more advanced levels. Chapter 8 covers the simulation of 3D illumination effects in 2D game scenes. Chapter 9 discusses physically based behavior simulations. Chapter 10 presents the basics of particle systems that are suitable for modeling explosions. Chapter 11 examines more advanced camera functionality including infinite scrolling through tiling and parallax.

Chapter 12 summarizes the book by leading you through the design of a complete game based on the game engine you have developed.

Code Samples

Every chapter in this book includes examples that let you interactively experiment with and learn the new materials. You can access the source code for all the projects, including the associated assets (images, audio clips, or fonts), by clicking the **Download Source Code** button located at www.apress.com/9781484273760. You should see a folder structure that is organized by chapter numbers. Within each folder are subfolders containing Visual Studio Code (VS Code) projects that correspond to sections of this book.

CHAPTER 1

Introducing 2D Game Engine Development with JavaScript

Video games are complex, interactive, multimedia software systems. They must, in real time, process player input, simulate the interactions of semiautonomous objects, and generate high-fidelity graphics and audio outputs, all while trying to keep players engaged. Attempts at building a video game can quickly become overwhelming with the need to be well versed in software development as well as in how to create appealing player experiences. The first challenge can be alleviated with a software library, or game engine, that contains a coherent collection of utilities and objects designed specifically for developing video games. The player engagement goal is typically achieved through careful gameplay design and fine-tuning throughout the video game development process. This book is about the design and development of a game engine; it will focus on implementing and hiding the mundane operations of the engine while supporting many complex simulations. Through the projects in this book, you will build a practical game engine for developing video games that are accessible across the Internet.

A game engine relieves game developers from having to implement simple routine tasks such as decoding specific key presses on the keyboard, designing complex algorithms for common operations such as mimicking shadows in a 2D world, and understanding nuances in implementations such as enforcing accuracy tolerance of a physics simulation. Commercial and well-established game engines such as *Unity*, *Unreal Engine*, and *Panda3D* present their systems through a graphical user interface (GUI). Not only does the friendly GUI simplify some of the tedious processes of game design such as creating and placing objects in a level, but more importantly, it ensures that

© Kelvin Sung, Jebediah Pavleas, Matthew Munson, and Jason Pace 2022
K. Sung et al., *Build Your Own 2D Game Engine and Create Great Web Games*,
https://doi.org/10.1007/978-1-4842-7377-7_1

these game engines are accessible to creative designers with diverse backgrounds who may find software development specifics distracting.

This book focuses on the core functionality of a game engine independent from a GUI. While a comprehensive GUI system can improve the end-user experience, the implementation requirements can also distract and complicate the fundamentals of a game engine. For example, issues concerning the enforcement of compatible data types in the user interface system, such as restricting objects from a specific class to be assigned as shadow receivers, are important to GUI design but are irrelevant to the core functionality of a game engine.

This book approaches game engine development from two important aspects: programmability and maintainability. As a software library, the interface of the game engine should facilitate programmability by game developers with well-abstracted utility methods and objects that hide simple routine tasks and support complex yet common operations. As a software system, the code base of the game engine should support maintainability with a well-designed infrastructure and well-organized source code systems that enable code reuse, ongoing system upkeep, improvement, and expansion.

This chapter describes the implementation technology and organization of this book. The discussion leads you through the steps of downloading, installing, and setting up the development environment, guides you to build your first HTML5 application, and uses this first application development experience to explain the best approach to reading and learning from this book.

The Technologies

The goal of building a game engine that allows games to be accessible across the World Wide Web is enabled by freely available technologies.

JavaScript is supported by virtually all web browsers because an interpreter is installed on almost every personal computer in the world. As a programming language, JavaScript is dynamically typed, supports inheritance and functions as first-class objects, and is easy to learn with well-established user and developer communities. With the strategic choice of this technology, video games developed based on JavaScript can be accessible by anyone over the Internet through appropriate web browsers. Therefore, JavaScript is one of the best programming languages for developing video games for the masses.

While JavaScript serves as an excellent tool for implementing the game logic and algorithms, additional technologies in the form of software libraries, or application programming interfaces (APIs), are necessary to support the user input and media output requirements. With the goal of building games that are accessible across the Internet through web browsers, HTML5 and WebGL provide the ideal complementary input and output APIs.

HTML5 is designed to structure and present content across the Internet. It includes detailed processing models and the associated APIs to handle user input and multimedia outputs. These APIs are native to JavaScript and are perfect for implementing browser-based video games. While HTML5 offers a basic Scalable Vector Graphics (SVG) API, it does not support the sophistication demanded by video games for effects such as real-time lighting, explosions, or shadows. The Web Graphics Library (WebGL) is a JavaScript API designed specifically for the generation of 2D and 3D computer graphics through web browsers. With its support for OpenGL Shading Language (GLSL) and the ability to access the graphics processing unit (GPU) on client machines, WebGL has the capability of producing highly complex graphical effects in real time and is perfect as the graphics API for browser-based video games.

This book is about the concepts and development of a game engine where JavaScript, HTML5, and WebGL are simply tools for the implementation. The discussion in this book focuses on applying the technologies to realize the required implementations and does not try to cover the details of the technologies. For example, in the game engine, inheritance is implemented with the JavaScript class functionality which is based on object prototype chain; however, the merits of prototype-based scripting languages are not discussed. The engine audio cue and background music functionalities are based on the HTML5 AudioContext interface, and yet its range of capabilities is not described. The game engine objects are drawn based on WebGL texture maps, while the features of the WebGL texture subsystem are not presented. The specifics of the technologies would distract from the game engine discussion. The key learning outcomes of the book are the concepts and implementation strategies for a game engine and not the details of any of the technologies. In this way, after reading this book, you will be able to build a similar game engine based on any comparable set of technologies such as C# and MonoGame, Java and JOGL, C++ and Direct3D, and so on. If you want to learn more about or brush up on JavaScript, HTML5, or WebGL, please refer to the references in the "Technologies" section at the end of this chapter.

Setting Up Your Development Environment

The game engine you are going to build will be accessible through web browsers that could be running on any operating system (OS). The development environment you are about to set up is also OS agnostic. For simplicity, the following instructions are based on a Windows 10 OS. You should be able to reproduce a similar environment with minor modifications in a Unix-based environment like MacOS or Ubuntu.

Your development environment includes an integrated development environment (IDE) and a runtime web browser that is capable of hosting the running game engine. The most convenient systems we have found is the Visual Studio Code (VS Code) IDE with the Google Chrome web browser as runtime environment. Here are the details:

- **IDE**: All projects in this book are based on VS Code IDE. You can download and install the program from `https://code. visualstudio.com/`.

- **Runtime environment**: You will execute your video game projects in the Google Chrome web browser. You can download and install this browser from `www.google.com/chrome/browser/`.

- **glMatrix math library**: This is a library that implements the foundational mathematical operations. You can download this library from `http://glMatrix.net/`. You will integrate this library into your game engine in Chapter 3, so more details will be provided there.

Notice that there are no specific system requirements to support the JavaScript programming language, HTML5, or WebGL. All these technologies are embedded in the web browser runtime environment.

Note   As mentioned, we chose the VS Code–based development environment because we found it to be the most convenient. There are many other alternatives that are also free, including and not limited to NetBeans, IntelliJ IDEA, Eclipse, and Sublime.

Downloading and Installing JavaScript Syntax Checker

We have found ESLint to be an effective tool in detecting potential JavaScript source code errors. You can integrate ESLint into VS Code with the following steps:

- Go to `https://marketplace.visualstudio.com/items?itemName=dbaeumer.vscode-eslint` and click install.

- You will be prompted to open VS Code and may need to click install again within the application.

The following are some useful references for working with ESLint:

- For instructions on how to work with ESLint, see `https://eslint.org/docs/user-guide/`.

- For details on how ESLint works, see `https://eslint.org/docs/developer-guide/`.

Downloading and Installing LiveServer

The LiveServer extension to the VS Code is required to run your game engine. It launches a web server locally on your computer through VS Code to host developed games. Much like ESLint, you can install LiveServer with the following steps:

- Go to `https://marketplace.visualstudio.com/items?itemName=ritwickdey.LiveServer` and click install.

- You will be prompted to open VS Code and may need to click install again within the application.

Working in the VS Code Development Environment

The VS Code IDE is easy to work with, and the projects in this book require only the editor. Relevant source code files organized under a parent folder are interpreted by VS Code as a project. To open a project, select File ➤ Open Folder and navigate and select the parent folder that contains the source code files of the project. Once a project is open, you need to become familiar with the basic windows of VS Code, as illustrated in Figure 1-1.

- **Explorer window**: This window displays the source code files of the project. If you accidentally close this window, you can recall it by selecting View ➤ Explorer.

- **Editor window**: This window displays and allows you to edit the source code of your project. You can select the source code file to work with by clicking once the corresponding file name in the Explorer window.

- **Output window**: This window is not used in our projects; feel free to close it by clicking the "x" icon on the top right of the window.

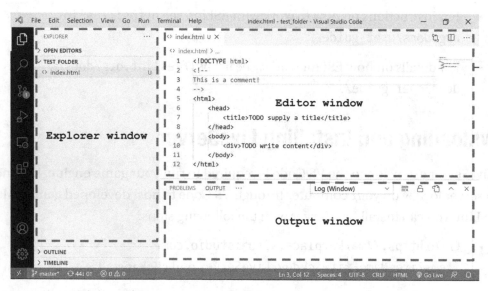

Figure 1-1. *The VS Code IDE*

Creating an HTML5 Project in VS Code

You are now ready to create your first HTML5 project:

- Using File Explorer, create a directory in the location where you would like to keep your projects. This directory will contain all source code files related to your projects. In VS Code, select File ➤ Open Folder and navigate to the directory you created.

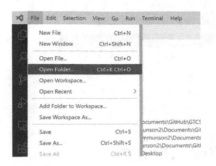

Figure 1-2. *Opening a project folder*

- VS Code will open the project folder. Your IDE should look similar to Figure 1-3; notice that the Explorer window is empty when your project folder is empty.

Figure 1-3. *An empty VS Code project*

- You can now create your first HTML file, `index.html`. Select File ➤ New File and name the file `index.html`. This will serve as the home or landing page when your application is launched.

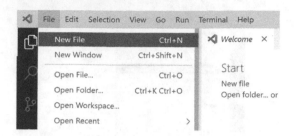

Figure 1-4. *Creating the* `index.html` *file*

- In the Editor window, enter the following text into your `index.html`:

```
<!DOCTYPE html>
<!--
This is a comment!
-->
<html>
    <head>
        <title>TODO supply a title</title>
    </head>
    <body>
        <div>TODO write content</div>
    </body>
</html>
```

The first line declares the file to be an HTML file. The block that follows within the `<!--` and `-->` tags is a comment block. The complementary `<html></html>` tags contain all the HTML code. In this case, the template defines the head and body sections. The head sets the title of the web page, and the body is where all the content for the web page will be located.

As illustrated in Figure 1-5, you can run this project by clicking the "Go Live" button in the bottom-right corner of your VS Code or by pressing Alt+L Alt+O. There is a chance that right after you entered the previous HTML code for the first time, the "Go Live" button may not appear. In this case, simply right-click the `index.html` file in the Explorer window, and click "Open with Live Server" menu item to launch the web page. After the first time, the "Go Live" button will appear in the lower-right region of the IDE, as illustrated in Figure 1-5.

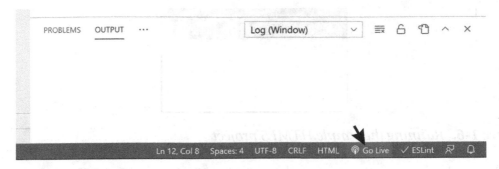

Figure 1-5. *Click the Go Live button to run a project*

Note   To run a project, the `index.html` file of that project must be opened in the editor when the "Go Live" button is clicked or when the Alt+L Alt+O keys are typed. This will become important in the subsequent chapters when there are other JavaScript source code files in the project.

Figure 1-6 shows an example of what the default project looks like when you run it. Notice that after the project begins to run, the "Go Live" button updates its label to show "Port:5500." You can click this button again to disconnect the IDE from the web page to observe the "Go Live" label again. Clicking the button one more time will rerun the project.

Figure 1-6. *Running the simple HTML5 project*

To stop the program, simply close the web page. You have successfully run your first HTML5 project. Through the development of this very simple project, you have familiarized yourself with the IDE environment.

Note   For debugging, we recommend the Chrome Developer tools. These tools can be accessed by typing Ctrl+Shift+I (or the F12 key) in the browser window when your project is running. To find out more about these tools, please refer to `https://developer.chrome.com/docs/devtools/`.

How to Use This Book

This book guides you through the development of a game engine by building projects similar to the one you have just experienced. Each chapter covers an essential component of a typical game engine, and the sections in each chapter describe the important concepts and implementation projects that construct the corresponding component. Throughout the text, the project from each section builds upon the results from the projects that precede it. While this makes it a little challenging to skip around in the book, it will give you practical experience and a solid understanding of how the different concepts relate. In addition, rather than always working with new and minimalistic projects, you gain experience with building larger and more interesting projects while integrating new functionality into your expanding game engine.

The projects start with demonstrating simple concepts, such as drawing a simple square, but evolve quickly into presenting more complex concepts, such as working with user-defined coordinate systems and implementing pixel-accurate collision detection. Initially, as you have experienced in building the first HTML5 application, you will be guided with detailed steps and complete source code listings. As you become familiar with the development environment and the technologies, the guides and source code listings accompanying each project will shift to highlight on the important implementation details. Eventually, as the complexity of the projects increases, the discussion will focus only on the vital and relevant issues, while straightforward source code changes will not be mentioned.

The final code base, which you will have developed incrementally over the course of the book, is a complete and practical game engine; it's a great platform on which you can begin building your own 2D games. This is exactly what the last chapter of the book does, leading you from the conceptualization to design to implementation of a casual 2D game.

There are several ways for you to follow along with this book. The most obvious is to enter the code into your project as you follow each step in the book. From a learning perspective, this is the most effective way to absorb the information presented; however, we understand that it may not be the most realistic because of the amount of code or debugging this approach may require. Alternatively, we recommend that you run and examine the source code of the completed project when you begin a new section. Doing so lets you preview the current section's project, gives you a clear idea of the end goal, and lets you see what the project is trying to achieve. You may also find the completed project code useful when you have problems while building the code yourself, because during difficult debugging situations, you can compare your code with the code of the completed project.

Note   We have found the WinMerge program (`http://winmerge.org/`) to be an excellent tool for comparing source code files and folders. Mac users can check out the FileMerge utility for a similar purpose.

Finally, after completing a project, we recommend that you compare the behavior of your implementation with the completed implementation provided. By doing so, you can observe whether your code is behaving as expected.

How Do You Make a Great Video Game?

While the focus of this book is on the design and implementation of a game engine, it is important to appreciate how different components can contribute to the creation of a fun and engaging video game. Beginning in Chapter 4, a "Game Design Considerations" section is included at the end of each chapter to relate the functionality of the engine component to elements of game design. This section presents the framework for these discussions.

It's a complex question, and there's no exact formula for making a video game that people will love to play, just as there's no exact formula for making a movie that people will love to watch. We've all seen big-budget movies that look great and feature top acting, writing, and directing talent bomb at the box office, and we've all seen big-budget games from major studios that fail to capture the imaginations of players. By the same token, movies by unknown directors can grab the world's attention, and games from small, unknown studios can take the market by storm.

While no explicit instructions exist for making a great game, a number of elements work together in harmony to create a final experience greater than the sum of its parts, and all game designers must successfully address each of them in order to produce something worth playing. The elements include the following:

- **Technical design**: This includes all game code and the game platform and is generally not directly exposed to players; rather, it forms the foundation and scaffolding for all aspects of the game experience. This book is primarily focused on issues related to the technical design of games, including specific tasks such as the lines of code required to draw elements on the screen and more architectural considerations such as determining the strategy for how and when to load assets into memory. Technical design issues impact the player experience in many ways (e.g., the number of times a player experiences "loading" delays during play or how many frames per second the game displays), but the technical design is typically invisible to players because it runs under what's referred to as the presentation layer or all of the audiovisual and/or haptic feedback the player encounters during play.

- **Game mechanic(s):** The game mechanic is an abstract description of what can be referred to as the foundation of play for a given game experience. Types of game mechanics include puzzles, dexterity challenges such as jumping or aiming, timed events, combat encounters, and the like. The game mechanic is a framework; specific puzzles, encounters, and game interactions are implementations of the framework. A real-time strategy (RTS) game might include a resource-gathering mechanic, for example, where the mechanic might be described as "Players are required to gather specific types of resources and combine them to build units which they can use in combat." The specific implementation of that mechanic (how players locate and extract the resources in the game, how they transport them from one place to another, and the rules for combining resources to produce units) is an aspect of systems design, level design, and the interaction model/game loop (described later in this section).

- **Systems design:** The internal rules and logical relationships that provide structured challenge to the core game mechanic are referred to as the game's systems design. Using the previous RTS example, a game might require players to gather a certain amount of metal ore and combine it with a certain amount of wood to make a game object; the specific rules for how many of each resource is required to make the objects and the unique process for creating the objects (e.g., objects can be produced only in certain structures on the player's base and take x number of minutes to appear after the player starts the process) are aspects of systems design. Casual games may have basic systems designs. A simple puzzle game like *Pull the Pin* from Popcore Games, for example, is a game with few systems and low complexity, while major genres like RTS games may have deeply complex and interrelated systems designs created and balanced by entire teams of designers. Game systems designs are often where the most hidden complexity of game design exists; as designers go through the exercise of defining all variables that contribute to an implementation of a game mechanic, it's easy to become lost in a sea of complexity and balance dependencies. Systems that appear fairly simple to players may require many components working together and balanced perfectly against each other, and underestimating system complexity is perhaps one of the biggest pitfalls encountered by new (and veteran!) game designers. Until you know what you're getting into, always assume the systems you create will prove to be considerably more complex than you anticipate.

- **Level design**: A game's level design reflects the specific ways each of the other eight elements combines within the context of individual "chunks" of gameplay, where players must complete a certain chunk of objectives before continuing to the next section (some games may have only one level, while others will have dozens). Level designs within a single game can all be variations of the same core mechanic and systems design (games like *Tetris* and *Bejeweled* are examples of games with many levels all focusing on the same mechanic), while other games will mix and match mechanics and systems designs for variety among levels. Most games feature one primary mechanic and a game-spanning approach to systems design and will add minor variations between levels to keep things feeling fresh (changing environments, changing difficulty, adding time limits, increasing complexity, and the like), although occasionally games will introduce new levels that rely on completely separate mechanics and systems to surprise players and hold their interest. Great level design in games is a balance between creating "chunks" of play that showcase the mechanic and systems design and changing enough between these chunks to keep things interesting for players as they progress through the game (but not changing so much between chunks that the gameplay feels disjointed and disconnected).

- **Interaction model**: The interaction model is the combination of keys, buttons, controller sticks, touch gestures, and so on, used to interact with the game to accomplish tasks and the graphical user interfaces that support those interactions within the game world. Some game theorists break the game's user interface (UI) design into a separate category (game UI includes things such as menu designs, item inventories, heads-up displays [HUDs]), but the interaction model is deeply connected to UI design, and it's a good practice to think of these two elements as inseparable. In the case of the RTS game referenced earlier, the interaction model includes the actions required to select objects in the game, to move those objects, to open menus and manage inventories, to save progress, to initiate combat, and to queue build tasks. The interaction model is completely independent of the mechanic and systems design and is concerned only with the physical actions the player must take to initiate behaviors (e.g., click mouse button, press key, move stick, scroll wheel); the UI is the audiovisual or haptic feedback connected to those actions (onscreen buttons, menus, statuses, audio cues, vibrations, and the like).

- **Game setting**: Are you on an alien planet? In a fantasy world? In an abstract environment? The game setting is a critical part of the game experience and, in partnership with the audiovisual design, turns what would otherwise be a disconnected set of basic interactions into an engaging experience with context. Game settings need not be elaborate to be effective; the perennially popular puzzle game *Tetris* has a rather simple setting with no real narrative wrapper, but the combination of abstract setting, audiovisual design, and level design is uniquely well matched and contributes significantly to the millions of hours players invest in the experience year after year.

- **Visual design**: Video games exist in a largely visual medium, so it's not surprising that companies frequently spend as much or more on the visual design of their games as they spend on the technical execution of the code. Large games are aggregations of thousands of visual assets, including environments, characters, objects, animations, and cinematics; even small casual games generally ship with hundreds or thousands of individual visual elements. Each object a player interacts with in the game must be a unique asset, and if that asset includes more complex animation than just moving it from one location on the screen to another or changing the scale or opacity, the object most likely will need to be animated by an artist. Game graphics need not be photorealistic or stylistically elaborate to be visually excellent or to effectively represent the setting (many games intentionally utilize a simplistic visual style), but the best games consider art direction and visual style to be core to the player

15

experience, and visual choices will be intentional and well matched to the game setting and mechanic.

- **Audio design**: This includes music and sound effects, ambient background sounds, and all sounds connected to player actions (select/use/swap item, open inventory, invoke menu, and the like). Audio design functions hand in hand with visual design to convey and reinforce game setting, and many new designers significantly underestimate the impact of sound to immerse players into game worlds. Imagine *Star Wars*, for example, without the music, the light saber sound effect, Darth Vader's breathing, or R2D2's characteristic beeps; the audio effects and musical score are as fundamental to the experience as the visuals.

- **Meta-game**: The meta-game centers on how individual objectives come together to propel players through the game experience (often via scoring, unlocking individual levels in sequence, playing through a narrative, and the like). In many modern games, the meta-game is the narrative arc or story; players often don't receive a "score" per se but rather reveal a linear or semi-linear story as they progress through game levels, driving forward to complete the story. Other games (especially social and competitive games) involve players "leveling up" their characters, which can happen as a result of playing through a game-spanning narrative experience or by simply venturing into the game world and undertaking individual challenges that grant experience points to characters. Other games, of course, continue focusing on scoring points or winning rounds against other players.

The magic of video games typically arises from the interplay between these nine elements, and the most successful games finely balance each as part of a unified vision to ensure a harmonious experience; this balance will always be unique to each individual effort and is found in games ranging from Nintendo's *Animal Crossing* to Rockstar's *Red Dead Redemption 2*. The core game mechanic in many successful games is often a variation on one or more fairly simple, common themes (*Pull the Pin*, for example, is a game based entirely on pulling virtual pins from a container to release colored balls), but the visual design, narrative context, audio effects, interactions, and progression system work together with the game mechanic to create a unique experience that's considerably more engaging than the sum of its individual parts, making players want to return to it again and again. Great games range from the simple to the complex, but they all feature an elegant balance of supporting design elements.

References

The examples in this book are created with the assumptions that you understand data encapsulation, inheritance, and basic data structures, such as linked lists and dictionaries, and are comfortable working with the fundamentals of algebra and geometry, particularly linear equations and coordinate systems. Many examples in this book apply and implement concepts in computer graphics and linear algebra. These concepts warrant much more in-depth examinations. Interested readers can learn more about these topics in other books.

- Computer graphics:

  - Marschner and Shirley. *Fundamentals of Computer Graphics*, 4th edition. CRC Press, 2016.

  - Angle and Shreiner. *Interactive Computer Graphics: A Top Down Approach with WebGL*, 7th edition. Pearson Education, 2014.

- Linear algebra:

  - Sung and Smith. *Basic Math for Game Development with Unity 3D: A Beginner's Guide to Mathematical Foundations*. Apress, 2019.

  - Johnson, Riess, and Arnold. *Introduction to Linear Algebra*, 5th edition. Addison-Wesley, 2002.

  - Anton and Rorres. *Elementary Linear Algebra: Applications Version*, 11th edition. Wiley, 2013.

Technologies

The following list offers links for obtaining additional information on technologies used in this book:

- **JavaScript**: www.w3schools.com/js

- **HTML5**: www.w3schools.com/html/html5_intro.asp

- **WebGL**: www.khronos.org/webgl

- **OpenGL**: www.opengl.org

- **Visual Studio Code**: https://code.visualstudio.com/

- **Chrome**: www.google.com/chrome

- **glMatrix**: http://glMatrix.net

- **ESLint**: www.eslint.org

CHAPTER 2

Working with HTML5 and WebGL

After completing this chapter, you will be able to

- Create a new JavaScript source code file for your simple game engine

- Draw a simple constant color square with WebGL

- Define JavaScript modules and classes to encapsulate and implement core game engine functionality

- Appreciate the importance of abstraction and the organization of your source code structure to support growth in complexity

Introduction

Drawing is one of the most essential functionalities common to all video games. A game engine should offer a flexible and programmer-friendly interface to its drawing system. In this way, when building a game, the designers and developers can focus on the important aspects of the game itself, such as mechanics, logic, and aesthetics.

WebGL is a modern JavaScript graphical application programming interface (API) designed for web browser–based applications that offers quality and efficiency via direct access to the graphics hardware. For these reasons, WebGL serves as an excellent base to support drawing in a game engine, especially for video games that are designed to be played across the Internet.

This chapter examines the fundamentals of drawing with WebGL, designs abstractions to encapsulate irrelevant details to facilitate programming, and builds the foundational infrastructure to organize a complex source code system to support future expansion.

© Kelvin Sung, Jebediah Pavleas, Matthew Munson, and Jason Pace 2022
K. Sung et al., *Build Your Own 2D Game Engine and Create Great Web Games*,
https://doi.org/10.1007/978-1-4842-7377-7_2

Note   The game engine you will develop in this book is based on the latest version of WebGL specification: version 2.0. For brevity, the term WebGL will be used to refer to this API.

Canvas for Drawing

To draw, you must first define and dedicate an area within the web page. You can achieve this easily by using the HTML canvas element to define an area for WebGL drawing. The canvas element is a container for drawing that you can access and manipulate with JavaScript.

The HTML5 Canvas Project

This project demonstrates how to create and clear a canvas element on a web page. Figure 2-1 shows an example of running this project, which is defined in the chapter2/2.1.html5_canvas folder.

The above is WebGL draw area!

Figure 2-1. *Running the HTML5 Canvas project*

The goals of the project are as follows:

- To learn how to set up the HTML canvas element

- To learn how to retrieve the canvas element from an HTML document for use in JavaScript

- To learn how to create a reference context to WebGL from the retrieved canvas element and manipulate the canvas through the WebGL context

Creating and Clearing the HTML Canvas

In this first project, you will create an empty HTML5 canvas and clear the canvas to a specific color with WebGL:

1. Create a new project by creating a new folder named html5_ canvas in your chosen directory and copying and pasting the index.html file you created in the previous project in Chapter 1.

Note   From this point on, when asked to create a new project, you should follow the process described previously. That is, create a new folder with the project's name and copy/paste the previous project's files. In this way, your new projects can expand upon your old ones while retaining the original functionality.

---

2. Open the index.html file in the editor by opening the html5_ canvas folder, expanding it if needed and clicking the index.html file, as illustrated in Figure 2-2.

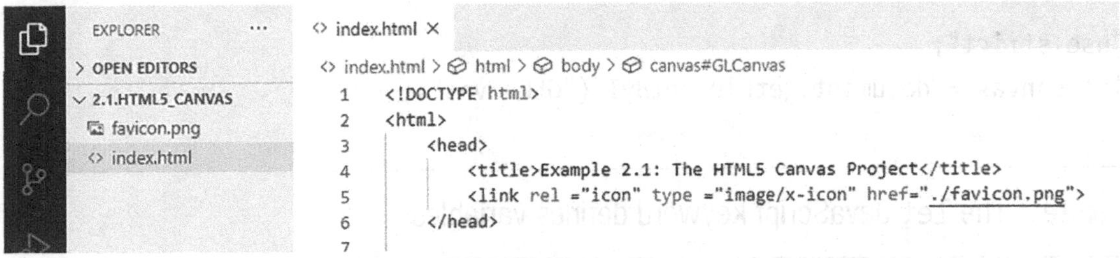

Figure 2-2. *Editing the index.html file in your project*

3. Create the HTML `canvas` for drawing by adding the following lines
    in the `index.html` file within the body element:

```
<canvas id="GLCanvas" width="640" height="480">
Your browser does not support the HTML5 canvas.
</canvas>
```

The code defines a `canvas` element named `GLCanvas` with the specified `width` and `height` attributes. As you will experience later, you will retrieve the reference to the `GLCanvas` to draw into this area. The text inside the element will be displayed if your browser does not support drawing with `WebGL`.

Note   The lines between the `<body>` and `</body>` tags are referred to as "within the body element." For the rest of this book, "within the `AnyTag` element" will be used to refer to any line between the beginning (`<AnyTag>`) and end (`</AnyTag>`) of the element.

---

4. Create a `script` element for the inclusion of JavaScript
    programming code, once again within the body element:

```
<script type="text/javascript">
    // JavaScript code goes here.
</script>
```

This takes care of the HTML portion of this project. You will now write JavaScript code for the remainder of the example:

5. Retrieve a reference to the `GLCanvas` in JavaScript code by adding
    the following line within the `script` element:

```
"use strict";
let canvas = document.getElementById("GLCanvas");
```

Note   The `let` JavaScript keyword defines variables.

The first line, "use strict", is a JavaScript directive indicating that the code should be executed in "strict mode", where the use of undeclared variables is a runtime error. The second line creates a new variable named canvas and references the variable to the GLCanvas drawing area.

Note   All local variable names begin with a lowercase letter, as in canvas.

---

6. Retrieve and bind a reference to the WebGL context to the drawing area by adding the following code:

```
let gl = canvas.getContext("webgl2") ||
        canvas.getContext("experimental-webgl2");
```

As the code indicates, the retrieved reference to the WebGL version 2 context is stored in the local variable named gl. From this variable, you have access to all the functionality of WebGL 2.0. Once again, in the rest of this book, the term WebGL will be used to refer to the WebGL version 2.0 API.

7. Clear the canvas drawing area to your favorite color through WebGL by adding the following:

```
if (gl !== null) {
    gl.clearColor(0.0, 0.8, 0.0, 1.0);
    gl.clear(gl.COLOR_BUFFER_BIT);
}
```

This code checks to ensure that the WebGL context is properly retrieved, sets the clear color, and clears the drawing area. Note that the clearing color is given in RGBA format, with floating-point values ranging from 0.0 to 1.0. The fourth number in the RGBA format is the alpha channel. You will learn more about the alpha channel in later chapters. For now, always assign 1.0 to the alpha channel. The specified color, (0.0, 0.8, 0.0, 1.0), has zero values for the red and blue channels and a 0.8, or 80 percent, intensity on the green channel. For this reason, the canvas area is cleared to a light green color.

8. Add a simple `write` command to the `document` to identify the `canvas` by inserting the following line:

```
document.write("<br><b>The above is WebGL draw area!</b>");
```

You can refer to the final source code in the `index.html` file in the `chapter2/2.1.html5_canvas` project. Run the project, and you should see a light green area on your browser window as shown in Figure 2-1. This is the 640×480 canvas drawing area you defined.

You can try changing the cleared color to white by setting the RGBA of `gl.clearColor()` to 1 or to black by setting the color to 0 and leaving the alpha value 1. Notice that if you set the alpha channel to 0, the canvas color will disappear. This is because a 0 value in the alpha channel represents complete transparency, and thus, you will "see through" the canvas and observe the background color of the web page. You can also try altering the resolution of the canvas by changing the 640×480 values to any number you fancy. Notice that these two numbers refer to the pixel counts and thus must always be integers.

Separating HTML and JavaScript

In the previous project, you created an HTML `canvas` element and cleared the area defined by the canvas using WebGL. Notice that all the functionality is clustered in the `index.html` file. As the project complexity increases, this clustering of functionality can quickly become unmanageable and negatively impact the programmability of your system. For this reason, throughout the development process in this book, after a concept is introduced, efforts will be spent on separating the associated source code into either well-defined source code files or classes in an object-oriented programming style. To begin this process, the HTML and JavaScript source code from the previous project will be separated into different source code files.

The JavaScript Source File Project

This project demonstrates how to logically separate the source code into appropriate files. You can accomplish this by creating a separate JavaScript source code file named `core.js` which implements the corresponding functionality in the `index.html` file. The web page will load the JavaScript source code as instructed by the code in the index.html file. As illustrated in Figure 2-3, this project looks identical as the previous project when running. The source code of this project is located in the chapter2/2.2.javascript_source_file folder.

The above is WebGL draw area!

Figure 2-3. *Running the JavaScript Source File project*

The goals of the project are as follows:

- To learn how to separate source code into different files
- To organize your code in a logical structure

Separate JavaScript Source Code File

This section details how to create and edit a new JavaScript source code file. You should familiarize yourself with this process because you'll create numerous source code files throughout this book.

1. Create a new HTML5 project titled `javascript_source_file`.
    Recall that a new project is created by creating a folder with the
    appropriate name, copying files from the previous project, and
    editing the `<Title>` element of the `index.html` to reflect the new
    project.

2. Create a new folder named `src` inside the project folder by
    clicking the new folder icon while hovering over the project folder,
    as illustrated in Figure 2-4. This folder will contain all of your
    source code.

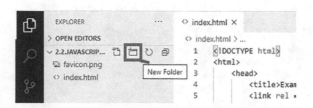

Figure 2-4. *Creating a new source code folder*

3. Create a new source code file within the `src` folder by right-
    clicking the `src` folder, as illustrated in Figure 2-5. Name the new
    source file `core.js`.

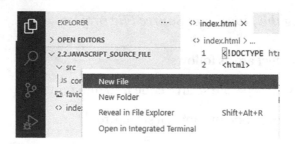

Figure 2-5. *Adding a new JavaScript source code file*

Note   In VS Code, you can create/copy/rename folders and files by using the
right-click menus in the Explorer window.

---

4. Open the new `core.js` source file for editing.

5. Define a variable for referencing the WebGL context, and add a function which allows you to access the variable:

```
"use strict";
let mGL = null;
function getGL() { return mGL; }
```

Note   Variables that are accessible throughout a file, or a module, have names that begin with lowercase "m", as in mGL.

---

6. Define the `initWebGL()` function to retrieve `GLCanvas` by passing in the proper canvas `id` as a parameter, bind the drawing area to the WebGL context, store the results in the defined `mGL` variable, and clear the drawing area:

```
function initWebGL(htmlCanvasID) {
    let canvas = document.getElementById(htmlCanvasID);

    mGL = canvas.getContext("webgl2") ||
        canvas.getContext("experimental-webgl2");

    if (mGL === null) {
        document.write("<br><b>WebGL 2 is not supported!</b>");
        return;
    }
    mGL.clearColor(0.0, 0.8, 0.0, 1.0);
}
```

Notice that this function is similar to the JavaScript source code you typed in the previous project. This is because all you are doing differently, in this case, is separating JavaScript source code from HTML code.

Note   All function names begin with a lowercase letter, as in initWebGL().

---

7. Define the clearCanvas() function to invoke the WebGL context to clear the canvas drawing area:

```
function clearCanvas() {
    mGL.clear(mGL.COLOR_BUFFER_BIT);
}
```

8. Define a function to carry out the initialization and clearing of the canvas area after the web browser has completed the loading of the index.html file:

```
window.onload = function() {
    initWebGL("GLCanvas");
    clearCanvas();
}
```

Load and Run JavaScript Source Code from index.html

With all the JavaScript functionality defined in the core.js file, you now need to load this file to operate on your web page through the index.html file:

1. Open the index.html file for editing.

2. Create the HTML canvas, GLCanvas, as in the previous project.

3. Load the core.js source code by including the following code within the head element:

```
<script type="module" src="./src/core.js"></script>
```

With this code, the core.js file will be loaded as part of the index.html defined web page. Recall that you have defined a function for window.onload and that function will be invoked when the loading of index.html is completed.

You can refer to the final source code in the core.js and index.html files in the chapter2/2.2.javascript_source_file project folder. Although the output from this project is identical to that from the previous project, the organization of your code will allow you to expand, debug, and understand the game engine as you continue to add new functionality.

Note   Recall that to run a project, you click the "Go Live" button on the lower right of the VS Code window, or type Alt+L Alt+O keys, while the associated `index.html` file is opened in the Editor window. In this case, the project will not run if you click the "Go Live" button while the `core.js` file is opened in the Editor window.

Observations

Examine your `index.html` file closely and compare its content to the same file from the previous project. You will notice that the `index.html` file from the previous project contains two types of information (HTML and JavaScript code) and that the same file from this project contains only the former, with all JavaScript code being extracted to `core.js`. This clean separation of information allows for easy understanding of the source code and improves support for more complex systems. From this point on, all JavaScript source code will be added to separate source code files.

Elementary Drawing with WebGL

In general, drawing involves geometric data and the instructions for processing the data. In the case of WebGL, the instructions for processing the data are specified in the OpenGL Shading Language (GLSL) and are referred to as shaders. In order to draw with WebGL, programmers must define the geometric data and GLSL shaders in the CPU and load both to the drawing hardware, or the graphics processing unit (GPU). This process involves a significant number of WebGL function calls. This section presents the WebGL drawing steps in detail.

It is important to focus on learning these basic steps and avoid being distracted by the less important WebGL configuration nuances such that you can continue to learn the overall concepts involved when building your game engine.

In the following project, you will learn about drawing with WebGL by focusing on the most elementary operations. This includes the loading of the simple geometry of a square from the CPU to the GPU, the creation of a constant color shader, and the basic instructions for drawing a simple square with two triangles.

The Draw One Square Project

This project leads you through the steps required to draw a single square on the canvas. Figure 2-6 shows an example of running this project, which is defined in the `chapter2/2.3.draw_one_square` folder.

Figure 2-6. *Running the Draw One Square project*

The goals of the project are as follows:

- To understand how to load geometric data to the GPU

- To learn about simple GLSL shaders for drawing with WebGL

- To learn how to compile and load shaders to the GPU

- To understand the steps required to draw with WebGL

- To demonstrate the implementation of a singleton-like JavaScript module based on simple source code files

Set Up and Load the Primitive Geometry Data

To draw efficiently with WebGL, the data associated with the geometry to be drawn, such as the vertex positions of a square, should be stored in the GPU hardware. In the following steps, you will create a contiguous buffer in the GPU, load the vertex positions of a unit square into the buffer, and store the reference to the GPU buffer in a variable. Learning from the previous project, the corresponding JavaScript code will be stored in a new source code file, vertex_buffer.js.

Note   A unit square is a 1×1 square centered at the origin.

---

1. Create a new JavaScript source file in the src folder and name it vertex_buffer.js.

2. Import all the exported functionality from the core.js file as core with the JavaScript import statement:

```
"use strict";
import * as core from "./core.js";
```

Note   With the JavaScript import and, soon to be encountered, export statements, features and functionalities defined in a file can be conveniently encapsulated and accessed. In this case, the functionality exported from core.js is imported in vertex_buffer.js and accessible via the module identifier, core. For example, as you will see, in this project, core.js defines and exports a getGL() function. With the given import statement, this function can be accessed as core.getGL() in the vertex_buffer.js file.

---

3. Declare the variable mGLVertexBuffer to store the reference to the WebGL buffer location. Remember to define a function for accessing this variable.

```
let mGLVertexBuffer = null;
function get() { return mGLVertexBuffer; }
```

4. Define the variable mVerticesOfSquare and initialize it with vertices of a unit square:

```
let mVerticesOfSquare = [
    0.5, 0.5, 0.0,
    -0.5, 0.5, 0.0,
    0.5, -0.5, 0.0,
    -0.5, -0.5, 0.0
];
```

In the code shown, each row of three numbers is the x-, y-, and z-coordinate position of a vertex. Notice that the z dimension is set to 0.0 because you are building a 2D game engine. Also notice that 0.5 is being used so that we define a square in 2D space which has sides equal to 1 and centered at the origin or a unit square.

5. Define the init() function to allocate a buffer in the GPU via the gl context, and load the vertices to the allocated buffer in the GPU:

```
function init() {
    let gl = core.getGL();

    // Step A: Create a buffer on the gl context for our vertex positions
    mGLVertexBuffer = gl.createBuffer();

    // Step B: Activate vertexBuffer
    gl.bindBuffer(gl.ARRAY_BUFFER, mGLVertexBuffer);

    // Step C: Loads mVerticesOfSquare into the vertexBuffer
    gl.bufferData(gl.ARRAY_BUFFER,
            new Float32Array(mVerticesOfSquare), gl.STATIC_DRAW);
}
```

This code first gets access to the WebGL drawing context through the core.getGL() function. After which, Step A creates a buffer on the GPU for storing the vertex positions of the square and stores the reference to the GPU buffer in the variable mGLVertexBuffer. Step B activates the newly created buffer, and step C loads the vertex position of the square into the activated buffer on the GPU. The keyword STATIC_DRAW informs the drawing hardware that the content of this buffer will not be changed.

Tip   Remember that the mGL variable accessed through the getGL() function is defined in the core.js file and initialized by the initWebGL() function. You will define an export statement in the core.js file to provide access to this function in the coming steps.

---

6.   Provide access to the init() and get() functions to the rest of your engine by exporting them with the following code:

```
export {init, get}
```

With the functionality of loading vertex positions defined, you are now ready to define and load the GLSL shaders.

Set Up the GLSL Shaders

The term shader refers to programs, or a collection of instructions, that run on the GPU. In the context of the game engine, shaders must always be defined in pairs consisting of a vertex shader and a corresponding fragment shader. The GPU will execute the vertex shader once per primitive vertex and the fragment shader once per pixel covered by the primitive. For example, you can define a square with four vertices and display this square to cover a 100×100 pixel area. To draw this square, WebGL will invoke the vertex shader 4 times (once for each vertex) and execute the fragment shader 10,000 times (once for each of the 100×100 pixels)!

In the case of WebGL, both the vertex and fragment shaders are implemented in the OpenGL Shading Language (GLSL). GLSL is a language with syntax that is similar to the C programming language and designed specifically for processing and displaying graphical primitives. You will learn sufficient GLSL to support the drawing for the game engine when required.

In the following steps, you will load into GPU memory the source code for both vertex and fragment shaders, compile and link them into a single shader program, and load the linked program into the GPU memory for drawing. In this project, the shader source code is defined in the index.html file, while the loading, compiling, and linking of the shaders are defined in the shader_support.js source file.

Note   The WebGL context can be considered as an abstraction of the GPU hardware. To facilitate readability, the two terms WebGL and GPU are sometimes used interchangeably.

Define the Vertex and Fragment Shaders

GLSL shaders are simply programs consisting of GLSL instructions:

1. Define the vertex shader by opening the index.html file, and within the head element, add the following code:

```
<script type="x-shader/x-vertex" id="VertexShader">
    // this is the vertex shader
    attribute vec3 aVertexPosition;  // Expects one vertex position
        // naming convention, attributes always begin with "a"
    void main(void) {
        // Convert the vec3 into vec4 for scan conversion and
        // assign to gl_Position to pass vertex to the fragment shader
        gl_Position = vec4(aVertexPosition, 1.0);
    }
    // End of vertex shader
</script>
```

Note   Shader attribute variables have names that begin with a lowercase "a", as in aVertexPosition.

The script element type is set to x-shader/x-vertex because that is a common convention for shaders. As you will see, the id field with the value VertexShader allows you to identify and load this vertex shader into memory.

The GLSL attribute keyword identifies per-vertex data that will be passed to the vertex shader in the GPU. In this case, the aVertexPosition attribute is of data type vec3 or an array of three floating-point numbers. As you will see in later steps, aVertexPosition will be set to reference the vertex positions for the unit square.

The gl_Position is a GLSL built-in variable, specifically an array of four floating-point numbers that must contain the vertex position. In this case, the fourth position of the array will always be 1.0. The code shows the shader converting the aVertexPosition into a vec4 and passing the information to WebGL.

2. Define the fragment shader in index.html by adding the following code within the head element:

```
<script type="x-shader/x-fragment" id="FragmentShader">
    // this is the fragment (or pixel) shader
    void main(void) {
        // for every pixel called (within the square) sets
        // constant color white with alpha-channel value of 1.0
        gl_FragColor = vec4(1.0, 1.0, 1.0, 1.0);
    }
    // End of fragment/pixel shader
</script>
```

Note the different type and id fields. Recall that the fragment shader is invoked once per pixel. The variable gl_FragColor is the built-in variable that determines the color of the pixel. In this case, a color of (1,1,1,1), or white, is returned. This means all pixels covered will be shaded to a constant white color.

With both the vertex and fragment shaders defined in the index.html file, you are now ready to implement the functionality to compile, link, and load the resulting shader program to the GPU.

Compile, Link, and Load the Vertex and Fragment Shaders

To maintain source code in logically separated source files, you will create shader support functionality in a new source code file, shader_support.js.

1. Create a new JavaScript file, shader_support.js.

2. Import functionality from the core.js and vertex_buffer.js files:

```
"use strict";  // Variables must be declared before used!
import * as core from "./core.js";  // access as core module
import * as vertexBuffer from "./vertex_buffer.js"; //vertexBuffer module
```

3. Define two variables, mCompiledShader and mVertexPositionRef, for referencing to the shader program and the vertex position attribute in the GPU:

```
let mCompiledShader = null;
let mVertexPositionRef = null;
```

4. Create a function to load and compile the shader you defined in the index.html:

```
function loadAndCompileShader(id, shaderType) {
    let shaderSource = null, compiledShader = null;

    // Step A: Get the shader source from index.html
    let shaderText = document.getElementById(id);
    shaderSource = shaderText.firstChild.textContent;

    let gl = core.getGL();
    // Step B: Create shader based on type: vertex or fragment
    compiledShader = gl.createShader(shaderType);

    // Step C: Compile the created shader
    gl.shaderSource(compiledShader, shaderSource);
    gl.compileShader(compiledShader);

    // Step D: check for errors and return results (null if error)
    // The log info is how shader compilation errors are displayed.
    // This is useful for debugging the shaders.
    if (!gl.getShaderParameter(compiledShader, gl.COMPILE_STATUS)) {
        throw new Error("A shader compiling error occurred: " +
                    gl.getShaderInfoLog(compiledShader));
    }

    return compiledShader;
}
```

Step A of the code finds shader source code in the index.html file using the id field you specified when defining the shaders, either VertexShader or FragmentShader. Step B creates a specified shader (either vertex or fragment) in the GPU. Step C specifies the source code and compiles the shader. Finally, step D checks and returns the reference to the compiled shader while throwing an error if the shader compilation is unsuccessful.

5.   You are now ready to create, compile, and link a shader program by defining the init() function:

```
function init(vertexShaderID, fragmentShaderID) {
    let gl = core.getGL();

    // Step A: load and compile vertex and fragment shaders
    let vertexShader = loadAndCompileShader(vertexShaderID,
                                        gl.VERTEX_SHADER);
    let fragmentShader = loadAndCompileShader(fragmentShaderID,
                                        gl.FRAGMENT_SHADER);

    // Step B: Create and link the shaders into a program.
    mCompiledShader = gl.createProgram();
    gl.attachShader(mCompiledShader, vertexShader);
    gl.attachShader(mCompiledShader, fragmentShader);
    gl.linkProgram(mCompiledShader);

    // Step C: check for error
    if (!gl.getProgramParameter(mCompiledShader, gl.LINK_STATUS)) {
        throw new Error("Error linking shader");
        return null;
    }

    // Step D: Gets reference to aVertexPosition attribute in the shader
    mVertexPositionRef = gl.getAttribLocation(mCompiledShader,
                                        "aVertexPosition");
}
```

Step A loads and compiles the shader code you defined in index.html by calling the loadAndCompileShader() function with the corresponding parameters. Step B attaches the compiled shaders and links the two shaders into a program. The reference to this program is stored in the variable mCompiledShader. After error checking in step C, step D locates and stores the reference to the aVertexPosition attribute defined in your vertex shader.

6. Define a function to allow the activation of the shader so that it can be used for drawing the square:

```
function activate() {
    // Step A: access to the webgl context
    let gl = core.getGL();

    // Step B: identify the compiled shader to use
    gl.useProgram(mCompiledShader);

    // Step C: bind vertex buffer to attribute defined in vertex shader
    gl.bindBuffer(gl.ARRAY_BUFFER, vertexBuffer.get());
    gl.vertexAttribPointer(this.mVertexPositionRef,
        3,              // each element is a 3-float (x,y.z)
        gl.FLOAT,       // data type is FLOAT
        false,          // if the content is normalized vectors
        0,              // number of bytes to skip in between elements
        0);             // offsets to the first element
    gl.enableVertexAttribArray(this.mVertexPositionRef);
}
```

In the code shown, step A sets the gl variable to the WebGL context through the core module. Step B loads the compiled shader program to the GPU memory, while step C binds the vertex buffer created in vertex_buffer.js to the aVertexPosition attribute defined in the vertex shader. The gl.vertexAttribPointer() function captures the fact that the vertex buffer was loaded with vertices of a unit square consisting of three floating-point values for each vertex position.

7. Lastly, provide access to the init() and activate() functions to the rest of the game engine by exporting them with the export statement:

```
export { init, activate }
```

Note   Notice that the loadAndCompileShader() function is excluded from the export statement. This function is not needed elsewhere and thus, following the good development practice of hiding local implementation details, should remain private to this file.

The shader loading and compiling functionality is now defined. You can now utilize and activate these functions to draw with WebGL.

Set Up Drawing with WebGL

With the vertex data and shader functionality defined, you can now execute the following steps to draw with WebGL. Recall from the previous project that the initialization and drawing code is defined in the core.js file. Now open this file for editing.

1. Import the defined functionality from vertex_buffer.js and shader_support.js files:

```
import * as vertexBuffer from "./vertex_buffer.js";
import * as simpleShader from "./shader_support.js";
```

2. Modify the initWebGL() function to include the initialization of the vertex buffer and the shader program:

```
function initWebGL(htmlCanvasID) {
    let canvas = document.getElementById(htmlCanvasID);

    // Get standard or experimental webgl and bind to the Canvas area
    // store the results to the instance variable mGL
    mGL = canvas.getContext("webgl2") ||
        canvas.getContext("experimental-webgl2");

    if (mGL === null) {
        document.write("<br><b>WebGL 2 is not supported!</b>");
        return;
    }
    mGL.clearColor(0.0, 0.8, 0.0, 1.0);  // set the color to be cleared

    // 1. initialize buffer with vertex positions for the unit square
    vertexBuffer.init(); // function defined in the vertex_buffer.js

    // 2. now load and compile the vertex and fragment shaders
    simpleShader.init("VertexShader", "FragmentShader");
        // the two shaders are defined in the index.html file
        // init() function is defined in shader_support.js file
}
```

As shown in the code, after successfully obtaining the reference to the WebGL context and setting the clear color, you should first call the init() function defined in vertex_buffer.js to initialize the GPU vertex buffer with the unit square vertices and then call the init() function defined in shader_support.js to load and compile the vertex and fragment shaders.

3.   Add a drawSquare() function for drawing the defined square:

```
function drawSquare() {
    // Step A: Activate the shader
    simpleShader.activate();

    // Step B. draw with the above settings
    mGL.drawArrays(mGL.TRIANGLE_STRIP, 0, 4);
}
```

This code shows the steps to draw with WebGL. Step A activates the shader program to use. Step B issues the WebGL draw command. In this case, you are issuing a command to draw the four vertices as two connected triangles that form a square.

4.   Now you just need to modify the window.onload function to call the newly defined drawSquare() function:

```
window.onload = function() {
    initWebGL("GLCanvas");   // Binds mGL context to WebGL functionality
    clearCanvas();           // Clears the GL area
    drawSquare();            // Draws one square
}
```

5.   Finally, provide access to the WebGL context to the rest of the engine by exporting the getGL() function. Remember that this function is imported and has been called to access the WebGL context in both vertex_buffer.js and simple_shader.js.

```
export {getGL}
```

Recall that the function that is bounded to window.onload will be invoked after index1.html has been loaded by the web browser. For this reason, WebGL will be initialized, the canvas cleared to light green, and a white square will be drawn. You can refer to the source code in the chapter2/2.3.draw_one_square project for the entire system described.

Observations

Run the project and you will see a white rectangle on a green canvas. What happened to the square? Remember that the vertex position of your 1×1 square was defined at locations (±0.5, ±0.5). Now observe the project output: the white rectangle is located in the middle of the green canvas covering exactly half of the canvas' width and height. As it turns out, WebGL draws vertices within the ±1.0 range onto the entire defined drawing area. In this case, the ±1.0 in the x dimension is mapped to 640 pixels, while the ±1.0 in the y dimension is mapped to 480 pixels (the created canvas dimension is 640×480). The 1x1 square is drawn onto a 640x480 area, or an area with an aspect ratio of 4:3. Since the 1:1 aspect ratio of the square does not match the 4:3 aspect ratio of the display area, the square shows up as a 4:3 rectangle. This problem will be resolved later in the next chapter.

You can try editing the fragment shader in `index.html` by changing the color set in the `gl_FragColor` function to alter the color of the white square. Notice that a value of less than 1 in the alpha channel does not result in the white square becoming transparent. Transparency of drawn primitives will be discussed in later chapters.

Finally, note that this project defines three separate files and hides information with the JavaScript import/export statements. The functionality defined in these files with the corresponding import and export statements is referred to as JavaScript modules. A module can be considered as a global singleton object and is excellent for hiding implementation details. The `loadAndCompileShader()` function in the `shader_support` module serves as a great example of this concept. However, modules are not well suited for supporting abstraction and specialization. In the next sections, you will begin to work with JavaScript classes to further encapsulate portions of this example to form the basis of the game engine framework.

Abstraction with JavaScript Classes

The previous project decomposed the drawing of a square into logical modules and implemented the modules as files containing global functions. In software engineering, this process is referred to as functional decomposition, and the implementation is referred to as procedural programming. Procedural programming often results in solutions that are well structured and easy to understand. This is why functional decomposition and procedural programming are often used to prototype concepts or to learn new techniques.

This project enhances the Draw One Square project with object-oriented analysis and programming to introduce data abstraction. As additional concepts are introduced and as the game engine complexity grows, proper data abstraction supports straightforward design, behavior specialization, and code reuse through inheritance.

The JavaScript Objects Project

This project demonstrates how to abstract the global functions from the Draw One Square project into JavaScript classes and objects. This object-oriented abstraction will result in a framework that offers manageability and expandability for subsequent projects. As illustrated in Figure 2-7, when running, this project displays a white rectangle in a greenish canvas, identical to that from the Draw One Square project. The source code to this project can be found in the chapter2/2.4.javascript_objects folder.

Figure 2-7. *Running the JavaScript Objects project*

The goals of the project are as follows:

- To separate the code for the game engine from the code for the game logic

- To understand how to build abstractions with JavaScript classes and objects

The steps for creating this project are as follows:

1. Create separate folders to organize the source code for the game engine and the logic of the game.

2. Define a JavaScript class to abstract the simple_shader and work with an instance of this class.

3. Define a JavaScript class to implement the drawing of one square, which is the logic of your simple game for now.

Source Code Organization

Create a new HTML5 project with VS Code by creating a new folder and adding a source code folder named src. Within src, create engine and my_game as subfolders, as illustrated in Figure 2-8.

Figure 2-8. *Creating* engine *and* my_game *under the* src *folder*

The src/engine folder will contain all the source code to the game engine, and the src/my_game folder will contain the source for the logic of your game. It is important to organize source code diligently because the complexity of the system and the number of files will increase rapidly as more concepts are introduced. A well-organized source code structure facilitates understanding and expansion.

Tip The source code in the `my_game` folder implements the game by relying on the functionality provided by the game engine defined in the `engine` folder. For this reason, in this book, the source code in the `my_game` folder is often referred to as the *client* of the game engine.

Abstracting the Game Engine

A completed game engine would include many self-contained subsystems to fulfill different responsibilities. For example, you may be familiar with or have heard of the geometry subsystem for managing the geometries to be drawn, the resource management subsystem for managing images and audio clips, the physics subsystem for managing object interactions, and so on. In most cases, the game engine would include one unique instance of each of these subsystems, that is, one instance of the geometry subsystem, of the resource management subsystem, of the physics subsystem, and so on.

These subsystems will be covered in later chapters of this book. This section focuses on establishing the mechanism and organization for implementing this single-instance or singleton-like functionality based on the JavaScript module you have worked with in the previous project.

Note All module and instance variable names begin with an "m" and are followed by a capital letter, as in `mVariable`. Though not enforced by JavaScript, you should never access a module or instance variable from outside the module/class. For example, you should never access `core.mGL` directly; instead, call the `core.getGL()` function to access the variable.

The Shader Class

Although the code in the `shader_support.js` file from the previous project properly implements the required functionality, the variables and functions do not lend themselves well to behavior specialization and code reuse. For example, in the cases when different types of shaders are required, it can be challenging to modify the implementation while achieving behavior and code reuse. This section follows the object-oriented design principles and defines a `SimpleShader` class to abstract the behaviors and hide the internal representations of shaders. Besides the ability to create multiple instances of the SimpleShader object, the basic functionality remains largely unchanged.

Note   Module identifiers begin with lower case, for example, core or vertexBuffer. Class names begin with upper case, for example, SimpleShader or MyGame.

---

1. Create a new source file in the src/engine folder and name the file simple_shader.js to implement the SimpleShader class.

2. Import both the core and vertex_buffer modules:

```
import * as core from "./core.js";
import * as vertexBuffer from "./vertex_buffer.js";
```

3. Declare the SimpleShader as a JavaScript class:

```
class SimpleShader {
    ... implementation to follow ...
}
```

4. Define the constructor within the SimpleShader class to load, compile, and link the vertex and fragment shaders into a program and to create a reference to the aVertexPosition attribute in the vertex shader for loading the square vertex positions from the WebGL vertex buffer for drawing:

```
constructor(vertexShaderID, fragmentShaderID) {
    // instance variables
    // Convention: all instance variables: mVariables
    this.mCompiledShader = null;  // ref to compiled shader in webgl
    this.mVertexPositionRef = null; // ref to VertexPosition in shader

    let gl = core.getGL();
    // Step A: load and compile vertex and fragment shaders
    this.mVertexShader = loadAndCompileShader(vertexShaderID,
                                    gl.VERTEX_SHADER);
```

```
    this.mFragmentShader = loadAndCompileShader(fragmentShaderID,
                                        gl.FRAGMENT_SHADER);

    // Step B: Create and link the shaders into a program.
    this.mCompiledShader = gl.createProgram();
    gl.attachShader(this.mCompiledShader, this.mVertexShader);
    gl.attachShader(this.mCompiledShader, this.mFragmentShader);
    gl.linkProgram(this.mCompiledShader);

    // Step C: check for error
    if (!gl.getProgramParameter(this.mCompiledShader, gl.LINK_STATUS)) {
        throw new Error("Error linking shader");
        return null;
    }

    // Step D: reference to aVertexPosition attribute in the shaders
    this.mVertexPositionRef = gl.getAttribLocation(
                            this.mCompiledShader, "aVertexPosition");
}
```

Notice that this constructor is essentially the same as the init() function in the shader_support.js module from the previous project.

Note   The JavaScript constructor keyword defines the constructor of a class.

---

5. Add a method to the SimpleShader class to activate the shader for drawing. Once again, similar to your activate() function in shader_support.js from previous project.

```
activate() {
    let gl = core.getGL();
    gl.useProgram(this.mCompiledShader);

    // bind vertex buffer
    gl.bindBuffer(gl.ARRAY_BUFFER, vertexBuffer.get());
    gl.vertexAttribPointer(this.mVertexPositionRef,
        3,              // each element is a 3-float (x,y.z)
        gl.FLOAT,       // data type is FLOAT
```

```
        false,          // if the content is normalized vectors
        0,              // number of bytes to skip in between elements
        0);             // offsets to the first element
    gl.enableVertexAttribArray(this.mVertexPositionRef);
}
```

6. Add a private method, which cannot be accessed from outside
   the simple_shader.js file, by creating a function outside the
   SimpleShader class to perform the actual loading and compiling
   functionality:

```
function loadAndCompileShader(id, shaderType) {
    let shaderSource = null, compiledShader = null;
    let gl = core.getGL();

    // Step A: Get the shader source from index.html
    let shaderText = document.getElementById(id);
    shaderSource = shaderText.firstChild.textContent;

    // Step B: Create shader based on type: vertex or fragment
    compiledShader = gl.createShader(shaderType);

    // Step C: Compile the created shader
    gl.shaderSource(compiledShader, shaderSource);
    gl.compileShader(compiledShader);

    // Step D: check for errors and return results (null if error)
    // The log info is how shader compilation errors are displayed
    // This is useful for debugging the shaders.
    if (!gl.getShaderParameter(compiledShader, gl.COMPILE_STATUS)) {
        throw new Error("A shader compiling error occurred: " +
                    gl.getShaderInfoLog(compiledShader));
    }

    return compiledShader;
}
```

Notice that this function is identical to the one you created in shader_support.js.

Note   The JavaScript # prefix that defines private members is not used in this book because the lack of visibility from subclasses complicates specialization of behaviors in inheritance.

---

7. Finally, add an export for the SimpleShader class such that it can be accessed and instantiated outside of this file:

```
export default SimpleShader;
```

Note   The default keyword signifies that the name SimpleShader cannot be changed by import statements.

The Core of the Game Engine: core.js

The core contains common functionality shared by the entire game engine. This can include one-time initialization of the WebGL (or GPU), shared resources, utility functions, and so on.

1. Create a copy of your core.js under the new folder src/engine.

2. Define a function to create a new instance of the SimpleShader object:

```
// The shader
let mShader = null;
function createShader() {
    mShader = new SimpleShader(
        "VertexShader",     // IDs of the script tag in the index.html
        "FragmentShader");  // 
}
```

3. Modify the initWebGL() function to focus on only initializing the
    WebGL as follows:

```
// initialize the WebGL
function initWebGL(htmlCanvasID) {
    let canvas = document.getElementById(htmlCanvasID);

    // Get standard or experimental webgl and binds to the Canvas area
    // store the results to the instance variable mGL
    mGL = canvas.getContext("webgl2") ||
          canvas.getContext("experimental-webgl2");

    if (mGL === null) {
        document.write("<br><b>WebGL 2 is not supported!</b>");
        return;
    }
}
```

4. Create an init() function to perform engine-wide system
    initialization, which includes initializing of WebGL and the vertex
    buffer and creating an instance of the simple shader:

```
function init(htmlCanvasID) {
    initWebGL(htmlCanvasID);   // setup mGL
    vertexBuffer.init();       // setup mGLVertexBuffer
    createShader();            // create the shader
}
```

5. Modify the clear canvas function to parameterize the color to be
    cleared to:

```
function clearCanvas(color) {
    mGL.clearColor(color[0], color[1], color[2], color[3]);
    mGL.clear(mGL.COLOR_BUFFER_BIT); // clear to the color set
}
```

6. Export the relevant functions for access by the rest of the game engine:

```
export { getGL, init, clearCanvas, drawSquare }
```

7. Finally, remove the `window.onload` function as the behavior of the actual game should be defined by the client of the game engine or, in this case, the `MyGame` class.

The `src/engine` folder now contains the basic source code for the entire game engine. Due to these structural changes to your source code, the game engine can now function as a simple library that provides functionality for creating games or a simple application programming interface (API). For now, your game engine consists of three files that support the initialization of WebGL and the drawing of a unit square, the `core` module, the `vertex_buffer` module, and the `SimpleShader` class. New source files and functionality will continue to be added to this folder throughout the remaining projects. Eventually, this folder will contain a complete and sophisticated game engine. However, the core library-like framework defined here will persist.

The Client Source Code

The `src/my_game` folder will contain the actual source code for the game. As mentioned, the code in this folder will be referred to as the *client* of the game engine. For now, the source code in the `my_game` folder will focus on drawing a simple square by utilizing the functionality of the simple game engine you defined.

1. Create a new source file in the `src/my_game` folder, or the *client* folder, and name the file `my_game.js`.

2. Import the `core` module as follows:

```
import * as engine from "../engine/core.js";
```

3. Define `MyGame` as a JavaScript class and add a `constructor` to initialize the game engine, clear the `canvas`, and draw the square:

```
class MyGame {
    constructor(htmlCanvasID) {
        // Step A: Initialize the game engine
        engine.init(htmlCanvasID);
```

```
        // Step B: Clear the canvas
        engine.clearCanvas([0, 0.8, 0, 1]);

        // Step C: Draw the square
        engine.drawSquare();
    }
}
```

4. Bind the creation of a new instance of the MyGame object to the
    window.onload function:

```
window.onload = function() {
    new MyGame('GLCanvas');
}
```

5. Finally, modify the index.html to load the game client rather than
    the engine core.js within the head element:

```
<script type="module" src="./src/my_game/my_game.js"></script>
```

Observations

Although you're accomplishing the same tasks as with the previous project, with this
project, you have created an infrastructure that supports subsequent modifications and
expansions of your game engine. You have organized your source code into separate and
logical folders, organized the singleton-like modules to implement core functionality
of the engine, and gained experience with abstracting the SimpleShader class that will
support future design and code reuse. With the engine now comprised of well-defined
modules and objects with clean interface methods, you can now focus on learning new
concepts, abstracting the concepts, and integrating new implementation source code
into your engine.

Separating GLSL from HTML

Thus far in your projects, the GLSL shader code is embedded in the HTML source code
of index.html. This organization means that new shaders must be added through the
editing of the index.html file. Logically, GLSL shaders should be organized separately

from HTML source files; logistically, continuously adding to index.html will result in a cluttered and unmanageable file that would become difficult to work with. For these reasons, the GLSL shaders should be stored in separate source files.

The Shader Source File Project

This project demonstrates how to separate the GLSL shaders into separate files. As illustrated in Figure 2-9, when running this project, a white rectangle is displayed on a greenish canvas, identical to the previous projects. The source code to this project is defined in the chapter2/2.5.shader_source_files folder.

Figure 2-9. *Running the Shader Source File project*

The goals of the project are as follows:

- To separate the GLSL shaders from the HTML source code

- To demonstrate how to load the shader source code files during runtime

Loading Shaders in SimpleShader

Instead of loading the GLSL shaders as part of the HTML document, the loadAndCompileShader() in SimpleShader can be modified to load the GLSL shaders as separate files:

1. Continue from the previous project, open the simple_shader.js file, and edit the loadAndCompileShader() function, to receive a file path instead of an HTML ID:

```
function loadAndCompileShader(filePath, shaderType)
```

2. Within the loadAndCompileShader() function, replace the HTML element retrieval code in step A with the following XMLHttpRequest to load a file:

```
let xmlReq, shaderSource = null, compiledShader = null;
let gl = core.getGL();

// Step A: Request the text from the given file location.
xmlReq = new XMLHttpRequest();
xmlReq.open('GET', filePath, false);
try {
    xmlReq.send();
} catch (error) {
    throw new Error("Failed to load shader: "
            + filePath
            + " [Hint: you cannot double click to run this project. "
            + "The index.html file must be loaded by a web-server.]");
    return null;
}
shaderSource = xmlReq.responseText;

if (shaderSource === null) {
    throw new Error("WARNING: Loading of:" + filePath + " Failed!");
    return null;
}
```

Notice that the file loading will occur synchronously where the web browser will actually stop and wait for the completion of the xmlReq.open() function to return with the content of the opened file. If the file should be missing, the opening operation will fail, and the response text will be null.

The synchronized "stop and wait" for the completion of xmlReq.open() function is inefficient and may result in slow loading of the web page. This shortcoming will be addressed in Chapter 4 when you learn about the asynchronous loading of game resources.

Note   The XMLHttpRequest() object requires a running web server to fulfill the HTTP get request. This means you will be able to test this project from within the VS Code with the installed "Go Live" extension. However, unless there is a web server running on your machine, you will not be able to run this project by double-clicking the index.html file directly. This is because there is no server to fulfill the HTTP get requests and the GLSL shader loading will fail.

With this modification, the SimpleShader constructor can now be modified to receive and forward file paths to the loadAndCompileShader() function instead of the HTML element IDs.

Extracting Shaders into Their Own Files

The following steps retrieve the source code of the vertex and fragment shaders from the index.html file and create separate files for storing them:

1. Create a new folder that will contain all of the GLSL shader source code files in the src folder, and name it glsl_shaders, as illustrated in Figure 2-10.

Figure 2-10.   *Creating the glsl_shaders folder*

2. Create two new text files within the `glsl_shaders` folder, and
    name them `simple_vs.glsl` and `white_fs.glsl` for simple vertex
    shader and white fragment shader.

Note   All GLSL shader source code files will end with the `.glsl` extension. The
`vs` in the shader file names signifies that the file contains a vertex shader, while `fs`
signifies a fragment shader.

---

3. Create the GLSL vertex shader source code by editing `simple_`
    `vs.glsl` and pasting the vertex shader code in the `index.html` file
    from the previous project:

```
attribute vec3 aVertexPosition;   // Vertex shader expects one position
void main(void) {
    // Convert the vec3 into vec4 for scan conversion and
    // assign to gl_Position to pass the vertex to the fragment shader
    gl_Position = vec4(aVertexPosition, 1.0);
}
```

4. Create the GLSL fragment shader source code by editing `white_`
    `fs.glsl` and pasting the fragment shader code in the `index.html`
    file from the previous project:

```
precision mediump float; // precision for float computation
void main(void) {
    // for every pixel called (within the square) sets
    // constant color white with alpha-channel value of 1.0
    gl_FragColor = vec4(1.0, 1.0, 1.0, 1.0);
}
```

Cleaning Up HTML Code

With vertex and fragment shaders being stored in separate files, it is now possible to
clean up the `index.html` file such that it contains only HTML code:

1. Remove all the GLSL shader code from index.html, such that this file becomes as follows:

```
<!DOCTYPE html>
<html>
    <head>
        <title>Example 2.5: The Shader Source File Project</title>
        <link rel ="icon" type ="image/x-icon" href="./favicon.png">
        <!-- there are javascript source code contained in
             the external source files
        -->
        <!-- Client game code -->
        <script type="module" src="./src/my_game/my_game.js"></script>
    </head>

    <body>
        <canvas id="GLCanvas" width="640" height="480">
            <!-- GLCanvas is the area we will draw in: a 640x480 area -->
            Your browser does not support the HTML5 canvas.
            <!-- this message will show only if WebGL clearing failed -->
        </canvas>
    </body>
</html>
```

Notice that index.html no longer contains any GLSL shader code and only a single reference to JavaScript code. With this organization, the index.html file can properly be considered as representing the web page where you do not need to edit this file to modify the shaders from now on.

2. Modify the createShader() function in core.js to load the shader files instead of HTML element IDs:

```
function createShader() {
    mShader = new SimpleShader(
        "src/glsl_shaders/simple_vs.glsl", // Path to VertexShader
        "src/glsl_shaders/white_fs.glsl"); // Path to FragmentShader
}
```

Source Code Organization

The separation of logical components in the engine source code has progressed to the following state:

- `index.html`: This is the file that contains the HTML code that defines the canvas on the web page for the game and loads the source code for your game.

- `src/glsl_shaders`: This is the folder that contains all the GLSL shader source code files that draws the elements of your game.

- `src/engine`: This is the folder that contains all the source code files for your game engine.

- `src/my_game`: This is the client folder that contains the source code for the actual game.

Changing the Shader and Controlling the Color

With GLSL shaders being stored in separate source code files, it is now possible to edit or replace the shaders with relatively minor changes to the rest of the source code. The next project demonstrates this convenience by replacing the restrictive constant white color fragment shader, `white_fs.glsl`, with a shader that can be parameterized to draw with any color.

The Parameterized Fragment Shader Project

This project replaces `white_fs.glsl` with a `simple_fs.glsl` that supports the drawing with any color. Figure 2-11 shows the output of running the Parameterized Fragment Shader project; notice that a red square replaces the white square from the previous projects. The source code for this project is defined in the `chapter2/2.6.parameterized_fragment_shader` folder.

Figure 2-11. *Running the Parameterized Fragment Shader project*

The goals of the project are as follows:

- To gain experience with creating a GLSL shader in the source code structure

- To learn about the uniform variable and define a fragment shader with the color parameter

Defining the simple_fs.glsl Fragment Shader

A new fragment shader needs to be created to support changing the pixel color for each draw operation. This can be accomplished by creating a new GLSL fragment shader in the src/glsl_shaders folder and name it simple_fs.glsl. Edit this file to add the following:

```
precision mediump float; // precision for float computation
// Color of pixel
uniform vec4 uPixelColor;
void main(void) {
    // for every pixel called sets to the user specified color
    gl_FragColor = uPixelColor;
}
```

Recall that the GLSL attribute keyword identifies data that changes for every vertex position. In this case, the uniform keyword denotes that a variable is constant for all the vertices. The uPixelColor variable can be set from JavaScript to control the eventual pixel color. The precision mediump keywords define the floating precisions for computations.

Note   Floating-point precision trades the accuracy of computation for performance. Please follow the references in Chapter 1 for more information on WebGL.

Modify the SimpleShader to Support the Color Parameter

The SimpleShader class can now be modified to gain access to the new uPixelColor variable:

1. Edit simple_shader.js and add a new instance variable for referencing the uPixelColor in the constructor:

```
this.mPixelColorRef = null; // pixelColor uniform in fragment shader
```

2. Add code to the end of the constructor to create the reference to the uPixelColor:

```
// Step E: Gets uniform variable uPixelColor in fragment shader
this.mPixelColorRef = gl.getUniformLocation(
                        this.mCompiledShader, "uPixelColor");
```

3. Modify the shader activation to allow the setting of the pixel color via the uniform4fv() function:

```
activate(pixelColor) {
    let gl = core.getGL();
    gl.useProgram(this.mCompiledShader);

    // bind vertex buffer
    gl.bindBuffer(gl.ARRAY_BUFFER, vertexBuffer.get());
    gl.vertexAttribPointer(this.mVertexPositionRef,
        3,              // each element is a 3-float (x,y.z)
        gl.FLOAT,       // data type is FLOAT
        false,          // if the content is normalized vectors
        0,              // number of bytes to skip in between elements
        0);             // offsets to the first element
    gl.enableVertexAttribArray(this.mVertexPositionRef);

    // load uniforms
    gl.uniform4fv(this.mPixelColorRef, pixelColor);
}
```

The gl.uniform4fv() function copies four floating-point values from the pixelColor float array to the WebGL location referenced by mPixelColorRef or the uPixelColor in the simple_fs.glsl fragment shader.

Drawing with the New Shader

To test simple_fs.glsl, modify the core.js module to create a SimpleShader with the new simple_fs and use the parameterized color when drawing with the new shader:

```
function createShader() {
    mShader = new SimpleShader(
        "src/glsl_shaders/simple_vs.glsl", // Path to the VertexShader
        "src/glsl_shaders/simple_fs.glsl"); // Path to the FragmentShader
}

function drawSquare(color) {
    // Step A: Activate the shader
    mShader.activate(color);
```

```
    // Step B: Draw with currently activated geometry and shader
    mGL.drawArrays(mGL.TRIANGLE_STRIP, 0, 4);
}
```

Lastly, edit the `constructor` of the MyGame class to include a color when drawing the square, in this case, red:

```
// Step C: Draw the square in red
engine.drawSquare([1, 0, 0, 1]);
```

Notice that a color value, an array of four floats, is now required with the new `simple_fs.glsl` (instead of `white_fs`) shader and that it is important to pass in the drawing color when activating the shader. With the new `simple_fs`, you can now experiment with drawing the squares with any desired color.

As you have experienced in this project, the source code structure supports simple and localized changes when the game engine is expanded or modified. In this case, only changes to the `simple_shader.js` file and minor modifications to `core.js` and the `my_game.js` were required. This demonstrates the benefit of proper encapsulation and source code organization.

Summary

By this point, the game engine is simple and supports only the initialization of WebGL and the drawing of one colored square. However, through the projects in this chapter, you have gained experience with the techniques required to build an excellent foundation for the game engine. You have also structured the source code to support further complexity with limited modification to the existing code base, and you are now ready to further encapsulate the functionality of the game engine to facilitate additional features. The next chapter will focus on building a proper framework in the game engine to support more flexible and configurable drawings.

CHAPTER 3

Drawing Objects in the World

After completing this chapter, you will be able to

- Create and draw multiple rectangular objects
- Control the position, size, rotation, and color of the created rectangular objects
- Define a coordinate system to draw from
- Define a target subarea on the canvas to draw to
- Work with abstract representations of Renderable objects, transformation operators, and cameras

Introduction

Ideally, a video game engine should provide proper abstractions to support designing and building games in meaningful contexts. For example, when designing a soccer game, instead of a single square with a fixed ±1.0 drawing range, a game engine should provide proper utilities to support designs in the context of players running on a soccer field. This high-level abstraction requires the encapsulation of basic operations with data hiding and meaningful functions for setting and receiving the desired results.

While this book is about building abstractions for a game engine, this chapter focuses on creating the fundamental abstractions to support drawing. Based on the soccer game example, the support for drawing in an effective game engine would likely include the ability to easily create the soccer players, control their size and orientations, and allow them to be moved and drawn on the soccer field. Additionally, to support

© Kelvin Sung, Jebediah Pavleas, Matthew Munson, and Jason Pace 2022
K. Sung et al., *Build Your Own 2D Game Engine and Create Great Web Games*,
https://doi.org/10.1007/978-1-4842-7377-7_3

proper presentation, the game engine must allow drawing to specific subregions on the canvas so that a distinct game status can be displayed at different subregions, such as the soccer field in one subregion and player statistics and scores in another subregion.

This chapter identifies proper abstraction entities for the basic drawing operations, introduces operators that are based on foundational mathematics to control the drawing, overviews the WebGL tools for configuring the canvas to support subregion drawing, defines JavaScript classes to implement these concepts, and integrates these implementations into the game engine while maintaining the organized structure of the source code.

Encapsulating Drawing

Although the ability to draw is one of the most fundamental functionalities of a game engine, the details of how drawings are implemented are generally a distraction to gameplay programming. For example, it is important to create, control the locations of, and draw soccer players in a soccer game. However, exposing the details of how each player is actually defined (by a collection of vertices that form triangles) can quickly overwhelm and complicate the game development process. Thus, it is important for a game engine to provide a well-defined abstraction interface for drawing operations.

With a well-organized source code structure, it is possible to gradually and systematically increase the complexity of the game engine by implementing new concepts with localized changes to the corresponding folders. The first task is to expand the engine to support the encapsulation of drawing such that it becomes possible to manipulate drawing operations as a logical entity or as an object that can be rendered.

Note   In the context of computer graphics and video games, the word *render* refers to the process of changing the color of pixels corresponding to an abstract representation. For example, in the previous chapter, you learned how to render a square.

The Renderable Objects Project

This project introduces the Renderable class to encapsulate the drawing operation. Over the next few projects, you will learn more supporting concepts to refine the implementation of the Renderable class such that multiple instances can be created and manipulated. Figure 3-1 shows the output of running the Renderable Objects project. The source code to this project is defined in the chapter3/3.1.renderable_objects folder.

Figure 3-1. *Running the Renderable Objects project*

The goals of the project are as follows:

- To reorganize the source code structure in anticipation for functionality increases

- To support game engine internal resource sharing

- To introduce a systematic interface for the game developer via the index.js file

- To begin the process of building a class to encapsulate drawing operations by first abstracting the related drawing functionality

- To demonstrate the ability to create multiple `Renderable` objects

Source Code Structure Reorganization

Before introducing additional functionality to the game engine, it is important to recognize some shortfalls of the engine source code organization from the previous project. In particular, take note of the following:

1. The `core.js` source code file contains the WebGL interface, engine initialization, and drawing functionalities. These should be modularized to support the anticipated increase in system complexity.

2. A system should be defined to support the sharing of game engine internal resources. For example, `SimpleShader` is responsible for interfacing from the game engine to the GLSL shader compiled fromthesimple_vs.glslandsimple_fs.glslsourcecodefiles.Since there is only one copy of the compiled shader, there only needs to be a single instance of the `SimpleShader` object. The game engine should facilitate this by allowing the convenient creation and sharing of the object.

3. As you have experienced, the JavaScript `export` statement can be an excellent tool for hiding detailed implementations. However, it is also true that determining which classes or modules to import from a number of files can be confusing and overwhelming in a large and complex system, such as the game engine you are about to develop. An easy to work with and systematic interface should be provided such that the game developer, users of the game engine, can be insulated from these details.

In the following section, the game engine source code will be reorganized to address these issues.

Define a WebGL-Specific Module

The first step in source code reorganization is to recognize and isolate functionality that is internal and should not be accessible by the clients of the game engine:

1. In your project, under the src/engine folder, create a new folder and name it core. Form this point forward, this folder will contain all functionality that is internal to the game engine and will not be exported to the game developers.

2. You can cut and paste the vertex_buffer.js source code file from the previous project into the src/engine/core folder. The details of the primitive vertices are internal to the game engine and should not be visible or accessible by the clients of the game engine.

3. Create a new source code file in the src/engine/core folder, name it gl.js, and define WebGL's initialization and access methods:

```
"use strict"

let mCanvas = null;
let mGL = null;

function get() { return mGL; }

function init(htmlCanvasID) {
    mCanvas = document.getElementById(htmlCanvasID);
    if (mCanvas == null)
        throw new Error("Engine init [" +
                        htmlCanvasID + "] HTML element id not found");

    // Get standard or experimental webgl and binds to the Canvas area
    // store the results to the instance variable mGL
    mGL = mCanvas.getContext("webgl2") ||
        mCanvas.getContext("experimental-webgl2");
```

```
    if (mGL === null) {
        document.write("<br><b>WebGL 2 is not supported!</b>");
        return;
    }
}

export {init, get}
```

Notice that the init() function is identical to the initWebGL() function in core.js from the previous project. Unlike the previous core.js source code file, the gl.js file contains only WebGL-specific functionality.

Define a System for Internal Shader Resource Sharing

Since only a single copy of the GLSL shader is created and compiled from the simple_vs.glsl and simple_fs.glsl source code files, only a single copy of SimpleShader object is required within the game engine to interface with the compiled shader. You will now create a simple resource sharing system to support future additions of different types of shaders.

Create a new source code file in the src/engine/core folder, name it shader_resources.js, and define the creation and accessing methods for SimpleShader.

Note   Recall from the previous chapter that the SimpleShader class is defined in the simple_shader.js file which is located in the src/engine folder. Remember to copy all relevant source code files from the previous project.

```
"use strict";

import SimpleShader from "../simple_shader.js";

// Simple Shader
let kSimpleVS = "src/glsl_shaders/simple_vs.glsl"; // to VertexShader
let kSimpleFS = "src/glsl_shaders/simple_fs.glsl"; // to FragmentShader
let mConstColorShader = null;
```

```
function createShaders() {
    mConstColorShader = new SimpleShader(kSimpleVS, kSimpleFS);
}

function init() {
    createShaders();
}
function getConstColorShader() { return mConstColorShader; }

export {init, getConstColorShader}
```

Note   Variables referencing constant values have names that begin with lowercase "k", as in kSimpleVS.

Since the shader_resources module is located in the src/engine/core folder, the defined shaders are shared within and cannot be accessed from the clients of the game engine.

Define an Access File for the Game Developer

You will define an engine access file, index.js, to implement the fundamental functions of the game engine and to serve a similar purpose as a C++ header file, the import statement in Java, or the using statement in C#, where functionality can be readily accessed without in-depth knowledge of the engine source code structure. That is, by importing index.js, the client can access all the components and functionality from the engine to build their game.

1. Create index.js file in the src/engine folder; import from gl. js, vertex_buffer.js, and shader_resources.js; and define the init() function to initialize the game engine by calling the corresponding init() functions of the three imported modules:

```
// local to this file only
import * as glSys from "./core/gl.js";
import * as vertexBuffer from "./core/vertex_buffer.js";
import * as shaderResources from "./core/shader_resources.js";
```

```
// general engine utilities
function init(htmlCanvasID) {
    glSys.init(htmlCanvasID);
    vertexBuffer.init();
    shaderResources.init();
}
```

2. Define the clearCanvas() function to clear the drawing canvas:

```
function clearCanvas(color) {
    let gl = glSys.get();
    gl.clearColor(color[0], color[1], color[2], color[3]);
    gl.clear(gl.COLOR_BUFFER_BIT); // clear to the color set
}
```

3. Now, to properly expose the Renderable symbol to the clients of the game engine, make sure to import such that the class can be properly exported. The Renderable class will be introduced in details in the next section.

```
// general utilities
import Renderable from "./renderable.js";
```

4. Finally, remember to export the proper symbols and functionality for the clients of the game engine:

```
export  default {
    // Util classes
    Renderable,

    // functions
    init, clearCanvas
}
```

With proper maintenance and update of this index.js file, the clients of your game engine, the game developers, can simply import from the index.js file to gain access to the entire game engine functionality without any knowledge of the source code structure. Lastly, notice that the glSys, vertexBuffer, and shaderResources internal functionality defined in the engine/src/core folder are not exported by index.js and thus are not accessible to the game developers.

The Renderable Class

At last, you are ready to define the Renderable class to encapsulate the drawing process:

1. Define the Renderable class in the game engine by creating a new source code file in the src/engine folder, and name the file renderable.js.

2. Open renderable.js, import from gl.js and shader_resources.js, and define the Renderable class with a constructor to initialize a reference to a shader and a color instance variable. Notice that the shader is a reference to the shared SimpleShader instance defined in shader_resources.

```
import * as glSys from "./core/gl.js";
import * as shaderResources from "./core/shader_resources.js";

class Renderable {
    constructor() {
        this.mShader = shaderResources.getConstColorShader();
        this.mColor = [1, 1, 1, 1]; // color of pixel
    }
    ... implementation to follow ...
}
```

3. Define a draw() function for Renderable:

```
draw() {
    let gl = glSys.get();
    this.mShader.activate(this.mColor);
    gl.drawArrays(gl.TRIANGLE_STRIP, 0, 4);
}
```

Notice that it is important to activate the proper GLSL shader in the GPU by calling the activate() function before sending the vertices with the gl.drawArrays() function.

4. Define the getter and setter functions for the color instance variable:

```
setColor(color) {this.mColor = color; }
getColor() { return this.mColor; }
```

71

5. Export the Renderable symbol as default to ensure this identifier
    cannot be renamed:

```
export default Renderable;
```

Though this example is simple, it is now possible to create and draw multiple instances of the Renderable objects with different colors.

Testing the Renderable Object

To test Renderable objects in MyGame, white and red instances are created and drawn as follows:

```
// import from engine/index.js for all engine symbols
import engine from "../engine/index.js";

class MyGame {
    constructor(htmlCanvasID) {

        // Step A: Initialize the webGL Context
        engine.init(htmlCanvasID);

        // Step B: Create the Renderable objects:
        this.mWhiteSq = new engine.Renderable();
        this.mWhiteSq.setColor([1, 1, 1, 1]);
        this.mRedSq = new engine.Renderable();
        this.mRedSq.setColor([1, 0, 0, 1]);

        // Step C: Draw!
        engine.clearCanvas([0, 0.8, 0, 1]);  // Clear the canvas

        // Step C1: Draw Renderable objects with the white shader
        this.mWhiteSq.draw();

        // Step C2: Draw Renderable objects with the red shader
        this.mRedSq.draw();
    }
}
```

Notice that the import statement is modified to import from the engine access file, index.js. Additionally, the MyGame constructor is modified to include the following steps:

1. Step A initializes the engine.

2. Step B creates two instances of Renderable and sets the colors of the objects accordingly.

3. Step C clears the canvas; steps C1 and C2 simply call the respective draw() functions of the white and red squares. Although both of the squares are drawn, for now, you are only able to see the last of the drawn squares in the canvas. Please refer to the following discussion for the details.

Observations

Run the project and you will notice that only the red square is visible! What happens is that both of the squares are drawn to the same location. Being the same size, the two squares simply overlap perfectly. Since the red square is drawn last, it overwrites all the pixels of the white square. You can verify this by commenting out the drawing of the red square (comment out the line mRedSq.draw()) and rerunning the project. An interesting observation to make is that objects that appear in the front are drawn last (the red square). You will take advantage of this observation much later when working with transparency.

This simple observation leads to your next task—to allow multiple instances of Renderable to be visible at the same time. Each instance of Renderable object needs to support the ability to be drawn at different locations, with different sizes and orientations so that they do not overlap one another.

Transforming a Renderable Object

A mechanism is required to manipulate the position, size, and orientation of a Renderable object. Over the next few projects, you will learn about how matrix transformations can be used to translate or move an object's position, scale the size of an object, and change the orientation or rotate an object on the canvas. These operations are the most intuitive ones for object manipulations. However, before the implementation of transformation matrices, a quick review of the operations and capabilities of matrices is required.

Matrices as Transform Operators

Before we begin, it is important to recognize that matrices and transformations are general topic areas in mathematics. The following discussion does not attempt to include a comprehensive coverage of these subjects. Instead, the focus is on a small collection of relevant concepts and operators from the perspective of what the game engine requires. In this way, the coverage is on how to utilize the operators and not the theories. If you are interested in the specifics of matrices and how they relate to computer graphics, please refer to the discussion in Chapter 1 where you can learn more about these topics by delving into relevant books on linear algebra and computer graphics.

A matrix is an m rows by n columns 2D array of numbers. For the purposes of this game engine, you will be working exclusively with 4×4 matrices. While a 2D game engine could get by with 3×3 matrices, a 4×4 matrix is used to support features that will be introduced in the later chapters. Among the many powerful applications, 4×4 matrices can be constructed as transform operators for vertex positions. The most important and intuitive of these operators are the translation, scaling, rotation, and identity operators.

- The translation operator T(tx,ty), as illustrated in Figure 3-2, translates or moves a given vertex position from (x, y) to (x+tx, y+ty). Notice that T(0,0) does not change the value of a given vertex position and is a convenient initial value for accumulating translation operations.

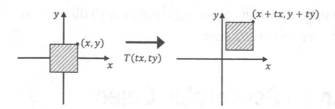

Figure 3-2. *Translating a square by T(tx, ty)*

- The scaling operator S(sx, sy), as illustrated by Figure 3-3, scales or resizes a given vertex position from (x, y) to (x×sx, y×sy). Notice that S(1, 1) does not change the value of a given vertex position and is a convenient initial value for accumulating scaling operations.

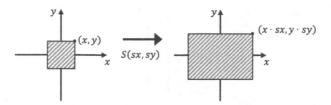

Figure 3-3. *Scaling a square by S(sx, sy)*

- The rotation operator R(θ), as illustrated in Figure 3-4, rotates a given vertex position with respect to the origin.

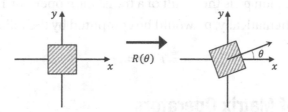

Figure 3-4. *Rotating a square by R(θ)*

In the case of rotation, R(0) does not change the value of a given vertex and is the convenient initial value for accumulating rotation operations. The values for θ are typically expressed in radians (and not degrees).

- The identity operator I does not affect a given vertex position. This operator is mostly used for initialization.

As an example, a 4×4 identity matrix looks like the following:

$$I = \begin{bmatrix} 1 & 0 & 0 & 0 \\ 0 & 1 & 0 & 0 \\ 0 & 0 & 1 & 0 \\ 0 & 0 & 0 & 1 \end{bmatrix}$$

Mathematically, a matrix transform operator operates on a vertex through a matrix-vector multiplication. To support this operation, a vertex position $p = (x, y, z)$ must be represented as a 4x1 vector as follows:

$$p = \begin{bmatrix} x \\ y \\ z \\ 1 \end{bmatrix}$$

Note   The z component is the third dimension, or the depth information, of a vertex position. In most cases, you should leave the z component to be 0.

For example, if position p' is the result of a translation operator T operating on the vertex position p, mathematically, p' would be computed by the following:

$$p' = T \times p = Tp$$

Concatenation of Matrix Operators

Multiple matrix operators can be *concatenated*, or combined, into a single operator while retaining the same transformation characteristics as the original operators. For example, you may want to apply the scaling operator S, followed by the rotation operator R, and finally the translation operator T, on a given vertex position, or to compute p' with the following:

$$p' = TRSp$$

Alternatively, you can compute a new operator M by concatenating all the transform operators, as follows:

$$M = TRS$$

And then operate M on vertex position p, as follows, to produce identical results:

$$p' = Mp$$

The M operator is a convenient and efficient way to record and reapply the results of multiple operators.

Finally, notice that when working with transformation operators, the order of operation is important. For example, a scaling operation followed by a translation operation is in general different from a translation followed by a scaling or, in general:

$$ST \neq TS$$

The glMatrix Library

The details of matrix operators and operations are nontrivial to say the least. Developing a complete matrix library is time-consuming and not the focus of this book. Fortunately, there are many well-developed and well-documented matrix libraries available in the public domain. The glMatrix library is one such example. To integrate this library into your source code structure, follow these steps:

1. Create a new folder under the src folder, and name the new folder lib.

2. Go to http://glMatrix.net, as shown in Figure 3-5, and download, unzip, and store the resulting glMatrix.js source file into the new lib folder.

Figure 3-5. *Downloading the glMatrix library*

All projects in this book are based on glMatrix version 2.2.2.

3. As a library that must be accessible by both the game engine and
    the client game developer, you will load the source file in the
    main index.html by adding the following before the loading of
    my_game.js:

```
<!-- external library -->
<script type="text/javascript" src="src/lib/gl-matrix.js"></script>

<!-- our game -->
<script type="module" src="./src/my_game/my_game.js"></script>
```

The Matrix Transform Project

This project introduces and demonstrates how to use transformation matrices as
operators to manipulate the position, size, and orientation of Renderable objects drawn
on the canvas. In this way, a Renderable can now be drawn to any location, with any
size and any orientation. Figure 3-6 shows the output of running the Matrix Transform
project. The source code to this project is defined in the chapter3/3.2.matrix_
transform folder.

Figure 3-6. *Running the Matrix Transform project*

The goals of the project are as follows:

- To introduce transformation matrices as operators for drawing a Renderable

- To understand how to work with the transform operators to manipulate a Renderable

Modify the Vertex Shader to Support Transforms

As discussed, matrix transform operators operate on vertices of geometries. The vertex shader is where all vertices are passed in from the WebGL context and is the most convenient location to apply the transform operations.

You will continue working with the previous project to support the transformation operator in the vertex shader:

1.   Edit `simple_vs.glsl` to declare a uniform 4×4 matrix:

Note   Recall from the discussion in Chapter 2 that glsl files contain OpenGL Shading Language (GLSL) instructions that will be loaded to and executed by the GPU. You can find out more about GLSL by referring to the WebGL and OpenGL references provided at the end of Chapter 1.

```
// to transform the vertex position
uniform mat4 uModelXformMatrix;
```

Recall that the `uniform` keyword in a GLSL shader declares a variable with values that do not change for all the vertices within that shader. In this case, the `uModelXformMatrix` variable is the transform operator for all the vertices.

Note   GLSL uniform variable names always begin with lowercase "u", as in `uModelXformMatrix`.

---

2.   In the `main()` function, apply the `uModelXformMatrix` to the currently referenced vertex position:

```
gl_Position = uModelXformMatrix * vec4(aVertexPosition, 1.0);
```

Notice that the operation follows directly from the discussion on matrix transformation operators. The reason for converting `aVertexPosition` to a `vec4` is to support the matrix-vector multiplication.

With this simple modification, the vertex positions of the unit square will be operated on by the `uModelXformMatrix` operator, and thus the square can be drawn to different locations. The task now is to set up `SimpleShader` to load the appropriate transformation operator into `uModelXformMatrix`.

Modify SimpleShader to Load the Transform Operator

Follow these steps:

1. Edit `simple_shader.js` and add an instance variable to hold the reference to the uModelXformMatrix matrix in the vertex shader:

```
this.mModelMatrixRef = null;
```

2. At the end of the `SimpleShader` constructor under step E, after setting the reference to uPixelColor, add the following code to initialize this reference:

```
// Step E: Gets a reference to uniform variables in fragment shader
this.mPixelColorRef = gl.getUniformLocation(
                    this.mCompiledShader, "uPixelColor");
this.mModelMatrixRef = gl.getUniformLocation(
                    this.mCompiledShader, "uModelXformMatrix");
```

3. Modify the `activate()` function to receive a second parameter, and load the value to uModelXformMatrix via mModelMatrixRef:

```
activate(pixelColor, trsMatrix) {
    let gl = glSys.get();
    gl.useProgram(this.mCompiledShader);

        ... identical to previous code ...

    // load uniforms
    gl.uniform4fv(this.mPixelColorRef, pixelColor);
    gl.uniformMatrix4fv(this.mModelMatrixRef, false, trsMatrix);
}
```

The `gl.uniformMatrix4fv()` function copies the values from `trsMatrix` to the vertex shader location identified by `this.mModelMatrixRef` or the uModelXfromMatrix operator in the vertex shader. The name of the variable, `trsMatrix`, signifies that it should be a matrix operator containing the concatenated result of translation (T), rotation (R), and scaling (S) or TRS.

Modify Renderable Class to Set the Transform Operator

Edit renderable.js to modify the draw() function to receive and to forward a transform operator to the mShader.activate() function to be loaded to the GLSL shader:

```
draw(trsMatrix) {
    let gl = glSys.get();
    this.mShader.activate(this.mColor, trsMatrix);
    gl.drawArrays(gl.TRIANGLE_STRIP, 0, 4);
}
```

In this way, when the vertices of the unit square are processed by the vertex shader, the uModelXformMatrix will contain the proper operator for transforming the vertices and thus drawing the square at the desired location, size, and rotation.

Testing the Transforms

Now that the game engine supports transformation, you need to modify the client code to draw with it:

1. Edit my_game.js; after step C, instead of activating and drawing the two squares, replace steps C1 and C2 to create a new identity transform operator, trsMatrix:

```
// create a new identify transform operator
let trsMatrix = mat4.create();
```

2. Compute the concatenation of matrices to a single transform operator that implements translation (T), rotation (R), and scaling (S) or TRS:

```
// Step D: compute the white square transform
mat4.translate(trsMatrix, trsMatrix, vec3.fromValues(-0.25, 0.25, 0.0));
mat4.rotateZ(trsMatrix, trsMatrix, 0.2);       // rotation is in radian
mat4.scale(trsMatrix, trsMatrix, vec3.fromValues(1.2, 1.2, 1.0));

// Step E: draw the white square with the computed transform
this.mWhiteSq.draw(trsMatrix);
```

Step D concatenates T(-0.25, 0.25), moving to the left and up; with R(0.2), rotating clockwise by 0.2 radians; and S(1.2, 1.2), increasing size by 1.2 times. The concatenation order applies the scaling operator first, followed by rotation, with translation being the last operation, or trsMatrix=TRS. In step E, the Renderable object is drawn with the trsMatrix operator or a 1.2×1.2 white rectangle slightly rotated and located somewhat to the upper left from the center.

3. Finally, step F defines the trsMatrix operator that to draw a 0.4×0.4 square that is rotated by 45 degrees and located slightly toward the lower right from the center of the canvas, and step G draws the red square:

```
// Step F: compute the red square transform
mat4.identity(trsMatrix); // restart
mat4.translate(trsMatrix, trsMatrix, vec3.fromValues(0.25, -0.25, 0.0));
mat4.rotateZ(trsMatrix, trsMatrix, -0.785);    // about -45-degrees
mat4.scale(trsMatrix, trsMatrix, vec3.fromValues(0.4, 0.4, 1.0));

// Step G: draw the red square with the computed transform
this.mRedSq.draw(trsMatrix);
```

Observations

Run the project, and you should see the corresponding white and red rectangles drawn on the canvas. You can gain some intuition of the operators by changing the values; for example, move and scale the squares to different locations with different sizes. You can try changing the order of concatenation by moving the corresponding line of code; for example, move mat4.scale() to before mat4.translate(). You will notice that, in general, the transformed results do not correspond to your intuition. In this book, you will always apply the transformation operators in the fixed TRS order. This ordering of transformation operators corresponds to typical human intuition. The TRS operation order is followed by most, if not all, graphical APIs and applications that support transformation operations.

Now that you understand how to work with the matrix transformation operators, it is time to abstract them and hide their details.

Encapsulating the Transform Operator

In the previous project, the transformation operators were computed directly based on the matrices. While the results were important, the computation involves distracting details and repetitive code. This project guides you to follow good coding practices to encapsulate the transformation operators by hiding the detailed computations with a class. In this way, you can maintain the modularity and accessibility of the game engine by supporting further expansion while maintaining programmability.

The Transform Objects Project

This project defines the Transform class to provide a logical interface for manipulating and hiding the details of working with the matrix transformation operators. Figure 3-7 shows the output of running the Matrix Transform project. Notice that the output of this project is identical to that from the previous project. The source code to this project is defined in the chapter3/3.3.transform_objects folder.

Figure 3-7. *Running the Transform Objects project*

The goals of the project are as follows:

- To create the Transform class to encapsulate the matrix transformation functionality

- To integrate the Transform class into the game engine

- To demonstrate how to work with Transform objects

The Transform Class

Continue working with the previous project:

1. Define the Transform class in the game engine by creating a new source code file in the src/engine folder, and name the file transform.js.

2. Define the constructor to initialize instance variables that correspond to the operators: mPosition for translation, mScale for scaling, and mRotationInRad for rotation.

```
class Transform {
    constructor() {
        this.mPosition = vec2.fromValues(0, 0);   // translation
        this.mScale = vec2.fromValues(1, 1);      // width (x), height (y)
        this.mRotationInRad = 0.0;                 // in radians!
    }
    ... implementation to follow ...
}
```

3. Add getters and setters for the values of each operator:

```
// Position getters and setters
setPosition(xPos, yPos) { this.setXPos(xPos); this.setYPos(yPos); }
getPosition() { return this.mPosition; }
// ... additional get and set functions for position not shown
// Size setters and getters
setSize(width, height) {
    this.setWidth(width);
    this.setHeight(height);
}
```

```
getSize() { return this.mScale; }
// ... additional get and set functions for size not shown
// Rotation getters and setters
setRotationInRad(rotationInRadians) {
    this.mRotationInRad = rotationInRadians;
    while (this.mRotationInRad > (2 * Math.PI)) {
        this.mRotationInRad -= (2 * Math.PI);
    }
}

setRotationInDegree(rotationInDegree) {
    this.setRotationInRad(rotationInDegree * Math.PI / 180.0);
}
// ... additional get and set functions for rotation not shown
```

4. Define the getTRSMatrix() function to compute and return the concatenated transform operator, TRS:

```
getTRSMatrix() {
    // Creates a blank identity matrix
    let matrix = mat4.create();

    // Step A: compute translation, for now z is always at 0.0
    mat4.translate(matrix, matrix,
                   vec3.fromValues(this.getXPos(), this.getYPos(), 0.0));
    // Step B: concatenate with rotation.
    mat4.rotateZ(matrix, matrix, this.getRotationInRad());
    // Step C: concatenate with scaling
    mat4.scale(matrix, matrix,
               vec3.fromValues(this.getWidth(), this.getHeight(), 1.0));

    return matrix;
}
```

This code is similar to steps D and F in my_game.js from the previous project. The concatenated operator TRS performs scaling first, followed by rotation, and lastly by translation.

5. Finally, remember to export the newly defined Transform class:

```
export default Transform;
```

The Transformable Renderable Class

By integrating the Transform class, a Renderable object can now have a position, size (scale), and orientation (rotation). This integration can be easily accomplished through the following steps:

1. Edit renderable.js and add a new instance variable to reference a Transform object in the constructor:

```
this.mXform = new Transform();      // transform operator for the object
```

2. Define an accessor for the transform operator:

```
getXform() { return this.mXform; }
```

3. Modify the draw() function to pass the trsMatrix operator of the mXform object to activate the shader before drawing the unit square:

```
draw() {
    let gl = glSys.get();
    this.mShader.activate(this.mColor, this.mXform.getTRSMatrix());
    gl.drawArrays(gl.TRIANGLE_STRIP, 0, 4);
}
```

With this simple modification, Renderable objects will be drawn with characteristics defined by the values of its own transformation operators.

Modify the Engine Access File to Export Transform

It is important to maintain the engine access file, index.js, up to date such that the newly defined Transform class can be accessed by the game developer:

1. Edit index.js; import from the newly define transform.js file:

```
// general utilities
import Transform from "./transform.js";
import Renderable from "./renderable.js";
```

2. Export Transform for client's access:

```
export default {
    // Util classes
    Transform, Renderable,

    // functions
    init, clearCanvas
}
```

Modify Drawing to Support Transform Object

To test the Transform and the improved Renderable classes, the MyGame constructor can be modified to set the transform operators in each of the Renderable objects accordingly:

```
// Step D: sets the white Renderable object's transform
this.mWhiteSq.getXform().setPosition(-0.25, 0.25);
this.mWhiteSq.getXform().setRotationInRad(0.2); // In Radians
this.mWhiteSq.getXform().setSize(1.2, 1.2);
// Step E: draws the white square (transform behavior in the object)
this.mWhiteSq.draw();

// Step F: sets the red square transform
this.mRedSq.getXform().setXPos(0.25); // alternative to setPosition
this.mRedSq.getXform().setYPos(-0.25);// setX/Y separately
this.mRedSq.getXform().setRotationInDegree(45);  // this is in Degree
this.mRedSq.getXform().setWidth(0.4); // alternative to setSize
this.mRedSq.getXform().setHeight(0.4);// set width/height separately
// Step G: draw the red square (transform in the object)
this.mRedSq.draw();
```

Run the project to observe identical output as from the previous project. You can now create and draw a `Renderable` at any location in the canvas, and the transform operator has now been properly encapsulated.

The Camera Transform and Viewports

When designing and building a video game, the game designers and programmers must be able to focus on the intrinsic logic and presentation. To facilitate these aspects, it is important that the designers and programmers can formulate solutions in a convenient dimension and space.

For example, continuing with the soccer game idea, consider the task of creating a soccer field. How big is the field? What is the unit of measurement? In general, when building a game world, it is often easier to design a solution by referring to the real world. In the real world, soccer fields are around 100 meters long. However, in the game or graphics world, units are arbitrary. So, a simple solution may be to create a field that is 100 units in meters and a coordinate space where the origin is located at the center of the soccer field. In this way, opposing sides of the fields can simply be determined by the sign of the x value, and drawing a player at location (0, 1) would mean drawing the player 1 meter to the right from the center of the soccer field.

A contrasting example would be when building a chess-like board game. It may be more convenient to design the solution based on a unitless n×n grid with the origin located at the lower-left corner of the board. In this scenario, drawing a piece at location (0, 1) would mean drawing the piece at the location one cell or unit toward the right from the lower-left corner of the board. As will be discussed, the ability to define specific coordinate systems is often accomplished by computing and working with a matrix representing the view from a camera.

In all cases, to support a proper presentation of the game, it is important to allow the programmer to control the drawing of the contents to any location on the canvas. For example, you may want to draw the soccer field and players to one subregion and draw a mini-map into another subregion. These axis-aligned rectangular drawing areas or subregions of the canvas are referred to as viewports.

In this section, you will learn about coordinate systems and how to use the matrix transformation as a tool to define a drawing area that conforms to the fixed ±1 drawing range of the WebGL.

Coordinate Systems and Transformations

A 2D coordinate system uniquely identifies every position on a 2D plane. All projects in this book follow the Cartesian coordinate system where positions are defined according to perpendicular distances from a reference point known as the *origin*, as illustrated in Figure 3-8. The perpendicular directions for measuring the distances are known as the *major axes*. In 2D space, these are the familiar x and y axes.

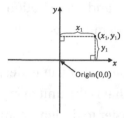

Figure 3-8. *Working with a 2D Cartesian coordinate system*

Modeling and Normalized Device Coordinate Systems

So far in this book, you have experience with two distinct coordinate systems. The first is the coordinate system that defines the vertices for the 1×1 square in the vertex buffer. This is referred to as the Modeling Coordinate System, which defines the Model Space. The Model Space is unique for each geometric object, as in the case of the unit square. The Model Space is defined to describe the geometry of a single model. The second coordinate system that you have worked with is the one that WebGL draws to, where the x-/y-axis ranges are bounded to ±1.0. This is known as the Normalized Device Coordinate (NDC) System. As you have experienced, WebGL always draws to the NDC space and that the contents in the ±1.0 range cover all the pixels in the canvas.

   The Modeling transform, typically defined by a matrix transformation operator, is the operation that transforms geometries from its Model Space into another coordinate space that is convenient for drawing. In the previous project, the `uModelXformMatrix` variable in `simple_vs.glsl` is the Modeling transform. As illustrated in Figure 3-9, in that case, the Modeling transform transformed the unit square into the WebGL's NDC space. The rightmost arrow annotated with the *Fixed Mapping* label in Figure 3-9 that points from *WebGL NDC* to *Canvas Coordinates* signifies that WebGL always displays the entire content of the NDC space in the canvas.

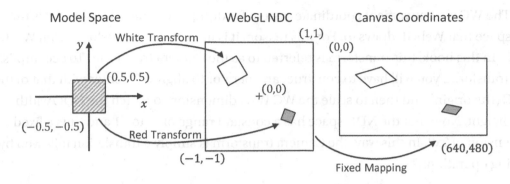

Figure 3-9. *Transforming the square from Model to NDC space*

The World Coordinate System

Although it is possible to draw to any location with the Modeling transform, the disproportional scaling that draws squares as rectangles is still a problem. In addition, the fixed -1.0 and 1.0 NDC space is not a convenient coordinate space for designing games. The World Coordinate (WC) System describes a convenient World Space that resolves these issues. For convenience and readability, in the rest of this book, WC will also be used to refer to the World Space that is defined by a specific World Coordinate System.

As illustrated in Figure 3-10, with a WC instead of the fixed NDC space, Modeling transforms can transform models into a convenient coordinate system that lends itself to game designs. For the soccer game example, the World Space dimension can be the size of the soccer field. As in any Cartesian coordinate system, the WC system is defined by a reference position and its width and height. The reference position can either be the lower-left corner or the center of the WC.

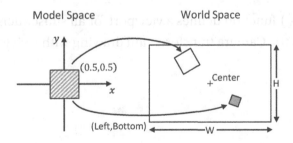

Figure 3-10. *Working with a World Coordinate (WC) System*

The WC is a convenient coordinate system for designing games. However, it is not the space that WebGL draws to. For this reason, it is important to transform from WC to NDC. In this book, this transform is referred to as the Camera transform. To accomplish this transform, you will have to construct an operator to align WC center with that of the NDC (the origin) and then to scale the WC WxH dimension to match the NDC width and height. Note that the NDC space has a constant range of -1 to +1 and thus a fixed dimension of 2x2. In this way, the Camera transform is simply a translation followed by a scaling operation:

$$M = S\left(\frac{2}{W}, \frac{2}{H}\right) T\left(-center.x, -center.y\right)$$

In this case, (center.x, center.y) and WxH are the center and the dimension of the WC system.

The Viewport

A viewport is an area to be drawn to. As you have experienced, by default, WebGL defines the entire canvas to be the viewport for drawing. Conveniently, WebGL provides a function to override this default behavior:

```
gl.viewport(
    x,      // x position of bottom-left corner of the area to be drawn
    y,      // y position of bottom-left corner of the area to be drawn
    width, // width of the area to be drawn
    height // height of the area to be drawn
);
```

The gl.viewport() function defines a viewport for all subsequent drawings. Figure 3-11 illustrates the Camera transform and drawing with a viewport.

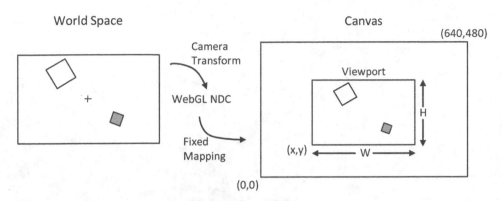

Figure 3-11. *Working with the WebGL viewport*

The Camera Transform and Viewport Project

This project demonstrates how to use the Camera transform to draw from any desired coordinate location to any subregion of the canvas or a viewport. Figure 3-12 shows the output of running the Camera Transform and Viewport project. The source code to this project is defined in the `chapter3/3.4.camera_transform_and_viewport` folder.

Figure 3-12. *Running the Camera Transform and Viewport project*

The goals of the project are as follows:

- To understand the different coordinate systems

- To experience working with a WebGL viewport to define and draw to different subregions within the canvas

- To understand the Camera transform

- To begin drawing to the user-defined World Coordinate System

You are now ready to modify the game engine to support the Camera transform to define your own WC and the corresponding viewport for drawing. The first step is to modify the shaders to support a new transform operator.

Modify the Vertex Shader to Support the Camera Transform

Relatively minor changes are required to add the support for the Camera transform:

1. Edit `simple_vs.glsl` to add a new `uniform` matrix operator to represent the Camera transform:

```
uniform mat4 uCameraXformMatrix;
```

2. Make sure to apply the operator on the vertex positions in the vertex shader program:

```
gl_Position = uCameraXformMatrix *
              uModelXformMatrix *
              vec4(aVertexPosition, 1.0);
```

Recall that the order of matrix operations is important. In this case, the uModelXformMatrix first transforms the vertex positions from Model Space to WC, and then the uCameraXformMatrix transforms from WC to NDC. The order of uModelxformMatrix and uCameraXformMatrix cannot be switched.

Modify SimpleShader to Support the Camera Transform

The SimpleShader object must be modified to access and pass the Camera transform matrix to the vertex shader:

1. Edit `simple_shader.js` and, in the constructor, add an instance variable for storing the reference to the Camera transform operator in `simple_vs.glsl`:

```
this.mCameraMatrixRef = null;
```

2. At the end of the SimpleShader constructor, retrieve the reference to the Camera transform operator, uCameraXformMatrix, after retrieving those for the uModelXformMatrix and uPixelColor:

```
// Step E: Gets reference to uniform variables in fragment shader
this.mPixelColorRef = gl.getUniformLocation(
                    this.mCompiledShader, "uPixelColor");
```

```
this.mModelMatrixRef = gl.getUniformLocation(
                        this.mCompiledShader, "uModelXformMatrix");
this.mCameraMatrixRef = gl.getUniformLocation(
                        this.mCompiledShader, "uCameraXformMatrix");
```

3. Modify the activate function to receive a Camera transform matrix and pass it to the shader:

```
activate(pixelColor, trsMatrix, cameraMatrix) {
    let gl = glSys.get();
    gl.useProgram(this.mCompiledShader);

    ... identical to previous code ...

    // load uniforms
    gl.uniform4fv(this.mPixelColorRef, pixelColor);
    gl.uniformMatrix4fv(this.mModelMatrixRef, false, trsMatrix);
    gl.uniformMatrix4fv(this.mCameraMatrixRef, false, cameraMatrix);
}
```

As you have seen previously, the gl.uniformMatrix4fv() function copies the content of cameraMatrix to the uCameraXformMatrix operator.

Modify Renderable to Support the Camera Transform

Recall that shaders are activated in the draw() function of the Renderable class; as such, Renderable must also be modified to receive and pass cameraMatrix to activate the shader:

```
draw(cameraMatrix) {
    let gl = glSys.get();
    this.mShader.activate(this.mColor,
                          this.mXform.getTRSMatrix(), cameraMatrix);
    gl.drawArrays(gl.TRIANGLE_STRIP, 0, 4);
}
```

It is now possible to set up a WC for drawing and define a subarea in the canvas to draw to.

Design the Scene

As illustrated in Figure 3-13, for testing purposes, a World Space (WC) will be defined to be centered at (20, 60) with a dimension of 20×10. Two rotated squares, a 5x5 blue square and a 2×2 red square, will be drawn at the center of the WC. To verify the coordinate bounds, a 1×1 square with a distinct color will be drawn at each of the WC corners.

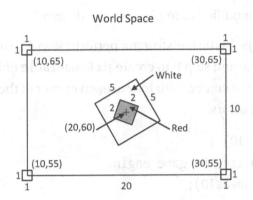

Figure 3-13. *Designing a WC to support drawing*

As illustrated in Figure 3-14, the WC will be drawn into a viewport with the lower-left corner located at (20, 40) and a dimension of 600×300 pixels. It is important to note that in order for squares to show up proportionally, the width-to-height aspect ratio of the WC must match that of the viewport. In this case, the WC has a 20:10 aspect ratio, and this 2:1 ratio matches that of the 600:300 of the viewport.

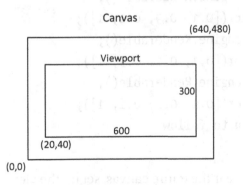

Figure 3-14. *Drawing the WC to the viewport*

Note that the details of the WC, centered at (20, 60) with dimension 20x10, and the viewport, lower-left corner at (20, 40) and dimension of 600x300, are chosen rather randomly. These are simply reasonable values that can demonstrate the correctness of the implementation.

Implement the Design

The MyGame class will be modified to implement the design:

1. Edit my_game.js. In the constructor, perform step A to initialize the game engine and step B to create six Renderable objects (two to be drawn at the center, with four at each corner of the WC) with corresponding colors.

```
constructor(htmlCanvasID) {
    // Step A: Initialize the game engine
    engine.init(htmlCanvasID);

    // Step B: Create the Renderable objects:
    this.mBlueSq = new engine.Renderable();
    this.mBlueSq.setColor([0.25, 0.25, 0.95, 1]);
    this.mRedSq = new engine.Renderable();
    this.mRedSq.setColor([1, 0.25, 0.25, 1]);
    this.mTLSq = new engine.Renderable();
    this.mTLSq.setColor([0.9, 0.1, 0.1, 1]);
    this.mTRSq = new engine.Renderable();
    this.mTRSq.setColor([0.1, 0.9, 0.1, 1]);
    this.mBRSq = new engine.Renderable();
    this.mBRSq.setColor([0.1, 0.1, 0.9, 1]);
    this.mBLSq = new engine.Renderable();
    this.mBLSq.setColor([0.1, 0.1, 0.1, 1]);
    ... implementation to follow ...
}
```

2. Steps C and D clear the entire canvas, set up the viewport, and clear the viewport to a different color:

```
// Step C: Clear the entire canvas first
engine.clearCanvas([0.9, 0.9, 0.9, 1]);
```

```
// get access to the gl connection to the GPU
let gl = glSys.get();

// Step D: Setting up Viewport
// Step D1: Set up the viewport: area on canvas to be drawn
gl.viewport(
    20,      // x position of bottom-left corner of the area to be drawn
    40,      // y position of bottom-left corner of the area to be drawn
    600,     // width of the area to be drawn
    300);    // height of the area to be drawn

// Step D2: set up the corresponding scissor area to limit clear area
gl.scissor(
    20,      // x position of bottom-left corner of the area to be drawn
    40,      // y position of bottom-left corner of the area to be drawn
    600,     // width of the area to be drawn
    300);    // height of the area to be drawn

// Step D3: enable scissor area, clear and then disable the scissor area
    gl.enable(gl.SCISSOR_TEST);
    engine.clearCanvas([0.8, 0.8, 0.8, 1.0]);  // clear the scissor area
    gl.disable(gl.SCISSOR_TEST);
```

Step D1 defines the viewport, and step D2 defines a corresponding scissor area. The scissor area tests and limits the area to be cleared. Since the testing involved in gl.scissor() is computationally expensive, it is disabled immediately after use.

3. Step E defines the WC with the Camera transform by concatenating the proper scaling and translation operators:

```
// Step E: Set up camera transform matrix
// assume camera position and dimension
let cameraCenter = vec2.fromValues(20, 60);
let wcSize = vec2.fromValues(20, 10);
let cameraMatrix = mat4.create();

// Step E1: after translation, scale to: -1 to 1: a 2x2 square at origin
mat4.scale(cameraMatrix, mat4.create(),
        vec3.fromValues(2.0/wcSize[0], 2.0/wcSize[1], 1.0));
```

```
// Step E2: first to perform is to translate camera center to origin
mat4.translate(cameraMatrix, cameraMatrix,
                  vec3.fromValues(-cameraCenter[0], -cameraCenter[1], 0));
```

Step E1 defines the scaling operator, S(2/W, 2/H), to scale the WC WxH to the NDC 2x2 dimension, and step E2 defines the translation operator, T(-center.x, -center.y), to align the WC with the NDC center. Note that the concatenation order implements the translation first followed by the scaling operator. This is precisely the Camera transform described earlier that defines the WC as follows:

    a. **Center**: (20,60)

    b. **Top-left corner**: (10, 65)

    c. **Top-right corner**: (30, 65)

    d. **Bottom-right corner**: (30, 55)

    e. **Bottom-left corner**: (10, 55)

Recall that the order of multiplication is important and that the order of scaling and translation operators cannot be swapped.

    4. Set up the slightly rotated 5x5 blue square at the center of WC, and draw with the Camera transform operator, cameraMatrix:

```
// Step F: Draw the blue square
// Center Blue, slightly rotated square
this.mBlueSq.getXform().setPosition(20, 60);
this.mBlueSq.getXform().setRotationInRad(0.2); // In Radians
this.mBlueSq.getXform().setSize(5, 5);
this.mBlueSq.draw(cameraMatrix);
```

    5. Now draw the other five squares, first the 2x2 in the center and one each at a corner of the WC:

```
// Step G: Draw the center and the corner squares
// center red square
this.mRedSq.getXform().setPosition(20, 60);
this.mRedSq.getXform().setSize(2, 2);
this.mRedSq.draw(cameraMatrix);
```

```
// top left
this.mTLSq.getXform().setPosition(10, 65);
this.mTLSq.draw(cameraMatrix);

// top right
this.mTRSq.getXform().setPosition(30, 65);
this.mTRSq.draw(cameraMatrix);

// bottom right
this.mBRSq.getXform().setPosition(30, 55);
this.mBRSq.draw(cameraMatrix);

// bottom left
this.mBLSq.getXform().setPosition(10, 55);
this.mBLSq.draw(cameraMatrix);
```

Run this project and observe the distinct colors at the four corners: the top left (mTLSq) in red, the top right (mTRSq) in green, the bottom right (mBRSq) in blue, and the bottom left (mBLSq) in dark gray. Change the locations of the corner squares to verify that the center positions of these squares are located in the bounds of the WC, and thus, only one quarter of the squares are actually visible. For example, set mBlSq to (12, 57) to observe the dark-gray square is actually four times the size. This observation verifies that the areas of the squares outside of the viewport/scissor area are clipped by WebGL.

Although lacking proper abstraction, it is now possible to define any convenient WC system and any rectangular subregions of the canvas for drawing. With the Modeling and Camera transformations, a game programmer can now design a game solution based on the semantic needs of the game and ignore the irrelevant WebGL NDC drawing range. However, the code in the MyGame class is complicated and can be distracting. As you have seen so far, the important next step is to define an abstraction to hide the details of Camera transform matrix computation.

The Camera

The Camera transform allows the definition of a WC. In the physical world, this is analogous to taking a photograph with the camera. The center of the viewfinder of your camera is the center of the WC, and the width and height of the world visible through the viewfinder are the dimensions of WC. With this analogy, the act of taking the photograph is equivalent to computing the drawing of each object in the WC. Lastly, the viewport describes the location to display the computed image.

The Camera Objects Project

This project demonstrates how to abstract the Camera transform and the viewport to hide the details of matrix computation and WebGL configurations. Figure 3-15 shows the output of running the Camera Objects project; notice the output of this project is identical to that from the previous project. The source code to this project is defined in the chapter3/3.5.camera_objects folder.

Figure 3-15. *Running the Camera Objects project*

The goals of the project are as follows:

- To define the Camera class to encapsulate the definition of WC and the viewport functionality

- To integrate the Camera class into the game engine

- To demonstrate how to work with a Camera object

The Camera Class

The Camera class must encapsulate the functionality defined by the scaling and translation operators in the MyGame constructor from the previous example. A clean and reusable class design should be completed with appropriate getter and setter functions.

1. Define the Camera class in the game engine by creating a new source file in the src/engine folder, and name the file camera.js.

2. Add the constructor for Camera:

```
class Camera {
    constructor(wcCenter, wcWidth, viewportArray) {
        // WC and viewport position and size
        this.mWCCenter = wcCenter;
        this.mWCWidth = wcWidth;
        this.mViewport = viewportArray;  // [x, y, width, height]

        // Camera transform operator
        this.mCameraMatrix = mat4.create();

        // background color
        this.mBGColor = [0.8, 0.8, 0.8, 1]; // RGB and Alpha
    }
    ... implementation to follow ...
}
```

The Camera defines the WC center and width, the viewport, the Camera transform operator, and a background color. Take note of the following:

    a.   The mWCCenter is a vec2 (vec2 is defined in the glMatrix library). It is a float array of two elements. The first element, index position 0, of vec2 is the x, and the second element, index position 1, is the y position.

    b.   The four elements of the viewportArray are the x and y positions of the lower-left corner and the width and height of the viewport, in that order. This compact representation of the viewport keeps the number of instance variables to a minimum and helps keep the Camera class manageable.

    c.   The mWCWidth is the width of the WC. To guarantee a matching aspect ratio between WC and the viewport, the height of the WC is always computed from the aspect ratio of the viewport and mWCWidth.

    d.   mBgColor is an array of four floats representing the red, green, blue, and alpha components of a color.

    3.   Outside of the Camera class definition, define enumerated indices for accessing the viewportArray:

```
const eViewport = Object.freeze({
    eOrgX: 0,
    eOrgY: 1,
    eWidth: 2,
    eHeight: 3
});
```

Note   Enumerated elements have names that begin with lowercase "e", as in eViewport and eOrgX.

---

4. Define the function to compute the WC height based on the aspect ratio of the viewport:

```
getWCHeight() {
    // viewportH/viewportW
    let ratio = this.mViewport[eViewport.eHeight] /
                this.mViewport[eViewport.eWidth];
    return this.getWCWidth() * ratio;
}
```

5. Add getters and setters for the instance variables:

```
setWCCenter(xPos, yPos) {
    this.mWCCenter[0] = xPos;
    this.mWCCenter[1] = yPos;
}
getWCCenter() { return this.mWCCenter; }
setWCWidth(width) { this.mWCWidth = width; }

setViewport(viewportArray) { this.mViewport = viewportArray; }
getViewport() { return this.mViewport; }

setBackgroundColor(newColor) { this.mBGColor = newColor; }
getBackgroundColor() { return this.mBGColor; }
```

6. Create a function to set the viewport and compute the Camera transform operator for this Camera:

```
// Initializes the camera to begin drawing
setViewAndCameraMatrix() {
    let gl = glSys.get();
    // Step A: Configure the viewport
    ... implementation to follow ...

    // Step B: compute the Camera Matrix
    ... implementation to follow ...
}
```

Note that this function is called setViewAndCameraMatrix() because it configures WebGL to draw to the desire viewport and sets up the Camera transform operator. The following explains the details of steps A and B.

7.   The code to configure the viewport under step A is as follows:

```
// Step A1: Set up the viewport: area on canvas to be drawn
gl.viewport(this.mViewport[0],  // x of bottom-left of area to be drawn
    this.mViewport[1],  // y of bottom-left of area to be drawn
    this.mViewport[2],  // width of the area to be drawn
    this.mViewport[3]); // height of the area to be drawn
// Step A2: set up the corresponding scissor area to limit the clear area
gl.scissor(this.mViewport[0], // x of bottom-left of area to be drawn
    this.mViewport[1], // y of bottom-left of area to be drawn
    this.mViewport[2], // width of the area to be drawn
    this.mViewport[3]);// height of the area to be drawn

// Step A3: set the color to be clear
gl.clearColor(this.mBGColor[0], this.mBGColor[1],
            this.mBGColor[2], this.mBGColor[3]);
// set the color to be cleared
// Step A4: enable scissor area, clear and then disable the scissor area
gl.enable(gl.SCISSOR_TEST);
gl.clear(gl.COLOR_BUFFER_BIT);
gl.disable(gl.SCISSOR_TEST);
```

Notice the similarity of these steps to the viewport setup code in MyGame of the previous example. The only difference is the proper references to the instance variables via this.

8.   The code to set up the Camera transform operator under step B is as follows:

```
// Step B: Compute the Camera Matrix
let center = this.getWCCenter();

// Step B1: after translation, scale to -1 to 1: 2x2 square at origin
mat4.scale(this.mCameraMatrix, mat4.create(),
        vec3.fromValues(2.0 / this.getWCWidth(),
                        2.0 / this.getWCHeight(), 1.0));
```

```
// Step B2: first translate camera center to the origin
mat4.translate(this.mCameraMatrix, this.mCameraMatrix,
               vec3.fromValues(-center[0], -center[1], 0));
```

Once again, this code is similar to the MyGame constructor from the previous example.

9. Define a function to access the computed camera matrix:

```
getCameraMatrix() { return this.mCameraMatrix; }
```

10. Finally, remember to export the newly defined Camera class:

```
export default Camera.
```

Modify Renderable to Support the Camera Class

The draw() function of the Renderable class must be modified to receive the newly defined Camera in order to access the computed camera matrix:

```
draw(camera) {
    let gl = glSys.get();
    this.mShader.activate(this.mColor, this.mXform.getTRSMatrix(),
                    camera.getCameraMatrix());
    gl.drawArrays(gl.TRIANGLE_STRIP, 0, 4);
}
```

Modify the Engine Access File to Export Camera

It is important to maintain the engine access file, index.js, up to date such that the newly defined Camera class can be accessed by the game developer:

1. Edit index.js; import from the newly define camera.js file:

```
// general utilities
import Camera from "./camera.js";
import Transform from "./transform.js";
import Renderable from "./renderable.js";
```

2. Export Camera for client's access:

```
export default {
    // Util classes
    Camera, Transform, Renderable,

    // functions
    init, clearCanvas
}
```

Test the Camera

With the Camera class properly defined, testing it from my_game.js is straightforward:

1. Edit my_game.js; after the initialization of the game engine in step A, create an instance of the Camera object with settings that define the WC and viewport from the previous project in step B:

```
class MyGame {
    constructor(htmlCanvasID) {
        // Step A: Initialize the game engine
        engine.init(htmlCanvasID);

        // Step B: Setup the camera
        this.mCamera = new engine.Camera(
            vec2.fromValues(20, 60),    // center of the WC
            20,                         // width of WC
            [20, 40, 600, 300]          // viewport:orgX, orgY, W, H
            );
        ... implementation to follow ...
}
```

2. Continue with the creation of the six Renderable objects and the clearing of the canvas in steps C and D:

```
// Step C: Create the Renderable objects:
this.mBlueSq = new engine.Renderable();
this.mBlueSq.setColor([0.25, 0.25, 0.95, 1]);
this.mRedSq = new engine.Renderable();
this.mRedSq.setColor([1, 0.25, 0.25, 1]);
```

```
this.mTLSq = new engine.Renderable();
this.mTLSq.setColor([0.9, 0.1, 0.1, 1]);
this.mTRSq = new engine.Renderable();
this.mTRSq.setColor([0.1, 0.9, 0.1, 1]);
this.mBRSq = new engine.Renderable();
this.mBRSq.setColor([0.1, 0.1, 0.9, 1]);
this.mBLSq = new engine.Renderable();
this.mBLSq.setColor([0.1, 0.1, 0.1, 1]);

// Step D: Clear the canvas
engine.clearCanvas([0.9, 0.9, 0.9, 1]);          // Clear the canvas
```

3. Now, call the setViewAndCameraMatrix() function of the Camera object in to configure the WebGL viewport and compute the camera matrix in step E, and draw all the Renderables using the Camera object in steps F and G.

```
// Step E: Starts the drawing by activating the camera
this.mCamera.setViewAndCameraMatrix();

// Step F: Draw the blue square
// Center Blue, slightly rotated square
this.mBlueSq.getXform().setPosition(20, 60);
this.mBlueSq.getXform().setRotationInRad(0.2); // In Radians
this.mBlueSq.getXform().setSize(5, 5);
this.mBlueSq.draw(this.mCamera);

// Step G: Draw the center and the corner squares
// center red square
this.mRedSq.getXform().setPosition(20, 60);
this.mRedSq.getXform().setSize(2, 2);
this.mRedSq.draw(this.mCamera);

// top left
this.mTLSq.getXform().setPosition(10, 65);
this.mTLSq.draw(this.mCamera);
```

```
// top right
this.mTRSq.getXform().setPosition(30, 65);
this.mTRSq.draw(this.mCamera);

// bottom right
this.mBRSq.getXform().setPosition(30, 55);
this.mBRSq.draw(this.mCamera);

// bottom left
this.mBLSq.getXform().setPosition(10, 55);
this.mBLSq.draw(this.mCamera);
```

The mCamera object is passed to the draw() function of the Renderable objects such that the Camera transform matrix operator can be retrieved and used to activate the shader.

Summary

In this chapter, you learned how to create a system that can support the drawing of many objects. The system is composed of three parts: the objects, the details of each object, and the display of the objects on the browser's canvas. The objects are encapsulated by the Renderable, which uses a Transform to capture its details—the position, size, and rotation. The particulars of displaying the objects are defined by the Camera, where objects at specific locations can be displayed at desirable subregions on the canvas.

You also learned that objects are all drawn relative to a World Space or WC, a convenient coordinate system. A WC is defined for scene compositions based on coordinate transformations. Lastly, the Camera transform is used to select which portion of the WC to actually display on the canvas within a browser. This can be achieved by defining an area that is viewable by the Camera and using the viewport functionality provided by WebGL.

As you built the drawing system, the game engine source code structure has been consistently refactored into abstracted and encapsulated components. In this way, the source code structure continues to support further expansion including additional functionality which will be discussed in the next chapter.

CHAPTER 4

Implementing Common Components of Video Games

After completing this chapter, you will be able to

- Control the position, size, and rotation of Renderable objects to construct complex movements and animations
- Receive keyboard input from the player to control and animate Renderable objects
- Work with asynchronous loading and unloading of external assets
- Define, load, and execute a simple game level from a scene file
- Change game levels by loading a new scene
- Work with sound clips for background music and audio cues

Introduction

In the previous chapters, a skeletal game engine was constructed to support basic drawing operations. Drawing is the first step to constructing your game engine because it allows you to observe the output while continuing to expand the game engine functionality. In this chapter, the two important mechanisms, interactivity and resource support, will be examined and added to the game engine. Interactivity allows the engine to receive and interpret player input, while resource support refers to the functionality of working with external files like the GLSL shader source code files, audio clips, and images.

© Kelvin Sung, Jebediah Pavleas, Matthew Munson, and Jason Pace 2022
K. Sung et al., *Build Your Own 2D Game Engine and Create Great Web Games*,
https://doi.org/10.1007/978-1-4842-7377-7_4

This chapter begins by introducing you to the game loop, a critical component that creates the sensation of real-time interaction and immediacy in nearly all video games. Based on the game loop foundation, player keyboard input will be supported via integrating the corresponding HTML5 functionality. A resource management infrastructure will be constructed from the ground up to support the efficient loading, storing, retrieving, and utilization of external files. Functionality for working with external text files (e.g., the GLSL shader source code files) and audio clips will be integrated with corresponding example projects. Additionally, game scene architecture will be derived to support the ability to work with multiple scenes and scene transitions, including scenes that are defined in external scene files. By the end of this chapter, your game engine will support player interaction via the keyboard, have the ability to provide audio feedback, and be able to transition between distinct game levels including loading a level from an external file.

The Game Loop

One of the most basic operations of any video game is the support of seemingly instantaneous interactions between the players' input and the graphical gaming elements. In reality, these interactions are implemented as a continuous running loop that receives and processes player input, updates the game state, and renders the game. This constantly running loop is referred to as the *game loop*.

To convey the proper sense of instantaneity, each cycle of the game loop must be completed within an average person's reaction time. This is often referred to as real time, which is the amount of time that is too short for humans to detect visually. Typically, real time can be achieved when the game loop is running at a rate of higher than 40–60 cycles in a second. Since there is usually one drawing operation in each game loop cycle, the rate of this cycle is also referred to as frames per second (FPS) or the frame rate. An FPS of 60 is a good target for performance. This is to say, your game engine must receive player input, update the game world, and then draw the game world all within 1/60th of a second!

The game loop itself, including the implementation details, is the most fundamental control structure for a game. With the main goal of maintaining real-time performance, the details of a game loop's operation are of no concern to the rest of the game engine. For this reason, the implementation of a game loop should be tightly encapsulated in the core of the game engine with its detailed operations hidden from other gaming elements.

Typical Game Loop Implementations

A game loop is the mechanism through which logic and drawing are continuously executed. A simple game loop consists of drawing all objects, processing the player input, and updating the state of those objects, as illustrated in the following pseudocode:

```
initialize();
while(game running) {
    draw();
    input();
    update();
}
```

As discussed, an FPS of 60 is required to maintain the sense of real-time interactivity. When the game complexity increases, one problem that may arise is when sometimes a single loop can take longer than 1/60th of a second to complete, causing the game to run at a reduced frame rate. When this happens, the entire game will appear to slow down. A common solution is to prioritize some operations over others. That is, the engine can be designed in such a way as to fixate the game loop on completing operations that the engine deems more vital while skipping others. Since correct input and updates are required for a game to function as designed, it is often the draw operation that is skipped when necessary. This is referred to as frame skipping, and the following pseudocode illustrates one such implementation:

```
elapsedTime = now;
previousLoop = now;
while(game running) {
    elapsedTime += now - previousLoop;
    previousLoop = now;

    draw();
    input();
    while( elapsedTime >= UPDATE_TIME_RATE ) {
        update();
        elapsedTime -= UPDATE_TIME_RATE;
    }
}
```

In the previous pseudocode listing, UPDATE_TIME_RATE is the required real-time update rate. When the elapsed time between the game loop cycle is greater than the UPDATE_TIME_RATE, update() will be called until it has caught up. This means that the draw() operation is essentially skipped when the game loop is running too slowly. When this happens, the entire game will appear to run slowly, with lagging gameplay input responses and skipped frames. However, the game logic will continue to function correctly.

Notice that the while loop that encompasses the update() function call simulates a fixed update time step of UPDATE_TIME_RATE. This fixed time step update allows for a straightforward implementation in maintaining a deterministic game state. This is an important component to make sure your game engine functions as expected whether running optimally or slowly.

To ensure the focus is solely on the understanding of the core game loop's draw and update operations, input will be ignored until the next project.

The Game Loop Project

This project demonstrates how to incorporate a game loop into your game engine and to support real-time animation by drawing and updating Renderable objects. You can see an example of this project running in Figure 4-1. The source code to this project is defined in the chapter4/4.1.game_loop folder.

Figure 4-1. *Running the Game Loop project*

The goals of the project are as follows:

- To understand the internal operations of a game loop

- To implement and encapsulate the operations of a game loop

- To gain experience with continuous draw and update to create animation

Implement the Game Loop Component

The game loop component is core to the game engine's functionality and thus should be located similar to that of `vertex_buffer`, as a file defined in the `src/engine/core` folder:

1. Create a new file for the loop module in the `src/engine/core` folder and name the file `loop.js`.

2. Define the following instance variables to keep track of frame
    rate, processing time in milliseconds per frame, the game loop's
    current run state, and a reference to the current scene as follows:

```
"use strict"
const kUPS = 60; // Updates per second
const kMPF = 1000 / kUPS; // Milliseconds per update.
// Variables for timing gameloop.
let mPrevTime;
let mLagTime;
// The current loop state (running or should stop)
let mLoopRunning = false;
let mCurrentScene = null;
let mFrameID = -1;
```

Notice that kUPS is the updates per second similar to the FPS discussed, and it is set
to 60 or 60 updates per second. The time available for each update is simply 1/60 of a
second. Since there are 1000 milliseconds in a second, the available time for each update
in milliseconds is 1000 * (1/60), or kMPF.

Note   When the game is running optimally, frame drawing and updates are both
maintained at the same rate; FPS and kUPS can be thought of interchangeably.
However, when lag occurs, the loop skips frame drawing and prioritizes updates.
In this case, FPS will decrease, while kUPS will be maintained.

---

3. Add a function to run the core loop as follows:

```
function loopOnce() {
    if (mLoopRunning) {
        // Step A: set up for next call to LoopOnce
        mFrameID = requestAnimationFrame(loopOnce);

        // Step B: now let's draw
        //         draw() MUST be called before update()
        //         as update() may stop the loop!
        mCurrentScene.draw();
```

```
        // Step C: compute time elapsed since last loopOnce was executed
        let currentTime = performance.now();
        let elapsedTime = currentTime - mPrevTime;
        mPrevTime = currentTime;
        mLagTime += elapsedTime;

        // Step D: update the game the appropriate number of times.
        //      Update only every kMPF (1/60 of a second)
        //      If lag larger then update frames, update until caught up.
        while ((mLagTime >= kMPF) && mLoopRunning) {
            mCurrentScene.update();
            mLagTime -= kMPF;
        }
    }
}
```

Note   The `performance.now()` is a JavaScript function that returns a
timestamp in milliseconds.

Notice the similarity between the pseudocode examined previously and the steps B, C, and D of the `loopOnce()` function, that is, the drawing of the scene or game in step B, the calculation of the elapsed time since last update in step C, and the prioritization of update if the engine is lagging behind.

The main difference is that the outermost while loop is implemented based on the HTML5 `requestAnimationFrame()` function call at step A. The `requestAnimationFrame()` function will, at an approximated rate of 60 times per second, invoke the function pointer that is passed in as its parameter. In this case, the `loopOnce()` function will be called continuously at approximately 60 times per second. Notice that each call to the `requestAnimationFrame()` function will result in exactly one execution of the corresponding `loopOnce()` function and thus draw only once. However, if the system is lagging, multiple updates can occur during this single frame.

Note   The `requestAnimationFrame()` function is an HTML5 utility provided by the browser that hosts your game. The precise behavior of this function is browser implementation dependent.

The `mLoopRunning` condition of the `while` loop in step D is a redundant check for now. This condition will become important in later sections when `update()` can call `stop()` to stop the loop (e.g., for level transitions or the end of the game).

---

4. Declare a function to `start` the game loop. This function initializes the game or scene, the frame time variables, and the loop running flag before calling the first `requestAnimationFrame()` with the `loopOnce` function as its parameter to begin the game loop.

```
function start(scene) {
    if (mLoopRunning) {
        throw new Error("loop already running")
    }

    mCurrentScene = scene;
    mCurrentScene.init();

    mPrevTime = performance.now();
    mLagTime = 0.0;
    mLoopRunning = true;
    mFrameID = requestAnimationFrame(loopOnce);
}
```

5. Declare a function to `stop` the game loop. This function simply stops the loop by setting `mLoopRunning` to `false` and cancels the last requested animation frame.

```
function stop() {
    mLoopRunning = false;
    // make sure no more animation frames
    cancelAnimationFrame(mFrameID);
}
```

6. Lastly, remember to export the desired functionality to the rest of the game engine, in this case just the start and stop functions:

```
export {start, stop}
```

Working with the Game Loop

To test the game loop implementation, your game class must now implement draw(), update(), and init() functions. This is because to coordinate the beginning and the continual operation of your game, these functions are being called from the core of the game loop—the init() function is called from loop.start(), while the draw() and update() functions are called from loop.loopOnce().

1. Edit your my_game.js file to provide access to the loop by importing from the module. Allowing game developer access to the game loop module is a temporary measure and will be corrected in later sections.

```
// Accessing engine internal is not ideal,
//      this must be resolved! (later)
import * as loop from "../engine/core/loop.js";
```

2. Replace the MyGame constructor with the following:

```
constructor() {
    // variables for the squares
    this.mWhiteSq = null;        // these are the Renderable objects
    this.mRedSq = null;

    // The camera to view the scene
    this.mCamera = null;
}
```

3. Add an initialization function to set up a camera and two Renderable objects:

```
init() {
    // Step A: set up the cameras
    this.mCamera = new engine.Camera(
        vec2.fromValues(20, 60),    // position of the camera
```

```
        20,                             // width of camera
        [20, 40, 600, 300]            // viewport (orgX, orgY, width, height)
        );
    this.mCamera.setBackgroundColor([0.8, 0.8, 0.8, 1]);
    // sets the background to gray

    // Step  B: Create the Renderable objects:
    this.mWhiteSq = new engine.Renderable();
    this.mWhiteSq.setColor([1, 1, 1, 1]);
    this.mRedSq = new engine.Renderable();
    this.mRedSq.setColor([1, 0, 0, 1]);

    // Step  C: Init the white Renderable: centered, 5x5, rotated
    this.mWhiteSq.getXform().setPosition(20, 60);
    this.mWhiteSq.getXform().setRotationInRad(0.2); // In Radians
    this.mWhiteSq.getXform().setSize(5, 5);

    // Step  D: Initialize the red Renderable object: centered 2x2
    this.mRedSq.getXform().setPosition(20, 60);
    this.mRedSq.getXform().setSize(2, 2);
}
```

4. Draw the scene as before by clearing the canvas, setting up the
    camera, and drawing each square:

```
draw() {
    // Step A: clear the canvas
    engine.clearCanvas([0.9, 0.9, 0.9, 1.0]); // clear to light gray

    // Step  B: Activate the drawing Camera
    this.mCamera.setViewAndCameraMatrix();

    // Step  C: Activate the white shader to draw
    this.mWhiteSq.draw(this.mCamera);

    // Step  D: Activate the red shader to draw
    this.mRedSq.draw(this.mCamera);
}
```

5.   Add an `update()` function to animate a moving white square and a pulsing red square:

```
update() {
    // Simple game: move the white square and pulse the red
    let whiteXform = this.mWhiteSq.getXform();
    let deltaX = 0.05;

    // Step A: Rotate the white square
    if (whiteXform.getXPos() > 30) // the right-bound of the window
        whiteXform.setPosition(10, 60);
    whiteXform.incXPosBy(deltaX);
    whiteXform.incRotationByDegree(1);

    // Step B: pulse the red square
    let redXform = this.mRedSq.getXform();
    if (redXform.getWidth() > 5)
        redXform.setSize(2, 2);
    redXform.incSizeBy(0.05);
}
```

Recall that the `update()` function is called at about 60 times per second, and each time the following happens:

- Step A for the white square: Increase the rotation by 1 degree, increase the x position by 0.05, and reset to 10 if the resulting x position is greater than 30.

- Step B for the red square: Increase the size by 0.05 and reset it to 2 if the resulting size is greater than 5.

- Since the previous operations are performed continuously at about 60 times a second, you can expect to see the following:

  a.   A white square rotating while moving toward the right and upon reaching the right boundary wrapping around to the left boundary

  b.   A red square increasing in size and reducing to a size of 2 when the size reaches 5, thus appearing to be pulsing

6. Start the game `loop` from the `window.onload` function. Notice that a reference to an instance of `MyGame` is passed to the `loop`.

```
window.onload = function () {
    engine.init("GLCanvas");
    let myGame = new MyGame();
    // new begins the game
    loop.start(myGame);
}
```

You can now run the project to observe the rightward-moving, rotating white square and the pulsing red square. You can control the rate of the movement, rotation, and pulsing by changing the corresponding values of the `incXPosBy()`, `incRotationByDegree()`, and `incSizeBy()` functions. In these cases, the positional, rotational, and size values are changed by a constant amount in a fixed time interval. In effect, the parameters to these functions are the rate of change, or the speed, `incXPosBy(0.05)`, is the rightward speed of 0.05 units per 1/60th of a second or 3 units per second. In this project, the width of the world is 20 units, and with the white square traveling at 3 units per second, you can verify that it takes slightly more than 6 seconds for the white square to travel from the left to the right boundary.

Notice that in the core of the `loop` module, it is entirely possible for the `requestAnimationFrame()` function to invoke the `loopOnce()` function multiple times within a single kMPF interval. When this happens, the `draw()` function will be called multiples times without any `update()` function calls. In this way, the game loop can end up drawing the same game state multiple times. Please refer to the following references for discussions of supporting extrapolations in the `draw()` function to take advantage of efficient game loops:

- `http://gameprogrammingpatterns.com/game-loop.html#play-catch-up`

- `http://gafferongames.com/game-physics/fix-your-timestep/`

To clearly describe each component of the game engine and illustrate how these components interact, this book does not support extrapolation of the `draw()` function.

Keyboard Input

It is obvious that proper support to receive player input is important to interactive video games. For a typical personal computing device such as a PC or a Mac, the two common input devices are the keyboard and the mouse. While keyboard input is received in the form of a stream of characters, mouse input is packaged with positional information and is related to camera views. For this reason, keyboard input is more straightforward to support at this point in the development of the engine. This section will introduce and integrate keyboard support into your game engine. Mouse input will be examined in the Mouse Input project of Chapter 7, after the coverage of supporting multiple cameras in the same game.

The Keyboard Support Project

This project examines keyboard input support and integrates the functionality into the game engine. The position, rotation, and size of the game objects in this project are under your input control. You can see an example of this project running in Figure 4-2. The source code to this project is defined in the chapter4/4.2.keyboard_support folder.

Figure 4-2. *Running the Keyboard Support project*

The controls of the project are as follows:

- **Right-arrow key**: Moves the white square toward the right and wraps it to the left of the game window

- **Up-arrow key**: Rotates the white square

- **Down-arrow key**: Increases the size of the red square and then resets the size at a threshold

The goals of the project are as follows:

- To implement an engine component to receive keyboard input

- To understand the difference between key state (if a key is released or pressed) and key event (when the key state changes)

- To understand how to integrate the input component in the game loop

Add an Input Component to the Engine

Recall that the loop component is part of the core of the game engine and should not be accessed by the client game developer. In contrast, a well-defined input module should support the client game developer to query keyboard states without being distracted by any details. For this reason, the input module will be defined in the src/engine folder.

1. Create a new file in the src/engine folder and name it input.js.

2. Define a JavaScript dictionary to capture the key code mapping:

```
"use strict"
// Key code constants
const keys = {
    // arrows
    Left: 37,
    Up: 38,
    Right: 39,
    Down: 40,

    // space bar
    Space: 32,

    // numbers
    Zero: 48,
    One: 49,
    Two: 50,
    Three: 51,
    Four: 52,
    Five : 53,
    Six : 54,
    Seven : 55,
    Eight : 56,
    Nine : 57,

    // Alphabets
    A : 65,
    D : 68,
    E : 69,
```

```
    F : 70,
    G : 71,
    I : 73,
    J : 74,
    K : 75,
    L : 76,
    Q : 81,
    R : 82,
    S : 83,
    W : 87,

    LastKeyCode: 222
}
```

Key codes are unique numbers representing each keyboard character. Note that there are up to 222 unique keys. In the listing, only a small subset of the keys, those that are relevant to this project, are defined in the dictionary.

Note   Key codes for the alphabets are continuous, starting from 65 for A and ending with 90 for Z. You should feel free to add any characters for your own game engine. For a complete list of key codes, see `www.cambiaresearch.com/articles/15/javascript-char-codes-key-codes`.

---

3.   Create array instance variables for tracking the states of every key:

```
// Previous key state
let mKeyPreviousState = []; // a new array
// The pressed keys.
let  mIsKeyPressed = [];
// Click events: once an event is set, it will remain there until polled
let  mIsKeyClicked = [];
```

All three arrays define the state of every key as a boolean. The `mKeyPreviousState` records the key states from the previous update cycle, and the `mIsKeyPressed` records the current state of the keys. The key code entries of these two arrays are true when the corresponding keyboard keys are pressed, and false otherwise. The `mIsKeyClicked` array captures key click events. The key code entries of this array are true only when the corresponding keyboard key goes from being released to being pressed in two consecutive update cycles.

It is important to note that KeyPress is the state of a key, while KeyClicked is an event. For example, if a player presses the *A* key for one second before releasing it, then the duration of that entire second KeyPress for *A* is true, while KeyClick for *A* is true only once—the update cycle right after the key is pressed.

4.   Define functions to capture the actual keyboard state changes:

```
// Event handler functions
function onKeyDown(event) {
    mIsKeyPressed[event.keyCode] = true;
}

function onKeyUp(event) {
    mIsKeyPressed[event.keyCode] = false;
}
```

When these functions are called, the key code from the parameter is used to record the corresponding keyboard state changes. It is expected that the caller of these functions will pass the appropriate key code in the argument.

5.   Add a function to initialize all the key states, and register the key event handlers with the browser. The window. addEventListener() function registers the onKeyUp/Down() event handlers with the browser such that the corresponding functions will be called when the player presses or releases keys on the keyboard.

```
function init() {
    let i;
    for (i = 0; i < keys.LastKeyCode; i++) {
        mIsKeyPressed[i] = false;
        mKeyPreviousState[i] = false;
        mIsKeyClicked[i] = false;
    }
```

```
    // register handlers
    window.addEventListener('keyup', onKeyUp);
    window.addEventListener('keydown', onKeyDown);
}
```

6. Add an update() function to derive the key click events. The update() function uses mIsKeyPressed and mKeyPreviousState to determine whether a key clicked event has occurred.

```
function update() {
    let i;
    for (i = 0; i < keys.LastKeyCode; i++) {
        mIsKeyClicked[i] = (!mKeyPreviousState[i]) && mIsKeyPressed[i];
        mKeyPreviousState[i] = mIsKeyPressed[i];
    }
}
```

7. Add public functions for inquires to current keyboard states to support the client game developer:

```
// Function for GameEngine programmer to test if a key is pressed down
function isKeyPressed(keyCode) {
    return mIsKeyPressed[keyCode];
}
function isKeyClicked(keyCode) {
    return mIsKeyClicked[keyCode];
}
```

8. Finally, export the public functions and key constants:

```
export {keys, init,
    update,
    isKeyClicked,
    isKeyPressed
}
```

Modify the Engine to Support Keyboard Input

To properly support input, before the game loop begins, the engine must initialize the mIsKeyPressed, mIsKeyClicked, and mKeyPreviousState arrays. To properly capture the player actions, during gameplay from within the core of the game loop, these arrays must be updated accordingly.

1. Input state initialization: Modify index.js by importing the input.js module, adding the initialization of the input to the engine init() function, and adding the input module to the exported list to allow access from the client game developer.

```
import * as input from "./input.js";

function init(htmlCanvasID) {
    glSys.init(htmlCanvasID);
    vertexBuffer.init();
    shaderResources.init();
    input.init();
}

export default {
    // input support
    input,

    // Util classes
    Camera, Transform, Renderable,

    // functions
    init, clearCanvas
}
```

2. To accurately capture keyboard state changes, the input component must be integrated with the core of the game loop. Include the input's update() function in the core game loop by adding the following lines to loop.js. Notice the rest of the code is identical.

```
import * as input from "../input.js";

function loopOnce() {
```

```
    if (mLoopRunning) {

        ... identical to previous code ...

        // Step D: update the game the appropriate number of times.
        //      Update only every kMPF (1/60 of a second)
        //      If lag larger then update frames, update until caught up.
        while ((mLagTime >= kMPF) && mLoopRunning) {
            input.update();
            mCurrentScene.update();
            mLagTime -= kMPF;
        }
    }
}
```

Test Keyboard Input

You can test the input functionality by modifying the Renderable objects in your MyGame class. Replace the code in the MyGame update() function with the following:

```
update() {
    // Simple game: move the white square and pulse the red

    let whiteXform = this.mWhiteSq.getXform();
    let deltaX = 0.05;

    // Step A: test for white square movement
    if (engine.input.isKeyPressed(engine.input.keys.Right)) {
        if (whiteXform.getXPos() > 30) { // right-bound of the window
            whiteXform.setPosition(10, 60);
        }
        whiteXform.incXPosBy(deltaX);
    }

    // Step  B: test for white square rotation
    if (engine.input.isKeyClicked(engine.input.keys.Up)) {
        whiteXform.incRotationByDegree(1);
    }
```

```
    let redXform = this.mRedSq.getXform();
    // Step  C: test for pulsing the red square
    if (engine.input.isKeyPressed(engine.input.keys.Down)) {
        if (redXform.getWidth() > 5) {
            redXform.setSize(2, 2);
        }
        redXform.incSizeBy(0.05);
    }
}
```

In the previous code, step A ensures that pressing and holding the right-arrow key will move the white square toward the right. Step B checks for the pressing and then the releasing of the up-arrow key event. The white square is rotated when such an event is detected. Notice that pressing and holding the up-arrow key will not generate continuously key press events and thus will not cause the white square to continuously rotate. Step C tests for the pressing and holding of the down-arrow key to pulse the red square.

You can run the project and include additional controls for manipulating the squares. For example, include support for the **WASD** keys to control the location of the red square. Notice once again that by increasing/decreasing the position change amount, you are effectively controlling the speed of the object's movement.

Note   The term "**WASD** keys" is used to refer to the key binding of the popular game controls: key W to move upward, A leftward, S downward, and D rightward.

Resource Management and Asynchronous Loading

Video games typically utilize a multitude of artistic assets, or resources, including audio clips and images. The required resources to support a game can be large. Additionally, it is important to maintain the independence between the resources and the actual game such that they can be updated independently, for example, changing the background audio without changing the game itself. For these reasons, game resources are typically stored externally on a system hard drive or a server across the network. Being stored external to the game, the resources are sometimes referred to as *external resources* or *assets*.

After a game begins, external resources must be explicitly loaded. For efficient memory utilization, a game should load and unload resources dynamically based on necessity. However, loading external resources may involve input/output device operations or network packet latencies and thus can be time intensive and potentially affect real-time interactivity. For these reasons, at any instance in a game, only a portion of resources are kept in memory, where the loading operations are strategically executed to avoid interrupting the game. In most cases, resources required in each level are kept in memory during the gameplay of that level. With this approach, external resource loading can occur during level transitions where players are expecting a new game environment and are more likely to tolerate slight delays for loading.

Once loaded, a resource must be readily accessible to support interactivity. The efficient and effective management of resources is essential to any game engine. Take note of the clear differentiation between resource management, which is the responsibility of a game engine, and the actual ownerships of the resources. For example, a game engine must support the efficient loading and playing of the background music for a game, and it is the game (or client of the game engine) that actually owns and supplies the audio file for the background music. When implementing support for external resource management, it is important to remember that the actual resources are not part of the game engine.

At this point, the game engine you have been building handles only one type of resource—the GLSL shader files. Recall that the SimpleShader object loads and compiles the simple_vs.glsl and simple_fs.glsl files in its constructor. So far, the shader file loading has been accomplished via synchronous XMLHttpRequest.open(). This synchronous loading is an example of inefficient resource management because no operations can occur while the browser attempts to open and load a shader file. An efficient alternative would be to issue an asynchronous load command and allow additional operations to continue while the file is being opened and loaded.

This section builds an infrastructure to support asynchronous loading and efficient accessing of the loaded resources. Based on this infrastructure, over the next few projects, the game engine will be expanded to support batch resource loading during scene transitions.

The Resource Map and Shader Loader Project

This project guides you to develop the resource_map component, an infrastructural module for resource management, and demonstrates how to work with this module to load shader files asynchronously. You can see an example of this project running in Figure 4-3. This project appears to be identical to the previous project, with the only difference being how the GLSL shaders are loaded. The source code to this project is defined in the chapter4/4.3.resource_map_and_shader_loader folder.

Figure 4-3. *Running the Resource Map and Shader Loader project*

The controls of the project are identical to the previous project as follows:

- **Right-arrow key:** Moves the white square toward the right and wraps it to the left of the game window

- **Up-arrow key:** Rotates the white square

- **Down-arrow key**: Increases the size of the red square and then resets the size at a threshold

The goals of the project are as follows:

- To understand the handling of asynchronous loading

- To build an infrastructure that supports future resource loading and accessing

- To experience asynchronous resource loading via loading of the GLSL shader files

---

Note   For more information about asynchronous JavaScript operations, you can refer to many excellent resources online, for example, `https://developer.mozilla.org/en-US/docs/Learn/JavaScript/Asynchronous`.

Add a Resource Map Component to the Engine

The `resource_map` engine component manages resource loading, storage, and retrieval after the resources are loaded. These operations are internal to the game engine and should not be accessed by the game engine client. As in the case of all core engine components, for example, the game loop, the source code file is created in the `src/engine/core` folder. The details are as follows.

1. Create a new file in the `src/engine/core` folder and name it `resource_map.js`.

2. Define the `MapEntry` class to support reference counting of loaded resources. Reference counting is essential to avoid multiple loading or premature unloading of a resource.

```
class MapEntry {
    constructor(data) {
        this.mData = data;
        this.mRefCount = 1;
    }
    decRef() { this.mRefCount--; }
```

```
incRef() { this. mRefCount++; }

set(data) { this.mData = data;}
data() { return this.mData; }

canRemove() { return (this.mRefCount == 0); }
}
```

3. Define a key-value pair map, mMap, for storing and retrieving of
   resources and an array, mOutstandingPromises, to capture all
   outstanding asynchronous loading operations:

```
let mMap = new Map();
let mOutstandingPromises = [];
```

Note A JavaScript Map object holds a collection of key-value pairs.

---

4. Define functions for querying the existence of, retrieving, and
   setting a resource. Notice that as suggested by the variable name
   of the parameter, path, it is expected that the full path to the
   external resource file will be used as the key for accessing the
   corresponding resource, for example, using the path to the
   src/glsl_shaders/simple_vs.glsl file as the key for accessing
   the content of the file.

```
function has(path) { return mMap.has(path) }
function get(path) {
    if (!has(path)) {
        throw new Error("Error [" + path + "]: not loaded");
    }
    return mMap.get(path).data();
}
function set(key, value) { mMap.get(key).set(value); }
```

5. Define functions to indicate that loading has been requested, increase the reference count of a loaded resource, and to properly unload a resource. Due to the asynchronous nature of the loading operation, a load request will result in an empty MapEntry which will be updated when the load operation is completed sometime in the future. Note that each unload request will decrease the reference count and may or may not result in the resource being unloaded.

```
function loadRequested(path) {
    mMap.set(path, new MapEntry(null));
}
function incRef(path) {
    mMap.get(path).incRef();
}
function unload(path) {
    let entry = mMap.get(path);
    entry.decRef();
    if (entry.canRemove())
        mMap.delete(path)
    return entry.canRemove();
}
```

6. Define a function to append an ongoing asynchronous loading operation to the mOutstandingPromises array

```
function pushPromise(p) { mOutstandingPromises.push(p); }
```

7. Define a loading function, loadDecodeParse(). If the resource is already loaded, the corresponding reference count is incremented. Otherwise, the function first issues a loadRequest() to create an empty MapEntry in mMap. The function then creates an HTML5 fetch promise, using the path to the resource as key, to asynchronously fetch the external resource, decode the network packaging, parse the results into a proper format, and update the results into the created MapEntry. This created promise is then pushed into the mOutstandingPromises array.

```
// generic loading function,
//    Step 1: fetch from server
//    Step 2: decodeResource on the loaded package
//    Step 3: parseResource on the decodedResource
//    Step 4: store result into the map
// Push the promised operation into an array
function loadDecodeParse(path, decodeResource, parseResource) {
    let fetchPromise = null;
    if (!has(path)) {
        loadRequested(path);
        fetchPromise =  fetch(path)
            .then(res => decodeResource(res) )
            .then(data => parseResource(data) )
            .then(data => { return set(path, data) } )
            .catch(err => { throw err });
        pushPromise(fetchPromise);
    } else {
        incRef(path);   // increase reference count
    }
    return fetchPromise;
}
```

Notice that the decoding and parsing functions are passed in as parameters and thus are dependent upon the actual resource type that is being fetched. For example, the decoding and parsing of simple text, XML (Extensible Markup Language)-formatted text, audio clips, and images all have distinct requirements. It is the responsibility of the actual resource loader to define these functions.

The HTML5 fetch() function returns a JavaScript promise object. A typical JavaScript promise object contains operations that will be completed in the future. A promise is fulfilled when the operations are completed. In this case, the fetchPromise is fulfilled when the path is properly fetched, decoded, parsed, and updated into the corresponding MapEntry. This promise is being kept in the mOutstandingPromises array. Note that by the end of the loadDecodeParse() function, the asynchronous fetch() loading operation is issued and ongoing but not guaranteed to be completed. In this way, the mOutstandingPromises is an array of ongoing and unfulfilled, or outstanding, promises.

8. Define a JavaScript `async` function to block the execution and wait for all outstanding promises to be fulfilled, or wait for all ongoing asynchronous loading operations to be completed:

```
// will block, wait for all outstanding promises complete
// before continue
async function waitOnPromises() {
    await Promise.all(mOutstandingPromises);
    mOutstandingPromises = []; // remove all
}
```

Note   The JavaScript `async`/`await` keywords are paired where only `async` functions can `await` for a `promise`. The `await` statement blocks and returns the execution back to the caller of the `async` function. When the `promise` being waited on is fulfilled, execution will continue to the end of the `async` function.

---

9. Finally, export functionality to the rest of the game engine:

```
export {has, get, set,
    loadRequested, incRef, loadDecodeParse,
    unload,
    pushPromise, waitOnPromises}
```

Notice that although the storage-specific functionalities—query, get, and set—are well defined, `resource_map` is actually not capable of loading any specific resources. This module is designed to be utilized by resource type–specific modules where the decoding and parsing functions can be properly defined. In the next subsection, a text resource loader is defined to demonstrate this idea.

Define a Text Resource Module

This section will define a `text` module that utilizes the `resource_map` module to load your text files asynchronously. This module serves as an excellent example of how to take advantage of the `resource_map` facility and allows you to replace the synchronous loading of GLSL shader files. Replacing synchronous with asynchronous loading support is a significant upgrade to the game engine.

1. Create a new folder in `src/engine/` and name it `resources`. This new folder is created in anticipation of the necessary support for many resource types and to maintain a clean source code organization.

2. Create a new file in the `src/engine/resources` folder and name it `text.js`.

3. Import the core resource management and reuse the relevant functionality from `resource_map`:

```
"use strict"
import * as map from "../core/resource_map.js";

// functions from resource_map
let unload = map.unload;
let has = map.has;
let get = map.get;
```

4. Define the text decoding and parsing functions for `loadDecodeParse()`. Notice that there are no requirements for parsing the loaded text, and thus, the text parsing function does not perform any useful operation.

```
function decodeText(data) {
    return data.text();
}
function parseText(text) {
    return text;
}
```

5. Define the `load()` function to call the `resource_map` `loadDecodeParse()` function to trigger the asynchronous `fetch()` operation:

```
function load(path) {
    return map.loadDecodeParse(path, decodeText, parseText);
}
```

6. Export the functionality to provide access to the rest of the game engine:

```
export {has, get, load, unload}
```

7. Lastly, remember to update the defined functionality for the client in the index.js:

```
import * as text from "./resources/text.js";

... identical to previous code ...

export default {
    // resource support
    text,

    ... identical to previous code ...
}
```

Load Shaders Asynchronously

The text resource module can now be used to assist the loading of the shader files asynchronously as plain-text files. Since it is impossible to predict when an asynchronous loading operation will be completed, it is important to issue the load commands *before* the resources are needed and to ensure that the loading operations are *completed* before proceeding to retrieve the resources.

Modify Shader Resources for Asynchronous Support

To avoid loading the GLSL shader files synchronously, the files must be loaded before the creation of a SimpleShader object. Recall that a single instance of SimpleShader object is created in the shader_resources module and shared among all Renderables. You can now asynchronously load the GLSL shader files before the creation of the SimpleShader object.

1. Edit shader_resources.js and import functionality from the text and resource_map modules:

```
import * as text from "../resources/text.js";
import * as map from "./resource_map.js";
```

2. Replace the content of the init() function. Define a JavaScript promise, loadPromise, to load the two GLSL shader files asynchronously, and when the loading is completed, trigger the calling of the createShaders() function. Store the loadPromise in the mOutstandingPromises array of the resource_map by calling the map.pushPromise() function:

```
function init() {
    let loadPromise = new Promise(
        async function(resolve) {
            await Promise.all([
                text.load(kSimpleFS),
                text.load(kSimpleVS)
            ]);
            resolve();
    }).then(
            function resolve() { createShaders(); }
    );
    map.pushPromise(loadPromise);
}
```

Notice that after the shader_resources init() function, the loading of the two GLSL shader files would have begun. At that point, it is not guaranteed that the loading operations are completed and the SimpleShader object may not have been created. However, the promise that is based on the completion of these operations is stored in the resource_map mOutstandingPromises array. For this reason, it is guaranteed that these operations must have completed by the end of the resource_map waitOnPromises() function.

Modify SimpleShader to Retrieve the Shader Files

With the understanding that the GLSL shader files are already loaded, the changes to the SimpleShader class are straightforward. Instead of synchronously loading the shader files in the loadAndCompileShader() function, the contents to these files can simply be retrieved via the text resource.

1. Edit the `simple_shader.js` file and add an `import` from the `text` module for retrieving the content of the GLSL shaders:

```
import * as text from "./resources/text.js";
```

2. Since no loading operations are required, you should change the `loadAndCompileShader()` function name to simply `compileShader()` and replace the file-loading commands by text resource retrievals. Notice that the synchronous loading operations are replaced by a single call to `text.get()` to retrieve the file content based on the `filePath` or the unique resource name for the shader file.

```
function compileShader(filePath, shaderType) {
    let shaderSource = null, compiledShader = null;
    let gl = glSys.get();

    // Step A: Access the shader textfile
    shaderSource = text.get(filePath);

    if (shaderSource === null) {
        throw new Error("WARNING:" + filePath + " not loaded!");
        return null;
    }

    ... identical to previous code ...
}
```

3. Remember that in the `SimpleShader` constructor, the calls to `loadAndCompileShader()` functions should be replaced by the newly modified `compileShader()` functions, as follows:

```
constructor(vertexShaderPath, fragmentShaderPath) {
    ... identical to previous code ...

    // Step A: load and compile vertex and fragment shaders
    this.mVertexShader = compileShader(vertexShaderPath,
                                    gl.VERTEX_SHADER);
```

```
    this.mFragmentShader = compileShader(fragmentShaderPath,
                                          gl.FRAGMENT_SHADER);

    ... identical to previous code ...
}
```

Wait for Asynchronous Loading to Complete

With outstanding loading operations and incomplete shader creation, a client's game cannot be initialized because without SimpleShader, Renderable objects cannot be properly created. For this reason, the game engine must wait for all outstanding promises to be fulfilled before proceeding to initialize the client's game. Recall that client's game initialization is performed in the game loop start() function, right before the beginning of the first loop iteration.

1. Edit the loop.js file and import from the resource_map module:

```
import * as map from "./resource_map.js";
```

2. Modify the start() function to be an async function such that it
    is now possible to issue await and hold the execution by calling
    map.waitOnPromises() to wait for the fulfilment of all outstanding
    promises:

```
async function start(scene) {
    if (mLoopRunning) {
        throw new Error("loop already running")
    }
    // Wait for any async requests before game-load
    await map.waitOnPromises();

    mCurrentScene = scene;
    mCurrentScene.init();

    mPrevTime = performance.now();
    mLagTime = 0.0;
    mLoopRunning = true;
    mFrameID = requestAnimationFrame(loopOnce);
}
```

Test the Asynchronous Shader Loading

You can now run the project with shaders being loaded asynchronously. Though the output and interaction experience are identical to the previous project, you now have a game engine that is much better equipped to manage the loading and accessing of external resources.

The rest of this chapter further develops and formalizes the interface between the client, MyGame, and the rest of the game engine. The goal is to define the interface to the client such that multiple game-level instances can be created and interchanged during runtime. With this new interface, you will be able to define what a game level is and allow the game engine to load any level in any order.

Game Level from a Scene File

The operations involved in initiating a game level from a scene file can assist in the derivation and refinement of the formal interface between the game engine and its client. With a game level defined in a scene file, the game engine must first initiate asynchronous loading, wait for the load completion, and then initialize the client for the game loop. These steps present a complete functional interface between the game engine and the client. By examining and deriving the proper support for these steps, the interface between the game engine and its client can be refined.

The Scene File Project

This project uses the loading of a scene file as the vehicle to examine the necessary public methods for a typical game level. You can see an example of this project running in Figure 4-4. This project appears and interacts identically to the previous project with the only difference being that the scene definition is asynchronously loaded from a file. The source code to this project is defined in the chapter4/4.4.scene_file folder.

Figure 4-4. *Running the Scene File project*

The controls of the project are identical to the previous project, as follows:

- **Right-arrow key**: Moves the white square toward the right and wraps it to the left of the game window

- **Up-arrow key**: Rotates the white square

- **Down-arrow key**: Increases the size of the red square and then resets the size at a threshold

The goals of the project are as follows:

- To introduce the protocol for supporting asynchronous loading of the resources of a game

- To develop the proper game engine support for the protocol

- To identify and define the public interface methods for a general game level

While the parsing and loading process of a scene file is interesting to a game engine designer, the client should never need to concern themselves with these details. This project aims at developing a well-defined interface between the engine and the client. This interface will hide the complexity of the engine internal core from the client and thus avoid situations such as requiring access to the loop module from MyGame in the first project of this chapter.

The Scene File

Instead of hard-coding the creation of all objects to a game in the init() function, the information can be encoded in a file, and the file can be loaded and parsed during runtime. The advantage of such encoding in an external file is the flexibility to modify a scene without the need to change the game source code, while the disadvantages are the complexity and time required for loading and parsing. In general, the importance of flexibility dictates that most game engines support the loading of game scenes from a file.

Objects in a game scene can be defined in many ways. The key decision factors are that the format can properly describe the game objects and be easily parsed. Extensible Markup Language (XML) is well suited to serve as the encoding scheme for scene files.

Define an XML Resource Module

In order to support an XML-encoded scene file, you first need to expand the engine to support the asynchronous loading of an XML file resource. Similar to the text resource module, an XML resource module should also be based on the resource_map: store the loaded XML content in mMap of the resource_map, and define the specifics for decoding and parsing for the calling of the loadDecodeParse() function of the resource_map.

1. Define a new file in the src/engine/resources folder and name it xml.js. Edit this file and import the core resource management functionality from the resource_map.

```
"use strict"
import * as map from "../core/resource_map.js";
// functions from resource_map
let unload = map.unload;
let has = map.has;
let get = map.get;
```

2. Instantiate an XML DOMParser, define the decoding and parsing
    functions, and call the loadDecodeParse() function of the
    resource_map with the corresponding parameters to initiate the
    loading of the XML file:

```
let mParser = new DOMParser();

function decodeXML(data) {
    return data.text();
}

function parseXML(text) {
    return mParser.parseFromString(text, "text/xml");
}

function load(path) {
    return map.loadDecodeParse(path, decodeXML, parseXML);
}
```

3. Remember to export the defined functionality:

```
export {has, get, load, unload}
```

4. Lastly, remember to export the defined functionality for the client
    in the index.js:

```
import * as xml from "./resources/xml.js";

... identical to previous code ...

export default {
    // resource support
    text, xml,

    ... identical to previous code ...
}
```

The newly defined xml module can be conveniently accessed by the client and used
in a similar fashion as the text module in loading external XML-encoded text files.

Note   The JavaScript DOMParser provides the ability to parse XML or HTML text strings.

Modify the Engine to Integrate Client Resource Loading

The scene file is an external resource that is being loaded by the client. With asynchronous operations, the game engine must stop and wait for the completion of the load process before it can initialize the game. This is because the game initialization will likely require the loaded resources.

Coordinate Client Load and Engine Wait in the Loop Module

Since all resource loading and storage are based on the same resource_map, the client issuing of the load requests and the engine waiting for the load completions can be coordinated in the loop.start() function as follows:

```
async function start(scene) {
    if (mLoopRunning) {
        throw new Error("loop already running")
    }
    mCurrentScene = scene;
    mCurrentScene.load();

    // Wait for any async requests before game-load
    await map.waitOnPromises();

    mCurrentScene.init();
    mPrevTime = performance.now();
    mLagTime = 0.0;
    mLoopRunning = true;
    mFrameID = requestAnimationFrame(loopOnce);
}
```

Note that this function is exactly two lines different from the previous project—mCurrentScene is assigned a reference to the parameter, and the client's load() function is called before the engine waits for the completion of all asynchronous loading operations.

Derive a Public Interface for the Client

Though slightly involved, the details of XML-parsing specifics are less important than the fact that XML files can now be loaded. It is now possible to use the asynchronous loading of an external resource to examine the required public methods for interfacing a game level to the game engine.

Public Methods of MyGame

While the game engine is designed to facilitate the building of games, the actual state of a game is specific to each individual client. In general, there is no way for the engine to anticipate the required operations to initialize, update, or draw any particular game. For this reason, such operations are defined to be part of the public interface between the game engine and the client. At this point, it is established that MyGame should define the following:

- constructor(): For declaring variables and defining constants.

- init(): For instantiating the variables and setting up the game scene. This is called from the loop.start() function before the first iteration of the game loop.

- draw()/update(): For interfacing to the game loop with these two functions being called continuously from within the core of the game loop, in the loop.loopOnce() function.

With the requirement of loading a scene file, or any external resources, two additional public methods should be defined:

- load(): For initiating the asynchronous loading of external resources, in this case, the scene file. This is called from the loop.start() function before the engine waits for the completion of all asynchronous loading operations.

- unload(): For unloading of external resources when the game has ended. Currently, the engine does not attempt to free up resources. This will be rectified in the next project.

Implement the Client

You are now ready to create an XML-encoded scene file to test external resource loading by the client and to interface to the client with game engine based on the described public methods.

Define a Scene File

Define a simple scene file to capture the game state from the previous project:

1. Create a new folder at the same level as the src folder and name it assets. This is the folder where all external resources, or assets, of a game will be stored including the scene files, audio clips, texture images, and fonts.

Tip It is important to differentiate between the src/engine/resources folder that is created for organizing game engine source code files and the assets folder that you just created for storing client resources. Although GLSL shaders are also loaded at runtime, they are considered as source code and will continue to be stored in the src/glsl_shaders folder.

---

2. Create a new file in the assets folder and name it scene.xml. This file will store the client's game scene. Add the following content. The listed XML content describes the same scene as defined in the init() functions from the previous MyGame class.

```
<MyGameLevel>

<!--  *** be careful!! comma (,) is not a supported syntax!!  -->
<!--  make sure there are no comma in between attributes -->
<!--  e.g., do NOT do:  PosX="20", PosY="30" -->
<!--  notice the "comma" between PosX and PosY: Syntax error! -->

    <!-- cameras -->
    <!-- Viewport: x, y, w, h -->
```

```
<Camera CenterX="20" CenterY="60" Width="20"
        Viewport="20 40 600 300"
        BgColor="0.8 0.8 0.8 1.0"
/>

<!-- Squares Rotation is in degree -->
<Square PosX="20" PosY="60" Width="5" Height="5"
        Rotation="30" Color="1 1 1 1" />
<Square PosX="20" PosY="60" Width="2" Height="2"
        Rotation="0"  Color="1 0 0 1" />
</MyGameLevel>
```

Tip   The JavaScript XML parser does not support delimiting attributes with commas.

Parse the Scene File

A specific parser for the listed XML scene file must be defined to extract the scene
information. Since the scene file is specific to a game, the parser should also be specific
to the game and be created within the my_game folder.

1. Create a new folder in the src/my_game folder and name it util.
   Add a new file in the util folder and name it scene_file_parser.js.
   This file will contain the specific parsing logic to decode the listed
   scene file.

2. Define a new class, name it SceneFileParser, and add a
   constructor with code as follows:

```
import engine from "../../engine/index.js";

class SceneFileParser {
    constructor (xml) {
        this.xml = xml
    }
    ... implementation to follow ...
}
```

Note that the xml parameter is the actual content of the loaded XML file.

151

Note   The following XML parsing is based on JavaScript XML API. Please refer to
`https://www.w3schools.com/xml` for more details.

---

3.   Add a function to the `SceneFileParser` to parse the details of the
Camera from the xml file you created:

```
parseCamera() {
    let camElm = getElm(this.xml, "Camera");
    let cx = Number(camElm[0].getAttribute("CenterX"));
    let cy = Number(camElm[0].getAttribute("CenterY"));
    let w = Number(camElm[0].getAttribute("Width"));
    let viewport = camElm[0].getAttribute("Viewport").split(" ");
    let bgColor = camElm[0].getAttribute("BgColor").split(" ");
    // make sure viewport and color are number
    let j;
    for (j = 0; j < 4; j++) {
        bgColor[j] = Number(bgColor[j]);
        viewport[j] = Number(viewport[j]);
    }

    let cam = new engine.Camera(
        vec2.fromValues(cx, cy),   // position of the camera
        w,                         // width of camera
        viewport                   // viewport (orgX, orgY, width, height)
        );
    cam.setBackgroundColor(bgColor);
    return cam;
}
```

The camera parser finds a camera element and constructs a `Camera` object with the
retrieved information. Notice that the viewport and background color are arrays of four
numbers. These are input as strings of four numbers delimited by spaces. Strings can be
split into arrays, which is the case here with the space delimiter. The JavaScript `Number()`
function ensures that all strings are converted into numbers.

4. Add a function to the SceneFileParser to parse the details of the squares from the xml file you created:

```
parseSquares(sqSet) {
    let elm = getElm(this.xml, "Square");
    let i, j, x, y, w, h, r, c, sq;
    for (i = 0; i < elm.length; i++) {
        x = Number(elm.item(i).attributes.getNamedItem("PosX").value);
        y = Number(elm.item(i).attributes.getNamedItem("PosY").value);
        w = Number(elm.item(i).attributes.getNamedItem("Width").value);
        h = Number(elm.item(i).attributes.getNamedItem("Height").value);
        r = Number(elm.item(i).attributes.getNamedItem("Rotation").value);
        c = elm.item(i).attributes.getNamedItem("Color").value.split(" ");
        sq = new engine.Renderable();
        // make sure color array contains numbers
        for (j = 0; j < 4; j++) {
            c[j] = Number(c[j]);
        }
        sq.setColor(c);
        sq.getXform().setPosition(x, y);
        sq.getXform().setRotationInDegree(r); // In Degree
        sq.getXform().setSize(w, h);
        sqSet.push(sq);
    }
}
```

This function parses the XML file to create Renderable objects to be placed in the array that is passed in as a parameter.

5. Add a function outside the SceneFileParser to parse for contents of an XML element:

```
function getElm(xmlContent, tagElm) {
    let theElm = xmlContent.getElementsByTagName(tagElm);
    if (theElm.length === 0) {
        console.error("Warning: Level element:[" +
```

```
                            tagElm + "]: is not found!");
    }
    return theElm;
}
```

6. Finally, export the SceneFileParser:

```
export default SceneFileParser;
```

Implement MyGame

The implementations of the described public functions for this project are as follows:

1. Edit my_game.js file and import the SceneFileParser:

```
import SceneFileParser from "./util/scene_file_parser.js";
```

2. Modify the MyGame constructor to define the scene file path, the array mSqSet for storing the Renderable objects, and the camera:

```
constructor() {
    // scene file name
    this.mSceneFile = "assets/scene.xml";
    // all squares
    this.mSqSet = [];          // these are the Renderable objects

    // The camera to view the scene
    this.mCamera = null;
}
```

3. Change the init() function to create objects based on the scene parser. Note the retrieval of the XML file content via the engine.xml.get() function where the file path to the scene file is used as the key.

```
init() {
    let sceneParser = new SceneFileParser(
                        engine.xml.get(this.mSceneFile));

    // Step A: Read in the camera
```

```
    this.mCamera = sceneParser.parseCamera();

    // Step B: Read all the squares
    sceneParser.parseSquares(this.mSqSet);
}
```

4. The draw and update functions are similar to the previous examples with the exception of referencing the corresponding array elements.

```
draw() {
    // Step A: clear the canvas
    engine.clearCanvas([0.9, 0.9, 0.9, 1.0]);

    this.mCamera.setViewAndCameraMatrix();
    // Step B: draw all the squares
    let i;
    for (i = 0; i < this.mSqSet.length; i++)
        this.mSqSet[i].draw(this.mCamera);
}
update() {
    // simple game: move the white square and pulse the red
    let xform = this.mSqSet[0].getXform();
    let deltaX = 0.05;

    // Step A: test for white square movement
    ... identical to previous code ...
    xform = this.mSqSet[1].getXform();
    // Step C: test for pulsing the red square
    ... identical to previous code ...
}
```

5. Lastly, define the functions to load and unload the scene file.

```
load() {
    engine.xml.load(this.mSceneFile);
}
```

```
unload() {
    // unload the scene file and loaded resources
    engine.xml.unload(this.mSceneFile);
}
```

You can now run the project and see that it behaves the same as the previous two projects. While this may not seem interesting, through this project, a simple and well-defined interface between the engine and the client has been derived where the complexities and details of each are hidden. Based on this interface, additional engine functionality can be introduced without the requirements of modifying any existing clients, and at the same time, complex games can be created and maintained independently from engine internals. The details of this interface will be introduced in the next project.

Before continuing, you may notice that the MyGame.unload() function is never called. This is because in this example the game loop never stopped cycling and MyGame is never unloaded. This issue will be addressed in the next project.

Scene Object: Client Interface to the Game Engine

At this point, in your game engine, the following is happening:

- The window.onload function initializes the game engine and calls the loop.start() function, passing in MyGame as a parameter.

- The loop.start() function, through the resource_map, waits for the completion of all asynchronous loading operations before it calls to initialize MyGame and starts the actual game loop cycle.

From this discussion, it is interesting to recognize that any object with the appropriately defined public methods can replace the MyGame object. Effectively, at any point, it is possible to call the loop.start() function to initiate the loading of a new scene. This section expands on this idea by introducing the Scene object for interfacing the game engine with its clients.

The Scene Objects Project

This project defines the Scene as an abstract superclass for interfacing with your game engine. From this project on, all client code must be encapsulated in subclasses of the abstract Scene class, and the game engine will be able to interact with these classes in a coherent and well-defined manner. You can see an example of this project running in Figure 4-5. The source code to this project is defined in the chapter4/4.5.scene_objects folder.

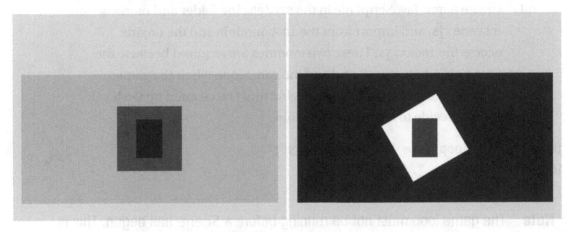

Figure 4-5. Running the Scene Objects project with both scenes

There are two distinct levels in this project: the MyGame level with a blue rectangle drawn above a red square over a gray background and the BlueLevel level with a red rectangle drawn above a rotated white square over a dark blue background. For simplicity, the controls for both levels are the same.

- **Left-/right-arrow key:** Move the front rectangle left and right

- **Q key:** Quits the game

Notice that on each level, moving the front rectangle toward the left to touch the left boundary will cause the loading of the other level. The MyGame level will cause BlueLevel to be loaded, and BlueLevel will cause the MyGame level to be loaded.

The goals of the project are as follows:

- To define the abstract Scene class to interface to the game engine

- To experience game engine support for scene transitions

- To create scene-specific loading and unloading support

The Abstract Scene Class

Based on the experience from the previous project, an abstract Scene class for encapsulating the interface to the game engine must at the very least define these functions: init(), draw(), update(), load(), and unload(). Missing from this list is the support for level transitions to start, advance to the next level, and, if desired, to stop the game.

1. Create a new JavaScript file in the src/engine folder and name it scene.js, and import from the loop module and the engine access file index.js. These two modules are required because the Scene object must start and end the game loop when the game level begins and ends, and the engine must be cleaned up if a level should decide to terminate the game.

```
import  * as loop from "./core/loop.js";
import engine from "./index.js";
```

Note   The game loop must not be running before a Scene has begun. This is because the required resources must be properly loaded before the update() function of the Scene can be called from the running game loop. Similarly, unloading of a level can only be performed after a game loop has stopped running.

---

2. Define JavaScript Error objects for warning the client in case of misuse:

```
const kAbstractClassError = new Error("Abstract Class")
const kAbstractMethodError = new Error("Abstract Method")
```

3. Create a new class named Scene and export it:

```
class Scene { ... implementation to follow ... }
export default Scene;
```

4. Implement the constructor to ensure only subclasses of the Scene class are instantiated:

```
constructor() {
    if (this.constructor === Scene) {
        throw kAbstractClassError
    }
}
```

5. Define scene transition functions: start(), next(), and stop(). The start() function is an async function because it is responsible for starting the game loop, which in turn is waiting for all the asynchronous loading to complete. Both the next() and the stop() functions stop the game loop and call the unload() function to unload the loaded resources. The difference is that the next() function is expected to be overwritten and called from a subclass where after unloading the current scene, the subclass can proceed to advance to the next level. After unloading, the stop() function assumes the game has terminated and proceeds to clean up the game engine.

```
async start() {
    await loop.start(this);
}

next() {
    loop.stop();
    this.unload();
}

stop() {
    loop.stop();
    this.unload();
    engine.cleanUp();
}
```

6. Define the rest of the derived interface functions. Notice that the Scene class is an abstract class because all of the interface functions are empty. While a subclass can choose to only implement a selective subset of the interface functions, the draw() and update() functions are not optional because together they form the central core of a level.

```
init() { /* to initialize the level (called from loop.start()) */ }
load() { /* to load necessary resources */ }
unload() { /* unload all resources */ }
// draw/update must be over-written by subclass
draw() { throw kAbstractMethodError; }
update() { throw kAbstractMethodError; }
```

Together these functions present a protocol to interface with the game engine. It is expected that subclasses will override these functions to implement the actual game behaviors.

Note   JavaScript does *not* support abstract classes. The language does not prevent a game programmer from instantiating a Scene object; however, the created instance will be completely useless, and the error message will provide them with a proper warning.

Modify Game Engine to Support the Scene Class

The game engine must be modified in two important ways. First, the game engine access file, index.js, must be modified to export the newly introduced symbols to the client as is done with all new functionality. Second, the Scene.stop() function introduces the possibility of stopping the game and handles the cleanup and resource deallocation required.

Export the Scene Class to the Client

Edit the `index.js` file to import from `scene.js` and export Scene for the client:

```
... identical to previous code ...
import Scene from "./scene.js";
... identical to previous code ...
export default {
    ... identical to previous code ...
    Camera, Scene, Transform, Renderable,
    ... identical to previous code ...
}
```

Implement Engine Cleanup Support

It is important to release the allocated resources when the game engine shuts down. The cleanup process is rather involved and occurs in the reverse order of system component initialization.

1. Edit **index.js** once again, this time to implement support for game engine cleanup. Import from the `loop` module, and then define and export the `cleanup()` function.

```
... identical to previous code ...
import * as loop from "./core/loop.js";
... identical to previous code ...
function cleanUp() {
    loop.cleanUp();
    input.cleanUp();
    shaderResources.cleanUp();
    vertexBuffer.cleanUp();
    glSys.cleanUp();
}
... identical to previous code ...
export default {
    ... identical to previous code ...
    init, cleanUp, clearCanvas
    ... identical to previous code ...
}
```

Note   Similar to other core engine internal components, such as `gl` or `vertex_buffer`, `loop` should not be accessed by the client. For this reason, `loop` module is imported but not exported by `index.js`, imported such that game loop cleanup can be invoked, not exported, such that the client can be shielded from irrelevant complexity within the engine.

Notice that none of the components have defined their corresponding cleanup functions. You will now remedy this. In each of the following cases, make sure to remember to export the newly defined `cleanup()` function when appropriate.

2. Edit `loop.js` to define and export a `cleanUp()` function to stop the game loop and unload the currently active scene:

```
... identical to previous code ...
function cleanUp() {
    if (mLoopRunning) {
        stop();
        // unload all resources
        mCurrentScene.unload();
        mCurrentScene = null;
    }
}
export {start, stop, cleanUp}
```

3. Edit `input.js` to define and export a `cleanUp()` function. For now, no specific resources need to be released.

```
... identical to previous code ...
function cleanUp() {}  // nothing to do for now
export {keys, init, cleanUp,
... identical to previous code ...
```

4. Edit `shader_resources.js` to define and export a `cleanUp()` function to clean up the created shader and unload its source code:

```
... identical to previous code ...
function cleanUp() {
    mConstColorShader.cleanUp();
    text.unload(kSimpleVS);
    text.unload(kSimpleFS);
}
export {init, cleanUp, getConstColorShader}
```

5. Edit `simple_shader.js` to define the `cleanUp()` function for the SimpleShader class to release the allocated WebGL resources:

```
cleanUp() {
    let gl = glSys.get();
    gl.detachShader(this.mCompiledShader, this.mVertexShader);
    gl.detachShader(this.mCompiledShader, this.mFragmentShader);
    gl.deleteShader(this.mVertexShader);
    gl.deleteShader(this.mFragmentShader);
    gl.deleteProgram(this.mCompiledShader);
}
```

6. Edit `vertex_buffer.js` to define and export a `cleanUp()` function to delete the allocated buffer memory:

```
... identical to previous code ...
function cleanUp() {
    if (mGLVertexBuffer !== null) {
        glSys.get().deleteBuffer(mGLVertexBuffer);
        mGLVertexBuffer = null;
    }
}
export {init, get, cleanUp}
```

7. Lastly, edit gl.js to define and export a cleanUp() function to inform the player that the engine is now shut down:

```
... identical to previous code ...
function cleanUp() {
    if ((mGL == null) || (mCanvas == null))
        throw new Error("Engine cleanup: system is not initialized.");
    mGL = null;
    // let the user know
    mCanvas.style.position = "fixed";
    mCanvas.style.backgroundColor = "rgba(200, 200, 200, 0.5)";
    mCanvas = null;
    document.body.innerHTML +=
            "<br><br><h1>End of Game</h1><h1>GL System Shut Down</h1>";
}
export {init, get, cleanUp}
```

Test the Scene Class Interface to the Game Engine

With the abstract Scene class definition and the resource management modifications to the game engine core components, it is now possible to stop an existing scene and load a new scene at will. This section cycles between two subclasses of the Scene class, MyGame and BlueLevel, to illustrate the loading and unloading of scenes.

For simplicity, the two test scenes are almost identical to the MyGame scene from the previous project. In this project, MyGame explicitly defines the scene in the init() function, while the BlueScene, in a manner identical to the case in the previous project, loads the scene content from the blue_level.xml file located in the assets folder. The content and the parsing of the XML scene file are identical to those from the previous project and thus will not be repeated.

The MyGame Scene

As mentioned, this scene defines in the init() function with identical content found in the scene file from the previous project. In the following section, take note of the definition and calls to next() and stop() functions.

1. Edit my_game.js to import from index.js and the newly defined
    blue_level.js. Note that with the Scene class support, you no
    longer need to import from the loop module.

```
import engine from "../engine/index.js";
import BlueLevel from "./blue_level.js";
```

2. Define MyGame to be a subclass of the engine Scene class, and
    remember to export MyGame:

```
class MyGame extends engine.Scene {
    ... implementation to follow ...
}
export default MyGame;
```

Note   The JavaScript extends keyword defines the parent/child relationship.

---

3. Define the constructor(), init(), and draw() functions. Note
    that the scene content defined in the init() function, with the
    exception of the camera background color, is identical to that of
    the previous project.

```
constructor() {
    super();
    // The camera to view the scene
    this.mCamera = null;

    // the hero and the support objects
    this.mHero = null;
    this.mSupport = null;
}

init() {
    // Step A: set up the cameras
    this.mCamera = new engine.Camera(
        vec2.fromValues(20, 60),    // position of the camera
```

```
    20,                            // width of camera
    [20, 40, 600, 300]            // viewport (orgX, orgY, width, height)
);
this.mCamera.setBackgroundColor([0.8, 0.8, 0.8, 1]);

// Step B: Create the support object in red
this.mSupport = new engine.Renderable();
this.mSupport.setColor([0.8, 0.2, 0.2, 1]);
this.mSupport.getXform().setPosition(20, 60);
this.mSupport.getXform().setSize(5, 5);

// Step C: Create the hero object in blue
this.mHero = new engine.Renderable();
this.mHero.setColor([0, 0, 1, 1]);
this.mHero.getXform().setPosition(20, 60);
this.mHero.getXform().setSize(2, 3);
}

draw() {
    // Step A: clear the canvas
    engine.clearCanvas([0.9, 0.9, 0.9, 1.0]);
    // Step  B: Activate the drawing Camera
    this.mCamera.setViewAndCameraMatrix();

    // Step  C: draw everything
    this.mSupport.draw(this.mCamera);
    this.mHero.draw(this.mCamera);
}
```

4. Define the update() function; take note of the this.next() call
   when the mHero object crosses the x=11 boundary from the right
   and the this.stop() call when the Q key is pressed.

```
update() {
    // let's only allow the movement of hero,
    // and if hero moves too far off, this level ends, we will
    // load the next level
    let deltaX = 0.05;
```

```
let xform = this.mHero.getXform();

// Support hero movements
if (engine.input.isKeyPressed(engine.input.keys.Right)) {
    xform.incXPosBy(deltaX);
    if (xform.getXPos() > 30) { // right-bound of the window
        xform.setPosition(12, 60);
    }
}

if (engine.input.isKeyPressed(engine.input.keys.Left)) {
    xform.incXPosBy(-deltaX);
    if (xform.getXPos() < 11) {  // left-bound of the window
        this.next();
    }
}

if (engine.input.isKeyPressed(engine.input.keys.Q))
    this.stop();   // Quit the game
}
```

5. Define the next() function to transition to the BlueLevel scene:

```
next() {
    super.next();   // this must be called!

    // next scene to run
    let nextLevel = new BlueLevel();   // next level to be loaded
    nextLevel.start();
}
```

Note   The super.next() call, where the super class can stop the game loop and cause the unloading of this scene, is necessary and absolutely critical in causing the scene transition.

---

6.   Lastly, modify the window.onload() function to replace access to the loop module with a client-friendly myGame.start() function:

```
window.onload = function () {
    engine.init("GLCanvas");

    let myGame = new MyGame();
    myGame.start();
}
```

The BlueLevel Scene

The BlueLevel scene is almost identical to the MyGame object from the previous project with the exception of supporting the new Scene class and scene transition:

1.   Create and edit blue_level.js file in the my_game folder to import from the engine index.js, MyGame, and SceneFileParser. Define and export BlueLevel to be a subclass of the engine.Scene class.

```
// Engine Core stuff
import engine from "../engine/index.js";

// Local stuff
import MyGame from "./my_game.js";
import SceneFileParser from "./util/scene_file_parser.js";

class BlueLevel extends engine.Scene {
    ... implementation to follow ...
}
export default BlueLevel
```

2.   Define the init(), draw(), load(), and unload() functions to be identical to those in the MyGame class from the previous project.

3.   Define the update() function similar to that of the MyGame scene. Once again, note the this.next() call when the object crosses the x=11 boundary from the right and the this.stop() call when the Q key is pressed.

```
update() {
    // For this very simple game, let's move the first square
    let xform = this.mSQSet[1].getXform();
    let deltaX = 0.05;

    /// Move right and swap over
    if (engine.input.isKeyPressed(engine.input.keys.Right)) {
        xform.incXPosBy(deltaX);
        if (xform.getXPos() > 30) { // right-bound of the window
            xform.setPosition(12, 60);
        }
    }

    // test for white square movement
    if (engine.input.isKeyPressed(engine.input.keys.Left)) {
        xform.incXPosBy(-deltaX);
        if (xform.getXPos() < 11) { // this is the left-boundary
            this.next(); // go back to my game
        }
    }

    if (engine.input.isKeyPressed(engine.input.keys.Q))
        this.stop();  // Quit the game
}
```

4. Lastly, define the next() function to transition to the MyGame
   scene. It is worth reiterating that the call to super.next() is
   necessary because it is critical to stop the game loop and unload
   the current scene before proceeding to the next scene.

```
next() {
    super.next();
    let nextLevel = new MyGame();  // load the next level
    nextLevel.start();
}
```

You can now run the project and view the scenes unloading and loading and quit the game at any point during the interaction. Your game engine now has a well-defined interface for working with its client. This interface follows the well-defined protocol of the Scene class.

- `constructor()`: For declaring variables and defining constants.

- `start()/stop()`: For starting a scene and stopping the game. These two methods are not meant to be overwritten by a subclass.

The following interface methods are meant to be overwritten by subclasses.

- `init()`: For instantiating the variables and setting up the game scene.

- `load()/unload()`: For initiating the asynchronous loading and unloading of external resources.

- `draw()/update()`: For continuously displaying the game state and receiving player input and implementing the game logic.

- `next()`: For instantiating and transitioning to the next scene. Lastly, as a final reminder, it is absolutely critical for the subclass to call the `super.next()` to stop the game loop and unload the scene.

Any objects that define these methods can be loaded and interacted with by your game engine. You can experiment with creating other levels.

Audio

Audio is an essential element of all video games. In general, audio effects in games fall into two categories. The first category is background audio. This includes background music or ambient effects and is often used to bring atmosphere or emotion to different portions of the game. The second category is sound effects. Sound effects are useful for all sorts of purposes, from notifying users of game actions to hearing the footfalls of your hero character. Usually, sound effects represent a specific action, triggered either by the user or by the game itself. Such sound effects are often thought of as an audio cue.

One important difference between these two types of audio is how you control them. Sound effects or cues cannot be stopped or have their volume adjusted once they have started; therefore, cues are generally short. On the other hand, background audio can be started and stopped at will. These capabilities are useful for stopping the background track completely and starting another one.

The Audio Support Project

This project has identical MyGame and the BlueLevel scenes to the previous project. You can move the front rectangle left or right with the arrow keys, the intersection with the left boundary triggers the loading of the other scene, and the Q key quits the game. However, in this version, each scene plays background music and triggers a brief audio cue when the left-/right-arrow key is pressed. Notice that the volume varies for each type of audio clip. The implementation of this project also reinforces the concept of loading and unloading of external resources and the audio clips themselves. You can see an example of this project running in Figure 4-6. The source code to this project is defined in the chapter4/4.6.audio_support folder.

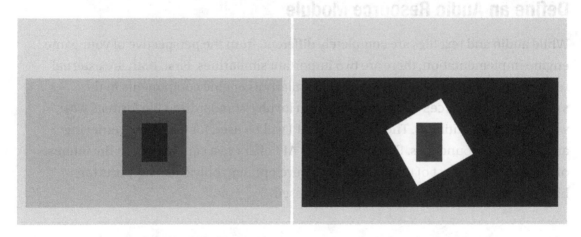

Figure 4-6. *Running the Audio Support project with both scenes*

The controls of the project are as follows:

- **Left-/right-arrow key**: Moves the front rectangle left and right to increase and decrease the volume of the background music

- **Q key:** Quits the game

The goals of the project are as follows:

- To add audio support to the resource management system

- To provide an interface to play audio for games

You can find the following audio files in the `assets/sounds` folder:

- `bg_clip.mp3`

- `blue_level_cue.wav`

- `my_game_cue.wav`

Notice that the audio files are in two formats, `mp3` and `wav`. While both are supported, audio files of these formats should be used with care. Files in `.mp3` format are compressed and are suitable for storing longer durations of audio content, for example, for background music. Files in `.wav` format are uncompressed and should contain only very short audio snippet, for example, for storing cue effects.

Define an Audio Resource Module

While audio and text files are completely different, from the perspective of your game engine implementation, there are two important similarities. First, both are external resources and thus will be implemented similarly as engine components in the `src/engine/resources` folder. Second, both involve standardized file formats with well-defined API utilities. The Web Audio API will be used for the actual retrieving and playing of sound files. Even though this API offers vast capabilities, in the interests of focusing on the rest of the game engine development, only basic supports for background audio and effect cues are discussed.

Note   Interested readers can learn more about the Web Audio API from `www.w3.org/TR/webaudio/`.

The latest policy for some browsers, including Chrome, is that audio will not be allowed to play until first interaction from the user. This means that the context creation will result in an initial warning from Chrome that is output to the runtime browser console. The audio will only be played after user input (e.g., mouse click or keyboard events).

---

1. In the `src/engine/resources` folder, create a new file and name it `audio.js`. This file will implement the module for the audio component. This component must support two types of functionality: loading and unloading of audio files and playing and controlling of the content of audio file for the game developer.

2. The loading and unloading are similar to the implementations of `text` and `xml` modules where the core resource management functionality is imported from `resource_map`:

```
"use strict";

import * as map from "../core/resource_map.js";
// functions from resource_map
let unload = map.unload;
let has = map.has;
```

3. Define the decoding and parsing functions, and call the `resource_map` `loadDecodeParse()` function to load an audio file. Notice that with the support from `resource_map` and the rest of the engine infrastructure, loading and unloading of external resources have become straightforward.

```
function decodeResource(data) { return data.arrayBuffer(); }
function parseResource(data) {
    return mAudioContext.decodeAudioData(data); }
function load(path) {
    return map.loadDecodeParse(path, decodeResource, parseResource);
}
```

4. With the loading functionality completed, you can now define the audio control and manipulation functions. Declare variables to maintain references to the Web Audio context and background music and to control volumes.

```
let mAudioContext = null;
let mBackgroundAudio = null;

// volume control support
let mBackgroundGain = null; // background volume
```

173

```
let mCueGain = null;        // cue/special effects volume
let mMasterGain = null;     // overall/master volume

let kDefaultInitGain = 0.1;
```

5. Define the init() function to create and store a reference to the
   Web Audio context in mAudioContext, and initialize the audio
   volume gain controls for the background, cue, and a master that
   affects both. In all cases, volume gain of a 0 corresponds to no
   audio and 1 means maximum loudness.

```
function init() {
    try {
        let AudioContext = window.AudioContext ||
                           window.webkitAudioContext;
        mAudioContext = new AudioContext();

        // connect Master volume control
        mMasterGain = mAudioContext.createGain();
        mMasterGain.connect(mAudioContext.destination);
        // set default Master volume
        mMasterGain.gain.value = kDefaultInitGain;

        // connect Background volume control
        mBackgroundGain = mAudioContext.createGain();
        mBackgroundGain.connect(mMasterGain);
        // set default Background volume
        mBackgroundGain.gain.value = 1.0;

        // connect Cuevolume control
        mCueGain = mAudioContext.createGain();
        mCueGain.connect(mMasterGain);
        // set default Cue volume
        mCueGain.gain.value = 1.0;
    } catch (e) {
        throw new Error("...");
    }
}
```

6. Define the `playCue()` function to play the entire duration of an
    audio clip with proper volume control. This function uses the
    audio file path as a resource name to find the loaded asset from
    the `resource_map` and then invokes the Web Audio API to play the
    audio clip. Notice that no reference to the `source` variable is kept,
    and thus once started, there is no way to stop the corresponding
    audio clip. A game should call this function to play short snippets
    of audio clips as cues.

```
function playCue(path, volume) {
    let source = mAudioContext.createBufferSource();
    source.buffer = map.get(path);
    source.start(0);

    // volume support for cue
    source.connect(mCueGain);
    mCueGain.gain.value = volume;
}
```

7. Define the functionality to play, stop, query, and control
    the volume of the background music. In this case, the
    `mBackgroundAudio` variable keeps a reference to the currently
    playing audio, and thus, it is possible to stop the clip or change its
    volume.

```
function playBackground(path, volume) {
    if (has(path)) {
        stopBackground();
        mBackgroundAudio = mAudioContext.createBufferSource();
        mBackgroundAudio.buffer = map.get(path);
        mBackgroundAudio.loop = true;
        mBackgroundAudio.start(0);

        // connect volume accordingly
        mBackgroundAudio.connect(mBackgroundGain);
        setBackgroundVolume(volume);
    }
}
```

```
function stopBackground() {
    if (mBackgroundAudio !== null) {
        mBackgroundAudio.stop(0);
        mBackgroundAudio = null;
    }
}

function isBackgroundPlaying() {
    return (mBackgroundAudio !== null);
}

function setBackgroundVolume(volume) {
    if (mBackgroundGain !== null) {
        mBackgroundGain.gain.value = volume;
    }
}

function incBackgroundVolume(increment) {
    if (mBackgroundGain !== null) {
        mBackgroundGain.gain.value += increment;

        // need this since volume increases when negative
        if (mBackgroundGain.gain.value < 0) {
            setBackgroundVolume(0);
        }
    }
}
```

8. Define functions for controlling the master volume, which adjusts the volume of both the cue and the background music:

```
function setMasterVolume(volume) {
    if (mMasterGain !== null) {
        mMasterGain.gain.value = volume;
    }
}
```

```
function  incMasterVolume(increment) {
    if (mMasterGain !== null) {
        mMasterGain.gain.value += increment;

        // need this since volume increases when negative
        if (mMasterGain.gain.value < 0) {
            mMasterGain.gain.value = 0;
        }
    }
}
```

9. Define a `cleanUp()` function to release the allocated HTML5
    resources:

```
function cleanUp() {
    mAudioContext.close();
    mAudioContext = null;
}
```

10. Remember to export the functions from this module:

```
export {init, cleanUp,
        has, load, unload,

        playCue,

        playBackground, stopBackground, isBackgroundPlaying,
        setBackgroundVolume, incBackgroundVolume,

        setMasterVolume, incMasterVolume
}
```

Export the Audio Module to the Client

Edit the `index.js` file to import from `audio.js`, initialize and cleanup the module
accordingly, and to export to the client:

```
... identical to previous code ...
import * as audio from "./resources/audio.js";
... identical to previous code ...
```

```
function init(htmlCanvasID) {
    glSys.init(htmlCanvasID);
    vertexBuffer.init();
    shaderResources.init();
    input.init();
    audio.init();
}

function cleanUp() {
    loop.cleanUp();
    audio.cleanUp();
    input.cleanUp();
    shaderResources.cleanUp();
    vertexBuffer.cleanUp();
    glSys.cleanUp();
}
... identical to previous code ...
export default {
    // resource support
    audio, text, xml
    ... identical to previous code ...
}
```

Testing the Audio Component

To test the audio component, you must copy the necessary audio files into your game project. Create a new folder in the assets folder and name it sounds. Copy the bg_clip. mp3, blue_level_cue.wav, and my_game_cue.wav files into the sounds folder. You will now need to update the MyGame and BlueLevel implementations to load and use these audio resources.

Change MyGame.js

Update MyGame scene to load the audio clips, play background audio, and cue the player when the arrow keys are pressed:

1. Declare constant file paths to the audio files in the constructor. Recall that these file paths are used as resource names for loading, storage, and retrieval. Declaring these as constants for later reference is a good software engineering practice.

```
constructor() {
    super();

    // audio clips: supports both mp3 and wav formats
    this.mBackgroundAudio = "assets/sounds/bg_clip.mp3";
    this.mCue = "assets/sounds/my_game_cue.wav";
    ... identical to previous code ...
}
```

2. Request the loading of audio clips in the load() function, and make sure to define the corresponding unload() function. Notice that the unloading of background music is preceded by stopping the music. In general, a resource's operations must be halted prior to its unloading.

```
load() {
    // loads the audios
    engine.audio.load(this.mBackgroundAudio);
    engine.audio.load(this.mCue);
}

unload() {
    // Step A: Game loop not running, unload all assets
    // stop the background audio
    engine.audio.stopBackground();

    // unload the scene resources
    engine.audio.unload(this.mBackgroundAudio);
    engine.audio.unload(this.mCue);
}
```

3.   Start the background audio at the end of the init() function.

```
init() {
    ... identical to previous code ...

    // now start the Background music ...
    engine.audio.playBackground(this.mBackgroundAudio, 1.0);
}
```

4.   In the update() function, cue the players when the right- and left-
     arrow keys are pressed, and increase and decrease the volume of
     the background music:

```
update() {
    ... identical to previous code ...
    // Support hero movements
    if (engine.input.isKeyPressed(engine.input.keys.Right)) {
        engine.audio.playCue(this.mCue, 0.5);
        engine.audio.incBackgroundVolume(0.05);
        xform.incXPosBy(deltaX);
        if (xform.getXPos() > 30) { // right-bound of the window
            xform.setPosition(12, 60);
        }
    }

    if (engine.input.isKeyPressed(engine.input.keys.Left)) {
        engine.audio.playCue(this.mCue, 1.5);
        engine.audio.incBackgroundVolume(-0.05);
        xform.incXPosBy(-deltaX);
        if (xform.getXPos() < 11) {  // left-bound of the window
            this.next();
        }
    }
    ... identical to previous code ...
}
```

Change BlueLevel.js

The changes to the BlueLevel scene are similar to those of the MyGame scene but with a different audio cue:

1. In the BlueLevel constructor, add the following path names to the audio resources:

```
constructor() {
    super();

    // audio clips: supports both mp3 and wav formats
    this.mBackgroundAudio = "assets/sounds/bg_clip.mp3";
    this.mCue = "assets/sounds/blue_level_cue.wav";
    ... identical to previous code ...
}
```

2. Modify the load() and unload() functions for the audio clips:

```
load() {
    engine.xml.load(this.mSceneFile);
    engine.audio.load(this.mBackgroundAudio);
    engine.audio.load(this.mCue);
}

unload() {
    // stop the background audio
    engine.audio.stopBackground();

    // unload the scene file and loaded resources
    engine.xml.unload(this.mSceneFile);
    engine.audio.unload(this.mBackgroundAudio);
    engine.audio.unload(this.mCue);
}
```

3. In the same manner as MyGame, start the background audio in the init() function and cue the player when the left and right keys are pressed in the update() function. Notice that in this case, the audio cues are played with different volume settings.

```
init() {
    ... identical to previous code ...

    // now start the Background music ...
    engine.audio.playBackground(this.mBackgroundAudio, 0.5);
}

update() {
    ... identical to previous code ...

    // Move right and swap over
    if (engine.input.isKeyPressed(engine.input.keys.Right)) {
        engine.audio.playCue(this.mCue, 0.5);
        xform.incXPosBy(deltaX);
        if (xform.getXPos() > 30) { // right-bound of the window
            xform.setPosition(12, 60);
        }
    }

    // Step A: test for white square movement
    if (engine.input.isKeyPressed(engine.input.keys.Left)) {
        engine.audio.playCue(this.mCue, 1.0);
        xform.incXPosBy(-deltaX);
        if (xform.getXPos() < 11) { // this is the left-boundary
            this.next(); // go back to my game
        }
    }
    ... identical to previous code ...
}
```

You can now run the project and listen to the wonderful audio feedback. If you press and hold the arrow keys, there will be many cues repeatedly played. In fact, there are so many cues echoed that the sound effects are blurred into an annoying blast. This serves as an excellent example illustrating the importance of using audio cues with care and ensuring each individual cue is nice and short. You can try tapping the arrow keys to listen to more distinct and pleasant-sounding cues, or you can simply replace the isKeyPressed() function with the isKeyClicked() function and listen to each individual cue.

Summary

In this chapter, you learned how several common components of a game engine come together. Starting with the ever-important game loop, you learned how it implements an input, update, and draw pattern in order to surpass human perception or trick our senses into believing that the system is continuous and running in real time. This pattern is at the heart of any game engine. You learned how full keyboard support can be implemented with flexibility and reusability to provide the engine with a reliable input component. Furthermore, you saw how a resource manager can be implemented to load files asynchronously and how scenes can be abstracted to support scenes being loaded from a file, which can drastically reduce duplication in the code. Lastly, you learned how audio support supplies the client with an interface to load and play both ambient background audio and audio cues.

These components separately have little in common but together make up the core fundamentals of nearly every game. As you implement these core components into the game engine, the games that are created with the engine will not need to worry about the specifics of each component. Instead, the games programmer can focus on utilizing the functionality to hasten and streamline the development process. In the next chapter, you will learn how to create the illusion of an animation with external images.

Game Design Considerations

In this chapter, we discussed the *game loop* and the technical foundation contributing to the connection between what the player does and how the game responds. If a player selects a square that's drawn on the screen and moves it from location A to location B by using the arrow keys, for example, you'd typically want that action to appear as a smooth motion beginning as soon as the arrow key is pressed, without stutters, delays, or noticeable lag. The game loop contributes significantly to what's known as *presence* in game design; presence is the player's ability to feel as if they're connected to the game world, and responsiveness plays a key role in making players feel connected. Presence is reinforced when actions in the real world (such as pressing arrow keys) seamlessly translate to responses in the game world (such as moving objects, flipping switches, jumping, and so on); presence is compromised when actions in the real world suffer translation errors such as delays and lag.

As mentioned in Chapter 1, effective game mechanic design can begin with just a few simple elements. By the time you've completed the *Keyboard Support* project in this chapter, for example, many of the pieces will already be in place to begin constructing game levels: you've provided players with the ability to manipulate two individual elements on the screen (the red and white squares), and all that remains in order to create a basic game loop is to design a causal chain using those elements that results in a new event when completed. Imagine the *Keyboard Support* project is your game: how might you use what's available to create a causal chain? You might choose to play with the relationship between the squares, perhaps requiring that the red square be moved completely within the white square in order to unlock the next challenge; once the player successfully placed the red square in the white square, the level would complete. This basic mechanic may not be quite enough on its own to create an engaging experience, but by including just a few of the other eight elements of game design (systems design, setting, visual design, music and audio, and the like), it's possible to turn this one basic interaction into an almost infinite number of engaging experiences and create that sense of presence for players. You'll add more game design elements to these exercises as you continue through subsequent chapters.

The *Resource Map and Shader Loader* project, the *Scene File* project, and the *Scene Objects* project are designed to help you begin thinking about architecting game designs from the ground up for maximum efficiency so that problems such as asset loading delays that detract from the player's sense of presence are minimized. As you begin designing games with multiple stages and levels and many assets, a resource management plan becomes essential. Understanding the limits of available memory and how to smartly load and unload assets can mean the difference between a great experience and a frustrating experience.

We experience the world through our senses, and our feeling of presence in games tends to be magnified as we include additional sensory inputs. The *Audio Support* project adds basic audio to our simple state-changing exercise from the *Scene Objects* project in the form of a constant background score to provide ambient mood and includes a distinct movement sound for each of the two areas. Compare the two experiences and consider how different they feel because of the presence of sound cues; although the visual and interaction experience is identical between the two, the *Audio Support* project begins to add some emotional cues because of the beat of the background score and the individual tones the rectangle makes as it moves. Audio is a powerful enhancement to interactive experiences and can dramatically increase a player's sense of presence in game environments, and as you continue through the chapters, you'll explore how audio contributes to game design in more detail.

CHAPTER 5

Working with Textures, Sprites, and Fonts

After completing this chapter, you will be able to

- Use any image or photograph as a texture representing characters or objects in your game

- Understand and use texture coordinates to identify a location on an image

- Optimize texture memory utilization by combining multiple characters and objects into one image

- Produce and control animations using sprite sheets

- Display texts of different fonts and sizes anywhere in your game

Introduction

Custom-composed images are used to represent almost all objects including characters, backgrounds, and even animations in most 2D games. For this reason, the proper support of image operations is core to 2D game engines. A game typically works with an image in three distinct stages: loading, rendering, and unloading.

Loading is the reading of the image from the hard drive of the web server into the client's system main memory, where it is processed and stored in the graphics subsystem. *Rendering* occurs during gameplay when the loaded image is drawn continuously to represent the respective game objects. *Unloading* happens when an image is no longer required by the game and the associated resources are reclaimed for future uses. Because of the slower response time of the hard drive and the potentially

185

© Kelvin Sung, Jebediah Pavleas, Matthew Munson, and Jason Pace 2022
K. Sung et al., *Build Your Own 2D Game Engine and Create Great Web Games*,
https://doi.org/10.1007/978-1-4842-7377-7_5

large amount of data that must be transferred and processed, loading images can take a noticeable amount of time. This, together with the fact that, just like the objects that images represent, the usefulness of an image is usually associated with individual game level, image loading and unloading operations typically occur during game-level transitions. To optimize the number of loading and unloading operations, it is a common practice to combine multiple lower-resolution images into a single larger image. This larger image is referred to as a *sprite sheet*.

To represent objects, images with meaningful drawings are pasted, or *mapped*, on simple geometries. For example, a horse in a game can be represented by a square that is mapped with an image of a horse. In this way, a game developer can manipulate the transformation of the square to control the horse. This mapping of images on geometries is referred to as *texture mapping* in computer graphics.

The illusion of movement, or animation, can be created by cycling through strategically mapping selected images on the same geometry. For example, during subsequent game loop updates, different images of the same horse with strategically drawn leg positions can be mapped on the same square to create the illusion that the horse is galloping. Usually, these images of different animated positions are stored in one sprite sheet or an animated sprite sheet. The process of sequencing through these images to create animation is referred to as *sprite animation* or *sprite sheet animation*.

This chapter first introduces you to the concept of texture coordinates such that you can understand and program with the WebGL texture mapping interface. You will then build a core texture component and the associated classes to support mapping with simple textures, working with sprite sheets that contain multiple objects, creating and controlling motions with animated sprite sheets, and extracting alphabet characters from a sprite sheet to display text messages.

Note   A texture is an image that is loaded into the graphics system and ready to be mapped onto a geometry. When discussing the process of texture mapping, "an image" and "a texture" are often used interchangeably. A pixel is a color location in an image and a *texel* is a color location in a texture.

Texture Mapping and Texture Coordinates

As discussed, texture mapping is the process of pasting an image on a geometry, just like putting a sticker on an object. In the case of your game engine, instead of drawing a constant color for each pixel occupied by the unit square, you will create GLSL shaders to strategically select texels from the texture and display the corresponding texel colors at the screen pixel locations covered by the unit square. The process of selecting a texel, or converting a group of texels into a single color, to be displayed to a screen pixel location is referred to as texture sampling. To render a texture-mapped pixel, the texture must be sampled to extract a corresponding texel color.

The process of mapping a texture of any resolution to a fixed-size geometry can be daunting. The Texture Coordinate System that specifies the Texture Space is designed to hide the resolution of textures to facilitate this mapping process. As depicted in Figure 5-1, the Texture Coordinate System is a normalized system defined over the entire texture with the origin located at the lower-left corner and (1,1) located at the top-right corner. This simple fact that the normalized 0 to 1 range is always defined over the entire texture regardless of the resolution is the elegance of the Texture Coordinate System. Given a texture of any resolution, (0.5, 0.5) is always the center, (0, 1) is always the top-left corner, and so on. Notice that in Figure 5-1 the horizontal axis is labeled as the u axis, and the vertical axis is labeled as the v axis. Oftentimes a texture coordinate, or the uv values associated with a texture coordinate, is used interchangeably to refer to a location in the Texture Coordinate System.

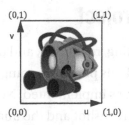

Figure 5-1. *The Texture Coordinate System and the corresponding uv values defined for all images*

Note   There are conventions that define the v axis increasing either upward or downward. In all examples of this book, you will program WebGL to follow the convention in Figure 5-1, with the v axis increasing upward.

To map a texture onto a unit square, you must define a corresponding uv value for each of the vertex positions. As illustrated in Figure 5-2, in addition to defining the value of the xy position for each of the four corners of the square, to map an image onto this square, a corresponding uv coordinate must also be defined. In this case, the top-left corner has xy=(-0.5, 0.5) and uv=(0, 1), the top-right corner has xy=(0.5, 0.5) and uv=(1, 1), and so on. Given this definition, it is possible to compute a unique uv value for any position inside the square by linearly interpolating the uv values defined at the vertices. For example, given the settings shown in Figure 5-2, you know that the midpoint along the top edge of the square maps to a uv of (0.5, 1.0) in Texture Space, the midpoint along the left edge maps to a uv of (0, 0.5), and so on.

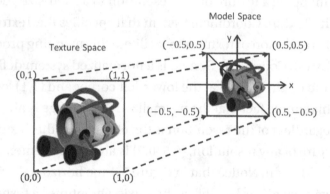

Figure 5-2. *Defining Texture Space uv values to map the entire image onto the geometry in Model Space*

The Texture Shaders Project

This project demonstrates the loading, rendering, and unloading of textures with WebGL. You can see an example of this project running in Figure 5-3 with the left and right screenshots from the two scenes implemented. Notice the natural-looking objects without white borders in the left screenshot and the images with white backgrounds in the right screenshot. This project will also highlight the differences between images with and without the alpha channel, or *transparency*. The source code to this project is defined in the chapter5/5.1.texture_shaders folder.

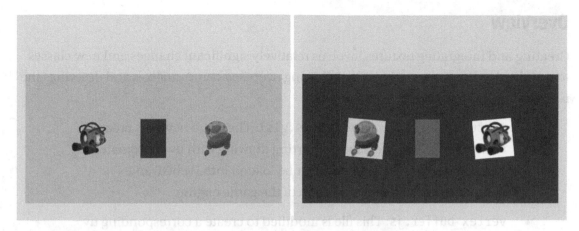

Figure 5-3. *Running the Texture Shaders project with both scenes*

The controls of the project are as follows, for both scenes:

- **Right-arrow key**: Moves the middle rectangle toward the right. If this rectangle passes the right window boundary, it will be wrapped to the left side of the window.

- **Left-arrow key**: Moves the middle rectangle toward the left. If this rectangle crosses the left window boundary, the game will transition to the next scene.

The goals of the project are as follows:

- To demonstrate how to define uv coordinates for geometries with WebGL

- To create a texture coordinate buffer in the graphics system with WebGL

- To build GLSL shaders to render the textured geometry

- To define the Texture core engine component to load and process an image into a texture and to unload a texture

- To implement simple texture tinting, a modification of all texels with a programmer-specified color

You can find the following external resource files in the assets folder: a scene-level file (blue_level.xml) and four images (minion_collector.jpg, minion_collector.png, minion_portal.jpg, and minion_portal.png).

Overview

Creating and integrating textures involves relatively significant changes and new classes to be added to the game engine. The following overview contextualizes and describes the reasons for the changes:

- texture_vs.glsl and texture_fs.glsl: These are new files created to define GLSL shaders for supporting drawing with uv coordinates. Recall that the GLSL shaders must be loaded into WebGL and compiled during the initialization of the game engine.

- vertex_buffer.js: This file is modified to create a corresponding uv coordinate buffer to define the texture coordinate for the vertices of the unit square.

- texture_shader.js: This is a new file that defines TextureShader as a subclass of SimpleShader to interface the game engine with the corresponding GLSL shaders (TextureVS and TextureFS).

- texture_renderable.js: This is a new file that defines TextureRenderable as a subclass of Renderable to facilitate the creation, manipulation, and drawing of multiple instances of textured objects.

- shader_resources.js: Recall that this file defines a single instance of SimpleShader to wrap over the corresponding GLSL shaders to be shared system wide by all instances of Renderable objects. In a similar manner, this file is modified to define an instance of TextureShader to be shared by all instances of TextureRenderable objects.

- gl.js: This file is modified to configure WebGL to support drawing with texture maps.

- texture.js: This is a new file that defines the core engine component that is capable of loading, activating (for rendering), and unloading texture images.

- my_game.js and blue_level.js: These game engine client files are modified to test the new texture mapping functionality.

Two new source code folders, `src/engine/shaders` and `src/engine/renderables`, are created for organizing the engine source code. These folders are created in anticipation of the many new shader and renderer types required to support the corresponding texture-related functionality. Once again, continuous source code reorganization is important in supporting the corresponding increase in complexity. A systematic and logical source code structure is critical in maintaining and expanding the functionality of large software systems.

Extension of SimpleShader/Renderable Architecture

Recall that the `SimpleShader/Renderable` object pair is designed to support the loading of relevant game engine data to the `SimpleVS/FS` GLSL shaders and to support instantiating multiple copies of `Renderable` geometries by the game engine clients. As illustrated in Figure 5-4, the horizontal dotted line separates the game engine from WebGL. Notice that the GLSL shaders, `SimpleVS` and `SimpleFS`, are modules in WebGL and outside the game engine. The `SimpleShader` object maintains references to all attributes and uniform variables in the GLSL shaders and acts as the conduit for sending all transformation and vertex information to the `SimpleVS/FS` shaders. Although not depicted explicitly in Figure 5-4, there is only one instance of the `SimpleShader` object created in the game engine, in `shader_resources`, and this instance is shared by all `Renderable` objects.

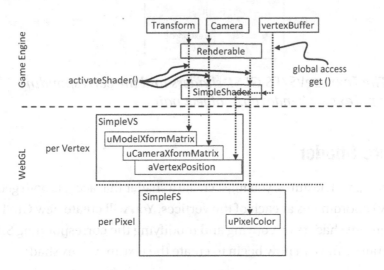

Figure 5-4. *The SimpleShader and Renderable architecture*

The proper support of texture mapping demands new GLSL vertex and fragment shaders and thus requires that a corresponding shader and renderable object pair be defined in the game engine. As illustrated in Figure 5-5, both the GLSL TextureVS/FS shaders and TextureShader/TextureRenderable object pair are extensions (or subclasses) to the corresponding existing objects. The TextureShader/TextureRenderable object pair extends from the corresponding SimpleShader/Renderable objects to forward texture coordinates to the GLSL shaders. The TextureVS/FS shaders are extensions to the corresponding SimpleVS/FS shaders to read texels from the provided texture map when computing pixel colors. Note that since GLSL does not support subclassing, the TextureVS/FS source code is copied from the SimpleVS/FS files.

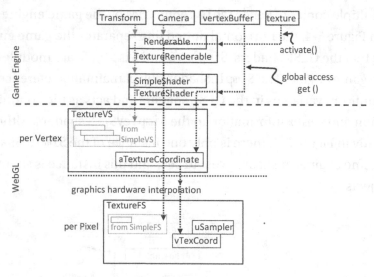

Figure 5-5. *The* TextureVS/FS *GLSL shaders and the corresponding* TextureShader/TextureRenderable *object pair*

GLSL Texture Shader

To support drawing with textures, you must create a shader that accepts both geometric (xy) and texture (uv) coordinates at each of the vertices. You will create new GLSL texture vertex and fragment shaders by copying and modifying the corresponding SimpleVS and SimpleFS programs. You can now begin to create the texture vertex shader.

1. Create a new file in the src/glsl_shaders folder and name it texture_vs.glsl.

2.   Add the following code to the `texture_vs.glsl` file:

```
attribute vec3 aVertexPosition; // expects one vertex position
attribute vec2 aTextureCoordinate; // texture coordinate attribute

// texture coordinate that maps image to the square
varying vec2 vTexCoord;

// to transform the vertex position
uniform mat4 uModelXformMatrix;
uniform mat4 uCameraXformMatrix;

void main(void) {
    // Convert the vec3 into vec4 for scan conversion and
    // transform by uModelXformMatrix and uCameraXformMatrix before
    // assign to gl_Position to pass the vertex to the fragment shader
    gl_Position = uCameraXformMatrix *
                  uModelXformMatrix *
                  vec4(aVertexPosition, 1.0);

    // pass the texture coordinate to the fragment shader
    vTexCoord = aTextureCoordinate;
}
```

You may notice that the TextureVS shader is similar to the SimpleVS shader, with only three additional lines of code:

a.   The first additional line adds the aTextureCoordinate attribute. This defines a vertex to include a vec3 (aVertexPosition, the xyz position of the vertex) and a vec2 (aTextureCoordinate, the uv coordinate of the vertex).

b.   The second declares the varying vTexCoord variable. The varying keyword in GLSL signifies that the associated variable will be linearly interpolated and passed to the fragment shader. As explained earlier and illustrated in Figure 5-2, uv values are defined only at vertex positions. In this case, the varying vTexCoord variable instructs the graphics hardware to linearly interpolate the uv values to compute the texture coordinate for each invocation of the fragment shader.

    c.   The third and final line assigns the vertex uv coordinate
values to the varying variable for interpolation and
forwarding to the fragment shader.

With the vertex shader defined, you can now create the associated fragment shader:

1. Create a new file in the src/glsl_shaders folder and name it
texture_fs.glsl.

2. Add the following code to the texture_fs.glsl file to declare
the variables. The sampler2D data type is a GLSL utility that is
capable of reading texel values from a 2D texture. In this case, the
uSampler object will be bound to a GLSL texture such that texel
values can be sampled for every pixel rendered. The uPixelColor
is the same as the one from SimpleFS. The vTexCoord is the
interpolated uv coordinate value for each pixel.

```
// The object that fetches data from texture.
// Must be set outside the shader.
uniform sampler2D uSampler;

// Color of pixel
uniform vec4 uPixelColor;

// "varying" keyword signifies that the texture coordinate will be
// interpolated and thus varies.
varying vec2 vTexCoord;
```

3. Add the following code to compute the color for each pixel:

```
void main(void)  {
    // texel color look up based on interpolated UV value in vTexCoord
    vec4 c = texture2D(uSampler, vec2(vTexCoord.s, vTexCoord.t));

    // tint the textured. transparent area defined by the texture
    vec3 r = vec3(c) * (1.0-uPixelColor.a) +
```

```
            vec3(uPixelColor) * uPixelColor.a;
    vec4 result = vec4(r, c.a);

    gl_FragColor = result;
}
```

The texture2D() function samples and reads the texel value from the texture that is associated with uSampler using the interpolated uv values from vTexCoord. In this example, the texel color is modified, or tinted, by a weighted sum of the color value defined in uPixelColor according to the *transparency* or the value of the corresponding alpha channel. In general, there is no agreed-upon definition for tinting texture colors. You are free to experiment with different ways to combine uPixelColor and the sampled texel color. For example, you can try multiplying the two. In the provided source code file, a few alternatives are suggested. Please do experiment with them.

Define and Set Up Texture Coordinates

Recall that all shaders share the same xy coordinate buffer of a unit square that is defined in the vertex_buffer.js file. In a similar fashion, a corresponding buffer must be defined to supply texture coordinates to the GLSL shaders.

1. Modify vertex_buffer.js to define both xy and uv coordinates for the unit square. As illustrated in Figure 5-2, the mTextureCoordinates variable defines the uv values for the corresponding four xy values of the unit square defined sequentially in mVerticesOfSquare. For example, (1, 1) are the uv values associated with the (0.5, 0.5, 0) xy position, (0, 1) for (-0.5, 0.5, 0), and so on.

```
// First: define the vertices for a square
let mVerticesOfSquare = [
    0.5, 0.5, 0.0,
    -0.5, 0.5, 0.0,
    0.5, -0.5, 0.0,
    -0.5, -0.5, 0.0
];
```

```
// Second: define the corresponding texture coordinates
let mTextureCoordinates = [
    1.0, 1.0,
    0.0, 1.0,
    1.0, 0.0,
    0.0, 0.0
];
```

2. Define the variable, mGLTextureCoordBuffer, to keep a reference
    to the WebGL buffer storage for the texture coordinate values of
    mTextureCoordinates and the corresponding getter function:

```
let mGLTextureCoordBuffer = null;
function getTexCoord() { return mGLTextureCoordBuffer; }
```

3. Modify the init() function to include a step D to initialize the
    texture coordinates as a WebGL buffer. Notice the initialization
    process is identical to that of the vertex xy coordinates
    except that the reference to the new buffer is stored in
    mGLTextureCoordBuffer and the transferred data are the uv
    coordinate values.

```
function init() {
    let gl = glSys.get();

    ... identical to previous code ...

    // Step  D: Allocate and store texture coordinates
    // Create a buffer on the gl context for texture coordinates
    mGLTextureCoordBuffer = gl.createBuffer();

    // Activate texture coordinate buffer
    gl.bindBuffer(gl.ARRAY_BUFFER, mGLTextureCoordBuffer);

    // Loads textureCoordinates into the mGLTextureCoordBuffer
    gl.bufferData(gl.ARRAY_BUFFER,
                new Float32Array(mTextureCoordinates), gl.STATIC_DRAW);
}
```

4. Remember to release the allocated buffer during final cleanup:

```
function cleanUp() {
    ... identical to previous code ...

    if (mGLTextureCoordBuffer !== null) {
        gl.deleteBuffer(mGLTextureCoordBuffer);
        mGLTextureCoordBuffer = null;
    }
}
```

5. Finally, remember to export the changes:

```
export {init, cleanUp, get, getTexCoord}
```

Interface GLSL Shader to the Engine

Just as the SimpleShader object was defined to interface to the SimpleVS and SimpleFS shaders, a corresponding shader object needs to be created in the game engine to interface to the TextureVS and TextureFS GLSL shaders. As mentioned in the overview of this project, you will also create a new folder to organize the growing number of different shaders.

1. Create a new folder called shaders in src/engine. Move the simple_shader.js file into this folder, and do not forget to update the reference path in index.js.

2. Create a new file in the src/engine/shaders folder and name it texture_shader.js.

```
class TextureShader extends SimpleShader {
    constructor(vertexShaderPath, fragmentShaderPath) {
        // Call super class constructor
        super(vertexShaderPath, fragmentShaderPath);

        // reference to aTextureCoordinate within the shader
        this.mTextureCoordinateRef = null;

        // get the reference of aTextureCoordinate within the shader
        let gl = glSys.get();
        this.mTextureCoordinateRef = gl.getAttribLocation(
```

```
                                        this.mCompiledShader,
                                        "aTextureCoordinate");
        this.mSamplerRef = gl.getUniformLocation(this.mCompiledShader,
                                                "uSampler");
}
... implementation to follow ...
```

In the listed code, take note of the following:

    a.   The defined TextureShader class is an extension, or subclass, to the SimpleShader class.

    b.   The constructor implementation first calls super(), the constructor of SimpleShader. Recall that the SimpleShader constructor will load and compile the GLSL shaders defined by the vertexShaderPath and fragmentShaderPath parameters and set mVertexPositionRef to reference the aVertexPosition attribute defined in the shader.

    c.   In the rest of the constructor, the mTextureCoordinateRef keeps a reference to the aTextureCoordinate attribute defined in the texture_vs.glsl.

    d.   In this way, both the vertex position (aVertexPosition) and texture coordinate (aTextureCoordinate) attributes are referenced by a JavaScript TextureShader object.

  3. Override the activate() function to enable the texture coordinate data. The superclass super.activate() function sets up the xy vertex position and passes the values of pixelColor, trsMatrix, and cameraMatrix to the shader. The rest of the code binds mTextureCoordinateRef, the texture coordinate buffer defined in the vertex_buffer module, to the aTextureCoordinate attribute in the GLSL shader and mSampler to texture unit 0 (to be detailed later).

```
// Overriding the Activation of the shader for rendering
activate(pixelColor, trsMatrix, cameraMatrix) {
    // first call the super class's activate
    super.activate(pixelColor, trsMatrix, cameraMatrix);
```

```
    // now our own functionality: enable texture coordinate array
    let gl = glSys.get();
    gl.bindBuffer(gl.ARRAY_BUFFER, this._getTexCoordBuffer());
    gl.vertexAttribPointer(this.mTextureCoordinateRef, 2,
                            gl.FLOAT, false, 0, 0);
    gl.enableVertexAttribArray(this.mTextureCoordinateRef);

    // bind uSampler to texture 0
    gl.uniform1i(this.mSamplerRef, 0);
        // texture.activateTexture() binds to Texture0
}
```

With the combined functionality of SimpleShader and TextureShader, after the activate() function call, both of the attribute variables (aVertexPosition and aTextureCoordinate) in the GLSL texture_vs shader are connected to the corresponding buffers in the WebGL memory.

Facilitate Sharing with shader_resources

In the same manner that SimpleShader is a reusable resource, only one instance of the TextureShader needs to be created, and this instance can be shared. The shader_resources module should be modified to reflect this.

1. In shader_resources.js, add the variables to hold a texture shader:

```
// Texture Shader
let kTextureVS = "src/glsl_shaders/texture_vs.glsl"; // VertexShader
let kTextureFS = "src/glsl_shaders/texture_fs.glsl"; // FragmentShader
let mTextureShader = null;
```

2. Define a function to retrieve the texture shader:

```
function getTextureShader() { return mTextureShader; }
```

3. Create the instance of texture shader in the createShaders() function:

```
function createShaders() {
    mConstColorShader = new SimpleShader(kSimpleVS, kSimpleFS);
    mTextureShader = new TextureShader(kTextureVS, kTextureFS);
}
```

4. Modify the init() function to append the loadPromise to include the loading of the texture shader source files:

```
function init() {
    let loadPromise = new Promise(
        async function(resolve) {
            await Promise.all([
                text.load(kSimpleFS),
                text.load(kSimpleVS),
                text.load(kTextureFS),
                text.load(kTextureVS)
            ]);
            resolve();
        }).then(
            function resolve() { createShaders(); }
        );
    map.pushPromise(loadPromise);
}
```

5. Remember to release newly allocated resources during cleanup:

```
function cleanUp() {
    mConstColorShader.cleanUp();
    mTextureShader.cleanUp();   .

    text.unload(kSimpleVS);
    text.unload(kSimpleFS);
    text.unload(kTextureVS);
    text.unload(kTextureFS);
}
```

6. Lastly, remember to export the newly defined functionality:

```
export {init, cleanUp, getConstColorShader, getTextureShader}
```

TextureRenderable Class

Just as the Renderable class encapsulates and facilitates the definition and drawing of multiple instances of SimpleShader objects, a corresponding TextureRenderable class needs to be defined to support the drawing of multiple instances of TextureShader objects.

Changes to the Renderable Class

As mentioned in the project overview, for the same reason as creating and organizing shader classes in the Shaders folder, a renderables folder should be created to organize the growing number of different kinds of Renderable objects. In addition, the Renderable class must be modified to support it being the base class of all Renderable objects.

1. Create the src/engine/renderables folder and move renderable.js into this folder. Remember to update index.js to reflect the file location change.

2. Define the _setShader() function to set the shader for the Renderable. This is a protected function which allows subclasses to modify the mShader variable to refer to the appropriate shaders for each corresponding subclass.

```
// this is private/protected
_setShader(s) { this.mShader = s; }
```

Note   Functions with names that begin with "_" are either private or protected and should not be called from outside of the class. This is a convention followed in this book and not enforced by JavaScript.

Define the TextureRenderable Class

You are now ready to define the TextureRenderable class. As noted, TextureRenderable is derived from and extends the Renderable class functionality to render texture mapped objects.

1. Create a new file in the src/engine/renderables folder and name it texture_renderable.js. Add the constructor. Recall that super() is a call to the superclass (Renderable) constructor; similarly, the super.setColor() and super._setShader() are calls to the superclass functions. As will be detailed when discussing the engine texture resource module, the myTexture parameter is the path to the file that contains the texture image.

```
class TextureRenderable extends Renderable {
    constructor(myTexture) {
        super();
        super.setColor([1, 1, 1, 0]); // Alpha 0: no texture tinting
        super._setShader(shaderResources.getTextureShader());
        this.mTexture = myTexture;   // cannot be a "null"
    }
... implementation to follow ...
```

2. Define a draw() function to append the function defined in the Renderable class to support textures. The texture.activate() function activates and allows drawing with the specific texture. The details of this function will be discussed in the following section.

```
draw(camera) {
    // activate the texture
    texture.activate(this.mTexture);
    super.draw(camera);
}
```

3. Define a getter and setter for the texture reference:

```
getTexture() { return this.mTexture; }
setTexture(newTexture) { this.mTexture = newTexture; }
```

4. Finally, remember to export the class:

```
export default TextureRenderable;
```

Texture Support in the Engine

To support drawing with textures, the rest of the game engine requires two main modifications: WebGL context configuration and a dedicated engine component to support operations associated with textures.

Configure WebGL to Support Textures

The configuration of WebGL context must be updated to support textures. In gl.js, update the init() function according to the following:

```
function init(htmlCanvasID) {
    mCanvas = document.getElementById(htmlCanvasID);
    if (mCanvas == null)
        throw new Error("Engine init [" +
                            htmlCanvasID + "] HTML element id not found");

    // the standard or experimental webgl and binds to the Canvas area
    // store the results to the instance variable mGL
    mGL = mCanvas.getContext("webgl2", {alpha: false}) ||
        mCanvas.getContext("experimental-webgl2", {alpha: false});

    if (mGL === null) {
        document.write("<br><b>WebGL 2 is not supported!</b>");
        return;
    }

    // Allows transparency with textures.
    mGL.blendFunc(mGL.SRC_ALPHA, mGL.ONE_MINUS_SRC_ALPHA);
    mGL.enable(mGL.BLEND);

    // Set images to flip y axis to match the texture coordinate space.
    mGL.pixelStorei(mGL.UNPACK_FLIP_Y_WEBGL, true);
}
```

The parameter passed to mCanvas.getContext() informs the browser that the canvas should be opaque. This can speed up the drawing of transparent content and images. The blendFunc() function enables transparencies when drawing images with the alpha channel. The pixelStorei() function defines the origin of the uv coordinate to be at the lower-left corner.

Create the Texture Resource Module

Similar to text and audio files, a new engine component must be defined to support the corresponding texture operations including loading from the server file system, storing via the WebGL context to the GPU memory, activating the texture buffer for drawing, and removing from the GPU:

1. Create a new file in the src/engine/resources folder and name it texture.js. This file will implement the Texture engine component.

2. Define the TextureInfo class to represent a texture in the game engine. The mWidth and mHeight are the pixel resolution of the texture image, and mGLTexID is a reference to the WebGL texture storage.

```
class TextureInfo {
    constructor(w, h, id) {
        this.mWidth = w;
        this.mHeight = h;
        this.mGLTexID = id;
    }
}
```

Note   For efficiency reasons, many graphics hardware only supports texture with image resolutions that are in powers of 2, such as 2x4 ($2^1 x 2^2$), or 4x16 ($2^2 x 2^4$), or 64x256 ($2^6 x 2^8$), and so on. This is also the case for WebGL. All examples in this book only work with textures with resolutions that are powers of 2.

---

3. Import the core resource management functionality from the resource_map:

```
import * as map from "../core/resource_map.js";
// functions from resource_map
let has = map.has;
let get = map.get;
```

4. Define a function to load an image asynchronously as a promise
    and push the promise to be part of the pending promises in the
    map. Distinct from the text and audio resources, JavaScript
    Image API supports straightforward image file loading, and
    the map.loadDecodeParse() is not required in this case. Once
    an image is loaded, it is passed to the processLoadedImage()
    function with its file path as the name.

```
// Loads a texture so that it can be drawn.
function load(textureName) {
    let image = new Image();
    let texturePromise = new Promise(
        function(resolve) {
            image.onload = resolve;
            image.src = textureName;
        }).then(
            function resolve() {
                processLoadedImage(textureName, image); }
        );
    map.pushPromise(texturePromise);
    return texturePromise;
}
```

5. Add an unload() function to clean up the engine and release
    WebGL resources:

```
// Remove the reference to allow associated memory
// to be available for subsequent garbage collection
function unload(textureName) {
    let texInfo = get(textureName);
    if (map.unload(textureName)) {
        let gl = glSys.get();
        gl.deleteTexture(texInfo.mGLTexID);
    }
}
```

6. Now define the processLoadedImage() function to convert the
    format of an image and store it to the WebGL context. The
    gl.createTexture() function creates a WebGL texture buffer
    and returns a unique ID. The texImage2D() function stores the
    image into the WebGL texture buffer, and generateMipmap()
    computes a mipmap for the texture. Lastly, a TextureInfo object
    is instantiated to refer to the WebGL texture and stored into the
    resource_map according to the file path to the texture image file.

```
function processLoadedImage(path, image) {
    let gl = glSys.get();

    // Generate a texture reference to the webGL context
    let textureID = gl.createTexture();

    // binds texture reference with current texture in the webGL
    gl.bindTexture(gl.TEXTURE_2D, textureID);

    // Loads texture to texture data structure with descriptive info.
    // Parameters:
    //   1: "binding point" or target the texture is being loaded to.
    //   2: Level of detail. Used for mipmapping. 0 is base texture level.
    //   3: Internal format. The composition of each element. i.e. pixels.
    //   4: Format of texel data. Must match internal format.
    //   5: The data type of the texel data.
    //   6: Texture Data.
    gl.texImage2D(gl.TEXTURE_2D, 0,
                  gl.RGBA, gl.RGBA, gl.UNSIGNED_BYTE, image);

    // Creates a mipmap for this texture.
    gl.generateMipmap(gl.TEXTURE_2D);

    // Tells WebGL done manipulating data at the mGL.TEXTURE_2D target.
    gl.bindTexture(gl.TEXTURE_2D, null);

    let texInfo = new TextureInfo(image.naturalWidth,
                                  image.naturalHeight, textureID);
    map.set(path, texInfo);
}
```

Note   A *mipmap* is a representation of the texture image that facilitates
high-quality rendering. Please consult a computer graphics reference book to
learn more about mipmap representation and the associated texture mapping
algorithms.

---

   7.   Define a function to activate a WebGL texture for drawing:

```
function activate(textureName) {
    let gl = glSys.get();
    let texInfo = get(textureName);

    // Binds texture reference to the current webGL texture functionality
    gl.activeTexture(gl.TEXTURE0);
    gl.bindTexture(gl.TEXTURE_2D, texInfo.mGLTexID);

    // To prevent texture wrapping
    gl.texParameteri(gl.TEXTURE_2D, gl.TEXTURE_WRAP_S, gl.CLAMP_TO_EDGE);
    gl.texParameteri(gl.TEXTURE_2D, gl.TEXTURE_WRAP_T, gl.CLAMP_TO_EDGE);

    // Handles how magnification and minimization filters will work.
    gl.texParameteri(gl.TEXTURE_2D, gl.TEXTURE_MAG_FILTER, gl.LINEAR);
    gl.texParameteri(gl.TEXTURE_2D, gl.TEXTURE_MIN_FILTER,
                     gl.LINEAR_MIPMAP_LINEAR);

    // For the texture to look "sharp" do the following:
    // gl.texParameteri(gl.TEXTURE_2D, gl.TEXTURE_MAG_FILTER,gl.NEAREST);
    // gl.texParameteri(gl.TEXTURE_2D, gl.TEXTURE_MIN_FILTER,gl.NEAREST);
}
```

   a.   The get() function locates the TextureInfo object from
        the resource_map based on the textureName. The located
        mGLTexID is used in the bindTexture() function to activate
        the corresponding WebGL texture buffer for rendering.

b.   The texParameteri() function defines the rendering behavior for the texture. The TEXTURE_WRAP_S/T parameters ensure that the texel values will not wrap around at the texture boundaries. The TEXTURE_MAG_FILTER parameter defines how to magnify a texture, in other words, when a low-resolution texture is rendered to many pixels in the game window. The TEXTURE_MIN_FILTER parameter defines how to minimize a texture, in other words, when a high-resolution texture is rendered to a small number of pixels.

c.   The LINEAR and LINEAR_MIPMAP_LINEAR configurations generate smooth textures by blurring the details of the original images, while the commented out NEAREST option will result in unprocessed textures best suitable for pixelated effects. Notice that in this case, color boundaries of the texture image may appear jagged.

Note   In general, it is best to use texture images with similar resolution as the number of pixels occupied by the objects in the game. For example, a square that occupies a 64x64 pixel space should ideally use a 64x64 texel texture.

---

8.   Define a function to deactivate a texture as follows. This function sets the WebGL context to a state of not working with any texture.

```
function deactivate() {
    let gl = glSys.get();
    gl.bindTexture(gl.TEXTURE_2D, null);
}
```

9.   Finally, remember to export the functionality:

```
export {has, get, load, unload,
    TextureInfo,
    activate, deactivate}
```

Export New Functionality to the Client

The last step in integrating texture functionality into the engine involves modifying
the engine access file, index.js. Edit index.js and add in the following import and
export statements to grant the client access to the texture resource module and the
TextureRenderable class:

```
... identical to previous code ...
import * as texture from "./resources/texture.js";
// renderables
import Renderable from "./renderables/renderable.js";
import TextureRenderable from "./renderables/texture_renderable.js";
... identical to previous code ...

export default {
    // resource support
    audio, text, xml, texture,

    // input support
    input,

    // Util classes
    Camera, Scene, Transform,

    // Renderables
    Renderable, TextureRenderable,

    // functions
    init, cleanUp, clearCanvas
}
```

Testing of Texture Mapping Functionality

With the described modifications, the game engine can now render constant color
objects as well as objects with interesting and different types of textures. The following
testing code is similar to that from the previous example where two scenes, MyGame and
BlueLevel, are used to demonstrate the newly added texture mapping functionality.
The main modifications include the loading and unloading of texture images and the
creation and drawing of TextureRenderable objects. In addition, the MyGame scene

highlights transparent texture maps with alpha channel using PNG images, and the BlueScene scene shows corresponding textures with images in the JPEG format.

As in all cases of building a game, it is essential to ensure that all external resources are properly organized. Recall that the assets folder is created specifically for the organization of external resources. Take note of the four new texture files located in the assets folder: minion_collector.jpg, minion_collector.png, minion_portal.jpg, and minion_portal.png.

Modify the BlueLevel Scene File to Support Textures

The blue_level.xml scene file is modified from the previous example to support texture mapping:

```
<MyGameLevel>

    <!-- cameras -->
            <!-- Viewport: x, y, w, h -->
    <Camera CenterX="20" CenterY="60" Width="20"
            Viewport="20 40 600 300"
            BgColor="0 0 1 1.0"/>

    <!-- The red rectangle -->
    <Square PosX="20" PosY="60" Width="2" Height="3"
            Rotation="0"  Color="1 0 0 1" />

    <!-- Textures Square -->
    <TextureSquare PosX="15" PosY="60" Width="3" Height="3"
                Rotation="-5" Color="1 0 0 0.3"
                Texture="assets/minion_portal.jpg" />

    <TextureSquare PosX="25" PosY="60" Width="3" Height="3"
                Rotation="5" Color="0 0 0 0"
                Texture="assets/minion_collector.jpg"/>
        <!-- without tinting, alpha should be 0 -->

</MyGameLevel>
```

The TextureSquare element is similar to Square with the addition of a Texture attribute that specifies which image file should be used as a texture map for the square. Note that as implemented in texture_fs.glsl, the alpha value of the Color element is used for tinting the texture map. The XML scene description is meant to support slight tinting of the `minion_portal.jpg` texture and no tinting of the `minion_collector.jpg` texture. This texture tinting effect can be observed in the right image of Figure 5-3. In addition, notice that both images specified are in the JPEG format. Since the JPEG format does not support the storing of alpha channel, the unused regions of the two images show up as white areas outside the portal and collector minions in the right image of Figure 5-3.

Modify SceneFileParser

The scene file parser, `scene_file_parser.js`, is modified to support the parsing of the updated `blue_scene.xml`, in particular, to parse Square elements into Renderable objects and TextureSquare elements into TextureRenderable objects. For details of the changes, please refer to the source code file in the `src/my_game/util` folder.

Test BlueLevel with JPEGs

The modifications to `blue_level.js` are in the constructor, `load()`, `unload()`, `next()`, and `init()` functions where the texture images are loaded and unloaded and new TextureRenderable objects are parsed:

1. Edit `blue_level.js` and modify the constructor to define constants to represent the texture images:

```
class BlueLevel extends engine.Scene {
    constructor() {
        super();
        // scene file name
        this.kSceneFile = "assets/blue_level.xml";

        // textures: (Note: jpg does not support transparency)
        this.kPortal = "assets/minion_portal.jpg";
        this.kCollector = "assets/minion_collector.jpg";

        // all squares
        this.mSqSet = [];        // these are the Renderable objects

        // The camera to view the scene
        this.mCamera = null;
    }
    ... implementation to follow ...
```

2. Initiate loading of the textures in the load() function:

```
load() {
    // load the scene file
    engine.xml.load(this.kSceneFile);

    // load the textures
    engine.texture.load(this.kPortal);
    engine.texture.load(this.kCollector);
}
```

3. Likewise, add code to clean up by unloading the textures in the unload() function:

```
unload() {
    // unload the scene file and loaded resources
    engine.xml.unload(this.kSceneFile);
    engine.texture.unload(this.kPortal);
    engine.texture.unload(this.kCollector);
}
```

4. Support loading of the next scene with the next() function:

```
next() {
    super.next();
    let nextLevel = new MyGame();  // load the next level
    nextLevel.start();
}
```

5. Parse the textured squares in the init() function:

```
init() {
    let sceneParser = new SceneFileParser(this.kSceneFile);

    // Step A: Read in the camera
    this.mCamera = sceneParser.parseCamera();
```

```
// Step B: Read all the squares and textureSquares
sceneParser.parseSquares(this.mSqSet);
sceneParser.parseTextureSquares(this.mSqSet);
}
```

6. Include appropriate code in the update() function to continuously change the tinting of the portal TextureRenderable, as follows:

```
update() {
    ... identical to previous code ...

    // continuously change texture tinting
    let c = this.mSqSet[1].getColor();
    let ca = c[3] + deltaX;
    if (ca > 1) {
        ca = 0;
    }
    c[3] = ca;
}
```

   a.   Index 1 of mSqSet is the portal TextureRenderable object, and index 3 of the color array is the alpha channel.

   b.   The listed code continuously increases and wraps the alpha value of the mColor variable in the TextureRenderable object. Recall that the values of this variable are passed to TextureShader and then loaded to the uPixelColor of TextureFS for tinting the texture map results.

   c.   As defined in the first TextureSquare element in the blue_ scene.xml file, the color defined for the portal object is red. For this reason, when running this project, in the blue level, the portal object appears to be blinking in red.

Test MyGame with PNGs

Similar to the BlueLevel scene, MyGame is a straightforward modification of the previous example with changes to load and unload texture images and to create TextureRenderable objects:

1. Edit my_game.js; modify the MyGame constructor to define texture image files and the variables for referencing the TextureRenderable objects:

```
class MyGame extends engine.Scene {
    constructor() {
        super();

        // textures:
        this.kPortal = "assets/minion_portal.png"; // with transparency
        this.kCollector = "assets/minion_collector.png";

        // The camera to view the scene
        this.mCamera = null;

        // the hero and the support objects
        this.mHero = null;
        this.mPortal = null;
        this.mCollector = null;
    }
```

2. Initiate the loading of the textures in the load() function:

```
load() {
    // loads the textures
    engine.texture.load(this.kPortal);
    engine.texture.load(this.kCollector);
}
```

3. Make sure you remember to unload the textures in unload():

```
unload() {
    // Game loop not running, unload all assets
    engine.texture.unload(this.kPortal);
    engine.texture.unload(this.kCollector);
}
```

4. Define the next() function to start the blue level:

```
next() {
    super.next();
    // starts the next level
    let nextLevel = new BlueLevel();  // next level to be loaded
    nextLevel.start();
}
```

5. Create and initialize the TextureRenderables objects in the init() function:

```
init() {
    // Step A: set up the cameras
    this.mCamera = new engine.Camera(
            vec2.fromValues(20, 60),   // position of the camera
            20,                        // width of camera
            [20, 40, 600, 300] // viewport (X, Y, width, height)
            );
    this.mCamera.setBackgroundColor([0.8, 0.8, 0.8, 1]);
    // sets the background to gray

    // Step B: Create the game objects
    this.mPortal = new engine.TextureRenderable(this.kPortal);
    this.mPortal.setColor([1, 0, 0, 0.2]);  // tints red
    this.mPortal.getXform().setPosition(25, 60);
    this.mPortal.getXform().setSize(3, 3);

    this.mCollector = new engine.TextureRenderable(this.kCollector);
    this.mCollector.setColor([0, 0, 0, 0]);  // No tinting
    this.mCollector.getXform().setPosition(15, 60);
    this.mCollector.getXform().setSize(3, 3);
```

```
    // Step C: Create the hero object in blue
    this.mHero = new engine.Renderable();
    this.mHero.setColor([0, 0, 1, 1]);
    this.mHero.getXform().setPosition(20, 60);
    this.mHero.getXform().setSize(2, 3);
}
```

Remember that the texture file path is used as the unique identifier in the resource_map. For this reason, it is essential for file texture loading and unloading and for the creation of TextureRenderable objects to refer to the same file path. In the given code, all three functions refer to the same constants defined in the constructor.

6. The modification to the draw() function draws the two new TextureRenderable objects by calling their corresponding draw() functions, while the modification to the update() function is similar to that of the BlueLevel discussed earlier. Please refer to the my_game.js source code file in the src/my_game folder for details.

When running the example for this project in the chapter5/5.1.texture_shaders folder, once again take note of the results of continuously changing the texture tinting—the blinking of the portal minion in red. In addition, notice the differences between the PNG-based textures in the MyGame level and the corresponding JPEG ones with white borders in the BlueLevel. It is visually more pleasing and accurate to represent objects using textures with the alpha (or transparency) channel. PNG is one of the most popular image formats that supports the alpha channel.

Observations

This project has been the longest and most complicated one that you have worked with. This is because working with texture mapping requires you to understand texture coordinates, the implementation cuts across many of the files in the engine, and the fact that actual images must be loaded, converted into textures, and stored/accessed via WebGL. To help summarize the changes, Figure 5-6 shows the game engine states in relation to the states of an image used for texture mapping and some of the main game engine operations.

The left column of Figure 5-6 identifies the main game engine states, from WebGL initialization to the initialization of a scene, to the game loop, and to the eventual unloading of the scene. The middle column shows the corresponding states of an image that will be used as a texture. Initially, this image is stored on the server file system. During the scene initialization, the `Scene.load()` function will invoke the `engine/resources/texture.load()` function to load the image and cause the loaded image to be processed by the `engine/resources/texture.processLoadedImage()` function into a corresponding WebGL texture to be stored in the GPU texture buffer. During the game loop cycle, the `TextureRenderable.draw()` function activates the appropriate WebGL texture via the `engine/resources/texture.activate()` function. This enables the corresponding GLSL fragment shader to sample from the correct texture during rendering. Finally, when a texture is no longer needed by the game, the `Scene.unload()` function will call `engine/resources/texture.unload()` to remove the loaded image from the system.

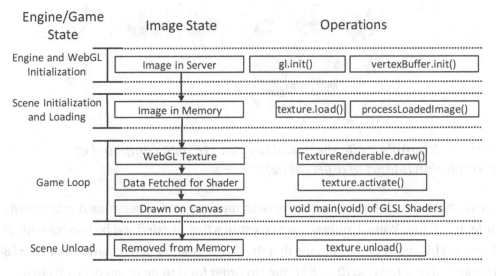

Figure 5-6. *Overview of the states of an image file and the corresponding WebGL texture*

Drawing with Sprite Sheets

As described earlier, a sprite sheet is an image that is composed of multiple lower-resolution images that individually represent different objects. Each of these individual images is referred to as a *sprite sheet element*. For example, Figure 5-7 is a sprite sheet with 13 elements from 4 different objects. Each of the top two rows contains five elements of the same object in different animated positions, and in the last row, there are three elements of different objects: the character Dye, the portal minion, and the collector minion. The artist or software program that created the sprite sheet must communicate the pixel locations of each sprite element to the game developer, in much the same way as illustrated in Figure 5-7.

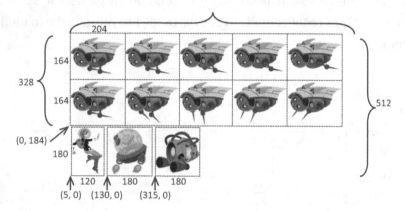

Figure 5-7. *Example sprite sheet:* `minion_sprite.png` *composed of lower-resolution images of different objects*

Sprite sheets are defined to optimize both memory and processing requirements. For example, recall that WebGL only supports textures that are defined by images with $2^x \times 2^y$ resolutions. This requirement means that the Dye character at a resolution of 120x180 must be stored in a 128x256 ($2^7 \times 2^8$) image in order for it to be created as a WebGL texture. Additionally, if the 13 elements of Figure 5-7 were stored as separate image files, then it would mean 13 slow file system accesses would be required to load all the images, instead of one single system access to load the sprite sheet.

The key to working with a sprite sheet and the associated elements is to remember that the texture coordinate uv values are defined over the 0 to 1 normalized range regardless of the actual image resolution. For example, Figure 5-8 focuses on the uv values of the collector minion in Figure 5-7, the rightmost sprite element on the third row. The top, center, and bottom rows of Figure 5-8 show coordinate values of the portal element.

- **Pixel positions**: The lower-left corner is (315, 0), and the upper-right corner is (495, 180).

- **UV values**: The lower-left corner is (0.308, 0.0), and the upper-right corner is (0.483, 0.352).

- **Use in Model Space**: Texture mapping of the element is accomplished by associating the corresponding uv values with the xy values at each vertex position.

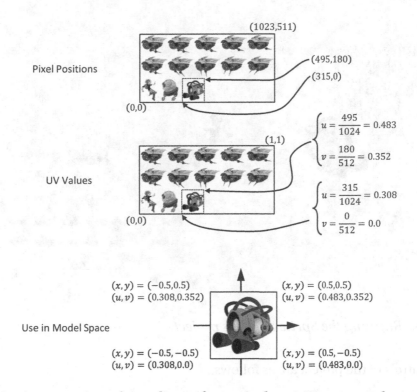

Figure 5-8. *A conversion of coordinate from pixel position to uv values and used for mapping on geometry*

The Sprite Shaders Project

This project demonstrates how to draw objects with sprite sheet elements by defining appropriate abstractions and classes. You can see an example of this project running in Figure 5-9. The source code to this project is defined in the chapter5/5.2.sprite_ shaders folder.

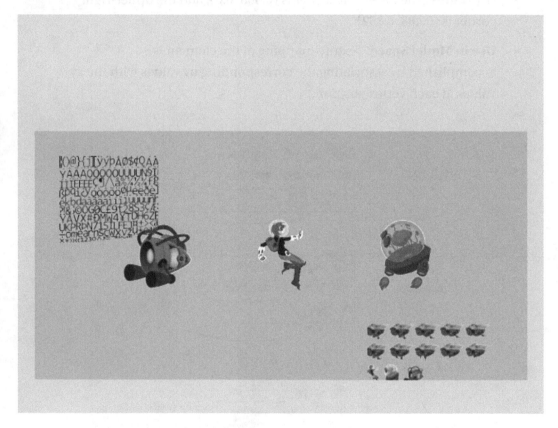

Figure 5-9. *Running the Sprite Shaders project*

The controls of the project are as follows:

- **Right-arrow key**: Moves the Dye character (the hero) right and loops to the left boundary when the right boundary is reached

- **Left-arrow key**: Moves the hero left and resets the position to the middle of the window when the left boundary is reached

The goals of the project are as follows:

- To gain a deeper understanding of texture coordinates

- To experience defining subregions within an image for texture mapping

- To draw squares by mapping from sprite sheet elements

- To prepare for working with sprite animation and bitmap fonts

You can find the following external resource files in the assets folder: consolas-72.png and minion_sprite.png. Notice that minion_sprite.png is the image shown in Figure 5-7.

As depicted in Figure 5-5, one of the main advantages and shortcomings of the texture support defined in the previous section is that the texture coordinate accessed via the getTexCoord() function is statically defined in the vertex_buffer.js file. This is an advantage because in those cases where an entire image is mapped onto a square, all instances of TextureShader objects can share the same default uv values. This is also a shortcoming because the static texture coordinate buffer does not allow working with different subregions of an image and thus does not support working with sprite sheet elements. As illustrated in Figure 5-10, the example from this section overcomes this shortcoming by defining a per-object texture coordinate in the SpriteShader and SpriteRenderable objects. Notice that there are no new GLSL shaders defined since their functionality remains the same as TextureVS/FS.

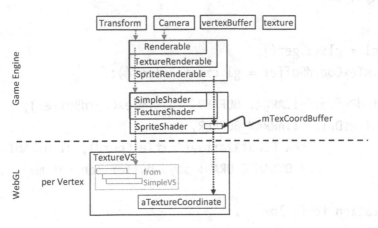

Figure 5-10. *Defining a texture coordinate buffer in the SpriteShader*

Interface GLSL Texture Shaders to the Engine with SpriteShader

Shaders supporting texture mapping with sprite sheet elements must be able to identify distinct subregions of an image. To support this functionality, you will implement the SpriteShader to define its own texture coordinate. Since this new shader extends the functionality of TextureShader, it is logical to implement it as a subclass.

1. Create a new file in the src/engine/shaders folder and name it sprite_shader.js.

2. Define the SpriteShader class and its constructor to extend the TextureShader class:

```
class SpriteShader extends TextureShader {
    constructor(vertexShaderPath, fragmentShaderPath) {
        // Call super class constructor
        super(vertexShaderPath, fragmentShaderPath);

        this.mTexCoordBuffer = null; // gl buffer with texture coordinate
        let initTexCoord = [
            1.0, 1.0,
            0.0, 1.0,
            1.0, 0.0,
            0.0, 0.0
        ];

        let gl = glSys.get();
        this.mTexCoordBuffer = gl.createBuffer();

        gl.bindBuffer(gl.ARRAY_BUFFER, this.mTexCoordBuffer);
        gl.bufferData(gl.ARRAY_BUFFER,
                    new Float32Array(initTexCoord), gl.DYNAMIC_DRAW);
                    // DYNAMIC_DRAW: says buffer content may change!
    }
... implementation to follow ...
```

SpriteShader defines its own texture coordinate buffer in WebGL, and the reference to this buffer is kept by mTexCoordBuffer. Notice that when creating this buffer in the WebGL bufferData() function, the DYNAMIC_DRAW option is specified. This is compared with the STATIC_DRAW option used in vertex_buffer.js when defining the system default texture coordinate buffer. The dynamic option informs the WebGL graphics system that the content to this buffer will be subjected to changes.

3. Define a function to set the WebGL texture coordinate buffer:

```
setTextureCoordinate(texCoord) {
    let gl = glSys.get();
    gl.bindBuffer(gl.ARRAY_BUFFER, this.mTexCoordBuffer);
    gl.bufferSubData(gl.ARRAY_BUFFER, 0, new Float32Array(texCoord));
}
```

Note that texCoord parameter is an array of eight floating-point numbers that specifies texture coordinate locations to the WebGL context. The format and content of this array are defined by the WebGL interface to be top-right, top-left, bottom-right, and bottom-left corners. In your case, these should be the four corners of a sprite sheet element.

4. Override the texture coordinate accessing function, _getTexCoordBuffer(), such that when the shader is activated, the locally allocated dynamic buffer is returned and not the global static buffer. Note that the activate() function is inherited from TextureShader.

```
_getTexCoordBuffer() {
    return this.mTexCoordBuffer;
}
```

5. Remember to export the class:

```
export default SpriteShader;
```

SpriteRenderable Class

Similar to the Renderable class (which are shaded with SimpleShader) and TextureRenderable class (which are shaded with TextureShader), a corresponding SpriteRenderable class should be defined to represent objects that will be shaded with SpriteShader:

1. Create a new file in the src/engine/renderables folder and name it sprite_renderable.js.

2. Define the SpriteRenderable class and constructor to extend from the TextureRenderable class. Notice that the four instance variables, mElmLeft, mElmRight, mElmTop, and mElmBottom, together identify a subregion within the Texture Space. These are the bounds of a sprite sheet element.

```
class SpriteRenderable extends TextureRenderable {
    constructor(myTexture) {
        super(myTexture);
        super._setShader(shaderResources.getSpriteShader());
        // sprite coordinate
        this.mElmLeft = 0.0;    // texture coordinate bound
        this.mElmRight = 1.0;   //   0-left, 1-right
        this.mElmTop = 1.0;     //   1-top   0-bottom
        this.mElmBottom = 0.0;  // of image
    }
... implementation to follow ...
```

3. Define an enumerated data type with values that identify corresponding offset positions of a WebGL texture coordinate specification array:

```
// texture coordinate array is an array of 8 floats where elements:
//  [0] [1]: is u/v coordinate of Top-Right
//  [2] [3]: is u/v coordinate of Top-Left
//  [4] [5]: is u/v coordinate of Bottom-Right
//  [6] [7]: is u/v coordinate of Bottom-Left
const eTexCoordArrayIndex = Object.freeze({
```

```
    eLeft: 2,
    eRight: 0,
    eTop: 1,
    eBottom: 5
});
```

Note   An enumerated data type has a name that begins with an "e", as in
eTexCoordArrayIndex.

---

4. Define functions to allow the specification of uv values for a sprite
    sheet element in both texture coordinate space (normalized between
    0 and 1) and with pixel positions (which are converted to uv values):

```
// specify element region by texture coordinate (between 0 to 1)
setElementUVCoordinate(left, right, bottom, top) {
    this.mElmLeft = left;
    this.mElmRight = right;
    this.mElmBottom = bottom;
    this.mElmTop = top;
}

// element region defined pixel positions (0 to image resolutions)
setElementPixelPositions(left, right, bottom, top) {
    let texInfo = texture.get(this.mTexture);
    // entire image width, height
    let imageW = texInfo.mWidth;
    let imageH = texInfo.mHeight;

    this.mElmLeft = left / imageW;
    this.mElmRight = right / imageW;
    this.mElmBottom = bottom / imageH;
    this.mElmTop = top / imageH;
}
```

Note that the setElementPixelPositions() function converts from pixel to texture
coordinate before storing the results with the corresponding instance variables.

5. Add a function to construct the texture coordinate specification
    array that is appropriate for passing to the WebGL context:

```
getElementUVCoordinateArray() {
    return [
        this.mElmRight,   this.mElmTop,              // x,y of top-right
        this.mElmLeft,    this.mElmTop,
        this.mElmRight,   this.mElmBottom,
        this.mElmLeft,    this.mElmBottom
    ];
}
```

6. Override the `draw()` function to load the specific texture
    coordinate values to WebGL context before the actual drawing:

```
draw(camera) {
    // set the current texture coordinate
    // activate the texture
    this.mShader.setTextureCoordinate(this.getElementUVCoordinateArray());
    super.draw(camera);
}
```

7. Finally, remember to export the class and the defined enumerated
    type:

```
export default SpriteRenderable;
export {eTexCoordArrayIndex}
```

Facilitate Sharing with shader_resources

Similar to `SimpleShader` and `TextureShader`, the `SpriteShader` is a resource that can be
shared. Thus, it should be added to the engine's `shaderResources`.

1. In the engine/core/shader_resources.js file, import SpriteShader,
    add a variable for storing, and define the corresponding getter
    function to access the shared SpriteShader instance:

```
import SpriteShader from "../shaders/sprite_shader.js";
let mSpriteShader = null;
function getSpriteShader() { return mSpriteShader; }
```

2.   Modify the `createShaders()` function to create the `SpriteShader`:

```
function createShaders() {
    mConstColorShader = new SimpleShader(kSimpleVS, kSimpleFS);
    mTextureShader = new TextureShader(kTextureVS, kTextureFS);
    mSpriteShader = new SpriteShader(kTextureVS, kTextureFS);
}
```

Notice that the `SpriteShader` actually wraps over the existing GLSL shaders defined in the `texture_vs.glsl` and `texture_fs.glsl` files. From the perspective of WebGL, the functionality of drawing with texture remains the same. The only difference with `SpriteShader` is that the texture's coordinate values are now programmable.

3.   Update the `cleanUp()` function for proper release of resources:

```
function cleanUp() {
    mConstColorShader.cleanUp();
    mTextureShader.cleanUp();
    mSpriteShader.cleanUp();

    ... identical to previous code ...
}
```

4.   Make sure to export the new functionality:

```
export {init, cleanUp,
    getConstColorShader, getTextureShader, getSpriteShader}
```

Export New Functionality to the Client

The last step in integrating sprite element functionality into the engine involves modifying the engine access file, `index.js`. Edit `index.js` and add in the following import and export statements to grant client access to `SpriteRenderable` and `eTexCoordArrayIndex`, the enumerated data type for accessing the WebGL texture coordinate array.

```
// renderables
import Renderable from "./renderables/renderable.js";
import TextureRenderable from "./renderables/texture_renderable.js";
```

```
import SpriteRenderable from "./renderables/sprite_renderable.js";
import { eTexCoordArrayIndex } from "./renderables/sprite_renderable.js";
... identical to previous code ...

export default {
    ... identical to previous code ...

    // Renderables
    Renderable, TextureRenderable, SpriteRenderable,

    // constants
    eTexCoordArrayIndex,

    // functions
    init, cleanUp, clearCanvas
}
```

Testing the SpriteRenderable

There are two important functionalities of sprite elements and texture coordinate that should be tested: the proper extraction, drawing, and controlling of a sprite sheet element as an object; and the changing and controlling of uv coordinate on an object. For proper testing of the added functionality, you must modify the my_game.js file.

1. The constructing, loading, unloading, and drawing of MyGame are similar to previous examples, so the details will not be repeated here. Please refer to the source code in the src/my_game folder for details.

2. Modify the init() function as follows.

```
init() {
    // Step A: set up the cameras
    this.mCamera = new engine.Camera(
        vec2.fromValues(20, 60),    // position of the camera
        20,                         // width of camera
        [20, 40, 600, 300]         // viewport (orgX, orgY, width, height)
    );
    this.mCamera.setBackgroundColor([0.8, 0.8, 0.8, 1]);
    // sets the background to gray
```

```
// Step B: Create the support objects
this.mPortal = new engine.SpriteRenderable(this.kMinionSprite);
this.mPortal.setColor([1, 0, 0, 0.2]);  // tints red
this.mPortal.getXform().setPosition(25, 60);
this.mPortal.getXform().setSize(3, 3);
this.mPortal.setElementPixelPositions(130, 310, 0, 180);

this.mCollector = new engine.SpriteRenderable(this.kMinionSprite);
this.mCollector.setColor([0, 0, 0, 0]);  // No tinting
this.mCollector.getXform().setPosition(15, 60);
this.mCollector.getXform().setSize(3, 3);
this.mCollector.setElementUVCoordinate(0.308, 0.483, 0, 0.352);

// Step C: Create the font and minion images using sprite
this.mFontImage = new engine.SpriteRenderable(this.kFontImage);
this.mFontImage.setColor([1, 1, 1, 0]);
this.mFontImage.getXform().setPosition(13, 62);
this.mFontImage.getXform().setSize(4, 4);

this.mMinion = new engine.SpriteRenderable(this.kMinionSprite);
this.mMinion.setColor([1, 1, 1, 0]);
this.mMinion.getXform().setPosition(26, 56);
this.mMinion.getXform().setSize(5, 2.5);

// Step D: Create hero object with texture from lower-left corner
this.mHero = new engine.SpriteRenderable(this.kMinionSprite);
this.mHero.setColor([1, 1, 1, 0]);
this.mHero.getXform().setPosition(20, 60);
this.mHero.getXform().setSize(2, 3);
this.mHero.setElementPixelPositions(0, 120, 0, 180);
}
```

a.   After the camera is set up in step A, notice that in step B both mPortal and mCollector are created based on the same image, kMinionSprite, with the respective setElementPixelPositions() and setElementUVCoordinate() calls to specify the actual sprite element to use for rendering.

b.   Step C creates two additional SpriteRenderable objects: mFontImage and mMinion. The sprite element uv coordinate settings are the defaults where the texture image will cover the entire geometry.

c.   Similar to step B, step D creates the hero character as a SpriteRenderable object based on the same kMinionSprite image. The sprite sheet element that corresponds to the hero is identified with the setElementPixelPositions() call.

Notice that in this example, four of the five SpriteRenderable objects created are based on the same kMinionSprite image.

3.   The update() function is modified to support the controlling of the hero object and changes to the uv values.

```
update() {
    // let's only allow the movement of hero,
    let deltaX = 0.05;
    let xform = this.mHero.getXform();

    // Support hero movements
    if (engine.input.isKeyPressed(engine.input.keys.Right)) {
        xform.incXPosBy(deltaX);
        if (xform.getXPos() > 30) { // right-bound of the window
            xform.setPosition(12, 60);
        }
    }

    if (engine.input.isKeyPressed(engine.input.keys.Left)) {
        xform.incXPosBy(-deltaX);
        if (xform.getXPos() < 11) {  // left-bound of the window
            xform.setXPos(20);
        }
    }

    // continuously change texture tinting
    let c = this.mPortal.getColor();
    let ca = c[3] + deltaX;
```

```
if (ca > 1) {
    ca = 0;
}
c[3] = ca;

// New update code for changing the sub-texture regions being shown"
let deltaT = 0.001;

// The font image:
// zoom into the texture by updating texture coordinate
// For font: zoom to the upper left corner by changing bottom right
let texCoord = this.mFontImage.getElementUVCoordinateArray();
// The 8 elements:
//      mTexRight,  mTexTop,         // x,y of top-right
//      mTexLeft,   mTexTop,
//      mTexRight,  mTexBottom,
//      mTexLeft,   mTexBottom
let b = texCoord[engine.eTexCoordArrayIndex.eBottom] + deltaT;
let r = texCoord[engine.eTexCoordArrayIndex.eRight] - deltaT;
if (b > 1.0) {
    b = 0;
}
if (r < 0) {
    r = 1.0;
}
this.mFontImage.setElementUVCoordinate(
    texCoord[engine.eTexCoordArrayIndex.eLeft],
    r,
    b,
    texCoord[engine.eTexCoordArrayIndex.eTop]
);
//

// The minion image:
// For minion: zoom to the bottom right corner by changing top left
texCoord = this.mMinion.getElementUVCoordinateArray();
// The 8 elements:
```

```
//      mTexRight,  mTexTop,              // x,y of top-right
//      mTexLeft,   mTexTop,
//      mTexRight,  mTexBottom,
//      mTexLeft,   mTexBottom
let t = texCoord[engine.eTexCoordArrayIndex.eTop] - deltaT;
let l = texCoord[engine.eTexCoordArrayIndex.eLeft] + deltaT;
if (l > 0.5) {
    l = 0;
}
if (t < 0.5) {
    t = 1.0;
}
this.mMinion.setElementUVCoordinate(
    l,
    texCoord[engine.eTexCoordArrayIndex.eRight],
    texCoord[engine.eTexCoordArrayIndex.eBottom],
    t
);
}
```

a. Observe that the keyboard control and the drawing of the hero object are identical to previous projects.

b. Notice the calls to setElementUVCoordinate() for mFontImage and mMinion. These calls continuously decrease and reset the V values that correspond to the bottom, the U values that correspond to the right for mFontImage, the V values that correspond to the top, and the U values that correspond to the left for mMinion. The end results are the continuous changing of texture and the appearance of a zooming animation on these two objects

Sprite Animations

In games, you often want to create animations that reflect the movements or actions of your characters. In the previous chapter, you learned about moving the geometries of these objects with transformation operators. However, as you have observed when controlling the hero character in the previous example, if the textures on these objects do not change in ways that correspond to the control, the interaction conveys the sensation of moving a static image rather than setting a character in motion. What is needed is the ability to create the illusion of animations on geometries when desired.

In the previous example, you observed from the mFontImage and mMinion objects that the appearance of an animation can be created by constantly changing the uv values on a texture-mapped geometry. As discussed at the beginning of this chapter, one way to control this type of animation is by working with an animated sprite sheet.

Overview of Animated Sprite Sheets

Recall that an animated sprite sheet is a sprite sheet that contains the sequence of images of an object in an animation, typically in one or more rows or columns. For example, in Figure 5-11 you can see a 2x5 animated sprite sheet that contains two separate animations organized in two rows. The animations depict an object retracting its spikes toward the right in the top row and extending them toward the left in the bottom row. In this example, the animations are separated into rows. It is also possible for an animated sprite sheet to define animations that are along columns. The organization of a sprite sheet and the details of element pixel locations are generally handled by its creator and must be explicitly communicated to the game developer for use in games.

Figure 5-11. *An animated sprite sheet organized into two rows representing two animated sequences of the same object*

233

Figure 5-12 shows that to achieve the animated effect of an object retracting its spikes toward the right, as depicted by the top row of Figure 5-11, you map the elements from the left to the right in the sequence 1, 2, 3, 4, 5. When these images are mapped onto the same geometry, sequenced, and looped in an appropriate rate, it conveys the sense that the object is indeed repeating the action of retracting its spikes. Alternatively, if the sequence is reversed where the elements are mapped in the right-to-left sequence, it would create the animation that corresponds to the object extending the spikes toward the left. It is also possible to map the sequence in a swing loop from left to right and then back from right to left. In this case, the animation would correspond to the object going through the motion of retracting and extending its spikes continuously.

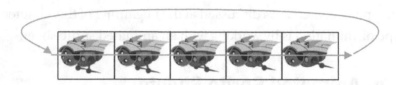

Figure 5-12. *A sprite animation sequence that loops*

The Sprite Animation Project

This project demonstrates how to work with an animated sprite sheet and generate continuous sprite animations. You can see an example of this project running in Figure 5-13. The project scene contains the objects from the previous scene plus two animated objects. The source code to this project is defined in the chapter5/5.3.sprite_animate_shaders folder.

Figure 5-13. *Running the Sprite Animate Shaders project*

The controls of the project are as follows:

- **Right-arrow key**: Moves the hero right; when crossing the right boundary, the hero is wrapped back to the left boundary

- **Left-arrow key**: Opposite movements of the right arrow key

- **Number 1 key**: Animates by showing sprite elements continuously from right to left

- **Number 2 key**: Animates by showing sprite elements moving back and forth continuously from left to right and right to left

- **Number 3 key**: Animates by showing sprite elements continuously from left to right

- **Number 4 key**: Increases the animation speed

- **Number 5 key**: Decreases the animation speed

The goals of the project are as follows:

- To understand animated sprite sheets

- To experience the creation of sprite animations

- To define abstractions for implementing sprite animations

You can find the same files as in the previous project in the `assets` folder.

SpriteAnimateRenderable Class

Sprite animation can be implemented by strategically controlling the uv values of a
`SpriteRenderable` to display the appropriate sprite element at desired time periods.
For this reason, only a single class, `SpriteAnimateRenderable`, needs to be defined to
support sprite animations.

For simplicity and ease of understanding, the following implementation assumes
that all sprite elements associated with an animation are always organized along the
same row. For example, in Figure 5-11, the rightward retraction and leftward extension
movements of the spikes are each organized along a row; neither spans more than
one single row, and neither is organized along a column. Animated sprite elements
organized along a column are not supported.

1. Create a new file in the `src/engine/renderables` folder and name
   it `sprite_animate_renderable.js`.

2. Define an enumerated data type for the three different sequences
   to animate:

```
// Assumption: first sprite is always the leftmost element.
const eAnimationType = Object.freeze({
    eRight: 0, // from left to right, when ended, start from left again
    eLeft: 1,  // from right animate left-wards,
    eSwing: 2  // left to right, then, right to left
});
```

The eAnimationType enum defines three modes for animation:

   a.   eRight starts at the leftmost element and animates by iterating toward the right along the same row. When the last element is reached, the animation continues by starting from the leftmost element again.

   b.   eLeft is the reverse of eRight; it starts from the right, animates toward the left, and continues by starting from the rightmost element after reaching the leftmost element.

   c.   eSwing is a continuous loop from left to right and then from right to left.

  3. Define the SpriteAnimateRenderable class to extend from SpriteRenderable and define the constructor:

```
class SpriteAnimateRenderable extends SpriteRenderable {
    constructor(myTexture) {
        super(myTexture);
        super._setShader(shaderResources.getSpriteShader());

        // All coordinates are in texture coordinate (UV between 0 to 1)
        // Information on the sprite element
        this.mFirstElmLeft = 0.0; // 0.0 is left corner of image
        this.mElmTop = 1.0;  // image top corner (from SpriteRenderable)
        this.mElmWidth = 1.0;
        this.mElmHeight = 1.0;
        this.mWidthPadding = 0.0;
        this.mNumElems = 1;   // number of elements in an animation

        // per animation settings
        this.mUpdateInterval = 1;   // how often to advance
        this.mAnimationType = eAnimationType.eRight;

        this.mCurrentAnimAdvance = -1;
        this.mCurrentElm = 0;
        this._initAnimation();
    }
... implementation to follow ...
```

The `SpriteAnimateRenderable` constructor defines three sets of variables:

a. The first set, including `mFirstElmLeft`, `mElmTop`, and so on, defines the location and dimensions of each sprite element and the number of elements in the animation. This information can be used to accurately compute the texture coordinate for each sprite element when the elements are ordered by rows and columns. Note that all coordinates are in texture coordinate space (0 to 1).

b. The second set stores information on how to animate, the `mAnimationType` of left, right, or swing, and how much time, `mUpdateInterval`, to wait before advancing to the next sprite element. This information can be changed during runtime to reverse, loop, or control the speed of a character's movement.

c. The third set, `mCurrentAnimAdvance` and `mCurrentElm`, describes offset for advancing and the current frame number. Both of these variables are in units of element counts and are not designed to be accessed by the game programmer because they are used internally to compute the next sprite element for display.

The `_initAnimation()` function computes the values of `mCurrentAnimAdvance` and `mCurrentElm` to initialize an animation sequence.

4. Define the `_initAnimation()` function to compute the proper vales for `mCurrentAnimAdance` and `mCurrentElm` according to the current animation type:

```
_initAnimation() {
        // Currently running animation
        this.mCurrentTick = 0;
        switch (this.mAnimationType) {
        case eAnimationType.eRight:
            this.mCurrentElm = 0;
```

```
            this.mCurrentAnimAdvance = 1; // either 1 or -1
            break;
        case eAnimationType.eSwing:
            this.mCurrentAnimAdvance = -1 * this.mCurrentAnimAdvance;
            this.mCurrentElm += 2 * this.mCurrentAnimAdvance;
            break;
        case eAnimationType.eLeft:
            this.mCurrentElm = this.mNumElems - 1;
            this.mCurrentAnimAdvance = -1; // either 1 or -1
            break;
    }
    this._setSpriteElement();
}
```

The mCurrentElm is the number of elements to offset from the leftmost, and mCurrentAnimAdvance records whether the mCurrentElm offset should be incremented (for rightward animation) or decremented (for leftward animation) during each update. The _setSpriteElement() function is called to set the uv values that correspond to the currently identified sprite element for displaying.

5. Define the _setSpriteElement() function to compute and load the uv values of the currently identified sprite element for rendering:

```
_setSpriteElement() {
    let left = this.mFirstElmLeft +
            (this.mCurrentElm * (this.mElmWidth+this.mWidthPadding));
    super.setElementUVCoordinate(left, left + this.mElmWidth,
                        this.mElmTop - this.mElmHeight, this.mElmTop);
}
```

The variable left is the left u value of mCurrentElm and is used to compute the right u value, with the assumption that all animation sequences are along the same row of sprite elements and that the top and bottom v values are constant where they do not change over a given animation sequence. These uv values are set to the super class SpriteRenderable for drawing.

6. Define a function to set the animation type. Note that the animation is always reset to start from the beginning when the animation type (left, right, or swing) is changed.

```
setAnimationType(animationType) {
    this.mAnimationType = animationType;
    this.mCurrentAnimAdvance = -1;
    this.mCurrentElm = 0;
    this._initAnimation();
}
```

7. Define a function for specifying a sprite animation sequence. The inputs to the function are in pixels and are converted to texture coordinates by dividing by the width and height of the image.

```
// Always set the leftmost element to be the first
setSpriteSequence(
    topPixel,    // offset from top-left
    leftPixel, // offset from top-left
    elmWidthInPixel,
    elmHeightInPixel,
    numElements,       // number of elements in sequence
    wPaddingInPixel   // left/right padding
) {
    let texInfo = texture.get(this.mTexture);
    // entire image width, height
    let imageW = texInfo.mWidth;
    let imageH = texInfo.mHeight;

    this.mNumElems = numElements;    // number of elements in animation
    this.mFirstElmLeft = leftPixel / imageW;
    this.mElmTop = topPixel / imageH;
    this.mElmWidth = elmWidthInPixel / imageW;
    this.mElmHeight = elmHeightInPixel / imageH;
    this.mWidthPadding = wPaddingInPixel / imageW;
    this._initAnimation();
}
```

8. Define functions to change animation speed, either directly or by an offset:

```
setAnimationSpeed(tickInterval) {
    this.mUpdateInterval = tickInterval; }
incAnimationSpeed(deltaInterval) {
    this.mUpdateInterval += deltaInterval; }
```

9. Define a function to advance the animation for each game loop update:

```
updateAnimation() {
    this.mCurrentTick++;
    if (this.mCurrentTick >= this.mUpdateInterval) {
        this.mCurrentTick = 0;
        this.mCurrentElm += this.mCurrentAnimAdvance;
        if ((this.mCurrentElm>=0) && (this.mCurrentElm<this.mNumElems)) {
            this._setSpriteElement();
        } else {
            this._initAnimation();
        }
    }
}
```

Each time the updateAnimation() function is called, the mCurrentTick counter is incremented, and when the number of ticks reaches the mUpdateInterval value, the animation is re-initialized by the _initAnimation() function. It is important to note that the time unit for controlling the animation is the number of times the updateAnimation() function is called and not the real-world elapsed time. Recall that the engine loop.loopOnce() function ensures system-wide updates to occur at kMPF intervals even when frame rate lags. The game engine architecture ensures the updateAnimation() function calls are kMPF milliseconds apart.

10. Finally, remember to export the defined class and enumerated animation type:

```
export default SpriteAnimateRenderable;
export {eAnimationType}
```

Export New Functionality to the Client

The last step in integrating animated sprite element functionality into the engine involves modifying the engine access file, index.js. Edit index.js and add in the following import and export statements to grant client access to SpriteAnimateRenderable and eAnimationType:

```
// renderables
import Renderable from "./renderables/renderable.js";
import SpriteRenderable from "./renderables/sprite_renderable.js";
import SpriteAnimateRenderable from
                          "./renderables/sprite_animate_renderable.js";
import { eTexCoordArrayIndex } from "./renderables/sprite_renderable.js";
import { eAnimationType } from
                          "./renderables/sprite_animate_renderable.js";
... identical to previous code ...

export default {
    ... identical to previous code ...

    // Renderables
    Renderable, TextureRenderable,
    SpriteRenderable, SpriteAnimateRenderable,

    // constants
    eTexCoordArrayIndex, eAnimationType,

    // functions
    init, cleanUp, clearCanvas
}
```

Testing Sprite Animation

The test cases for the SpriteAnimateRenderable object must demonstrate the game programmer's control over the modes (left, right, swing) and speed of animation. The MyGame object is modified to accomplish these purposes.

1. The constructing, loading, unloading, and drawing of MyGame are similar to the previous example and the details are not repeated.

2. In the init() function, add code to create and initialize the SpriteAnimateRenderable objects between steps C and D:

```
init() {
    ... identical to previous code ...

    // The right minion
    this.mRightMinion = new engine.SpriteAnimateRenderable(
                            this.kMinionSprite);
    this.mRightMinion.setColor([1, 1, 1, 0]);
    this.mRightMinion.getXform().setPosition(26, 56.5);
    this.mRightMinion.getXform().setSize(4, 3.2);
    this.mRightMinion.setSpriteSequence(
        512, 0,   // first element pixel positions: top: 512 left: 0
        204, 164, // widthxheight in pixels
        5,        // number of elements in this sequence
        0);       // horizontal padding in between
    this.mRightMinion.setAnimationType(engine.eAnimationType.eRight);
    this.mRightMinion.setAnimationSpeed(50);
    // the left minion
    this.mLeftMinion = new engine.SpriteAnimateRenderable(
                            this.kMinionSprite);
    this.mLeftMinion.setColor([1, 1, 1, 0]);
    this.mLeftMinion.getXform().setPosition(15, 56.5);
    this.mLeftMinion.getXform().setSize(4, 3.2);
    this.mLeftMinion.setSpriteSequence(
        348, 0,   // first element pixel positions: top: 164 left: 0
        204, 164, // widthxheight in pixels
        5,        // number of elements in this sequence
```

```
    0);         // horizontal padding in between
    this.mLeftMinion.setAnimationType(engine.eAnimationType.eRight);
    this.mLeftMinion.setAnimationSpeed(50);

    ... identical to previous code ...
}
```

The SpriteAnimateRenderable objects are created in similar ways as SpriteRenderable objects with a sprite sheet as the texture parameter. In this case, it is essential to call the setSpriteSequence() function to identify the elements involved in the animation including the location, dimension, and total number of elements.

3. The update() function must invoke the SpriteAnimateRenderable object's updateAnimation() function to advance the sprite animation:

```
update() {
    ... identical to previous code ...

    // remember to update the minion's animation
    this.mRightMinion.updateAnimation();
    this.mLeftMinion.updateAnimation();

    // Animate left on the sprite sheet
    if (engine.input.isKeyClicked(engine.input.keys.One)) {
        this.mRightMinion.setAnimationType(engine.eAnimationType.eLeft);
        this.mLeftMinion.setAnimationType(engine.eAnimationType.eLeft);
    }

    // swing animation
    if (engine.input.isKeyClicked(engine.input.keys.Two)) {
        this.mRightMinion.setAnimationType(engine.eAnimationType.eSwing);
        this.mLeftMinion.setAnimationType(engine.eAnimationType.eSwing);
    }

    // Animate right on the sprite sheet
    if (engine.input.isKeyClicked(engine.input.keys.Three)) {
        this.mRightMinion.setAnimationType(engine.eAnimationType.eRight);
        this.mLeftMinion.setAnimationType(engine.eAnimationType.eRight);
    }
```

```
    // decrease duration of each sprite element to speed up animation
    if (engine.input.isKeyClicked(engine.input.keys.Four)) {
        this.mRightMinion.incAnimationSpeed(-2);
        this.mLeftMinion.incAnimationSpeed(-2);
    }

    // increase duration of each sprite element to slow down animation
    if (engine.input.isKeyClicked(engine.input.keys.Five)) {
        this.mRightMinion.incAnimationSpeed(2);
        this.mLeftMinion.incAnimationSpeed(2);
    }

    ... identical to previous code ...
}
```

The keys 1, 2, and 3 change the animation type, and keys 4 and 5 change the animation speed. Note that the limit of the animation speed is the update rate of the game loop.

Fonts and Drawing of Text

A valuable tool that many games use for a variety of tasks is text output. Drawing of text messages is an efficient way to communicate to the user as well as you, the developer. For example, text messages can be used to communicate the game's story, the player's score, or debugging information during development. Unfortunately, WebGL does not support the drawing of text. This section briefly introduces bitmap fonts and introduces FontRenderable objects to support the drawing of texts.

Bitmap Fonts

A font must be defined such that individual characters can be extracted for the drawing of text messages. A bitmap font, as the name implies, is a simple map describing which bit (or pixel) must be switched on to represent characters in the font. Combining all characters of a bitmap font into a single image and defining an accompanied decoding description document provide a straightforward solution for drawing text output. For example, Figure 5-14 shows a bitmap font sprite where all the defined characters are tightly organized into the same image. Figure 5-15 is a snippet of the accompanying decoding description in XML format.

Figure 5-14. *An example bitmap font sprite image*

```
<?xml version="1.0"?>
<font>
  <info face="Consolas" size="24" bold="0" italic="0" charset="" unicode="1" stretchH="100" smooth="1" aa="1"
padding="0,0,0,0" spacing="1,1" outline="0"/>
  <common lineHeight="24" base="19" scaleW="256" scaleH="128" pages="1" packed="0" alphaChnl="0" redChnl="3"
greenChnl="3" blueChnl="3"/>
  <pages>
    <page id="0" file="Consolas-24-NoKerning_0.png" />
  </pages>
  <chars count="193">
    <char id="0" x="252" y="35" width="3" height="1" xoffset="-1" yoffset="23" xadvance="11" page="0" chnl="15" />
    <char id="13" x="254" y="0" width="0" height="1" xoffset="0" yoffset="23" xadvance="0" page="0" chnl="15" />
    <char id="32" x="17" y="38" width="3" height="1" xoffset="-1" yoffset="23" xadvance="11" page="0" chnl="15" />
```

Figure 5-15. *A snippet of the XML file with the decoding information for the bitmap font image shown in Figure 5-14*

Notice that the decoding information as shown in Figure 5-15 uniquely defines the uv coordinate positions for each character in the image, as shown in Figure 5-14. In this way, displaying individual characters from a bitmap font sprite image can be performed in a straightforward manner by the SpriteRenderable objects.

Note   There are many bitmap font file formats. The format used in this book is the AngleCode BMFont–compatible font in XML form. BMFont is an open source software that converts vector fonts, such as TrueType and OpenType, into bitmap fonts. See www.angelcode.com/products/bmfont/ for more information.

The Font Support Project

This project demonstrates how to draw text from a bitmap font using the SpriteRenderable object. You can see an example of this project running in Figure 5-16. The source code to this project is defined in the chapter5/5.4.font_support folder.

Figure 5-16. Running the Font Support project

The controls of the project are as follows:

- **Number keys 0, 1, 2, and 3**: Select the Consolas, 16, 24, 32, or 72 fonts, respectively, for size modification.

- **Up/down key while holding down X/Y key**: Increases or decreases (arrow keys) the width (X key) or the height (Y key) of the selected font.

- **Left- and right-arrow keys**: Move the hero left or right. The hero wraps if it exits the bounds.

247

The goals of the project are as follows:

- To understand bitmap fonts

- To gain a basic understanding of drawing text strings in a game

- To implement text drawing support in your game engine

You can find the following external resource files in the assets folder: consolas-72.png and minion_sprite.png. In the assets/fonts folder are the bitmap font sprite image files and the associated XML files that contain the decoding information: consolas-16.fnt, consolas-16.png, consolas-24.fnt, consolas-24. png, consolas-32.fnt, consolas-32.png, consolas-72.fnt, consolas-72.png, segment7-96.fnt, segment7-96.png, system-default-font.fnt, and system-default-font.png.

Notice that the .fnt and .png files are paired. The former contains decoding information for the latter. These file pairs must be included in the same folder for the engine to load the font properly. system-default-font is the default font for the game engine, and it is assumed that this font is always present in the asset/fonts folder.

Note   The actions of parsing, decoding, and extracting of character information from the .fnt files are independent from the foundational operations of a game engine. For this reason, the details of these operations are not presented. If you are interested, you should consult the source code.

Loading and Storing Fonts in the Engine

Loading font files is special because fonts are defined in pairs: the .fnt file that contains decoding information and the corresponding .png sprite image file. However, since the .fnt file is an XML file and the .png file is a simple texture image, the loading of these two types of files is already supported by the engine. The details of loading and storing fonts in the engine are encapsulated by a new engine component, font.

1. Create a new file in the src/engine/resources folder and name it font.js.

2. Import the resource management functionality from the xml module
    for loading the .fnt file and the texture module for the .png sprite
    image file, and define local constants for these file extensions:

```
import * as xml from "./xml.js";
import * as texture from "./texture.js";

let kDescExt = ".fnt";   // extension for the bitmap font description
let kImageExt = ".png";  // extension for the bitmap font image
```

3. Define a class for storing uv coordinate locations and the size
    associated with a character. This information can be computed
    based on the contents from the .fnt file.

```
class CharacterInfo {
    constructor() {
        // in texture coordinate (0 to 1) maps to the entire image
        this.mTexCoordLeft = 0;
        this.mTexCoordRight = 1;
        this.mTexCoordBottom = 0;
        this.mTexCoordTop = 0;

        // nominal char size, 1 is "standard width/height" of a char
        this.mCharWidth = 1;
        this.mCharHeight = 1;
        this.mCharWidthOffset = 0;
        this.mCharHeightOffset = 0;

        // reference of char width/height ratio
        this.mCharAspectRatio = 1;
    }
}
```

4. Define two functions to return proper extensions based on a path
    with no file extension. Note that fontName is a path to the font
    files but without any file extensions. For example, assets/fonts/
    system-default-font is the string and the two functions identify
    the two associated .fnt and .png files.

```
function descName(fontName) { return fontName+kDescExt;}
function imageName(fontName) { return fontName+kImageExt;}
```

5. Define the load() and unload() functions. Notice that two file
   operations are actually invoked in each: one for the .fnt and the
   second for the .png files.

```
function load(fontName) {
    xml.load(descName(fontName));
    texture.load(imageName(fontName));
}

function unload(fontName) {
    xml.unload(descName(fontName));
    texture.unload(imageName(fontName));
}
```

6. Define a function to inquire the loading status of a given font:

```
function has(fontName) {
    return texture.has(imageName(fontName)) &&
            xml.has(descName(fontName));
}
```

7. Define a function to compute CharacterInfo based on the
   information presented in the .fnt file:

```
function getCharInfo(fontName, aChar) {
    ... details omitted for lack of relevancy

    returnInfo = new CharacterInfo();

    // computes and fills in the contents of CharacterInfo
    ... details omitted for lack of relevancy

    return returnInfo;
};
```

Details of decoding and extracting information for a given
character are omitted because they are unrelated to the rest of the
game engine implementation.

Note   For details of the .fnt format information, please refer to www. angelcode.com/products/bmfont/doc/file_format.html.

8. Finally, remember to export the functions from this module:

```
export {has, load, unload,
        imageName, descName,
        CharacterInfo,
        getCharInfo
}
```

Adding a Default Font to the Engine

A default system font should be provided by the game engine for the convenience of the game programmer. To accomplish this, an engine utility should be defined to load and initialize default resources to be shared with the game developer. Recall that the shader_ resources module in the src/engine/core folder is defined to support engine-wide sharing of shaders. This pattern can be duplicated for sharing of default resources with the client. A default_resources module can be defined in the src/engine/resources folder to accomplish this sharing.

1. Create a file in the src/engine/resources folder and name it default_resources.js, import functionality from the font and resource_map modules, and define a constant string and its getter function for the path to the default system font:

```
import * as font from "./font.js";
import * as map from "../core/resource_map.js";

// Default font
let kDefaultFont = "assets/fonts/system_default_font";
var getDefaultFont = function() { return kDefaultFont; }
```

2. Define an `init()` function to issue the default system font
    loading request in a JavaScript `Promise` and append the `Promise`
    to the array of outstanding load requests in the `resource_map`.
    Recall that the `loop.start()` function in the `loop` module waits
    for the fulfillment of all `resource_map` loading promises before
    starting the game loop. For this reason, as in the case of all other
    asynchronously loaded resources, by the time the game loop
    begins, the default system font will have been properly loaded.

```
function init() {
    let loadPromise = new Promise(
      async function (resolve) {
          await Promise.all([
              font.load(kDefaultFont)
          ]);
          resolve();
      }).then(
          function resolve() { /* nothing to do for font */ }
      );
    map.pushPromise(loadPromise);
}
```

3. Define the `cleanUp()` function to release all allocated resources,
    in this case, unload the font:

```
// unload all resources
function cleanUp() {
    font.unload(kDefaultFont);
}
```

4. Lastly, remember to export all defined functionality:

```
export {
    init, cleanUp,

    // default system font name: this is guaranteed to be loaded
    getDefaultFontName
}
```

Defining a FontRenderable Object to Draw Texts

The defined font module is capable of loading font files and extracting per-character uv coordinate and size information. With this functionality, the drawing of a text string can be accomplished by identifying each character in the string, retrieving the corresponding texture mapping information, and rendering the character using a SpriteRenderable object. The FontRenderable object will be defined to accomplish this.

1. Create a new file in the src/engine/renderables folder and name it font_renderable.js.

2. Define the FontRenderable class and its constructor to accept a string as its parameter:

```
class FontRenderable {
    constructor(aString) {
        this.mFontName = defaultResources.getDefaultFontName();
        this.mOneChar = new SpriteRenderable(
                        font.imageName(this.mFontName));
        this.mXform = new Transform(); // to move this object around
        this.mText = aString;
    }
... implementation to follow ...
```

a. The aString variable is the message to be drawn.

b. Notice that FontRenderable objects do not customize the behaviors of SpriteRenderable objects. Rather, it relies on a SpriteRenderable object to draw each character in the string. For this reason, FontRenderable is not a subclass of but instead contains an instance of the SpriteRenderable object, the mOneChar variable.

3. Define the draw() function to parse and draw each character in the string using the mOneChar variable:

```
draw(camera) {
    // we will draw the text string by calling mOneChar for each of the
    // chars in the mText string.
```

```
    let widthOfOneChar = this.mXform.getWidth() / this.mText.length;
    let heightOfOneChar = this.mXform.getHeight();
    let yPos = this.mXform.getYPos();

    // center position of the first char
    let xPos = this.mXform.getXPos() -
                (widthOfOneChar / 2) + (widthOfOneChar * 0.5);
    let charIndex, aChar, charInfo, xSize, ySize, xOffset, yOffset;
    for (charIndex = 0; charIndex < this.mText.length; charIndex++) {
        aChar = this.mText.charCodeAt(charIndex);
        charInfo = font.getCharInfo(this.mFontName, aChar);

        // set the texture coordinate
        this.mOneChar.setElementUVCoordinate(
            charInfo.mTexCoordLeft, charInfo.mTexCoordRight,
            charInfo.mTexCoordBottom, charInfo.mTexCoordTop);

        // now the size of the char
        xSize = widthOfOneChar * charInfo.mCharWidth;
        ySize = heightOfOneChar * charInfo.mCharHeight;
        this.mOneChar.getXform().setSize(xSize, ySize);

        // how much to offset from the center
        xOffset = widthOfOneChar * charInfo.mCharWidthOffset * 0.5;
        yOffset = heightOfOneChar * charInfo.mCharHeightOffset * 0.5;

        this.mOneChar.getXform().setPosition(xPos-xOffset, yPos-yOffset);

        this.mOneChar.draw(camera);

        xPos += widthOfOneChar;
    }
}
```

The dimension of each character is defined by widthOfOneChar and heightOfOneChar where the width is simply dividing the total FontRenderable width by the number of characters in the string. The for loop then performs the following operations:

- a. Extracts each character in the string

- b. Calls the getCharInfo() function to receive the character's uv values and size information in charInfo

- c. Uses the uv values from charInfo to identify the sprite element location for mOneChar (by calling and passing the information to the mOneChar.setElementUVCoordinate() function)

- d. Uses the size information from charInfo to compute the actual size (xSize and ySize) and location offset for the character (xOffset and yOffset) and draws the character mOneChar with the appropriate settings

4. Implement the getters and setters for the transform, the text message to be drawn, the font to use for drawing, and the color:

```
getXform() { return this.mXform; }
getText() { return this.mText; }

setText(t) {
    this.mText = t;
    this.setTextHeight(this.getXform().getHeight());
}

getFontName() { return this.mFontName; }
setFontName(f) {
    this.mFontName = f;
    this.mOneChar.setTexture(font.imageName(this.mFontName));
}

setColor(c) { this.mOneChar.setColor(c); }
getColor() { return this.mOneChar.getColor(); }
```

5. Define the setTextHeight() function to define the height of the message to be output:

```
setTextHeight(h) {
    let charInfo = font.getCharInfo(this.mFontName, "A".charCodeAt(0));
    let w = h * charInfo.mCharAspectRatio;
    this.getXform().setSize(w * this.mText.length, h);
}
```

Notice that the width of the entire message to be drawn is automatically computed based on the message string length and maintaining the character width to height aspect ratio.

6. Finally, remember to export the defined class:

```
export default FrontRenderable;
```

Note   FontRenderable does not support the rotation of the entire message. Text messages are always drawn horizontally from left to right.

Initialize, Cleaning, and Export Font Functionality

As in all engine functionality, it is important to update the engine access file, index.js, to grant access to the game developer. In this case, it is also essential to initialize and clean up resources associated with the default system font.

1. Edit index.js to import functionality from the font and default_resources modules and the FontRenderable class:

```
// resources
import * as audio from "./resources/audio.js";
import * as text from "./resources/text.js";
import * as xml from "./resources/xml.js";
import * as texture from "./resources/texture.js";
import * as font from "./resources/font.js";
import * as defaultResources from "./resources/default_resources.js";

... identical to previous code ...
```

```
// renderables
import Renderable from "./renderables/renderable.js";
import SpriteRenderable from "./renderables/sprite_renderable.js";
import SpriteAnimateRenderable from
                    "./renderables/sprite_animate_renderable.js";
import FontRenderable from "./renderables/font_renderable.js";
... identical to previous code ...
```

2. Add default resources initialization and cleanup in the engine
   init() and cleanUp() functions:

```
function init(htmlCanvasID) {
    glSys.init(htmlCanvasID);
    vertexBuffer.init();
    input.init();
    audio.init();
    shaderResources.init();
    defaultResources.init();
}

function cleanUp() {
    loop.cleanUp();
    shaderResources.cleanUp();
    defaultResources.cleanUp();
    audio.cleanUp();
    input.cleanUp();
    vertexBuffer.cleanUp();
    glSys.cleanUp();
}
```

3. Remember to export the newly defined functionality:

```
export default {
    // resource support
    audio, text, xml, texture, font, defaultResources,

    ... identical to previous code ...
```

257

```
// Renderables
Renderable, TextureRenderable,
SpriteRenderable, SpriteAnimateRenderable, FontRenderable,

... identical to previous code ...
}
```

Testing Fonts

You can now modify the MyGame scene to print messages with the various fonts found in the assets folder:

4. In the my_game.js file, modify the constructor to define corresponding variables for printing the messages, and modify the draw() function to draw all objects accordingly. Please refer to the src/my_game/my_game.js file for the details of the code.

5. Modify the load() function to load the textures and fonts. Once again, notice that the font paths, for example, assets/fonts/consolas-16, do not include file name extensions. Recall that this path will be appended with .fnt and .png, where two separate files will be loaded to support the drawing of fonts.

```
load() {
    // Step A: loads the textures
    engine.texture.load(this.kFontImage);
    engine.texture.load(this.kMinionSprite);

    // Step B: loads all the fonts
    engine.font.load(this.kFontCon16);
    engine.font.load(this.kFontCon24);
    engine.font.load(this.kFontCon32);
    engine.font.load(this.kFontCon72);
    engine.font.load(this.kFontSeg96);
}
```

6.   Modify the `unload()` function to unload the textures and fonts:

```
unload() {
    engine.texture.unload(this.kFontImage);
    engine.texture.unload(this.kMinionSprite);

    // unload the fonts
    engine.font.unload(this.kFontCon16);
    engine.font.unload(this.kFontCon24);
    engine.font.unload(this.kFontCon32);
    engine.font.unload(this.kFontCon72);
    engine.font.unload(this.kFontSeg96);
}
```

7.   Define a private `_initText()` function to set the color, location, and height of a `FontRenderable` object. Modify the `init()` function to set up the proper WC system and initialize the fonts. Notice the calls to `setFont()` function to change the font type for each message.

```
_initText(font, posX, posY, color, textH) {
    font.setColor(color);
    font.getXform().setPosition(posX, posY);
    font.setTextHeight(textH);
}

init() {
    // Step A: set up the cameras
    this.mCamera = new engine.Camera(
        vec2.fromValues(50, 33),    // position of the camera
        100,                        // width of camera
        [0, 0, 600, 400]            // viewport (orgX, orgY, width, height)
    );
    this.mCamera.setBackgroundColor([0.8, 0.8, 0.8, 1]);
    // sets the background to gray

    // Step B: Create the font and minion images using sprite
    this.mFontImage = new engine.SpriteRenderable(this.kFontImage);
```

```
this.mFontImage.setColor([1, 1, 1, 0]);
this.mFontImage.getXform().setPosition(15, 50);
this.mFontImage.getXform().setSize(20, 20);

// The right minion
this.mMinion = new engine.SpriteAnimateRenderable(
                        this.kMinionSprite);
this.mMinion.setColor([1, 1, 1, 0]);
this.mMinion.getXform().setPosition(15, 25);
this.mMinion.getXform().setSize(24, 19.2);
this.mMinion.setSpriteSequence(512, 0,  // first element: top, left
    204, 164,      // widthxheight in pixels
    5,             // number of elements in this sequence
    0);.           // horizontal padding in between
this.mMinion.setAnimationType(engine.eAnimationType.eSwing);
this.mMinion.setAnimationSpeed(15);
// show each element for mAnimSpeed updates

// Step D: Create hero object with texture from lower-left corner
this.mHero = new engine.SpriteRenderable(this.kMinionSprite);
this.mHero.setColor([1, 1, 1, 0]);
this.mHero.getXform().setPosition(35, 50);
this.mHero.getXform().setSize(12, 18);
this.mHero.setElementPixelPositions(0, 120, 0, 180);

// Create the fonts
this.mTextSysFont = new engine.FontRenderable("System Font: in Red");
this._initText(this.mTextSysFont, 50, 60, [1, 0, 0, 1], 3);

this.mTextCon16 = new engine.FontRenderable("Consolas 16: in black");
this.mTextCon16.setFontName(this.kFontCon16);
this._initText(this.mTextCon16, 50, 55, [0, 0, 0, 1], 2);

this.mTextCon24 = new engine.FontRenderable("Consolas 24: in black");
this.mTextCon24.setFontName(this.kFontCon24);
this._initText(this.mTextCon24, 50, 50, [0, 0, 0, 1], 3);

this.mTextCon32 = new engine.FontRenderable("Consolas 32: in white");
```

```
    this.mTextCon32.setFontName(this.kFontCon32);
    this._initText(this.mTextCon32, 40, 40, [1, 1, 1, 1], 4);

    this.mTextCon72 = new engine.FontRenderable("Consolas 72: in blue");
    this.mTextCon72.setFontName(this.kFontCon72);
    this._initText(this.mTextCon72, 30, 30, [0, 0, 1, 1], 6);

    this.mTextSeg96 = new engine.FontRenderable("Segment7-92");
    this.mTextSeg96.setFontName(this.kFontSeg96);
    this._initText(this.mTextSeg96, 30, 15, [1, 1, 0, 1], 7);

    this.mTextToWork = this.mTextCon16;
}
```

8. Modify the update() function with the following:

```
update() {
    ... identical to previous code ...
    // choose which text to work on
    if (engine.input.isKeyClicked(engine.input.keys.Zero)) {
        this.mTextToWork = this.mTextCon16;
    }
    if (engine.input.isKeyClicked(engine.input.keys.One)) {
        this.mTextToWork = this.mTextCon24;
    }
    if (engine.input.isKeyClicked(engine.input.keys.Three)) {
        this.mTextToWork = this.mTextCon32;
    }
    if (engine.input.isKeyClicked(engine.input.keys.Four)) {
        this.mTextToWork = this.mTextCon72;
    }
    let deltaF = 0.005;
    if (engine.input.isKeyPressed(engine.input.keys.Up)) {
        if (engine.input.isKeyPressed(engine.input.keys.X)) {
            this.mTextToWork.getXform().incWidthBy(deltaF);
        }
```

```
        if (engine.input.isKeyPressed(engine.input.keys.Y)) {
            this.mTextToWork.getXform().incHeightBy(deltaF);
        }
        this.mTextSysFont.setText(
                this.mTextToWork.getXform().getWidth().toFixed(2) + "x" +
                this.mTextToWork.getXform().getHeight().toFixed(2));
    }

    if (engine.input.isKeyPressed(engine.input.keys.Down)) {
        if (engine.input.isKeyPressed(engine.input.keys.X)) {
            this.mTextToWork.getXform().incWidthBy(-deltaF);
        }
        if (engine.input.isKeyPressed(engine.input.keys.Y)) {
            this.mTextToWork.getXform().incHeightBy(-deltaF);
        }
        this.mTextSysFont.setText(
                this.mTextToWork.getXform().getWidth().toFixed(2) + "x" +
                this.mTextToWork.getXform().getHeight().toFixed(2));
    }
}
```

The listed code shows that you can perform the following operations during runtime:

a. Select which FontRenderable object to work with based on keyboard 0 to 4 input.

b. Control the width and height of the selected FontRenderable object when both the left/right arrow and X/Y keys are pressed.

You can now interact with the Font Support project to modify the size of each of the displayed font message and to move the hero toward the left and right.

Summary

In this chapter, you learned how to paste, or texture map, images on unit squares to better represent objects in your games. You also learned how to identify a selected subregion of an image and texture map to the unit square based on the normalize-ranged Texture Coordinate System. The chapter then explained how sprite sheets can reduce the time required for loading texture images while facilitating the creation of animations. This knowledge was then generalized and applied to the drawing of bitmap fonts.

The implementation of texture mapping and sprite sheet rendering takes advantage of an important aspect of game engine architecture: the `SimpleShader`/`Renderable` object pair where JavaScript `SimpleShader` objects are defined to interface with corresponding GLSL shaders and `Renderable` objects to facilitate the creation and interaction with multiple object instances. For example, you created `TextureShader` to interface with `TextureVS` and `TextureFS` GLSL shaders and created `TextureRenderable` for the game programmers to work with. This same pattern is repeated for `SpriteShader` and `SpriteRenderable`. The experience from `SpriteShader` objects paired with `SpriteAnimateRenderable` shows that, when appropriate, the same shader object can support multiple renderable object types in the game engine. This `SimpleShader`/`Renderable` pair implementation pattern will appear again in Chapter 8, when you learn to create 3D illumination effects.

At the beginning of this chapter, your game engine supports the player manipulating objects with the keyboard and the drawing of these objects in various sizes and orientations. With the functionality from this chapter, you can now represent these objects with interesting images and create animations of these objects when desired. In the next chapter, you will learn about defining and supporting behaviors for these objects including pseudo autonomous behaviors such as chasing and collision detections.

Game Design Considerations

In Chapter 4, you learned how responsive game feedback is essential for making players feel connected to a game world and that this sense of connection is known as *presence* in game design. As you move through future chapters in this book, you'll notice that most game design is ultimately focused on enhancing the sense of presence in one way or another, and you'll discover that visual design is one of the most important contributors to presence. Imagine, for example, a game where an object controlled by the player (also known as the *hero* object) must maneuver through a 2D platformer-style game world; the player's goal might be to use the mouse and keyboard to jump the hero between individual surfaces rendered in the game without falling through gaps that exist between those surfaces. The visual representation of the hero and other objects in the environment determines how the player identifies with the game setting, which in turn determines how effectively the game creates presence: Is the hero represented as a living creature or just an abstract shape like a square or circle? Are the surfaces represented as building rooftops, as floating rocks on an alien planet, or simply as abstract rectangles? There is no right or wrong answer when it comes to selecting a visual representation or game setting, but it is important to design a visual style for all game elements that feels unified and integrated into whatever game setting you choose (e.g., abstract rectangle platforms may negatively impact presence if your game setting is a tropical rainforest).

The *Texture Shaders* project demonstrated how `.png` images with transparency, more effectively integrate game elements into the game environment than formats like `.jpg` that don't support transparency. If you move the hero (represented here as simply a rectangle) to the right, nothing on the screen changes, but if you move the hero to the left, you'll eventually trigger a state change that alters the displayed visual elements as you did in the *Scene Objects* project from Chapter 4. Notice how much more effectively the robot sprites are integrated into the game scene when they're `.png` files with transparency on the gray background compared to when they're `.jpg` images without transparency on the blue background.

The *Sprite Shaders* project introduces a hero that more closely matches other elements in the game setting: you've replaced the rectangle from the *Texture Shaders* project with a humanoid figure stylistically matched to the flying robots on the screen, and the area of the rectangular hero image not occupied by the humanoid figure is transparent. If you were to combine the hero from the Sprite Shaders project with the screen-altering action in the *Texture Shaders* project, imagine that as the hero moves toward the robot on the right side of the screen, the robot might turn red when the hero gets too close. The coded events are still simple at this point, but you can see how the visual design and a few simple triggered actions can already begin to convey a game setting and enhance presence.

Note that as game designers we often become enamored with highly detailed and elaborate visual designs, and we begin to believe that higher fidelity and more elaborate visual elements are required to make the best games; this drive for ever-more powerful graphics is the familiar race that many AAA games engage in with their competition.

While it's true that game experiences and the sense of presence can be considerably enhanced when paired with excellent art direction, excellence does not always require elaborate and complex. Great art direction relies on developing a unified visual language where all elements harmonize with each other and contribute to driving the game forward and that harmony can be achieved with anything from simple shapes and colors in a 2D plane to hyperreal 3D environments and every combination in between.

Adding animated motion to the game's visual elements can further enhance game presence because animation brings a sense of cinematic dynamism to gameplay that further connects players to the game world. We typically experience motion in our world as interconnected systems; when you walk across the room, for example, you don't just glide without moving your body but move different parts of your body together in different ways. By adding targeted animations to objects onscreen that cause those objects to behave in ways you might expect complex systems to move or act, you connect players in a more immersive and convincing way to what's going on in the game world. The *Sprite Animation* project demonstrates how animation increases presence by allowing you to articulate the flying robot's spikes, controlling direction and speed. Imagine again combining the *Sprite Animation* project with the earlier projects in this chapter; as the hero moves closer to the robot, it might first turn red, eventually triggering the robot's animations and moving it either toward or away from the player. Animations often come fairly late in the game design process because it's usually necessary to first have the game mechanic and other systems well defined to avoid time-consuming changes that may be required as environments and level designs are updated. Designers typically use simple placeholder assets in the early stages of development, adding polished and animated final assets only when all of the other elements of gameplay have been finalized to minimize the need for rework.

As was the case with visual design, the animation approach need not be complex to be effective. While animation needs to be intentional and unified and should feel smooth and stutter-free unless it's intentionally designed to be otherwise, a wide degree of artistic license can be employed in how movement is represented onscreen.

The *Font Support* project introduced you to game fonts. While fonts rarely have a direct impact on gameplay, they can have a dramatic impact on presence. Fonts are a form of visual communication, and the style of the font is often as important as the words it conveys in setting tone and mood and can either support or detract from the game setting and visual style. Pay particular attention to the fonts displayed in this project, and note how the yellow font conveys a digital feeling that's matched to the science fiction–inspired visual style of the hero and robots, while the Consolas font family with its round letterforms feels a bit out of place with this game setting (sparse though the game setting may still be). As a more extreme example, imagine how disconnected a flowing calligraphic script font (the type typically used in high-fantasy games) would appear in a futuristic game that takes place on a spaceship.

There are as many visual style possibilities for games as there are people and ideas, and great games can feature extremely simple graphics. Remember that excellent game design is a combination of the nine contributing elements (return to the introduction if you need to refresh your memory), and the most important thing to keep in mind as a game designer is maintaining focus on how each of those elements harmonizes with and elevates the others to create something greater than the sum of its parts.

CHAPTER 6

Defining Behaviors and Detecting Collisions

After completing this chapter, you will be able to

- Implement autonomous behaviors such as target-locked chasing and gradual turning

- Collide textured objects accurately

- Understand the efficiency concerns of pixel-accurate collision

- Program with pixel-accurate collision effectively and efficiently

Introduction

By this point, your game engine is capable of implementing games in convenient coordinate systems as well as presenting and animating objects that are visually appealing. However, there is a lack of abstraction support for the behaviors of objects. You can see the direct results of this shortcoming in the init() and update() functions of the MyGame objects in all the previous projects: the init() function is often crowded with mundane per-game object settings, while the update() function is often crowded with conditional statements for controlling objects, such as checking for key presses for moving the hero.

A well-designed system should hide the initialization and controls of individual objects with proper object-oriented abstractions or classes. An abstract GameObject class should be introduced to encapsulate and hide the specifics of its initialization and behaviors. There are two main advantages to this approach. First, the init() and update() functions of a game level can focus on managing individual game object and

© Kelvin Sung, Jebediah Pavleas, Matthew Munson, and Jason Pace 2022
K. Sung et al., *Build Your Own 2D Game Engine and Create Great Web Games*,
https://doi.org/10.1007/978-1-4842-7377-7_6

the interactions of these objects without being clustered with details specific to different types of objects. Second, as you have experienced with the Renderable and SimpleShader class hierarchies, proper object-oriented abstraction creates a standardized interface and facilitates code sharing and reuse.

As you transition from working with the mere drawing of objects (in other words, Renderable) to programming with the behavior of objects (in other words, GameObject), you will immediately notice that for the game to be entertaining or fun, the objects need to interact. Interesting behaviors of objects, such as facing or evading enemies, often require the knowledge of the relative positions of other objects in the game. In general, resolving relative positions of all objects in a 2D world is nontrivial. Fortunately, typical video games require the knowledge of only those objects that are in close proximity to each other or are about to collide or have collided.

An efficient but somewhat crude approximation to detect collision is to compute the bounds of an object and approximate object collisions based on colliding bounding boxes. In the simplest cases, bounding boxes are rectangular boxes with edges that are aligned with the x/y axes. These are referred to as axis-aligned bounding boxes or AABBs. Because of the axis alignments, it is computationally efficient to detect when two AABBs overlap or when collision is about to occur.

Many 2D game engines can also detect the actual collision between two textured objects by comparing the location of pixels from both objects and detecting the situation when at least one of the nontransparent pixels overlaps. This computationally intensive process is known as per-pixel-accurate collision detection, pixel-accurate collision, or per-pixel collision.

This chapter begins by introducing the GameObject class to provide a platform for abstracting game object behaviors. The GameObject class is then generalized to introduce common behavior attributes including speed, movement direction, and target-locked chasing. The rest of the chapter focuses on deriving an efficient per-pixel accurate collision implementation that supports both textured and animated sprite objects.

Game Objects

As mentioned, an abstraction that encapsulates the intrinsic behavior of typical game objects should be introduced to minimize the clustering of code in the init() and update() functions of a game level and to facilitate reuse. This section introduces the simple GameObject class to illustrate how the cleaner and uncluttered init() and update() functions clearly reflect the in-game logic and to demonstrate how the basic platform for abstracting object behaviors facilitates design and code reuse.

The Game Objects Project

This project defines the simple GameObject class as the first step in building an abstraction to represent actual objects with behaviors in a game. You can see an example of this project running in Figure 6-1. Notice the many minions charging from right to left and wrapping around when they reach the left boundary. This project leads you to create the infrastructure to support the many minions while keeping the logic in the MyGame level simple. The source code to this project is defined in the chapter6/6.1.game_objects folder.

Figure 6-1. *Running the Game Objects project*

The controls of the project are as follows:

- **WASD keys**: Move the hero up, left, down, and right

The goals of the project are as follows:

- To begin defining the GameObject class to encapsulate object behaviors in games

- To demonstrate the creation of subclasses to the GameObject class to maintain the simplicity of the MyGame level update() function

- To introduce the GameObjectSet class demonstrating support for a set of homogenous objects with an identical interface

You can find the following external resource file in the assets folder: minion_sprite.png; you'll also find the fonts folder that contains the default system fonts. Note that, as shown in Figure 6-2, the minion_sprite.png image file has been updated from the previous project to include two extra sprite elements: the DyePack and the Brain minion.

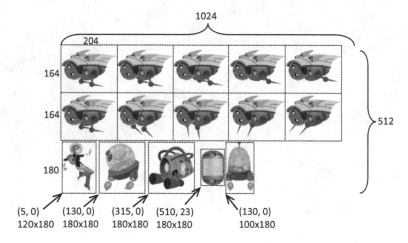

Figure 6-2. *The new sprite elements of the* minion_sprite.png *image*

Define the GameObject Class

The goal is to define a logical abstraction to encapsulate all relevant behavioral characteristics of a typical object in a game including the ability to control positions, drawing, and so on. As in the case for the Scene objects in the earlier chapter, the main result is to provide a well-defined interface governing the functions that subclasses implement. The more sophisticated behaviors will be introduced in the next section. This example only demonstrates the potential of the GameObject class with minimal behaviors defined.

1. Add a new folder src/engine/game_objects for storing GameObject-related files.

2. Create a new file in this folder, name it game_object.js, and add the following code:

```
class GameObject {
    constructor(renderable) {
        this.mRenderComponent = renderable;
    }

    getXform() { return this.mRenderComponent.getXform(); }

    getRenderable() { return this.mRenderComponent; }

    update() {   }

    draw(aCamera) {
        this.mRenderComponent.draw(aCamera);
    }
}

export default GameObject;
```

With the assessors to the Renderable and Transform objects defined, all GameObject instances can be drawn and have defined locations and sizes. Note that the update() function is designed for subclasses to override with per object–specific behaviors, and thus, it is left empty.

Manage Game Objects in Sets

Because most games consist of many interacting objects, it is useful to define a utility class to support working with a set of GameObject instances:

1. Create a new file in the src/engine/game_objects folder and name it game_object_set.js. Define the GameObjectSet class and the constructor to initialize an array for holding GameObject instances.

```
class GameObjectSet {
    constructor() {
        this.mSet = [];
    }

... implementation to follow ...

export default GameObjectSet;
```

2. Define functions for managing the set membership:

```
size() { return this.mSet.length; }
getObjectAt(index) { return this.mSet[index]; }
addToSet(obj) { this.mSet.push(obj); }
removeFromSet(obj) {
    let index = this.mSet.indexOf(obj);
    if (index > -1)
        this.mSet.splice(index, 1);
}
```

3. Define functions to update and draw each of the GameObject instances in the set:

```
update() {
    let i;
    for (i = 0; i < this.mSet.length; i++) {
        this.mSet[i].update();
    }
}
```

```
draw(aCamera) {
    let i;
    for (i = 0; i < this.mSet.length; i++) {
        this.mSet[i].draw(aCamera);
    }
}
```

Export the Classes to the Client

The last step in integrating any new functionality into the engine involves modifying the engine access file, index.js. Edit index.js and add the following import and export statements to grant the client access to the GameObject and GameObjectSet classes:

... identical to previous code ...

```
// game objects
import GameObject from "./game_objects/game_object.js";
import GameObjectSet from "./game_objects/game_object_set.js";
```

... identical to previous code ...

```
export default {
    ... identical to previous code ...

    // Game Objects
    GameObject, GameObjectSet,

    ... identical to previous code ...
}
```

Note   This process of import/export classes via the engine access file, index.js, must be repeated for every newly defined functionality. Henceforth, only a reminder will be provided and the straightforward code change will not be shown again.

Test the GameObject and GameObjectSet

The goals of this project are to ensure proper functioning of the new GameObject class, to demonstrate customization of behaviors by individual object types, and to observe a cleaner MyGame implementation clearly reflecting the in-game logic. To accomplish these goals, three object types are defined: DyePack, Hero, and Minion. Before you begin to examine the detailed implementation of these objects, follow good source code organization practice and create a new folder src/my_game/objects for storing the new object types.

The DyePack GameObject

The DyePack class derives from the GameObject class to demonstrate the most basic example of a GameObject: an object that has no behavior and is simply drawn to the screen.

Create a new file in the src/my_game/objects folder and name it dye_pack.js. Import from the engine access file, index.js, to gain access to all of the game engine functionality. Define DyePack as a subclass of GameObject and implement the constructor as follows:

```
import engine from "../../engine/index.js";
class DyePack extends engine.GameObject {
    constructor(spriteTexture) {
        super(null);
        this.kRefWidth = 80;
        this.kRefHeight = 130;
        this.mRenderComponent =
                            new engine.SpriteRenderable(spriteTexture);
        this.mRenderComponent.setColor([1, 1, 1, 0.1]);
        this.mRenderComponent.getXform().setPosition(50, 33);
        this.mRenderComponent.getXform().setSize(
                            this.kRefWidth / 50, this.kRefHeight / 50);
        this.mRenderComponent.setElementPixelPositions(510,595,23,153);
    }
}
export default DyePack;
```

Notice that even without specific behaviors, the DyePack is implementing code that used to be found in the init() function of the MyGame level. In this way, the DyePack object hides specific geometric information and simplifies the MyGame level.

Note   The need to import from the engine access file, index.js, is true for almost all client source code file and will not be repeated.

The Hero GameObject

The Hero class supports direct user keyboard control. This object demonstrates hiding of game object control logic from the update() function of MyGame.

1. Create a new file in the src/my_game/objects folder and name it hero.js. Define Hero as a subclass of GameObject, and implement the constructor to initialize the sprite UV values, size, and position. Make sure to export and share this class.

```
class Hero extends engine.GameObject {
    constructor(spriteTexture) {
        super(null);
        this.kDelta = 0.3;

        this.mRenderComponent =
                        new engine.SpriteRenderable(spriteTexture);
        this.mRenderComponent.setColor([1, 1, 1, 0]);
        this.mRenderComponent.getXform().setPosition(35, 50);
        this.mRenderComponent.getXform().setSize(9, 12);
        this.mRenderComponent.setElementPixelPositions(0, 120, 0, 180);
}
}

... implementation to follow ...

export default Hero;
```

2. Add a function to support the update of this object by user keyboard control. The Hero object moves at a kDelta rate based on WASD input from the keyboard.

```
update() {
    // control by WASD
    let xform = this.getXform();
    if (engine.input.isKeyPressed(engine.input.keys.W)) {
        xform.incYPosBy(this.kDelta);
    }
    if (engine.input.isKeyPressed(engine.input.keys.S)) {
        xform.incYPosBy(-this.kDelta);
    }
    if (engine.input.isKeyPressed(engine.input.keys.A)) {
        xform.incXPosBy(-this.kDelta);
    }
    if (engine.input.isKeyPressed(engine.input.keys.D)) {
            xform.incXPosBy(this.kDelta);
    }
}
```

The Minion GameObject

The Minion class demonstrates that simple autonomous behavior can also be hidden:

1. Create a new file in the src/my_game/objects folder and name
    it minion.js. Define Minion as a subclass of GameObject, and
    implement the constructor to initialize the sprite UV values, sprite
    animation parameters, size, and position as follows:

```
class Minion extends engine.GameObject {
    constructor(spriteTexture, atY) {
        super(null);
        this.kDelta = 0.2;

        this.mRenderComponent =
                    new engine.SpriteAnimateRenderable(spriteTexture);

        this.mRenderComponent.setColor([1, 1, 1, 0]);
        this.mRenderComponent.getXform().setPosition(
                                            Math.random() * 100, atY);
        this.mRenderComponent.getXform().setSize(12, 9.6);
```

```
    // first element pixel position: top-left 512 is top of image
    // 0 is left of the image
    this.mRenderComponent.setSpriteSequence(512, 0,
        204, 164,    // width x height in pixels
        5,           // number of elements in this sequence
        0);          // horizontal padding in between
    this.mRenderComponent.setAnimationType(
                                        engine.eAnimationType.eSwing);
    this.mRenderComponent.setAnimationSpeed(15);
    // show each element for mAnimSpeed updates
    }

    ... implementation to follow ...


}
export default Minion;
```

2. Add a function to update the sprite animation, support the simple
   right-to-left movements, and provide the wrapping functionality:

```
update() {
    // remember to update this.mRenderComponent's animation
    this.mRenderComponent.updateAnimation();

    // move towards the left and wraps
    let xform = this.getXform();
    xform.incXPosBy(-this.kDelta);

    // if fly off to the left, re-appear at the right
    if (xform.getXPos() < 0) {
        xform.setXPos(100);
        xform.setYPos(65 * Math.random());
    }
}
```

The MyGame Scene

As in all cases, the MyGame level is implemented in the my_game.js file. With the three specific GameObject subclasses defined, follow these steps:

1. In addition to the engine access file, index.js, in order to gain access to the newly defined objects, the corresponding source code must be imported:

```
import engine from "../engine/index.js";

// user stuff
import DyePack from "./objects/dye_pack.js";
import Minion from "./objects/minion.js";
import Hero from "./objects/hero.js";
```

Note   As is the case for other import/export statements, unless there are other specific reasons, this reminder will not be shown again.

---

2. The constructor and the load(), unload(), and draw() functions are similar as in previous projects, so the details are not shown here.

3. Edit the init() function and add the following code:

```
init() {
    ... identical to previous code ...

    // Step B: The dye pack: simply another GameObject
    this.mDyePack = new DyePack(this.kMinionSprite);

    // Step C: A set of Minions
    this.mMinionset = new engine.GameObjectSet();
    let i = 0, randomY, aMinion;
    // create 5 minions at random Y values
    for (i = 0; i < 5; i++) {
        randomY = Math.random() * 65;
```

```
        aMinion = new Minion(this.kMinionSprite, randomY);
        this.mMinionset.addToSet(aMinion);
    }

    // Step D: Create the hero object
    this.mHero = new Hero(this.kMinionSprite);

    // Step E: Create and initialize message output
    this.mMsg = new engine.FontRenderable("Status Message");
    this.mMsg.setColor([0, 0, 0, 1]);
    this.mMsg.getXform().setPosition(1, 2);
    this.mMsg.setTextHeight(3);
}
```

The details of step A, the creation of the camera and initialization of the background color, are not shown because they are identical to previous projects. Steps B, C, and D show the instantiation of the three object types, with step C showing the creation and insertion of the right-to-left moving Minion objects into the mMinionset, an instance of the GameObjectSet class. Notice that the init() function is free from the clustering of setting each object's textures, geometries, and so on.

4. Edit the update() function to update the game state:

```
update() {
    this.mHero.update();
    this.mMinionset.update();
    this.mDyePack.update();
}
```

With the well-defined behaviors for each object type abstracted, the clean update() function clearly shows that the game consists of three noninteracting objects.

Observation

You can now run the project and notice that the slightly more complex movements of six minions are accomplished with much cleaner init() and update() functions. The init() function consists of only logic and controls for placing created objects in the game world and does not include any specific settings for different object types. With the Minion object defining its motion behaviors in its own update() function, the logic in the

MyGame update() function can focus on the details of the level. Note that the structure of this function clearly shows that the three objects are updated independently and do not interact with each other.

Note   Throughout this book, in almost all cases, MyGame classes are designed to showcase the engine functionality. As a result, the source code organization in most MyGame classes may not represent the best practices for implementing games.

Creating a Chase Behavior

A closer examination of the previous project reveals that though there are quite a few minions moving on the screen, their motions are simple and boring. Even though there are variations in speed and direction, the motions are without purpose or awareness of other game objects in the scene. To support more sophisticated or interesting movements, a GameObject needs to be aware of the locations of other objects and determine motion based on that information.

Chasing behavior is one such example. The goal of a chasing object is usually to catch the game object that it is targeting. This requires programmatic manipulation of the front direction and speed of the chaser such that it can hone in on its target. However, it is generally important to avoid implementing a chaser that has perfect aim and always hits its target—because if the player is unable to avoid being hit, the game becomes impossibly difficult. Nonetheless, this does not mean you should not implement a perfect chaser if your game design requires it. You will implement a chaser in the next project.

Vectors and the associated operations are the foundation for implementing object movements and behaviors. Before programming with vectors, a quick review is provided. As in the case of matrices and transform operators, the following discussion is not meant to be a comprehensive coverage of vectors. Instead, the focus is on the application of a small collection of concepts that are relevant to the implementation of the game engine. This is not a study of the theories behind the mathematics. If you are interested in the specifics of vectors and how they relate to games, please refer to the discussion in Chapter 1 where you can learn more about these topics in depth by delving into relevant books on linear algebra and games.

Vectors Review

Vectors are used across many fields of study, including mathematics, physics, computer science, and engineering. They are particularly important in games; nearly every game uses vectors in one way or another. Because they are used so extensively, this section is devoted to understanding and utilizing vectors in games.

Note   For an introductory and comprehensive coverage of vectors, you can refer to www.storyofmathematics.com/vectors. For more detailed coverage of vector applications in games, you can refer to *Basic Math for Game Development with Unity 3D: A Beginner's Guide to Mathematical Foundations*, Apress, 2019.

One of the most common uses for vectors is to represent an object's displacement and direction or *velocity*. This can be done easily because a vector is defined by its size and direction. Using only this small amount of information, you can represent attributes such as the velocity or acceleration of an object. If you have the position of an object, its direction, and its velocity, then you have sufficient information to move it around the game world without user input.

Before going any further, it is important to review the concepts of a vector, starting with how you can define one. A vector can be specified using two points. For example, given the arbitrary positions $P_a = (x_a, y_a)$ and $P_b = (x_b, y_b)$, you can define the vector from P_a to P_b or $\vec{V}_{ab}$ as $P_b - P_a$. You can see this represented in the following equations and Figure 6-3:

- $P_a = (x_a, y_a)$
- $P_b = (x_b, y_b)$
- $\vec{V}_{ab} = P_b - P_a = (x_b - x_a, \, y_b - y_a)$

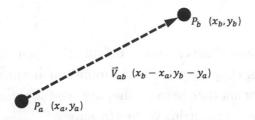

Figure 6-3. *A vector defined by two points*

Now that you have a vector $\vec{V}_{ab}$, you can easily determine its length (or size) and direction. A vector's length is equal to the distance between the two points that created it. In this example, the length of $\vec{V}_{ab}$ is equal to the distance between P_a and P_b, while the direction of $\vec{V}_{ab}$ goes from P_a toward P_b.

Note   The size of a vector is often referred to as its length or *magnitude*.

In the gl-matrix library, the vec2 object implements the functionality of a 2D vector. Conveniently, you can also use the vec2 object to represent 2D points or positions in space. In the preceding example, P_a, P_b, and $\vec{V}_{ab}$ can all be implemented as instances of the vec2 object. However, $\vec{V}_{ab}$ is the only mathematically defined vector. P_a and P_b represent positions or points used to create a vector.

Recall that a vector can also be normalized. A *normalized* vector (also known as a *unit vector*) always has a size of 1. You can see a normalized vector by the following function, as shown in Figure 6-4. Notice that the mathematical symbol for a regular vector is $\vec{V}_a$ and for a normalized vector is $\hat{V}_a$:

- *vec2.normalized*$\left(\vec{V}_a\right)$: Normalizes vector $\vec{V}_a$ and stores the results to the vec2 object

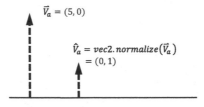

Figure 6-4. *A vector being normalized*

Vectors to a position can also be rotated. If, for example, the vector $\vec{V} = (x_v, y_v)$ represents the direction from the origin to the position (x_v, y_v) and you want to rotate it by θ, then, as illustrated in Figure 6-5, you can use the following equations to derive x_r and y_r:

- $x_r = x_v \cos \theta - y_v \sin \theta$

- $y_r = x_v \sin \theta + y_v \cos \theta$

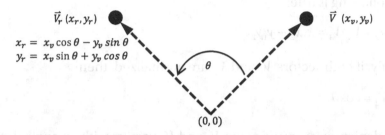

Figure 6-5. *A vector from the origin to the position (x_v, y_v) being rotated by the angle theta*

Note   JavaScript trigonometric functions, including the `Math.sin()` and `Math.cos()` functions, assume input to be in radians and not degrees. Recall that 1 degree is equal to $\dfrac{\pi}{180}$ radians.

It is always important to remember that vectors are defined by their direction and size. In other words, two vectors can be equal to each other independent of the locations of the vectors. Figure 6-6 shows two vectors $\vec{V}_a$ and $\vec{V}_{bc}$ that are located at different positions but have the same direction and magnitude and thus are equal to each other. In contrast, the vector $\vec{V}_d$ is not the same because its direction and magnitude are different from the others.

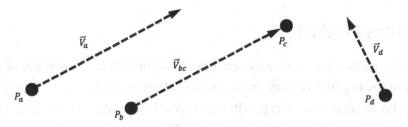

Figure 6-6. *Three vectors represented in 2D space with two vectors equal to each other*

The Dot Product

The dot product of two normalized vectors provides you with the means to find the angle between those vectors. For example, given the following:

- $\vec{V_1} = (x_1, y_1)$
- $\vec{V_2} = (x_2, y_2)$

Then the following is true:

- $\vec{V_1} \cdot \vec{V_2} = \vec{V_2} \cdot \vec{V_1} = x_1 x_2 + y_1 y_2$.

Additionally, if both vectors $\vec{V_1}$ and $\vec{V_2}$ are normalized, then

- $\hat{V_1} \cdot \hat{V_2} = \cos\theta$

Figure 6-7 depicts an example of the $\vec{V_1}$ and $\vec{V_2}$ vectors with an angle θ in between them. It is also important to recognize that if $\vec{V_1} \cdot \vec{V_2} = 0$, then the two vectors are perpendicular.

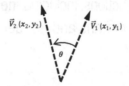

Figure 6-7. *The angle between two vectors, which can be found through the dot product*

Note   If you need to review or refresh the concept of a dot product, please refer to www.mathsisfun.com/algebra/vectors-dot-product.html.

The Cross Product

The cross product of two vectors produces a vector that is *orthogonal*, or perpendicular, to both of the original vectors. In 2D games, where the 2D dimensions lie flat on the screen, the result of the cross product is a vector that points either inward (toward the screen) or outward (away from the screen). This may seem odd because it is not intuitive that crossing two vectors in 2D or the x/y plane results in a vector that lies in the third dimension or along the z axis. However, the resulting vector in the third dimension carries crucial information. For example, the direction of this vector in the third dimension can be used to determine whether the game object needs to rotate in the clockwise or counterclockwise direction. Take a closer look at the following:

- $\vec{V}_1 = (x_1, y_1)$
- $\vec{V}_2 = (x_2, y_2)$

Given the previous, the following is true:

- $\vec{V}_3 = \vec{V}_1 \times \vec{V}_2$ is a vector perpendicular to both $\vec{V}_1$ and $\vec{V}_2$.

Additionally, you know that the cross product of two vectors on the x/y plane results in a vector in the z direction. When $\vec{V}_1 \times \vec{V}_2 > 0$, you know that $\vec{V}_1$ is in the clockwise direction from $\vec{V}_2$; similarly, when $\vec{V}_1 \times \vec{V}_2 < 0$, you know that $\vec{V}_1$ is in the counterclockwise direction. Figure 6-8 should help clarify this concept.

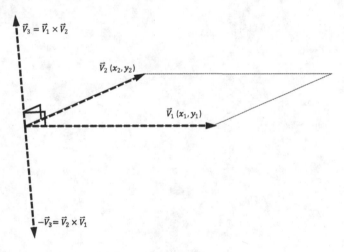

Figure 6-8. *The cross product of two vectors*

Note   If you need to review or refresh the concept of a cross product, please refer to www.mathsisfun.com/algebra/vectors-cross-product.html.

The Front and Chase Project

This project implements more interesting and sophisticated behaviors based on the vector concepts that have been reviewed. Instead of constant and aimless motions, you will experience the process of defining and varying the front direction of an object and guiding an object to chase after another object in the scene. You can see an example of this project running in Figure 6-9. The source code to this project is defined in the chapter6/6.2.front_and_chase folder.

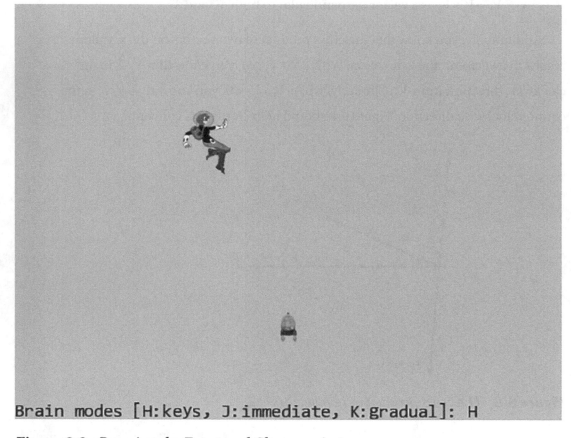

Brain modes [H:keys, J:immediate, K:gradual]: H

Figure 6-9. *Running the Front and Chase project*

The controls of the project are as follows:

- **WASD keys:** Moves the Hero object

- **Left-/right-arrow keys:** Change the front direction of the Brain object when it is under user control

- **Up-/down-arrow keys**: Increase/decrease the speed of the `Brain` object

- **H key**: Switches the `Brain` object to be under user arrow keys control

- **J key**: Switches the `Brain` object to always point at and move toward the current `Hero` object position

- **K key**: Switches the `Brain` object to turn and move gradually toward the current `Hero` object position

The goals of the project are as follows:

- To experience working with speed and direction

- To practice traveling along a predefined direction

- To implement algorithms with vector dot and cross products

- To examine and implement chasing behavior

You can find the same external resource files as in the previous project in the `assets` folder.

Add Vector Rotation to the gl-matrix Library

The `gl-matrix` library does not support rotating a position in 2D space. This can be rectified by adding the following code to the `gl-matrix.js` file in the `lib` folder:

```
vec2.rotate = function(out, a, c){
    var r=[];
    // perform rotation
    r[0] = a[0]*Math.cos(c) - a[1]*Math.sin(c);
    r[1] = a[0]*Math.sin(c) + a[1]*Math.cos(c);
    out[0] = r[0];
    out[1] = r[1];
    return r;
};
```

Note   This modification to the `gl-matrix` library must be present in all projects from this point forward.

Modify GameObject to Support Interesting Behaviors

The GameObject class abstracts and implements the desired new object behaviors:

1. Edit the game_object.js file and modify the GameObject constructor to define visibility, front direction, and speed:

```
constructor(renderable) {
    this.mRenderComponent = renderable;
    this.mVisible = true;
    this.mCurrentFrontDir = vec2.fromValues(0, 1); // front direction
    this.mSpeed = 0;
}
```

2. Add assessor and setter functions for the instance variables:

```
getXform() { return this.mRenderComponent.getXform(); }

setVisibility(f) { this.mVisible = f; }
isVisible() { return this.mVisible; }

setSpeed(s) { this.mSpeed = s; }
getSpeed() { return this.mSpeed; }
incSpeedBy(delta) { this.mSpeed += delta; }

setCurrentFrontDir(f) { vec2.normalize(this.mCurrentFrontDir, f); }
getCurrentFrontDir() { return this.mCurrentFrontDir; }

getRenderable() { return this.mRenderComponent; }
```

3. Implement a function to rotate the front direction toward a position, p:

```
rotateObjPointTo(p, rate) {
    // Step A: determine if reached the destination position p
    let dir = [];
    vec2.sub(dir, p, this.getXform().getPosition());
    let len = vec2.length(dir);
    if (len < Number.MIN_VALUE) {
        return; // we are there.
    }
```

```
vec2.scale(dir, dir, 1 / len);
// Step B: compute the angle to rotate
let fdir = this.getCurrentFrontDir();
let cosTheta = vec2.dot(dir, fdir);

if (cosTheta > 0.999999) { // almost exactly the same direction
    return;
}

// Step C: clamp the cosTheta to -1 to 1
// in a perfect world, this would never happen! BUT ...
if (cosTheta > 1) {
    cosTheta = 1;
} else {
    if (cosTheta < -1) {
        cosTheta = -1;
    }
}

// Step D: compute whether to rotate clockwise, or counterclockwise
let dir3d = vec3.fromValues(dir[0], dir[1], 0);
let f3d = vec3.fromValues(fdir[0], fdir[1], 0);
let r3d = [];
vec3.cross(r3d, f3d, dir3d);

let rad = Math.acos(cosTheta);  // radian to roate
if (r3d[2] < 0) {
    rad = -rad;
}

// Step E: rotate the facing direction with the angle and rate
rad *= rate;  // actual angle need to rotate from Obj's front
vec2.rotate(this.getCurrentFrontDir(),this.getCurrentFrontDir(),rad);
this.getXform().incRotationByRad(rad);
}
```

The `rotateObjPointTo()` function rotates the `mCurrentFrontDir` to point to the destination position p at a rate specified by the parameter `rate`. Here are the details of each operation:

a. Step A computes the distance between the current object and the destination position p. If this value is small, it means current object and the target position are close. The function returns without further processing.

b. Step B, as illustrated in Figure 6-10, computes the dot product to determine the angle θ between the current front direction of the object (`fdir`) and the direction toward the destination position p (`dir`). If these two vectors are pointing in the same direction (cosθ is almost 1 or θ almost zero), the function returns.

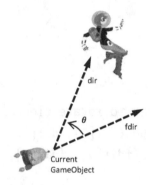

Figure 6-10. *A GameObject (`Brain`) chasing a target (`Hero`)*

c. Step C checks for the range of `cosTheta`. This is a step that must be performed because of the inaccuracy of floating-point operations in JavaScript.

d. Step D uses the results of the cross product to determine whether the current `GameObject` should be turning clockwise or counterclockwise to face toward the destination position p.

e. Step E rotates `mCurrentFrontDir` and sets the rotation in the `Transform` of the `Renderable` object. It is important to recognize the two separate object rotation controls. The `Transform` controls the rotation of what is being drawn, and `mCurrentFrontDir` controls the direction of travel. In this

290

case, the two are synchronized and thus must be updated
with the new value simultaneously.

4. Add a function to update the object's position with its direction
    and speed. Notice that if the mCurrentFrontDir is modified by the
    rotateObjPointTo() function, then this update() function will
    move the object toward the target position p, and the object will
    behave as though it is chasing the target.

```
update() {
    // simple default behavior
    let pos = this.getXform().getPosition();
    vec2.scaleAndAdd(pos, pos,this.getCurrentFrontDir(),this.getSpeed());
}
```

5. Add a function to draw the object based on the visibility setting:

```
draw(aCamera) {
    if (this.isVisible()) {
        this.mRenderComponent.draw(aCamera);
    }
}
```

Test the Chasing Functionality

The strategy and goals of this test case are to create a steerable Brain object to
demonstrate traveling along a predefined front direction and to direct the Brain to chase
after the Hero to demonstrate the chasing functionality.

Define the Brain GameObject

The Brain object will travel along its front direction under the control of the user's left-/
right-arrow keys for steering:

1. Create a new file in the src/my_game/objects folder and name
    it brain.js. Define Brain as a subclass of GameObject, and
    implement the constructor to initialize the appearance and
    behavior parameters.

```
class Brain extends engine.GameObject {
    constructor(spriteTexture) {
        super(null);
        this.kDeltaDegree = 1;
        this.kDeltaRad = Math.PI * this.kDeltaDegree / 180;
        this.kDeltaSpeed = 0.01;
        this.mRenderComponent =
                            new engine.SpriteRenderable(spriteTexture);
        this.mRenderComponent.setColor([1, 1, 1, 0]);
        this.mRenderComponent.getXform().setPosition(50, 10);
        this.mRenderComponent.getXform().setSize(3, 5.4);
        this.mRenderComponent.setElementPixelPositions(600, 700, 0, 180);

        this.setSpeed(0.05);
    }

    ... implementation to follow ...
}
export default Brain;
```

2. Override the update() function to support the user steering and
    controlling the speed. Notice that the default update() function in
    the GameObject must be called to support the basic traveling of the
    object along the front direction according to its speed.

```
update() {
    super.update();
    let xf = this.getXform();
    let fdir = this.getCurrentFrontDir();
    if (engine.input.isKeyPressed(engine.input.keys.Left)) {
        xf.incRotationByDegree(this.kDeltaDegree);
        vec2.rotate(fdir, fdir, this.kDeltaRad);
    }
    if (engine.input.isKeyPressed(engine.input.keys.Right)) {
        xf.incRotationByRad(-this.kDeltaRad);
        vec2.rotate(fdir, fdir, -this.kDeltaRad);
    }
```

```
    if (engine.input.isKeyClicked(engine.input.keys.Up)) {
        this.incSpeedBy(this.kDeltaSpeed);
    }
    if (engine.input.isKeyClicked(engine.input.keys.Down)) {
        this.incSpeedBy(-this.kDeltaSpeed);
    }
}
```

The MyGame Scene

Modify the MyGame scene to test the Brain object movement. In this case, except for
the update() function, the rest of the source code in my_game.js is similar to previous
projects. For this reason, only the details of the update() function are shown:

```
update() {
    let msg = "Brain [H:keys J:imm K:gradual]: ";
    let rate = 1;

    this.mHero.update();

    switch (this.mMode) {
        case 'H':
            this.mBrain.update();  // player steers with arrow keys
            break;
        case 'K':
            rate = 0.02;    // gradual rate
            // In gradual mode, the following should also be executed
        case 'J':
            this.mBrain.rotateObjPointTo(
                this.mHero.getXform().getPosition(), rate);

            // the default GameObject: only move forward
            engine.GameObject.prototype.update.call(this.mBrain);
            break;
    }

    if (engine.input.isKeyClicked(engine.input.keys.H)) {
        this.mMode = 'H';
    }
```

```
    if (engine.input.isKeyClicked(engine.input.keys.J)) {
        this.mMode = 'J';
    }
    if (engine.input.isKeyClicked(engine.input.keys.K)) {
        this.mMode = 'K';
    }
    this.mMsg.setText(msg + this.mMode);
}
```

In the update() function, the switch statement uses mMode to determine how to update the Brain object. In the cases of J and K modes, the Brain object turns toward the Hero object position with the rotateObjPointTo() function call. While in the H mode, the Brain object's update() function is called for the user to steer the object with the arrow keys. The final three if statements simply set the mMode variable according to user input.

Note that in the cases of J and K modes, in order to bypass the user control logic after the rotateObjPointTo(), the update() function being called is the one defined by the GameObject and not by the Brain.

Note   The JavaScript syntax, ClassName.prototype.FunctionName. call(anObj), calls FunctionName defined by ClassName, where anObj is a subclass of ClassName.

Observation

You can now try running the project. Initially, the Brain object is under the user's control. You can use the left- and right-arrow keys to change the front direction of the Brain object and experience steering the object. Pressing the J key causes the Brain object to immediately point and move toward the Hero object. This is a result of the default turn rate value of 1.0. The K key causes a more natural behavior, where the Brain object continues to move forward and gradually turns to move toward the Hero object. Feel free to change the values of the rate variable or modify the control value of the Brain object. For example, change the kDeltaRad or kDeltaSpeed to experiment with different settings for the behavior.

Collisions Between GameObjects

In the previous project, the Brain object would never stop traveling. Notice that under the J and K modes, the Brain object would orbit or rapidly flip directions when it reaches the target position. The Brain object is missing the critical ability to detect that it has collided with the Hero object, and as a result, it never stops moving. This section describes axis-aligned bounding boxes (AABBs), one of the most straightforward tools for approximating object collisions, and demonstrates the implementation of collision detection based on AABB.

Axis-Aligned Bounding Box (AABB)

An AABB is an x/y axis–aligned rectangular box that bounds a given object. The term *x/y axis aligned* refers to the fact that the four sides of an AABB are parallel either to the horizontal x axis or to the vertical y axis. Figure 6-11 shows an example of representing the bounds to the Hero object by the lower-left corner (mLL), width, and height. This is a fairly common way to represent an AABB because it uses only one position and two floating-point numbers to represent the dimensions.

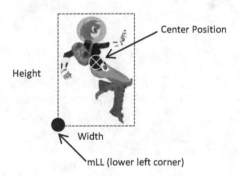

Figure 6-11.   The lower-left corner and size of the bounds for an object

It is interesting to note that in addition to representing the bounds of an object, bounding boxes can be used to represent the bounds of any given rectangular area. For example, recall that the WC visible through the Camera is a rectangular area with the camera's position located at the center and the WC width/height defined by the game developer. An AABB can be defined to represent the visible WC rectangular area, or the WC window, and used for detecting collision between the WC window and GameObject instances in the game world.

Note   In this book, AABB and "bounding box" are used interchangeably.

The Bounding Box and Collisions Project

This project demonstrates how to define a bounding box for a GameObject instance and detect collisions between two GameObject instances based on their bounding boxes. It is important to remember that bounding boxes are axes aligned, and thus, the solution presented in this section does not support collision detections between rotated objects. You can see an example of this project running in Figure 6-12. The source code to this project is defined in the chapter6/6.3.bbox_and_collisions folder.

Figure 6-12. *Running the Bounding Box and Collisions project*

The controls of the project are identical to the previous project:

- **WASD keys**: Moves the Hero object

- **Left-/right-arrow keys**: Change the front direction of the Brain object when it is under user control

- **Up-/down-arrow keys**: Increase/decrease the speed of the Brain object

- **H key**: Switches the Brain object to be under user arrow keys control

- **J key**: Switches the Brain object to always point at and move toward the current Hero object position

- **K key**: Switches the Brain object to turn and move gradually toward the current Hero object position

The goals of the project are as follows:

- To understand the implementation of the bounding box class

- To experience working with the bounding box of a GameObject instance

- To compute and work with the bounds of a Camera WC window

- To program with object collisions and object and camera WC window collisions

You can find the same external resource files as in the previous project in the assets folder.

Define a Bounding Box Class

Define a BoundingBox class to represent the bounds of a rectangular area:

1. Create a new file in the src/engine folder; name it bounding_box.js. First, define an enumerated data type with values that identify the colliding sides of a bounding box.

```
const eBoundCollideStatus = Object.freeze({
    eCollideLeft: 1,
    eCollideRight: 2,
    eCollideTop: 4,
```

```
      eCollideBottom: 8,
      eInside: 16,
      eOutside: 0
});
```

Notice that each enumerated value has only one nonzero bit. This allows the enumerated values to be combined with the bitwise-or operator to represent a multisided collision. For example, if an object collides with both the top and left sides of a bounding box, the collision status will be eCollideLeft | eCollideTop = 1 | 4 = 5.

2. Now, define the BoundingBox class and the constructor with instance variables to represent a bound, as illustrated in Figure 6-11. Notice that the eBoundCollideStatus must also be exported such that the rest of the engine, including the client, can also have access.

```
class BoundingBox {
    constructor(centerPos, w, h) {
        this.mLL = vec2.fromValues(0, 0);
        this.setBounds(centerPos, w, h);
    }

    ... implementation to follow ...
}

export {eBoundCollideStatus}
export default BoundingBox;
```

3. The setBounds() function computes and sets the instance variables of the bounding box:

```
setBounds(centerPos, w, h) {
    this.mWidth = w;
    this.mHeight = h;
    this.mLL[0] = centerPos[0] - (w / 2);
    this.mLL[1] = centerPos[1] - (h / 2);
}
```

4. Define a function to determine whether a given position, (x, y), is
    within the bounds of the box:

```
containsPoint(x, y) {
    return ((x > this.minX()) && (x < this.maxX()) &&
        (y > this.minY()) && (y < this.maxY())));
}
```

5. Define a function to determine whether a given bound intersects
    with the current one:

```
intersectsBound(otherBound) {
    return ((this.minX() < otherBound.maxX()) &&
        (this.maxX() > otherBound.minX()) &&
        (this.minY() < otherBound.maxY()) &&
        (this.maxY() > otherBound.minY()));
}
```

6. Define a function to compute the intersection status between a
    given bound and the current one:

```
boundCollideStatus(otherBound) {
    let status = eBoundCollideStatus.eOutside;

    if (this.intersectsBound(otherBound)) {
        if (otherBound.minX() < this.minX()) {
            status |= eBoundCollideStatus.eCollideLeft;
        }
        if (otherBound.maxX() > this.maxX()) {
            status |= eBoundCollideStatus.eCollideRight;
        }
        if (otherBound.minY() < this.minY()) {
            status |= eBoundCollideStatus.eCollideBottom;
        }
        if (otherBound.maxY() > this.maxY()) {
            status |= eBoundCollideStatus.eCollideTop;
        }
```

```
        // if the bounds intersects and yet none of the sides overlaps
        // otherBound is completely inside thisBound
        if (status === eBoundCollideStatus.eOutside) {
            status = eBoundCollideStatus.eInside;
        }
    }
    return status;
}
```

Notice the subtle yet important difference between the `intersectsBound()` and `boundCollideStatus()` functions where the former is capable of returning only a `true` or `false` condition while the latter function encodes the colliding sides in the returned status.

7. Implement the functions that return the X/Y values to the min and max bounds of the bounding box:

```
minX() { return this.mLL[0]; }
maxX() { return this.mLL[0] + this.mWidth; }
minY() { return this.mLL[1]; }
maxY() { return this.mLL[1] + this.mHeight; }
```

Lastly, remember to update the engine access file, `index.js`, to forward the newly defined functionality to the client.

Use the BoundingBox in the Engine

The newly defined functionality will be used to detect collisions between objects and between objects and the WC bounds. In order to accomplish this, the `GameObject` and `Camera` classes must be modified.

1. Edit game_object.js to import the newly defined functionality and modify the `GameObject` class; implement the `getBBox()` function to return the bounding box of the unrotated `Renderable` object:

```
import BoundingBox from "../bounding_box.js";
class GameObject {
    ... identical to previous code ...
```

```
    getBBox() {
        let xform = this.getXform();
        let b = new BoundingBox(
                          xform.getPosition(),
                          xform.getWidth(),
                          xform.getHeight());
        return b;
    }
    ... identical to previous code ...
}
```

2. Edit camera.js to import from bounding box, and modify the
   Camera class to compute the collision status between the bounds
   of a Transform object (typically defined in a Renderable object)
   and that of the WC window:

```
import BoundingBox from "./bounding_box.js";
class Camera {
    ... identical to previous code ...
    collideWCBound(aXform, zone) {
        let bbox = new BoundingBox(
                          aXform.getPosition(),
                          aXform.getWidth(),
                          aXform.getHeight());
        let w = zone * this.getWCWidth();
        let h = zone * this.getWCHeight();
        let cameraBound = new BoundingBox(this.getWCCenter(), w, h);
        return cameraBound.boundCollideStatus(bbox);
    }
}
```

Notice that the zone parameter defines the relative size of WC that should be used
in the collision computation. For example, a zone value of 0.8 would mean computing
for intersection status based on 80 percent of the current WC window size. Figure 6-13
shows how the camera collides with an object.

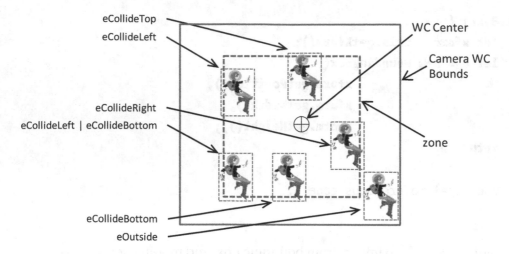

Figure 6-13. *Camera WC bounds colliding with the bounds defining a Transform object*

Test Bounding Boxes with MyGame

The goal of this test case is to verify the correctness of the bounding box implementation in detecting object-object and object-camera intersections. Once again, with the exception of the update() function, the majority of the code in the my_game.js file is similar to the previous projects and is not repeated here. The update() function is modified from the previous project to test for bounding box intersections.

```
update() {
    ... identical to previous code ...

    switch (this.mMode) {
        case 'H':
            this.mBrain.update();  // player steers with arrow keys
            break;
        case 'K':
            rate = 0.02;    // gradual rate
            // no break here on purpose
        case 'J':
            // stop the brain when it touches hero bound
            if (!hBbox.intersectsBound(bBbox)) {
                this.mBrain.rotateObjPointTo(
```

```
                    this.mHero.getXform().getPosition(), rate);
            // the default GameObject: only move forward
            engine.GameObject.prototype.update.call(this.mBrain);
        }
        break;
    }

    // Check for hero going outside 80% of the WC Window bound
    let status = this.mCamera.collideWCBound(this.mHero.getXform(), 0.8);

    ... identical to previous code ...

    this.mMsg.setText(msg + this.mMode + " [Hero bound=" + status + "]");
}
```

In the switch statement's J and K cases, the modification tests for bounding box collision between the Brain and Hero objects before invoking Brain. rotateObjPointTo() and update() to cause the chasing behavior. In this way, the Brain object will stop moving as soon as it touches the bound of the Hero object. In addition, the collision results between the Hero object and 80 percent of the camera WC window are computed and displayed.

Observation

You can now run the project and observe that the Brain object, when in autonomous mode (J or K keys), stops moving as soon as it touches the Hero object. When you move the Hero object around, observe the Hero bound output message begins to echo WC window collisions before the Hero object actually touches the WC window bounds. This is a result of the 0.8, or 80 percent, parameter passed to the mCamera.collideWCBound() function, configuring the collision computation to 80 percent of the current WC window size. When the Hero object is completely within 80 percent of the WC window bounds, the output Hero bound value is 16 or the value of eboundcollideStatus.eInside. Try moving the Hero object to touch the top 20 percent of the window bound, and observe the Hero bound value of 4 or the value of eboundcollideStatus.eCollideTop. Now move the Hero object toward the top-left corner of the window, and observe the Hero bound value of 5 or eboundcollideStatus.eCollideTop | eboundcollideStatus.eCollideLeft. In this way, the collision status is a bitwise-or result of all the colliding bounds.

Per-Pixel Collisions

In the previous example, you saw the results of bounding box collision approximation. Namely, the `Brain` object's motion stops as soon as its bounds overlap that of the `Hero` object. This is much improved over the original situation where the `Brain` object never stops moving. However, as illustrated in Figure 6-14, there are two serious limitations to the bounding box–based collisions.

1. The `BoundingBox` object introduced in the previous example does not account for rotation. This is a well-known limitation for AABB: although the approach is computationally efficient, it does not support rotated objects.

2. The two objects do not actually collide. The fact that the bounds of two objects overlap does not automatically equate to the two objects colliding.

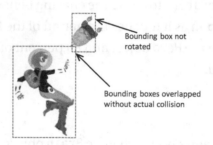

Bounding box not rotated

Bounding boxes overlapped without actual collision

Figure 6-14. *Limitation with bounding box–based collision*

In this project, you will implement per-pixel-accurate collision detection, pixel-accurate collision detection, or per-pixel collision detection, to detect the overlapping of nontransparent pixels of two colliding objects. However, keep in mind that this is *not* an end-all solution. While the per-pixel collision detection is precise, the trade-off is potential performance costs. As an image becomes larger and more complex, it also has more pixels that need to be checked for collisions. This is in contrast to the constant computation cost required for bounding box collision detection.

The Per-Pixel Collisions Project

This project demonstrates how to detect collision between a large textured object, the Collector minion and a small textured object, the Portal minion. Both of the textures contain transparent and nontransparent areas. A collision occurs only when the nontransparent pixels overlap. In this project, when a collision occurs, a yellow DyePack appears at the collision point. You can see an example of this project running in Figure 6-15. The source code to this project is defined in the chapter6/6.4.per_pixel_collisions folder.

Figure 6-15. Running the Per-Pixel Collisions project

The controls of the project are as follows:

- **Arrow keys:** Move the small textured object, the Portal minion
- **WASD keys:** Move the large textured object, the Collector minion

The goals of the project are as follows:

- To demonstrate how to detect nontransparent pixel overlap

- To understand the pros and cons of using per-pixel-accurate collision detection

---

Note   A "transparent" pixel is one you can see through completely and, in the case of this engine, has an alpha value of 0. A "nontransparent" pixel has a greater than 0 alpha value, or the pixel does not completely block what is behind it; it may or may not occlude. An "opaque" pixel occludes what is behind it, is "nontransparent," and has an alpha value of 1. For example, notice that you can "see through" the top region of the `Portal` object. These pixels are nontransparent but not opaque and should cause a collision when an overlap occurs based on the parameters defined by the project.

You can find the following external resources in the `assets` folder: the `fonts` folder that contains the default system fonts, `minion_collector.png`, `minion_portal.png`, and `minion_sprite.png`. Note that `minion_collector.png` is a large, 1024x1024 image, while `minion_portal.png` is a small, 64x64 image; `minion_sprite.png` defines the DyePack sprite element.

Overview of Per-Pixel Collision Algorithm

Before moving forward, it is important to identify the requirements for detecting a collision between two textured objects. Foremost is that the texture itself needs to contain an area of transparency in order for this type of collision detection to provide any increase in accuracy. Without transparency in the texture, you can and should use a simple bounding box collision detection. If one or both of the textures contain transparent areas, then you'll need to handle two cases of collision. The first case is to check whether the bounds of the two objects collide. You can see this reflected in Figure 6-16. Notice how the bounds of the objects overlap, yet none of the nontransparent colored pixels are touching.

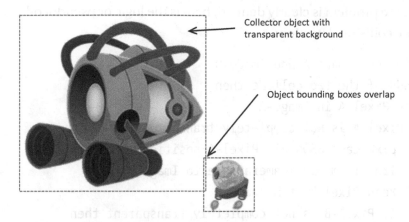

Figure 6-16. *Overlapping bounding boxes without actual collision*

The next case is to check whether the nontransparent pixels of the textures overlap. Take a look at Figure 6-17. Nontransparent pixels from the textures of the `Collector` and `Portal` objects are clearly in contact with one another.

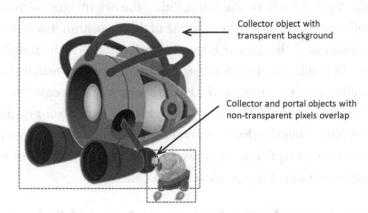

Figure 6-17. *Pixel collision occurring between the large texture and the small texture*

Now that the problem is clearly defined, here is the logic or pseudocode for per-pixel-accurate collision detection:

```
Given two images, Image-A and Image-B
If the bounds of the two collide then
   For each Pixel-A in Image-A
       If Pixel-A is not completely transparent
           pixelCameraSpace = Pixel-A position in camera space
           Transform pixelCameraSpace to Image-B space
           Read Pixel-B from Image-B
           If Pixel-B is not completely transparent then
               A collision has occurred
```

The per-pixel transformation to Image-B space from `pixelCameraSpace` is required because collision checking must be carried out within the same coordinate space.

Notice that in the algorithm Image-A and Image-B are exchangeable. That is, when testing for collision between two images, it does not matter which image is Image-A or Image-B. The collision result will be the same. Either the two images do overlap, or they do not. Additionally, pay attention to the runtime of this algorithm. Each pixel within Image-A must be processed; thus, the runtime is O(N), where N is the number of pixels in Image-A or Image-A's resolution. For this reason, for performance reason, it is important to choose the smaller of the two images (the `Portal` minion in this case) as Image-A.

At this point, you can probably see why the performance of pixel-accurate collision detection is concerning. Checking for these collisions during every update with many high-resolution textures can quickly bog down performance. You are now ready to examine the implementation of per-pixel-accurate collision.

Modify Texture to Load a Texture as an Array of Colors

Recall that the `Texture` component reads image files from the server file system, loads the images to the GPU memory, and processes the images into WebGL textures. In this way, texture images are stored on the GPU and are not accessible by the game engine which is running on the CPU. To support per-pixel collision detection, the color information must be retrieved from the GPU and stored in the CPU. The `Texture` component can be modified to support this requirement.

1. In the `texture.js` file, expand the `TextureInfo` object to include a
    new variable for storing the color array of a file texture:

```
class TextureInfo {
    constructor(w, h, id) {
        this.mWidth = w;
        this.mHeight = h;
        this.mGLTexID = id;
        this.mColorArray = null;
    }
}
```

2. Define and export a function to retrieve the color array from the
    GPU memory:

```
function getColorArray(textureName) {
    let gl = glSys.get();
    let texInfo = get(textureName);
    if (texInfo.mColorArray === null) {
        // create framebuffer bind to texture and read the color content
        let fb = gl.createFramebuffer();
        gl.bindFramebuffer(gl.FRAMEBUFFER, fb);
        gl.framebufferTexture2D(gl.FRAMEBUFFER,
                        gl.COLOR_ATTACHMENT0,
                        gl.TEXTURE_2D, texInfo.mGLTexID, 0);
        if (gl.checkFramebufferStatus(gl.FRAMEBUFFER) ===
            gl.FRAMEBUFFER_COMPLETE) {
            let pixels = new Uint8Array(
                        texInfo.mWidth * texInfo.mHeight * 4);
            gl.readPixels(0, 0, texInfo.mWidth, texInfo.mHeight,
                gl.RGBA, gl.UNSIGNED_BYTE, pixels);
            texInfo.mColorArray = pixels;
        } else {
            throw new Error("...");
            return null;
        }
```

```
        gl.bindFramebuffer(gl.FRAMEBUFFER, null);
        gl.deleteFramebuffer(fb);
    }
    return texInfo.mColorArray;
}

export {has, get, load, unload,

    TextureInfo,

    activate, deactivate,

    getColorArray
}
```

The getColorArray() function creates a WebGL FRAMEBUFFER, fills the buffer with the desired texture, and retrieves the buffer content into the CPU memory referenced by texInfo.mColorArray.

Modify TextureRenderable to Support Per-Pixel Collision

The TextureRenderable is the most appropriate class for implementing the per-pixel collision functionality. This is because TextureRenderable is the base class for all classes that render textures. Implementation in this base class means all subclasses can inherit the functionality with minimal additional changes.

As the functionality of the TextureRenderable class increases, so will the complexity and size of the implementation source code. For readability and expandability, it is important to maintain the size of source code files. An effective approach is to separate the source code of a class into multiple files according to their functionality.

Organize the Source Code

In the following steps, the TextureRenderable class will be separated into three source code files: texture_renderable_main.js for implementing the basic functionality from previous projects, texture_renderable_pixel_collision.js for implementing the newly introduced per-pixel-accurate collision, and texture_renderable.js for serving as the class access point.

1. Rename `texture_renderable.js` to `texture_renderable_main.js`. This file defines the basic functionality of the TextureRenderable class.

2. Create a new file in `src/engine/renderables` and name it `texture_renderable_pixel_collision.js`. This file will be used to extend the TextureRenderable class functionality in supporting per-pixel-accurate collision. Add in the following code to import from the Texture module and the basic TextureRenderable class, and reexport the TextureRenderable class. For now, this file does not serve any purpose; you will add in the appropriate extending functions in the following subsection.

```
"use strict";
import TextureRenderable from "./texture_renderable_main.js";
import * as texture from "../resources/texture.js";

... implementation to follow ...

export default TextureRenderable;
```

3. Create a new `texture_renderable.js` file to serve as the TextureRenderable access point by adding the following code:

```
"use strict";
import TextureRenderable from "./ texture_renderable_pixel_collision.js";
export default TextureRenderable;
```

With this structure, the `texture_renderable_main.js` file implements all the basic functionality and exports to `texture_renderable_pixel_collision.js`, which appends additional functionality to the TextureRenderable class. Finally, `texture_renderable.js` imports the extended functions from `texture_renderable_pixel_collision.js`. The users of the TextureRenderable class can simply import from `texture_renderable.js` and will have access to all of the defined functionality.

In this way, from the perspective of the game developer, `texture_renderable.js` serves as the access point to the TextureRenderable class and hides the details of the implementation source code structure. At the same time, from the perspective of you as the engine developer, complex implementations are separated into source code files with names indicating the content achieving readability of each individual file.

Define Access to the Texture Color Array

Recall that you began this project by first editing the Texture module to retrieve, from the GPU to the CPU, the color array that represents a texture. You must now edit TextureRenderable to gain access to this color array.

1. Edit the texture_renderable_main.js file, and modify the constructor to add instance variables to hold texture information, including a reference to the retrieved color array, for supporting per-pixel collision detection and for later subclass overrides:

```
class TextureRenderable extends Renderable {
    constructor(myTexture) {
        super();
        // Alpha of 0: switch off tinting of texture
        super.setColor([1, 1, 1, 0]);
        super._setShader(shaderResources.getTextureShader());

        this.mTexture = null;
        // these two instance variables are to cache texture information
        // for supporting per-pixel accurate collision
        this.mTextureInfo = null;
        this.mColorArray = null;
        // defined for subclass to override
        this.mElmWidthPixels = 0;
        this.mElmHeightPixels = 0;
        this.mElmLeftIndex = 0;
        this.mElmBottomIndex = 0;

        // texture for this object, cannot be a "null"
        this.setTexture(myTexture);
    }
```

2. Modify the setTexture() function to initialize the instance variables accordingly:

```
setTexture(newTexture) {
    this.mTexture = newTexture;
    // these two instance variables are to cache texture information
```

```
    // for supporting per-pixel accurate collision
    this.mTextureInfo = texture.get(newTexture);
    this.mColorArray = null;
    // defined for one sprite element for subclass to override
    // For texture_renderable, one sprite element is the entire texture
    this.mElmWidthPixels = this.mTextureInfo.mWidth;
    this.mElmHeightPixels = this.mTextureInfo.mHeight;
    this.mElmLeftIndex = 0;
    this.mElmBottomIndex = 0;
}
```

Note that by default, the mColorArry is initialized to null. For CPU memory optimization, the color array is fetched from the GPU only for textures that participate in per-pixel collision. The mElmWidthPixels and mElmHeightPixels variables are the width and height of the texture. These variables are defined for later subclass overrides such that the algorithm can support the collision of sprite elements.

Implement Per-Pixel Collision

You are now ready to implement the per-pixel collision algorithm in the newly created texture_renderable_pixel_collision.js file.

1. Edit the texture_renderable_pixel_collision.js file, and define a new function for the TextureRenderable class to set the mColorArray:

```
TextureRenderable.prototype.setColorArray = function() {
    if (this.mColorArray === null) {
        this.mColorArray = texture.getColorArray(this.mTexture);
    }
}
```

Note   JavaScript classes are implemented based on prototype chains. After class construction, instance methods can be accessed and defined via the prototype of the class or aClass.prototype.method. For more information on JavaScript classes and prototypes, please refer to https://developer.mozilla.org/en-US/docs/Web/JavaScript/Inheritance_and_the_prototype_chain.

---

2. Define a new function to return the alpha value, or the transparency, of any given pixel (x, y):

```
TextureRenderable.prototype._pixelAlphaValue = function(x, y) {
    x = x * 4;
    y = y * 4;
    return this.mColorArray[(y * this.mTextureInfo.mWidth) + x + 3];
}
```

Notice that mColorArray is a 1D array where colors of pixels are stored as four floats and organized by rows.

3. Define a function to compute the WC position (returnWCPos) of a given pixel (i, j):

```
TextureRenderable.prototype._indexToWCPosition =
function(returnWCPos, i, j) {
    let x = i * this.mXform.getWidth() / this.mElmWidthPixels;
    let y = j * this.mXform.getHeight() / this.mElmHeightPixels;
    returnWCPos[0] = this.mXform.getXPos() +
                     (x - (this.mXform.getWidth() * 0.5));
    returnWCPos[1] = this.mXform.getYPos() +
                     (y - (this.mXform.getHeight() * 0.5));
}
```

4. Now, implement the inverse of the previous function, and use a WC position (wcPos) to compute the texture pixel indices (returnIndex):

```
TextureRenderable.prototype._wcPositionToIndex =
function(returnIndex, wcPos) {
    // use wcPos to compute the corresponding returnIndex[0 and 1]
    let delta = [];
    vec2.sub(delta, wcPos, this.mXform.getPosition());
    returnIndex[0] = this.mElmWidthPixels *
                     (delta[0] / this.mXform.getWidth());
    returnIndex[1] = this.mElmHeightPixels *
                     (delta[1] / this.mXform.getHeight());
```

```
    // recall that xForm.getPosition() returns center, yet
    // Texture origin is at lower-left corner!
    returnIndex[0] += this.mElmWidthPixels / 2;
    returnIndex[1] += this.mElmHeightPixels / 2;

    returnIndex[0] = Math.floor(returnIndex[0]);
    returnIndex[1] = Math.floor(returnIndex[1]);
}
```

5. Now it is possible to implement the outlined per-pixel collision
    algorithm:

```
TextureRenderable.prototype.pixelTouches = function(other, wcTouchPos) {
    let pixelTouch = false;
    let xIndex = 0, yIndex;
    let otherIndex = [0, 0];

    while ((!pixelTouch) && (xIndex < this.mElmWidthPixels)) {
        yIndex = 0;
        while ((!pixelTouch) && (yIndex < this.mElmHeightPixels)) {
            if (this._pixelAlphaValue(xIndex, yIndex) > 0) {
                this._indexToWCPosition(wcTouchPos, xIndex, yIndex);
                other._wcPositionToIndex(otherIndex, wcTouchPos);
                if ((otherIndex[0] >= 0) &&
                    (otherIndex[0] < other.mElmWidthPixels) &&
                    (otherIndex[1] >= 0) &&
                    (otherIndex[1] < other.mElmHeightPixels)) {
                    pixelTouch = other._pixelAlphaValue(
                                        otherIndex[0], otherIndex[1]) > 0;
                }
            }
            yIndex++;
        }
        xIndex++;
    }
    return pixelTouch;
}
```

The parameter other is a reference to the other TextureRenderable object that is being tested for collision. If pixels do overlap between the objects, the returned value of wcTouchPos is the first detected colliding position in the WC space. Notice that the nested loops terminate as soon as one-pixel overlap is detected or when pixelTouch becomes true. This is an important feature for efficiency concerns. However, this also means that the returned wcTouchPos is simply one of the many potentially colliding points.

Support Per-Pixel Collision in GameObject

Edit the game_object.js file to add the pixelTouches() function to the GameObject class:

```
pixelTouches(otherObj, wcTouchPos) {
    // only continue if both objects have getColorArray defined
    // if defined, should have other texture intersection support!
    let pixelTouch = false;
    let myRen = this.getRenderable();
    let otherRen = otherObj.getRenderable();

    if ((typeof myRen.pixelTouches === "function") &&
        (typeof otherRen.pixelTouches === "function")) {
        let otherBbox = otherObj.getBBox();
        if (otherBbox.intersectsBound(this.getBBox())) {
            myRen.setColorArray();
            otherRen.setColorArray();
            pixelTouch = myRen.pixelTouches(otherRen, wcTouchPos);
        }
        return pixelTouch;
    }
}
```

This function checks to ensure that the objects are colliding and delegates the actual per-pixel collision to the TextureRenderable objects. Notice the intersectsBound() function for a bounding box intersection check before invoking the potentially expensive TextureRenderable.pixelTouches() function.

Test the Per-Pixel Collision in MyGame

As illustrated in Figure 6-15, the testing of per-pixel collision is rather straightforward, involving three instances of GameObject: the large Collector minion, the small Portal minion, and the DyePack. The Collector and Portal minions are controlled by the arrow and WASD keys, respectively. The details of the implementation of MyGame are similar to the previous projects and are not shown.

The noteworthy code fragment is the collision testing in the update() function, as shown here:

```
update() {
    let msg = "No Collision";

    this.mCollector.update(engine.input.keys.W, engine.input.keys.S,
            engine.input.keys.A, engine.input.keys.D);
    this.mPortal.update(engine.input.keys.Up, engine.input.keys.Down,
            engine.input.keys.Left, engine.input.keys.Right);

    let h = [];

    // Portal's resolution is 1/16 x 1/16 that of Collector!
    // VERY EXPENSIVE!!
    // if (this.mCollector.pixelTouches(this.mPortal, h)) {

    if (this.mPortal.pixelTouches(this.mCollector, h)) {
        msg = "Collided!: (" + h[0].toPrecision(4) + ".." +
                h[1].toPrecision(4) + ")";
        this.mDyePack.setVisibility(true);
        this.mDyePack.getXform().setXPos(h[0]);
        this.mDyePack.getXform().setYPos(h[1]);
    } else {
        this.mDyePack.setVisibility(false);
    }
    this.mMsg.setText(msg);

}
```

Observation

You can now test the collision accuracy by moving the two minions and intersecting them at different locations (e.g., top colliding with the bottom, left colliding with the right) or moving them such that there are large overlapping areas. Notice that it is rather difficult, if not impossible, to predict the actual reported intersection position (position of the DyePack). It is important to remember that the per-pixel collision function is mainly a function that returns true or false indicating whether there is a collision. You cannot rely on this function to compute the actual collision positions.

Lastly, try switching to calling the Collector.pixelTouches() function to detect collisions. Notice the less than real-time performance! In this case, the computation cost of the Collector.pixelTouches() function is 16×16=256 times that of the Portal.pixelTouches() function.

Generalized Per-Pixel Collisions

In the previous section, you saw the basic operations required to achieve per-pixel-accurate collision detection. However, as you may have noticed, the previous project applies only when the textures are aligned along the x/y axes. This means that your implementation does not support collisions between rotated objects.

This section explains how you can achieve per-pixel-accurate collision detection when objects are rotated. The fundamental concepts of this project are the same as in the previous project; however, this version involves working with vector decomposition, and a quick review can be helpful.

Vector Review: Components and Decomposition

Recall that two perpendicular directions can be used to decompose a vector into corresponding components. For example, Figure 6-18 contains two normalized vectors, or the component vectors, that can be used to decompose the vector $\vec{V} = (2, 3)$: the normalized component vectors $\hat{i} = (1, 0)$ and $\hat{j} = (0, 1)$ decompose the vector $\vec{V}$ into the components $2\hat{i}$ and $3\hat{j}$.

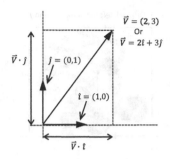

Figure 6-18. *The decomposition of vector* $\vec{V}$

In general, as illustrated in Figure 6-19, given the normalized perpendicular component vectors $\hat{L}$ and $\hat{M}$ and any vector $\vec{V}$, the following formulae are always true:

$$\vec{V}=\left(\vec{V}\cdot\hat{i}\right)\hat{i}+\left(\vec{V}\cdot\hat{j}\right)\hat{j}$$

$$\vec{V}=\left(\vec{V}\cdot\hat{L}\right)\hat{L}+\left(\vec{V}\cdot\hat{M}\right)\hat{M}$$

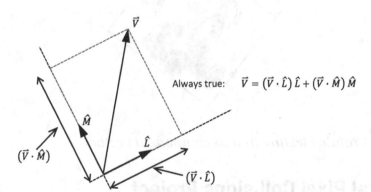

Figure 6-19. *Decomposing a vector by two normalized component vectors*

Vector decomposition is relevant to this project because of the rotated image axes. Without rotation, an image can be referenced by the familiar normalized perpendicular set of vectors along the default x axis ($\hat{i}$) and y axis ($\hat{j}$). You handled this case in the previous project. You can see an example of this in Figure 6-20.

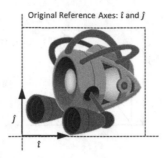

Figure 6-20. *An axes-aligned texture*

However, after the image has been rotated, the reference vector set no longer resides along the x/y axes. Therefore, the collision computation must take into account the newly rotated axes $\hat{L}$ and $\hat{M}$, as shown in Figure 6-21.

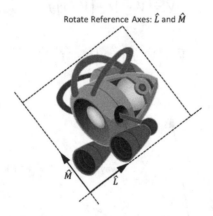

Figure 6-21. *A rotated texture and its component vectors*

The General Pixel Collisions Project

This project demonstrates how to detect a collision between two rotated TextureRenderable objects with per-pixel accuracy. Similar to the previous project, a yellow DyePack object (as a test confirmation) will be displayed at the detected colliding position. You can see an example of this project running in Figure 6-22. The source code to this project is defined in the chapter6/6.5.general_pixel_collisions folder.

Figure 6-22. *Running the General Pixel Collisions project*

The controls of the project are as follows:

- **Arrow keys**: Move the small textured object, the `Portal` minion

- **P key**: Rotates the small textured object, the `Portal` minion

- **WASD keys**: Move the large textured object, the `Collector` minion

- **E key**: Rotates the large textured object, the `Collector` minion

The goals of the project are as follows:

- To access pixels of a rotated image via vector decomposition

- To support per-pixel-accurate collision detection between two rotated textured objects

You can find the same external resource files as in the previous project in the assets folder.

Modify Pixel Collision to Support Rotation

1. Edit the texture_renderable_pixel_collision.js file and modify the _indexToWCPosition() function:

```
TextureRenderable.prototype._indexToWCPosition =
function (returnWCPos, i, j, xDir, yDir) {
    let x = i * this.mXform.getWidth() / this.mElmWidthPixels;
    let y = j * this.mXform.getHeight() / this.mElmHeightPixels;
    let xDisp = x - (this.mXform.getWidth() * 0.5);
    let yDisp = y - (this.mXform.getHeight() * 0.5);
    let xDirDisp = [];
    let yDirDisp = [];

    vec2.scale(xDirDisp, xDir, xDisp);
    vec2.scale(yDirDisp, yDir, yDisp);
    vec2.add(returnWCPos, this.mXform.getPosition(), xDirDisp);
    vec2.add(returnWCPos, returnWCPos, yDirDisp);
}
```

In the listed code, xDir and yDir are the $\hat{L}$ and $\hat{M}$ normalized component vectors. The variables xDisp and yDisp are the displacements to be offset along xDir and yDir, respectively. The returned value of returnWCPos is a simple displacement from the object's center position along the xDirDisp and yDirDisp vectors. Note that xDirDisp and yDirDisp are the scaled xDir and yDir vectors.

2. In a similar fashion, modify the _wcPositionToIndex() function to support the rotated normalized vector components:

```
TextureRenderable.prototype._wcPositionToIndex =
function (returnIndex, wcPos, xDir, yDir) {
    // use wcPos to compute the corresponding returnIndex[0 and 1]
    let delta = [];
    vec2.sub(delta, wcPos, this.mXform.getPosition());
    let xDisp = vec2.dot(delta, xDir);
```

```
let yDisp = vec2.dot(delta, yDir);
returnIndex[0] = this.mElmWidthPixels *
                    (xDisp / this.mXform.getWidth());
returnIndex[1] = this.mElmHeightPixels *
                    (yDisp / this.mXform.getHeight());

// recall that xForm.getPosition() returns center, yet
// Texture origin is at lower-left corner!
returnIndex[0] += this.mElmWidthPixels / 2;
returnIndex[1] += this.mElmHeightPixels / 2;

returnIndex[0] = Math.floor(returnIndex[0]);
returnIndex[1] = Math.floor(returnIndex[1]);
}
```

3. The pixelTouches() function needs to be modified to compute
    the rotated normalized component vectors:

```
TextureRenderable.prototype.pixelTouches = function (other, wcTouchPos) {
    let pixelTouch = false;
    let xIndex = 0, yIndex;
    let otherIndex = [0, 0];

    let xDir = [1, 0];
    let yDir = [0, 1];
    let otherXDir = [1, 0];
    let otherYDir = [0, 1];
    vec2.rotate(xDir, xDir, this.mXform.getRotationInRad());
    vec2.rotate(yDir, yDir, this.mXform.getRotationInRad());
    vec2.rotate(otherXDir, otherXDir, other.mXform.getRotationInRad());
    vec2.rotate(otherYDir, otherYDir, other.mXform.getRotationInRad());

    while ((!pixelTouch) && (xIndex < this.mElmWidthPixels)) {
        yIndex = 0;
        while ((!pixelTouch) && (yIndex < this.mElmHeightPixels)) {
            if (this._pixelAlphaValue(xIndex, yIndex) > 0) {
                this._indexToWCPosition(wcTouchPos,
                                        xIndex, yIndex, xDir, yDir);
```

```
                other._wcPositionToIndex(otherIndex, wcTouchPos,
                                         otherXDir, otherYDir);
                if ((otherIndex[0] >= 0) &&
                    (otherIndex[0] < other.mElmWidthPixels) &&
                    (otherIndex[1] >= 0) &&
                    (otherIndex[1] < other.mElmHeightPixels)) {
                    pixelTouch = other._pixelAlphaValue(
                                  otherIndex[0], otherIndex[1]) > 0;
                }
            }
            yIndex++;
        }
        xIndex++;
    }
    return pixelTouch;
}
```

The variables xDir and yDir are the rotated normalized component vectors $\hat{L}$ and $\hat{M}$ of this TextureRenderable object, while otherXDir and otherYDir are those of the colliding object. These vectors are used as references for computing transformations from texture index to WC and from WC to texture index.

Modify GameObject to Support Rotation

Recall that the GameObject class first tests for the bounding-box collision between two objects before it actually invokes the much more expensive per-pixel collision computation. As illustrated in Figure 6-14, the BoundingBox object does not support object rotation correctly, and the following code remedies this shortcoming:

```
pixelTouches(otherObj, wcTouchPos) {
    // only continue if both objects have getColorArray defined
    // if defined, should have other texture intersection support!
    let pixelTouch = false;
    let myRen = this.getRenderable();
    let otherRen = otherObj.getRenderable();

    if ((typeof myRen.pixelTouches === "function") &&
```

```
        (typeof otherRen.pixelTouches === "function")) {
    if ((myRen.getXform().getRotationInRad() === 0) &&
        (otherRen.getXform().getRotationInRad() === 0)) {
        // no rotation, we can use bbox ...
        let otherBbox = otherObj.getBBox();
        if (otherBbox.intersectsBound(this.getBBox())) {
            myRen.setColorArray();
            otherRen.setColorArray();
            pixelTouch = myRen.pixelTouches(otherRen, wcTouchPos);
        }
    } else {
        // One or both are rotated, compute an encompassing circle
        // by using the hypotenuse as radius
        let mySize = myRen.getXform().getSize();
        let otherSize = otherRen.getXform().getSize();
        let myR = Math.sqrt(0.5*mySize[0]*0.5*mySize[0] +
                            0.5*mySize[1]*0.5*mySize[1]);
        let otherR = Math.sqrt(0.5*otherSize[0]*0.5*otherSize[0] +
                               0.5*otherSize[1]*0.5*otherSize[1]);
        let d = [];
        vec2.sub(d, myRen.getXform().getPosition(),
                    otherRen.getXform().getPosition());
        if (vec2.length(d) < (myR + otherR)) {
            myRen.setColorArray();
            otherRen.setColorArray();
            pixelTouch = myRen.pixelTouches(otherRen, wcTouchPos);
        }
    }
    }
}
    return pixelTouch;
}
```

The listed code shows that if either of the colliding objects is rotated, then two encompassing circles are used to determine whether the objects are sufficiently close for the expensive per-pixel collision computation. The two circles are defined with radii equal to the hypotenuse of the x/y size of the corresponding TextureRenderable objects.

The per-pixel collision detection is invoked only if the distance between these two circles is less than the sum of the radii.

Test Generalized Per-Pixel Collision

The code for testing the rotated TextureRenderable objects is essentially identical to that from the previous project, with the exception of the two added controls for rotations. The details of the implementation are not shown. You can now run the project, rotate the two objects, and observe the accurate collision results.

Per-Pixel Collisions for Sprites

The previous project implicitly assumes that the Renderable object is covered by the entire texture map. This assumption means that the per-pixel collision implementation does not support sprite or animated sprite objects. In this section, you will remedy this deficiency.

The Sprite Pixel Collisions Project

This project demonstrates how to move an animated sprite object around the screen and perform per-pixel collision detection with other objects. The project tests for the correctness between collisions of TextureRenderable, SpriteRenderable, and SpriteAnimateRenderable objects. You can see an example of this project running in Figure 6-23. The source code to this project is defined in the chapter6/6.6.sprite_pixel_collisions folder.

L/R: Left or Right Minion; H: Dye; B: Brain]: H

Figure 6-23. *Running the Sprite Pixel Collisions project*

The controls of the project are as follows:

- **Arrow and P keys**: Move and rotate the `Portal` minion

- **WASD keys**: Move the `Hero`

- **L, R, H, B keys**: Select the target for colliding with the `Portal` minion

The goal of the project is as follows:

- To generalize the per-pixel collision implementation for sprite and animated sprite objects

You can find the following external resource files in the `assets` folder: the `fonts` folder that contains the default system fonts, `minion_sprite.png`, and `minion_portal.png`.

Implement Per-Pixel Collision for SpriteRenderable

Edit sprite_renderable.js to implement the per-pixel-specific support for
SpriteRenderable objects:

1. Modify the SpriteRenderable constructor to call the _
    setTexInfo() function to initialize per-pixel collision parameters;
    this function is defined in the next step:

```
constructor(myTexture) {
    super(myTexture);
    super._setShader(shaderResources.getSpriteShader());
    // sprite coordinate
    // bounds of texture coordinate (0 is left, 1 is right)
    this.mElmLeft = 0.0;
    this.mElmRight = 1.0;
    this.mElmTop = 1.0;      //   1 is top and 0 is bottom of image
    this.mElmBottom = 0.0; //

    // sets info to support per-pixel collision
    this._setTexInfo();
}
```

2. Define the _setTexInfo() function to override instance variables
    defined in the TextureRenderable superclass. Instead of the
    entire texture image, the instance variables now identify the
    currently active sprite element.

```
_setTexInfo() {
    let imageW = this.mTextureInfo.mWidth;
    let imageH = this.mTextureInfo.mHeight;

    this.mElmLeftIndex = this.mElmLeft * imageW;
    this.mElmBottomIndex = this.mElmBottom * imageH;

    this.mElmWidthPixels = ((this.mElmRight - this.mElmLeft)*imageW)+1;
    this.mElmHeightPixels = ((this.mElmTop - this.mElmBottom)*imageH)+1;
}
```

Notice that instead of the dimension of the entire texture map, mElmWidthPixel and mElmHeightPixel now contain pixel values that correspond to the dimension of a single sprite element in the sprite sheet.

3. Remember to call the _setTexInfo() function when the current sprite element is updated in the setElementUVCoordinate() and setElementPixelPositions() functions:

```
setElementUVCoordinate(left, right, bottom, top) {
    this.mElmLeft = left;
    this.mElmRight = right;
    this.mElmBottom = bottom;
    this.mElmTop = top;
    this._setTexInfo();
}

setElementPixelPositions(left, right, bottom, top) {
    // entire image width, height
    let imageW = this.mTextureInfo.mWidth;
    let imageH = this.mTextureInfo.mHeight;

    this.mElmLeft = left / imageW;
    this.mElmRight = right / imageW;
    this.mElmBottom = bottom / imageH;
    this.mElmTop = top / imageH;
    this._setTexInfo();
}
```

Support Accesses to Sprite Pixels in TextureRenderable

Edit the texture_renderable_pixel_collision.js file, and modify the _pixelAlphaValue() function to support pixel accesses with a sprite element index offset:

```
TextureRenderable.prototype._pixelAlphaValue = function (x, y) {
    y += this.mElmBottomIndex;
    x += this.mElmLeftIndex;
    x = x * 4;
    y = y * 4;
    return this.mColorArray[(y * this.mTextureInfo.mWidth) + x + 3];
}
```

Test Per-Pixel Collision for Sprites in MyGame

The code for testing this project is a simple modification from previous projects, and the details are not listed. It is important to note the different object types in the scene.

- **Portal minion**: A simple TextureRenderable object

- **Hero and Brain**: SpriteRenderable objects where the textures shown on the geometries are sprite elements defined in the minion_sprite. png sprite sheet

- **Left and Right minions**: SpriteAnimateRenderable objects with sprite elements defined in the top two rows of the minion_sprite. pnganimated sprite sheet

Observation

You can now run this project and observe the correct results from the collisions of the different object types:

1. Try moving the Hero object and observe how the Brain object constantly seeks out and collides with it. This is the case of collision between two SpriteRenderable objects.

2. Press the L/R keys and then move the Portal minion with the WASD keys to collide with the Left or Right minions. Remember that you can rotate the Portal minion with the P key. This is the case of collision between TextureRenderable and SpriteAnimatedRenderable objects.

3. Press the H key and then move the Portal minion to collide with the Hero object. This is the case of collision between TextureRenderable and SpriteRenderable objects.

4. Press the B key and then move the Portal minion to collide with the Brain object. This is the case of collision between rotated TextureRenderable and SpriteRenderable objects.

Summary

This chapter showed you how to encapsulate common behaviors of objects in games and demonstrated the benefits of the encapsulation in the forms of a simpler and better organized control logic in the client's MyGame test levels. You reviewed vectors in 2D space. A vector is defined by its direction and magnitude. Vectors are convenient for describing displacements (velocities). You reviewed some foundational vector operations, including normalization of a vector and how to calculate both dot and cross products. You worked with these operators to implement the front-facing direction capability and create simple autonomous behaviors such as pointing toward a specific object and chasing.

The need for detecting object collisions became a prominent omission as the behaviors of objects increased in sophistication. The axis-aligned bounding boxes, or AABBs, were introduced as a crude, yet computationally efficient solution for approximating object collisions. You learned the algorithm for per-pixel-accurate collision detection and that its accuracy comes at the cost of performance. You now understand how to mitigate the computational cost in two ways. First, you invoke the pixel-accurate procedure only when the objects are sufficiently close to each other, such as when their bounding boxes collide. Second, you invoke the pixel iteration process based on the texture with a lower resolution.

When implementing pixel-accurate collision, you began with tackling the basic case of working with axis-aligned textures. After that implementation, you went back and added support for collision detection between rotated textures. Finally, you generalized the implementation to support collisions between sprite elements. Solving the easiest case first lets you test and observe the results and helps define what you might need for the more advanced problems (rotation and subregions of a texture in this case).

At the beginning of this chapter, your game engine supported interesting sophistication in drawing ranging from the abilities to define WC space, to view the WC space with the Camera object, and to draw visually pleasing textures and animations on objects. However, there was no infrastructure for supporting the behaviors of the objects. This shortcoming resulted in clustering of initialization and control logic in the client-level implementations. With the object behavior abstraction, mathematics, and collision algorithms introduced and implemented in this chapter, your game engine functionality is now better balanced. The clients of your game engine now have tools for encapsulating specific behaviors and detecting collisions. The next chapter reexamines and enhances the functionality of the `Camera` object. You will learn to control and manipulate the `Camera` object and work with multiple `Camera` objects in the same game.

Game Design Considerations

Chapters 1–5 introduced foundation techniques for drawing, moving, and animating objects on the screen. The *Scene Objects* project from Chapter 4 described a simple interaction behavior and showed you how to change the game screen based on the location of a rectangle: recall that moving the rectangle to the left boundary caused the level to visually change, while the *Audio Support* project added contextual sound to reinforce the overall sense of presence. Although it's possible to build an intriguing (albeit simple) puzzle game using only the elements from Chapters 1 to 5, things get much more interesting when you can integrate object detection and collision triggers; these behaviors form the basis for many common game mechanics and provide opportunities to design a wide range of interesting gameplay scenarios.

Starting with the *Game Objects* project, you can see how the screen elements start working together to convey the game setting; even with the interaction in this project limited to character movement, the setting is beginning to resolve into something that conveys a sense of place. The hero character appears to be flying through a moving scene populated by a number of mechanized robots, and there's a small object in the center of the screen that you might imagine could become some kind of special pickup.

Even at this basic stage of development it's possible to brainstorm game mechanics that could potentially form the foundation for a full game. If you were designing a simple game mechanic based on only the screen elements found in the *Game Objects* project, what kind of behaviors would you choose and what kind of actions would you require the player to perform? As one example, imagine that the hero character must avoid colliding with the flying robots and that perhaps some of the robots will detect and pursue the hero in an attempt to stop the player's progress; maybe the hero is also penalized in some way if they come into contact with a robot. Imagine perhaps that the small object in the center of the screen allows the hero to be invincible for a fixed period of time and that we've designed the level to require temporary invincibility to reach the goal, thus creating a more complex and interesting game loop (e.g., avoid the pursuing robots to reach the power up, activate the power up and become temporarily invincible, use invincibility to reach the goal). With these few basic interactions, we've opened opportunities to explore mechanics and level designs that will feel very familiar from many different kinds of games, all with just the inclusion of the object detection, chase, and collision behaviors covered in Chapter 6. Try this design exercise yourself using just the elements shown in the *Game Objects* project: What kinds of simple conditions and behaviors might you design to make your experience unique? How many ways can you think of to use the small object in the center of the screen? The final design project in Chapter 12 will explore these themes in greater detail.

This is also a good opportunity to brainstorm some of the other nine elements of game design discussed in Chapter 1. What if the game wasn't set in space with robots? Perhaps the setting is in a forest, or under water, or even something completely abstract. How might you incorporate audio to enhance the sense of presence and reinforce the game setting? You'll probably be surprised by the variety of settings and scenarios you come up with. Limiting yourself to just the elements and interactions covered through Chapter 6 is actually a beneficial exercise as design constraints often help the creative process by shaping and guiding your ideas. Even the most advanced video games typically have a fairly basic set of core game loops as their foundation.

The *Vectors: Front and Chase* project is interesting from both a game mechanic and presence perspective. Many games, of course, require objects in the game world to detect the hero character and will either chase or try to avoid the player (or both if the object has multiple states). The project also demonstrates two different approaches to chase behavior, instant and smooth pursuit, and the game setting will typically influence which behavior you choose to implement. The choice between instant and smooth pursuit is a great example of subtle behaviors that can significantly influence the sense of presence. If you were designing a game where ships were interacting on the ocean, for example, you would likely want their pursuit behavior to take real-world inertia and momentum into consideration because ships can't instantly turn and respond to changes in movement; rather, they move smoothly and gradually, demonstrating a noticeable delay in how quickly they can respond to a moving target. Most objects in the physical world will display the same inertial and momentum constraint to some degree, but there are also situations where you may want game objects to respond directly to path changes (or, perhaps, you want to intentionally flout real-world physics and create a behavior that isn't based on the limitations of physical objects). The key is to always be intentional about your design choices, and it's good to remember that virtually no implementation details are too small to be noticed by players.

The *Bounding Box and Collisions* project introduces the key element of detection to your design arsenal, allowing you to begin including more robust cause-and-effect mechanics that form the basis for many game interactions. Chapter 6 discusses the trade-offs of choosing between the less precise but more performant bounding box collision detection method and the precise but resource-intensive per-pixel detection method. There are many situations where the bounding-box approach is sufficient, but if players perceive collisions to be arbitrary because the bounding boxes are too different from the actual visual objects, it can negatively impact the sense of presence. Detection and collision are even more powerful design tools when coupled with the result from the Per-Pixel Collisions project. Although the dye pack in this example was used to indicate the first point of collision, you can imagine building interesting causal chains around a new object being produced as the result of two objects colliding (e.g., player pursues object, player collides with object, object "drops" a new object that enables the player to do something they couldn't do before). Game objects that move around the game screen will typically be animated, of course, so the *Sprite Pixel Collisions* project describes how to implement collision detection when the object boundaries aren't stationary.

With the addition of the techniques in Chapter 6, you now have a critical mass of behaviors that can be combined to create truly interesting game mechanics covering the spectrum from action games to puzzlers. Of course, game mechanic behaviors are only one of the nine elements of game design and typically aren't sufficient on their own to create a magical gameplay experience: the setting, visual style, meta-game elements, and the like all have something important to contribute. The good news is that creating a memorable game experience need not be as elaborate as you often believe and great games continue being produced based on relatively basic combinations of the behaviors and techniques covered in Chapters 1–6. The games that often shine the brightest aren't always the most complex, but rather they're often the games where every aspect of each of the nine elements of design is intentional and working together in harmony. If you give the appropriate attention and focus to all aspects of the game design, you're on a great track to produce something great whether you're working on your own or you're part of a large team.

CHAPTER 7

Manipulating the Camera

After completing this chapter, you will be able to

- Implement operations that are commonly employed in manipulating a camera

- Interpolate values between old and new to create a smooth transition

- Understand how some motions or behaviors can be described by simple mathematical formulations

- Build games with multiple camera views

- Transform positions from the mouse-clicked pixel to the World Coordinate (WC) position

- Program with mouse input in a game environment with multiple cameras

Introduction

Your game engine is now capable of representing and drawing objects. With the basic abstraction mechanism introduced in the previous chapter, the engine can also support the interactions and behaviors of these objects. This chapter refocuses the attention on controlling and interacting with the Camera object that abstracts and facilitates the presentation of the game objects on the canvas. In this way, your game engine will be able to control and manipulate the presentation of visually appealing game objects with well-structured behaviors.

Figure 7-1 presents a brief review of the Camera object abstraction that was introduced in Chapter 3. The Camera object allows the game programmer to define a World Coordinate (WC) window of the game world to be displayed into a viewport on the HTML canvas. The WC window is the bounds defined by a WC center and a

© Kelvin Sung, Jebediah Pavleas, Matthew Munson, and Jason Pace 2022
K. Sung et al., *Build Your Own 2D Game Engine and Create Great Web Games*,
https://doi.org/10.1007/978-1-4842-7377-7_7

dimension of $W_{wc} \times H_{wc}$. A viewport is a rectangular area on the HTML canvas with the lower-left corner located at (V_x, V_y) and a dimension of $W_v \times H_v$. The Camera object's setViewAndCameraMatrix() function encapsulates the details and enables the drawing of all game objects inside the WC window bounds to be displayed in the corresponding viewport.

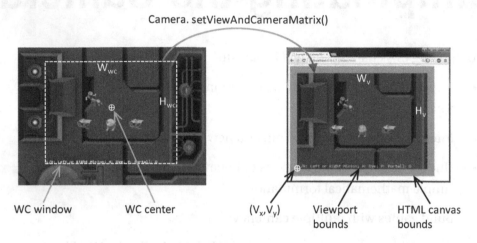

Figure 7-1. *Review of WC parameters that define a Camera object*

Note   In this book, the WC window or WC bounds are used to refer to the WC window bounds.

'The Camera object abstraction allows the game programmer to ignore the details of WC bounds and the HTML canvas and focus on designing a fun and entertaining gameplay experience. Programming with a Camera object in a game level should reflect the use of a physical video camera in the real world. For example, you may want to pan the camera to show your audiences the environment, you may want to attach the camera on an actress and share her journey with your audience, or you may want to play the role of a director and instruct the actors in your scene to stay within the visual ranges of the camera. The distinct characteristics of these examples, such as panning or following a character's view, are the high-level functional specifications. Notice that in the real world you do not specify coordinate positions or bounds of windows.

This chapter introduces some of the most commonly encountered camera manipulation operations including clamping, panning, and zooming. Solutions in the form of interpolation will be derived to alleviate annoying or confusing abrupt transitions resulting from the manipulation of cameras. You will also learn about supporting multiple camera views in the same game level and working with mouse input.

Camera Manipulations

In a 2D world, you may want to clamp or restrict the movements of objects to be within the bounds of a camera, to pan or move the camera, or to zoom the camera into or away from specific areas. These high-level functional specifications can be realized by strategically changing the parameters of the Camera object: the WC center and the $W_{wc} \times H_{wc}$ of the WC window. The key is to create convenient functions for the game developers to manipulate these values in the context of the game. For example, instead of increasing/decreasing the width/height of the WC windows, zoom functions can be defined for the programmer.

The Camera Manipulations Project

This project demonstrates how to implement intuitive camera manipulation operations by working with the WC center, width, and height of the Camera object. You can see an example of this project running in Figure 7-2. The source code to this project is defined in the chapter7/7.1.camera_manipulations folder.

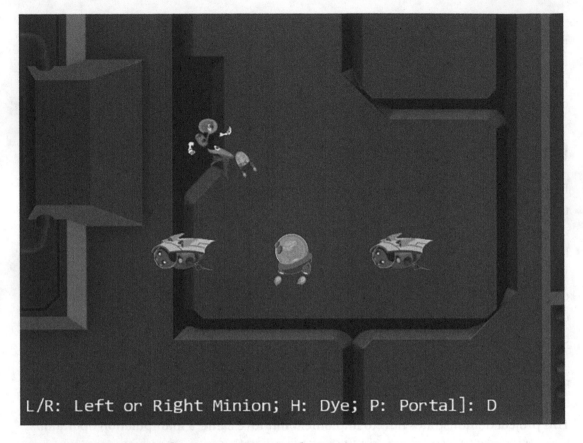

L/R: Left or Right Minion; H: Dye; P: Portal]: D

Figure 7-2. *Running the Camera Manipulations project*

The controls of the project are as follows:

- **WASD keys**: Move the Dye character (the Hero object). Notice that the camera WC window updates to follow the Hero object when it attempts to move beyond 90 percent of the WC bounds.

- **Arrow keys**: Move the Portal object. Notice that the Portal object cannot move beyond 80 percent of the WC bounds.

- **L/R/P/H keys**: Select the Left minion, Right minion, Portal object, or Hero object to be the object in focus; the L/R keys also set the camera to center on the Left or Right minion.

- **N/M keys**: Zoom into or away from the center of the camera.

- **J/K keys**: Zoom into or away while ensuring the constant relative position of the currently in-focus object. In other words, as the camera zooms, the positions of all objects will change except that of the in-focus object.

The goals of the project are as follows:

- To experience some of the common camera manipulation operations

- To understand the mapping from manipulation operations to the corresponding camera parameter values that must be altered

- To implement camera manipulation operations

You can find the following external resources in the assets folder: the fonts folder that contains the default system fonts and three texture images (minion_portal.png, minion_sprite.png, and bg.png). The Portal object is represented by the first texture image, the remaining objects are sprite elements of minion_sprite.png, and the background is a large TextureRenderable object texture mapped with bg.png.

Organize the Source Code

To accommodate the increase in functionality and the complexity of the Camera class you will create a separate folder for storing the related source code files. Similar to the case of dividing the complicated source code of TextureRenderable into multiple files, in this project the Camera class implementation will be separated into three files.

- camera_main.js for implementing the basic functionality from previous projects

- camera_manipulation.js for supporting the newly introduced manipulation operations

- camera.js for serving as the class access point

The implementation steps are as follows:

1. Create a new folder called cameras in src/engine. Move the camera.js file into this folder and rename it to camera_main.js.

2. Create a new file in src/engine/cameras and name it camera_
manipulation.js. This file will be used to extend the Camera class
functionality in supporting manipulations. Add in the following
code to import and export the basic Camera class functionality.
For now, this file does not contain any useful source code and
thus does not serve any purpose. You will define the appropriate
extension functions in the following subsection.

```
import Camera from "./camera_main.js";

// new functionality to be defined here in the next subsection

export default Camera;
```

3. Create a new camera.js to serve as the Camera access point by
adding the following code:

```
import Camera from "./camera_manipulation.js";
export default Camera;
```

With this structure of the source code files, camera_main.js implements all the
basic functionality and exports to camera_manipulation.js that defines additional
functionality for the Camera class. Finally, camera.js imports the extended functions
from camera_manipulation.js. The users of the Camera class can simply import from
camera.js and will have access to all of the defined functionality. This allows camera.
js to serve as the access point to the Camera class while hiding the details of the
implementation source code structure.

Support Clamping to Camera WC Bounds

Edit camera_main.js to import bounding box functionality and define a function to clamp
the bounds associated with a Transform object to the camera WC bound:

```
import * as glSys from "../core/gl.js";
import BoundingBox from "../bounding_box.js";
import { eBoundCollideStatus } from "../bounding_box.js";

... identical to previous code ...

clampAtBoundary(aXform, zone) {
```

```
    let status = this.collideWCBound(aXform, zone);
    if (status !== eBoundCollideStatus.eInside) {
        let pos = aXform.getPosition();
        if ((status & eBoundCollideStatus.eCollideTop) !== 0) {
            pos[1] = (this.getWCCenter())[1] +
                        (zone * this.getWCHeight() / 2) -
                        (aXform.getHeight() / 2);
        }
        if ((status & eBoundCollideStatus.eCollideBottom) !== 0) {
            pos[1] = (this.getWCCenter())[1] -
                        (zone * this.getWCHeight() / 2) +
                        (aXform.getHeight() / 2);
        }
        if ((status & eBoundCollideStatus.eCollideRight) !== 0) {
            pos[0] = (this.getWCCenter())[0] +
                        (zone * this.getWCWidth() / 2) -
                        (aXform.getWidth() / 2);
        }
        if ((status & eBoundCollideStatus.eCollideLeft) !== 0) {
            pos[0] = (this.getWCCenter())[0] -
                        (zone * this.getWCWidth() / 2) +
                        (aXform.getWidth() / 2);
        }
    }
    return status;
}
```

The aXform object can be the Transform of a GameObject or Renderable object. The clampAtBoundary() function ensures that the bounds of the aXform remain inside the WC bounds of the camera by clamping the aXform position. The zone variable defines a percentage of clamping for the WC bounds. For example, a 1.0 would mean clamping to the exact WC bounds, while a 0.9 means clamping to a bound that is 90 percent of the current WC window size. It is important to note that the clampAtBoundary() function operates only on bounds that collide with the camera WC bounds. For example, if the aXform object has its bounds that are completely outside of the camera WC bounds, it will remain outside.

Define Camera Manipulation Operations in camera_manipulation.js File

Recall that you have created an empty `camera_manipulation.js` source code file. You are now ready to edit this file and define additional functions on the `Camera` class to manipulate the camera.

1. Edit `camera_manipulate.js`. Ensure you are adding code between the initial import and final export of the `Camera` class functionality.

2. Import the bounding box collision status, and define the `panWidth()` function to pan the camera based on the bounds of a `Transform` object. This function is complementary to the `clampAtBoundary()` function, where instead of changing the `aXform` position, the camera is moved to ensure the proper inclusion of the `aXform` bounds. As in the case of the `clampAtBoundary()` function, the camera will not be changed if the `aXform` bounds are completely outside the tested WC bounds area.

```
import { eBoundCollideStatus } from "../bounding_box.js";

Camera.prototype.panWith = function (aXform, zone) {
    let status = this.collideWCBound(aXform, zone);
    if (status !== eBoundCollideStatus.eInside) {
        let pos = aXform.getPosition();
        let newC = this.getWCCenter();

        if ((status & eBoundCollideStatus.eCollideTop) !== 0) {
            newC[1] = pos[1]+(aXform.getHeight() / 2) -
                    (zone * this.getWCHeight() / 2);
        }
        if ((status & eBoundCollideStatus.eCollideBottom) !== 0) {
            newC[1] = pos[1] - (aXform.getHeight() / 2) +
                    (zone * this.getWCHeight() / 2);
        }
```

```
        if ((status & eBoundCollideStatus.eCollideRight) !== 0) {
            newC[0] = pos[0] + (aXform.getWidth() / 2) -
                    (zone * this.getWCWidth() / 2);
        }
        if ((status & eBoundCollideStatus.eCollideLeft) !== 0) {
            newC[0] = pos[0] - (aXform.getWidth() / 2) +
                    (zone * this.getWCWidth() / 2);
        }
    }
}
```

3. Define camera panning functions panBy() and panTo() by appending to the Camera class prototype. These two functions change the camera WC center by adding a delta to it or moving it to a new location.

```
Camera.prototype.panBy = function (dx, dy) {
    this.mWCCenter[0] += dx;
    this.mWCCenter[1] += dy;
}

Camera.prototype.panTo = function (cx, cy) {
    this.setWCCenter(cx, cy);
}
```

4. Define functions to zoom the camera with respect to the center or a target position:

```
Camera.prototype.zoomBy = function (zoom) {
    if (zoom > 0) {
        this.setWCWidth(this.getWCWidth() * zoom);
    }
}

Camera.prototype.zoomTowards = function (pos, zoom) {
    let delta = [];
    vec2.sub(delta, pos, this.mWCCenter);
    vec2.scale(delta, delta, zoom - 1);
    vec2.sub(this.mWCCenter, this.mWCCenter, delta);
```

```
    this.zoomBy(zoom);
}
```

The zoomBy() function zooms with respect to the center of the camera, and the
zoomTowards() function zooms with respect to a world coordinate position. If the zoom
variable is greater than 1, the WC window size becomes larger, and you will see more of
the world in a process we intuitively know as zooming out. A zoom value of less than 1
zooms in. Figure 7-3 shows the results of zoom=0.5 for zooming with respect to the center
of WC and with respect to the position of the Hero object.

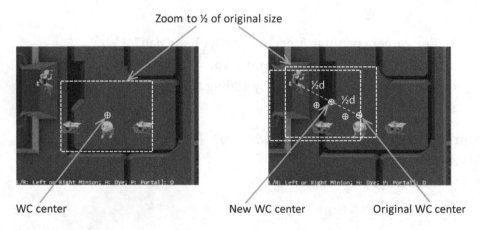

Figure 7-3. *Zooming toward the WC Center and toward a target position*

Manipulating the Camera in MyGame

There are two important functionalities to be tested: panning and zooming. The only
notable changes to the MyGame class are in the update() function. The init(), load(),
unload(), and draw() functions are similar to previous projects and can be found in the
project source code.

```
update() {
    let zoomDelta = 0.05;
    let msg = "L/R: Left or Right Minion; H: Dye; P: Portal]: ";

    // ... code to update each object not shown

    // Brain chasing the hero
    let h = [];
```

```
if (!this.mHero.pixelTouches(this.mBrain, h)) {
    this.mBrain.rotateObjPointTo(
                this.mHero.getXform().getPosition(), 0.01);
    engine.GameObject.prototype.update.call(this.mBrain);
}

// Pan camera to object
if (engine.input.isKeyClicked(engine.input.keys.L)) {
    this.mFocusObj = this.mLMinion;
    this.mChoice = 'L';
    this.mCamera.panTo(this.mLMinion.getXform().getXPos(),
                    this.mLMinion.getXform().getYPos());
}
if (engine.input.isKeyClicked(engine.input.keys.R)) {
    this.mFocusObj = this.mRMinion;
    this.mChoice = 'R';
    this.mCamera.panTo(this.mRMinion.getXform().getXPos(),
                    this.mRMinion.getXform().getYPos());
}
if (engine.input.isKeyClicked(engine.input.keys.P)) {
    this.mFocusObj = this.mPortal;
    this.mChoice = 'P';
}
if (engine.input.isKeyClicked(engine.input.keys.H)) {
    this.mFocusObj = this.mHero;
    this.mChoice = 'H';
}

// zoom
if (engine.input.isKeyClicked(engine.input.keys.N)) {
    this.mCamera.zoomBy(1 - zoomDelta);
}
if (engine.input.isKeyClicked(engine.input.keys.M)) {
    this.mCamera.zoomBy(1 + zoomDelta);
}
if (engine.input.isKeyClicked(engine.input.keys.J)) {
```

```
        this.mCamera.zoomTowards(
                        this.mFocusObj.getXform().getPosition(),
                        1 - zoomDelta);
    }
    if (engine.input.isKeyClicked(engine.input.keys.K)) {
        this.mCamera.zoomTowards(
                        this.mFocusObj.getXform().getPosition(),
                        1 + zoomDelta);
    }

    // interaction with the WC bound
    this.mCamera.clampAtBoundary(this.mBrain.getXform(), 0.9);
    this.mCamera.clampAtBoundary(this.mPortal.getXform(), 0.8);
    this.mCamera.panWith(this.mHero.getXform(), 0.9);

    this.mMsg.setText(msg + this.mChoice);
}
```

In the listed code, the first four if statements select the in-focus object, where L and R keys also re-center the camera by calling the panTo() function with the appropriate WC positions. The second set of four if statements control the zoom, either toward the WC center or toward the current in-focus object. Then the function clamps the Brain and Portal objects to within 90 percent and 80 percent of the WC bounds, respectively. The function finally ends by panning the camera based on the transform (or position) of the Hero object.

You can now run the project and move the Hero object with the WASD keys. Move the Hero object toward the WC bounds to observe the camera being pushed. Continue pushing the camera with the Hero object; notice that because of the clampAtBoundary() function call, the Portal object will in turn be pushed such that it never leaves the camera WC bounds. Now press the L/R key to observe the camera center switching to the center on the Left or Right minion. The N/M keys demonstrate straightforward zooming with respect to the center. To experience zooming with respect to a target, move the Hero object toward the top left of the canvas and then press the H key to select it as the zoom focus. Now, with your mouse pointer pointing at the head of the Hero object, you can press the K key to zoom out first and then the J key to zoom back in. Notice that as you zoom, all objects in the scene change positions except the areas around the Hero object.

Zooming into a desired region of a world is a useful feature for game developers with many applications. You can experience moving the Hero object around while zooming into/away from it.

Interpolation

It is now possible to manipulate the camera based on high-level functions such as pan or zoom. However, the results are often sudden or visually incoherent changes to the rendered image, which may result in annoyance or confusion. For example, in the previous project, the L or R key causes the camera to re-center with a simple assignment of new WC center values. The abrupt change in camera position results in the sudden appearance of a seemingly new game world. This is not only visually distracting but can also confuse the player as to what has happened.

When new values for camera parameters are available, instead of assigning them and causing an abrupt change, it is desirable to morph the values gradually from the old to the new over time or *interpolate* the values. For example, as illustrated in Figure 7-4, at time t_1, a parameter with the old value is to be assigned a new one. In this case, instead of updating the value abruptly, interpolation will change the value gradually over time. It will compute the intermediate results with decreasing values and complete the change to the new value at a later time t_2.

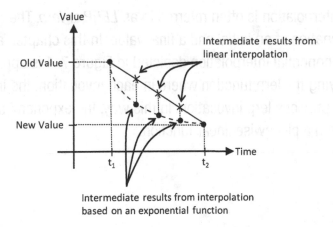

Figure 7-4. *Interpolating values based on linear and exponential functions*

Figure 7-4 shows that there are multiple ways to interpolate values over time. For example, linear interpolation computes intermediate results according to the slope of the line connecting the old and new values. In contrast, an exponential function may compute intermediate results based on percentages from previous values. In this way, with linear interpolation, a camera position would move from an old to new position with a constant speed similar to a moving (or panning) a camera at some constant speed. In comparison, the interpolation based on the given exponential function would move the camera position rapidly at first and then slow down quickly over time giving a sensation of moving and focusing the camera on a new target.

Human motions and movements typically follow the exponential interpolation function. For example, try turning your head from facing the front to facing the right or moving your hand to pick up an object on your desk. Notice that in both cases, you began with a relatively quick motion and slowed down significantly when the destination is in close proximity. That is, you probably started by turning your head quickly and slowed down rapidly as your view approaches your right side, and it is likely your hand started moving quickly toward the object and slowed down significantly when the hand is almost reaching the object. In both of these examples, your displacements followed the exponential interpolation function as depicted in Figure 7-4, quick changes followed by a rapid slow down as the destination approaches. This is the function you will implement in the game engine because it mimics human movements and is likely to seem natural to human players.

Note   Linear interpolation is often referred to as *LERP* or *lerp*. The result of lerp is the linear combination of an initial and a final value. In this chapter, and in almost all cases, the exponential interpolation depicted in Figure 7-4 is approximated by repeatedly applying the lerp function where in each invocation, the initial value is the result of the previous lerp invocation. In this way, the exponential function is approximated with a piecewise linear function.

This section introduces the Lerp and LerpVec2 utility classes to support smooth and gradual camera movements resulting from camera manipulation operations.

The Camera Interpolations Project

This project demonstrates the smoother and visually more appealing interpolated results from camera manipulation operations. You can see an example of this project running in Figure 7-5. The source code to this project is defined in the chapter7/7.2.camera_interpolations folder.

Figure 7-5. *Running the Camera Interpolations project*

The controls of the project are identical to the previous project:

- **WASD keys**: Move the Dye character (the Hero object). Notice that the camera WC window updates to follow the Hero object when it attempts to move beyond 90 percent of the WC bounds.

- **Arrow keys**: Move the Portal object. Notice that the Portal object cannot move beyond 80 percent of the WC bounds.

- **L/R/P/H keys**: Select the Left minion, Right minion, Portal object, or Hero object to be the object in focus. The L/R keys also set the camera to focus on the Left or Right minion.

- **N/M keys**: Zoom into or away from the center of the camera.

- **J/K keys**: Zoom into or away while ensuring constant relative position of the currently in-focus object. In other words, as the camera zooms, the positions of all objects will change except that of the in-focus object.

The goals of the project are as follows:

- To understand the concept of interpolation between given values

- To implement interpolation supporting gradual camera parameter changes

- To experience interpolated changes in camera parameters

As in previous projects, you can find external resource files in the assets folder.

Interpolation as a Utility

Similar to the Transform class supporting transformation functionality and the BoundingBox class supporting collision detection, a Lerp class can be defined to support interpolation of values. To keep the source code organized, a new folder should be defined to store these utilities.

Create the src/engine/utils folder and move the transform.js and bounding_box.js files into this folder.

The Lerp Class

Define the Lerp class to compute interpolation between two values:

1. Create a new file in the src/engine/utils folder, name it lerp.
   js, and define the constructor. This class is designed to interpolate
   values from mCurrentValue to mFinalValue in the duration of
   mCycles. During each update, intermediate results are computed
   based on the mRate increment on the difference between
   mCurrentValue and mFinalValue, as shown next.

```
class Lerp {
    constructor(value, cycles, rate) {
        this.mCurrentValue = value;     // begin value of interpolation
        this.mFinalValue = value;       // final value of interpolation
        this.mCycles = cycles;
        this.mRate = rate;

        // Number of cycles left for interpolation
        this.mCyclesLeft = 0;
    }

    ... implementation to follow ...
}
```

2. Define the function that computes the intermediate results:

```
// subclass should override this function for non-scalar values
_interpolateValue() {
    this.mCurrentValue = this.mCurrentValue + this.mRate *
                    (this.mFinalValue - this.mCurrentValue);
}
```

Note that the _interpolateValue() function computes a
result that linearly interpolates between mCurrentValue and
mFinalValue. In this way, mCurrentValue will be set to the
intermediate value during each iteration approximating an
exponential curve as it approaches the value of the mFinalValue.

3. Define a function to configure the interpolation. The mRate
    variable defines how quickly the interpolated result approaches
    the final value. A mRate of 0.0 will result in no change at all, where
    1.0 causes instantaneous change. The mCycle variable defines the
    duration of the interpolation process.

```
config(stiffness, duration) {
    this.mRate = stiffness;
    this.mCycles = duration;
}
```

4. Define relevant getter and setter functions. Note that the
    setFinal() function both sets the final value and triggers a new
    round of interpolation computation.

```
get() { return this.mCurrentValue; }

setFinal(v) {
    this.mFinalValue = v;
    this.mCyclesLeft = this.mCycles;      // will trigger interpolation
}
```

5. Define the function to trigger the computation of each
    intermediate result:

```
update() {
    if (this.mCyclesLeft <= 0) { return; }

    this.mCyclesLeft--;
    if (this.mCyclesLeft === 0) {
        this.mCurrentValue = this.mFinalValue;
    } else {
        this._interpolateValue();
    }
}
```

6. Finally, make sure to export the defined class:

```
export default Lerp;
```

The LerpVec2 Class

Since many of the camera parameters are vec2 objects (e.g., the WC center position), it is important to generalize the Lerp class to support the interpolation of vec2 objects:

1. Create a new file in the src/engine/utils folder, name it lerp_vec2.js, and define its constructor:

```
class LerpVec2 extends Lerp {
    constructor(value, cycle, rate) {
        super(value, cycle, rate);
    }

    ... implementation to follow ...
}
```

2. Override the _interpolateValue() function to compute intermediate results for vec2:

```
_interpolateValue() {
    vec2.lerp(this.mCurrentValue, this.mCurrentValue,
                            this.mFinalValue, this.mRate);
}
```

The vec2.lerp() function defined in the gl-matrix.js file computes the vec2 components for x and y. The computation involved is identical to the _interpolateValue() function in the Lerp class.

Lastly, remember to update the engine access file, index.js, to forward the newly defined Lerp and LerpVec2 functionality to the client.

Represent Interpolated Intermediate Results with CameraState

The state of a Camera object must be generalized to support gradual changes of interpolated intermediate results. The CameraState class is introduced to accomplish this purpose.

1. Create a new file in the src/engine/cameras folder, name it camera_state.js, import the defined Lerp functionality, and define the constructor:

```
import Lerp from "../utils/lerp.js";
import LerpVec2 from "../utils/lerp_vec2.js";

class CameraState {
    constructor(center, width) {
        this.kCycles = 300;  // cycles to complete the transition
        this.kRate = 0.1;     // rate of change for each cycle
        this.mCenter = new LerpVec2(center, this.kCycles, this.kRate);
        this.mWidth = new Lerp(width, this.kCycles, this.kRate);
    }

    ... implementation to follow ...
}

export default CameraState;
```

> Observe that mCenter and mWidth are the only variables required to support camera panning (changing of mCenter) and zooming (changing of mWidth). Both of these variables are instances of the corresponding Lerp classes and are capable of interpolating and computing intermediate results to achieve gradual changes.

2. Define the getter and setter functions:

```
getCenter() { return this.mCenter.get(); }
getWidth() { return this.mWidth.get(); }

setCenter(c) { this.mCenter.setFinal(c); }
setWidth(w) { this.mWidth.setFinal(w); }
```

3. Define the update function to trigger the interpolation computation:

```
update() {
    this.mCenter.update();
    this.mWidth.update();
}
```

4. Define a function to configure the interpolation:

```
config(stiffness, duration) {
    this.mCenter.config(stiffness, duration);
    this.mWidth.config(stiffness, duration);
}
```

The stiffness variable is the mRate of Lerp. It defines how quickly the interpolated intermediate results should converge to the final value. As discussed in the Lerp class definition, this is a number between 0 and 1, where 0 means the convergence will never happen and a 1 means instantaneous convergence. The duration variable is the mCycle of Lerp. It defines the number of update cycles it takes for the results to converge. This must be a positive integer value.

Note that as the sophistication of the engine increases, so does the complexity of the supporting code. In this case, you have designed an internal utility class, CameraState, for storing the internal state of a Camera object to support interpolation. This is an internal engine operation. There is no reason for the game programmer to access this class, and thus, the engine access file, index.js, should not be modified to forward the definition.

Integrate Interpolation into Camera Manipulation Operations

The Camera class in camera_main.js must be modified to represent the WC center and width using the newly defined CameraState:

1. Edit the camera_main.js file and import the newly defined CameraState class:

```
import CameraState from "./camera_state.js";
```

2. Modify the Camera constructor to replace the center and width variables with an instance of CameraState:

```
constructor(wcCenter, wcWidth, viewportArray) {
    this.mCameraState = new CameraState(wcCenter, wcWidth);

    ... identical to previous code ...
}
```

3. Now, edit the camera_manipulation.js file to define the functions to update and configure the interpolation functionality of the CameraState object:

```
Camera.prototype.update = function () {
    this.mCameraState.update();
}

// For LERP function configuration
Camera.prototype.configLerp = function (stiffness, duration) {
    this.mCameraState.config(stiffness, duration);
}
```

4. Modify the panBy() camera manipulation function to support the CameraState object as follows:

```
Camera.prototype.panBy = function (dx, dy) {
    let newC = vec2.clone(this.getWCCenter());
    newC[0] += dx;
    newC[1] += dy;
    this.mCameraState.setCenter(newC);
}
```

5. Update panWith() and zoomTowards() functions to receive and set WC center to the newly defined CameraState object:

```
Camera.prototype.panWith = function (aXform, zone) {
    let status = this.collideWCBound(aXform, zone);
    if (status !== eBoundCollideStatus.eInside) {
        let pos = aXform.getPosition();
        let newC = vec2.clone(this.getWCCenter());
        if ((status & eBoundCollideStatus.eCollideTop) !== 0)

        ... identical to previous code ...

        this.mCameraState.setCenter(newC);
    }
}
```

```
Camera.prototype.zoomTowards = function (pos, zoom) {
    ... identical to previous code ...
    this.zoomBy(zoom);
    this.mCameraState.setCenter(newC);
}
```

Testing Interpolation in MyGame

Recall that the user controls of this project are identical to that from the previous project. The only difference is that in this project, you can expect gradual and smooth transitions between different camera settings. To observe the proper interpolated results, the camera update() function must be invoked at each game scene update.

```
update() {
    let zoomDelta = 0.05;
    let msg = "L/R: Left or Right Minion; H: Dye; P: Portal]: ";

    this.mCamera.update();  // for smoother camera movements

    ... identical to previous code ...
}
```

The call to update the camera for computing interpolated intermediate results is the only change in the my_game.js file. You can now run the project and experiment with the smooth and gradual changes resulting from camera manipulation operations. Notice that the interpolated results do not change the rendered image abruptly and thus maintain the sense of continuity in space from before and after the manipulation commands. You can try changing the stiffness and duration variables to better appreciate the different rates of interpolation convergence.

Camera Shake and Object Oscillation Effects

In video games, shaking the camera can be a convenient way to convey the significance or mightiness of events, such as the appearance of an enemy boss or the collisions between large objects. Similar to the interpolation of values, the camera shake movement can also be modeled by straightforward mathematical formulations.

Consider how a camera shake may occur in a real-life situation. For instance, while shooting with a video camera, say you are surprised or startled by someone or that something collided with you. Your reaction will probably be slight disorientation followed by quickly refocusing on the original targets. From the perspective of the camera, this reaction can be described as an initial large displacement from the original camera center followed by quick adjustments to re-center the camera. Mathematically, as illustrated in Figure 7-6, damped simple harmonic motions, which can be represented with the damping of trigonometric functions, can be used to describe these types of displacements.

Note that straight mathematical formulation is precise with perfect predictability. Such formulation can be suitable for describing regular, normal, or expected behaviors, for example, the bouncing of a ball or the oscillation of a pendulum. A shaking effect should involve slight chaotic and unpredictable randomness, for example, the stabilization of the coffee-carrying hand after an unexpected collision or, as in the previous example, the stabilization of the video camera after being startled. Following this reasoning, in this section, you will define a general damped oscillation function and then inject pseudo-randomness to simulate the slight chaos to achieve the shake effect.

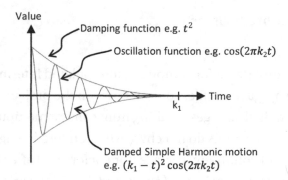

Figure 7-6. *The displacements of a damped simple harmonic motion*

The Camera Shake and Object Oscillate Project

This project demonstrates how to implement damped simple harmonic motion to simulate object oscillation and the injection of pseudo-randomness to create a camera shake effect. You can see an example of this project running in Figure 7-7. This project is identical to the previous project except for an additional command to create object oscillation and camera shake effects. The source code to this project is defined in the chapter7/7.3.camera_shake_and_object_oscillate folder.

Figure 7-7. *Running the Camera Shake and Object Oscillate project*

The following is the new control of this project:

- **Q key**: Initiates the positional oscillation of the Dye character and the camera shake effects.

The following controls are identical to the previous project:

- **WASD keys**: Move the Dye character (the Hero object). Notice that the camera WC window updates to follow the Hero object when it attempts to move beyond 90 percent of the WC bounds.

- **Arrow keys**: Move the Portal object. Notice that the Portal object cannot move beyond 80 percent of the WC bounds.

- **L/R/P/H keys**: Select the Left minion, Right minion, Portal object, or Hero object to be the object in focus. The L/R keys also set the camera to focus on the Left or Right minion.

- **N/M keys**: Zoom into or away from the center of the camera.

- **J/K keys**: Zoom into or away while ensuring constant relative position of the currently in-focus object. In other words, as the camera zooms, the positions of all objects will change except that of the in-focus object.

The goals of the project are as follows:

- To gain some insight into modeling displacements with simple mathematical functions

- To experience the oscillate effect on an object

- To experience the shake effect on a camera

- To implement oscillations as damped simple harmonic motion and to introduce pseudo-randomness to create the camera shake effect

As in previous projects, you can find external resource files in the `assets` folder.

Abstract the Shake Behavior

The ability to shake the camera is a common and dynamic behavior in many games. However, it is important to recognize that the shake behavior can be applied to more than just the camera. That is, the shaking effect can be abstracted as the perturbation (shaking) of numerical value(s) such as a size, a point, or a position. In the case of camera shake, it just so happened that the numerical values being shaken represent the x and y positions of the camera. For this reason, the shake and associated supports should be general utility functions of the game engine so that they can be applied by the game developer to any numerical values. The following are the new utilities that will be defined:

- `Oscillate`: The base class that implements simple harmonic oscillation of a value over time

- `Shake`: An extension of the `Oscillate` class that introduces randomness to the magnitudes of the oscillations to simulate slight chaos of the shake effect on a value

- `ShakeVec2`: An extension of the `Shake` class that expands the `Shake` behavior to two values such as a position

Create the Oscillate Class to Model Simple Harmonic Motion

Because all of the described behaviors depend on simple oscillation, this should be implemented first;

1. Create a new file in the src/engine/utils folder and name it oscillate.js. Define a class named Oscillate and add the following code to construct the object:

```
class Oscillate {
    constructor(delta, frequency, duration) {
        this.mMag = delta;

        this.mCycles = duration; // cycles to complete the transition
        this.mOmega = frequency * 2 * Math.PI; // Converts to radians
        this.mNumCyclesLeft = duration;
    }

    ... implementation to follow ...
}

export default Oscillate;
```

> The delta variable represents the initial displacements before damping, in WC space. The frequency parameter specifies how much to oscillate with a value of 1 representing one complete period of a cosine function. The duration parameter defines how long to oscillate in units of game loop updates.

2. Define the damped simple harmonic motion:

```
_nextDampedHarmonic() {
    // computes (Cycles) * cos(Omega * t)
    let frac = this.mNumCyclesLeft / this.mCycles;
    return frac * frac * Math.cos((1 - frac) * this.mOmega);
}
```

> Refer to Figure 7-8. mNumCyclesLeft is the number of cycles left in the oscillation, or k-t, and the frac variable, $\frac{k-t}{k}$, is the damping factor. This function returns a value between -1 and 1 and can be scaled as needed.

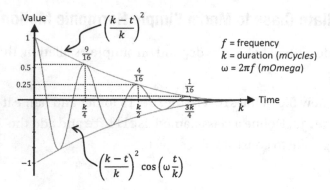

Figure 7-8. *The damped simple harmonic motion that specifies value oscillation*

3. Define a protected function to retrieve the value of the next damped harmonic motion. This function may seem trivial and unnecessary. However, as you will observe in the next subsection, this function allows a shake subclass to overwrite and inject randomness.

```
// local/protected methods
_nextValue() {
    return (this._nextDampedHarmonic());
}
```

4. Define functions to check for the end of the oscillation and for restarting the oscillation:

```
done() { return (this.mNumCyclesLeft <= 0); }
reStart() { this.mNumCyclesLeft = this.mCycles; }
```

5. Lastly, define a public function to trigger the calculation of oscillation. Notice that the computed oscillation result must be scaled by the desired magnitude, mMag:

```
getNext() {
    this.mNumCyclesLeft--;
    let v = 0;
    if (!this.done()) {
        v = this._nextValue();
    }
    return (v * this.mMag);
}
```

362

Create the Shake Class to Randomize an Oscillation

You can now extend the oscillation behavior to convey a sense of shaking by introducing pseudo-randomness into the effect.

1. Create a new file, shake.js, in the src/engine/utils folder. Define the Shake class to extend Oscillate and add the following code to construct the object:

```
import Oscillate from "./oscillate.js";

class Shake extends Oscillate {
    constructor(delta, frequency, duration) {
        super(delta, frequency, duration);
    }

    ... implementation to follow ...
}

export default Shake;
```

2. Overwrite the _nextValue() to randomize the sign of the oscillation results as follows. Recall that the _nextValue() function is called from the public getNext() function to retrieve the oscillating value. While the results from the damped simple harmonic oscillation continuously and predictably decrease in magnitude, the associated signs of the values are randomized causing sudden and unexpected discontinuities conveying a sense of chaos from the results of a shake.

```
_nextValue() {
    let v = this._nextDampedHarmonic();
    let fx = (Math.random() > 0.5) ? -v : v;
    return fx;
}
```

Create the ShakeVec2 Class to Model the Shaking of a vec2, or a Position

You can now generalize the shake effect to support the shaking of two values simultaneously. This is a useful utility because positions in 2D games are two-value entities and positions are convenient targets for shake effects. For example, in this project, the shaking of the camera position, a two-value entity, simulates the camera shake effect.

The ShakeVec2 class extends the Shake class to support the shaking of a vec2 object, shaking the values in both the x and y dimensions. The x-dimension shaking is supported via an instance of the Shake object, while the y dimension is supported via the Shake class functionality that is defined in the super class.

1. Create a new file, shake_vec2.js, in the src/engine/utils folder. Define the ShakeVec2 class to extend the Shake class. Similar to the constructor parameters of the Shake super classes, the deltas and freqs parameters are 2D, or vec2, versions of magnitude and frequency for shaking in the x and y dimensions. In the constructor, the xShake instance variable keeps track of shaking effect in the x dimension. Note the y-component parameters, array indices of 1, in the super() constructor invocation. The Shake super class keeps track of the shaking effect in the y dimension.

```
class ShakeVec2 extends Shake {
    constructor(deltas, freqs, duration) {
        super(deltas[1], freqs[1], duration);  // super in y-direction
        this.xShake = new Shake(deltas[0], freqs[0], duration);
    }

    ... implementation to follow ...
}

export default ShakeVec2;
```

2. Extend the reStart() and getNext() functions to support the second dimension:

```
reStart() {
    super.reStart();
    this.xShake.reStart();
}
```

```
getNext() {
    let x = this.xShake.getNext();
    let y = super.getNext();
    return [x, y];
}
```

Lastly, remember to update the engine access file, index.js, to forward the newly defined Oscillate, Shake, and ShakeVec2 functionality to the client.

Define the CameraShake Class to Abstract the Camera Shaking Effect

With the defined ShakeVec2 class, it is convenient to apply the displacements of a pseudo-random damped simple harmonic motion on the position of the Camera. However, the Camera object requires an additional abstraction layer.

1. Create a new file, camera_shake.js, in the src/engine/cameras folder, and define the constructor to receive the camera state, the state parameter, and shake configurations: deltas, freqs, and shakeDuration. The parameter state is of datatype CameraState, consisting of the camera center position and width.

```
import ShakeVec2 from "../utils/shake_vec2.js";

class CameraShake {
    // state is the CameraState to be shaken
    constructor(state, deltas, freqs, shakeDuration) {
        this.mOrgCenter = vec2.clone(state.getCenter());
        this.mShakeCenter = vec2.clone(this.mOrgCenter);
        this.mShake = new ShakeVec2(deltas, freqs, shakeDuration);
    }

    ... implementation to follow ...
}
export default CameraShake;
```

2. Define the function that triggers the displacement computation for accomplishing the shaking effect. Notice that the shake results are offsets from the original position. The given code adds this offset to the original camera center position.

365

```
update() {
    let delta = this.mShake.getNext();
    vec2.add(this.mShakeCenter, this.mOrgCenter, delta);
}
```

3. Define utility functions: inquire if shaking is done, restart the
    shaking, and getter/setter functions.

```
done() { return this.mShake.done(); }
reShake() {this.mShake.reStart();}
getCenter() { return this.mShakeCenter; }
setRefCenter(c) {
    this.mOrgCenter[0] = c[0];
    this.mOrgCenter[1] = c[1];
}
```

Similar to CameraState, CameraShake is also a game engine internal utility and should not be exported to the client game programmer. The engine access file, index.js, should not be updated to export this class.

Modify the Camera to Support Shake Effect

With the proper CameraShake abstraction, supporting the shaking of the camera simply means initiating and updating the shake effect:

1. Modify camera_main.js and camera_manipulation.js to import
    camera_shake.js as shown:

```
import CameraShake from "./camera_shake.js";
```

2. In camera_main.js, modify the Camera constructor to initialize a
    CameraShake object:

```
constructor(wcCenter, wcWidth, viewportArray) {
    this.mCameraState = new CameraState(wcCenter, wcWidth);
    this.mCameraShake = null;

    ... identical to previous code ...
}
```

3. Modify step B of the setViewAndCameraMatrix() function to use the CameraShake object's center if it is defined:

```
setViewAndCameraMatrix() {
    ... identical to previous code ...

    // Step B: Compute the Camera Matrix
    let center = [];
    if (this.mCameraShake !== null) {
        center = this.mCameraShake.getCenter();
    } else {
        center = this.getWCCenter();
    }

    ... identical to previous code ...
}
```

4. Modify the camera_manipulation.js file to add support to initiate and restart the shake effect:

```
Camera.prototype.shake = function (deltas, freqs, duration) {
    this.mCameraShake = new CameraShake(this.mCameraState,
                                        deltas, freqs, duration);
}

// Restart the shake
Camera.prototype.reShake = function () {
    let success = (this.mCameraShake !== null);
    if (success)
        this.mCameraShake.reShake();
    return success;
}
```

5. Continue working with the camera_manipulation.js file, and modify the update() function to trigger a camera shake update if one is defined:

```
Camera.prototype.update = function () {
    if (this.mCameraShake !== null) {
        if (this.mCameraShake.done()) {
```

367

```
            this.mCameraShake = null;
        } else {
            this.mCameraShake.setRefCenter(this.getWCCenter());
            this.mCameraShake.update();
        }
    }
    this.mCameraState.update();
}
```

Testing the Camera Shake and Oscillation Effects in MyGame

The my_game.js file only needs to be modified slightly in the init() and update() functions to support triggering the oscillation and camera shake effects with the Q key:

1. Define a new instance variable for creating oscillation or bouncing effect on the Dye character:

```
init() {
    ... identical to previous code ...

    // create an Oscillate object to simulate motion
    this.mBounce = new engine.Oscillate(2, 6, 120);
                                    // delta, freq, duration
}
```

2. Modify the update() function to trigger the bouncing and camera shake effects with the Q key. In the following code, note the advantage of well-designed abstraction. For example, the camera shake effect is opaque where the only information a programmer needs to specify is the actual shake behavior, that is, the shake magnitude, frequency, and duration. In contrast, the oscillating or bouncing effect of the Dye character position is accomplished by explicitly inquiring and using the mBounce results.

```
update() {
    ... identical to previous code ...

    if (engine.input.isKeyClicked(engine.input.keys.Q)) {
        if (!this.mCamera.reShake())
            this.mCamera.shake([6, 1], [10, 3], 60);
```

```
        // also re-start bouncing effect
        this.mBounce.reStart();
    }

    if (!this.mBounce.done()) {
        let d = this.mBounce.getNext();
        this.mHero.getXform().incXPosBy(d);
    }

    this.mMsg.setText(msg + this.mChoice);
}
```

You can now run the project and experience the pseudo-random damped simple harmonic motion that simulates the camera shake effect. You can also observe the oscillation of the Dye character's x position. Notice that the displacement of the camera center position will undergo interpolation and thus result in a smoother final shake effect. You can try changing the parameters when creating the mBounce object or when calling the mCamera.shake() function to experiment with different oscillation and shake configurations. Recall that in both cases the first two parameters control the initial displacements and the frequency (number of cosine periods) and the third parameter is the duration of how long the effects should last.

Multiple Cameras

Video games often present the players with multiple views into the game world to communicate vital or interesting gameplay information, such as showing a mini-map to help the player navigate the world or providing a view of the enemy boss to warn the player of what is to come.

In your game engine, the Camera class abstracts the graphical presentation of the game world according to the source and destination areas of drawing. The source area of the drawing is the WC window of the game world, and the destination area is the viewport region on the canvas. This abstraction already effectively encapsulates and supports the multiple view idea with multiple Camera instances. Each view in the game can be handled with a separate instance of the Camera object with distinct WC window and viewport configurations.

The Multiple Cameras Project

This project demonstrates how to represent multiple views in the game world with multiple Camera objects. You can see an example of this project running in Figure 7-9. The source code to this project is defined in the chapter7/7.4.multiple_cameras folder.

Figure 7-9. *Running the Multiple Cameras project*

The controls of the project are identical to the previous project:

- **Q key**: Initiates the positional oscillation of the Dye character and the camera shake effects.

- **WASD keys**: Move the Dye character (the Hero object). Notice that the camera WC window updates to follow the Hero object when it attempts to move beyond 90 percent of the WC bounds.

- **Arrow keys**: Move the Portal object. Notice that the Portal object cannot move beyond 80 percent of the WC bounds.

- **L/R/P/H keys**: Select the Left minion, Right minion, Portal object, or Hero object to be the object in focus. The L/R keys also set the camera to focus on the Left or Right minion.

- **N/M keys**: Zoom into or away from the center of the camera.

- **J/K keys**: Zoom into or away while ensuring the constant relative position of the currently in-focus object. In other words, as the camera zooms, the positions of all objects will change except that of the in-focus object.

The goals of the project are as follows:

- To understand the camera abstraction for presenting views into the game world

- To experience working with multiple cameras in the same game level

- To appreciate the importance of interpolation configuration for cameras with specific purposes

As in previous projects, you can find external resource files in the assets folder.

Modify the Camera

The Camera object will be slightly modified to allow the drawing of the viewport with a bound. This will allow easy differentiation of camera views on the canvas.

1. Edit camera_main.js and modify the Camera constructor to allow programmers to define a bound number of pixels to surround the viewport of the camera:

```
constructor(wcCenter, wcWidth, viewportArray, bound) {
    this.mCameraState = new CameraState(wcCenter, wcWidth);
    this.mCameraShake = null;

    this.mViewport = [];  // [x, y, width, height]
    this.mViewportBound = 0;
    if (bound !== undefined) {
```

```
        this.mViewportBound = bound;
    }
    this.mScissorBound = [];  // use for bounds
    this.setViewport(viewportArray, this.mViewportBound);

    // Camera transform operator
    this.mCameraMatrix = mat4.create();

    // background color
    this.mBGColor = [0.8, 0.8, 0.8, 1]; // RGB and Alpha
}
```

Please refer to the setViewport() function that follows. By default, bound is assumed to be zero, and the camera will draw to the entire mViewport. When being nonzero, the bound number of pixels that surround the mViewport will be left as the background color, thereby allowing easy differentiation of multiple viewports on the canvas.

2. Define the setViewport() function:

```
setViewport(viewportArray, bound) {
    if (bound === undefined) {
        bound = this.mViewportBound;
    }
    // [x, y, width, height]
    this.mViewport[0] = viewportArray[0] + bound;
    this.mViewport[1] = viewportArray[1] + bound;
    this.mViewport[2] = viewportArray[2] - (2 * bound);
    this.mViewport[3] = viewportArray[3] - (2 * bound);
    this.mScissorBound[0] = viewportArray[0];
    this.mScissorBound[1] = viewportArray[1];
    this.mScissorBound[2] = viewportArray[2];
    this.mScissorBound[3] = viewportArray[3];
}
```

Recall that when setting the camera viewport, you invoke the gl.scissor() function to define an area to be cleared and the gl.viewport() function to identify the target area for drawing. Previously, the scissor and viewport bounds are identical, whereas in this case, notice that the actual mViewport bounds are the bound number of pixels smaller than the mScissorBound. These settings allow the mScissorBound to identify the area to be cleared to background color, while the mViewport bounds define the actual canvas area for drawing. In this way, the bound number of pixels around the viewport will remain the background color.

3. Define the getViewport() function to return the actual bounds that are reserved for this camera. In this case, it is the mScissorBound instead of the potentially smaller viewport bounds.

```
getViewport() {
    let out = [];
    out[0] = this.mScissorBound[0];
    out[1] = this.mScissorBound[1];
    out[2] = this.mScissorBound[2];
    out[3] = this.mScissorBound[3];
    return out;
}
```

4. Modify the setViewAndCameraMatrix() function to bind scissor bounds with mScissorBound instead of the viewport bounds:

```
setViewAndCameraMatrix() {
    let gl = glSys.get();
    ... identical to previous code ...
    // Step A2: set up corresponding scissor area to limit clear area
    gl.scissor(this.mScissorBound[0], // x of bottom-left corner
        this.mScissorBound[1], // y position of bottom-left corner
        this.mScissorBound[2], // width of the area to be drawn
        this.mScissorBound[3]);// height of the area to be drawn

    ... identical to previous code ...
}
```

Testing Multiple Cameras in MyGame

The MyGame level must create multiple cameras, configure them properly, and draw each independently. For ease of demonstration, two new Camera objects will be created, one to focus on the Hero object and one to focus on the chasing Brain object. As in the previous examples, the implementation of the MyGame level is largely identical. In this example, some portions of the init(), draw(), and update() functions are modified to handle the multiple Camera objects and are highlighted.

1. Modify the init() function to define three Camera objects. Both the mHeroCam and mBrainCam define a two-pixel boundary for their viewports, with the mHeroCam boundary defined to be gray (the background color) and with mBrainCam white. Notice the mBrainCam object's stiff interpolation setting informing the camera interpolation to converge to new values in ten cycles.

```
init() {
    // Step A: set up the cameras
    this.mCamera = new engine.Camera(
        vec2.fromValues(50, 36), // position of the camera
        100,                     // width of camera
        [0, 0, 640, 480]         // viewport (orgX, orgY, width, height)
    );
    this.mCamera.setBackgroundColor([0.8, 0.8, 0.8, 1]);
    // sets the background to gray

    this.mHeroCam = new engine.Camera(
        vec2.fromValues(50, 30), // update each cycle to point to hero
        20,
        [490, 330, 150, 150],
        2                                // viewport bounds
     );
    this.mHeroCam.setBackgroundColor([0.5, 0.5, 0.5, 1]);

    this.mBrainCam = new engine.Camera(
        vec2.fromValues(50, 30),  // update each cycle to point to brain
        10,
```

```
    [0, 330, 150, 150],
    2                                    // viewport bounds
);
this.mBrainCam.setBackgroundColor([1, 1, 1, 1]);
this.mBrainCam.configLerp(0.7, 10);

... identical to previous code ...
}
```

2. Define a helper function to draw the world that is common to all three cameras:

```
_drawCamera(camera) {
    camera.setViewAndCameraMatrix();
    this.mBg.draw(camera);
    this.mHero.draw(camera);
    this.mBrain.draw(camera);
    this.mPortal.draw(camera);
    this.mLMinion.draw(camera);
    this.mRMinion.draw(camera);
}
```

3. Modify the MyGame object draw() function to draw all three cameras. Take note of the mMsg object only being drawn to mCamera, the main camera. For this reason, the echo message will appear only in the viewport of the main camera.

```
draw() {
    // Step A: clear the canvas
    engine.clearCanvas([0.9, 0.9, 0.9, 1.0]); // clear to light gray

    // Step  B: Draw with all three cameras
    this._drawCamera(this.mCamera);
    this.mMsg.draw(this.mCamera);   // only draw status in main camera
    this._drawCamera(this.mHeroCam);
    this._drawCamera(this.mBrainCam);

}
```

4. Modify the update() function to pan the mHeroCam and mBrainCam
    with the corresponding objects and to move the mHeroCam
    viewport continuously:

Note   Viewports typically do not change their positions during gameplays. For
testing purposes, the following code moves the mHeroCam viewport continuously
from left to right in the canvas.

```
update() {
    let zoomDelta = 0.05;
    let msg = "L/R: Left or Right Minion; H: Dye; P: Portal]: ";

    this.mCamera.update();  // for smoother camera movements
    this.mHeroCam.update();
    this.mBrainCam.update();

    ... identical to previous code ...

    // set the hero and brain cams
    this.mHeroCam.panTo(this.mHero.getXform().getXPos(),
                        this.mHero.getXform().getYPos());
    this.mBrainCam.panTo(this.mBrain.getXform().getXPos(),
                         this.mBrain.getXform().getYPos());

    // Move the hero cam viewport just to show it is possible
    let v = this.mHeroCam.getViewport();
    v[0] += 1;
    if (v[0] > 500) {
        v[0] = 0;
    }
    this.mHeroCam.setViewport(v);

    this.mMsg.setText(msg + this.mChoice);
}
```

You can now run the project and notice the three different viewports displayed on
the HTML canvas. The two-pixel-wide bounds around the mHeroCam and mBrainCam
viewports allow easy visual parsing of the three views. Observe that the mBrainCam

viewport is drawn on top of the mHeroCam. This is because in the MyGame.draw() function, the mBrainCam is drawn last. The last drawn object always appears on the top. You can move the Hero object to observe that mHeroCam follows the hero and experience the smooth interpolated results of panning the camera.

Now try changing the parameters to the mBrainCam.configLerp() function to generate smoother interpolated results, such as by setting the stiffness to 0.1 and the duration to 100 cycles. Note how it appears as though the camera is constantly trying to catch up to the Brain object. In this case, the camera needs a stiff interpolation setting to ensure the main object remains in the center of the camera view. For a much more drastic and fun effect, you can try setting mBrainCam to have much smoother interpolated results, such as with a stiffness value of 0.01 and a duration of 200 cycles. With these values, the camera can never catch up to the Brain object and will appear as though it is wandering aimlessly around the game world.

Mouse Input Through Cameras

The mouse is a pointing input device that reports position information in the Canvas Coordinate space. Recall from the discussion in Chapter 3 that the Canvas Coordinate space is simply a measurement of pixel offsets along the x/y axes with respect to the lower-left corner of the canvas. Remember that the game engine defines and works with the WC space where all objects and measurements are specified in WC. For the game engine to work with the reported mouse position, this position must be transformed from Canvas Coordinate space to WC.

The drawing on the left side of Figure 7-10 shows an example of a mouse position located at (mouseX, mouseY) on the canvas. The drawing on the right side of Figure 7-10 shows that when a viewport with the lower-left corner located at (V_x, V_y) and a dimension of $W_v \times H_v$ is defined within the canvas, the same (mouseX, mouseY) position can be represented as a position in the viewport as (mouseDCX, mouseDCY) where

- mouseDCX = mouseX − V_x

- mouseDCY = mouseY − V_y

In this way, (mouseDCX, mouseDCY) is the offset from the (V_x, V_y), the lower-left corner of the viewport.

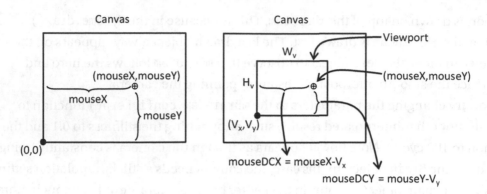

Figure 7-10. *Mouse position on canvas and viewport*

The left drawing in Figure 7-11 shows that the Device Coordinate (DC) space defines a pixel position within a viewport with offsets measured with respect to the lower-left corner of the viewport. For this reason, the DC space is also referred to as the pixel space. The computed (mouseDCX, mouseDCY) position is an example of a position in DC space. The right drawing in Figure 7-11 shows that this position can be transformed into the WC space with the lower-left corner located at (minWCX, minWCY) and a dimension of $W_{wc} \times H_{wc}$ according to these formulae:

- $\text{mouseWCX} = \text{minWCX} + \left(\text{mouseDCX} \times \dfrac{W_{wc}}{W_v} \right)$

- $\text{mouseWCY} = \text{minWCY} + \left(\text{mouseDCY} \times \dfrac{H_{wc}}{H_v} \right)$

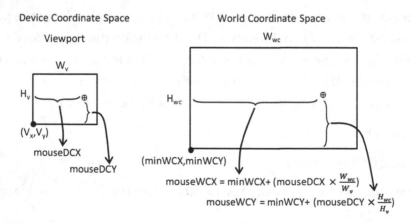

Figure 7-11. *Mouse position in viewport DC space and WC space*

With the knowledge of how to transform positions from the Canvas Coordinate space to the WC space, it is now possible to implement mouse input support in the game engine.

The Mouse Input Project

This project demonstrates mouse input support in the game engine. You can see an example of this project running in Figure 7-12. The source code to this project is defined in the chapter7/7.5.mouse_input folder.

Figure 7-12. Running the Mouse Input project

The new controls of this project are as follows:

- **Left mouse button clicked in the main Camera view**: Drags the Portal object

- **Middle mouse button clicked in the HeroCam view**: Drags the Hero object

- **Right/middle mouse button clicked in any view**: Hides/shows the Portal object

The following controls are identical to the previous project:

- **Q key**: Initiates the positional oscillation of the Dye character and the camera shake effects

- **WASD keys**: Move the Dye character (the Hero object) and push the camera WC bounds

- **Arrow keys**: Move the Portal object

- **L/R/P/H keys**: Select the in-focus object with L/R keys refocusing the camera to the Left or Right minion

- **N/M and J/K keys**: Zoom into or away from the center of the camera or the in-focus object

The goals of the project are as follows:

- To understand the Canvas Coordinate space to WC space transform

- To appreciate the importance of differentiating between viewports for mouse events

- To implement transformation between coordinate spaces

- To support and experience working with mouse input

As in previous projects, you can find external resource files in the assets folder.

Modify index.js to Pass Canvas ID to Input Component

To receive mouse input information, the input component needs to have access to the HTML canvas. Edit index.js and modify the init() function to pass the htmlCamvasID to the input component during initialization.

```
... identical to previous code ...

// general engine utilities
function init(htmlCanvasID) {
    glSys.init(htmlCanvasID);
    vertexBuffer.init();
    input.init(htmlCanvasID);
    audio.init();
    shaderResources.init();
    defaultResources.init();
}

... identical to previous code ...
```

Implement Mouse Support in input.js

Similar to the keyboard input, you should add mouse support to the input module by editing input.js:

1. Edit input.js and define the constants to represent the three mouse buttons:

```
// mouse button enums
const eMouseButton = Object.freeze({
    eLeft: 0,
    eMiddle: 1,
    eRight: 2
});
```

2. Define the variables to support mouse input. Similar to keyboard input, mouse button states are arrays of three boolean elements, each representing the state of the three mouse buttons.

```
let mCanvas = null;
let mButtonPreviousState = [];
let mIsButtonPressed = [];
let mIsButtonClicked = [];
let mMousePosX = -1;
let mMousePosY = -1;
```

3. Define the mouse movement event handler:

```
function onMouseMove(event) {
    let inside = false;
    let bBox = mCanvas.getBoundingClientRect();
    // In Canvas Space now. Convert via ratio from canvas to client.
    let x = Math.round((event.clientX - bBox.left) *
                        (mCanvas.width / bBox.width));
    let y = Math.round((event.clientY - bBox.top) *
                        (mCanvas.height / bBox.height));

    if ((x >= 0) && (x < mCanvas.width) &&
        (y >= 0) && (y < mCanvas.height)) {
        mMousePosX = x;
        mMousePosY = mCanvas.height - 1 - y;
        inside = true;
    }
    return inside;
}
```

Notice that the mouse event handler transforms a raw pixel position into the Canvas Coordinate space by first checking whether the position is within the bounds of the canvas and then flipping the y position such that the displacement is measured with respect to the lower-left corner.

4. Define the mouse button click handler to record the button event:

```
function onMouseDown(event) {
    if (onMouseMove(event)) {
        mIsButtonPressed[event.button] = true;
    }
}
```

5. Define the mouse button release handler to facilitate the detection of a mouse button click event. Recall from the keyboard input discussion in Chapter 4 that in order to detect the button up event, you should test for a button state that was previously released and currently clicked. The mouseUp() handler records the released state of a mouse button.

```
function onMouseUp(event) {
    onMouseMove(event);
    mIsButtonPressed[event.button] = false;
}
```

6. Modify the init() function to receive the canvasID parameter and initialize mouse event handlers:

```
function init(canvasID) {
    let i;

    // keyboard support
    ... identical to previous code ...

    // Mouse support
    for (i = 0; i < 3; i++) {
        mButtonPreviousState[i] = false;
        mIsButtonPressed[i] = false;
        mIsButtonClicked[i] = false;
    }
    window.addEventListener('mousedown', onMouseDown);
    window.addEventListener('mouseup', onMouseUp);
    window.addEventListener('mousemove', onMouseMove);
    mCanvas = document.getElementById(canvasID);
}
```

7. Modify the update() function to process mouse button state changes in a similar fashion to the keyboard. Take note of the mouse-click condition that a button that was previously not clicked is now clicked.

```
function update() {
    let i;
    // update keyboard input state
    ... identical to previous code ...

    // update mouse input state
    for (i = 0; i < 3; i++) {
        mIsButtonClicked[i] = (!mButtonPreviousState[i]) &&
```

```
                            mIsButtonPressed[i];
    mButtonPreviousState[i] = mIsButtonPressed[i];
    }
}
```

8. Define the functions to retrieve mouse position and mouse button
    states:

```
function isButtonPressed(button) { return mIsButtonPressed[button]; }
function isButtonClicked(button) { return mIsButtonClicked[button]; }

function getMousePosX() { return mMousePosX; }
function getMousePosY() { return mMousePosY; }
```

9. Lastly, remember to export the newly defined functionality:

```
export {
    keys, eMouseButton,

    init, cleanUp, update,

    // keyboard
    isKeyClicked, isKeyPressed,

    // mouse
    isButtonClicked, isButtonPressed, getMousePosX, getMousePosY
}
```

Modify the Camera to Support Viewport to WC Space Transform

The Camera class encapsulates the WC window and viewport and thus should be
responsible for transforming mouse positions. Recall that to maintain readability,
the Camera class source code files are separated according to functionality. The basic
functions of the class are defined in camera_main.js. The camera_manipulate.js file
imports from camera_main.js and defines additional manipulation functions. Lastly, the
camera.js file imports from camera_manipulate.js to include all the defined functions
and exports the Camera class for external access.

This chaining of imports from subsequent source code files to define additional
functions will continue for the Camera class, with camera_input.js defining input
functionality:

1. Create a new file in the src/engine/cameras folder and name it camera_input.js. This file will expand the Camera class by defining the mouse input support functions. Import the following files:

    - camera_manipulation.js for all the defined functions for the Camera class

    - eViewport constants for accessing the viewport array

    - input module to access the mouse-related functions

```
import Camera from "./camera_manipulation.js";
import { eViewport } from "./camera_main.js";
import * as input from "../input.js";

... implementation to follow ...

export default Camera;
```

2. Define functions to transform mouse positions from Canvas Coordinate space to the DC space, as illustrated in Figure 7-10:

```
Camera.prototype._mouseDCX = function () {
    return input.getMousePosX() - this.mViewport[eViewport.eOrgX];
}

Camera.prototype._mouseDCY = function() {
    return input.getMousePosY() - this.mViewport[eViewport.eOrgY];
}
```

3. Define a function to determine whether a given mouse position is within the viewport bounds of the camera:

```
Camera.prototype.isMouseInViewport = function () {
    let dcX = this._mouseDCX();
    let dcY = this._mouseDCY();
    return ((dcX >= 0) && (dcX < this.mViewport[eViewport.eWidth]) &&
            (dcY >= 0) && (dcY < this.mViewport[eViewport.eHeight]));
}
```

4. Define the functions to transform the mouse position into the WC
    space, as illustrated in Figure 7 11:

```
Camera.prototype.mouseWCX = function () {
    let minWCX = this.getWCCenter()[0] - this.getWCWidth() / 2;
    return minWCX + (this._mouseDCX() *
            (this.getWCWidth() / this.mViewport[eViewport.eWidth]));
}

Camera.prototype.mouseWCY = function () {
    let minWCY = this.getWCCenter()[1] - this.getWCHeight() / 2;
    return minWCY + (this._mouseDCY() *
            (this.getWCHeight() / this.mViewport[eViewport.eHeight]));
}
```

Lastly, update the Camera class access file to properly export the newly defined
input functionality. This is accomplished by editing the camera.js file and replacing the
import from camera_manipulate.js with camera_input.js:

```
import Camera from "./camera_input.js";
export default Camera;
```

Testing the Mouse Input in MyGame

The main functionality to be tested includes the abilities to detect which view
should receive the mouse input, react to mouse button state changes, and transform
mouse-click pixel positions to the WC space. As in previous examples, the my_game.
js implementation is largely similar to previous projects. In this case, only the
update() function contains noteworthy changes that work with the new mouse input
functionality.

```
update() {
    ... identical to previous code ...

    msg = "";
    // testing the mouse input
    if (engine.input.isButtonPressed(engine.input.eMouseButton.eLeft)) {
        msg += "[L Down]";
```

```
        if (this.mCamera.isMouseInViewport()) {
            this.mPortal.getXform().setXPos(this.mCamera.mouseWCX());
            this.mPortal.getXform().setYPos(this.mCamera.mouseWCY());
        }
    }

    if (engine.input.isButtonPressed(engine.input.eMouseButton.eMiddle)){
        if (this.mHeroCam.isMouseInViewport()) {
            this.mHero.getXform().setXPos(this.mHeroCam.mouseWCX());
            this.mHero.getXform().setYPos(this.mHeroCam.mouseWCY());
        }
    }
    if (engine.input.isButtonClicked(engine.input.eMouseButton.eRight)) {
        this.mPortal.setVisibility(false);
    }

    if (engine.input.isButtonClicked(engine.input.eMouseButton.eMiddle)){
        this.mPortal.setVisibility(true);
    }

    msg += " X=" + engine.input.getMousePosX() +
           " Y=" + engine.input.getMousePosY();
    this.mMsg.setText(msg);
}
```

The camera.isMouseInViewport() condition is checked when the viewport context is important, as in the case of a left mouse button click in the main camera view or a middle mouse button click in the mHeroCam view. This is in contrast to a right or middle mouse button click for setting the visibility of the Portal object. These two mouse clicks will cause execution no matter where the mouse position is.

You can now run the project and verify the correctness of the transformation to WC space. Click and drag with left mouse button in the main view, or middle mouse button in the mHeroCam view, to observe the accurate movement of the corresponding object as they follow the changing mouse position. The left or middle mouse button drag actions in the wrong views have no effect on the corresponding objects. For example, a left mouse button drag in the mHeroCam or mBrainCam view has no effect on the Portal object. However, notice that the right or middle mouse button click controls the visibility of the Portal object, independent of the location of the mouse pointer. Be aware that the browser maps the right mouse button click to a default pop-up menu. For this reason, you should avoid working with right mouse button clicks in your games.

Summary

This chapter was about controlling and interacting with the Camera object. You have learned about the most common camera manipulation operations including clamping, panning, and zooming. These operations are implemented in the game engine with utility functions that map the high-level specifications to actual WC window bound parameters. The sudden, often annoying, and potentially confusing movements from camera manipulations are mitigated with the introduction of interpolation. Through the implementation of the camera shake effect, you have discovered that some movements can be modeled by simple mathematical formulations. You have also experienced the importance of effective Camera object abstraction in supporting multiple camera views. The last section guided you through the implementation of transforming a mouse position from the Canvas Coordinate space to the WC space.

In Chapter 5, you found out how to represent and draw an object with a visually appealing image and control the animation of this object. In Chapter 6, you read about how to define an abstraction to encapsulate the behaviors of an object and the fundamental support required to detect collisions between objects. This chapter was about the "directing" of these objects: what should be visible, where the focus should be, how much of the world to show, how to ensure smooth transition between foci, and how to receive input from the mouse. With these capabilities, you now have a well-rounded game engine framework that can represent and draw objects, model and manage the behaviors of the objects, and control how, where, and what objects are shown.

The following chapters will continue to examine object appearance and behavior at more advanced levels, including creating lighting and illumination effects in a 2D world and simulating and integrating behaviors based on simple classical mechanics.

Game Design Considerations

You've learned the basics of object interaction, and it's a good time to start thinking about creating your first simple game mechanic and experimenting with the logical conditions and rules that constitute well-formed gameplay experiences. Many designers approach game creation from the top-down (meaning they start with an idea for an implementation of a specific genre like a real-time strategy, tower defense, or role-playing game), which we might expect in an industry like video games where the creators typically spend quite a bit of time as content consumers before transitioning into content makers. Game studios often reinforce this top-down design approach, assigning new staff to work under seasoned leads to learn best practices for whatever genre that particular studio works in. This has proven effective for training designers who can competently iterate on known genres, but it's not always the best path to develop well-rounded creators who can design entirely new systems and mechanics from the ground-up.

The aforementioned might lead us to ask, "What makes gameplay well formed?" At a fundamental level, a game is an interactive experience where rules must be learned and applied to achieve a specified outcome; all games must meet this minimum criterion, including card, board, physical, video, and other game types. Taking it a step further, a good game is an interactive experience with rules people enjoy learning and applying to achieve an outcome they feel invested in. There's quite a bit to unpack in this brief definition, of course, but as a general rule, players will enjoy a game more when the rules are discoverable, consistent, and make logical sense and when the outcome feels like a satisfactory reward for mastering those rules. This definition applies to both individual game mechanics and entire game experiences. To use a metaphor, it can be helpful to think of game designs as being built with letters (interactions) that form words (mechanics) that form sentences (levels) that ultimately form readable content (genres). Most new designers attempt to write novels before they know the alphabet, and everyone has played games where the mechanics and levels felt at best like sentences written with poor grammar and at worst like unsatisfying, random jumbles of unintelligible letters.

Over the next several chapters, you'll learn about more advanced features in 2D game engines, including simulations of illumination and physical behaviors. You'll also be introduced to a set of design techniques enabling you to deliver a complete and well-formed game level, integrating these techniques and utilizing more of the nine elements of game design discussed in Chapter 4 in an intentional way and working from the ground-up to deliver a unified experience. In the earliest stages of design exploration, it's often helpful to focus only on creating and refining the basic game mechanics and interaction model; at this stage, try to avoid thinking about setting, meta-game, systems design, and the like (these will be folded into the design as it progresses).

The first design technique we'll explore is a simple exercise that allows you to start learning the game design alphabet: an "escape the room" scenario with one simple mechanic, where you must accomplish a task in order to unlock a door and claim a reward. This exercise will help you develop insight into creating well-formed and logical rules that are discoverable and consistent, which is much easier to accomplish when the tasks are separated into basic interactions. You've already explored the beginnings of potential rule-based scenarios in earlier projects: recall the Keyboard Support project from Chapter 4, which suggested you might have players move a smaller square completely into the boundary of a larger square in order to trigger some kind of behavior. How might that single interaction (or "letter of the game alphabet") combine to form a game mechanic (or "word") that makes sense? Figure 7-13 sets the stage for the locked room puzzle.

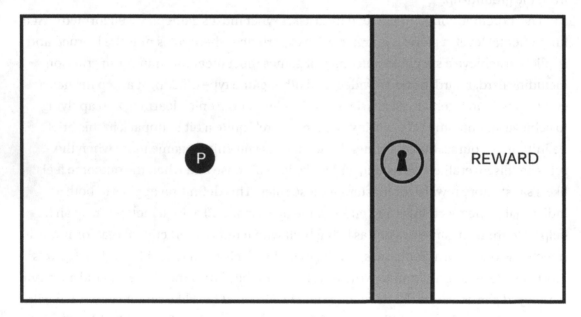

Figure 7-13. *The image represents a single game screen divided into three areas. A playable area on the left with a hero character (the circle marked with a P), an impassable barrier marked with a lock icon, and a reward area on the right*

The screen represented in Figure 7-13 is a useful starting place when exploring new mechanics. The goal for this exercise is to create one logical challenge that a player must complete to unlock the barrier and reach the reward. The specific nature of the task can be based on a wide range of elemental mechanics: it might involve jumping or shooting, puzzle solving, narrative situations, or the like. The key is to keep this first iteration simple (this first challenge should have a limited number of components contributing to the solution) and discoverable (players must be able to experiment and learn the rules of engagement so they can intentionally solve the challenge). You'll add complexity and interest to the mechanic in later iterations, and you'll see how elemental mechanics can be evolved to support many kinds of game types.

Figure 7-14 sets the stage for a logical relationship mechanic where players must interact with objects in the environment to learn the rules.

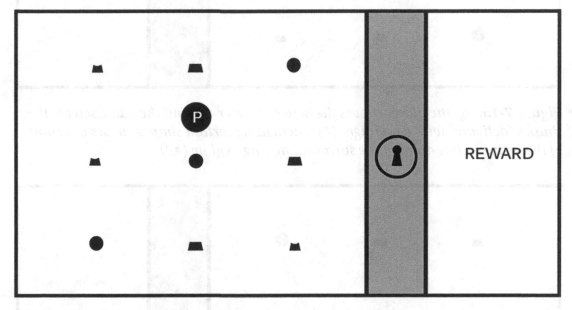

Figure 7-14. *The game screen is populated with an assortment of individual objects*

It's not immediately apparent just by looking at Figure 7-14 what the player needs to do to unlock the barrier, so they must experiment in order to learn the rules by which the game world operates; it's this experimentation that forms the core element of a game mechanic driving players forward through the level, and the mechanic will be more or less satisfying based on the discoverability and logical consistency of its rules. In this example, imagine that as the player moves around the game screen, they notice that when the hero character interacts with an object, it always "activates" with a highlight, as shown in Figure 7-15, and sometimes causes a section of the lock icon and one-third of the ring around the lock icon to glow. Some shapes, however, will not cause the lock and ring to glow when activated, as shown in Figure 7-16.

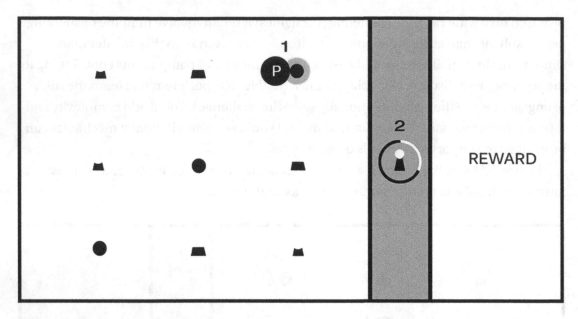

Figure 7-15. *As the player moves the hero character around the game screen, the shapes "activate" with a highlight (#1); activating certain shapes causes a section of the lock and one-third of the surrounding ring to glow (#2)*

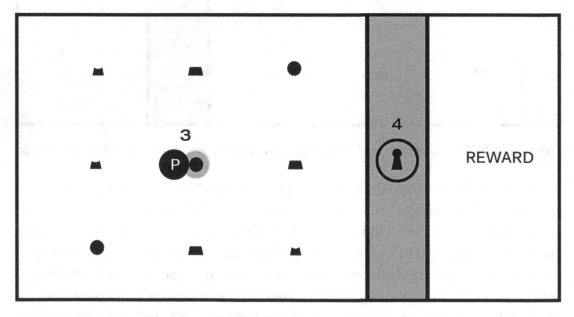

Figure 7-16. *Activating some shapes (#3) will not cause the lock and ring to glow (#4)*

Astute players will learn the rules for this puzzle fairly quickly. Can you guess what they might be just from looking at Figures 7-15 and 7-16? If you're feeling stuck, Figure 7-17 should provide enough information to solve the puzzle.

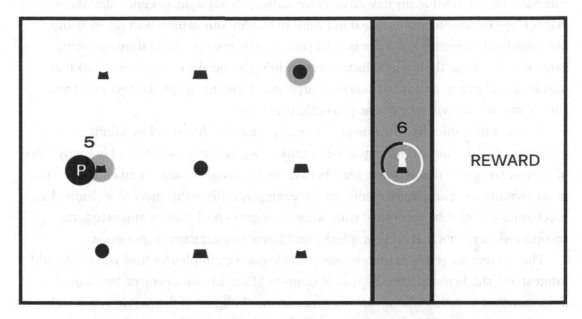

Figure 7-17. *After the first object was activated (the circle in the upper right) and caused the top section of the lock and first third of the ring to glow, as shown in Figure 7-15, the second object in the correct sequence (#5) caused the middle section of the lock and second third of the ring to glow (#6)*

You (and players) should now have all required clues to learn the rules of this mechanic and solve the puzzle. There are three shapes the player can interact with and only one instance of each shape per row; the shapes are representations of the top, middle, and bottom of the lock icon, and as shown in Figure 7-15, activating the circle shape caused the corresponding section of the lock to glow. Figure 7-16, however, did not cause the corresponding section of the lock to glow, and the difference is the "hook" for this mechanic: sections of the lock must be activated in the correct relative position: top in the top row, middle in the middle row, bottom on the bottom (you might also choose to require that players activate them in the correct sequence starting with the top section, although that requirement is not discoverable just from looking at Figures 7-15 to 7-17).

Congratulations, you've now created a well-formed and logically consistent (if simple) puzzle, with all of the elements needed to build a larger and more ambitious level! This unlocking sequence is a game mechanic without narrative context: the game screen is intentionally devoid of game setting, visual style, or genre alignment at this stage of design because we don't want to burden our exploration yet with any preconceived expectations. It can benefit you as a designer to spend time exploring game mechanics in their purest form before adding higher-level game elements like narrative and genre, and you'll likely be surprised at the unexpected directions, these simple mechanics will take you as you build them out.

Simple mechanics like the one in this example can be described as "complete a multistage task in the correct sequence to achieve a goal" and are featured in many kinds of games; any game that requires players to collect parts of an object and combine them in an inventory to complete a challenge, for example, utilizes this mechanic. Individual mechanics can also be combined with other mechanics and game features to form compound elements that add complexity and flavor to your game experience.

The camera exercises in this chapter provide good examples for how you might add interest to a single mechanic; the simple Camera Manipulations project, for example, demonstrates a method for advancing game action. Imagine in the previous example that after a player receives a reward for unlocking the barrier, they move the hero object to the right side of the screen and advance to a new "room" or area. Now imagine how gameplay would change if the camera advanced the screen at a fixed rate when the level started; the addition of autoscrolling changes this mechanic considerably because the player must solve the puzzle and unlock the barrier before the advancing barrier pushes the player off the screen. The first instance creates a leisurely puzzle-solving game experience, while the latter increases the tension considerably by giving the player a limited amount of time to complete each screen. In an autoscrolling implementation, how might you lay out the game screen to ensure the player had sufficient time to learn the rules and solve the puzzle?

The Multiple Cameras project can be especially useful as a mini-map that provides information about places in the game world not currently displayed on the game screen; in the case of the previous exercise, imagine that the locked barrier appeared somewhere else in the game world other than the player's current screen and that a secondary camera acting as a mini-map displayed a zoomed out view of the entire game world map. As the game designer, you might want to let the player know when they complete a task that allows them to advance and provide information about where they need to go next, so in this case, you might flash a beacon on the mini-map calling attention to the barrier that just unlocked and showing the player where to go. In the context of our "game design is like a written language" metaphor, adding additional elements like camera behavior to enhance or extend a simple mechanic is one way to begin forming "adjectives" that add interest to the basic nouns and verbs we've been creating from the letters in the game design alphabet.

A game designer's primary challenge is typically to create scenarios that require clever experimentation while maintaining logical consistency; it's perfectly fine to frustrate players by creating devious scenarios requiring creative problem solving (we call this "good" frustration), but it's generally considered poor design to frustrate players by creating scenarios that are logically inconsistent and make players feel that they succeeded in a challenge only by random luck ("bad" frustration). Think back to the games you've played that have resulted in bad frustration: where did they go wrong, and what might the designers have done to improve the experience?

The locked room scenario is a useful design tool because it forces you to construct basic mechanics, but you might be surprised at the variety of scenarios that can result from this exercise. Try a few different approaches to the locked room puzzle and see where the design process takes you, but keep it simple. For now, stay focused on one-step events to unlock the room that require players to learn only one rule. You'll revisit this exercise in the next chapter and begin creating more ambitious mechanics that add additional challenges.

CHAPTER 8

Implementing Illumination and Shadow

After completing this chapter, you will be able to

- Understand the parameters of simple illumination models

- Define infrastructure supports for working with multiple light sources

- Understand the basics of diffuse reflection and normal mapping

- Understand the basics of specular reflection and the Phong illumination model

- Implement GLSL shaders to simulate diffuse and specular reflection and the Phong illumination model

- Create and manipulate point, directional, and spotlights

- Simulate shadows with the WebGL stencil buffer

Introduction

Up until now in the game engine, you have implemented mostly functional modules in order to provide the fundamentals required for many types of 2D games. That is, you have developed engine components and utility classes that are designed to support the actual gameplay directly. This is a great approach because it allows you to systematically expand the capabilities of your engine to allow more types of games and gameplay. For instance, with the topics covered thus far, you can implement a variety of different games including puzzle games, top-down space shooters, and even simple platform games.

© Kelvin Sung, Jebediah Pavleas, Matthew Munson, and Jason Pace 2022
K. Sung et al., *Build Your Own 2D Game Engine and Create Great Web Games*,
https://doi.org/10.1007/978-1-4842-7377-7_8

An illumination model, or a lighting model, is a mathematical formulation that describes the color and brightness of a scene based on approximating light energy reflecting off the surfaces in the scene. In this chapter, you will implement an illumination model that indirectly affects the types of gameplay your game engine can support and the visual fidelity that can be achieved. This is because illumination support from a game engine can be more than a simple aesthetic effect. When applied creatively, illumination can enhance gameplay or provide a dramatic setting for your game. For example, you could have a scene with a torch light that illuminates an otherwise dark pathway for the hero, with the torch flickering to communicate a sense of unease or danger to the player. Additionally, while the lighting model is based on light behaviors in the physical world, in your game implementation, the lighting model allows surreal or physically impossible settings, such as an oversaturated light source that displays bright or iridescent colors or even a negative light source that absorbs visible energy around it.

When implementing illumination models commonly present in game engines, you will need to venture into concepts in 3D space to properly simulate light. As such, the third dimension, or depth, must be specified for the light sources to cast light energy upon the game objects, or the Renderable objects, which are flat 2D geometries. Once you consider concepts in 3D, the task of implementing a lighting model becomes much more straightforward, and you can apply knowledge from computer graphics to properly illuminate a scene.

A simplified variation of the Phong illumination model that caters specifically to the 2D aspect of your game engine will be derived and implemented. However, the principles of the illumination model remain the same. If you desire more information or a further in-depth analysis of the Phong illumination model, please refer to the recommended reference books from Chapter 1.

Overview of Illumination and GLSL Implementation

In general, an illumination model is one or a set of mathematical equations describing how humans observe the interaction of light with object materials in the environment. As you can imagine, an accurate illumination model that is based on the physical world can be highly complex and computationally expensive. The Phong illumination model captures many of the interesting aspects of light/material interactions with a relatively simple equation that can be implemented efficiently. The projects in this chapter guide you in understanding the fundamental elements of the Phong illumination model in the following order:

- **Ambient light**: Reviews the effects of lights in the absence of explicit light sources

- **Light source**: Examines the effect of illumination from a single light source

- **Multiple light sources**: Develop game engine infrastructure to support multiple light sources

- **Diffuse reflection and normal maps**: Simulate light reflection from matte or diffuse surfaces

- **Specular light and material**: Models light reflecting off shinning surfaces and reaching the camera

- **Light source types**: Introduce illumination based on different types of light sources

- **Shadow**: Approximates the results from light being blocked

Together, the projects in this chapter build a powerful tool for adding visual intricacy into your games. In order to properly render and display the results of illumination, the associated computation must be performed for each affected pixel. Recall that the GLSL fragment shader is responsible for computing the color of each pixel. In this way, each fundamental element of the Phong illumination model can be implemented as additional functionality to existing or new GLSL fragment shaders. In all projects of this chapter, you will begin by working with the GLSL fragment shader.

Ambient Light

Ambient light, often referred to as background light, allows you to see objects in the environment when there are no explicit light sources. For example, in the dark of night, you can see objects in a room even though all lights are switched off. In the real world, light coming from the window, from underneath the door, or from the background illuminates the room for you. A realistic simulation of the background light illumination, often referred to as indirect illumination, is algorithmically complex and can be computationally expensive. Instead, in computer graphics and most 2D games, ambient lighting is approximated by adding a constant color, or the ambient light, to every object within the current scene or world. It is important to note that while ambient lighting can provide the desired results, it is only a rough approximation and does not mimic real-world indirect lighting.

The Global Ambient Project

This project demonstrates how to implement ambient lighting within your scenes by defining a global ambient color and a global ambient intensity for drawing each Renderable object. You can see an example of this project running in Figure 8-1. The source code of this project is located in the chapter8/8.1.global_ambient folder.

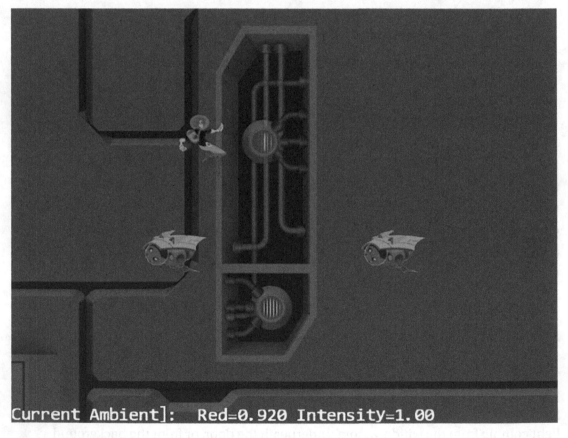

Figure 8-1. *Running the Global Ambient project*

The controls of the project are as follows:

- **Left mouse button**: Increases the global red ambient

- **Middle mouse button**: Decreases the global red ambient

- **Left-/right-arrow keys**: Decrease/increase the global ambient intensity

The goals of the project are as follows:

- To experience the effects of ambient lighting

- To understand how to implement a simple global ambient illumination across a scene

- To refamiliarize yourself with the `SimpleShader`/`Renderable` pair structure to interface to GLSL shaders and the game engine

You can find the following external resources in the `assets` folder. The `fonts` folder contains the default system fonts and two texture images: `minion_sprite.png`, which defines the sprite elements for the hero and the minions, and `bg.png`, which defines the background.

Modifying the GLSL Shaders

A good place to start when implementing new shaders or shading functionality for the game engine is the GLSL shader. The GLSL code creation or modification allows you to implement the actual functional details, which, in turn, serves as the requirements for expanding the engine. For example, in this project, you will begin by adding ambient lighting functionality to all existing GLSL shaders. The support for this newly added functionality then becomes the requirements that guide the modifications to the rest of the engine. You will observe this implementation pattern for all of the examples in this chapter. Thus, to begin, integrate the global ambient into your `simple_fs.glsl`.

1. Modify the fragment shader `simple_fs.glsl` by defining two new uniform variables `uGlobalAmbientColor` and `uGlobalAmbientIntensity` and multiplying these variables with the `uPixelColor` when computing the final color for each pixel:

```
precision mediump float;

// Color of pixel
uniform vec4 uPixelColor;
uniform vec4 uGlobalAmbientColor;  // this is shared globally
uniform float uGlobalAmbientIntensity;  // this is shared globally

void main(void) {
    // for every pixel called sets to the user specified color
    gl_FragColor = uPixelColor * uGlobalAmbientIntensity *
                              uGlobalAmbientColor;

}
```

2. Similarly, modify the texture fragment shader texture_fs.glsl by adding the uniform variables uGlobalAmbientColor and uGlobalAmbientIntensity. Multiply these two variables with the sampled texture color to create the background lighting effect.

```
uniform sampler2D uSampler;

// Color of pixel
uniform vec4 uPixelColor;
uniform vec4 uGlobalAmbientColor;  // this is shared globally
uniform float uGlobalAmbientIntensity;  // this is shared globally

varying vec2 vTexCoord;

void main(void)  {
    // texel color look up based on interpolated UV value in vTexCoord
    vec4 c = texture2D(uSampler, vec2(vTexCoord.s, vTexCoord.t));
    c = c * uGlobalAmbientIntensity * uGlobalAmbientColor;

    ... identical to previous code ...
}
```

Defining as Global Shared Resources

Ambient lighting affects the entire scene, and thus, the associated variables must be global and shared. In this case, the two variables, a color (ambient color) and a floating point (intensity of the color), should be globally accessible to the rest of the engine and to the clients. The defaultResources module is perfectly suited for this purpose. Edit the src/engine/resources/default_resources.js file and define the color and intensity variables, their corresponding getters and setters, and remember to export the functionality.

```
import * as font from "./font.js";
import * as map from "../core/resource_map.js";

// Global Ambient color
let mGlobalAmbientColor = [0.3, 0.3, 0.3, 1];
let mGlobalAmbientIntensity = 1;
function getGlobalAmbientIntensity() { return mGlobalAmbientIntensity; }
function setGlobalAmbientIntensity(v) { mGlobalAmbientIntensity = v; }
function getGlobalAmbientColor() { return mGlobalAmbientColor; }
function setGlobalAmbientColor(v) {
    mGlobalAmbientColor = vec4.fromValues(v[0], v[1], v[2], v[3]); }

... identical to previous code ...

export {
    init, cleanUp,

    // default system font name: this is guaranteed to be loaded
    getDefaultFontName,

    // Global ambient: intensity and color
    getGlobalAmbientColor, setGlobalAmbientColor,
    getGlobalAmbientIntensity, setGlobalAmbientIntensity
}
```

Modifying SimpleShader

With global ambient color and intensity now implemented in the GLSL shaders, you need to modify the rest of the game engine to support the newly defined functionality. Recall that simple_fs.glsl is referenced by the SimpleShader class and that texture_fs.glsl is referenced by the TextureShader class. Since TextureShader is a subclass of SimpleShader, the newly defined GLSL functionality in texture_fs.glsl will be supported with appropriate SimpleShader modifications.

1. Modify the `simple_shader.js` file in the `src/engine/shaders` folder to import from the `defaultResources` module for accessing the global ambient light effects variables:

```
import * as defaultResources from "../resources/default_resources.js";
```

2. Define two new instance variables in the constructor for storing the references or locations of the ambient color and intensity variables in the GLSL shader:

```
this.mGlobalAmbientColorRef = null;
this.mGlobalAmbientIntensityRef = null;
```

3. In step E of the `SimpleShader` constructor, call the WebGL `getUniformLocation()` function to query and store the locations of the uniform variables for ambient color and intensity in the GLSL shader:

```
// Step E: Gets references to the uniform variables
this.mPixelColorRef = gl.getUniformLocation(
                                this.mCompiledShader, "uPixelColor");
this.mModelMatrixRef = gl.getUniformLocation(
                                this.mCompiledShader, "uModelXformMatrix");
this.mCameraMatrixRef = gl.getUniformLocation(
                                this.mCompiledShader, "uCameraXformMatrix");
this.mGlobalAmbientColorRef = gl.getUniformLocation(
                                this.mCompiledShader, "uGlobalAmbientColor");
this.mGlobalAmbientIntensityRef = gl.getUniformLocation(
                                this.mCompiledShader, "uGlobalAmbientIntensity");
```

4. In the `activate()` function, retrieve the global ambient color and intensity values from the `defaultResources` module and pass to the corresponding uniform variables in the GLSL shader. Notice the data type-specific WebGL function names for setting uniform variables. As you can probably guess, `uniform4fv` corresponds to `vec4`, which is the color storage, and `uniform1f` corresponds to a float, which is the intensity.

```
activate(pixelColor, trsMatrix, cameraMatrix) {
    let gl = glSys.get();

    ... identical to previous code ...

    // load uniforms
    gl.uniformMatrix4fv(this.mCameraMatrixRef, false, cameraMatrix);
    gl.uniform4fv(this.mGlobalAmbientColorRef,
                    defaultResources.getGlobalAmbientColor());
    gl.uniform1f(this.mGlobalAmbientIntensityRef,
                    defaultResources.getGlobalAmbientIntensity());
}
```

Testing the Ambient Illumination

You can now define the MyGame class to verify the correctness of the newly defined ambient lighting effect. In anticipation of upcoming complexities in testing, the MyGame class source code will be separated into multiple files similar to your experience working with the Camera class in Chapter 7. All files implementing MyGame will have a name that begins with my_game and ends with an indication of the associated functionality defined in the file. For example, in later examples, my_game_light.js indicates that the file implements light source-related logic. For this project, similar to the Camera class naming scheme, the basic functionality of MyGame class will be implemented in my_game_main.js, and the access will be via the file my_game.js.

1. Create the MyGame class access file in src/my_game. For now, the MyGame functionality should be imported from the basic class implementation file, my_game_main.js. With full access to the MyGame class, it is convenient to define the webpage onload() function in this file.

```
import engine from "../engine/index.js";
import MyGame from "./my_game_main.js";

window.onload = function () {
    engine.init("GLCanvas");

    let myGame = new MyGame();
    myGame.start();
}
```

2. Create my_game_main.js; import from the engine access file, index.js, and from Hero and Minion; and remember to export the MyGame functionality. Now, as in all previous cases, define MyGame as a subclass of engine.Scene with the constructor that initializes instance variables to null.

```
import engine from "../engine/index.js";

// user stuff
import Hero from "./objects/hero.js";
import Minion from "./objects/minion.js";

class MyGame extends engine.Scene {
    constructor() {
        super();
        this.kMinionSprite = "assets/minion_sprite.png";
        this.kBg = "assets/bg.png";

        // The camera to view the scene
        this.mCamera = null;
        this.mBg = null;

        this.mMsg = null;

        // the hero and the support objects
        this.mHero = null;
        this.mLMinion = null;
        this.mRMinion = null;
    }

    ... implementation to follow ...

}

export default MyGame;
```

3. Load and unload the background and the minions:

```
load() {
    engine.texture.load(this.kMinionSprite);
    engine.texture.load(this.kBg);
}

unload() {
    engine.texture.unload(this.kMinionSprite);
    engine.texture.unload(this.kBg);
}
```

4. Initialize the camera and scene objects with corresponding values
    to ensure proper scene view at startup. Note the simple elements
    in the scene, the camera, the large background, a Hero, the left
    and right Minion objects, and the status message.

```
init() {
    // Step A: set up the cameras
    this.mCamera = new engine.Camera(
        vec2.fromValues(50, 37.5), // position of the camera
        100,                       // width of camera
        [0, 0, 640, 480]           // viewport (orgX, orgY, width, height)
    );
    this.mCamera.setBackgroundColor([0.8, 0.8, 0.8, 1]);
    // sets the background to gray

    let bgR = new engine.SpriteRenderable(this.kBg);
    bgR.setElementPixelPositions(0, 1900, 0, 1000);
    bgR.getXform().setSize(190, 100);
    bgR.getXform().setPosition(50, 35);
    this.mBg = new engine.GameObject(bgR);

    this.mHero = new Hero(this.kMinionSprite);

    this.mLMinion = new Minion(this.kMinionSprite, 30, 30);
    this.mRMinion = new Minion(this.kMinionSprite, 70, 30);
```

```
    this.mMsg = new engine.FontRenderable("Status Message");
    this.mMsg.setColor([1, 1, 1, 1]);
    this.mMsg.getXform().setPosition(1, 2);
    this.mMsg.setTextHeight(3);
}
```

5. Define the draw() function. As always, draw the status message last such that it will not be covered by any other object.

```
draw() {
    // Clear the canvas
    engine.clearCanvas([0.9, 0.9, 0.9, 1.0]); // clear to light gray

    // Set up the camera and draw
    this.mCamera.setViewAndCameraMatrix();
    this.mBg.draw(this.mCamera);
    this.mHero.draw(this.mCamera);
    this.mLMinion.draw(this.mCamera);
    this.mRMinion.draw(this.mCamera);

    this.mMsg.draw(this.mCamera);    // draw last
}
```

6. Lastly, implement the update() function to update all objects and receive controls over global ambient color and intensity:

```
update() {
    let deltaAmbient = 0.01;
    let msg = "Current Ambient]: ";

    this.mCamera.update();   // ensure proper interpolated movement
    this.mLMinion.update(); // ensure sprite animation
    this.mRMinion.update();
    this.mHero.update();   // allow keyboard control to move
    this.mCamera.panWith(this.mHero.getXform(), 0.8);

    let v = engine.defaultResources.getGlobalAmbientColor();
    if (engine.input.isButtonPressed(engine.input.eMouseButton.eLeft))
        v[0] += deltaAmbient;
```

```
    if (engine.input.isButtonPressed(engine.input.eMouseButton.eMiddle))
        v[0] -= deltaAmbient;

    if (engine.input.isKeyPressed(engine.input.keys.Left))
        engine.defaultResources.setGlobalAmbientIntensity(
                engine.defaultResources.getGlobalAmbientIntensity() -
                                                    deltaAmbient);

    if (engine.input.isKeyPressed(engine.input.keys.Right))
        engine.defaultResources.setGlobalAmbientIntensity(
                engine.defaultResources.getGlobalAmbientIntensity() +
                                                    deltaAmbient);

    msg += " Red=" + v[0].toPrecision(3) + " Intensity=" +
        engine.defaultResources.getGlobalAmbientIntensity().toPrecision(3);
    this.mMsg.setText(msg);
}
```

Observations

You can now run the project and observe the results. Notice that the initial scene is dark. This is because the RGB values for the global ambient color were all initialized to 0.3. Since the ambient color is multiplied by the color sampled from the textures, the results are similar to applying a dark tint across the entire scene. The same effect can be accomplished if the RGB values were set to 1.0 and the intensity was set 0.3 because the two sets of values are simply multiplied.

Before moving onto the next project, try fiddling with the ambient red channel and the ambient intensity to observe their effects on the scene. By pressing the right-arrow key, you can increase the intensity of the entire scene and make all objects more visible. Continue with this increment and observe that when the intensity reaches values beyond 15.0, all colors in the scene converge toward white or begin to oversaturate. Without proper context, oversaturation can be a distraction. However, it is also true that strategically creating oversaturation on selective objects can be used to indicate significant events, for example, triggering a trap. The next section describes how to create and direct a light source to illuminate selected objects.

Light Source

Examine your surroundings and you can observe many types of light sources, for example, your table lamp, light rays from the sun, or an isolated light bulb. The isolated light bulb can be described as a point that emits light uniformly in all directions or a point light. The point light is where you will begin to analyze light sources.

Fundamentally, a point light illuminates an area or radius around a specified point. In 3D space, this region of illumination is simply a sphere, referred to as a volume of illumination. The volume of illumination of a point light is defined by the position of the light, or the center of the sphere, and the distance that the light illuminates, or the radius of the sphere. To observe the effects of a light source, objects must be present and within the volume of illumination.

As mentioned in the introduction of this chapter, the 2D engine will need to venture into the third dimension to properly simulate the propagation of light energy. Now, consider your 2D engine; thus far, you have implemented a system in which everything is in 2D. An alternative way is to interpret that the engine defines and renders everything on a single plane where z = 0 and objects are layered by drawing order. On this system, you are going to add light sources that reside in 3D.

To observe the effects of a light source, its illumination volume must overlap an object on the XY plane where your objects are defined. Figure 8-2 shows the volume of illumination from a simple point light located at z = 10 intersecting a plane at z = 0. This intersection results in an illuminated circle on the plane. The next project implements Figure 8-2 where you will examine light sources with an object-oriented approach while adhering to the expectations of how a light illuminates a scene. This can be achieved through the definition of a Light object to represent a light source.

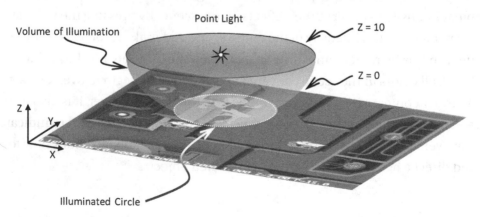

Figure 8-2. *Point light and the corresponding volume of illumination in 3D*

GLSL Implementation and Integration into the Game Engine

Recall that the engine interfaces to the GLSL shaders with the corresponding subclasses of the SimpleShader/Renderable pairs. SimpleShader and its subclasses interface to the GLSL shaders and Renderable, and its subclasses provide programmers with the convenience of manipulating many copies of geometries with the same shader type. For example, texture_vs.glsl and texture_fs.glsl are interfaced to the game engine via the TextureShader object, and the TextureRenderable objects allow game programmers to create and manipulate multiple instances of geometries shaded by the texture_vs/fs shaders. Figure 8-3 depicts that the next project extends this architecture to implement point light illumination. The Light class encapsulates the attributes of a point light including position, radius, and color. This information is forwarded to the GLSL fragment shader, light_fs, via the LightShader/LightRenderable pair for computing the appropriate pixel colors. The GLSL vertex shader, texture_vs, is reused because light source illumination involves the same information to be processed at each vertex.

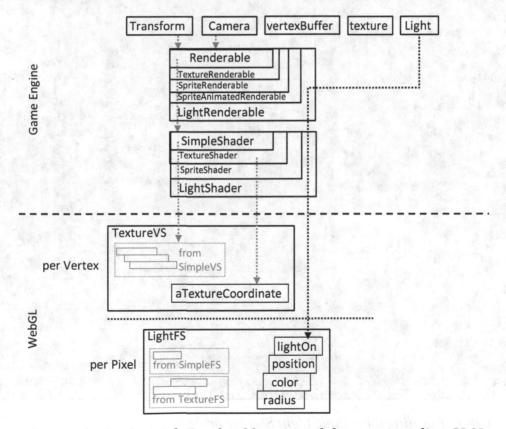

Figure 8-3. *LightShader/LightRenderable pair and the corresponding GLSL LightShader*

Finally, it is important to remember that the GLSL fragment shader is invoked once for every pixel covered by the corresponding geometry. This means that the GLSL fragment shaders you are about to create will be invoked many times per frame, probably in the range of hundreds of thousands or even millions. Considering the fact that the game loop initiates redrawing at a real-time rate, or around 60 frame redraws per second, the GLSL fragment shaders will be invoked many millions of times per second! The efficiency of the implementation is important for a smooth experience.

The Simple Light Shader Project

This project demonstrates how to implement and illuminate with a simple point light. You can see an example of this project running in Figure 8-4. The source code of this project is located in the chapter8/8.2.simple_light_shader folder.

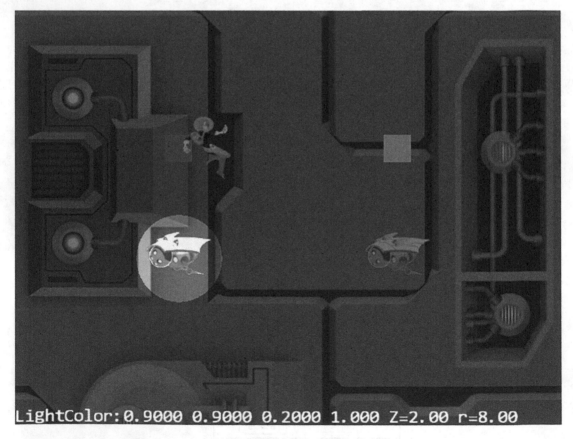

Figure 8-4. *Running the Simple Light Shader project*

The controls of the project are as follows:

- **WASD keys**: Move the hero character on the screen

- **WASD keys + left mouse button**: Move the hero character and the light source around the screen

- **Left-/right-arrow key**: Decreases/increases the light intensity

- **Z/X key**: Increases/decreases the light Z position

- **C/V key**: Increases/decreases the light radius

The goals of the project are as follows:

- To understand how to simulate the illumination effects from a point light

- To observe point light illumination

- To implement a GLSL shader that supports point light illumination

Creating the GLSL Light Fragment Shader

As with the previous section, the implementation will begin with the GLSL shader. It is not necessary to define a new GLSL vertex shader as the per vertex information and computation involved are identical to that of texture_vs. A new GLSL fragment shader must be defined to compute the illuminated circle.

1. In the src/glsl_shaders folder, create a new file and name it light_fs.glsl.

2. Refer to texture_fs.glsl and copy all uniform and varying variables. This is an important step because the light_fs fragment shader will interface to the game engine via the LightShader class. The LightShader class, in turn, will be implemented as a subclass of TextureShader, where the existence of these variables is assumed.

```
precision mediump float;

// The object that fetches data from texture.
// Must be set outside the shader.
uniform sampler2D uSampler;
```

```
// Color of pixel
uniform vec4 uPixelColor;
uniform vec4 uGlobalAmbientColor; // this is shared globally
uniform float uGlobalAmbientIntensity;

// "varying" keyword signifies that the texture coordinate will be
// interpolated and thus varies.
varying vec2 vTexCoord;

... implementation to follow ...
```

3. Now, define the variables to support a point light: on/off switch, color, position, and radius. It is important to note that the position and radius are in units of pixels.

```
// Light information
uniform bool uLightOn;
uniform vec4 uLightColor;
uniform vec3 uLightPosition;   // in pixel space!
uniform float uLightRadius;    // in pixel space!
```

4. Implement the light illumination in the main() function as follows:

   a. Step A, sample the texture color and apply the ambient color and intensity.

   b. Step B, perform the light source illumination. This is accomplished by determining if the computation is required—testing if the light is switched on and if the pixel is nontransparent. If both are favorable, the distance between the light position and the current pixel is compared with the light radius to determine if the pixel is inside the volume of illumination. Note that gl_FragCord.xyz is the GLSL-defined variable for current pixel position and that this computation assumes pixel-space units. When all conditions are favorable, the color of the light is accumulated to the final results.

    c. The last step is to apply the tint and to set the final color via
       gl_FragColor.

```
void main(void) {
    // Step A: sample the texture and apply ambient
    vec4 textureMapColor = texture2D(uSampler,
                                        vec2(vTexCoord.s, vTexCoord.t));
    vec4 lgtResults = uGlobalAmbientIntensity * uGlobalAmbientColor;

    // Step B:  decide if the light should illuminate
    if (uLightOn && (textureMapColor.a > 0.0)) {
        float dist = length(uLightPosition.xyz - gl_FragCoord.xyz);
        if (dist <= uLightRadius)
            lgtResults += uLightColor;
    }
    lgtResults *= textureMapColor;

    // Step C: tint texture leave transparent area defined by texture
    vec3 r = vec3(lgtResults) * (1.0-uPixelColor.a) +
            vec3(uPixelColor) * uPixelColor.a;
    vec4 result = vec4(r, textureMapColor.a);

    gl_FragColor = result;
}
```

Defining a Light Class

With the GLSL light_fs shader defined, you can now define a class to encapsulate a point light source for the game engine:

1. Create a new lights folder in the src/engine folder. In the lights folder, add a new file and name it lights.js.

2. Edit lights.js to create the Light class, and define the constructor to initialize the light color, position, radius, and on/off status. Remember to export the class.

```
class Light {

    constructor() {
        this.mColor = vec4.fromValues(0.1, 0.1, 0.1, 1);  // light color
        this.mPosition = vec3.fromValues(0, 0, 5); // WC light position
        this.mRadius = 10;   // effective radius in WC
        this.mIsOn = true;
    }

    ... implementation to follow ...

}
export default Light;
```

3. Define the getters and setters for the instance variables:

```
// simple setters and getters
setColor(c) { this.mColor = vec4.clone(c); }
getColor() { return this.mColor; }

set2DPosition(p) {
    this.mPosition = vec3.fromValues(p[0], p[1], this.mPosition[2]); }
setXPos(x) { this.mPosition[0] = x; }
setYPos(y) { this.mPosition[1] = y; }
setZPos(z) { this.mPosition[2] = z; }
getPosition() { return this.mPosition; }

setRadius(r) { this.mRadius = r; }
getRadius() { return this.mRadius; }

setLightTo(isOn) { this.mIsOn = isOn; }
isLightOn() { return this.mIsOn; }
```

Lastly, remember to update the engine access file, index.js, to forward the newly defined functionality to the client.

Defining the LightShader Class

The LightShader class subclasses from the SpriteShader to encapsulate the communication of the values that are specific to the uniform variables defined for a point light source in the light_fs fragment shader. In this way, the LightShader class can serve as a convenient interface for the GLSL fragment shader.

1. In the src/engine/shaders folder, create a new file and name it light_shader.js.

2. Define the LightShader class to be a subclass of SpriteShader. In the constructor, define the necessary variables to support sending the information associated with a point light to the light_fs fragment shader. The point light information in the engine is stored in mLight, while the reference to the Camera is important to convert all information from WC to pixel space. The last four lines of the constructor query to obtain the reference locations to the uniform variables in light_fs. Don't forget to export the class.

```
import SpriteShader from "./sprite_shader.js";
import * as glSys from "../core/gl.js";

class LightShader extends SpriteShader {
    constructor(vertexShaderPath, fragmentShaderPath) {
        // Call super class constructor
        super(vertexShaderPath, fragmentShaderPath);

        // glsl uniform position references
        this.mColorRef = null;
        this.mPosRef = null;
        this.mRadiusRef = null;
        this.mIsOnRef = null;

        this.mLight = null;  // the light source in the Game Engine
        this.mCamera = null; // camera to draw, need for WC to DC xform
        //
        // create the references to these uniforms in the LightShader
        let shader = this.mCompiledShader;
        let gl = glSys.get();
```

417

```
        this.mColorRef = gl.getUniformLocation(shader, "uLightColor");
        this.mPosRef = gl.getUniformLocation(shader, "uLightPosition");
        this.mRadiusRef = gl.getUniformLocation(shader, "uLightRadius");
        this.mIsOnRef = gl.getUniformLocation(shader, "uLightOn");
    }

    ... implementation to follow ...

}
export default LightShader;
```

3. Define a simple setter function to associate a light and camera
    with the shader:

```
setCameraAndLight(c, l) {
    this.mCamera = c;
    this.mLight = l;
}
```

4. Override the activate() function to append the new functionality
    of loading the point light information in mLight when the light is
    present. Notice that you still call the activate() function of the
    super class to communicate the rest of the values to the uniform
    variables of the light_fs fragment shader.

```
activate(pixelColor, trsMatrix, cameraMatrix) {
    // first call the super class' activate
    super.activate(pixelColor, trsMatrix, cameraMatrix);

    if (this.mLight !== null) {
        this._loadToShader();
    } else {
        glSys.get().uniform1i(this.mIsOnRef, false); // switch off light!
    }
}
```

5. Implement the _loadToShader() function to communicate the values of the point light to the uniform variables in the shader. Recall that this communication is performed via the references created in the constructor and the set uniform functions. It is important to note that the camera provides the new coordinate space transformation functionality of wcPosToPixel() and wcSizeToPixel(). These two functions ensure corresponding values in the light_fs are in pixel space such that relevant computations such as distances between positions can be performed. The implementation of these functions will be examined shortly.

```
_loadToShader(aCamera) {
    let gl = glSys.get();
    gl.uniform1i(this.mIsOnRef, this.mLight.isLightOn());
    if (this.mLight.isLightOn()) {
        let p = this.mCamera.wcPosToPixel(this.mLight.getPosition());
        let r = this.mCamera.wcSizeToPixel(this.mLight.getRadius());
        let c = this.mLight.getColor();

        gl.uniform4fv(this.mColorRef, c);
        gl.uniform3fv(this.mPosRef, vec3.fromValues(p[0], p[1], p[2]));
        gl.uniform1f(this.mRadiusRef, r);
    }
}
```

Defining the LightRenderable Class

With LightShader defined to interface to the GLSL light_fs shader, you can now focus on defining a new Renderable class for the game programmer. It is important that a light can shine on and illuminate all Renderable types, including those with texture and animated sprites. For this reason, the new class must encapsulate all existing Renderable functionality and be a subclass of SpriteAnimateRenderable. You can think of this new class as a SpriteAnimateRenderable that can be illuminated by a Light object.

1. Create a new file in the src/engine/renderables folder and name it light_renderable.js.

2. Define the LightRenderable class to extend SpriteAnimateRenderable, set the shader to reference the new LightShader, and initialize a Light reference in the constructor. This is the light that shines and illuminates the SpriteAnimateRenderable. Don't forget to export the class.

```
import SpriteAnimateRenderable from "./sprite_animate_renderable.js";
import * as defaultShaders from "../core/shader_resources.js";

class LightRenderable extends SpriteAnimateRenderable {

    constructor(myTexture) {
        super(myTexture);
        super._setShader(defaultShaders.getLightShader());

        // here is the light source
        this.mLight = null;
    }

    ... implementation to follow ...

}
export default LightRenderable;
```

3. Define a draw function to pass the camera and illuminating light source to the LightShader before invoking the superclass draw() function to complete the drawing:

```
draw(camera) {
    this.mShader.setCameraAndLight(camera, this.mLight);
    super.draw(camera);
}
```

4. Lastly, simply add the support to get and set the light:

```
getLight() { return this.mLight; }
addLight(l) { this.mLight = l; }
```

Before moving on, remember to update the engine access file, index.js, to forward the newly defined functionality to the client.

Defining a Default LightShader Instance

As discussed, when you first defined TextureShader (Chapter 5), only a single instance is required for each shader type, and all the shaders are always hidden from the game programmer by a corresponding Renderable type. Each instance of the shader type is created during engine initialization by the shaderResources module in the src/engine/core folder.

You can now modify the engine to support the initializing, loading, and unloading of a LightShader object to be shared engine-wide:

1. Edit shader_resources.js in the src/engine/core folder to import LightShader; define the path to the GLSL source code, a corresponding variable and access function for the shader:

```
... identical to previous code ...
import LightShader from "../shaders/light_shader.js";

// Light Shader
let kLightFS = "src/glsl_shaders/light_fs.glsl"; // FragmentShader
let mLightShader = null;

function getLightShader() { return mLightShader; }
```

2. Create a new instance of light shader in the createShaders() function:

```
function createShaders() {
    mConstColorShader = new SimpleShader(kSimpleVS, kSimpleFS);
    mTextureShader = new TextureShader(kTextureVS, kTextureFS);
    mSpriteShader = new SpriteShader(kTextureVS, kTextureFS);
    mLineShader =  new LineShader(kSimpleVS, kLineFS);
    mLightShader = new LightShader(kTextureVS, kLightFS);
}
```

3. Load the light shader GLSL source code in the init() function:

```
function init() {
    let loadPromise = new Promise(
        async function(resolve) {
            await Promise.all([
```

```
            text.load(kSimpleFS),
            text.load(kSimpleVS),
            text.load(kTextureFS),
            text.load(kTextureVS),
            text.load(kLineFS),
            text.load(kLightFS)
        ]);
        resolve();
    }).then(
        function resolve() { createShaders(); }
    );
    map.pushPromise(loadPromise);
}
```

4. Remember to release GLSL resources and unload the source code during cleanup:

```
function cleanUp() {
    mConstColorShader.cleanUp();
    mTextureShader.cleanUp();
    mSpriteShader.cleanUp();
    mLineShader.cleanUp();
    mLightShader.cleanUp();

    text.unload(kSimpleVS);
    text.unload(kSimpleFS);
    text.unload(kTextureVS);
    text.unload(kTextureFS);
    text.unload(kLineFS);
    text.unload(kLightFS);
}
```

5. Lastly, export the access function to allow sharing of the created instance in the engine:

```
export {init, cleanUp,
    getConstColorShader, getTextureShader,
    getSpriteShader, getLineShader, getLightShader}
```

Modifying the Camera

The Camera utility functions, such as wcPosToPixel(), are invoked multiple times while rendering the LightShader object. These functions compute the transformation between WC and pixel space. This transformation requires the computation of intermediate values, for example, lower-left corner of WC window, that do not change during each rendering invocation. To avoid repeated computation of these values, a per-render invocation cache should be defined for the Camera object.

Defining a Per-Render Cache for the Camera

Define a per-render cache to store intermediate values that are required to support shading operations:

1. Edit camera_main.js and define a PerRenderCache class; in the constructor, define variables to hold the ratio between the WC space and the pixel space as well as the origin of the Camera. These are intermediate values required for computing the transformation from WC to pixel space, and these values do not change once rendering begins.

```
class PerRenderCache {
    // Information to be updated once per render for efficiency concerns
    constructor() {
        this.mWCToPixelRatio = 1;  // WC to pixel transformation
        this.mCameraOrgX = 1; // Lower-left corner of camera in WC
        this.mCameraOrgY = 1;
    }
}
```

2. Modify the Camera class to instantiate a new PerRenderCache object. It is important to note that this variable represents local caching of information and should be hidden from the rest of the engine.

```
constructor(wcCenter, wcWidth, viewportArray, bound) {

    ... identical to previous code ...
```

423

```
    // per-rendering cached information
    // needed for computing transforms for shaders
    // updated each time in SetupViewProjection()
    this.mRenderCache = new PerRenderCache();
        // SHOULD NOT be used except
        // xform operations during the rendering
        // Client game should not access this!
}
```

3. Initialize the per-render cache in the setViewAndCameraMatrix() function by adding a step B3 to calculate and set the cache based on the Camera viewport width, world width, and world height:

```
setViewAndCameraMatrix() {

    ... identical to previous code ...

    // Step B2: first operation is to translate camera center to origin
    mat4.translate(this.mCameraMatrix, this.mCameraMatrix,
                    vec3.fromValues(-center[0], -center[1], 0));

    // Step B3: compute and cache per-rendering information
    this.mRenderCache.mWCToPixelRatio =
                    this.mViewport[eViewport.eWidth] / this.getWCWidth();
    this.mRenderCache.mCameraOrgY = center[1] - (this.getWCHeight() / 2);
    this.mRenderCache.mCameraOrgX = center[0] - (this.getWCWidth() / 2);
}
```

Notice that the PerRenderCache class is completely local to the camera_main.js file. It is important to hide and carefully handle complex local caching functionality.

Adding Camera Transform Functions

Now that the per-render cache is defined and properly initialized, you can extend the functionality of the camera to support transformations from WC to pixel space. For code readability and maintainability, this functionality will be implemented in a separate file. Another important note is that since you are converting from WC to pixel space and pixel space has no z axis, you need to calculate a *fake* z value for the pixel space coordinate.

1. Edit the Camera access file, `camera.js`, to import from the file, `camera_xform.js`, which will contain the latest functionality additions, the WC to pixel space transform support:

```
import Camera from "./camera_xform.js";
export default Camera;
```

2. In the src/engine/cameras folder, create a new file and name it `camera_xform.js`. Import from `camera_input.js` such that you can continue to add new functionality to the Camera class, and do not forget to export.

```
import Camera from "./camera_input.js";
import { eViewport } from "./camera_main.js";

... implementation to follow ...

export default Camera;
```

3. Create a function to approximate a fake pixel space z value by scaling the input parameter according to the `mWCToPixelRatio` variable:

```
Camera.prototype.fakeZInPixelSpace = function (z) {
    return z * this.mRenderCache.mWCToPixelRatio;
}
```

4. Define a function to convert from WC to pixel space by subtracting the camera origin followed by scaling with the `mWCToPixelRatio`. The 0.5 offset at the end of the x and y conversion ensures that you are working with the center of the pixel rather than a corner.

```
Camera.prototype.wcPosToPixel = function (p) {  // p is a vec3, fake Z
    // Convert the position to pixel space
    let x = this.mViewport[eViewport.eOrgX] +
            ((p[0] - this.mRenderCache.mCameraOrgX) *
            this.mRenderCache.mWCToPixelRatio) + 0.5;
    let y = this.mViewport[eViewport.eOrgY] +
            ((p[1] - this.mRenderCache.mCameraOrgY) *
```

```
                this.mRenderCache.mWCToPixelRatio) + 0.5;
    let z = this.fakeZInPixelSpace(p[2]);
    return vec3.fromValues(x, y, z);
}
```

5. Lastly, define a function for converting a length from WC to pixel space by scaling with the mWCToPixelRatio variable:

```
Camera.prototype.wcSizeToPixel = function (s) {  //
    return (s * this.mRenderCache.mWCToPixelRatio) + 0.5;
}
```

Testing the Light

The MyGame level must be modified to utilize and test the newly defined light functionality.

Modifying the Hero and Minion

Modify the Hero and Minion classes to accommodate the new LightRenderable object:

1. Edit the hero.js file in the src/my_game/objects folder; in the constructor, replace the SpriteRenderable with a LightRenderable instantiation:

```
constructor(spriteTexture) {
    super(null);
    this.kDelta = 0.3;
    this.mRenderComponent = new engine.LightRenderable(spriteTexture);
    ... identical to previous code ...
}
```

2. Edit the minion.js file in the src/my_game/objects folder; in the constructor, replace the SpriteRenderable with a LightRenderable instantiation:

```
constructor(spriteTexture, atX, atY) {
    super(null);
    this.kDelta = 0.2;
```

```
    this.mRenderComponent = new engine.LightRenderable(spriteTexture);
    ... identical to previous code ...
}
```

Modifying the MyGame Object

With the implementation of the light completed and the game objects properly updated, you can now modify the MyGame level to display and test the light source. Because of the simplistic and repetitive nature of the code changes in the my_game_main.js file of adding variables for the new objects, initializing the objects, drawing the objects, and updating the objects, the details will not be shown here.

Observations

With the project now complete, you can run it and examine the results. There are a few observations to take note of. First is the fact that the illuminated results from the light source look like a circle. As depicted in Figure 8-2, this is the illuminated circle of the point light on the z = 0 plane where your objects are located. Press the Z or X key to increase or decrease the light's z position to observe that the illuminated circle decreases and increases in size as a result of intersection area changes. The sphere/plane intersection result can be verified when you continue to increase/decrease the z position. The illuminated circle will eventually begin to decrease in size and ultimately disappear completely when the sphere is moved more than its radius away from the z=0 plane.

You can also press the C or V key to increase or decrease the point light radius to increase or decrease the volume of illumination, and observe the corresponding changes in the illuminated circle radius.

Now, press the WASD keys along with the left mouse button to move the Hero and observe that the point light always follow the Hero and properly illuminates the background. Notice that the light source illuminates the left minion, the hero, and the background but not the other three objects in the scene. This is because the right minion and the red and green blocks are not LightRenderable objects and thus cannot be illuminated by the defined light source.

Multiple Light Sources and Distance Attenuation

In the previous project, a single point light source was defined with the capability of illuminating a spherical volume. This type of light source is useful in many games, but it is restrictive to be limited to only a single light source. The engine should support the illumination from multiple light sources to fulfill the design needs of different games. This shortcoming is remedied in the next project with general support for multiple light sources. The implementation principle for multiple lights remains the same as the previous project, with the modification of replacing the single light source with an array of lights. As illustrated in Figure 8-5, a new Light object will be defined, while the LightRenderable object will be modified to support an array of the Light objects. The LightShader object will define an array of ShaderLightAtIndex objects that are capable of communicating light source information to the uLights array in the GLSL light_fs fragment shader for illumination computations.

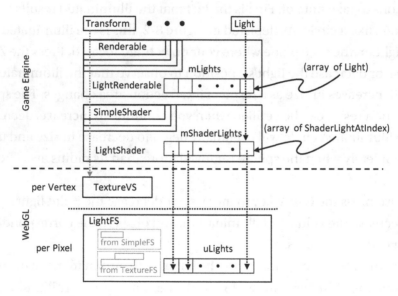

Figure 8-5. *Support for multiple light sources*

The point light illumination results from the previous project can be improved. You have observed that at its boundary, the illuminated circle disappears abruptly with a sharp brightness transition. This sudden disappearance of illumination results does not reflect real life where effects from a given light source decrease gradually over distance instead of switching off abruptly. A more visually pleasing light illumination result should show an illuminated circle where the illumination results at the boundary disappear gradually. This gradual decrease of light illumination effect over distance is referred to as distance attenuation. It is a common practice to approximate distant attenuation with quadratic functions because they produce effects that resemble the real world. In general, distance attenuation can be approximated in many ways, and it is often refined to suit the needs of the game.

In the following, you will implement a near and far cutoff distance, that is, two distances from the light source at which the distance attenuation effect will begin and end. These two values give you control over a light source to show a fully illuminated center area with illumination drop-off occurring only at a specified distance. Lastly, a light intensity will be defined to allow the dimming of light without changing its color. With these additional parameters, it becomes possible to define dramatically different effects. For example, you can have a soft, barely noticeable light that covers a wide area or an oversaturated glowing light that is concentrated over a small area in the scene.

The Multiple Lights Project

This project demonstrates how to implement multiple point lights within a single scene. It also demonstrates how to increase the sophistication of your point light model so that they are more flexible to serve a wider variety of purposes. You can see an example of this project running in Figure 8-6. The source code of this project is located in the chapter8/8.3.multiple_lights folder.

Selected Light=0 On(true) P(21 58 5.0) R(20.0/50.0) I(5.

Figure 8-6. *Running the Multiple Lights project*

The controls of the project are as follows:

- **WASD keys**: Move the hero character on the screen

- **Number keys 0, 1, 2, and 3**: Select the corresponding light source

- **Arrow keys**: Move the currently selected light

- **Z/X keys**: Increase/decrease the light z position

- **C/V and B/N keys**: Increase/decrease the near and far cutoff distances of the selected light

- **K/L keys**: Increase/decrease the intensity of the selected light

- **H key**: Toggles the selected light on/off

The goals of the project are as follows:

- To build the infrastructure for supporting multiple light sources in the engine and GLSL shaders

- To understand and examine the distance attenuation effects of light

- To experience controlling and manipulating multiple light sources in a scene

Modifying the GLSL Light Fragment Shader

The light_fs fragment shader needs to be modified to support the distance attenuation, cutoffs, and multiple light sources:

1. In the light_fs.glsl file, remove the light variables that were added for a single light and add a struct for light information that holds the position, color, near-distance, far-distance, intensity, and on/off variables. With the struct defined, add a uniform array of lights to the fragment shader. Notice that a #define has been added to hold the number of light sources to be used.

Note   GLSL requires array sizes and the number of loop iterations to be constants. The kGLSLuLightArraySize is the constant for light array size and the corresponding loop iteration control. Feel free to change this value to define as many lights as the hardware can support. For example, you can try increasing the number of lights to 50 and then test and measure the performance.

```
// Light information
#define kGLSLuLightArraySize 4
    // GLSL Fragment shader requires loop control
    // variable to be a constant number. This number 4
    // says, this fragment shader will _ALWAYS_ process
    // all 4 light sources.
    // **********WARNING*********************
    // This number must correspond to the constant with
    // the same name defined in LightShader.js file.
```

```
    // **********WARNING**************************
    // To change this number MAKE SURE: to update the
    //     kGLSLuLightArraySize
    // defined in LightShader.js file.
struct Light {
    vec3 Position;    // in pixel space!
    vec4 Color;
    float Near;       // distance in pixel space
    float Far;        // distance in pixel space
    float Intensity;
    bool IsOn;
};
uniform Light uLights[kGLSLuLightArraySize];
        // Maximum array of lights this shader supports
```

2. Define LightEffect() function to compute the illumination
    results from a light source. This function uses the distance
    between the light and the current pixel to determine whether the
    pixel lies within the near radius, in between near and far radii, or
    farther than the far radius. If the pixel position lies within the near
    radius, there is no attenuation, so the strength is set to 1. If the
    position is in between the near and far radii, then the strength is
    modulated by a quadratic function. A distance of greater than the
    far radius will result in no illumination from the corresponding
    light source, or a strength of 0.

```
vec4 LightEffect(Light lgt) {
    vec4 result = vec4(0);
    float strength = 0.0;
    float dist = length(lgt.Position.xyz - gl_FragCoord.xyz);
    if (dist <= lgt.Far) {
        if (dist <= lgt.Near)
            strength = 1.0;  //  no attenuation
        else {
            // simple quadratic drop off
            float n = dist - lgt.Near;
```

```
            float d = lgt.Far - lgt.Near;
            strength = smoothstep(0.0, 1.0, 1.0-(n*n)/(d*d));
                            // blended attenuation
        }
    }
    result = strength * lgt.Intensity * lgt.Color;
    return result;
}
```

3. Modify the main function to iterate through all the defined light
   sources and call the LightEffect() function to calculate and
   accumulate the contribution from the corresponding light in the
   array:

```
void main(void) {
    // simple tint based on uPixelColor setting
    vec4 textureMapColor = texture2D(uSampler,
                                vec2(vTexCoord.s, vTexCoord.t));
    vec4 lgtResults = uGlobalAmbientIntensity * uGlobalAmbientColor;

    // now decide if we should illuminate by the light
    if (textureMapColor.a > 0.0) {
        for (int i=0; i<kGLSLuLightArraySize; i++) {
            if (uLights[i].IsOn) {
                lgtResults +=  LightEffect(uLights[i]);
            }
        }
    }
    lgtResults *= textureMapColor;

    ... identical to previous code ...
}
```

Modifying the Light Class

The game engine Light object must be modified to reflect the newly added properties in
the light_fs fragment shader: near and far attenuations and intensity.

1. Modify the Lights.js constructor to define variables for the new properties:

```
constructor() {
    this.mColor = vec4.fromValues(0.1, 0.1, 0.1, 1);  // light color
    this.mPosition = vec3.fromValues(0, 0, 5); // light position in WC
    this.mNear = 5;  // effective radius in WC
    this.mFar = 10;  // within near is full on, outside far is off
    this.mIntensity = 1;
    this.mIsOn = true;
}
```

2. Define the corresponding get and set accessors for the variables. Note that the radius variable has been generalized and replaced by the near and far cutoff distances.

```
setNear(n) { this.mNear = n; }
getNear() { return this.mNear; }

setFar(f) { this.mFar = f; }
getFar() { return this.mFar; }

setIntensity(i) { this.mIntensity = i; }
getIntensity() { return this.mIntensity; }

setLightTo(on) { this.mIsOn = on; }
```

Defining the LightSet Class

You will define a LightSet class to facilitate the working with a collection of Light objects. In the src/engine/lights folder, create a new file and name it light_set.js. Define the basic interface for working with a set of Light objects.

```
class LightSet {
    constructor() { this.mSet = []; }

    numLights() { return this.mSet.length; }

    getLightAt(index) { return this.mSet[index]; }
```

```
    addToSet(light) { this.mSet.push(light); }
}
export default LightSet;
```

Lastly, don't forget to export the class and remember to update the engine access file, index.js, to forward the newly defined functionality to the client.

Defining the ShaderLightAt Class

Define the ShaderLightAt class to send information from a Light object to an element in the uLights array in the light_fs GLSL fragment shader:

1. In the src/engine/shaders folder, create a new file and name it shader_light_at.js; define the ShaderLightAt class and the constructor to receive a shader and an index to the uLight array. Don't forget to export the class.

```
import * as glSys from "../core/gl.js";

class ShaderLightAt {
    constructor(shader, index) {
        this._setShaderReferences(shader, index);
    }

    ... implementation to follow ...
}
export default ShaderLightAt;
```

2. Implement the _setShaderReferences() function to set the light property references to a specific index in the uLights array in the light_fs fragment shader:

```
_setShaderReferences(aLightShader, index) {
    let gl = glSys.get();
    this.mColorRef = gl.getUniformLocation(
                        aLightShader, "uLights[" + index + "].Color");
    this.mPosRef = gl.getUniformLocation(
                        aLightShader, "uLights[" + index + "].Position");
    this.mNearRef = gl.getUniformLocation(
                        aLightShader, "uLights[" + index + "].Near");
```

```
    this.mFarRef = gl.getUniformLocation(
                        aLightShader, "uLights[" + index + "].Far");
    this.mIntensityRef = gl.getUniformLocation(
                        aLightShader, "uLights[" + index + "].Intensity");
    this.mIsOnRef = gl.getUniformLocation(
                        aLightShader, "uLights[" + index + "].IsOn");
}
```

3. Implement the `loadToShader()` function to push the properties of a light to the `light_fs` fragment shader. Notice that this function is similar to the `_loadToShader()` function defined in the `light_shader.js` file from previous project. The important difference is that in this case, light information is loaded to a specific array index.

```
loadToShader(aCamera, aLight) {
    let gl = glSys.get();
    gl.uniform1i(this.mIsOnRef, aLight.isLightOn());
    if (aLight.isLightOn()) {
        let p = aCamera.wcPosToPixel(aLight.getPosition());
        let n = aCamera.wcSizeToPixel(aLight.getNear());
        let f = aCamera.wcSizeToPixel(aLight.getFar());
        let c = aLight.getColor();
        gl.uniform4fv(this.mColorRef, c);
        gl.uniform3fv(this.mPosRef, vec3.fromValues(p[0], p[1], p[2]));
        gl.uniform1f(this.mNearRef, n);
        gl.uniform1f(this.mFarRef, f);
        gl.uniform1f(this.mIntensityRef, aLight.getIntensity());
    }
}
```

4. Define a simple function to update the on/off status of the light in the array of the `light_fs` fragment shader:

```
switchOffLight() {
    let gl = glSys.get();
    gl.uniform1i(this.mIsOnRef, false);
}
```

Note that the ShaderLightAt class is defined for loading a light to a specific array element in the GLSL fragment shader. This is an internal engine operation. There is no reason for the game programmer to access this class, and thus, the engine access file, index.js, should not be modified to forward the definition of this class.

Modifying the LightShader Class

You must now modify the LightShader object to properly handle the communication between the Light object and the array of lights in the light_fs fragment shader:

1. Begin by editing the light_shader.js file, importing ShaderLightAt, and *removing* the _loadToShader() function. The actual loading of light information to the light_fs fragment shader is now handled by the newly defined ShaderLightAt objects.

```
import ShaderLightAt from "./shader_light_at.js";
```

2. Modify the constructor to define mLights, which is an array of ShaderLightAt objects to correspond to the uLights array defined in the light_fs fragment shader. It is important to note that the mLights and uLights arrays must be the exact same size.

```
constructor(vertexShaderPath, fragmentShaderPath) {
    // Call super class constructor
    super(vertexShaderPath, fragmentShaderPath);

    this.mLights = null;  // lights from the Renderable
    this.mCamera = null;  // camera to draw, need for WC to DC xform

    //*******WARNING**************
    // MUST correspond to GLSL uLight[] array size (for LightFS.glsl)
    //*******WARNING********************
    this.kGLSLuLightArraySize = 4;  // must be the same as LightFS.glsl
    this.mShaderLights = [];
    let i, ls;
    for (i = 0; i < this.kGLSLuLightArraySize; i++) {
        ls = new ShaderLightAt(this.mCompiledShader, i);
        this.mShaderLights.push(ls);
    }
}
```

3. Modify the activate() function to iterate and load the contents of
    each ShaderLightAt object to the light_fs shader by calling the
    corresponding loadToShader() function. Recall that the GLSL
    fragment shader requires the for-loop control variable to be a
    constant. This implies that all elements of the uLights array will
    be processed on each light_fs invocation. For this reason, it is
    important to ensure all unused lights are switched off. This is
    ensured by the last while loop in the following code:

```
activate(pixelColor, trsMatrix, cameraMatrix) {
    // first call the super class' activate
    super.activate(pixelColor, trsMatrix, cameraMatrix);

    // now push the light information to the shader
    let numLight = 0;
    if (this.mLights !== null) {
        while (numLight < this.mLights.length) {
            this.mShaderLights[numLight].loadToShader(
                                this.mCamera, this.mLights[numLight]);
            numLight++;
        }
    }
    // switch off the left over ones.
    while (numLight < this.kGLSLuLightArraySize) {
        this.mShaderLights[numLight].switchOffLight(); // off the un-use
        numLight++;
    }
}
```

4. Rename the setCameraAndLight() function to
    setCameraAndLights(); in addition to setting the corresponding
    variables, check to ensure that the light array size is not greater
    than the defined array size in the light_fs fragment shader.
    Lastly, remember to update the corresponding function name in
    sprite_shader.js.

```
setCameraAndLights(c, l) {
    this.mCamera = c;
    this.mLights = l;
    if (this.mLights.length > this.kGLSLuLightArraySize)
        throw new Error ("Error: " ...);
}
```

Modifying the LightRenderable Class

You can now modify the LightRenderable class to support multiple light sources:

1. In the LightRenderable constructor, replace the single light
    reference variable with an array:

```
constructor(myTexture) {
    super(myTexture);
    super._setShader(defaultShaders.getLightShader());

    // the light sources
    this.mLights = [];
}
```

2. Make sure to update the draw function to reflect the change to
    multiple light sources:

```
draw(camera) {
    this.mShader.setCameraAndLights(camera, this.mLights);
    super.draw(camera);
}
```

3. Define the corresponding accessor functions for the light array:

```
getLightAt(index) { return this.mLights[index]; }
addLight(l) { this.mLights.push(l); }
```

Testing the Light Sources with MyGame

With proper integration for multiple lights support in the engine, you can now modify
MyGame to test your implementation and examine the results. In addition to adding
multiple lights to the scene, you will be adding the ability to control the properties of

each light. In order to maintain readability, you will divide the light instantiation and controls into separate files. To avoid redundancy and repetitive code listings, the details to the straightforward implementations are not shown.

1. Modify the my_game_main.js file in the src/my_game folder to reflect the changes to the constructor, initialize function, draw function, and update function. All these changes revolve around handling multiple lights through a light set.

2. In the src/my_game folder, create the new file my_game_lights. js to import MyGame class from my_game_main.js and to add functionality to instantiate and initialize the lights.

3. In the src/my_game folder, create the new file my_game_light_ control.js to import from my_game_lights.js and to continue to add controls of the lights to MyGame.

4. Modify my_game.js to import from my_game_light_control.js ensuring access to all of the newly defined functionality.

Observations

Run the project to examine the implementation. Try selecting the lights with the 0, 1, 2, and 3 keys and toggling the selected light on/off. Notice that the game programmer has control over which light illuminates which of the objects: all lights illuminate the background, while the hero is illuminated only by lights 0 and 3, the left minion is illuminated only by lights 1 and 3, and the right minion is illuminated only by lights 2 and 3.

Move the Hero object with the WASD keys to observe how the illumination changes as it is moved through the near and far radii of light source 0. With light source 0 selected (type 0), press the C key to increase the near radius of the light. Notice that as the near radius approaches the value of the far, the illuminated circle boundary edge also becomes sharper. Eventually, when near radius is greater than far radius, you can once again observe the sudden brightness change at the boundary. You are observing the violation of the implicit assumption of the underlying illumination model that the near is always less than the far radius. This exact situation can be created by decreasing the far radius with the N key.

You can move the light sources with the arrow keys to observe the additive property of lights. Experiment with changing the light source's z position and its near/far values to observe how similar illumination effects can be accomplished with different z/near/far settings. In particular, try adjusting light intensities with the K/L keys to observe the effects of oversaturation and barely noticeable lighting. You can continue to press the L key till the intensity becomes negative to create a source that removes color from the scene. The two constant color squares are in the scene to confirm that nonilluminated objects can still be rendered.

Diffuse Reflection and Normal Mapping

You can now place or move many light sources and control the illumination or shading at targeted regions. However, if you run the previous project and move one of the light sources around, you may notice some peculiar effects. Figure 8-7 highlights these effects by comparing the illumination results from the previous project on the left to an illumination that you probably expect on the right. Now, refer to the image on the left. First, take note of the general uniform lighting within the near cutoff region where the expected brighter spot around the position of the point light source cannot be observed. Second, examine the vertical faces of the geometric block and take note of the bright illumination on the bottom face that is clearly behind, or *pointing away from*, the light source. Both of these peculiarities are absent from the right image in Figure 8-7.

Although visually odd, results from the left image of Figure 8-7 are to be expected in a 2D world. The vertical faces are only artist renditions, and your illumination calculation does not consider the geometric contours suggested by the image content. This restriction of illumination in a flat 2D world is remedied in this section with the introduction of diffuse reflection and normal mapping to approximate normal vectors of surfaces.

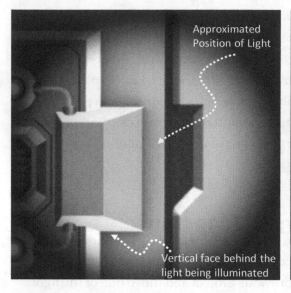
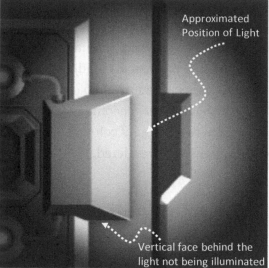

Figure 8-7. *Left: from previous project. Right: expected illumination*

As illustrated by the left drawing in Figure 8-8, a surface normal vector, a surface normal, or a normal vector is the vector that is perpendicular to a given surface element. The right drawing of Figure 8-8 shows that in 3D space, the surface normal vectors of an object describe the shape or contour of the object.

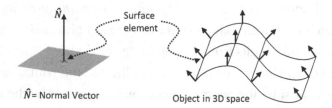

Figure 8-8. *Surface normal vectors of an object*

A human's observation of light illumination is the result of visible energy from light sources reflecting off object surfaces and reaching the eyes. A diffuse, matte, or Lambertian surface reflects light energy uniformly in all directions. Examples of diffuse surfaces include typical printer papers or matte-painted surfaces. Figure 8-9 shows a light source illuminating three diffuse surface element positions, A, B, and C. First, notice that the direction from the position being illuminated toward the light source is defined as the light vector, $\hat{L}$, at the position. It is important to note that the direction of the $\hat{L}$ vector is always toward the light source and that this is a normalized vector with a magnitude of 1.

Figure 8-9 also illustrates the diffuse illumination, or magnitude of diffuse reflection, with examples. Position A cannot receive any energy from the given light source because its normal vector, $\hat{N}$, is perpendicular to its light vector $\hat{L}$, or $\hat{N} \cdot \hat{L} = 0$. Position B can receive all the energy because its normal vector is pointing in the same direction as its light vector, or $\hat{N} \cdot \hat{L} = 1$. In general, as exemplified by position C, the proportion of light energy received and reflected by a diffuse surface is proportional to the cosine of the angle between its normal and the light vector, or $\hat{N} \cdot \hat{L}$. In an illumination model, the term with the $\hat{N} \cdot \hat{L}$ computation is referred to as the diffuse, or Lambertian, component.

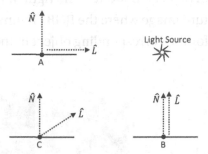

Figure 8-9. *Normal and light vectors and diffuse illumination*

The human vision system deduces 3D geometric shape contours based significantly on $\hat{N} \cdot \hat{L}$, or the diffuse component. For example, Figure 8-10 shows a sphere and torus (doughnut shape object) with (the left images) and without (the right images) the corresponding diffuse components. Clearly, in both cases, the 3D contour of the objects is captured by the left versions of the image with the diffuse component.

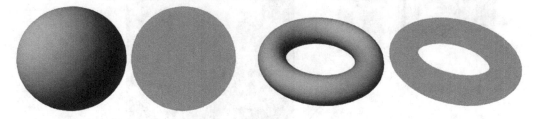

Figure 8-10. *Examples of 3D objects with and without diffuse component*

In a 2D world, as in the case of your game engine, all objects are represented as 2D images, or textures. Since all objects are 2D textured images defined on the xy plane, the normal vectors for all the objects are the same: a vector in the z direction. This lack of distinct normal vectors for objects implies that it is not possible to compute a distinct diffuse component for objects. Fortunately, similar to how texture mapping addresses the limitation of each geometry having only a single color, normal mapping can resolve the issue of each geometry having only a single normal vector.

Figure 8-11 shows the idea behind normal mapping where in addition to the color texture image, a corresponding normal texture image is required. The left image of Figure 8-11 is a typical color texture image, and the two right images are zoomed images of the highlighted square on the left image. Notice once again that two images are involved in normal mapping: the color texture image where the RGB channels of the texture record the color of objects (bottom of the right image of Figure 8-11) and a corresponding normal texture image where the RGB channels record the x, y, and z values of the normal vector for the corresponding object in the color texture (top of the right image).

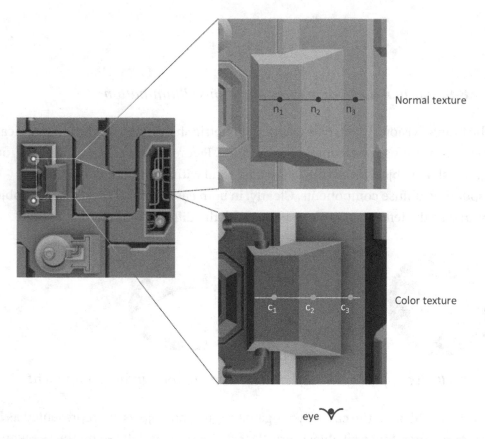

Figure 8-11. *Normal mapping with two texture images: the normal and the color texture*

Figure 8-12 captures the view of the three corresponding positions labeled on the right images of Figure 8-11, the positions n_1, n_2, and n_3 on the normal texture and the corresponding positions c_1, c_2, and c_3 on the color texture, to illustrate the details of normal mapping. The bottom layer of Figure 8-12 shows that the color texture records colors and the colors c_1, c_2, and c_3 are sampled at those three positions. The middle layer of Figure 8-12 shows that the RGB components of the normal texture record the normal vector xyz values of objects at the corresponding color texture positions. The top layer of Figure 8-12 shows that when illuminated by a light source, with the $\hat{N} \cdot \hat{L}$ term properly computed and displayed, the human vision system will perceive a sloped contour.

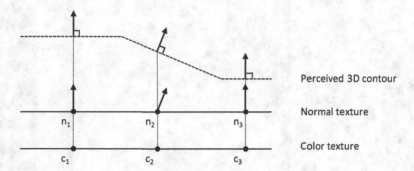

Figure 8-12. *Normal mapping with two texture images: the normal and the color texture*

In summary, a normal texture map or a normal map is a texture map that stores normal vector information rather than the usual color information. Each texel of a normal map encodes the xyz values of a normal vector in the RGB channels. In lieu of displaying the normal map texels as you would with a color texture, the texels are used purely for calculating how the surface would interact with light. In this way, instead of a constant normal vector pointing in the z direction, when a square is normal mapped, the normal vector of each pixel being rendered will be defined by texels from the normal map and can be used for computing the diffuse component. For this reason, the rendered image will display contours that resemble the shapes encoded in the normal map.

In the previous project, you expanded the engine to support multiple light sources. In this section, you will define the `IllumShader` class to generalize a `LightShader` to support the computation of the diffuse component based on normal mapping.

The Normal Maps and Illumination Shaders Project

This project demonstrates how to integrate normal mapping into your game engine and use the results to compute the diffuse component of objects. You can see an example of this project running in Figure 8-13. The source code of this project is located in the chapter8/8.4.normal_maps_and_illumination_shaders folder.

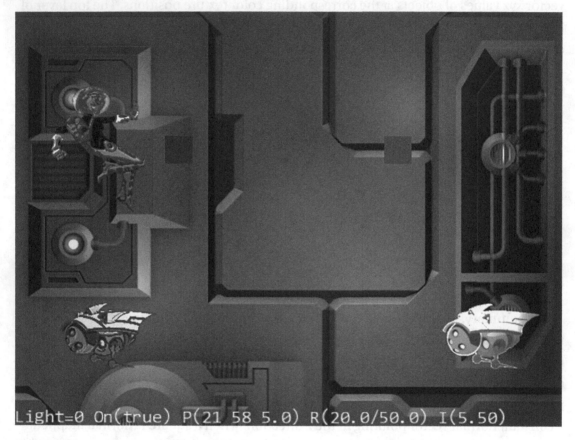

Light=0 On(true) P(21 58 5.0) R(20.0/50.0) I(5.50)

Figure 8-13. *Running the Normal Maps and Illumination Shaders project*

The controls of the project are identical to the previous project:

- **WASD keys**: Move the hero character on the screen

- **Number keys 0, 1, 2, and 3**: Select the corresponding light source

- **Arrow keys**: Move the currently selected light

- **Z/X key**: Increases/decreases the light z position

- **C/V and B/N keys**: Increases/decreases the near and far cutoff distances of the selected light

- **K/L key**: Increases/decreases the intensity of the selected light

- **H key**: Toggles the selected light on/off

The goals of the project are as follows:

- To understand and work with normal maps

- To implement normal maps as textures in the game engine

- To implement GLSL shaders that support diffuse component illumination

- To examine the diffuse, $\hat{N} \cdot \hat{L}$, component in an illumination model

You can find the following external resource files in the `assets` folder. The `fonts` folder contains the default system fonts, two texture images, and two corresponding normal maps for the texture images, `minion_sprite.png` and `bg.png`, and the corresponding normal maps, `minion_sprite_normal.png` and `bg_normal.png`. As in previous projects, the objects are sprite elements of `minion_sprite.png`, and the background is represented by `bg.png`.

Note   The `minion_sprite_normal.png` normal map is generated algorithmically from `http://cpetry.github.io/NormalMap-Online/` based on the `minion_sprite.png` image.

Creating the GLSL Illumination Fragment Shader

As with the previous projects, your normal map integration will begin with the implementation of the GLSL shader. Note that this new shader will be remarkably similar to your `light_fs.glsl` but with the inclusion of normal mapping and diffuse computation support. To ensure the support for simple lighting without normal mapping, you will create a new GLSL fragment shader.

1. Begin by copying from light_fs.glsl and pasting to a new file, illum_fs.glsl, in the src/glsl_shaders folder.

2. Edit the illum_fs.glsl file and add a sampler2D object, uNormalSampler, to sample the normal map:

```
uniform sampler2D uSampler;
uniform sampler2D uNormalSampler;
```

```
... identical to the variables declared in light_fs.glsl ...
```

3. Modify the LightEffect() function to receive a normal vector parameter, N. This normal vector N is assumed to be normalized with a magnitude of 1 and will be used in the diffuse component $\hat{N} \cdot \hat{L}$ computation. Enter the code to compute the $\hat{L}$ vector, remember to normalize the vector, and use the result of $\hat{N} \cdot \hat{L}$ to scale the light strength accordingly.

```
vec4 LightEffect(Light lgt, vec3 N) {
    vec4 result = vec4(0);
    float strength = 0.0;
    vec3 L = lgt.Position.xyz - gl_FragCoord.xyz;
    float dist = length(L);
    if (dist <= lgt.Far) {
        if (dist <= lgt.Near) {
            ... identical to previous code ...
        }
        L = L / dist; // To normalize L
            // Not calling normalize() function to avoid re-computing
            // "dist". This is computationally more efficient.
        float NdotL = max(0.0, dot(N, L));
        strength *= NdotL;
    }
    result = strength * lgt.Intensity * lgt.Color;
    return result;
}
```

4. Edit the main() function to sample from both the color texture with
    uSampler and the normal texture with uNormalSampler. Remember
    that the normal map provides you with a vector that represents the
    normal vector of the surface element at that given position. Because
    the xyz normal vector values are stored in the 0 to 1 RGB color
    format, the sampled normal map results must be scaled and offset
    to the -1 to 1 range. In addition, recall that texture uv coordinates
    can be defined with the v direction increasing upward or downward.
    In this case, depending on the v direction of the normal map, you
    may also have to flip the y direction of the sampled normal map
    values. The normalized normal vector, N, is then passed on to the
    LightEffect() function for the illumination calculations.

```
void main(void) {
    // simple tint based on uPixelColor setting
    vec4 textureMapColor = texture2D(uSampler, vTexCoord);
    vec4 normal = texture2D(uNormalSampler, vTexCoord); // same UV
    vec4 normalMap = (2.0 * normal) - 1.0;

    //
    // normalMap.y = -normalMap.y;  // flip Y
    //    depending on the normal map you work with,
    //    this may or may not be flipped
    //
    vec3 N = normalize(normalMap.xyz);

    vec4 lgtResult = uGlobalAmbientColor * uGlobalAmbientIntensity;

    // now decide if we should illuminate by the light
    if (textureMapColor.a > 0.0) {
        for (int i=0; i<kGLSLuLightArraySize; i++) {
            if (uLights[i].IsOn) {
                lgtResult += LightEffect(uLights[i], N);
            }
        }
    }
    ... identical to previous code ...
}
```

> **Note**   Normal maps can be created in a variety of different layouts where x or y might need to be flipped in order to properly represent the desired surface geometries. It depends entirely upon the tool or artist that created the map.

Defining the IllumShader Class

With the `Illum_fs` fragment shader supporting normal maps, you can create the JavaScript `IllumShader` class to interface with it:

1. In the src/engine/shaders folder, create illum_shader.js, and define `IllumShader` to be a subclass of `LightShader` to take advantage of the functionality related to light sources. In the constructor, define a variable, `mNormalSamplerRef`, to maintain the reference to the normal sampler in the `illum_fs` fragment shader. Don't forget to export the class.

```
import LightShader from "./light_shader.js";
import * as glSys from "../core/gl.js";

class IllumShader extends LightShader {
    constructor(vertexShaderPath, fragmentShaderPath) {
        super(vertexShaderPath, fragmentShaderPath);
        let gl = glSys.get();
        // reference to the normal map sampler
        this.mNormalSamplerRef = gl.getUniformLocation(
                            this.mCompiledShader, "uNormalSampler");
    }
    ... implementation to follow ...
}
export default IllumShader;
```

2. Override and extend the `activate()` function to binding the normal texture sampler reference to WebGL texture unit 1. You may recall from Chapter 5 that `TextureShader` binds the color texture sampler to texture unit 0. By binding normal mapping to texture unit 1,

the WebGL texture system can work concurrently with two active textures: units 0 and 1. As will be discussed in the next subsection, it is important to configure WebGL, via the texture module, to activate the appropriate texture units for the corresponding purpose: color vs. normal texture mapping.

```
activate(pixelColor, trsMatrix, cameraMatrix) {
    // first call the super class' activate
    super.activate(pixelColor, trsMatrix, cameraMatrix);
    let gl = glSys.get();
    gl.uniform1i(this.mNormalSamplerRef, 1); // binds to texture unit 1
    // do not need to set up texture coordinate buffer
    // as we are going to use the ones from the sprite texture
    // in the fragment shader
}
```

Note   WebGL supports simultaneous activation of multiple texture units during rendering. Depending on the GPU, a minimum of eight texture units can be active simultaneously during a single rendering pass. In this book, you will activate only two of the texture units during rendering: one for color texture and the other for normal texture.

Modifying the Texture Module

So far, you have been binding the color texture map to WebGL texture unit 0. With the addition of the normal texture, the binding to the unit of WebGL texture system must now be parameterized. Fortunately, this is a straightforward change.

Modify the texture module by opening texture.js in the src/engine/resources folder. Edit the activate() function to accept a second parameter, the WebGL texture unit to bind to. Notice that this is an optional parameter with the default value set to texture unit 0. This is such that no changes are required for any of the existing calls to the activate() function.

```
function activate(textureName, textureUnit = glSys.get().TEXTURE0) {
    let gl = glSys.get();
    let texInfo = get(textureName);

    // Binds texture reference to current webGL texture functionality
    gl.activeTexture(textureUnit);  // activate the WebGL texture unit
    gl.bindTexture(gl.TEXTURE_2D, texInfo.mGLTexID);

    ... identical to previous code ...
}
```

Creating the IllumRenderable Class

You can now define the illumination Renderable class to leverage the newly created illumination shader:

1. Begin by creating illum_renderable.js in the src/engine/ renderables folder, defining the IllumRenderable class to subclass from LightRenderable, and initializing a mNormalMap instance variable to record the normal map ID. The IllumRenderable object works with two texture maps: myTexture for color texture map and myNormalMap for normal mapping. Note that these two texture maps share the same texture coordinates defined in mTexCoordBuffer in the SpriteShader. This sharing of texture coordinate implicitly assumes that the geometry of the object is depicted in the color texture map and the normal texture map is derived to capture the contours of the object, which is *almost* always the case. Lastly, don't forget to export the class.

```
import * as texture from "../resources/texture.js";
import * as glSys from "../core/gl.js";
import LightRenderable from "./light_renderable.js";
import * as defaultShaders from "../core/shader_resources.js";

class IllumRenderable extends LightRenderable {
    constructor(myTexture, myNormalMap) {
        super(myTexture);
        super._setShader(defaultShaders.getIllumShader());
```

```
        // here is the normal map resource id
        this.mNormalMap = myNormalMap;

        // Normal map texture coordinate is same as sprite sheet
        // This means, the normal map MUST be based on the sprite sheet
    }
    ... implementation to follow ...
}

export default IllumRenderable;
```

Note   Once again, it is important to reiterate that the normal texture map is an image that must be created explicitly by an artist or algorithmically by an appropriate program. Using a regular color texture map image as a normal texture map will not work in general.

---

2.   Next, override the draw() function to activate the normal map before calling the draw() method of the super class. Notice the second argument of the texture.activate() function call where the WebGL texture unit 1 is explicitly specified. In this way, with IllumShader linking uNormalSampler to WebGL texture unit 1 and illum_fs sampling the uNormalSampler as a normal map, your engine now supports proper normal mapping.

```
draw(camera) {
    texture.activate(this.mNormalMap, glSys.get().TEXTURE1);
    // Here the normal map texture coordinate is copied from those of
    // the corresponding sprite sheet
    super.draw(camera);
}
```

Lastly, remember to update the engine access file, index.js, to forward the newly defined functionality to the client.

Defining a Default IllumShader Instance

Similar to all other shaders in the engine, a default instance of the `IllumShader` must be defined to be shared. The code involved in defining the default `IllumShader` instance is identical to that of `LightShader` presented earlier in this chapter, with the straightforward exception of substituting the corresponding variable names and data type. Please refer to the "Defining a Default LightShader Instance" subsection and the `shader_resources.js` source code file in the `src/engine/core` folder for details.

Testing the Normal Map

Testing the newly integrated normal map functionality must include the verification that the non-normal mapped simple color texture is working correctly. To accomplish this, the background, hero, and left minion will be created as the newly defined `IllumRenderable` object, while the right minion will remain a `LightRenderable` object.

Modifying the Hero and the Minion

The `Hero` and `Minion` objects should be instantiated as the newly defined `IllumRenderable` object:

1. Edit `hero.js` in `src/my_game/objects` to modify the constructor of the `Hero` class to instantiate the game object with an `IllumRenderable`:

```
constructor(spriteTexture, normalMap) {
    super(null);
    this.kDelta = 0.3;
    this.mRenderComponent = new engine.IllumRenderable(
                                    spriteTexture, normalMap);
    this.mRenderComponent.setColor([1, 1, 1, 0]);
    ... identical to previous code ...
}
```

2. In the same folder, edit `minion.js` to modify the constructor of `Minion` class to conditionally instantiate the game object with either a `LightRenderable` or an `IllumRenderable` when the normal texture map is present:

```
constructor(spriteTexture, normalMap, atX, atY) {
    super(null);
    this.kDelta = 0.2;

    if (normalMap === null) {
        this.mRenderComponent = new engine.LightRenderable(
                                            spriteTexture);
    } else {
        this.mRenderComponent = new engine.IllumRenderable(
                                            spriteTexture, normalMap);
    }

    ... identical to previous code ...
}
```

Modifying MyGame

You can now modify MyGame to test and display your implementation of the illumination shader. Modify the my_game_main.js file in the src/my_game folder to load and unload the new normal maps and to create the Hero and Minion objects with the normal map files. As previously, the involved changes are straightforward and relatively minimal; as such, the details are not shown here.

Observations

With the project now completed, you can run it and check your results to observe the effects of diffuse illumination. Notice that the Hero, left Minion, and the background objects are illuminated with a diffuse computation and appear to provide more depth from the lights. There is much more variation of colors and shades across these objects.

You can verify that the peculiar effects observed on the left image of Figure 8-7 is resolved. For a clearer observation, switch off all other lights (type the light number followed the H key) except leaving light 2 switched on. Now, move the light position (with the arrow keys) to illuminate the geometric block behind the Hero character; you can move it away with the WASD keys. Verify that you are viewing similar results to those in the right image of Figure 8-7. You should be able to clearly observe the brightest spot that corresponds to the point light position. Additionally, take note that the bottom face on the block is only illuminated when the light position is *in front of* the face or when the diffuse term, $\hat{N} \cdot \hat{L}$, is positive.

In general, as you move the light source, observe faces with vertical orientations, for example, the side faces of the geometric block or gaps. As the light position moves across such a boundary, the sign of the $\hat{N} \cdot \hat{L}$ term would flip, and the corresponding surface illumination would undergo drastic changes (from dark to lit, or vice versa). For a more dramatic result, lower the z height of the light (with the X key) to a value lower than 5. With the normal map and diffuse computation, you have turned a static background image into a background that is defined by complex 3D geometric shapes. Try moving the other light sources and observe the illumination changes on all the objects as the light sources move across them.

Lastly, the slightly pixelated and rough appearances of the Hero and left Minion attest to the fact that the normal maps for these objects are generated algorithmically from the corresponding color images and that the maps are not created by an artist.

Specular Reflection and Materials

The diffuse lighting you have implemented is suitable for simulating the illumination of matte surfaces such as typical printer papers, many painted interior walls, or even a traditional blackboard. The Phong illumination model extends this simple diffuse lighting by introducing a specular term to simulate the reflection of the light source across a shiny surface. Figure 8-14 shows an example of three spheres, a simple matte sphere, a sphere with moderate specular highlights, and a highly polished sphere. The highlights on the two spheres to the right are results of the Phong specular term.

Figure 8-14. *Specularity and shininess of objects*

Figure 8-15 illustrates that given a shiny or reflective surface like a polished floor or a polished plastic, the reflection of the light source will be visible when the eye, or the camera, is in the reflection direction of the light source. This reflection of the light source across a shiny surface is referred to as *specular reflection, specular highlight*, or *specularity*.

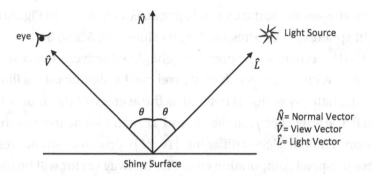

Figure 8-15. *Specularity: the reflection of the light source*

From real-life experience, you know that specular highlights are visible even when the eye's viewing direction is not perfectly aligned with the reflection direction of the light source. As illustrated in Figure 8-16, where the $\hat{R}$ vector is the reflection direction of the light vector $\hat{L}$, the specular highlight on an object is visible even when the viewing direction $\hat{V}$ is not perfectly aligned with the $\hat{R}$ vector. Real-life experience also informs you that the further away $\hat{V}$ is from $\hat{R}$, or the larger the angle-α is, the less likely you will observe the light reflection. In fact, you know that when α is zero, you would observe the maximum light reflection, and when α is 90° or when $\hat{V}$ and $\hat{R}$ are perpendicular, you would observe zero light reflection.

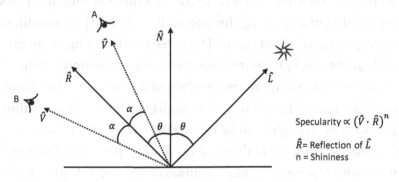

Figure 8-16. *The Phong specularity model*

The Phong illumination model simulates the characteristics of specularity with a $\left(\hat{V}\cdot\hat{R}\right)^{n}$ term. When $\hat{V}$ and $\hat{R}$ are aligned, or when $\alpha=0°$, the specularity term evaluates to 1, and the term drops off to 0 according to the cosine function when the separation between $\hat{V}$ and $\hat{R}$ increases to 90° or when $\alpha=90°$. The power n, referred to as shininess, describes how rapidly the specular highlight rolls off as α increases. The larger the n value, the faster the cosine function decreases as α increases, the faster the specular highlight drops off, and the glossier the surface would appear. For example, in Figure 8-14, the left, middle, and right spheres have corresponding n values of 0, 5, and 30.

While the $\left(\hat{V}\cdot\hat{R}\right)^{n}$ term models specular highlight effectively, the cost involved in computing the $\hat{R}$ vector for every shaded pixel can be significant. As illustrated in Figure 8-17, $\hat{H}$, the halfway vector, is defined as the average of the $\hat{L}$ and $\hat{V}$ vectors. It is observed that β, the angle between the $\hat{N}$ and $\hat{H}$, can also be used to characterize specular reflection. Though slightly different, $\left(\hat{N}\cdot\hat{H}\right)^{n}$ produces similar results as $\left(\hat{V}\cdot\hat{R}\right)^{n}$ with less per-pixel computation cost. The halfway vector will be used to approximate specularity in your implementation.

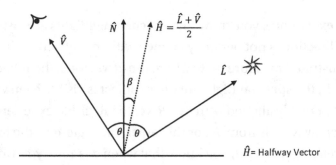

Figure 8-17. *The halfway vector*

As illustrated in Figure 8-18, the variation of the Phong illumination model that you will implement consists of simulating the interaction of three participating elements in the scene through three distinct terms. The three participating elements are the global ambient lighting, the light source, and the material property of the object to be illuminated. The previous examples have explained the first two: the global ambient lighting and the light source. In this way, to support the Phong illumination model, the material property of an object can be represented by K_a, K_d, K_s, and n. These stand for three colors, representing the ambient, diffuse, and specular reflectivity, and a floating-point number representing the shininess of an object. With the global ambient light intensity, I_a, and color, C_a, and the light source intensity, I_L, and color, C_L, the three terms of the Phong illumination model are as follows:

- **The ambient term**: $I_a C_a K_a$
- **The diffuse term**: $I_L C_L K_d \left(\hat{N} \cdot \hat{L} \right)$
- **The specular term**: $I_L C_L K_s \left(\hat{N} \cdot \hat{H} \right)^n$

Note that the first two terms, the ambient and diffuse terms, have been covered in the previous examples. The `illum_fs` GLSL fragment shader from the previous example implements these two terms with a light distance attenuation and without the K_a and K_d material properties. This project guides you to build the support for per-object material property and complete the Phong illumination model implementation in the `illum_fs` GLSL shader with the engine support in the `IllumShader/IllumRenderable` object pair.

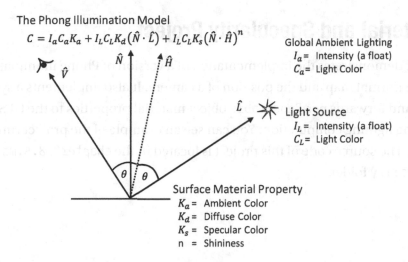

Figure 8-18.   *The Phong illumination model*

Integration of Material in the Game Engine and GLSL Shaders

To implement the Phong illumination model, a `Material` class that encapsulates the surface material property in Figure 8-18 must be defined and referenced by each `IllumRenderable` object that is to be shaded by the corresponding `illum_fs` fragment shader. Figure 8-19 illustrates that in your implementation, a new `ShaderMaterial` object will be defined and referenced in the `IllumShader` to load the content of the `Material` object to the `illum_fs` GLSL fragment shader.

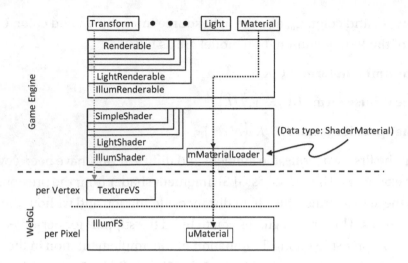

Figure 8-19. *Support for material*

The Material and Specularity Project

This project demonstrates the implementation of a version of Phong illumination model utilizing the normal map and the position of a camera. It also implements a system that stores and forwards per-Renderable object material properties to the GLSL shader for the Phong lighting computation. You can see an example of the project running in Figure 8-20. The source code of this project is located in the chapter8/8.5.material_ and_specularity folder.

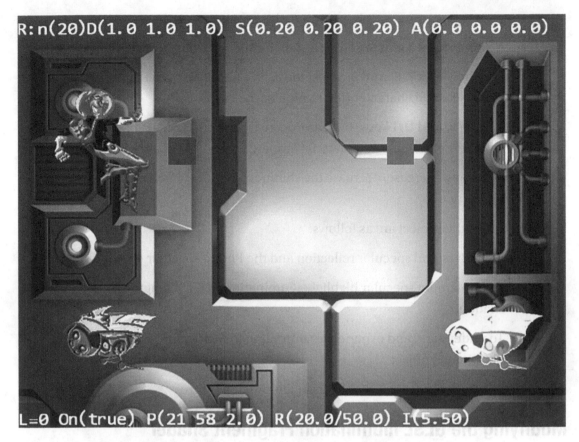

R:n(20)D(1.0 1.0 1.0) S(0.20 0.20 0.20) A(0.0 0.0 0.0)

L=0 On(true) P(21 58 2.0) R(20.0/50.0) I(5.50)

Figure 8-20. *Running the Material and Specularity project*

The main controls of the project are identical to the previous project:

- **WASD keys**: Move the hero character on the screen

Lighting controls:

- **Number keys 0, 1, 2, and 3**: Select the corresponding light source

- **Arrow keys**: Move the currently selected light

- **Z/X key**: Increases/decreases the light z position

- **C/V and B/N keys**: Increase/decrease the near and far cutoff distances of the selected light

- **K/L key**: Increases/decreases the intensity of the selected light

- **H key**: Toggles the selected light on/off

461

The material property controls are new to this project:

- **Number keys 5 and 6**: Select the left minion and the hero

- **Number keys 7, 8, and 9**: Select the K_a, K_d, and K_s material properties of the selected character (left minion or the hero)

- **E/R, T/Y, and U/I keys**: Increase/decrease the red, green, and blue channels of the selected material property

- **O/P keys**: Increase/decrease the shininess of the selected material property

The goals of the project are as follows:

- To understand specular reflection and the Phong specular term

- To implement specular highlight illumination in GLSL fragment shaders

- To understand and experience controlling the `Material` of an illuminated object

- To examine specular highlights in illuminated images

Modifying the GLSL Illumination Fragment Shader

As in the previous projects, you will begin with implementing the actual illumination model in the GLSL `illum_fs` fragment shader:

1. Edit the `illum_fs.glsl` file and define a variable, `uCameraPosition`, for storing the camera position. This position is used to compute the $\hat{V}$ vector, the viewing direction. Now, create a material `struct` and a corresponding variable, `uMaterial`, for storing the per-object material properties. Note the correspondence between the variable names Ka, Kd, Ks, and n and the terms in the Phong illumination model in Figure 8-18.

```
// for supporting a simple Phong-like illumination model
uniform vec3 uCameraPosition; // for computing the V-vector
// material properties
struct Material {
```

```
    vec4 Ka;     // simple boosting of color
    vec4 Kd;     // Diffuse
    vec4 Ks;     // Specular
    float Shininess; // this is the "n"
};
uniform Material uMaterial;
```

2. To support readability, mathematical terms in the illumination
   model will be defined into separate functions. You will begin by
   defining the DistanceDropOff() function to perform the exact
   same near/far cutoff computation as in the previous project.

```
// Computes the L-vector, returns strength
float DistanceDropOff(Light lgt, float dist) {
    float strength = 0.0;
    if (dist <= lgt.Far) {
        if (dist <= lgt.Near)
            strength = 1.0;  //  no attenuation
        else {
            // simple quadratic drop off
            float n = dist - lgt.Near;
            float d = lgt.Far - lgt.Near;
            strength = smoothstep(0.0, 1.0, 1.0-(n*n)/(d*d));
                            // blended attenuation
        }
    }
    return strength;
}
```

3. Define the function to compute the diffuse term. Notice that the
   texture map color is applied to the diffuse term.

```
vec4 DiffuseResult(vec3 N, vec3 L, vec4 textureMapColor) {
    return uMaterial.Kd * max(0.0, dot(N, L)) * textureMapColor;
}
```

4. Define the function to compute the specular term. The $\hat{V}$ vector, V, is computed by normalizing the results of subtracting uCameraPosition from the current pixel position, gl_FragCoord. It is important to observe that this operation is performed in the pixel space, and the IllumShader/IllumRenderable object pair must transform the WC camera position to pixel space before sending over the information.

```
vec4 SpecularResult(vec3 N, vec3 L) {
    vec3 V = normalize(uCameraPosition - gl_FragCoord.xyz);
    vec3 H = (L + V) * 0.5;
    return uMaterial.Ks * pow(max(0.0, dot(N, H)), uMaterial.Shininess);
}
```

5. Now you can implement the Phong illumination model to accumulate the diffuse and specular terms. Notice that lgt.Intensity, I_L, and lgt.Color, C_L, in Figure 8-18 are factored out and multiplied to the sum of diffuse and specular results. The scaling by the light strength based on near/far cutoff computation, strength, is the only difference between this implementation and the diffuse/specular terms listed in Figure 8-18.

```
vec4 ShadedResult(Light lgt, vec3 N, vec4 textureMapColor) {
    vec3 L = lgt.Position.xyz - gl_FragCoord.xyz;
    float dist = length(L);
    L = L / dist;
    float strength = DistanceDropOff(lgt, dist);
    vec4  diffuse = DiffuseResult(N, L, textureMapColor);
    vec4  specular = SpecularResult(N, L);
    vec4 result = strength * lgt.Intensity *
                              lgt.Color * (diffuse + specular);
    return result;
}
```

6. Complete the implementation in the `main()` function by
    accounting for the ambient term and looping over all defined light
    sources to accumulate for `ShadedResults()`. The bulk of the main
    function is similar to the one in the `illum_fs.glsl` file from the
    previous project. The only important differences are highlighted
    in bold.

```
void main(void)  {
    ... identical to previous code ...
    vec3 N = normalize(normalMap.xyz);

    vec4 shadedResult = uGlobalAmbientIntensity *
                        uGlobalAmbientColor * uMaterial.Ka;

    // now decide if we should illuminate by the light
    if (textureMapColor.a > 0.0) {
        for (int i=0; i<kGLSLuLightArraySize; i++) {
            if (uLights[i].IsOn) {
                shadedResult += ShadedResult(
                                uLights[i], N, textureMapColor);
            }
        }
    }

    ... identical to previous code ...
}
```

Defining the Material Class

As described, a simple `Material` class is required to encapsulate the per-Renderable
material property for the Phong illumination model:

1. Create `material.js` in the `src/engine` folder, define the `Material`
    class, and in the constructor, initialize the variables as defined in
    the surface material property in Figure 8-18. Notice that ambient,
    diffuse, and specular (`Ka`, `Kd`, and `Ks`) are colors, while shininess is
    a floating-point number.

```
class Material {
    constructor() {
        this.mKa = vec4.fromValues(0.0, 0.0, 0.0, 0);
        this.mKs = vec4.fromValues(0.2, 0.2, 0.2, 1);
        this.mKd = vec4.fromValues(1.0, 1.0, 1.0, 1);
        this.mShininess = 20;
    }
    ... implementation to follow ...
}

export default Material;
```

2.   Provide straightforward get and set accessors to the variables:

```
setAmbient(a) { this.mKa = vec4.clone(a); }
getAmbient() { return this.mKa; }

setDiffuse(d) { this.mKd = vec4.clone(d); }
getDiffuse() { return this.mKd; }

setSpecular(s) { this.mKs = vec4.clone(s); }
getSpecular() { return this.mKs; }

setShininess(s) { this.mShininess = s; }
getShininess() { return this.mShininess; }
```

Note that the Material class is designed to represent material properties of Renderable objects and must be accessible to the game programmer. As such, remember to update the engine access file, index.js, to forward the newly defined functionality to the client.

Defining the ShaderMaterial Class

Similar to defining the ShaderLightAt class to pass light source information at an array index to GLSL fragment shader, a new ShaderMaterial class should be defined to communicate the contents of Material to the GLSL illum_fs shader. Similar to the implementation of ShaderLightAt, the ShaderMaterial class will also be defined in the src/engine/shaders folder.

1. Create shader_material.js in the src/engine/shaders folder,
   define ShaderMaterial class, and in the constructor, initialize
   the variables as references to the ambient, diffuse, specular, and
   shininess in the illum_fs GLSL shader.

```
import * as glSys from "../core/gl.js";

class ShaderMaterial {
    constructor(aIllumShader) {
        let gl = glSys.get();
        this.mKaRef = gl.getUniformLocation(
                                    aIllumShader, "uMaterial.Ka");
        this.mKdRef = gl.getUniformLocation(
                                    aIllumShader, "uMaterial.Kd");
        this.mKsRef = gl.getUniformLocation(
                                    aIllumShader, "uMaterial.Ks");
        this.mShineRef = gl.getUniformLocation(
                            aIllumShader, "uMaterial.Shininess");
    }
    ... implementation to follow ...
}

export default ShaderMaterial;
```

2. Define the loadToShader() function to push the content of a
   Material to the GLSL shader:

```
loadToShader(aMaterial) {
    let gl = glSys.get();
    gl.uniform4fv(this.mKaRef, aMaterial.getAmbient());
    gl.uniform4fv(this.mKdRef, aMaterial.getDiffuse());
    gl.uniform4fv(this.mKsRef, aMaterial.getSpecular());
    gl.uniform1f(this.mShineRef, aMaterial.getShininess());
}
```

Similar to the ShaderLightAt class, the ShaderMaterial class is defined for loading
a material to the GLSL fragment shader. This is an internal engine operation. There is
no reason for the game programmer to access this class, and thus, the engine access file,
index.js, should not be modified to forward the definition of this class.

Modifying the IllumShader Class

Recall that the IllumShader class is the engine's interface to the corresponding GLSL illum_fs fragment shader. Now the IllumShader class must be modified to support the newly defined Phong illumination functionality in illum_fs. This support can be accomplished by modifying the IllumShader to define a ShaderMaterial object to load the contents of a Material object to the illum_fs fragment shader.

1. Edit illum_shader.js in src/engine/shaders to import ShaderMaterial, and modify the constructor to define new variables, mMaterial and mCameraPos, to support Phong illumination computation. Then define the variables mMaterialLoader and mCameraPosRef for keeping references and for loading the corresponding contents to the uniform variables in the shader.

```
import ShaderMaterial from "./shader_material.js";
constructor(vertexShaderPath, fragmentShaderPath) {
    // Call super class constructor
    super(vertexShaderPath, fragmentShaderPath);

    // this is the material property of the Renderable
    this.mMaterial = null;
    this.mMaterialLoader = new ShaderMaterial(this.mCompiledShader);

    let gl = glSys.get();
    // Reference to the camera position
    this.mCameraPos = null;  // points to a vec3
    this.mCameraPosRef = gl.getUniformLocation(
                            this.mCompiledShader, "uCameraPosition");

    // reference to the normal map sampler
    this.mNormalSamplerRef = gl.getUniformLocation(
                            this.mCompiledShader, "uNormalSampler");
}
```

2. Modify the `activate()` function to load the material and camera position to the `illum_fs` fragment shader:

```
activate(pixelColor, trsMatrix, cameraMatrix) {
    // first call the super class' activate
    super.activate(pixelColor, trsMatrix, cameraMatrix);
    let gl = glSys.get();
    gl.uniform1i(this.mNormalSamplerRef, 1); // binds to texture unit 1

    this.mMaterialLoader.loadToShader(this.mMaterial);
    gl.uniform3fv(this.mCameraPosRef, this.mCameraPos);
}
```

3. Define the `setMaterialAndCameraPos()` function to set the corresponding variables for Phong illumination computation:

```
setMaterialAndCameraPos(m, p) {
    this.mMaterial = m;
    this.mCameraPos = p;
}
```

Modifying the IllumRenderable Class

You can now modify the `IllumRenderable` class to include a material property and to properly support `IllumShader`. This is a straightforward change.

1. Edit `illum_renderable.js` in the `src/engine/renderables` folder, and modify the constructor to instantiate a new `Material` object:

```
import Material from "../material.js";
constructor(myTexture, myNormalMap) {
    ... identical to previous code ...

    // Material for this Renderable
    this.mMaterial = new Material();
}
```

2. Update the draw() function to set the material and camera
    position to the shader before the actual rendering. Notice that in
    thecalltocamera.getWCCenterInPixelSpace(),thecameraposition
    is properly transformed into pixel space.

```
draw(camera) {
    texture.activate(this.mNormalMap, glSys.get().TEXTURE1);
    this.mShader.setMaterialAndCameraPos(
        this.mMaterial, camera.getWCCenterInPixelSpace());
    super.draw(camera);
}
```

3. Define a simple accessor for the material object:

```
getMaterial() { return this.mMaterial; }
```

Modifying the Camera Class

As you have seen in the illum_fs fragment shader implementation, the camera position
required for computing the $\hat{V}$ vector must be in pixel space. The Camera object must be
modified to provide such information. Since the Camera object stores its position in WC
space, this position must be transformed to pixel space for each IllumRenderable object
rendered.

There may be a large number of IllumRenderable objects in a scene, and the camera
position cannot be changed once rendering begins. These observations suggest that the
pixel space camera position should be computed once and cached for each drawing cycle.
The PerRenderCache class, defined in the *Simple Light Shader* Project specifically for
caching per-drawing cycle information, is ideal for caching the pixel space camera position.

1. Edit the camera_main.js file and add a vec3 to the
    PerRenderCache to cache the camera's position in pixel space:

```
class PerRenderCache {
    // Information to be updated once per render for efficiency concerns
    constructor() {
        this.mWCToPixelRatio = 1;  // WC to pixel transformation
        this.mCameraOrgX = 1; // Lower-left corner of camera in WC
        this.mCameraOrgY = 1;
        this.mCameraPosInPixelSpace = vec3.fromValues(0, 0, 0);
```

```
    }
}
```

2. In the `Camera` constructor, define a z variable to simulate the distance between the `Camera` object and the rest of the `Renderable` objects. This third piece of information represents depth and is required for the illumination computation.

```
This.kCameraZ = 10; // this is for illumination computation
```

3. In step B4 of the `setViewAndCameraMatrix()` function, call the `wcPosToPixel()` function to transform the camera's position to 3D pixel space and cache the computed results:

```
// Step B4: compute and cache per-rendering information
this.mRenderCache.mWCToPixelRatio =
                    this.mViewport[eViewport.eWidth] / this.getWCWidth();
this.mRenderCache.mCameraOrgX = center[0] - (this.getWCWidth() / 2);
this.mRenderCache.mCameraOrgY = center[1] - (this.getWCHeight() / 2);
let p = this.wcPosToPixel(this.getWCCenter());
this.mRenderCache.mCameraPosInPixelSpace[0] = p[0];
this.mRenderCache.mCameraPosInPixelSpace[1] = p[1];
this.mRenderCache.mCameraPosInPixelSpace[2] =
                    this.fakeZInPixelSpace(this.kCameraZ);
```

4. Define the accessor for the camera position in pixel space:

```
getWCCenterInPixelSpace() {
    return this.mRenderCache.mCameraPosInPixelSpace; }
```

Testing Specular Reflection

You can now test your implementation of the Phong illumination model and observe the effects of altering an object's material property and specularity. Since the background, Hero, and left `Minion` are already instances of the `IllumRenderable` object, these three objects will now exhibit specularity. To ensure prominence of specular reflection, the specular material property, Ks, of the background object is set to bright red in the `init()` function.

A new function, _selectCharacter(), is defined to allow the user to work with the material property of either the Hero or the left Minion object. The file my_game_material_control.js implements the actual user interaction for controlling the selected material property.

Observations

You can run the project and interactively control the material property of the currently selected object (type keys 5 to select the left Minion and 6 for the Hero). By default, the material property of the Hero object is selected. You can try changing the diffuse RGB components by pressing the E/R, T/Y, or U/I keys. Notice that you can press multiple keys simultaneously to change multiple color channels at the same time.

The normal map of the background image is carefully generated and thus is best for examining specularity effects. You can observe red highlights along vertical boundaries in the background image. If you are unsure, pay attention to the top right region of the background image, select light 3 (type the 3 key), and toggle the on/off switch (typing the H key). Notice that as the light toggles from off to on, the entire top right region becomes brighter with a red highlight along the vertical boundary. This red highlight is the reflection of light 3 toward the camera. Now, with light 3 switched on, move it toward the left and right (the left-/right-arrow keys). Observe how the highlight intensifies and then fades as results of the angle between the halfway vector, $\hat{H}$, and the face normal vector, $\hat{N}$, change.

You can also adjust the material to observe specularity on the Hero. Now, select the Hero object (type the 6 key), decrease its diffuse material property (press R, Y, and I keys at the same time) to around 0.2, and increase the specularity property (type 9 to select Specular, and then press E, T, and U keys at the same time) to values beyond 1. With this setting, the diffused term is reduced and specular highlight emphasized, you can observe a dark Hero figure with bright highlight spots. If you are unsure, try toggling light 0 (type the 0 key) on/off (type the H key). At this point, you can press and hold the P key to decrease the value of the shininess, n. As the n value decreases, you can observe the increase in the sizes of the highlighted spots coupled with decrease in the brightness of these spots. As depicted by the middle sphere of Figure 8-14, a smaller n value corresponds to a less polished surface which typically exhibits highlights that are larger in area but with less intensity.

Relatively small objects, such as the Hero, do not occupy many pixels; the associated highlight is likely to span even smaller number of pixels and can be challenging to observe. Specular highlights can convey subtle and important effects; however, its usage can also be challenging to master.

Light Source Types

At this point, your game engine supports the illumination by many instances of a single type of light, a point light. A point light behaves much like a lightbulb in the real world. It illuminates from a single position with near and far radii where objects can be fully, partially, or not lit at all by the light. There are two other light types that are popular in most game engines: the directional light and the spotlight.

A directional light, in contrast to the point light, does not have a light position or a range. Rather, it illuminates everything in a specific direction. While these characteristics may not seem intuitive, they are perfect for general background lighting. This is the case in the real world. During the day, the general environment is illuminated by the sun where rays from the sun can conveniently be modeled as a directional light. The light rays from the sun, from the perspective of the earth, are practically parallel coming from a fixed direction, and these rays illuminate everything. A directional light is a simple light type that requires only a direction variable and has no distance drop-off. The directional lights are typically used as global lights that illuminate the entire scene.

A spotlight models a desk lamp with a cone-shape lampshade. As illustrated in Figure 8-21, a spotlight is a point light encompassed by a cone pointing in a specific direction, the light direction, with angular attenuation parameters for the inner and outer cone angles. Similar to the near and far radii of the distance attenuation, objects inside the inner cone angle are fully lit, outside the outer cone angle are not lit, and in between the two angles are partially lit. Just as in the case of a point light, a spotlight is often used for creating illumination effects in specific regions of a game scene. The spotlight, with directional and angular attenuation parameters, offers finer controls for simulating effects that are local to specific areas in a game.

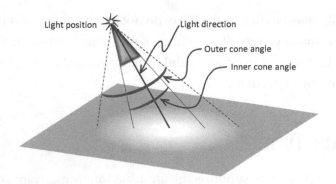

Figure 8-21. *A spotlight and its parameters*

Note   In illustrative diagrams, like Figure 8-21, for clarity purposes, light directions are usually represented by lines extending from the light position toward the environment. These lines are usually for illustrative purposes and do not carry mathematical meanings. These illustrative diagrams are contrasted with vector diagrams that explain illumination computations, like Figures 8-15 and 8-16. In vector diagrams, all vectors always point away from the position being illuminated and are assumed to be normalized with a magnitude of 1.

The Directional and Spotlights Project

This project demonstrates how to integrate directional lights and spotlights into your engine to support a wider range of illumination effects. You can see an example of the project running in Figure 8-22. The source code of this project is located in the chapter8/8.6.directional_and_spotlights folder.

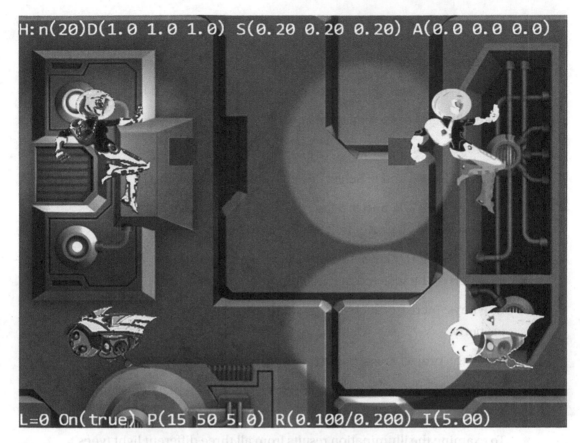

Figure 8-22. *Running the Directional and Spotlights project*

The controls of the project are as follows:

- **WASD keys**: Move the hero character on the screen

Lighting controls:

- **Number keys 0, 1, 2, and 3**: Select the corresponding light source.

- **Arrow keys**: Move the currently selected light; note that this has no effect on the directional light (light 1).

- **Arrow keys with spacebar pressed**: Change the direction of the currently selected light; note that this has no effect on the point light (light 0).

- **Z/X key**: Increases/decreases the light z position; note that this has no effect on the directional light (light 1).

- **C/V and B/N keys**: Increase/decrease the inner and outer cone angles of the selected light; note that these only affect the two spotlights in the scene (lights 2 and 3).

- **K/L key**: Increases/decreases the intensity of the selected light.

- **H key**: Toggles the selected light on/off.

Material property controls:

- **Number keys 5 and 6**: Select the left minion and the hero

- **Number keys 7, 8, and 9**: Select the K_a, K_d, and K_s material properties of the selected character (left minion or the hero)

- **E/R, T/Y, and U/I keys**: Increase/decrease the red, green, and blue channels of the selected material property

- **O/P keys**: Increase/decrease the shininess of the selected material property

The goals of the project are as follows:

- To understand the two additional light types: directional lights and spotlights

- To examine the illumination results from all three different light types

- To experience controlling the parameters of all three light types

- To support the three different light types in the engine and GLSL shaders

Supporting New Light Types in GLSL Fragment Shaders

As with the previous projects, the integration of the new functionality will begin with the GLSL shader. You must modify the GLSL IllumShader and LightShader fragment shaders to support the two new light types.

Modifying the GLSL Illumination Fragment Shader

Recall that the IllumShader simulates the Phong illumination model based on a point light. This will be expanded to support the two new light types.

1. Begin by editing illum_fs.glsl and defining constants for the three light types. Notice that to support proper communications between the GLSL shader and the engine, these constants must have identical values as the corresponding enumerated data defined in the light.js file.

```
#define ePointLight        0
#define eDirectionalLight  1
#define eSpotLight         2
    // ******** WARNING ******
    // The above enumerated values must be identical to
    // Light.eLightType values defined in Light.js
    // ******** WARNING ******
```

2. Expand the light struct to accommodate the new light types. While the directional light requires only a Direction variable, a spotlight requires a Direction, inner and outer angles, and a DropOff variable. As will be detailed next, instead of the actual angle values, the cosines of the inner and outer angles are stored in the struct to facilitate efficient implementation. The DropOff variable controls how rapidly light drops off between the inner and outer angles of the spotlight. The LightType variable identifies the type of light that is being represented in the struct.

```
struct Light {
    vec3 Position;  // in pixel space!
    vec3 Direction;     // Light direction
    vec4 Color;
    float Near;
    float Far;
    float CosInner;    // Cosine of inner cone angle for spotlight
    float CosOuter;    // Cosine of outer cone angle for spotlight
    float Intensity;
    float DropOff;    // for spotlight
    bool  IsOn;
    int LightType;    // One of ePoint, eDirectional, or eSpot
};
```

3. Define an `AngularDropOff()` function to compute the angular attenuation for the spotlight:

```
float AngularDropOff(Light lgt, vec3 lgtDir, vec3 L) {
    float strength = 0.0;
    float cosL = dot(lgtDir, L);
    float num = cosL - lgt.CosOuter;
    if (num > 0.0) {
        if (cosL > lgt.CosInner)
            strength = 1.0;
        else {
            float denom = lgt.CosInner - lgt.CosOuter;
            strength = smoothstep(0.0, 1.0, pow(num/denom, lgt.DropOff));
        }
    }
    return strength;
}
```

The parameter lgt is a spotlight in the `Light struct`, lgtDir is the direction of the spotlight (or `Light.Direction` normalized), and L is the light vector of the current position to be illuminated. Note that since the dot product of normalized vectors is the cosine of the angle between the vectors, it is convenient to represent all angular displacements by their corresponding cosine values and to perform the computations based on cosines of the angular displacements. Figure 8-23 illustrates the parameters involved in angular attenuation computation.

Note   The `lgtDir` is the direction of the spotlight, while the light vector, **L**, is the vector from the position being illumined to the position of the spotlight.

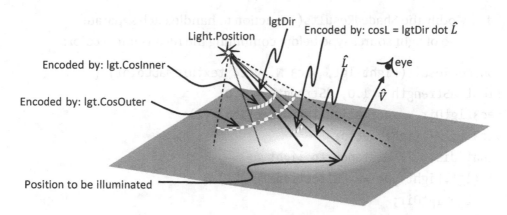

Figure 8-23. *Computing the angular attenuation of a spotlight*

Note   The following code is based on cosine of angular displacements. It is important to remember that given two angles α and β, where both are between 0 and 180 degrees, if $\alpha > \beta$, then, $\cos \alpha < \cos \beta$.

---

a. The cosL is the dot product of L with lgtDir; it records the angular displacement of the position currently being illuminated.

b. The num variable stores the difference between cosL and cosOuter. A negative num would mean that the position currently being illuminated is outside the outer cone where the position will not be lit and thus no further computation is required.

c. If the point to be illuminated is within the inner cone, cosL would be greater than lgt.CosInner, and full strength of the light, 1.0, will be returned.

d. If the point to be illuminated is in between the inner and outer cone angles, use the smoothstep() function to compute the effective strength from the light.

4.   Modify the ShadedResults() function to handle each separate
     case of light source type before combining the results into a color:

```
vec4 ShadedResult(Light lgt, vec3 N, vec4 textureMapColor) {
    float aStrength = 1.0, dStrength = 1.0;
    vec3 lgtDir = -normalize(lgt.Direction.xyz);
    vec3 L; // light vector
    float dist; // distance to light
    if (lgt.LightType == eDirectionalLight) {
        L = lgtDir;
    } else {
        L = lgt.Position.xyz - gl_FragCoord.xyz;
        dist = length(L);
        L = L / dist;
    }
    if (lgt.LightType == eSpotLight) {
        // spotlight: do angle dropoff
        aStrength = AngularDropOff(lgt, lgtDir, L);
    }
    if (lgt.LightType != eDirectionalLight) {
        // both spot and point light has distance dropoff
        dStrength = DistanceDropOff(lgt, dist);
    }
    vec4  diffuse = DiffuseResult(N, L, textureMapColor);
    vec4  specular = SpecularResult(N, L);
    vec4 result = aStrength * dStrength *
                  lgt.Intensity * lgt.Color * (diffuse + specular);
    return result;
}
```

Modifying the GLSL Light Fragment Shader

You can now modify the GLSL light_fs fragment shader to support the two new light
types. The modifications involved are remarkably similar to the changes made for illum_
fs, where constant values that correspond to light types are defined, the Light struct is

extended to support directional and spotlights, and the angular and distant attenuation functions are defined to properly compute the strengths from the light. Please refer to the light_fs.glsl source code file for details of the implementation.

Modifying the Light Class

You must extend the Light class to support the parameters of the two new light types:

1. Edit light.js in the src/engine/lights folder to define and export an enumerated data type for the different light types. It is important that the enumerated values correspond to the constant values defined in the GLSL illum_fs and light_fs shaders.

```
// **** WARNING: The following enumerate values must be identical to
// the values of
//
//    ePointLight, eDirectionalLight, eSpotLight
//
// defined in LightFS.glsl and IllumFS.glsl
const eLightType = Object.freeze({
    ePointLight: 0,
    eDirectionalLight: 1,
    eSpotLight: 2
});

export { eLightType }
```

2. Modify the constructor to define and initialize the new variables that correspond to the parameters of directional light and spotlight.

```
constructor() {
    this.mColor = vec4.fromValues(1, 1, 1, 1);  // light color
    this.mPosition = vec3.fromValues(0, 0, 5); // light position in WC
    this.mDirection = vec3.fromValues(0, 0, -1); // in WC
    this.mNear = 5;   // effective radius in WC
    this.mFar = 10;
    this.mInner = 0.1;   // in radian
```

```
    this.mOuter = 0.3;
    this.mIntensity = 1;
    this.mDropOff = 1;  //
    this.mLightType = eLightType.ePointLight;
    this.mIsOn = true;
}
```

3. Define the get and set accessors for the new variables. The exhaustive listing of these functions is not shown here. Please refer to the light.js source code file for details.

Modifying the ShaderLightAt Class

Recall that the ShaderLightAt class is responsible for loading the values from a light source to the GLSL fragment shader. This object must be refined to support the new light source parameters that correspond to directional lights and spotlights.

1. Edit shader_light_at.js to import the eLightType enumerated type from light.js:

```
import { eLightType } from "../lights/light.js";
```

2. Modify the _setShaderReferences() function to set the references to the newly added light properties:

```
_setShaderReferences(aLightShader, index) {
    let gl = glSys.get();
    this.mColorRef = gl.getUniformLocation(
                        aLightShader, "uLights[" + index + "].Color");
    this.mPosRef = gl.getUniformLocation(
                        aLightShader, "uLights[" + index + "].Position");
    this.mDirRef = gl.getUniformLocation(
                        aLightShader, "uLights[" + index + "].Direction");
    this.mNearRef = gl.getUniformLocation(
                        aLightShader, "uLights[" + index + "].Near");
    this.mFarRef = gl.getUniformLocation(
                        aLightShader, "uLights[" + index + "].Far");
    this.mInnerRef = gl.getUniformLocation(
                        aLightShader, "uLights[" + index + "].CosInner");
```

```
    this.mOuterRef = gl.getUniformLocation(
                    aLightShader, "uLights[" + index + "].CosOuter");
    this.mIntensityRef = gl.getUniformLocation(
                    aLightShader, "uLights[" + index + "].Intensity");
    this.mDropOffRef = gl.getUniformLocation(
                    aLightShader, "uLights[" + index + "].DropOff");
    this.mIsOnRef = gl.getUniformLocation(
                        aLightShader, "uLights[" + index + "].IsOn");
    this.mLightTypeRef = gl.getUniformLocation(
                    aLightShader, "uLights[" + index + "].LightType");
}
```

3. Modify the loadToShader() function to load the newly added
   light variables for the directional light and spotlight. Notice that
   depending upon the light type, the values of some variables
   may not be transferred to the GLSL shader. For example, the
   parameters associated with angular attenuation, the inner
   and outer angles, and the drop-off will be transferred only for
   spotlights.

```
loadToShader(aCamera, aLight) {
    let gl = glSys.get();
    gl.uniform1i(this.mIsOnRef, aLight.isLightOn());

    // Process a light only when it is switched on
    if (aLight.isLightOn()) {

        ... identical to previous code ...

        gl.uniform1f(this.mFarRef, f);
        gl.uniform1f(this.mInnerRef, 0.0);
        gl.uniform1f(this.mOuterRef, 0.0);
        gl.uniform1f(this.mIntensityRef, aLight.getIntensity());
        gl.uniform1f(this.mDropOffRef, 0);
        gl.uniform1i(this.mLightTypeRef, aLight.getLightType());

        // Point light does not need the direction
        if (aLight.getLightType() === eLightType.ePointLight) {
            gl.uniform3fv(this.mDirRef, vec3.fromValues(0, 0, 0));
```

```
        } else {
            // either spot or directional lights: must compute direction
            let d = aCamera.wcDirToPixel(aLight.getDirection());
            gl.uniform3fv(this.mDirRef, vec3.fromValues(d[0],d[1],d[2]));
            if (aLight.getLightType() === eLightType.eSpotLight) {
                gl.uniform1f(this.mInnerRef,
                            Math.cos(0.5 * aLight.getInner()));
                gl.uniform1f(this.mOuterRef,
                            Math.cos(0.5 * aLight.getOuter()));
                gl.uniform1f(this.mDropOffRef, aLight.getDropOff());
            }
        }
    }
}
```

Note, for `mInnerRef` and `mOuterRef`, the cosines of half the angles are actually computed and passed. Inner and outer angles are the total angular spreads of the spotlight where the half of these angles describe the angular displacements from the light direction. For this reason, cosines of the half angles will actually be used in the computations. This optimization relieves the GLSL fragment shaders from recomputing the cosine of these angles on every invocation.

Modifying the Camera Transform Class

Directional lights and spotlights require a light direction, and the GLSL `illum_fs` and `light_fs` shaders expect this direction to be specified in pixel space. Edit the `camera_xform.js` file of the Camera object to define the `wcDirToPixel()` function to transform a direction from WC to pixel space.

```
Camera.prototype.wcDirToPixel = function (d) {  // d:vec3 direction in WC
    // Convert the position to pixel space
    let x = d[0] * this.mRenderCache.mWCToPixelRatio;
    let y = d[1] * this.mRenderCache.mWCToPixelRatio;
    let z = d[2];
    return vec3.fromValues(x, y, z);
}
```

Testing the New Light Types

The main goals of the MyGame level are to test and provide functionality for manipulating the new light types. The modifications involved are straightforward; my_game_lights.js is modified to create all three light types, and my_game_light_control.js is modified to support the manipulation of the direction of the selected light when the arrow and space keys are pressed simultaneously. The implementation of these simple changes is not shown here. Please refer to the source code files for details.

Observations

You can run the project and interactively control the lights to examine the corresponding effects. There are four light sources defined, each illuminating all objects in the scene. Light source 0 is a point light, 1 is a directional light, and 2 and 3 are spotlights.

You can examine the effect from a directional light by typing the 1 key to select the light. Now hold the spacebar while taking turns pressing the left/right or up/down keys to swing the direction of the directional light. You will notice drastic illumination changes on the boundary edges of the 3D geometric shapes in the background image, together with occasional prominent red spots of specular reflections. Now, type the H key to switch off the directional light and observe the entire scene becomes darker. Without any kinds of attenuation, directional lights can be used as effective tools for brightening the entire scene.

Type the 2 or 3 key to select one of the spotlights, once again, by holding the spacebar while taking turns pressing the left/right or up/down keys to swing the direction of the spotlight. With the spotlight, you will observe the illuminated region swinging and changing shapes between a circle (when the spotlight is pointing perpendicularly toward the background image) and different elongated ellipses. The arrow keys will move the illuminated region around. Try experimenting with the C/V and B/N keys to increase/decrease the inner and outer cone angles. Notice that if you set the inner cone angle to be larger than the outer one, the boundary of the illuminated region becomes sharp where lighting effects from the spotlight will drop off abruptly. You can consider switching off the direction light, light 1, for a clearer observation of the spotlight effects.

Try experimenting with the different light settings, including overlapping the light illumination regions and setting the light intensities, the K and L keys, to negative numbers. While impossible in the physical world, negative intensity lights are completely valid options in a game world.

Shadow Simulation

Shadow is the result of light being obstructed or occluded. As an everyday phenomenon, shadow is something you observe but probably do not give much thought to. However, shadow plays a vital role in the visual perception system of humans. For example, the shadows of objects convey important cues of relative sizes, depths, distances, orderings, and so on. In video games, proper simulation of shadows can increase the quality of appearance and fidelity. For example, you can use shadows to properly convey the distance between two game objects or the height that the hero is jumping.

Shadows can be simulated by determining the visibility between the position to be illuminated and each of the light source positions in the environment. A position is in shadow with respect to a light source if something occludes it from the light source or the position is not visible from the light sourc. Computationally, this is an expensive operation because general visibility determination is an $O(n)$ operation, where n is the number of objects in the scene, and this operation must be performed for every pixel being illuminated. Algorithmically, this is a challenging problem because the solutions for visibility must be available within the fragment shader during illumination computation, again, for every pixel being illuminated.

Because of the computation and algorithmic challenges, instead of simulating shadow according to the physical world, many videogames approximate or create shadow-like effects for only selected objects based on dedicated hardware resources. In this section, you will learn about approximating shadows by selecting dedicated shadow casters and receivers based on the WebGL stencil buffer.

Figure 8-24 shows an example where a game wants to cast the shadow of the Hero object on the minion and yet not on the background. In this case, the background object will not participate in the shadow computation and thus will not receive the shadow.

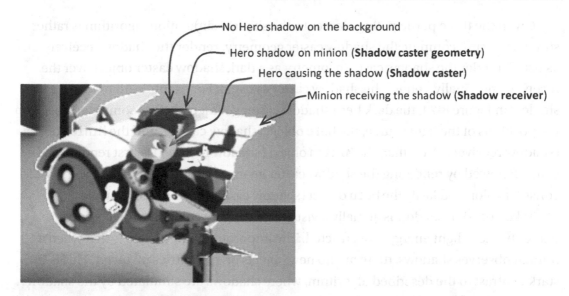

Figure 8-24. *Hero casting shadow on the minion but not on the background*

To properly simulate and render the shadow in Figure 8-24, as illustrated in Figure 8-25, there are three important elements.

- **Shadow caster**: This is the object that causes the shadow. In the Figure 8-24 example, the Hero object is the shadow caster.

- **Shadow receiver**: This is the object that the shadow appears on. In the Figure 8-24 example, the Minion object is the shadow receiver.

- **Shadow caster geometry**: This is the actual shadow, in other words, the darkness on the shadow receiver because of the occlusion of light. In the Figure 8-24 example, the dark imprint of the hero appearing on the minion behind the actual hero object is the shadow caster geometry.

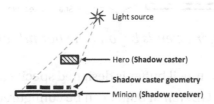

Figure 8-25. *The three participating elements of shadow simulation: the caster, the caster geometry, and the receiver*

Given the three participating elements, the shadow simulation algorithm is rather straightforward: compute the shadow caster geometry, render the shadow receiver as usual, render the shadow caster geometry as a dark shadow caster object over the receiver, and, finally, render the shadow caster as usual. For example, to render the shadow in Figure 8-24, the dark hero shadow caster geometry is first computed based on the positions of the light source, the Hero object (shadow caster), and the Minion object (shadow receiver). After that, the Minion object (shadow receiver) is first rendered as usual, followed by rendering the shadow caster geometry as the Hero object with a dark constant color, and lastly the Hero object (shadow caster) is rendered as usual.

Take note that shadow is actually a visual effect where colors on objects appear darker because light energy is obstructed. The important point to note is that when a human observes shadows, there are no new objects or geometries involved. This is in stark contrast to the described algorithm, where shadows are simulated by the shadow caster geometry, a dark color object. This dark color object does not actually exist in the scene. It is algorithmically created to approximate the visual perception of light being occluded. This creation and rendering of extra geometry to simulate the results of human visual perception, while interesting, has its own challenges.

As depicted in Figure 8-26, the illusion of shadow breaks down when the shadow caster geometry extends beyond the bounds of the shadow receiver. Such situations must be properly resolved in order for shadow to appear genuine. An example of proper handling of this situation can be observed in Figure 8-24; the top portion of the hero helmet shadow extends beyond the bounds of the minion and is not drawn.

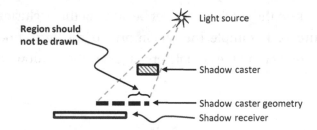

Figure 8-26. *Shadow caster extends beyond the bounds of shadow receiver*

Fortunately, the WebGL stencil buffer is designed specifically to resolve these types of situations. The WebGL stencil buffer can be configured as a 2D array of on/off switches with the same pixel resolution as the canvas that is displayed on the web browser. With this configuration, when stencil buffer checking is enabled, the pixels in the canvas that can be drawn on will be only those with corresponding stencil buffer pixels that are switched on.

Figure 8-27 uses an example to illustrate this functionality. In this example, the middle layer is the stencil buffer with all pixels initialized to off except for the pixels in the white triangular region being initialized to on. When the stencil buffer checking is enabled, the drawing of the top layer image will result in only a triangular region appearing in the canvas (bottom layer). This triangular region is formed by pixels that correspond to the on positions of the triangle in the stencil buffer. In this way, the stencil buffer acts exactly like a stencil over the canvas where only the on regions can be drawn on.

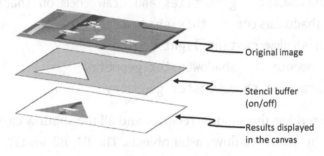

Original image

Stencil buffer
(on/off)

Results displayed
in the canvas

Figure 8-27. *The WebGL stencil buffer*

With the support of the WebGL stencil buffer, shadow simulation can now be specified accordingly by identifying all shadow receivers and by grouping corresponding shadow casters with each receiver. In the Figure 8-24 example, the Hero object is grouped as the shadow caster of the minion shadow receiver. In this example, for the background object to receive a shadow from the hero, it must be explicitly identified as a shadow receiver, and the Hero object must be grouped with it as a shadow caster. Notice that without explicitly grouping the minion object as a shadow caster of the background shadow receiver, the minion will not cast a shadow on the background.

As will be detailed in the following implementation discussion, the transparencies of the shadow casters and receivers and the intensity of the casting light source can all affect the generation of shadows. It is important to recognize that this shadow simulation is actually an algorithmic creation with effects that can be used to approximate human perception. This procedure does not describe how shadows are formed in the real world, and it is entirely possible to create unrealistic dramatic effects such as casting transparent or blue-colored shadows.

The Shadow Simulation Algorithm

The shadow simulation and rendering algorithm can now be outlined as follows:

```
Given a shadowReceiver
    A: Draw the shadowReceiver to the canvas as usual

    // Stencil op to enable the region for drawing on the shadowCaster
    B1: Initialize all stencil buffer pixels to off
    B2: Switch on stencil buffer pixels correspond to shadowReceiver
    B3: Enable stencil buffer checking

    // Compute shadowCaster geometries and draw them on shadowReceiver
    C: For each shadowCaster of this shadowReceiver
      D: For each shadow casting light source
            D1: Compute the shadowCaster geometry
            D2: Draw the shadowCaster geometry
```

The listed code renders the shadow receiver and all the shadow caster geometries without rendering the actual shadow caster objects. The B1, B2, and B3 steps switch on the stencil buffer pixels that correspond to the shadow receiver. This is similar to switching on the pixels that are associated with the white triangle in Figure 8-27, enabling the region that can be drawn. The loops of steps C and D point out that a separate geometry must be computed for each shadow casting light source. By the time step D1 draws the shadow caster geometry, with the stencil buffer containing the shadow receiver imprint and checking enabled, only pixels occupied by the shadow receiver will be enabled to be drawn on in the canvas.

The Shadow Shaders Project

This project demonstrates how to implement and integrate the shadow simulation algorithm into your game engine. You can see an example of the project running in Figure 8-28. The source code of this project is located in the chapter8/8.7.shadow_shaders folder.

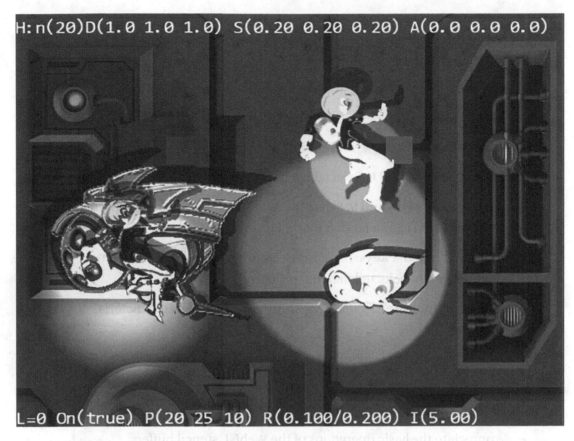

Figure 8-28. *Running the Shadow Shaders project*

The controls of this project are identical to the previous project:

- **WASD keys**: Move the hero character on the screen

Lighting controls:

- **Number keys 0, 1, 2, and 3**: Select the corresponding light source

- **Arrow keys**: Move the currently selected light; note that this has no effect on the directional light (light 1).

- **Arrow keys with spacebar pressed**: Change the direction of the currently selected light; note that this has no effect on the point light (light 0).

- **Z/X key**: Increases/decreases the light z position; note that this has no effect on the directional light (light 1).

- **C/V and B/N keys**: Increase/decrease the inner and outer cone angles of the selected light; note that these only affect the two spotlights in the scene (lights 2 and 3).

- **K/L key**: Increases/decreases the intensity of the selected light.

- **H key**: Toggles the selected light on/off.

Material property controls:

- **Number keys 5 and 6**: Select the left minion and the hero

- **Number keys 7, 8, and 9**: Select the K_a, K_d, and K_s material properties of the selected character (left minion or the hero)

- **E/R, T/Y, and U/I keys**: Increase/decrease the red, green, and blue channels of the selected material property

- **O/P keys**: Increase/decrease the shininess of the selected material property

The goals of the project are as follows:

- Understand shadows can be approximated by algorithmically defining and rendering explicit geometries

- Appreciate the basic operations of the WebGL stencil buffer

- Understand the simulation of shadows with shadow caster and receiver

- Implement the shadow simulation algorithm based on the WebGL stencil buffer

Creating GLSL Fragment Shaders

Two separate GLSL fragment shaders are required to support the rendering of shadow, one for drawing the shadow caster geometry onto the canvas and one for drawing the shadow receiver into the stencil buffer.

Defining the GLSL Shadow Caster Fragment Shader

The GLSL shadow_caster_fs fragment shader supports the drawing of the shadow caster geometries. Refer to Figure 8-25; the shadow caster geometry is the piece of geometry that fakes being the shadow of the shadow caster. This geometry is typically scaled by the engine according to its distance from the shadow caster; the further from the caster, the larger this geometry.

In the fragment shader, this geometry should be rendered as a dark-colored object to create the illusion of it being a shadow. Note that one shadow caster geometry is required for each shadow casting light source; as such, the fragment shader only supports one light source. Finally, the degree of darkness of this object depends on the effective strength of the shadow casting light sources, and thus, the fragment shader must define functionality to compute strengths from each type of light sources.

1. Inthesrc/glsl_shadersfolder,createafileshadow_caster_fs.glsl. Since all light types can cast shadow, existing light structures must be supported. Now, copy the Light struct and light type constants from light_fs (not shown). These data structure and constants must be exactly the same such that the corresponding interfacing shader in the engine can reuse existing utilities that support LightShader. The only difference is since a shadow caster geometry must be defined for each light source, the uLight array size is exactly 1 in this case.

2. Define constants for shadow rendering. The kMaxShadowOpacity is how opaque shadows should be, and kLightStrengthCutOff is a cutoff threshold where a light with intensity less than this value will not cast shadows.

```
#define kMaxShadowOpacity 0.7  // max of shadow opacity
#define kLightStrengthCutOff 0.05 // any less will not cause shadow
```

3. To properly support shadow casting from the three different light types, AngularDropOff() and DistanceDropOff(), functions must also be defined in exactly the same manner as those in light_fs (and illum_fs). You can copy these functions from light_fs. Note that since there is only one light source in the uLight array, you can remove the light parameter from these functions and

refer directly to uLight[0] in the computation. This parameter
replacement is the only modification required, and thus, the code
is not shown here.

4.   Remember that shadow is observed because of light occlusion
and is independent from the color of the light source. Now, modify
the LightStrength() function to compute the light strength
arriving at the position to be illuminated instead of a shaded color.

```
float LightStrength() {
    float aStrength = 1.0, dStrength = 1.0;
    vec3 lgtDir = -normalize(uLights[0].Direction.xyz);
    vec3 L; // light vector
    float dist; // distance to light
    if (uLights[0].LightType == eDirectionalLight) {
        L = lgtDir;
    } else {
        L = uLights[0].Position.xyz - gl_FragCoord.xyz;
        dist = length(L);
        L = L / dist;
    }
    if (uLights[0].LightType == eSpotLight) {
        // spotlight: do angle dropoff
        aStrength = AngularDropOff(lgtDir, L);
    }
    if (uLights[0].LightType != eDirectionalLight) {
        // both spot and point light has distance dropoff
        dStrength = DistanceDropOff(dist);
    }
    float result = aStrength * dStrength;
    return result;
}
```

Comparing the listed LightStrength() with the same function in light_fs, there are
two main differences. First, the function does not consider the color of the light and returns
a float, the aggregated strength of the light source. Second, since the uLight array is of size 1,
the function removed the Light parameter and referred to uLight[0] in the computation.

5. Compute the color of the shadow in the main() function based
    on the strength of the light source. Notice that no shadows will be
    cast if the light intensity is less than kLightStrengthCutOff and
    that the actual color of the shadow is not exactly black or opaque.
    Instead, it is a blend of the programmer-defined uPixelColor and
    the sampled transparency from the texture map.

```
void main(void)
{
    vec4 texFragColor = texture2D(uSampler, vTexCoord);
    float lgtStrength = LightStrength();
    if (lgtStrength < kLightStrengthCutOff)
        discard;
    vec3 shadowColor = lgtStrength * uPixelColor.rgb;
    shadowColor *= uPixelColor.a * texFragColor.a;
    gl_FragColor = vec4(shadowColor,
                        kMaxShadowOpacity * lgtStrength * texFragColor.a);
}
```

Defining the GLSL Shadow Receiver Fragment Shader

The GLSL shadow_receiver_fs fragment shader is the shader for drawing the shadow
receiver into the stencil buffer. Take note that the stencil buffer is configured as an on/
off buffer where any value returned in gl_FragColor will switch the corresponding pixel to
on. For this reason, transparent receiver fragments must be discarded.

1. Under the src/glsl_shaders folder, create shadow_receiver_
    fs.glsl, and define a sampler2D object to sample the color
    texture map of the shadow receiver object. In addition, define
    the constant kSufficientlyOpaque to be the threshold where
    fragments with less opacity will be treated as transparent and
    discarded. Stencil buffer pixels that correspond to discarded
    fragments will remain off and thus will not be able to receive
    shadow geometries.

```
// The object that fetches data from texture.
// Must be set outside the shader.
uniform sampler2D uSampler;
```

```
uniform vec4 uPixelColor;

// "varying" signifies that the texture coordinate will be
// interpolated and thus varies.
varying vec2 vTexCoord;

#define kSufficientlyOpaque        0.1
```

Note that to facilitate engine shader class code reuse, the variable names of uSampler and vTexCoord must not be changed. These correspond to the variable names defined in texture_fs.glsl, and the game engine can use the existing SpriteShader to facilitate the loading of information to this shader.

2. Implement the main() function to sample the texture of shadow receiver object and test for opacity threshold in determining if shadow could be received:

```
void main(void)
{
    vec4 texFragColor = texture2D(uSampler, vTexCoord);
    if (texFragColor.a < kSufficientlyOpaque)
        discard;
    else
        gl_FragColor = vec4(1, 1, 1, 1);

}
```

Interfacing the GLSL Shadow Shaders to the Engine

With two new GLSL shaders defined, you may expect that it is necessary to define two corresponding SimpleShader/Renderable pairs to facilitate the communications. This is not the case for two reasons:

- First, only one new engine shader type is required for supporting shadow_caster_fs. With the strategic variable naming in the shadow_receiver_fs shader, the existing SpriteShader object can be used to communicate with the shadow_receiver_fs GLSL fragment shader.

- Second, no new Renderable classes are required. The Renderable classes are designed to support the drawing and manipulation of game objects with the corresponding shaders. In this way, Renderable objects are visible to the players. In the case of shadow shaders, shadow_caster_fs draws shadow caster geometries, and shadow_receiver_fs draws the shadow receiver geometry into the stencil butter. Notice that neither of the shaders is designed to support drawing of objects that are visible to the players. For these reasons, there is no need for the corresponding Renderable objects.

Creating the Shadow Caster Shader

A JavaScript SimpleShader subclass must be defined to facilitate the loading of information from the game engine to the GLSL shader. In this case, a ShadowCasterShader needs to be defined to communicate with the GLSL shadow_caster_fs fragment shader.

1. Under the src/engine/shaders folder, create shadow_caster_shader.js; define the ShadowCasterShader class to inherit from SpriteShader. Since each shadow caster geometry is created by one casting light source, define a single light source for the shader.

```
import SpriteShader from "./sprite_shader.js";
import ShaderLightAt from "./shader_light_at.js";

class ShadowCasterShader extends SpriteShader {
    // constructor
    constructor(vertexShaderPath, fragmentShaderPath) {
        super(vertexShaderPath, fragmentShaderPath);

        this.mLight = null;  // The light that casts the shadow
        this.mCamera = null;

        // GLSL Shader must define uLights[1] (size of 1)!!
        this.mShaderLight = new ShaderLightAt(this.mCompiledShader, 0);
    }
    ... implementation to follow ...
}
export default ShadowCasterShader;
```

2. Override the `activate()` function to ensure the single light source is properly loaded to the shader:

```
// Overriding the activation of the shader for rendering
activate(pixelColor, trsMatrix, cameraMatrix) {
    // first call the super class' activate
    super.activate(pixelColor, trsMatrix, cameraMatrix);
    this.mShaderLight.loadToShader(this.mCamera, this.mLight);
}
```

3. Define a function to set the current camera and light source for this shader:

```
setCameraAndLights(c, l) {
    this.mCamera = c;
    this.mLight = l;
}
```

Instantiating Default Shadow Caster and Receiver Shaders

Default instances of engine shaders must be created to connect to the newly defined GLSL shader caster and receiver fragment shaders:

1. Modify `shader_resources.js` in the `src/engine/core` folder to import `ShadowCasterShader`, and define the constants and variables for the two new shadow-related shaders.

```
import ShadowCasterShader from "../shaders/shadow_caster_shader.js";
let kShadowReceiverFS = "src/glsl_shaders/shadow_receiver_fs.glsl";
let mShadowReceiverShader = null;
let kShadowCasterFS = "src/glsl_shaders/shadow_caster_fs.glsl";
let mShadowCasterShader = null;
```

2. Edit the `createShaders()` function to define engine shaders to interface to the new GLSL fragment shaders. Notice that both of the engine shaders are based on the `texture_vs` GLSL vertex shader. In addition, as discussed, a new instance of the engine `SpriteShader` is created to interface to the `shadow_receiver_fs` GLSL fragment shader.

```
function createShaders() {
    ... identical to previous code ...
    mIllumShader = new IllumShader(kTextureVS, kIllumFS);
    mShadowCasterShader = new ShadowCasterShader(
                                    kTextureVS, kShadowCasterFS);
    mShadowReceiverShader = new SpriteShader(
                                    kTextureVS, kShadowReceiverFS);
}
```

3. The rest of the modifications to the shader_resources.js file are
    routine, including defining accessors, loading and unloading the
    GLSL source code files, cleaning up the shaders, and exporting
    the accessors. The detailed listings of these are not included here
    because you saw similar changes on many occasions. Please refer
    to the source code file for the actual implementations.

Configuring and Supporting WebGL Buffers

Three modifications are necessary to integrate WebGL stencil buffer into the game
engine. First, the WebGL stencil buffer must be enabled and properly configured.
Second, functions must be defined to support the drawing with stencil buffer. Third,
buffer must be properly cleared before each drawing cycle.

1. Edit the gl.js file in the src/engine/core folder to enable and
    configure WebGL stencil buffer during engine initialization.
    In the init() function, add the request for the allocation
    and configuration of stencil and depth buffers during WebGL
    initialization. Notice that the depth buffer, or z buffer, is also
    allocated and configured. This is necessary for proper shadow
    caster support, where a shadow caster must be in front of a
    receiver, or with a larger z depth in order to cast shadow on the
    receiver.

```
function init(htmlCanvasID) {
    ... identical to previous code ...
    mGL = mCanvas.getContext("webgl2",
                   {alpha: false, depth: true, stencil: true}) ||
        mCanvas.getContext("experimental-webgl2",
                   {alpha: false, depth: true, stencil: true});

    ... identical to previous code ...

    // make sure depth testing is enabled
    mGL.enable(mGL.DEPTH_TEST);
    mGL.depthFunc(mGL.LEQUAL);
}
```

2. Continue working with gl.js; define functions to begin, end, and
   disable drawing with the stencil buffer. Remember to export these
   new stencil buffer support functions.

```
function beginDrawToStencil(bit, mask) {
    mGL.clear(mGL.STENCIL_BUFFER_BIT);
    mGL.enable(mGL.STENCIL_TEST);
    mGL.colorMask(false, false, false, false);
    mGL.depthMask(false);
    mGL.stencilFunc(mGL.NEVER, bit, mask);
    mGL.stencilOp(mGL.REPLACE, mGL.KEEP, mGL.KEEP);
    mGL.stencilMask(mask);
}

function endDrawToStencil(bit, mask) {
    mGL.depthMask(mGL.TRUE);
    mGL.stencilOp(mGL.KEEP, mGL.KEEP, mGL.KEEP);
    mGL.stencilFunc(mGL.EQUAL, bit, mask);
    mGL.colorMask(true, true, true, true);
}

function disableDrawToStencil() { mGL.disable(mGL.STENCIL_TEST); }
```

3. Edit the engine access file, `index.js`, in the `src/engine` folder to clear the stencil and depth buffers when clearing the canvas in the `clearCanvas()` function:

```
function clearCanvas(color) {
    ... identical to previous code ...
    gl.clear(gl.COLOR_BUFFER_BIT | gl.STENCIL_BUFFER_BIT |
            gl.DEPTH_BUFFER_BIT);
}
```

Defining Shadow Support for Game Developers

As described when defining `ShadowCasterShader`, `Renderable` classes should not be defined to pair with the shadow caster and receiver shaders as that would allow game developers the capabilities to manipulate the algorithmically created objects as regular game objects. Instead, the `ShadowCaster` and `ShadowReceiver` classes are introduced to allow the game developers to create shadows without granting access to manipulate the underlying geometries.

Defining the Shadow Caster Class

Instead of the familiar `Renderable` class hierarchy, the `ShadowCaster` class is defined to encapsulate the functionality of the implicitly defined shadow caster geometry. Recall from Figure 8-25, the shadow caster geometry is derived algorithmically for each shadow casting light sources based on the positions of the shadow caster, a `Renderable`, and the shadow receiver, another `Renderable`, objects.

To support receiving shadows on an animated sprite element, the shadow receiver must be of `SpriteRenderable` or its subclasses. The shadow casting `Renderable` object must be able to receive light sources and thus is must be of `LightRenderable` or its subclasses. A `ShadowCaster` object maintains references to the actual shadow casting and receiving `Renderable` objects and defines the algorithm to compute and render shadow caster geometries for each of the light sources referenced by the caster `LightRenderable` object. The details of the `ShadowCaster` class are as follows:

1. Create the `src/engine/shadows` folder for organizing shadow-related support files and the `shadow_caster.js` file in the folder.

2. Define the ShadowCaster class and the constructor to initialize
    the instance variables and constants required for caster geometry
    computations:

```
import * as shaderResources from "../core/shader_resources.js";
import SpriteRenderable from "../renderables/sprite_renderable.js";
import Transform from "../utils/transform.js";
import { eLightType } from "../lights/light.js";

// shadowCaster: GameObject referencing at least a LightRenderable
// shadowReceiver: GameObject referencing at least a SpriteRenderable
class ShadowCaster {
    constructor(shadowCaster, shadowReceiver) {
        this.mShadowCaster = shadowCaster;
        this.mShadowReceiver = shadowReceiver;
        this.mCasterShader = shaderResources.getShadowCasterShader();
        this.mShadowColor = [0, 0, 0, 0.2];
        this.mSaveXform = new Transform();

        this.kCasterMaxScale = 3;    // Max amount a caster will be scaled
        this.kVerySmall = 0.001;     //
        this.kDistanceFudge = 0.01; // to avoid caster-receiver overlap
        this.kReceiverDistanceFudge = 0.6;
                // Factor to reduce the projected caster geometry size
    }

    setShadowColor(c) {
        this.mShadowColor = c;
    }

    ... implementation to follow ...
}

export default ShadowCaster;
```

The mShadowCaster is a reference to the shadow caster GameObject with at
least a LightRenderable, and the mShadowReceiver is a GameObject with at least
a SpriteRenderable render component. As will be detailed in the next step,
mCasterShader, mShadowColor, and mSaveXform are variables to support the rendering of
shadow caster geometries.

3. Implement the draw() function to compute and draw a shadow caster geometry for each of the light sources that illuminates the Renderable object of mShadowCaster:

```
draw(aCamera) {
    let casterRenderable = this.mShadowCaster.getRenderable();
    // Step A: save caster xform/shader/color. Set caster to shadow color
    this.mShadowCaster.getXform().cloneTo(this.mSaveXform);
    let s = casterRenderable.swapShader(this.mCasterShader);
    let c = casterRenderable.getColor();
    casterRenderable.setColor(this.mShadowColor);
    let l, lgt;
    // Step B: loop through each light, if shadow casting is on
    //         compute the proper shadow offset
    for (l = 0; l < casterRenderable.getNumLights(); l++) {
        lgt = casterRenderable.getLightAt(l);
        if (lgt.isLightOn() && lgt.isLightCastShadow()) {
            // Step C: turn caster into caster geometry
            //         draws as SpriteRenderable
            this.mSaveXform.cloneTo(this.mShadowCaster.getXform());
            if (this._computeShadowGeometry(lgt)) {
                this.mCasterShader.setCameraAndLights(aCamera, lgt);
                SpriteRenderable.prototype.draw.call(
                                        casterRenderable, aCamera);
            }
        }
    }
    // Step D: restore the original shadow caster
    this.mSaveXform.cloneTo(this.mShadowCaster.getXform());
    casterRenderable.swapShader(s);
    casterRenderable.setColor(c);
}
```

The `casterRenderable` is the `Renderable` object that is actually casting the shadow. The following are the four main steps of the `draw()` function:

    a.   Step A saves the caster `Renderable` state, transform, shader, and color, and sets it into a shadow caster geometry by setting its shader to a `ShadowCasterShader` (`mCasterShader`) and its color to that of shadow color.

    b.   Step B iterates through all light sources illuminating the `casterRenderable` and looks for lights that are switched on and casting shadow.

    c.   Step C, for each shadow producing light, calls the `_computeShadowGeometry()` function to compute an appropriately size and positioned shadow caster geometry and renders it as a `SpriteRenderable`. With the replaced `ShadowCasterShader` and shadow color, the rendered geometry appears as the shadow of the actual `casterRenderable`.

    d.   Step D restores the state of the `casterRenderable`.

   4.   Define the `_computeShadowGeometry()` function to compute the shadow caster geometry based on the `mShadowCaster`, the `mShadowReceiver`, and a casting light source. Although slightly intimidating in length, the following function can be logically separated into four regions. The first region declares and initializes the variables. The second and third regions are the two cases of the `if` statement that handle the computation of transform parameters for directional and point/spotlights. The last region sets the computed parameters to the transform of the caster geometry, `cxf`.

```
_computeShadowGeometry(aLight) {
    // Region 1: declaring variables
    let cxf = this.mShadowCaster.getXform();
    let rxf = this.mShadowReceiver.getXform();
    // vector from light to caster
    let lgtToCaster = vec3.create();
```

```
let lgtToReceiverZ;
let receiverToCasterZ;
let distToCaster, distToReceiver; // along the lgtToCaster vector
let scale;
let offset = vec3.fromValues(0, 0, 0);

receiverToCasterZ = rxf.getZPos() - cxf.getZPos();
if (aLight.getLightType() === eLightType.eDirectionalLight) {
    // Region 2: Processing a directional light
    if (((Math.abs(aLight.getDirection()))[2]) < this.kVerySmall) ||
        ((receiverToCasterZ * (aLight.getDirection())[2]) < 0)) {
        return false;    // direction light casting side way or
        // caster and receiver on different sides of light in Z
    }
    vec3.copy(lgtToCaster, aLight.getDirection());
    vec3.normalize(lgtToCaster, lgtToCaster);

    distToReceiver = Math.abs(receiverToCasterZ / lgtToCaster[2]);
                                    // measured along lgtToCaster
    scale = Math.abs(1 / lgtToCaster[2]);
} else {
    // Region 3: Processing a point or spot light
    vec3.sub(lgtToCaster, cxf.get3DPosition(), aLight.getPosition());
    lgtToReceiverZ = rxf.getZPos() - (aLight.getPosition())[2];

    if ((lgtToReceiverZ * lgtToCaster[2]) < 0) {
        return false;  // caster and receiver
                        // on different sides of light in Z
    }

    if ((Math.abs(lgtToReceiverZ) < this.kVerySmall) ||
        ((Math.abs(lgtToCaster[2]) < this.kVerySmall))) {
        // almost the same Z, can't see shadow
        return false;
    }
    distToCaster = vec3.length(lgtToCaster);
    vec3.scale(lgtToCaster, lgtToCaster, 1 / distToCaster);
                                    // normalize lgtToCaster
```

505

```
        distToReceiver = Math.abs(receiverToCasterZ / lgtToCaster[2]);
                                        // measured along lgtToCaster
        scale = (distToCaster +
                (distToReceiver * this.kReceiverDistanceFudge)) /
            distToCaster;
    }
    vec3.scaleAndAdd(offset, cxf.get3DPosition(),
                    lgtToCaster, distToReceiver + this.kDistanceFudge);

    // Region 4: Setting casterRenderable xform
    cxf.setRotationInRad(cxf.getRotationInRad());
    cxf.setPosition(offset[0], offset[1]);
    cxf.setZPos(offset[2]);
    cxf.setWidth(cxf.getWidth() * scale);
    cxf.setHeight(cxf.getHeight() * scale);

    return true;
}
```

The aLight parameter is the casting light source. The goals of this function are
to compute and set the shadow caster geometry transform, cxf, by using the aLight
to project the shadow caster onto the shadow receiver. As illustrated in Figure 8-29,
there are two cases to consider for the size of the projected caster geometry. First, for a
directional light source, the projected size is a constant. Second, for a point or spotlight,
the projected size is a function of distance to the receiver. These are the two cases,
Regions 2 and 3, of the if statement with the following details:

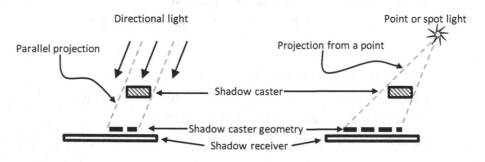

Figure 8-29. *Computing the shadow caster geometry*

a. **Region 2**: Computes parallel projection according to the directional light. The `if` statement within this region is to ensure no shadow is computed when the light direction is parallel to the xy plan or when the light is in the direction from the shadow receiver toward the shadow caster. Notice that for dramatic effects, the shadow caster geometry will be moderately scaled.

b. **Region 3**: Computes projection from the point or spotlight position. The two `if` statements within this region are to ensure that the shadow caster and receiver are on the same side of the light position, and for the purpose of maintaining mathematical stability, neither is very close to the light source.

c. **Region 4**: Uses the computed `distToReceiver` and `scale` to set the transform of the shadow caster or `cxf`.

The `ShadowCaster` object is meant for game developers to define and work with shadow. So, remember to update the engine access file, `index.js`, to forward the newly defined functionality to the client.

Defining the Shadow Receiver Class

Recall from Figure 8-25, `ShadowReceiver` is the object where the shadow of the caster object will appear. As illustrated in Figure 8-26, the `ShadowReceiver` must draw itself into the stencil buffer to ensure shadow caster geometry will only appear over pixels that are occupied by the `ShadowReceiver` object.

1. Create a new file, `shadow_receiver.js`, in the `src/engine/ shadows` folder; define the `ShadowReceiver` class. In the constructor, initialize the constants and variables necessary for receiving shadows. As discussed, the `mReceiver` is a `GameObject` with at least a `SpriteRenderable` reference and is the actual receiver of the shadow. Notice that `mShadowCaster` is an array of `ShadowCaster` objects. These objects will cast shadows on the `mReceiver`.

```
import * as shaderResources from "../core/shader_resources.js";
import ShadowCaster from "./shadow_caster.js";
import * as glSys from "../core/gl.js";
```

```
class ShadowReceiver {
    constructor(theReceiverObject) {
        this.kShadowStencilBit = 0x01;    // stencil bit for shadow
        this.kShadowStencilMask = 0xFF;  // The stencil mask
        this.mReceiverShader = shaderResources.getShadowReceiverShader();

        this.mReceiver = theReceiverObject;

        // To support shadow drawing
        this.mShadowCaster = [];          // array of ShadowCasters
    }

    ... implementation to follow ...
}
export default ShadowReceiver;
```

2. Define the addShadowCaster() function to add a game object as a
   shadow caster for this receiver:

```
addShadowCaster(lgtRenderable) {
    let c = new ShadowCaster(lgtRenderable, this.mReceiver);
    this.mShadowCaster.push(c);
}
// for now, cannot remove shadow casters
```

3. Define the draw() function to draw the receiver and all the
   shadow caster geometries:

```
draw(aCamera) {
    let c;

    // Step A: draw receiver as a regular renderable
    this.mReceiver.draw(aCamera);

    // Step B: draw receiver into stencil to enable corresponding pixels
    glSys.beginDrawToStencil(this.kShadowStencilBit,
                             this.kShadowStencilMask);
    //        Step B1: swap receiver shader to a ShadowReceiverShader
    let s = this.mReceiver.getRenderable().swapShader(
                        this.mReceiverShader);
```

```
//          Step B2: draw the receiver again to the stencil buffer
this.mReceiver.draw(aCamera);
this.mReceiver.getRenderable().swapShader(s);
glSys.endDrawToStencil(this.kShadowStencilBit,
                       this.kShadowStencilMask);

// Step C: draw shadow color to pixels with stencil switched on
for (c = 0; c < this.mShadowCaster.length; c++) {
    this.mShadowCaster[c].draw(aCamera);
}

// switch off stencil checking
glSys.disableDrawToStencil();
}
```

This function implements the outlined shadow simulation algorithm and does not draw the actual shadow caster. Notice that the mReceiver object is drawn twice, in steps A and B2. Step A, the first draw() function, renders the mReceiver to the canvas as usual. Step B enables the stencil buffer for drawing where all subsequent drawings will be directed to switching on stencil buffer pixels. For this reason, the draw() function at step B2 uses the ShadowReceiverShader and switches on all pixels in the stencil buffer that corresponds to the mReceiver object. With the proper stencil buffer setup, in step C, the draw() function calls to the mShadowCaster will draw the corresponding shadow caster geometries only into the pixels that are covered by the receiver.

Lastly, once again, the ShadowReceiver object is designed for the client game developers to create shadows. So, remember to update the engine access file, index.js, to forward the newly defined functionality to the client.

Updating Engine Support

With the new objects defined and engine configured, some of the existing engine classes must be modified to support the new shadow operations. The following summarizes the required changes without listing the straightforward changes. Please refer to the source code file for the actual implementation details.

- renderable.js: Both the ShadowCaster and ShadowReceiver objects require the ability to swap the shaders to render the objects for shadow simulation purpose. This swapShader() function is best realized in the root of the Renderable hierarchy.

509

- light.js: The Light source now defines mCastShadow, a boolean variable, and the associated getter and setter, indicating if the light should cast shadow.

- camera_main.js: The Camera WC center must now be located at some z distance away. A kCameraZ constant is defined for this purpose and used in the mCameraMatrix computation in the setViewAndCameraMatrix() function.

- transform.js: The Transform class must be modified to support being cloneTo() and the manipulation of a z-depth value.

Testing the Shadow Algorithm

There are two important aspects to testing the shadow simulation. First, you must understand how to program and create shadow effects based on the implementation. Second, you must verify that Renderable objects can serve as shadow casters and receivers. The MyGame level test case is similar to the previous project with the exception of the shadow setup and drawing.

Setting Up the Shadow

The proper way of setting up the shadow system is to create all ShadowCaster objects and then create and add to the ShadowReceiver objects. The my_game_shadow.js file defines the _setupShadow() function to demonstrate this.

```
MyGame.prototype._setupShadow = function () {
        // mLgtMinion has a LightRenderable
    this.mLgtMinionShadow = new engine.ShadowReceiver(this.mLgtMinion);
    this.mLgtMinionShadow.addShadowCaster(this.mIllumHero);
    this.mLgtMinionShadow.addShadowCaster(this.mLgtHero);

        // mIllumMinion has a SpriteAnimateRenderable
    this.mMinionShadow = new engine.ShadowReceiver(this.mIllumMinion);
    this.mMinionShadow.addShadowCaster(this.mIllumHero);
    this.mMinionShadow.addShadowCaster(this.mLgtHero);
    this.mMinionShadow.addShadowCaster(this.mLgtMinion);
```

```
      // mBg has a IllumRenderable
   this.mBgShadow = new engine.ShadowReceiver(this.mBg);
   this.mBgShadow.addShadowCaster(this.mLgtHero);
   this.mBgShadow.addShadowCaster(this.mIllumMinion);
   this.mBgShadow.addShadowCaster(this.mLgtMinion); }
```

The _setupShadow() function is called at the end of the MyGame.init() function, when all other GameObject instances are properly created and initialized. This function demonstrates that different types of Renderable objects can serve as shadow receivers.

- LightRenderable: mLgtMinionShadow is created with mLgtMinon as a receiver, which has a reference to a LightRenderable object.

- IllumRenderable: mBgShadow and mMinionShadow are created with mBg and mIllumMinion being the receivers where both have references to IllumRenderable object.

Note that in order to observe shadow on an object, an explicit corresponding ShadowReceiver must be created and followed by explicitly adding ShadowCaster objects to the receiver. For example, mLgtMinionShadow defines the mLgtMinion object to be a receiver, where only the mIllumHero and mLgtHero will cast shadows on this object. Lastly, notice that mLgtMinon and mIllumMinion are both receivers and casters of shadows.

Drawing the Shadow

In 2D drawings, objects are drawn by overwriting the previously drawn objects. For this reason, it is important to draw the shadow receivers and the shadow caster geometries before drawing the shadow casters. The following my_game.draw() function in my_game_main.js illustrates the important drawing order of objects:

```
draw() {
   // Clear the canvas
   engine.clearCanvas([0.9, 0.9, 0.9, 1.0]); // clear to light gray

   // Set up the camera and draw
   this.mCamera.setViewAndCameraMatrix();
```

```
        // always draw shadow receivers first!
        this.mBgShadow.draw(this.mCamera); // also draws the receiver object
        this.mMinionShadow.draw(this.mCamera);
        this.mLgtMinionShadow.draw(this.mCamera);

        this.mBlock1.draw(this.mCamera);
        this.mIllumHero.draw(this.mCamera);
        this.mBlock2.draw(this.mCamera);
        this.mLgtHero.draw(this.mCamera);

        this.mMsg.draw(this.mCamera);    // draw last
        this.mMatMsg.draw(this.mCamera);
}
```

It is important to note the draw ordering. All three shadow receivers are drawn first. Additionally, among the three receivers, the mBgShadow object is the actual background and thus is the first being drawn. Recall that in the definition of the ShadowReceiver class, the draw() function also draws the receiver object. For this reason, there is no need to call the draw() function of mLgtMinion, mIllumMinion, and mBg objects.

The rest of the MyGame level is largely similar to previous projects and is not listed here. Please refer to the source code for the details.

Observations

You can now run the project and observe the shadows. Notice the effect of the stencil buffer where the shadow from the mIllumHero object is cast onto the minion and yet not on the background. Press the WASD keys to move both of the Hero objects. Observe how the shadows offer depth and distance cues as they move with the two hero objects. The mLgtHero on the right is illuminated by all four lights and thus casts many shadows. Try selecting and manipulating each of the lights, such as moving or changing the direction or switching the light on/off to observe the effects on the shadows. You can even try changing the color of the shadow (in shadow_caster.js) to something dramatic, such as to bright blue [0, 0, 5, 1], and observe shadows that could never exist in the real world.

Summary

This chapter guided you to develop a variation of the simple yet complete Phong illumination model for the game engine. The examples were organized to follow the three terms of the Phong illumination model: ambient, diffuse, and specular. The coverage of light sources was strategically intermixed to ensure proper illumination can be observed for every topic discussed.

The first example in this chapter on ambient illumination introduced the idea of interactively controlling and fine-tuning the color of the scene. The following two examples on light sources presented the notion that illumination, an algorithmic approach to color manipulation, can be localized and developed in the engine infrastructure for supporting the eventual Phong illumination model. The example on diffuse reflection and normal mapping was critical because it enabled illumination computation based on simple physical models and simulation of an environment in 3D.

The Phong illumination model and the need for a per-object material property were presented in the specular reflection example. The halfway vector version of the Phong illumination model was implemented to avoid computing the light source reflection vector for each pixel. The light source type project demonstrated how subtle but important illumination variations can be accomplished by simulating different light sources in the real world. Finally, the last example explained that accurate shadow computation is nontrivial and introduced an approximation algorithm. The resulting shadow simulation, though inaccurate from a real-world perspective and with limitations, can be aesthetically appealing and is able to convey many of the same vital visual cues.

The first four chapters of this book introduced the basic foundations and components of a game engine. Chapters 5, 6, and 7 extended the core engine functionality to support drawing, game object behaviors, and camera controls, respectively. This chapter complements Chapter 5 by bringing the engine's capability in rendering higher-fidelity scenes to a new level. Over the next three chapters, this complementary pattern will be repeated. Chapter 9 will introduce physical behavior simulation, Chapter 10 will discuss particle effects, and Chapter 11 will complete the engine development with more advanced support for the camera including tiling and parallax.

Game Design Considerations

The work you did in the "*Game Design Considerations*" section of Chapter 7 to create a basic well-formed game mechanic will ultimately need to be paired with the other elements of game design to create something that feels satisfying for players. In addition to the basic game loop, you'll need to think about your game's systems, setting, and meta-game and how they'll help determine the kinds of levels you design. As you begin to define the setting, you'll begin exploring ideas for visual and audio design.

As is the case with most visual art, games rely in no small measure on effectively using lighting to convey setting. A horror game taking place in a graveyard at midnight will typically use a very different lighting model and color palette than a game focusing on upbeat, happy themes. Many people think that lighting applies primarily to games created in 3D engines that are capable of simulating realistic light and shadow, but the notion of lighting applies to most 2D game environments as well; consider the example presented by Playdead studio's 2D side-scrolling platform game *Limbo*, as shown in Figure 8-30.

Figure 8-30. *Playdead and Double Eleven's Limbo, a 2D side-scrolling game making clever use of background lighting and chiaroscuro techniques to convey tension and horror. Lighting can be both programmatically generated and designed into the color palettes of the images themselves by the visual artist and is frequently a combination of the two (image copyright Playdead media; please see www.playdead.com/limbo for more information)*

Lighting is also often used as a core element of the game loop in addition to setting the mood; a game where the player is perhaps navigating in the dark with a virtual flashlight is an obvious example, but lights can also indirectly support game mechanics by providing important information about the game environment. Red pulsing lights often signal dangerous areas, certain kinds of green environment lights might signal either safe areas or areas with deadly gas, flashing lights on a map can help direct players to important locations, and the like.

In the *Simple Global Ambient* project, you saw the impact that colored environment lighting has on the game setting. In that project, the hero character moves in front of a background of metallic panels, tubes, and machinery, perhaps the exterior of a space ship. The environment light is red and can be pulsed—notice the effect on mood when the intensity is set to a comparatively low 1.5 vs. when it's set to something like a supersaturated 3.5, and imagine how the pulsing between the two values might convey a story or increase tension. In the *Simple Light Shader* project, a light was attached to the hero character (a point light in this case), and you can imagine that the hero must navigate the environment to collect objects to complete the level that are visible only when illuminated by the light (or perhaps activate objects that switch on only when illuminated).

The *Multiple Lights* project illustrated how various light sources and colors can add considerable visual interest to an environment (sometimes referred to as localized environment lighting). Varying the types, intensities, and color values of lights often makes environments appear more alive and engaging because the light you encounter in the real world typically originates from many different sources. The other projects in this chapter all served to similarly enhance the sense of presence in the game level; as you work with diffuse shaders, normal maps, specularity, different light types, and shadows, consider how you might integrate some or all of these techniques into a level's visual design to make game objects and environments feel more vibrant and interesting.

Before you begin thinking about how lighting and other design elements might enhance the game setting and visual style, let us return for a moment to the simple game mechanic project from the "Game Design Considerations" section of Chapter 7 and consider how you might think about adding lighting to the mechanic to make the puzzle more engaging. Figure 8-31 begins with the basic mechanic from the end of the exercise.

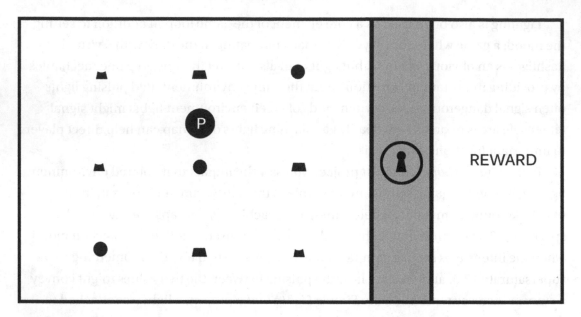

Figure 8-31. *The simple game mechanic project, without lighting. Recall that the player controls the circle labeled with a P and must activate each of the three sections of the lock in proper sequence to disengage the barrier and reach the reward*

For the next phase of the simple game mechanic project, how might you integrate light directly into the game loop so that it becomes part of gameplay? As with the previous exercise, minimizing complexity and limiting yourself to one addition or evolution to the current game loop at a time will help prevent the design from becoming overburdened or too complex. Start this phase of the exercise by considering all the different ways that light might impact the current game screen. You might choose to have a dark environment where the player sees only shadowy shapes unless illuminating an area with a flashlight, you might use colored light to change the visible color of illuminated objects, or you might use something like an X-ray or ultraviolet beam to reveal information about the objects that wouldn't be seen with the naked eye. For this example, you'll add one additional dimension to the simple sequence mechanic: a light beam that reveals hidden information about the objects, as shown in Figure 8-32.

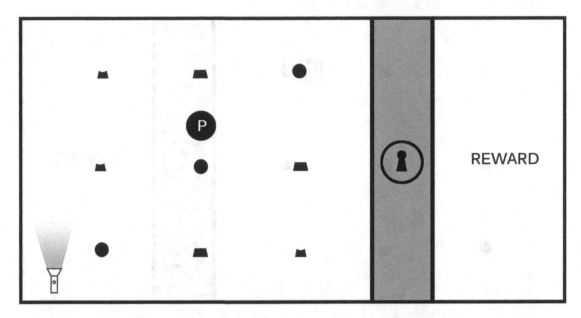

Figure 8-32. *The addition of a movable "flashlight" that shines a special beam*

In the first iteration of this game loop, the design required players to activate each segment of the lock in both the correct relative position (top on top, middle in the middle, bottom on bottom) and the correct order (top-middle-bottom). The interaction design provided consistent visual feedback for both correct and incorrect moves that allowed the player to understand the rules of play, and with some experimentation, astute players will deduce the proper sequence required to unlock the barrier. Now imagine how the addition of a special light beam might take the gameplay in a new direction: building on the basic notion of sequencing, you can create an increasingly clever puzzle requiring players to first discover the flashlight in the environment and experiment with it as a tool before making any progress on the lock. Imagine perhaps that the player can still directly activate the shapes when the hero character touches them even without the flashlight (triggering the highlight ring around the object as was the case in the first iteration, as shown in Figure 8-33), but that direct interaction is insufficient to activate the corresponding area of the lock unless the flashlight first reveals the secret clues required to understand the puzzle. Figure 8-34 shows the flashlight moved to illuminate one of the objects with its beam, revealing a single white dot.

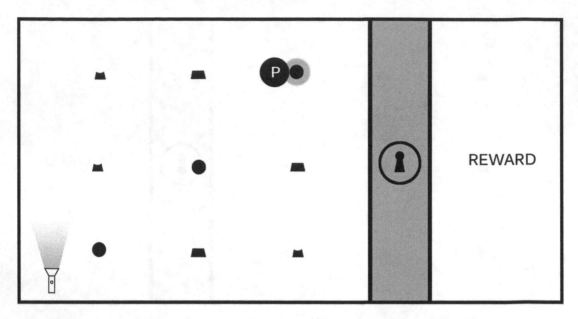

Figure 8-33. *The player is able to directly activate the objects as in the first iteration of the mechanic, but the corresponding section of the lock now remains inactive*

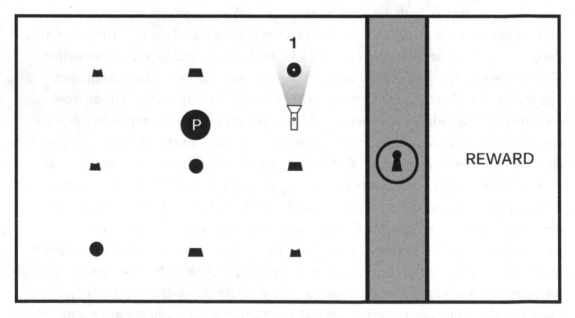

Figure 8-34. *The player moves the flashlight under one of the shapes to reveal a hidden clue (#1)*

From the gameplay point of view, any object in a game environment can be used as a tool; your job as a designer is to ensure the tool follows consistent, logical rules the player can first understand and then predictively apply to achieve their goal. In this case, it's reasonable to assume that players will explore the game environment looking for tools or clues; if the flashlight is an active object, players will attempt to learn how it functions in the context of the level.

The game loop in our sample project is evolving with the flashlight but uses the same basic sequencing principles and feedback metaphors. When the player reveals the secret symbol on the object with the flashlight, the player can begin the unlocking sequence by activating the object only when the symbol is visible. The new design requires players to activate each of the three objects corresponding to each section of the lock in the correct order, in this case from one dot to three dots; when all objects in a section are activated in order, that section of the lock will light up just as it did in the first iteration. Figures 8-35 to 8-37 show the new sequence using the flashlight beam.

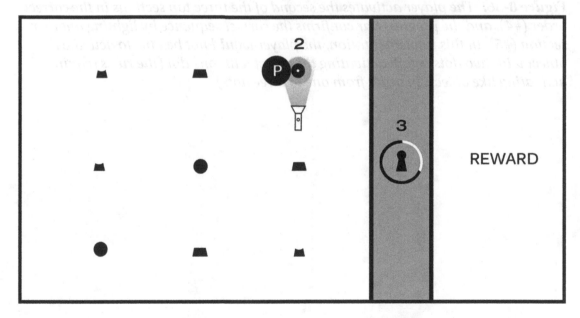

Figure 8-35. *With the flashlight revealing the hidden symbol, the player can now activate the object (#2), and a progress bar (#3) on the lock indicates the player is on the right track to complete a sequence*

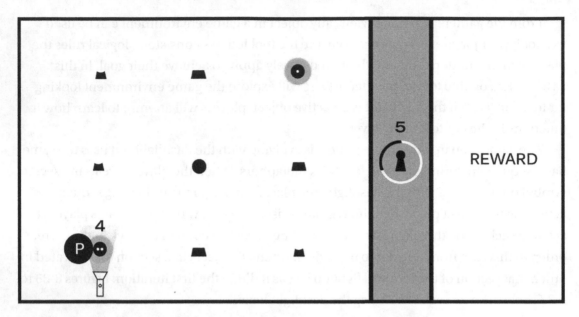

Figure 8-36. *The player activates the second of the three top sections in the correct order (#4), and the progress bar confirms the correct sequence by lighting another section (#5). In this implementation, the player would not be able to activate the object with two dots before activating the object with one dot (the rules require activating like objects in order from one to three dots)*

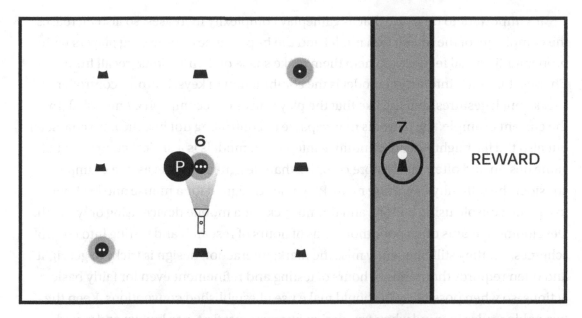

Figure 8-37. *The third of the three top sections is revealed with the flashlight beam and activated by the player (#6), thereby activating the top section of the lock (#7). Once the middle and lower sections of the lock have been similarly activated, the barrier is disabled and players can claim the reward*

Note that you've changed the feedback players receive slightly from the first iteration of the game loop: you originally used the progress bar to signal overall progress toward unlocking the barrier, but you're now using it to signal overall progress toward unlocking each section of the lock. The flashlight introduces an extra step into the causal chain leading to the level solution, and you've now taken a one-step elemental game loop and made something considerably more complex and challenging while maintaining logical consistency and following a set of rules that players can first learn and then predictively apply. In fact, the level is beginning to typify the kind of puzzle found in many adventure games: the game screen was a complex environment filled with a number of movable objects; finding the flashlight and learning that its beam reveals hidden information about objects in the game world would become part of the game setting itself.

It's important to be aware that as gameplay complexity increases, so also increases the complexity of the interaction model and the importance of providing players with proper audiovisual feedback to help them make sense of their actions (recall from Chapter 1 that the interaction model is the combination of keys, buttons, controller sticks, touch gestures, and the like that the player uses to accomplish game tasks). In the current example, the player is now capable of controlling not just the hero character but also the flashlight. Creating intuitive interaction models is a critical component of game design and often much more complex than designers realize; as one example, consider the difficulty in porting many PC games designed for a mouse and keyboard to a game console using buttons and thumb sticks or a mobile device using only touch. Development teams often pour thousands of hours of research and testing into control schemes, yet they still frequently miss the mark; interaction design is tricky to get right and often requires thousands of hours of testing and refinement even for fairly basic actions, so when possible, you should make use of established conventions. Keep the two golden rules in mind when you design interactions: first, use known and tested patterns when possible unless you have a compelling reason to ask players to learn something new; second, keep the number of unique actions players must remember to a minimum. Decades of user testing have clearly shown that players don't enjoy relearning basic key combinations for tasks that are similar across titles (which is why so many games have standardized on WASD for movement, e.g.), and similar data is available showing how easily players can become overwhelmed when you ask them to remember more than a few simple unique button combinations. There are exceptions, of course; many classic arcade fighting games, for example, use dozens of complex combinations, but those genres are targeted to a specific kind of player who considers mastering button combinations to be a fundamental component of what makes an experience fun. As a general rule, most players prefer to keep interaction complexity as streamlined and simple as possible if it's not an intentional component of play.

There are a number of ways to deal with controlling multiple objects. The most common pattern for our flashlight would likely be for the player to "equip" it; perhaps if the player moves over the flashlight and clicks the left mouse button, it becomes a new ability for the player that can be activated by pressing one of the keyboard keys or by clicking the right mouse button. Alternately, perhaps the hero character can move around the game screen freely with the WASD keys, while other active objects like the flashlight are first selected with a left-mouse-click and then moved by holding the left mouse button and dragging them into position. There are similarly a variety of ways to provide the player with contextual feedback that will help teach the puzzle logic and rules (in this case, we're using the ring around the lock as a progress bar to confirm players are following the correct sequence). As you experiment with various interaction and feedback models, it's always a good idea to review how other games have handled similar tasks, paying particular attention to things you believe to work especially well.

In the next chapter, you'll investigate how your game loop can evolve once again by applying simple physics to objects in the game world.

CHAPTER 9

Simulating the World with RigidShapes

After completing this chapter, you will be able to

- Recognize the significant computational complexity and cost of simulating real-world physical interactions

- Understand that typical game engine physics components approximate physical interaction based on simple geometries such as circles and rectangles

- Implement accurate collisions of circle and rectangular geometric shapes

- Approximate Newtonian motion formulation with Symplectic Euler Integration

- Resolve interpenetrating collisions based on a numerically stable relaxation method

- Compute and implement responses to collisions that resemble the behavior of rigid bodies in the real world

Introduction

In a game engine, the functionality of simulating energy transfer is often referred to as the physics, physics system, physics component, or physics engine. Game engine physics components play an important role in many types of games. The range of topics within physics for games is broad and includes but is not limited to areas such as rigid body, soft body, fluid dynamics, and vehicle physics. Believable physical behaviors

© Kelvin Sung, Jebediah Pavleas, Matthew Munson, and Jason Pace 2022
K. Sung et al., *Build Your Own 2D Game Engine and Create Great Web Games*,
https://doi.org/10.1007/978-1-4842-7377-7_9

and interactions of game objects have become key elements of many modern PC and console games, as well as, more recently, browser and smartphone games, for example, the bouncing of a ball, the wiggling of a jelly block, the ripples on a lake, or the skidding of a car. The proper simulation and realistic renditions of these are becoming common expectations.

Unfortunately, accurate simulations of the real world can involve details that are overwhelming and require in-depth disciplinary knowledge where the underlying mathematical models can be complicated and the associated computational costs prohibitive. For example, the skid of a car depends on its speed, the tire properties, etc.; the ripples on a lake depend on its cause, the size of the lake, etc.; the wiggle of a jelly block depends on its density, the initial deformation, etc. Even in the very simple case, the bounce of a ball depends on its material, the state of inflation, and, theoretically, even on the particle concentrations of the surrounding air. Modern game engine physics components address these complexities by restricting the types of physical interaction and simplifying the requirements for the simulation computation.

Physics engines typically restrict and simulate isolated types of physical interaction and do not support general combinations of interaction types. For example, the proper simulation of a ball bouncing (rigid body) often will not support the ball colliding and jiggling a jelly block (soft body) or accurately simulate the ripple effects caused by the ball interaction with fluid (fluid dynamics). That is, typically a rigid body physics engine does not support interactions with soft body objects, fluids, or vehicles. In the same manner, a soft body physics engine usually does not allow interactions with rigid body or other types of physical objects.

Additionally, physics engines typically approximate a vastly simplified interaction model while focusing mainly on attaining visually convincing results. The simplifications are usually in the forms of assumptions on object geometry and physical properties with restrictive interaction rules applied to a selective subset in the game world. For example, a rigid body physics engine typically simplifies the interactions of objects in the following ways:

- Assumes objects are continuous geometries with uniformly distributed mass where the center of mass is located at the center of the geometric shape

- Approximates object material properties with straightforward bounciness and friction

- Dictates that objects do not change shape during interactions
- Limits the simulation to a selective subset of objects in the game scene

Based on this set of assumptions, a rigid body physics simulation, or a rigid body simulation, is capable of capturing and reproducing many familiar real-world physical interactions such as objects bouncing, falling, and colliding, for example, a fully inflated bouncing ball or a simple *Lego* block bouncing off of a desk and landing on a hardwood floor. These types of rigid body physical interactions can be reliably simulated in real time as long as deformation does not occur during collisions.

Objects with uniformly distributed mass that do not change shape during interactions can be applicable to many important and useful scenarios in games. In general, rigid body physics engines are excellent for simulating moving objects coming into contact with one another such as a bowling ball colliding with pins or a cannon ball hitting an armored plate. However, it is important to recognize that with the given set of assumptions, a rigid body physics simulation does not support the following:

- Objects consisting of multiple geometric parts, for example, an arrow
- Objects with nontrivial material properties, for example, magnetism
- Objects with nonuniform mass distribution, for example, a baseball bat
- Objects that change shapes during collision, for example, rubber balls

Of all real-world physical object interaction types, rigid body interaction is the best understood, most straightforward to approximate solutions for, and least challenging to implement. This chapter focuses only on rigid body simulation.

Chapter Overview

Similar to illumination functionality, the physics component of a game engine is also a large and complex area of game engine design, architecture, and implementation. With this in mind, you will develop the rigid body physics component based on the same approach for all the previous game engine components. That is analyzing, understanding, and implementing individual steps to gradually realize the core functionality of the component. In the case of the physics component, the main ideas that encompass the rigid body simulation include the following:

- **Rigid shape and bounds**: Define the `RigidShape` class to support an optimized simulation by performing computation on separate and simple geometries instead of the potentially complex `Renderable` objects. This topic will be covered by the first project, the Rigid Shapes and Bounds project.

- **Collision detection**: Examines and implements the mathematics to accurately collide circle and rectangle `RigidShape` objects. An important concept is that in the digital world, rigid shapes can and often do overlap, and it is essential to retain the details of this overlapping event in a `CollisionInfo` object. The topics covered on collision detection will be discussed by three separate projects, each focusing on a unique collision interaction. They include

  - The collisions between circle shapes: the Circle Collisions and CollisionInfo project

  - The collisions between rectangle shapes: the Rectangle Collisions project

  - The collisions between rectangle and circle shapes: the Rectangle and Circle Collisions project

- **Movement**: Approximates integrals that describe motions in a world that is updated at fixed intervals. The topic on motion will be covered by the Rigid Shape Movements project.

- **Interpenetration of colliding objects**: Addresses the interpenetration between colliding rigid shapes with a numerically stable solution to incrementally correct the situation. This topic is presented in the Collision Position Correction project.

- **Collision resolution**: Models the responses to collision with the Impulse Method. The Impulse Method will be covered in two projects, first the simpler case without rotations in the Collision Resolution project and finally with considerations for rotation in the Collision Angular Resolution project.

Rigid Shapes and Bounds

The computation involved in simulating the interactions between arbitrary rigid shapes can be algorithmically complicated and computationally costly. For these reasons, rigid body simulations are typically based on a limited set of simple geometric shapes, for example, rigid circles and rectangles. In typical game engines, these simple rigid shapes can be attached to geometrically complex game objects for an approximated simulation of the physical interactions between those game objects, for example, attaching rigid circles on spaceships and performing rigid body physics simulations on the rigid circles to approximate the physical interactions between the spaceships.

From real-world experience, you know that simple rigid shapes can interact with one another only when they come into physical contact. Algorithmically, this observation is translated into detecting collisions between rigid shapes. For a proper simulation, every shape must be tested for collision with every other shape. In this way, the collision testing is an $O(n^2)$ operation, where n is the number of shapes that participate in the simulation. As an optimization for this costly operation, rigid shapes are often bounded by a simple geometry, for example, a circle, where the potentially expensive collision computation is only invoked when the bounds of the shapes overlap.

The Rigid Shapes and Bounds Project

This project introduces the RigidShape classes with a simple circular bound for collision optimization. The defined RigidShape class will be integrated into the game engine where each GameObject object will have references to both a Renderable and a RigidShape object. The Renderable object will be drawn showing the players a visually pleasing gaming element, while the RigidShape will be processed in the rigid shape simulation approximating the behavior of the GameObject object. You can see an example of this project running in Figure 9-1. The source code to this project is defined in chapter9/9.1.rigid_shapes_and_bounds.

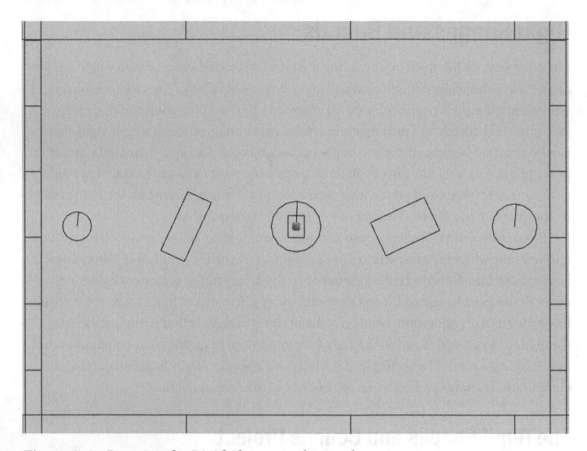

Figure 9-1. *Running the Rigid Shapes and Bounds project*

The controls of the project are as follows:

- **Behavior controls**:
  - **G key**: Randomly create a new rigid circle or rectangle
- **Draw controls**:
  - **T key**: Toggles textures on all objects
  - **R key**: Toggles the drawing of RigidShape
  - **B key**: Toggles the drawing of the bound on each RigidShape
- **Object controls**:
  - **Left-/right-arrow key**: Sequences through and selects an object
  - **WASD keys**: Move the selected object.

- **Z/X key**: Rotates the selected object.

- **Y/U key**: Increases/decreases `RigidShape` size of the selected object; this does not change the size of the corresponding `Renderable` object.

The goals of the project are as follows:

- To define the `RigidShape` classes and integrate with `GameObject`

- To demonstrate that a `RigidShape` represents a corresponding `Renderable` geometry on the same `GameObject`

- To lay the foundation for building a rigid shape physics simulator

- To define an initial scene for testing the physics component

In addition to the system `font` folder, you can find the following external resource files in the `assets` folder:

- `minion_sprite.png` is for the minion and hero objects.

- `platform.png` and `wall.png` are the horizontal and vertical boarder objects in the test scene.

- `target.png` is displayed over the currently selected object.

Setting up Implementation Support

You will begin building this project by first setting up implementation support. First, organize the engine source code structure with new folders for anticipation of increases in complexity. Second, define debugging utilities for visualization and verification of correctness. Third, extend library support for rotating rigid shapes.

Organizing the Engine Source Code

In anticipation for the new components, in the `src/engine` folder, create the `components` folder and move the `input.js` component source code file into this folder. This folder will contain the source code for physics and other components to be introduced in later chapters. You will have to edit `camera_input.js`, `loop.js`, and `index.js` to update the source code file location change of `input.js`.

Supporting Debug Drawing

It is important to note that only a Renderable object, typically referenced by a
GameObject, is actually visible in the game world. Rigid shapes do not actually exist in
the game world; they are defined to approximate the simulation of physical interactions
of corresponding Renderable objects. In order to support proper debugging and
verification of correctness, it is important to be able to draw and visualize the rigid
shapes.

1. In the src/core folder, create debug_draw.js, import from
   LineRenderable, and define supporting constants and variables for
   drawing simple shapes as line segments:

```
import LineRenderable from "../renderables/line_renderable.js";

let kDrawNumCircleSides = 16;     // approx circumference as line segments
let mUnitCirclePos = [];
let mLine = null;
```

2. Define the init() function to initialize the objects for drawing.
   The mUnitCirclePos are positions on the circumference of a unit
   circle, and mLine variable is the line object that will be used for
   drawing.

```
function init() {
    mLine = new LineRenderable();
    mLine.setPointSize(5);   // make sure when shown, its visible
    let deltaTheta = (Math.PI * 2.0) / kDrawNumCircleSides;
    let theta = deltaTheta;
    let i, x, y;
    for (i = 1; i <= kDrawNumCircleSides; i++) {
        let x = Math.cos(theta);
        let y = Math.sin(theta);
        mUnitCirclePos.push([x, y]);
        theta = theta + deltaTheta;
    }
}
```

3. Define the drawLine(), drawCrossMarker(), drawRectangle(), and drawCircle() functions to draw the corresponding shape based on the defined mLine object. The source code for these functions is not relevant to the physics simulation and is not shown. Please refer to the project source code folder for details.

4. Remember to export the defined functions:

```
export {
    init,
    drawLine, drawCrossMarker, drawCircle, drawRectangle
}
```

Initialing the Debug Drawing Functionality

Edit loop.js, import from debug_draw.js, and call the init() function after all asynchronous loading promises are fulfilled in start():

import * as debugDraw from "./debug_draw.js";

... identical to previous code ...

```
async function start(scene) {
    ... identical to previous code ...

    // Wait for any async requests before game-load
    await map.waitOnPromises();
```
    // With all resources loaded, it is now possible to initialize
    // system internal functions that depend on shaders, etc.
    debugDraw.init(); // drawing support for rigid shapes, etc.

    ... identical to previous code ...
```
}
```

> **Note**   A valid alternative for initializing debug drawing is in the
> createShaders() function of the shader_resources module after all the
> shaders are created. However, importing from debug_draw.js in shader_
> resources.js would create a circular import: debug_draw imports from
> LineRenderable that attempts to import from shader_resources.

Updating the gl-matrix Library

The gl-matrix library supports vertex translations with its vec2 addition and vertex
scaling with its vec2 scalar multiplication but does not support vertex rotations. Edit src/
lib/gl-matrix.js file, and define the vec2.rotateWRT() function to support rotating a vertex
position, pt, by angle with respect to the ref position. Following the convention of glmatrix, the first parameter of the function, out, returns the results of the operation.

```
vec2.rotateWRT = function(out, pt, angle, ref) {
    var r=[];

    vec2.subtract(r, pt, ref);
    vec2.rotate(r, r, angle);
    vec2.add(r, r, ref);
    out[0] = r[0];
    out[1] = r[1];

    return r;
};
```

Defining the RigidShape Base Class

You are now ready to define RigidShape to be the base class for the rectangle and circle
rigid shapes. This base class will encapsulate all the functionality that is common to the
two shapes.

1. Start by creating a new subfolder, rigid_shapes, in src/engine. In
    this folder, create rigid_shape.js, import from debug_draw, and
    define drawing colors and the RigidShape class.

```
import * as debugDraw from "../core/debug_draw.js";

let kShapeColor = [0, 0, 0, 1];
let kBoundColor = [1, 1, 1, 1];

class RigidShape {

    ... implementation to follow ...

}

export default RigidShape;
```

2. Define the constructor to include instance variables shared by all subclasses. The xf parameter is typically a reference to the Transform of the Renderable represented by this RigidShape. The mType variable will be initialized by subclasses to differentiate between shape types, for example, circle vs. rectangle. The mBoundRadius is the radius of the circular bound for collision optimization, and mDrawBounds indicates if the circular bound should be drawn.

```
constructor(xf) {
    this.mXform = xf;
    this.mType = "";

    this.mBoundRadius = 0;
    this.mDrawBounds = false;
}
```

3. Define appropriate getter and setter functions for the instance variables:

```
getType() { return this.mType; }

getCenter() { return this.mXform.getPosition(); }
getBoundRadius() { return this.mBoundRadius; }

toggleDrawBound() { this.mDrawBounds = !this.mDrawBounds; }
setBoundRadius(r) { this.mBoundRadius = r; }
```

```
setTransform(xf) { this.mXform = xf; }
setPosition(x, y) { this.mXform.setPosition(x, y); }
adjustPositionBy(v, delta) {
    let p = this.mXform.getPosition();
    vec2.scaleAndAdd(p, p, v, delta);
}

_shapeColor() { return kShapeColor; }
_boundColor() { return kBoundColor; }
```

4. Define the boundTest() function to determine if the circular
    bounds of two shapes have overlapped. As illustrated in
    Figure 9-2, a collision between two circles can be determined by
    comparing the sum of the two radii, rSum, with the distance, dist,
    between the centers of the circles. Once again, this is a relatively
    efficient operation designed to precede the costlier accurate
    collision computation between two shapes.

```
boundTest(otherShape) {
    let vFrom1to2 = [0, 0];
    vec2.subtract(vFrom1to2, otherShape.mXform.getPosition(),
                  this.mXform.getPosition());
    let rSum = this.mBoundRadius + otherShape.mBoundRadius;
    let dist = vec2.length(vFrom1to2);
    if (dist > rSum) {
        // not overlapping
        return false;
    }
    return true;
}
```

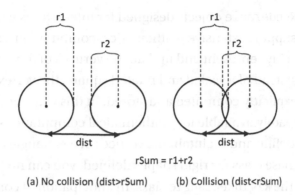

Figure 9-2. *Circle collision detection: (a) No collision. (b) Collision detected*

5. Define the update() and draw() functions. For now, update()
    is empty. When enabled, the draw() function draws the circular
    bound and an "X" marker at the center of the bound.

```
update() { // nothing for now }

draw(aCamera) {
    if (!this.mDrawBounds)
        return;
    debugDraw.drawCircle(aCamera, this.mXform.getPosition(),
                    this.mBoundRadius, this._boundColor());
    debugDraw.drawCrossMarker(aCamera, this.mXform.getPosition(),
                    this.mBoundRadius * 0.2, this._boundColor());
}
```

Defining the RigidRectangle Class

Renderable objects encode geometric information of a shape based on a Transform
operator being applied on the unit square. For example, a rotated rectangle is encoded
as a scaled and rotated unit square. As you have experienced, this representation, where
vertices of the unit square remain constant together with the matrix transformation
support from the GLSL vertex shader, is effective and efficient for supporting the drawing
of transformed shapes.

RigidShapes are Renderable objects designed for interactions where the underlying representation must support extensive mathematical computations. In this case, it is more efficient to explicitly represent and update the vertices of the underlying geometric shape. For example, instead of a scaled and rotated square, the vertex positions of the rectangle can be explicitly computed and stored. In this way, the actual vertex positions are always readily available for mathematical computations. For this reason, RigidRectangle will define and maintain the vertices of a rectangle explicitly.

With the abstract base class for rigid shapes defined, you can now create the first concrete rigid shape, the RigidRectangle class. In anticipation of complex collision functions, the implementation source code will be separated into multiple files. For now, create the rigid_rectangle.js as the access file, and import from the rigid_rectangle_main.js which will implement the core RigidRectangle functionality.

1. In the src/rigid_shapes folder, create rigid_rectangle.js to import from rigid_rectangle_main.js and to export the RigidRectangle class. This is the RigidRectangle class access file where users of this class should import from.

```
import RigidRectangle from "./rigid_rectangle_main.js";
export default RigidRectangle;
```

2. Now, create rigid_rectangle_main.js in the src/rigid_shapes folder to import RigidShape and debugDraw, and define RigidRectangle to be a subclass of RigidShape.

```
import RigidShape from "./rigid_shape.js";
import * as debugDraw from "../core/debug_draw.js";

class RigidRectangle extends RigidShape {

    ... implementation to follow ...

}
export default RigidRectangle;
```

3. Define the constructor to initialize the rectangle dimension, mWidth by mHeight, and mType. It is important to recognize that the vertex positions of the rigid rectangle are controlled by the Transform referenced by mXform. In contrast, the width and height dimensions are defined independently by mWidth

and mHeight. This dimension separation allows the designer
to determine how tightly a RigidRectangle should wrap the
corresponding Renderable. Notice that the actual vertex and face
normal of the shape are computed in the setVertices() and
computeFaceNormals() functions. The definition of face normal
will be detailed in the following steps:

```
constructor(xf, width, height) {
    super(xf);
    this.mType = "RigidRectangle";
    this.mWidth = width;
    this.mHeight = height;
    this.mBoundRadius = 0;
    this.mVertex = [];
    this.mFaceNormal = [];

    this.setVertices();
    this.computeFaceNormals();
}
```

4. Define the setVertices() function to set the vertex positions
   based on the dimension defined by mXform. As illustrated in
   Figure 9-3, the vertices on the rectangle is defined as index 0 being
   the top-left, 1 being top-right, 2 being bottom-right, and index 3
   corresponds to the bottom-left vertex position.

```
setVertices() {
    this.mBoundRadius = Math.sqrt(this.mWidth * this.mWidth +
                                    this.mHeight * this.mHeight) / 2;
    let center = this.mXform.getPosition();
    let hw = this.mWidth / 2;
    let hh = this.mHeight / 2;
    // 0--TopLeft;1--TopRight;2--BottomRight;3--BottomLeft
    this.mVertex[0] = vec2.fromValues(center[0] - hw, center[1] - hh);
    this.mVertex[1] = vec2.fromValues(center[0] + hw, center[1] - hh);
    this.mVertex[2] = vec2.fromValues(center[0] + hw, center[1] + hh);
    this.mVertex[3] = vec2.fromValues(center[0] - hw, center[1] + hh);
}
```

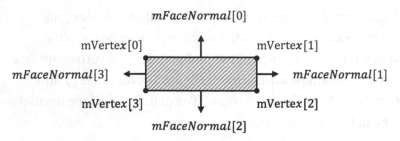

Figure 9-3. *The vertices and face normals of a rectangle*

5. Define the computeFaceNormals() function. Figure 9-3 shows that
    the face normals of a rectangle are vectors that are perpendicular
    to the edges and point away from the center of the rectangle.
    In addition, notice the relationship between the indices of the
    face normals and the corresponding vertices. Face normal index
    0 points in the same direction as the vector from vertex 2 to 1.
    This direction is perpendicular to the edge formed by vertices 0
    and 1. In this way, the face normal of index 0 is perpendicular to
    the first edge, and so on. Notice that the face normal vectors are
    normalized with length of 1. The face normal vectors will be used
    later for determining collisions.

```
computeFaceNormals() {
    // 0--Top;1--Right;2--Bottom;3--Left
    // mFaceNormal is normal of face toward outside of rectangle
    for (let i = 0; i < 4; i++) {
        let v = (i + 1) % 4;
        let nv = (i + 2) % 4;
        this.mFaceNormal[i] = vec2.clone(this.mVertex[v]);
        vec2.subtract(this.mFaceNormal[i],
                    this.mFaceNormal[i], this.mVertex[nv]);
        vec2.normalize(this.mFaceNormal[i], this.mFaceNormal[i]);
    }
}
```

6. Define the dimension and position manipulation functions. In all cases, the vertices and face normals must be recomputed (rotateVertices() calls computeFaceNormals()) and that it is critical to ensure that the vertex positions and the state of mXform are consistent.

```
incShapeSizeBy(dt) {
    this.mHeight += dt;
    this.mWidth += dt;
    this.setVertices();
    this.rotateVertices();
}

setPosition(x, y) {
    super.setPosition(x, y);
    this.setVertices();
    this.rotateVertices();
}

adjustPositionBy(v, delta) {
    super.adjustPositionBy(v, delta);
    this.setVertices();
    this.rotateVertices();
}

setTransform(xf) {
    super.setTransform(xf);
    this.setVertices();
    this.rotateVertices();
}

rotateVertices() {
    let center = this.mXform.getPosition();
    let r = this.mXform.getRotationInRad();
    for (let i = 0; i < 4; i++) {
        vec2.rotateWRT(this.mVertex[i], this.mVertex[i], r, center);
    }
    this.computeFaceNormals();
}
```

7. Now, define the draw() function to draw the edges of the
    rectangle as line segments, and the update() function to update
    the vertices of the rectangle. The vertices and face normals must
    be recomputed because, as you may recall from the RigidShape
    base class constructor discussion, the mXfrom is a reference
    to the Transform of a Renderable object; the game may have
    manipulated the position or the rotation of the Transform.
    To ensure RigidRectangle consistently reflect the potential
    Transform changes, the vertices and face normals must be
    recomputed at each update.

```
draw(aCamera) {
    super.draw(aCamera);   // the cross marker at the center
    debugDraw.drawRectangle(aCamera, this.mVertex, this._shapeColor());
}

update() {
    super.update();
    this.setVertices();
    this.rotateVertices();
}
```

Lastly, remember to update the engine access file, index.js, to forward the newly
defined functionality to the client.

Defining the RigidCircle Class

You can now implement the RigidCircle class with a similar overall structure to that of
RigidRectangle:

1. In the src/rigid_shapes folder, create rigid_circle.js
    to import from rigid_circle_main.js and to export the
    RigidCircle class. This is the RigidCircle class access file where
    users of this class should import from.

```
import RigidCircle from "./rigid_circle_main.js";
export default RigidCircle;
```

2. Now, create `rigid_circle_main.js` in the `src/rigid_shapes` folder to import `RigidShape` and `debugDraw`, and define `RigidCircle` to be a subclass of `RigidShape`:

```
import RigidShape from "./rigid_shape.js";
import * as debugDraw from "../core/debug_draw.js";

class RigidCircle extends RigidShape {

    ... implementation to follow ...

}
export default RigidCircle;
```

3. Define the constructor to initialize the circle radius, `mRadius`, and `mType`. Similar to the dimension of a `RigidRectangle`, the radius of `RigidCircle` is defined by `mRadius` and is independent from the size defined by the `mXfrom`. Note that the radii of the `RigidCircle`, `mRadius`, and the circular bound, `mBoundRadius`, are defined separately. This is to ensure future alternatives to separate the two.

```
constructor(xf, radius) {
    super(xf);
    this.mType = "RigidCircle";
    this.mRadius = radius;
    this.mBoundRadius = radius;
}
```

4. Define the getter and setter of the dimension:

```
getRadius() { return this.mRadius; }

incShapeSizeBy(dt) {
    this.mRadius += dt;
    this.mBoundRadius = this.mRadius;
}
```

5. Define the function to draw the circle as a collection of line
    segments along the circumference. To properly visualize the
    rotation of the circle, a bar is drawn from the center to the rotated
    vertical circumference position.

```
draw(aCamera) {
    let p = this.mXform.getPosition();
    debugDraw.drawCircle(aCamera, p, this.mRadius,
                            this._shapeColor());

    let u = [p[0], p[1] + this.mBoundRadius];
    // angular motion
    vec2.rotateWRT(u, u, this.mXform.getRotationInRad(), p);
    debugDraw.drawLine(aCamera, p, u,
                        false, this._shapeColor()); // show rotation

    super.draw(aCamera);   // draw last to be on top
}
```

Lastly, remember to update the engine access file, index.js, to forward the newly
defined functionality to the client.

Modifying the GameObject Class to Integrate RightShape

Recall from the discussions in Chapter 6, the GameObject class is designed to
encapsulate the visual appearance and behaviors of objects in the game scene. The
visual appearance of a GameObject is defined by the referenced Renderable object.
Thus far, the behaviors of a GameObject have been defined and implemented as part
of the GameObject class in the forms of an ad hoc traveling speed, mSpeed, and simple
autonomous behavior, rotateObjPointTo(). You can now replace these ad hoc parameters
with the upcoming systematic physics component support.

1. Edit GameObject.js to remove the support for speed, mSpeed,
    as well as the corresponding setter and getter functions and the
    rotateObjPointTo() function. Through the changes in the rest
    of this chapter, the game object behaviors will be supported
    by the rigid body physics simulation. Make sure to leave the
    other variables and functions alone; they are defined to support
    appearance and to detect texture overlaps, pixelTouches().

2. In the constructor, define new instance variables to reference to a
    RigidShape and to provide drawing options:

```
class GameObject {
    constructor(renderable) {
        this.mRenderComponent = renderable;
        this.mVisible = true;
        this.mCurrentFrontDir = vec2.fromValues(0, 1); // front direction
        this.mRigidBody = null;
        this.mDrawRenderable = true;
        this.mDrawRigidShape = false;
    }
    ... implementation to follow ...
}
```

3. Define getter and setter for mRigidBody and functions for toggling
    drawing options:

```
getRigidBody() { return this.mRigidBody; }
setRigidBody(r) { this.mRigidBody = r; }

toggleDrawRenderable() { this.mDrawRenderable = !this.mDrawRenderable; }
toggleDrawRigidShape() { this.mDrawRigidShape = !this.mDrawRigidShape; }
```

4. Refine the draw() and update() functions to respect the drawing
    options and to delegate GameObject behavior update to the
    RigidShape class:

```
draw(aCamera) {
    if (this.isVisible()) {
        if (this.mDrawRenderable)
            this.mRenderComponent.draw(aCamera);
        if ((this.mRigidBody !== null) && (this.mDrawRigidShape))
            this.mRigidBody.draw(aCamera);
    }
}
```

```
update() {
    // simple default behavior
    if (this.mRigidBody !== null)
        this.mRigidBody.update();
}
```

5. Edit the game_object_set.js file to modify the GameObjectSet class to support the toggling of different drawing options for the entire set:

```
... identical to previous code ...

    toggleDrawRenderable() {
        let i;
        for (i = 0; i < this.mSet.length; i++) {
            this.mSet[i].toggleDrawRenderable();
        }
    }

    toggleDrawRigidShape() {
        let i;
        for (i = 0; i < this.mSet.length; i++) {
            this.mSet[i].toggleDrawRigidShape();
        }
    }

    toggleDrawBound() {
        let i;
        for (i = 0; i < this.mSet.length; i++) {
            let r = this.mSet[i].getRigidBody()
            if (r !== null)
                r.toggleDrawBound();
        }
    }
```

Testing of RigidShape Functionality

RigidShape is designed to approximate and to participate on behalf of a Renderable object in the rigid shape simulation. For this reason, it is essential to create and test different combinations of RigidShape types, which includes circles and rectangles, with all combinations of Renderable types, more specifically, TextureRenderable, SpriteRenderable, and SpriteAnimateRenderable. The proper functioning of these combinations can demonstrate the correctness of the RigidShape implementation and allow you to visually examine the suitability as well as the limitations of approximating Renderable objects with simple circles and rectangles.

The overall structure of the test program, MyGame, is largely similar to previous projects where the details of the source code can be distracting and is not listed here. Instead, the following describes the tested objects and how these objects fulfill the specified requirements. As always, the source code files are located in src/my_game folder, and the supporting object classes are located in src/my_game/objects folder.

The testing of imminent collisions requires the manipulation of the positions and rotations of each object. The WASDObj class, implemented in wasd_obj.js, defines the WASD keys movement and Z/X keys rotation control of a GameObject. The Hero class, a subclass of WASDObj implemented in hero.js, is a GameObject with a SpriteRenderable and a RigidRectangle. The Minion class, also a subclass of WASDObj in minion.js, is a GameObject with SpriteAnimateRenderable and is wrapped by either a RigidCircle or a RigidRectangle. Based on these supporting classes, the created Hero and Minion objects encompass different combinations of Renderable and RigidShape types allowing you to visually inspect the accuracy of representing complex textures with different RigidShapes.

The vertical and horizontal bounds in the game scene are GameObject instances with TextureRenderable and RigidRectangle created by the wallAt() and platformAt() functions defined in my_game_bounds.js file. The constructor, init(), draw(), update(), etc., of MyGame are defined in the my_game_main.js file with largely identical functionality as in previous testing projects.

Observations

You can now run the project and observe the created RigidShape objects. Notice that by default, only RigidShape objects are drawn. You can verify this by typing the T key to toggle on the drawing of the Renderable objects. Notice how the textures of the Renderable objects are bounded by the corresponding RigidShape instances.

You can type the R key to toggle off the drawing of the RigidShape objects. Normally, this is what the players of a game will observe, with only the Renderable and without the RigidShape objects being drawn. Since the focus of this chapter is on the rigid shapes and the simulation of their interactions, the default is to show the RigidShape and not the Renderable objects.

Now type the T and R keys again to toggle back the drawing of RigidShape objects. The B key shows the circular bounds of the shapes. The more accurate and costly collision computations to be discussed in the next few sections will only be incurred between objects when these bounds overlap.

You can try using the WASD key to move the currently selected object around, by default with the Hero in the center. The Z/X and Y/U keys allow you to rotate and change the dimension of the Hero. Toggle on the texture, with the T key, to verify that rotation and movement are applied to both the Renderable and its corresponding RigidShape and that the Y/U keys only change the dimension of the RigidShape. This allows the designer to control over how tightly to wrap the Renderable with the corresponding RigidShape. You can type the left-/right-arrow keys to select and work with any of the objects in the scene. Finally, the G key creates new Minion objects with either a RigidCircle or a RigidRectangle.

Lastly, notice that you can move any selected object to any location, including overlapping with another RigidShape object. In the real world, the overlapping, or interpenetration, of rigid shape objects can never occur, while in the simulated digital world, this is an issue that must be addressed. With the functionality of the RigidShape classes verified, you can now examine how to compute the collision between these shapes.

Collision Detection

In order to simulate the interactions of rigid shapes, you must first detect which of the shapes are in physical contact with one another or which are the shapes that have collided. In general, there are two important issues to be addressed when working with rigid shape collisions: computation cost and the situations when the shapes overlap, or interpenetrate. In the following, the broad and narrow phase methods are explained as an approach to alleviate the computational cost, and collision information is introduced to record interpenetration conditions such that they can be resolved. This and the next two subsections detail the collision detection algorithms and implementations of circle-circle, rectangle-rectangle, and circle-rectangle collisions.

Broad and Narrow Phase Methods

As discussed when introducing the circular bounds for RigidShape objects, in general, every object must be tested for collision with every other object in the game scene. For example, if you want to detect the collisions between five objects, A, B, C, D, and E, you must perform four detection computations for the first object, A, against objects B, C, D, and E. With A and B's results computed, next you must perform three collision detections between the second object B, against objects C, D, and E; followed by two collisions for the third object, C; and then, finally, one for the fourth object, D. The fifth object, E, has already been tested against the other four. This testing process, while thorough, has its drawbacks. Without dedicated optimizations, you must perform $O(n^2)$ operations to detect the collisions between n objects.

In rigid shape simulation, a detailed collision detection algorithm involving intensive computations is required. This is because accurate results must be computed to support effective interpenetration resolution and realistic collision response simulation. A broad phase method optimizes this computation by exploiting the proximity of objects to rule out those that are physically far apart from each other and thus, clearly, cannot possibly collide. This allows the detailed and computationally intensive algorithm, or the narrow phase method, to be deployed for objects that are physically close to each other.

A popular broad phase method uses axis-aligned bounding boxes (AABBs) or bounding circles to approximate the proximity of objects. As detailed in Chapter 6, AABBs are excellent for approximating objects that are aligned with the major axes, but have limitations when objects are rotated. As you have observed from running the previous project with the B key typed, a bounding circle is a circle that centers around and completely bounds an object. By performing the straightforward bounding box/circle intersection computations, it becomes possible to focus only on objects with overlapping bounds as the candidates for narrow phase collision detection operations.

There are other broad phase methods that organize objects either with a spatial structure such as a uniform grid or a quad-tree or into coherent groups such as hierarchies of bounding colliders. Results from broad phase methods are typically fed into mid phase and finally narrow phase collision detection methods. Each phase narrows down candidates for the eventual collision computation, and each subsequent phase is incrementally more accurate and more expensive.

549

Collision Information

In addition to reporting if objects have collided, a collision detection algorithm should also compute and return information that can be used to resolve and respond to the collision. As you have observed when testing the previous project, it is possible for RigidShape objects to overlap in space, or interpenetrate. Since real-world rigid shape objects cannot interpenetrate, recording the details and resolving RigidShape overlaps is of key importance.

As illustrated in Figure 9-4, the essential information of a collision and interpenetration include collision depth, normal, start, and end. The collision depth is the smallest amount that the objects interpenetrated where the collision normal is the direction along which the collision depth is measured. The start and end are the beginning and end positions of the interpenetration defined for the convenience of drawing the interpenetration as a line segment. It is always true that any interpenetration of convex objects can be resolved by moving the colliding objects along the collision normal by the collision depth magnitude or the distance from the start to the end position.

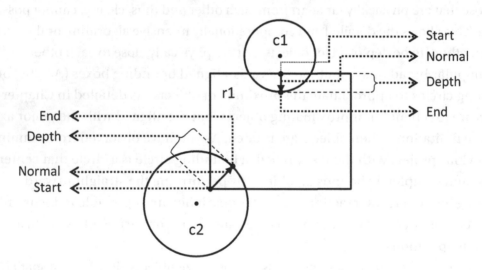

Figure 9-4. *Collision information*

The Circle Collisions and CollisionInfo Project

This project builds the infrastructure for computing and working with collision information based on collisions between circles. You can see an example of this project running in Figure 9-5. The source code to this project is defined in chapter9/9.2.circle_collisions_and_colllision_info.

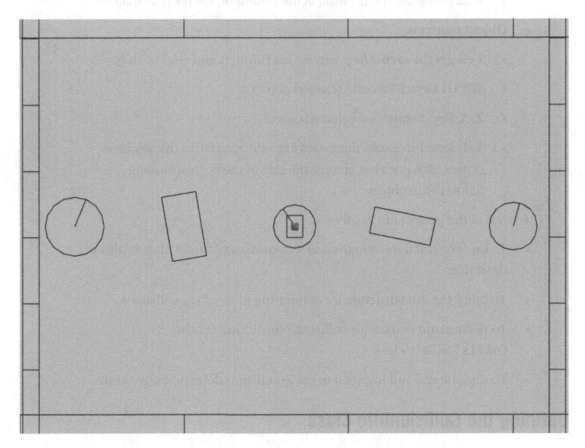

Figure 9-5. *Running the CollisionInfo and Circle Collisions project*

The controls of the project are identical to the previous project with a single addition of C key command in draw control:

- **Behavior controls**:
  - **G key**: Randomly create a new rigid circle or rectangle

- **Draw controls**:
  - **C key**: Toggles the drawing of all `CollisionInfo`
  - **T key**: Toggles textures on all objects
  - **R key**: Toggles the drawing of `RigidShape`
  - **B key**: Toggles the drawing of the bound on each `RigidShape`
- **Object controls**:
  - **Left-/right-arrow key**: Sequences through and selects an object.
  - **WASD keys**: Move the selected object.
  - **Z/X key**: Rotates the selected object.
  - **Y/U key**: Increases/decreases `RigidShape` size of the selected object; this does not change the size of the corresponding `Renderable` object.

The goals of the project are as follows:

- To understand the strengths and weaknesses of broad phase collision detection
- To build the infrastructure for computing inter-circle collisions
- To define and work with collision conditions via the `CollisionInfo` class
- To understand and implement circle collision detection algorithm

Defining the CollisionInfo Class

A new class must be defined to record `RigidShape` interpenetration situations as illustrated in Figure 9-4:

1. In the `src/engine/rigid_shape` folder, create the `collision_info.js` file, import from `debugDraw`, declare the drawing color to be magenta, and define the `CollisionInfo` class:

```
import * as debugDraw from "../core/debug_draw.js";

let kInfoColor = [1, 0, 1, 1]; // draw the info in magenta
```

```
class CollisionInfo {
    ... implementation to follow ...
}

export default CollisionInfo;
```

2. Define the constructor with instance variables that correspond to those illustrated in Figure 9-4 for collision depth, normal, and start and end positions:

```
constructor() {
    this.mDepth = 0;
    this.mNormal = vec2.fromValues(0, 0);
    this.mStart = vec2.fromValues(0, 0);
    this.mEnd = vec2.fromValues(0, 0);
}
```

3. Define the getter and setter for the variables:

```
getDepth() { return this.mDepth; }
setDepth(s) { this.mDepth = s; }

getNormal() { return this.mNormal; }
setNormal(s) { this.mNormal = s; }

getStart() { return this.mStart; }
getEnd() { return this.mEnd; }

setInfo(d, n, s) {
    this.mDepth = d;
    this.mNormal[0] = n[0];
    this.mNormal[1] = n[1];
    this.mStart[0] = s[0];
    this.mStart[1] = s[1];
    vec2.scaleAndAdd(this.mEnd, s, n, d);
}
```

4. Create a function to flip the direction of the collision normal. This function will be used to ensure that the normal is always pointing toward the object that is being tested for collision.

```
changeDir() {
    vec2.scale(this.mNormal, this.mNormal, -1);
    let n = this.mStart;
    this.mStart = this.mEnd;
    this.mEnd = n;
}
```

5. Define a `draw()` function to visualize the start, end, and collision normal in magenta:

```
draw(aCamera) {
    debugDraw.drawLine(aCamera, this.mStart, this.mEnd, true, kInfoColor);
}
```

Lastly, remember to update the engine access file, `index.js`, to forward the newly defined functionality to the client.

Modifying the RigidShape Classes

RigidShape classes must be updated to support collisions. Since the abstract base shape, RigidShape, does not contain actual geometric information, the actual collision functions must be implemented in the rectangle and circle classes.

Modifying the RigidRectangle Class

For readability, collision support will be implemented in a separate source code file, `rigid_rectangle_collision.js`:

1. Modify `rigid_rectangle.js` to import from the new source code file:

```
import RigidRectangle from "./rigid_rectangle_collision.js";
export default RigidRectangle;
```

2. In the `src/engine/rigid_shapes` folder, create the `rigid_rectangle_collision.js` file, import `CollisionInfo` and `RigidRectangle`, and define the `collisionTest()` function to always return a collision failed status. Collisions with RigidRectangle shape will always fail until the next subsection.

```
RigidRectangle.prototype.collisionTest =
function (otherShape, collisionInfo) {
    let status = false;
    if (otherShape.mType === "RigidCircle") {
        status = false;
    } else {
        status = false;
    }
    return status;
}
```

3. Remember to export the extended RigidRectangle class for the clients:

```
export default RigidRectangle;
```

Modifying the RigidCircle Class

Modify the RigidCircle source code files in exactly the same manner as that of RigidRectangle: edit rigid_circle.js to import from rigid_circle_collision.js. Now, you are ready to implement circle-circle collision detection.

1. In the src/engine/rigid_shape folder, create the rigid_circle_collision.js file, import RigidCircle, and define the collisionTest() function to always return a collision failed status if the otherShape is not a RigidCircle; otherwise, call and return the status of collideCircCirc(). For now, a RigidCircle does not know how to collide with a RigidRectangle.

```
import RigidCircle from "./rigid_circle_main.js";

RigidCircle.prototype.collisionTest =
function (otherShape, collisionInfo) {
    let status = false;
    if (otherShape.mType === "RigidCircle") {
        status = this.collideCircCirc(this, otherShape, collisionInfo);
    } else {
```

```
        status = false;
    }
    return status;
}
```

2. Define the `collideCircCirc()` function to detect the collision
    between two circles and to compute the corresponding collision
    information when a collision is detected. There are three cases
    to the collision detection: no collision (step 1), collision with
    centers of the two circles located at different positions (step 2),
    and collision with the two centers located at exactly the same
    position (step 3). The following code shows step 1, the detection of
    no collision; notice that this code also corresponds to the cases as
    illustrated in Figure 9-2.

```
RigidCircle.prototype.collideCircCirc= function (c1, c2, collisionInfo) {
    let vFrom1to2 = [0, 0];
    // Step 1: Determine if the circles overlap
    vec2.subtract(vFrom1to2, c2.getCenter(), c1.getCenter());
    let rSum = c1.mRadius + c2.mRadius;
    let dist = vec2.length(vFrom1to2);
    if (dist > Math.sqrt(rSum * rSum)) {
        // not overlapping
        return false;
    }
    ... implementation of Steps 2 and 3 to follow ...
}
```

3. When a collision is detected, if the two circle centers are located
    at different positions (step 2), the collision depth and normal can
    be computed as illustrated in Figure 9-6. Since `c2` is the reference
    to the other `RigidShape`, the collision normal is a vector pointing
    from `c1` toward `c2` or in the same direction as `vFrom1to2`. The
    collision depth is the difference between `rSum` and `dist`, and the
    start position for `c1` is simply `c2`-radius distance away from the
    center of `c2` along the negative `mFrom1to2` direction.

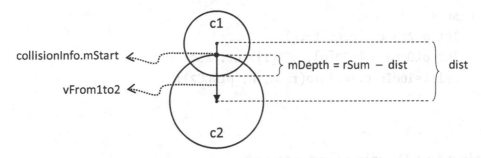

Figure 9-6. *Details of a circle-circle collision*

```
// Step 1: refer to previous step
if (dist !== 0) {
    // Step 2: Colliding circle centers are at different positions
    vec2.normalize(vFrom1to2, vFrom1to2);
    let vToC2 = [0, 0];
    vec2.scale(vToC2, vFrom1to2, -c2.mRadius);
    vec2.add(vToC2, c2.getCenter(), vToC2);
    collisionInfo.setInfo(rSum - dist, vFrom1to2, vToC2);
}
... implementation of Step 3 to follow ...
```

4. The last case for two colliding circles is when both circle centers are located at exactly the same position (step 3). In this case, the collision normal is defined to be the negative y direction, and the collision depth is simply the larger of the two radii.

```
// Step 1: refer to previous step
if (dist !== 0) {
    // Step 2: refer to previous step
} else {
    let n = [0, -1];
    // Step 3: Colliding circle centers are at exactly the same position
    if (c1.mRadius > c2.mRadius) {
        let pC1 = c1.getCenter();
        let ptOnC1 = [pC1[0], pC1[1] + c1.mRadius];
        collisionInfo.setInfo(rSum, n, ptOnC1);
```

```
    } else {
        let pC2 = c2.getCenter();
        let ptOnC2 = [pC2[0], pC2[1]+ c2.mRadius];
        collisionInfo.setInfo(rSum, n, ptOnC2);
    }
}
```

Defining the Physics Component

You can now define the physics component to trigger the collision detection
computations:

1. In the src/engine/components folder, create the physics.js
   file, import CollisionInfo and declare variables to support
   computations that are local to this file.

2. Define the collideShape() function to trigger the collision
   detection computation. Take note the two tests prior to the actual
   calling of shape collisionTest(). First, check to ensure the two
   shapes are not actually the same object. Second, call to the broad
   phase boundTest() method to determine the proximity of the
   shapes. Notice that the last parameter, infoSet, when defined
   will contain all CollisionInfo objects for all successful collisions.
   This is defined to support visualizing the CollisionInfo objects
   for verification and debugging purposes.

```
function collideShape(s1, s2, infoSet = null) {
    let hasCollision = false;
    if (s1 !== s2) {
        if (s1.boundTest(s2)) {
            hasCollision = s1.collisionTest(s2, mCInfo);
            if (hasCollision) {
                // make sure mCInfo is always from s1 towards s2
                vec2.subtract(mS1toS2, s2.getCenter(), s1.getCenter());
                if (vec2.dot(mS1toS2, mCInfo.getNormal()) < 0)
                    mCInfo.changeDir();
```

```
            // for showing off collision mCInfo!
            if (infoSet !== null) {
                infoSet.push(mCInfo);
                mCInfo = new CollisionInfo();
            }
        }
    }
}
    return hasCollision;
}
```

3. Define utility functions to support the game developer:
    processSet() to perform collision determination between all
    objects in the same GameObjectSet, processObjToSet() to check
    between a given GameObject and objects of a GameObjectSet, and
    processSetToSet() to check between all objects in two different
    GameObjectSets.

```
// collide all objects in the GameObjectSet with themselves
function processSet(set, infoSet = null) {
    let i = 0, j = 0;
    let hasCollision = false;

    for (i = 0; i < set.size(); i++) {
        let s1 = set.getObjectAt(i).getRigidBody();
        for (j = i + 1; j < set.size(); j++) {
            let s2 = set.getObjectAt(j).getRigidBody();
            hasCollision = collideShape(s1, s2, infoSet) || hasCollision;
        }
    }
    return hasCollision;
}

// collide a given GameObject with a GameObjectSet
function processObjToSet(obj, set, infoSet = null) {
    let j = 0;
```

```
    let hasCollision = false;
    let s1 = obj.getRigidBody();
    for (j = 0; j < set.size(); j++) {
        let s2 = set.getObjectAt(j).getRigidBody();
        hasCollision = collideShape(s1, s2, infoSet) || hasCollision;
    }
    return hasCollision;
}

// collide between all objects in two different GameObjectSets
function processSetToSet(set1, set2, infoSet = null){
    let i = 0, j = 0;
    let hasCollision = false;
    for (i = 0; i < set1.size(); i++) {
        let s1 = set1.getObjectAt(i).getRigidBody();
        for (j = 0; j < set2.size(); j++) {
            let s2 = set2.getObjectAt(j).getRigidBody();
            hasCollision = collideShape(s1, s2, infoSet) || hasCollision;
        }
    }
    return hasCollision;
}
```

4. Now, export all the defined functionality:

```
export {
    // collide two shapes
    collideShape,

    // Collide
    processSet, processObjToSet, processSetToSet
}
```

Lastly, remember to update the engine access file, index.js, to forward the newly defined functionality to the client.

Modifying the MyGame to Test Circle Collisions

The modifications required for testing the newly defined collision functionality is rather straightforward:

1. Edit my_game_main.js; in the constructor, define the array for storing CollisionInfo and a new flag indicating if CollisionInfo should be drawn:

```
constructor() {
    super();
    ... identical to previous code ...
    this.mCollisionInfos = [];
    ... identical to previous code ...

    // Draw controls
    this.mDrawCollisionInfo = true;  // showing of collision info
    ... identical to previous code ...
}
```

2. Modify the update() function to trigger the collision tests:

```
update() {
    ... identical to previous code ...
    if (this.mDrawCollisionInfo)
        this.mCollisionInfos = [];
    else
        this.mCollisionInfos = null;
    engine.physics.processObjToSet(this.mHero,
                this.mPlatforms, this.mCollisionInfos);
    engine.physics.processSetToSet(this.mAllObjs,
                this.mPlatforms, this.mCollisionInfos);
    engine.physics.processSet(this.mAllObjs, this.mCollisionInfos);
}
```

3. Modify the draw() function to draw the created CollisionInfo array when defined:

```
draw() {
    ... identical to previous code ...

    if (this.mCollisionInfos !== null) {
        for (let i = 0; i < this.mCollisionInfos.length; i++)
            this.mCollisionInfos[i].draw(this.mCamera);
        this.mCollisionInfos = [];
    }
    ... identical to previous code ...
}
```

4. Remember to update the drawControlUpdate() function to support the C key for toggling of the drawing of the CollisionInfo objects:

```
drawControlUpdate() {
    let i;
    if (engine.input.isKeyClicked(engine.input.keys.C)) {
        this.mDrawCollisionInfo = !this.mDrawCollisionInfo;
    }
    ... identical to previous code ...
}
```

Observations

You can now run the project to examine your collision implementation between RigidCircle shapes in the form of the resulting CollisionInfo objects. Remember that you have only implemented circle-circle collisions. Now, use the left-/right-arrow keys to select and work with a RigidCircle object. Use the WASD keys to move this object around to observe the magenta line segment representing the collision normal and depth when it overlaps with another RigidCircle. Try typing the Y/U keys to verify the correctness of CollisionInfo for shapes with different radii. Now, type the G key to create a few more RigidCircle objects. Try moving the selected object and increase its size such that it collides with multiple `RigidCircle` objects simultaneously and observe that a proper `CollisionInfo` is computed for every collision. Finally, note that you can toggle the drawing of `CollisionInfo` with the C key.

You have now implemented circle collision detection, built the required engine infrastructure to support collisions, and verified the correctness of the system. You are now ready to learn about Separating Axis Theorem (SAT) and implement a derived algorithm to detect collisions between rectangles.

Separating Axis Theorem

The Separating Axis Theorem (SAT) is the foundation for one of the most popular algorithms used for detecting collision between general convex shapes in 2D. Since the derived algorithm can be computationally intensive, it is typically preceded with an initial pass of the broad phase method. The SAT states that

> *Two convex polygons are not colliding if there exists a line (or axis) that is perpendicular to one of the given edges of the two polygons that when projecting all edges of the two polygons onto this axis results in no overlaps of the projected edges.*

In other words, given two convex shapes in 2D space, iterate through all of the edges of the convex shapes, one at a time. For each of the edges, derive a line (or axis) that is perpendicular to the edge, project all the edges of the two convex shapes onto this line, and compute for the overlaps of the projected edges. If you can find one of the perpendicular lines where none of the projected edges overlaps, then the two convex shapes do not collide.

Figure 9-7 illustrates this description using two axis-aligned rectangles. In this case, there are two lines that are perpendicular to the edges of the two given shapes, the X and Y axes.

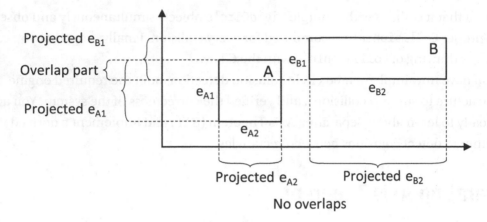

Figure 9-7. *A line where projected edges do not overlap*

When projecting all of the edges of the shapes onto these two lines/axes, note that the projection results on the Y axis overlap, while there is no overlap on the X axis. Since there exists one line that is perpendicular to one of the rectangle edges where the projected edges do not overlap, the SAT concludes that the two given rectangles do not collide.

The main strength of algorithms derived from the SAT is that for non-colliding shapes it has an early exit capability. As soon as an axis with no overlapping projected edge is detected, an algorithm can report no collision and does not need to continue with the testing for other axes. In the case of Figure 9-7, if the algorithm began with processing the X axis, there would be no need to perform the computation for the Y axis.

A Simple SAT-Based Algorithm

Algorithms derived based on the SAT typically consist of four steps. Note that this algorithm is applicable for detecting collisions between any convex shapes. For clarity, in the following explanation, each step is accompanied with a simple example consisting of two rectangles:

- **Step 1. Compute face normals**: Compute the perpendicular axes or face normals for projecting the edges. Using rectangles as an example, Figure 9-8 illustrates that there are four edges, and each edge has a corresponding perpendicular axis. For example, A1 is the corresponding axis for and thus is perpendicular to the edge e_{A1}. Note that in your `RigidRectangle` class, `mFaceNormal`, or face normals, are the perpendicular axes A1, A2, A3, and A4.

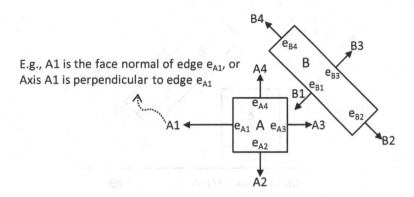

Figure 9-8. *Rectangle edges and face normals*

- **Step 2. Project vertices**: Project each of the vertices of the two convex shapes onto the face normals. For the given rectangle example, Figure 9-9 illustrates projecting all vertices onto the A1 axis from Figure 9-8.

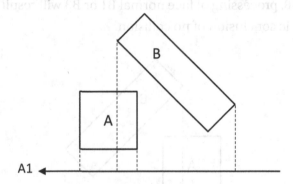

Figure 9-9. *Project each vertex onto face normals (shows A1)*

- **Step 3. Identify bounds**: Identifies the min and max bounds for the projected vertices of each convex shape. Continue with the rectangle example; Figure 9-10 shows the min and max positions for each of the two rectangles. Notice that the min/max positions are defined with respect to the direction of the given axis.

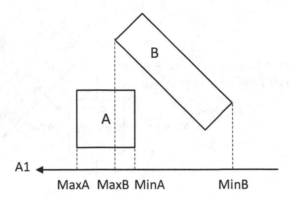

Figure 9-10. *Identify the min and max bound positions for each rectangle*

- **Step 4. Determine overlaps**: Determines if the two min/max bounds
  overlap. Figure 9-11 shows that the two projected bounds do indeed
  overlap. In this case, the algorithm cannot conclude and must
  proceed to process the next face normal. Notice that as illustrated
  in Figure 9-8, processing of face normal B1 or B3 will result in a
  deterministic conclusion of no collision.

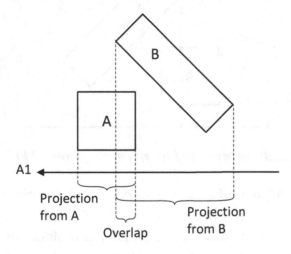

Figure 9-11. *Test for overlaps of projected edges (shows A1)*

The given algorithm is capable of determining if a collision has occurred with no
additional information. Recall that after detecting a collision, the physics engine must
also resolve potential interpenetration and derive a response for the colliding shapes.
Both of these computations require additional information—the collision information as

introduced in Figure 9-4. The next section introduces an efficient SAT-based algorithm that computes support points to both inform the true/false outcome of the collision detection and serve as the basis for deriving collision information.

An Efficient SAT Algorithm: The Support Points

As illustrated in Figure 9-12, a support point for a face normal of shape A is defined to be the vertex position on shape B where the vertex has the most negative distant from the corresponding edge of shape A. The vertex S_{A1} on shape B has the largest negative distant from edge e_{A1} when measured along the A1 direction, and thus, S_{A1} is the support point for face normal A1. The negative distance signifies that the measurement is directional and that a support point must be in the reversed direction from the face normal.

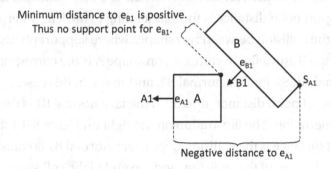

Figure 9-12. *Support points of face normals*

In general, the support point for a given face normal may be different during every update cycle and thus must be recomputed during each collision invocation. In addition, and very importantly, it is entirely possible for a face normal to not have a defined support point.

Support Point May Not Exist for a Face Normal

A support point is defined only when the measured distance along the face normal has a negative value. For example, in Figure 9-12, the face normal B1 of shape B does not have a corresponding support point on shape A. This is because all vertices on shape A are positive distances away from the corresponding edge e_{B1} when measured along B1. The positive distances signify that all vertices of shape A are in front of the edge e_{B1}. In other words, the entire shape A is in front of the edge e_{B1} of shape B; and thus, the two shapes are not physically touching; and thus, they are not colliding.

It follows that, when computing the collision between two shapes, if any of the face normals does not have a corresponding support point, then the two shapes are not colliding. Once again, the early exit capability is an important advantage—the algorithm can return a decision as soon as the first case of undefined support point is detected.

For convenience of discussion and implementation, the distance between a support point and the corresponding edge is referred to as the support point distance, and this distance is computed as a positive number. In this way, the support point distance is actually measured along the negative face normal direction. This will be the convention followed in the rest of the discussions in this book.

The Axis of Least Penetration and Collision Information

When support points are defined for all face normals of a convex shape, the face normal of the smallest support point distance is the axis leading to the least interpenetration. Figure 9-13 shows the collision between two shapes where support points for all of the face normals of shape B are defined: vertex S_{B1} on shape A is the corresponding support point for face normal B1, S_{B2} for face normal B2, and so on. In this case, S_{B1} has the smallest corresponding support point distance, and thus, the face normal B1 is the axis that leads to the least interpenetration. The illustration on the right on Figure 9-13 shows that in this case, support point distance is the collision depth, face normal B1 is collision normal, support point S_{B1} is the start of the collision, and the end of the collision can be readily computed; it is simply S_{B1} offset by collision depth in the collision normal direction.

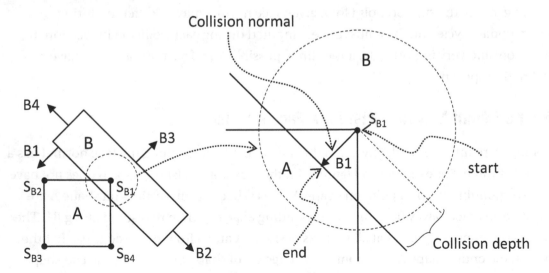

Figure 9-13. *Axis of least penetration and the corresponding collision information*

The Algorithm

With the background description, the efficient SAT-based algorithm to compute the collision between two convex shapes, A and B, can be summarized as

```
Compute the support points for all the face normals on shape-A
    If any of the support points is not defined, there is no collision
    If all support points defined, compute the axis of least penetration
Compute the support points for all the face normals on shape-B
    If any of the support points is not defined, there is no collision
    If all support points defined, compute the axis of least penetration
```

The collision information is simply the smaller collision depth from the earlier two results. You are now ready to implement the support point SAT algorithm.

The Rectangle Collisions Project

This project will guide you through the implementation of the support point SAT algorithm. You can see an example of this project running in Figure 9-14. The source code to this project is defined in chapter9/9.3.rectangle_collisions.

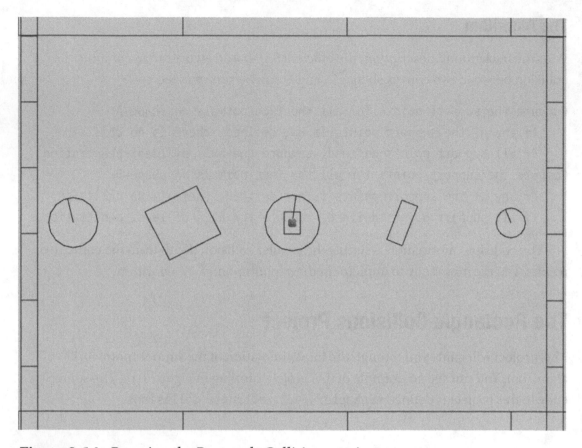

Figure 9-14. *Running the Rectangle Collisions project*

The controls of the project are identical to the previous project:

- **Behavior controls**:

  - **G key**: Randomly create a new rigid circle or rectangle

- **Draw controls**:

  - **C key**: Toggles the drawing of all `CollisionInfo`

  - **T key**: Toggles textures on all objects

  - **R key**: Toggles the drawing of `RigidShape`

  - **B key**: Toggles the drawing of the bound on each `RigidShape`

- **Object controls**:

  - **Left-/right-arrow key**: Sequences through and selects an object.

  - **WASD keys**: Move the selected object.

  - **Z/X key**: Rotates the selected object.

  - **Y/U key**: Increases/decreases `RigidShape` size of the selected object; this does not change the size of the corresponding `Renderable` object.

The goals of the project are as follows:

- To gain insights into and implement the support point SAT algorithm

- To continue with completing narrow phase collision detection implementation.

After this project, your game engine will be able to collide between circle shapes and between rectangle shapes while still not supporting collisions between circle and rectangle shapes. This will be one step closer to completing the implementation of narrow phase collision detection for rigid shapes. The remaining functionality, detecting circle-rectangle collisions, will be covered in the next subsection.

Implementing the Support Point SAT

With the collision detection infrastructure from the previous project completed, the only modification required is to append the new functionality to the `RigidRectangle` class. Recall that the source code file `rigid_rectangle_collision.js` was created for the implementation of rectangle collision.

1. In the `src/engine/rigid_shapes` folder, edit `rigid_rectangle_collision.js` to define local variables. These are temporary storage during computations; they are statically allocated and reused to avoid the cost of repeated dynamic allocation during each invocation.

```
class SupportStruct {
    constructor() {
        this.mSupportPoint = null;
```

```
        this.mSupportPointDist = 0;
    }
}

// temp work area to save memory allocations
let mTmpSupport = new SupportStruct();
let mCollisionInfoR1 = new CollisionInfo();
let mCollisionInfoR2 = new CollisionInfo();
```

2. Create a new function findSupportPoint() to compute a support
point based on, dir, the negated face normal direction, ptOnEdge,
a position on the given edge (e.g., a vertex). The listed code
marches through all the vertices; compute vToEdge, the vector
from vertices to ptOnEdge; project this vector onto the input dir;
and record the largest positive projected distant. Recall that dir is
the negated face normal direction, and thus, the largest positive
distant corresponds to the furthest vertex position. Note that it is
entirely possible for all of the projected distances to be negative. In
such cases, all vertices are in front of the input dir, a support point
does not exist for the given edge, and thus, the two rectangles do
not collide.

```
RigidRectangle.prototype.findSupportPoint = function (dir, ptOnEdge) {
    // the longest project length
    let vToEdge = [0, 0];
    let projection;

    mTmpSupport.mSupportPointDist = -Number.MAX_VALUE;
    mTmpSupport.mSupportPoint = null;
    // check each vector of other object
    for (let i = 0; i < this.mVertex.length; i++) {
        vec2.subtract(vToEdge, this.mVertex[i], ptOnEdge);
        projection = vec2.dot(vToEdge, dir);

        // find the longest distance with certain edge
        // dir is -n direction, so the distance should be positive
        if ((projection > 0) &&
            (projection > mTmpSupport.mSupportPointDist)) {
```

```
        mTmpSupport.mSupportPoint = this.mVertex[i];
        mTmpSupport.mSupportPointDist = projection;
    }
  }
}
```

3. With the ability to locate a support point for any face normal, the next step is the find the axis of least penetration with the findAxisLeastPenetration() function. Recall that the axis of least penetration is the support point with the least support point distant. The listed code loops over the four face normals, finds the corresponding support point and support point distance, and records the shortest distance. The while loop signifies that if a support point is not defined for any of the face normals, then the two rectangles do not collide.

```
RigidRectangle.prototype.findAxisLeastPenetration = function (otherRect,
collisionInfo) {
    let n;
    let supportPoint;

    let bestDistance = Number.MAX_VALUE;
    let bestIndex = null;

    let hasSupport = true;
    let i = 0;

    let dir = [0, 0];
    while ((hasSupport) && (i < this.mFaceNormal.length)) {
        // Retrieve a face normal from A
        n = this.mFaceNormal[i];

        // use -n as direction and the vertex on edge i as point on edge
        vec2.scale(dir, n, -1);
        let ptOnEdge = this.mVertex[i];
        // find the support on B
        // the point has longest distance with edge i
        otherRect.findSupportPoint(dir, ptOnEdge);
        hasSupport = (mTmpSupport.mSupportPoint !== null);
```

```
        // get the shortest support point depth
        if ((hasSupport) && (mTmpSupport.mSupportPointDist < bestDistance)) {
            bestDistance = mTmpSupport.mSupportPointDist;
            bestIndex = i;
            supportPoint = mTmpSupport.mSupportPoint;
        }
        i = i + 1;
    }
    if (hasSupport) {
        // all four directions have support point
        let bestVec = [0, 0];
        vec2.scale(bestVec, this.mFaceNormal[bestIndex], bestDistance);
        let atPos = [0, 0];
        vec2.add(atPos, supportPoint, bestVec);
        collisionInfo.setInfo(bestDistance, this.mFaceNormal[bestIndex],
        atPos);
    }
    return hasSupport;
}
```

4. You can now implement the collideRectRect() function by computing the axis of least penetration with respect to each of the two rectangles and choosing the smaller of the two results:

```
Rectangle.prototype.collideRectRect = function (r1, r2, collisionInfo) {
    var status1 = false;
    var status2 = false;
    // find Axis of Separation for both rectangle
    status1 = r1.findAxisLeastPenetration(r2, collisionInfoR1);
    if (status1) {
        status2 = r2.findAxisLeastPenetration(r1, collisionInfoR2);
        if (status2) {
            // if rectangles overlap, the shorter normal is the normal
            if (collisionInfoR1.getDepth()<collisionInfoR2.getDepth()) {
                var depthVec = collisionInfoR1.getNormal().scale(
                                            collisionInfoR1.getDepth());
```

```
        collisionInfo.setInfo(collisionInfoR1.getDepth(),
                        collisionInfoR1.getNormal(),
                        collisionInfoR1.mStart.subtract(depthVec));
    } else {
        collisionInfo.setInfo(collisionInfoR2.getDepth(),
                        collisionInfoR2.getNormal().scale(-1),
                        collisionInfoR2.mStart);
    }
  }
}
return status1 && status2;
}
```

5. Complete the implementation by modifying the collisionTest()
   function to call the newly defined collideRectRect() function to
   compute the collision between two rectangles:

```
RigidRectangle.prototype.collisionTest =
function (otherShape, collisionInfo) {
    let status = false;
    if (otherShape.mType === "RigidCircle") {
        status = false;
    } else {
        status = this.collideRectRect(this, otherShape, collisionInfo);
    }
    return status;
}
```

Observations

You can now run the project to test your implementation. You can use the left-/right-
arrow keys to select any rigid shape and use the WASD keys to move the selected object.
Once again, you can observe the magenta collision information between overlapping
rectangles or overlapping circles. Remember that this line shows the least amount of
positional correction needed to ensure that there is no overlap between the shapes. Type
the Z/X keys to rotate and the Y/U keys to change the size of the selected object, and
observe how the collision information changes accordingly.

At this point, only circle-circle and rectangle-rectangle collisions are supported, so when circles and rectangles overlap, there are no collision information shown. This will be resolved in the next project.

Collision Between Rectangles and Circles

The support point algorithm does not work with circles because a circle does not have identifiable vertex positions. Instead, you will implement an algorithm that detects collisions between a rectangle and a circle according to the relative position of the circle's center with respect to the rectangle.

Before discussing the actual algorithm, as illustrated in Figure 9-15, it is convenient to recognize that the area outside an edge of a rectangle can be categorized into three distinct regions by extending the connecting edges. In this case, the dotted lines separated the area outside the given edge into RG1, the region to the left/top; RG2, the region to the right/bottom; and RG3, the region immediately outside of the given edge.

With this background, the collision between a rectangle and a circle can be detected as follows:

- **Step A**: Compute the edge on the rectangle that is closest to the circle center.

- **Step B**: If the circle center is inside the rectangle, collision is detected.

- **Step C**: If circle center is outside

    - **Step C1**: If in Region RG1, distance between the circle center and top vertex determines if a collision has occurred.

    - **Step C2**: If in Region RG2, distance between the circle center and bottom vertex determines if a collision has occurred.

    - **Step C3**: If in Region RG3, perpendicular distance between the center and the edge determines if a collision has occurred.

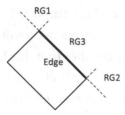

Figure 9-15. *The three regions outside a given edge of a rectangle*

The Rectangle and Circle Collisions Project

This project guides you in implementing the described rectangle-circle collision detection algorithm. You can see an example of this project running in Figure 9-16. The source code to this project is defined in `chapter9/9.4.rectangle_and_circle_collisions`.

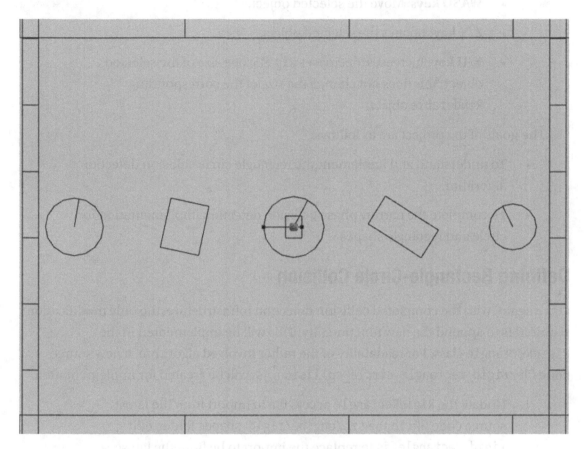

Figure 9-16. *Running the Rectangle and Circle Collisions project*

The controls of the project are identical to the previous project:

- **Behavior controls**:
  - **G key**: Randomly creates a new rigid circle or rectangle
- **Draw controls**:
  - **C key**: Toggles the drawing of all `CollisionInfo`
  - **T key**: Toggles textures on all objects

- **R key**: Toggles the drawing of `RigidShape`

- **B key**: Toggles the drawing of the bound on each `RigidShape`

- **Object controls**:

  - **Left-/right-arrow key**: Sequences through and selects an object.

  - **WASD keys**: Move the selected object.

  - **Z/X key**: Rotates the selected object.

  - **Y/U key**: Increases/decreases `RigidShape` size of the selected object; this does not change the size of the corresponding `Renderable` object.

The goals of the project are as follows:

- To understand and implement the rectangle circle collision detection algorithm

- To complete the narrow phase collision detection implementation for circle and rectangle shapes

Defining Rectangle-Circle Collision

Once again, with the completed collision detection infrastructure, the only modification required is to append the new functionality. This will be implemented in the `RigidRectangle` class. For readability of the rather involved algorithm, a new source code file, `rigid_rectangle_circle_collision.js`, will be created for implementation.

1. Update the `RigidRectangle` access file to import from the latest source code file. In the `src/engine/rigid_shapes` folder, edit `rigid_rectangle.js` to replace the import to be from the latest source code file.

```
import RigidRectangle from "./rigid_rectangle_circle_collision.js";
export default RigidRectangle;
```

2. In the same folder, create the `rigid_rectangle_circle_collision.js` file to import from `rigid_rectangle_collision.js` such that new collision function can be appended to the class:

```
import RigidRectangle from "./rigid_rectangle_collision.js";
```

3. Define a new function, checkCircRectVertex(), to process
    regions RG1 and RG2. As illustrated in the left diagram of
    Figure 9-17, the parameter v1 is the vector from vertex position
    to circle center. The right diagram of Figure 9-17 shows that a
    collision occurs when dist, the length of v1, is less than r, the
    radius. In this case, the collision depth is simply the difference
    between r and dist.

```
RigidRectangle.prototype.checkCircRectVertex =
function(v1, cirCenter, r, info) {
    // the center of circle is in corner region of mVertex[nearestEdge]
    let dist = vec2.length(v1);
    // compare the distance with radius to decide collision
    if (dist > r)
        return false;
    let radiusVec = [0, 0];
    let ptAtCirc = [0, 0];
    vec2.scale(v1, v1, 1/dist); // normalize
    vec2.scale(radiusVec, v1, -r);
    vec2.add(ptAtCirc, cirCenter, radiusVec);
    info.setInfo(r - dist, v1, ptAtCirc);
    return true;
}
```

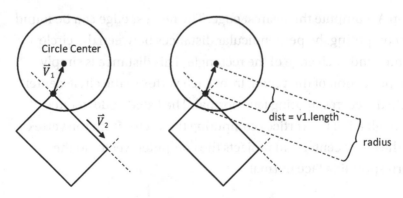

Figure 9-17. *Left: condition when center is in region RG1. Right: the
corresponding collision information*

4. Define collideRectCirc() function to detect the collision between a rectangle and a circle. The following code shows the declaration of local variables and the five major steps, A to C3, that must be performed. The details of each steps are discussed in the rest of this subsection.

```
RigidRectangle.prototype.collideRectCirc =
function (otherCir, collisionInfo) {
    let outside = false;
    let bestDistance = -Number.MAX_VALUE;
    let nearestEdge = 0;
    let vToC = [0, 0];
    let projection = 0;
    let i = 0;
    let cirCenter = otherCir.getCenter();

    ... Step A: Compute nearest edge, handle if center is inside ...
    if (!outside) {
        ... Step B: Circle center is inside rectangle ...
        return;
    }
    ... Steps C1 to C3: Circle center is outside rectangle ...
    return true;
};
```

5. Step A, compute the nearest edge. The nearest edge can be found by computing the perpendicular distances between the circle center and each edge of the rectangle. This distance is simply the projection of the vector, from each vertex to the circle center, onto the corresponding face normal. The listed code iterates through all of the vertices computing the vector from the vertex to the circle center and projects the computed vector to the corresponding face normal.

```
// Step A: Compute the nearest edge
while ((!outside) && (i<4)) {
    // find the nearest face for center of circle
    vec2.subtract(vToC, cirCenter, this.mVertex[i]);
    projection = vec2.dot(vToC, this.mFaceNormal[i]);
    if (projection > bestDistance) {
        outside = (projection > 0); // if projection < 0, inside
        bestDistance = projection;
        nearestEdge = i;
    }
    i++;
}
```

As illustrated in the left diagram of Figure 9-18, when the circle center is inside the rectangle, all vertex to center vectors will be in the opposite directions of their corresponding face normals and thus will result in negative projected lengths. This is in contrast to the right diagram of Figure 9-18, when the center is outside of the rectangle. In this case, at least one of the projected lengths will be positive. For this reason, the "nearest projected distance" is the one with the least negative value and thus is actually the largest number.

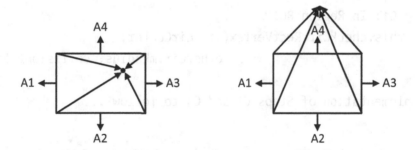

Figure 9-18. *Left: center inside the rectangle will result in all negative projected length. Right: center outside the rectangle will result in at least one positive projected length*

6. Step B, if the circle center is inside the rectangle, then collision is detected and the corresponding collision information can be computed and returned:

```
if (!outside) { // inside
    // Step B: The center of circle is inside of rectangle
    vec2.scale(radiusVec,this.mFaceNormal[nearestEdge],otherCir.mRadius);
    dist = otherCir.mRadius - bestDistance; // bestDist is -ve
    vec2.subtract(ptAtCirc, cirCenter, radiusVec);
    collisionInfo.setInfo(dist, this.mFaceNormal[nearestEdge], ptAtCirc);
    return true;
}
```

7. Step C1, determine and process if the circle center is in Region
    RG1. As illustrated in the left diagram of Figure 9-17, Region RG1
    can be detected when v1, the vector between the center and
    vertex, is in the opposite direction of v2, the direction of the edge.
    This condition is computed in the following listed code:

```
let v1 = [0, 0], v2 = [0, 0];
vec2.subtract(v1, cirCenter, this.mVertex[nearestEdge]);
vec2.subtract(v2, this.mVertex[(nearestEdge + 1) % 4],
                  this.mVertex[nearestEdge]);
let dot = vec2.dot(v1, v2);
```

```
if (dot < 0) {
    // Step C1: In Region RG1
    return this.checkCircRectVertex(v1, cirCenter,
                                    otherCir.mRadius, collisionInfo);
} else {
    ... implementation of Steps C2 and C3 to follow ...
}
```

8. Steps C2 and C3, differentiate and process for Regions RG2 and
    RG3. The listed code performs complementary computation
    for the other vertex on the same rectangle edge for Region RG2.
    The last region for the circle center to be located in would be
    the area immediately outside the nearest edge. In this case, the
    bestDistance computed previously in step A is the distance
    between the circle center and the given edge. If this distance is
    less than the circle radius, then a collision has occurred.

```
if (dot < 0) {
    // Step C1: In Region RG1
    ... identical to previous code ...
} else {
    // Either in Region RG2 or RG3
    // v1 is from right vertex of face to center of circle
    // v2 is from right vertex of face to left vertex of face
    vec2.subtract(v1, cirCenter, this.mVertex[(nearestEdge + 1) % 4]);
    vec2.scale(v2, v2, -1);
    dot = vec2.dot(v1, v2);
    if (dot < 0) {
        // Step C2: In Region RG2
        return this.checkCircRectVertex(v1, cirCenter,
                          otherCir.mRadius, collisionInfo);
    } else {
        // Step C3: In Region RG3
        if (bestDistance < otherCir.mRadius) {
            vec2.scale(radiusVec,
                    this.mFaceNormal[nearestEdge], otherCir.mRadius);
            dist = otherCir.mRadius - bestDistance;
            vec2.subtract(ptAtCirc, cirCenter, radiusVec);
            collisionInfo.setInfo(dist,
                            this.mFaceNormal[nearestEdge], ptAtCirc);
            return true;
        } else {
            return false;
        }
    }
}
}
```

Calling the Newly Defined Function

The last step is to invoke the newly defined function. Note that the collision function
should be called when a circle comes into contact with a rectangle, as well as when a
rectangle comes into contact with a circle. For this reason, you must modify both the
RigidRectangle class in rigid_rectangle_collision.js and the RigidCircle class in
rigid_circle_collision.js.

583

1. In the src/engine/rigid_shapes folder, edit rigid_rectangle_
    collision.js, and modify the collisionTest() function to call
    the newly defined collideRectCirc() when the parameter is a
    circle shape:

```
RigidRectangle.prototype.collisionTest =
function (otherShape, collisionInfo) {
    let status = false;
    if (otherShape.mType === "RigidCircle") {
        status = this.collideRectCirc(otherShape, collisionInfo);
    } else {
        status = this.collideRectRect(this, otherShape, collisionInfo);
    }
    return status;
}
```

2. In the same folder, edit rigid_circle_collision.js, modify
    the collisionTest() function to call the newly defined
    collideRectCirc() when the parameter is a rectangle shape:

```
RigidCircle.prototype.collisionTest =
function (otherShape, collisionInfo) {
    let status = false;
    if (otherShape.mType === "RigidCircle") {
        status = this.collideCircCirc(this, otherShape, collisionInfo);
    } else {
        status = otherShape.collideRectCirc(this, collisionInfo);
    }
    return status;
}
```

Observations

You can now run the project to test your implementation. You can create new rectangles
and circles, move, and rotate them to observe the corresponding collision information.

You have finally completed the narrow phase collision detection implementation
and can begin to examine the motions of these rigid shapes.

Movement

Movement is the description of how object positions change in the simulated world. Mathematically, movement can be formulated in many ways. In Chapter 6, you experienced working with movement where you continuously accumulated a displacement to the position of an object. As illustrated in the following equation and in Figure 9-19, you have been working with describing movement based on constant displacements.

- $p_{new} = p_{current} + displacement$

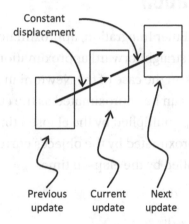

Figure 9-19. *Movement based on constant displacements*

Movement that is governed by the constant displacement formulation becomes restrictive when it is necessary to change the amount to be displaced over time. Newtonian mechanics address this restriction by considering time in the movement formulations, as seen in the following equations:

- $v_{new} = v_{current} + \int a(t)dt$
- $p_{new} = p_{current} + \int v(t)dt$

These two equations represent Newtonian-based movements where v(t) is the velocity that describes the change in position over time and a(t) is the acceleration that describes the change in velocity over time.

Notice that both velocity and acceleration are vector quantities encoding both the magnitude and direction. The magnitude of a velocity vector defines the speed, and the normalized velocity vector identifies the direction that the object is traveling. An acceleration vector lets you know whether an object is speeding up or slowing down as well as the changes in the object's traveling directions. Acceleration is changed by the forces acting upon an object. For example, if you were to throw a ball into the air, the gravitational force would affect the object's acceleration over time, which in turn would change the object's velocity.

Explicit Euler Integration

The Euler method, or Explicit Euler Integration, approximates integrals based on initial values. This is one of the most straightforward approximations for integrals. As illustrated in the following two equations, in the case of the Newtonian movement formulation, the new velocity, v_{new}, of an object can be approximated as the current velocity, $v_{current}$, plus the current acceleration, $a_{current}$, multiplied by the elapsed time. Similarly, the object's new position, p_{new}, can be approximated by the object's current position, $p_{current}$, plus the current velocity, $v_{current}$, multiplied by the elapsed time.

- $v_{new} = v_{current} + a_{current} * dt$

- $p_{new} = p_{current} + v_{current} * dt$

The left diagram of Figure 9-20 illustrates a simple example of approximating movements with Explicit Euler Integration. Notice that the new position, p_{new}, is computed based on the current velocity, $v_{current}$, while the new velocity, v_{new}, is computed to move the position for the next update cycle.

Figure 9-20. *Explicit (left) and Symplectic (right) Euler Integration*

Symplectic Euler Integration

You will implement the Semi-implicit Euler Integration or Symplectic Euler Integration. With Symplectic Euler Integration, instead of current results, intermediate results are used in subsequent approximations and thus better simulate the actual movement. The following equations show Symplectic Euler Integration. Notice that it is nearly identical to the Euler Method except that the new velocity, v_{new}, is being used when calculating the new position, p_{new}. This essentially means that the velocity for the next frame is being used to calculate the position of this frame.

- $v_{new} = v_{current} + a_{current} * dt$

- $p_{new} = p_{current} + v_{new} * dt$

The right diagram of Figure 9-20 illustrates that with the Symplectic Euler Integration, the new position p_{new} is computed based on the newly computed velocity, v_{new}.

The Rigid Shape Movements Project

You are now ready to implement Symplectic Euler Integration to approximate movements. The fixed time step, dt, formulation conveniently allows the integral to be evaluated once per update cycle. This project will guide you through working with the RigidShape class to support movement approximation with the Symplectic Euler Integration. You can see an example of this project running in Figure 9-21. The source code to this project is defined in chapter9/9.5.rigid_shape_movements.

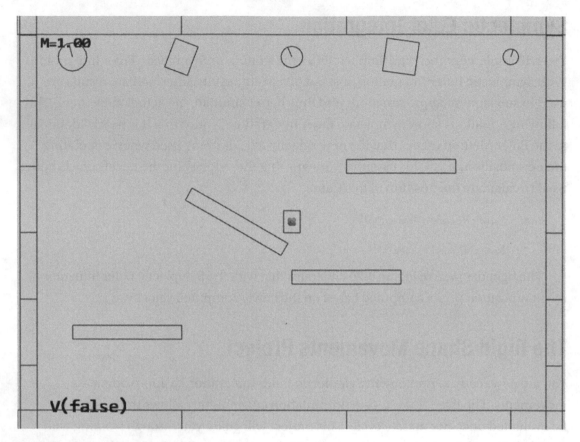

Figure 9-21. *Running the Rigid Shape Movements project*

The controls of the project are the same as previous with additional commands to control the behaviors and the mass of selected object:

- **Behavior controls**:

    - **V key**: Toggles motion of all objects

    - **H key**: Injects random velocity to all objects

    - **G key**: Randomly creates a new rigid circle or rectangle

- **Draw controls**:

    - **C key**: Toggles the drawing of all CollisionInfo

    - **T key**: Toggles textures on all objects

    - **R key**: Toggles the drawing of RigidShape

    - **B key**: Toggles the drawing of the bound on each RigidShape

- **Object controls**:
  - **Left-/right-arrow key**: Sequences through and selects an object.
  - **WASD keys**: Move the selected object.
  - **Z/X key**: Rotates the selected object.
  - **Y/U key**: Increases/decreases RigidShape size of the selected object; this does not change the size of the corresponding Renderable object.
  - **Up-/down-arrow key + M**: Increase/decrease the mass of the selected object.

The goals of the project are as follows:

- To complete the implementation of RigidShape classes to include relevant physical attributes
- To implement movement approximation based on Symplectic Euler Integration

In addition to implementing Symplectic Euler Integration, this project also guides you to define attributes required for collision simulation and response, such as mass, inertia, friction, etc. As will be explained, each of these attributes will play a part in the simulation of object collision responses. This straightforward information is presented here to avoid distracting discussion of the more complex concepts to be covered in the subsequent projects.

In the rest of this section, you will first define relevant physical attributes to complete the RigidShape implementation. After that, you will focus on building Symplectic Euler Integration support for approximating movements.

Completing the RigidShape Implementation

As mentioned, in order to allow focused discussions of the more complex concepts in the later sections, the attributes for supporting collisions and the corresponding supporting functions are introduced in this project. These attributes are defined in the rigid shape classes.

Modifying the RigidShape Class

Edit rigid_shape.js in the src/engine/rigid_shape folder:

1. In the constructor of the RigidShape class, define variables representing acceleration, velocity, angular velocity, mass, rotational inertia, restitution (bounciness), and friction. Notice that the inverse of the mass value is actually stored for computation efficiency (by avoiding an extra division during each update). Additionally, notice that a mass of zero is used to represent a stationary object.

```
class RigidShape {
    constructor(xf) {
        this.mXform = xf;
        this.mAcceleration = physics.getSystemAcceleration();
        this.mVelocity = vec2.fromValues(0, 0);
        this.mType = "";

        this.mInvMass = 1;
        this.mInertia = 0;

        this.mFriction = 0.8;
        this.mRestitution = 0.2;

        this.mAngularVelocity = 0;

        this.mBoundRadius = 0;

        this.mDrawBounds = false;
    }
```

2. Define the setMass() function to set the mass of the object. Once again, for computational efficiency, the inverse of the mass is stored. Setting the mass of an object to zero or negative is a signal that the object is stationary with zero acceleration and will not participate in any movement computation. Notice that when the mass of an object is changed, you would

need to call `updateInertia()` to update its rotational inertia, `mInertial`. Rotational inertia is geometric shape specific, and the implementation of `updateIntertia()` is subclass specific.

```
setMass(m) {
    if (m > 0) {
        this.mInvMass = 1 / m;
        this.mAcceleration = physics.getSystemAcceleration();
    } else {
        this.mInvMass = 0;
        this.mAcceleration = [0, 0];  // to ensure object does not move
    }
    this.updateInertia();
}
```

3. Define getter and setter functions for all of the other corresponding variables. These functions are straightforward and are not listed here.

4. For the convenience of debugging, define a function `getCurrentState()` to retrieve variable values as text and a function `userSetsState()` to allow interactive manipulations of the variables:

```
getCurrentState() {
    let m = this.mInvMass;
    if (m !== 0)
        m = 1 / m;

    return "M=" + m.toFixed(kPrintPrecision) +
        "(I=" + this.mInertia.toFixed(kPrintPrecision) + ")" +
        " F=" + this.mFriction.toFixed(kPrintPrecision) +
        " R=" + this.mRestitution.toFixed(kPrintPrecision);
}

userSetsState() {
    // keyboard control
    let delta = 0;
```

```
    if (input.isKeyPressed(input.keys.Up)) {
        delta = kRigidShapeUIDelta;
    }
    if (input.isKeyPressed(input.keys.Down)) {
        delta = -kRigidShapeUIDelta;
    }
    if (delta !== 0) {
        if (input.isKeyPressed(input.keys.M)) {
            let m = 0;
            if (this.mInvMass > 0)
                m = 1 / this.mInvMass;
            this.setMass(m + delta * 10);
        }
        if (input.isKeyPressed(input.keys.F)) {
            this.mFriction += delta;
            if (this.mFriction < 0)
                this.mFriction = 0;
            if (this.mFriction > 1)
                this.mFriction = 1;
        }
        if (input.isKeyPressed(input.keys.R)) {
            this.mRestitution += delta;
            if (this.mRestitution < 0)
                this.mRestitution = 0;
            if (this.mRestitution > 1)
                this.mRestitution = 1;
        }
    }
}
```

Modifying the RigidCircle Class

As mentioned, the rotational inertia, `mInertial`, is specific to geometric shape and must be modified by the corresponding classes:

1. Edit rigid_circle_main.js in the src/engine/rigid_
    shapes folder to modify the RigidCircle class to define the
    updateInertia() function. This function calculates the rotational
    inertia of a circle when its mass has changed.

```
updateInertia() {
    if (this.mInvMass === 0) {
        this.mInertia = 0;
    } else {
        // this.mInvMass is inverted!!
        // Inertia=mass * radius^2
        this.mInertia = (1 / this.mInvMass) *
                        (this.mRadius * this.mRadius) / 12;
    }
};
```

2. Update the RigidCircle constructor and incShapeSize()
    function to call the updateInertia() function:

```
constructor(xf, radius) {
    super(xf);
    ... identical to previous code ...
    this.updateInertia();
}

incShapeSizeBy(dt) {
    ... identical to previous code ...
    this.updateInertia();
}
```

Modifying the RigidRectangle Class

Modifications similar to the RigidCircle class must be defined for the RigidRectangle
class:

1. Edit rigid_rectangle_main.js in the src/engine/rigid_shapes
    folder to define the updateInertia() function:

```
updateInertia() {
    // Expect this.mInvMass to be already inverted!
    if (this.mInvMass === 0)
        this.mInertia = 0;
    else {
        // inertia=mass*width^2+height^2
        this.mInertia = (1 / this.mInvMass) *
                        (this.mWidth * this.mWidth +
                         this.mHeight * this.mHeight) / 12;
        this.mInertia = 1 / this.mInertia;
    }
}
```

2. Similar to the RigidCircle class, update the constructor and incShapeSize() function to call the updateInertia() function:

```
constructor(xf, width, height) {
    super(xf);
    ... identical to previous code ...
    this.updateInertia();
}

incShapeSizeBy(dt) {
    ... identical to previous code ...
    this.updateInertia();
}
```

Defining System Acceleration and Motion Control

With the RigidShape implementation completed, you are now ready to define the support for movement approximation.

Define a system-wide acceleration and motion control by adding appropriate variables and access functions to physics.js in the src/engine/components folder. Remember to export the newly defined functionality.

```
let mSystemAcceleration = [0, -20];   // system-wide default acceleration
let mHasMotion = true;
```

```
// getters and setters
function getSystemAcceleration() {
    return vec2.clone(mSystemAcceleration);
}
function setSystemAcceleration(x, y) {
    mSystemAcceleration[0] = x;
    mSystemAcceleration[1] = y;
}

function getHasMotion() { return mHasMotion; }
function toggleHasMotion() { mHasMotion = !mHasMotion; }

... identical to previous code ...

export {
    // Physics system attributes
    getSystemAcceleration, setSystemAcceleration,

    getHasMotion, toggleHasMotion,

    ... identical to previous code ...
}
```

Accessing the Fixed Time Interval

In your game engine, the fixed time step, dt, is simply the time interval in between the
calls to the loopOnce() function in the game loop component. Now, edit loop.js in the
src/engine/core folder to define and export the update time interval.

```
const kUPS = 60; // Updates per second
const kMPF = 1000 / kUPS; // Milliseconds per update.
const kSPU = 1/kUPS; // seconds per update

... identical to previous code ...

function getUpdateIntervalInSeconds() { return kSPU; }

... identical to previous code ...

export {getUpdateIntervalInSeconds}
```

Implementing Symplectic Euler Integration in the RigidShape class

You can now implement the Symplectic Euler Integration movement approximation in the rigid shape classes. Since this movement behavior is common to all types of rigid shapes, the implementation should be located in the base class, RigidShape.

1. In the src/engine/rigid_shapes folder, edit rigid_shape.js to define the travel() function to implement Symplectic Euler Integration for movement. Notice how the implementation closely follows the listed equations where the updated velocity is used for computing the new position. Additionally, notice the similarity between linear and angular motion where the location (either a position or an angle) is updated by a displacement that is derived from the velocity and time step. Rotation will be examined in detail in the last section of this chapter.

```
travel() {
    let dt = loop.getUpdateIntervalInSeconds();

    // update velocity by acceleration
    vec2.scaleAndAdd(this.mVelocity,
                     this.mVelocity, this.mAcceleration, dt);
    // p  = p + v*dt  with new velocity
    let p = this.mXform.getPosition();
    vec2.scaleAndAdd(p, p, this.mVelocity, dt);

    this.mXform.incRotationByRad(this.mAngularVelocity * dt);
}
```

2. Modify the update() function to invoke travel() when the object is not stationary, mInvMass of 0, and when motion of the physics component is switched on:

```
update() {
    if (this.mInvMass === 0)
        return;
```

```
    if (physics.getHasMotion())
        this.travel();
}
```

Modifying MyGame to Test Movements

The modification to the MyGame class involves supporting new user commands for
toggling system-wide motion, injecting random velocity, and setting the scene stationary
boundary objects to rigid shapes with zero mass. The injecting of random velocity is
implemented by the randomizeVelocity() function defined in my_game_bounds.js file.

All updates to the MyGame class are straightforward. To avoid unnecessary distraction,
the details are not shown. As always, you can refer to the source code files in the src/
my_game folder for implementation details.

Observations

You can now run the project to test your implementation. In order to properly observe
and track movements of objects, initially motion is switched off. You can type the V key
to enable motion when you are ready. When motion is toggled on, you can observe a
natural-looking free-falling movement for all objects. You can type G to create more
objects and observe similar free-fall movements of the created objects.

Notice that when the objects fall below the lower platform, they are regenerated in
the central region of the scene with a random initial upward velocity. Observe the objects
move upward until the y component of the velocity reaches zero, and then they begin to fall
downward as a result of gravitational acceleration. Typing the H key injects new random
upward velocities to all objects resulting in objects decelerating while moving upward.

Try typing the C key to observe the computed collision information when objects
overlap or interpenetrate. Pay attention and note that interpenetration occurs frequently
as objects travel through the scene. You are now ready to examine and implement how
to resolve object interpenetration in the next section.

Interpenetration of Colliding Objects

The fixed update time step introduced in the previous project means that the actual
location of an object in a continuous motion is approximated by a discrete set of
positions. As illustrated in Figure 9-22, the movement of the rectangular object is

approximated by placing the object at the three distinct positions over three update cycles. The most notable ramification of this approximation is in the challenges when determining collisions between objects.

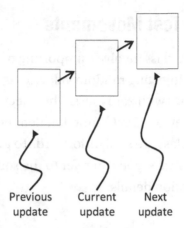

Figure 9-22. *A rigid rectangle in continuous motion*

You can see one such challenge in Figure 9-22. Imagine a thin wall existed in the space between the current and the next update. You would expect the object to collide and stop by the wall in the next update. However, if the wall was sufficiently thin, the object would appear to pass right through the wall as it jumped from one position to the next. This is a common problem faced in many game engines. A general solution for these types of problems can be algorithmically complex and computationally intensive. It is typically the job of the game designer to mitigate and avoid this problem with well-designed (e.g., appropriate size) and well-behaved (e.g., appropriate traveling speed) game objects.

Figure 9-23 shows another, and more significant, collision-related challenge resulting from fixed update time steps. In this case, before the time step, the objects are not touching. After the time step, the results of the movement approximation place the two objects where they partly overlap. In the real world, if the two objects are rigid shapes or solids, then the overlap, or interpenetration, would never occur. For this reason, this situation must be properly resolved in a rigid shape physics simulation. This is where details of a collision must be computed such that interpenetrating situations like these can be properly resolved.

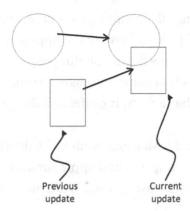

Previous
update

Current
update

Figure 9-23. *The interpenetration of colliding objects*

Collision Position Correction

In the context of game engines, collision resolution refers to the process that determines object responses after a collision, including strategies to resolve the potential interpenetration situations that may have occurred. Notice that in the real world, interpenetration of rigid objects can never occur since collisions are strictly governed by the laws of physics. As such, resolutions of interpenetrations are relevant only in a simulated virtual world where movements are approximated and impossible situations may occur. These situations must be resolved algorithmically where both the computational cost and resulting visual appearance should be acceptable.

In general, there are three common methods for responding to interpenetrating collisions. The first is to simply displace the objects from one another by the depth of penetration. This is known as the Projection Method since you simply move positions of objects such that they no longer overlap. While this is simple to calculate and implement, it lacks stability when many objects are in proximity and overlap with each other. In this case, the simple resolution of one pair of interpenetrating objects can result in new penetrations with other nearby objects. However, the Projection Method is still often implemented in simple engines or games with simple object interaction rules. For example, in a game of Pong, the ball never comes to rest on the paddles or walls and remains in continuous motion by bouncing off any object it collides with. The Projection Method is perfect for resolving collisions for these types of simple object interactions.

The second method, the Impulse Method, uses object velocities to compute and apply impulses to cause the objects to move in the opposite directions at the point of collision. This method tends to slow down colliding objects rapidly and converges to relatively stable solutions. This is because impulses are computed based on the transfer of momentum, which in turn has a damping effect on the velocities of the colliding objects.

The third method, the Penalty Method, models the depth of object interpenetration as the degree of compression of a spring and approximates an acceleration to apply forces to separate the objects. This last method is the most complex and challenging to implement.

For your engine, you will be combining the strengths of the Projection and Impulse Methods. The Projection Method will be used to separate the interpenetrating objects, while the Impulse Method will be used to compute impulses to reduce the object velocities in the direction that caused the interpenetration. As described, the simple Projection Method can result in an unstable system, such as objects that sink into each other when stacked. You will overcome this instability by implementing a relaxation loop where, in a single update cycle, interpenetrated objects are separated incrementally via repeated applications of the Projection Method.

With a relaxation loop, each application of the Projection Method is referred to as a relaxation iteration. During each relaxation iteration, the Projection Method reduces the interpenetration incrementally by a fixed percentage of the total penetration depth. For example, by default, the engine sets relaxation iterations to 15, and each relaxation iteration reduces the interpenetration by 80 percent. This means that within one update function call, after the movement integration approximation, the collision detection and resolution procedures will be executed 15 times. While costly, the repeated incremental separation ensures a stable system.

The Collision Position Correction Project

This project will guide you through the implementation of the relaxation iterations to incrementally resolve inter-object interpenetrations. You are going to use the collision information computed from previous project to correct the position of the colliding objects. You can see an example of this project running in Figure 9-24. The source code to this project is defined in chapter9/9.6.collision_position_correction.

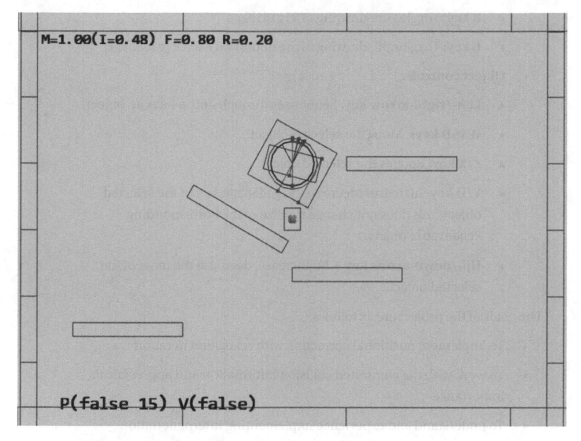

Figure 9-24. *Running the Collision Position Correction project*

The controls of the project are identical to the previous project with a single addition of the P key command in behavior control:

- **Behavior controls**:

  - **P key**: Toggles penetration resolution for all objects

  - **V key**: Toggles motion of all objects

  - **H key**: Injects random velocity to all objects

  - **G key**: Randomly creates a new rigid circle or rectangle

- **Draw controls**:

  - **C key**: Toggles the drawing of all `CollisionInfo`

  - **T key**: Toggles textures on all objects

- **R key**: Toggles the drawing of `RigidShape`

- **B key**: Toggles the drawing of the bound on each `RigidShape`

- **Object controls**:

  - **Left-/right-arrow key**: Sequences through and selects an object.

  - **WASD keys**: Move the selected object.

  - **Z/X key**: Rotates the selected object.

  - **Y/U key**: Increases/decreases `RigidShape` size of the selected object; this does not change the size of the corresponding `Renderable` object.

  - **Up-/down-arrow key + M**: Increase/decrease the mass of the selected object.

The goals of the project are as follows:

- To implement positional correction with relaxation iteration

- To work with the computed collision information and appreciate its importance

- To understand and experience implementing interpenetration resolution

Updating the Physics Component

The previous projects have established the required simulation infrastructure including the completion of the `RigidShape` implementation. You can now focus on the details of positional correction logic which is localized and hidden in the core of the physics component in the `physics.js` file in the `src/engine/components` folder.

1. Edit `physics.js` to define variables and the associated getters and setters for positional correction rate, relaxation loop count, and, toggling the positional correction computation. Make sure to export the newly defined functions.

```
let mPosCorrectionRate = 0.8;  // % separation to project objects
let mRelaxationCount = 15;        // number of relaxation iterations

let mCorrectPosition = true;
```

```
function getPositionalCorrection() { return mCorrectPosition; }
function togglePositionalCorrection() {
    mCorrectPosition = !mCorrectPosition;
}

function getRelaxationCount() { return mRelaxationCount; }
function incRelaxationCount(dc) { mRelaxationCount += dc; }

... identical to previous code ...

export {
    ... identical to previous code ...

    togglePositionalCorrection,
    getPositionalCorrection,

    getRelaxationCount,
    incRelaxationCount
}
```

2. Define the positionalCorrection() function to move and
    reduce the overlaps between objects by the predefined rate,
    mPosCorrectionRate. To properly support object momentum
    in the simulation, the amount in which each object moves is
    inversely proportional to their masses. That is, upon collision,
    an object with a larger mass will be moved by an amount that is
    less than the object with a smaller mass. Notice that the direction
    of movement is along the collision normal as defined in by the
    collisionInfo object.

```
function positionalCorrection(s1, s2, collisionInfo) {
    if (!mCorrectPosition)
        return;

    let s1InvMass = s1.getInvMass();
    let s2InvMass = s2.getInvMass();

    let num = collisionInfo.getDepth() /
                (s1InvMass + s2InvMass) * mPosCorrectionRate;
    let correctionAmount = [0, 0];
```

```
    vec2.scale(correctionAmount, collisionInfo.getNormal(), num);
    s1.adjustPositionBy(correctionAmount, -s1InvMass);
    s2.adjustPositionBy(correctionAmount, s2InvMass);
}
```

3. Modify the `collideShape()` function to perform positional correction when a collision is detected. Notice that collision detection is performed only when at least one of the objects is with nonzero masses.

```
function collideShape(s1, s2, infoSet = null) {
    ... identical to previous code ...
    if ((s1 !== s2) &&
        ((s1.getInvMass() !== 0) || (s2.getInvMass() !== 0))) {
        if (s1.boundTest(s2)) {
            hasCollision = s1.collisionTest(s2, mCInfo);
            if (hasCollision) {
                vec2.subtract(mS1toS2, s2.getCenter(), s1.getCenter());
                if (vec2.dot(mS1toS2, mCInfo.getNormal()) < 0)
                    mCInfo.changeDir();
                positionalCorrection(s1, s2, mCInfo);

                ... identical to previous code ...
    }
    return hasCollision;
}
```

4. Integrate a loop in all three utility functions, `processObjToSet()`, `processSetToSet()`, and `processSet()`, to execute relaxation iterations when performing the positional corrections:

```
function processObjToSet(obj, set, infoSet = null) {
    let j = 0, r = 0;
    let hasCollision = false;
    let s1 = obj.getRigidBody();
    for (r = 0; r < mRelaxationCount; r++) {
        for (j = 0; j < set.size(); j++) {
            let s2 = set.getObjectAt(j).getRigidBody();
```

```
            hasCollision = collideShape(s1, s2, infoSet) || hasCollision;
        }
    }
    return hasCollision;
}
function processSetToSet(set1, set2, infoSet = null) {
    let i = 0, j = 0, r = 0;
    let hasCollision = false;
    for (r = 0; r < mRelaxationCount; r++) {
        ... identical to previous code ...
    }
    return hasCollision;
}

// collide all objects in the GameObjectSet with themselves
function processSet(set, infoSet = null) {
    let i = 0, j = 0, r = 0;
    let hasCollision = false;
    for (r = 0; r < mRelaxationCount; r++) {
        ... identical to previous code ...
    }
    return hasCollision;
}
```

Testing Positional Correction in MyGame

The MyGame class must be modified to support the new P key command, to toggle off
initial motion, positional correction, and to spawn initial objects in the central region of
the game scene to guarantee initial collisions. These modifications are straightforward
and details are not shown. As always, you can refer to the source code files in the src/
my_game folder for implementation details.

Observations

You can now run the project to test your implementation. Notice that by default, motion
is off, positional correction is off, and showing of collision information is on. For these
reasons, you will observe the created rigid shapes clumping in the central region of the
game scene with many associated magenta collision information.

Now, type the P key and observe all of the shapes being pushed apart with all overlaps resolved. You can type the G key to create additional shapes and observe the shapes continuously push each other aside to ensure no overlaps. A fun experiment to perform is to toggle off positional correction, followed by typing the G key to create a large number of overlapping shapes and then to type the P key to observe the shapes pushing each other apart.

If you switch on motion with the V key, you will first observe all objects free falling as a result of the gravitational force. These objects will eventually come to a rest on one of the stationary platforms. Next, you will observe the magenta collision depth increasing continuously in the vertical direction. This increase in size is a result of the continuously increasing downward velocity as a result of the downward gravitational acceleration. Eventually, the downward velocity will grow so large that in one update the object will move past and appear to fall right through the platform. What you are observing is precisely the situation discussed in Figure 9-22. The next subsection will discuss responses to collision and address this ever-increasing velocity.

Lastly, notice that the utility functions defined in the physics component, the `processSet()`, `processObjToSet()`, and `processSetToSet()`, these are designed to detect and resolve collisions. While useful, these functions are not designed to report on if a collision has occurred—a common operation supported by typical physics engines. To avoid distraction from the rigid shape simulation discussion, functions to support simple collision detection without responses are not presented. At this point, you have the necessary knowledge to define such functions, and it is left as an exercise for you to complete.

Collision Resolution

With a proper positional correction system, you can now begin implementing collision resolution and support behaviors that resemble real-world situations. In order to focus on the core functionality of a collision resolution system, including understanding and implementing the Impulse Method and ensuring system stability, you will begin by examining collision responses without rotations. After the mechanics behind simple impulse resolution are fully understood and implemented, the complications associated with angular impulse resolutions will be examined in the next section.

In the following discussion, the rectangles and circles will not rotate as a response to collisions. However, the concepts and implementation described can be generalized in a straightforward manner to support rotational collision responses. This project is designed to help you understand the basic concepts of impulse-based collision resolutions.

The Impulse Method

You will formulate the solution for the Impulse Method by first reviewing how a circle can bounce off of a wall and other circles in a perfect world. This will subsequently be used to derive an approximation for an appropriate collision response. Note that the following discussion focuses on deriving the formulation for the Impulse Method and does not attempt to present a review on Newtonian mechanics. Here is a brief review of some of the relevant terms:

- **Mass**: Is the amount of matter in an object or how dense an object is.

- **Force**: Is any interaction or energy imparted on an object that will change the motion of that object.

- **Relative velocity**: Is the difference in velocity between two traveling shapes.

- **Coefficient of restitution**: The ratio of relative velocity from after and before a collision. This is a measurement of how much kinetic energy remains after an object bounces off another, or bounciness.

- **Coefficient of friction**: The ratio of the force of friction between two bodies. In your very simplistic implementation, friction is applied directly to slow down linear motion or rotation.

- **Impulse**: Accumulated force over time that can cause a change in the velocity. For example, resulting from a collision.

Note   Object rotations are described by their angular velocities and will be examined in the next section. In the rest of this section, the term velocity is used to refer to the movements of objects or their linear velocity.

Components of Velocity in a Collision

Figure 9-25 illustrates a circle A in three different stages. At stage 1, the circle is traveling at velocity $\vec{V}_1$ toward the wall on its right. At stage 2, the circle is colliding with the wall, and at stage 3, the circle has been reflected and is traveling away from the wall with velocity $\vec{V}_2$.

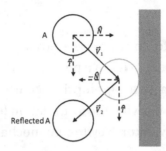

Figure 9-25. *Collision between a circle and a wall in a perfect world*

Mathematically, this collision and the response can be described by decomposing the initial velocity, $\vec{V}_1$, into the components that are perpendicular and parallel to the colliding wall. In general, the perpendicular direction to a collision is referred to as the collision normal, $\hat{N}$, and the direction that is tangential to the collision position is the collision tangent $\hat{T}$. This decomposition can be seen in the following equation:

- $$\vec{V}_1 = \left(\vec{V}_1 \cdot \hat{N}\right)\hat{N} + \left(\vec{V}_1 \cdot \hat{T}\right)\hat{T}$$

In a perfect world with no friction and no loss of kinetic energy, a collision will not affect the component along the tangent direction while the normal component will simply be reversed. In this way, the reflected vector $\vec{V}_2$ can be expressed as a linear combination of the normal and tangent components of $\vec{V}_1$ as follows:

- $$\vec{V}_2 = -\left(\vec{V}_1 \cdot \hat{N}\right)\hat{N} + \left(\vec{V}_1 \cdot \hat{T}\right)\hat{T}$$

Notice the negative sign in front of the $\hat{N}$ component. You can see in Figure 9-25 that the $\hat{N}$ component for vector $\vec{V}_2$ points in the opposite direction to that of $\vec{V}_1$ as a result of the collision. Additionally, notice that in the tangent direction $\hat{T}$, $\vec{V}_2$ continues to point in the same direction. This is because the tangent component is parallel to the wall and is unaffected by the collision. This analysis is true in general for any collisions in a perfect world with no friction and no loss of kinetic energy.

Relative Velocity of Colliding Shapes

The decomposition of vectors into the normal and tangent directions of the collision can also be applied to the general case of when both of the colliding shapes are in motion. For example, Figure 9-26 illustrates two traveling circle shapes, A and B, coming into a collision.

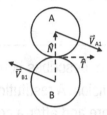

Figure 9-26. *Collision between two traveling circles*

In the case of Figure 9-26, before the collision, object A is traveling with velocity $\vec{V}_{A1}$, while object B with velocity $\vec{V}_{B1}$. The normal direction of the collision, $\hat{N}$, is defined to be the vector between the two circle centers, and the tangent direction of the collision, $\hat{T}$, is the vector that is tangential to both of the circles at the point of collision. To resolve this collision, the velocities for objects A and B after the collision, $\vec{V}_{A2}$ and $\vec{V}_{B2}$, must be computed.

The post-collision velocities are determined based on the relative velocity between the two shapes. The relative velocity between shapes A and B is defined as follows:

- $\vec{V}_{AB1} = \vec{V}_{A1} - \vec{V}_{B1}$

The collision vector decomposition can now be applied to the normal and tangent directions of the relative velocity where the relative velocity after the collision is $\vec{V}_{AB2}$:

- $$\vec{V}_{AB2} \cdot \hat{N} = -e\left(\vec{V}_{AB1} \cdot \hat{N}\right) \qquad \textbf{(1)}$$

- $$\vec{V}_{AB2} \cdot \hat{T} = f\left(\vec{V}_{AB1} \cdot \hat{T}\right) \qquad \textbf{(2)}$$

The restitution, e, and friction, f, coefficients model the real-world situation where some kinetic energy is changed to some other forms of energy during the collision. The negative sign of Equation (1) signifies that after the collision, objects will travel in the direction that is opposite to the initial collision normal direction. Equation (2) says that after the collision, friction will scale back the magnitude where objects will continue to travel in the same tangent direction only at a lower velocity. Notice that all variables on the right-hand side of Equations (1) and (2) are defined, as they are known at the time of collision. It is important to remember that

- $\vec{V}_{AB2} = \vec{V}_{A2} - \vec{V}_{B2}$

where the goal is to derive a solution for $\vec{V}_{A2}$ and $\vec{V}_{B2}$, the individual velocities of the colliding objects after a collision. You are now ready to model a solution to approximate $\vec{V}_{A2}$ and $\vec{V}_{B2}$.

Note   The restitution coefficient, e, describes bounciness or the proportion of the velocity that is retained after a collision. A restitution value of 1.0 would mean that speeds will be the same from before and after a collision. In contrast, friction is intuitively associated with the proportion lost or the slow down after a collision. For example, a friction coefficient of 1.0 would mean infinite friction where a velocity of zero will result from a collision. For consistency of the formulae, the coefficient f in Equation (2) is actually 1 minus the intuitive friction coefficient.

The Impulse

Accurately describing a collision involves complex considerations including factors like energy-changing form, or frictions resulting from different material properties, etc. Without considering these advanced issues, a simplistic description of a collision that occurs on a shape is a constant mass object changing its velocity from $\vec{V}_{A1}$ to $\vec{V}_{A2}$ after contacting with another object. Conveniently, this is the definition of an impulse, as can be seen in the following:

- $\vec{J} = m_A \vec{V}_{A2} - m_A \vec{V}_{A1}$

or when solving for $\vec{V}_{A2}$

- $\vec{V}_{A2} = \vec{V}_{A1} + \dfrac{\vec{J}}{m_A}$ (3)

Remember that the same impulse also causes the velocity change in object B, only in the opposite direction:

- $$\vec{J} = -\left(m_B \vec{V}_{B2} - m_B \vec{V}_{B1}\right)$$

or when solving for $\vec{V}_{B2}$

- $$\vec{V}_{B2} = \vec{V}_{B1} - \frac{\vec{J}}{m_B} \qquad\qquad (4)$$

Take a step back from the math and think about what this formula states. It makes intuitive sense. The equation states that the change in velocity is inversely proportional to the mass of an object. In other words, the more mass an object has, the less its velocity will change after a collision. The Impulse Method implements this observation.

Recall that Equations (1) and (2) describe the relative velocity after collision according to the collision normal and tangent directions independently. The impulse, being a vector, can also be expressed as a linear combination of components in the collision normal and tangent directions, j_N and j_T:

- $$\vec{J} = j_N \hat{N} + j_T \hat{T}$$

Substituting this expression into Equations (3) and (4) results in the following:

- $$\vec{V}_{A2} = \vec{V}_{A1} + \frac{j_N}{m_A}\hat{N} + \frac{j_T}{m_A}\hat{T} \qquad\qquad (5)$$

- $$\vec{V}_{B2} = \vec{V}_{B1} - \frac{j_N}{m_B}\hat{N} - \frac{j_T}{m_B}\hat{T} \qquad\qquad (6)$$

Note that j_N and j_T are the only unknowns in these two equations where the rest of the terms are either defined by the user or can be computed based on the geometric shapes. That is, the quantities $\vec{V}_{A1}$, $\vec{V}_{B1}$, m_A, and m_B are defined by the user, and $\hat{N}$ and $\hat{T}$ can be computed.

Note   The $\hat{N}$ and $\hat{T}$ vectors are normalized and perpendicular to each other. For this reason, the vectors have a value of 1 when dotted with themselves and a value of 0 when dotted with each other.

611

Normal Component of the Impulse

The normal component of the impulse, j_N, can be solved by performing a dot product with the $\hat{N}$ vector on both sides of Equations (5) and (6):

- $$\vec{V}_{A2} \cdot \hat{N} = \left(\vec{V}_{A1} + \frac{j_N}{m_A} \hat{N} + \frac{j_T}{m_A} \hat{T} \right) \cdot \hat{N} = \vec{V}_{A1} \cdot \hat{N} + \frac{j_N}{m_A}$$

- $$\vec{V}_{B2} \cdot \hat{N} = \left(\vec{V}_{B1} - \frac{j_N}{m_B} \hat{N} - \frac{j_T}{m_B} \hat{T} \right) \cdot \hat{N} = \vec{V}_{B1} \cdot \hat{N} - \frac{j_N}{m_B}$$

Subtracting the preceding two equations results in the following:

- $$\left(\vec{V}_{A2} - \vec{V}_{B2} \right) \cdot \hat{N} = \left(\vec{V}_{A1} - \vec{V}_{B1} \right) \cdot \hat{N} + j_N \left(\frac{1}{m_A} + \frac{1}{m_B} \right)$$

Recall that $\left(\vec{V}_{A2} - \vec{V}_{B2} \right)$ is simply $\vec{V}_{AB2}$ and that $\left(\vec{V}_{A1} - \vec{V}_{B1} \right)$ is $\vec{V}_{AB1}$, and this equation simplifies to the following:

- $$\vec{V}_{AB2} \cdot \hat{N} = \vec{V}_{AB1} \cdot \hat{N} + j_N \left(\frac{1}{m_A} + \frac{1}{m_B} \right)$$

Substituting Equation (1) for the left-hand side derives the following equation:

- $$-e\left(\vec{V}_{AB1} \cdot \hat{N} \right) = \vec{V}_{AB1} \cdot \hat{N} + j_N \left(\frac{1}{m_A} + \frac{1}{m_B} \right)$$

Collecting terms and solving for j_N, the impulse in the normal direction, result in the following:

- $$j_N = \frac{-(1+e)\left(\vec{V}_{AB1} \cdot \hat{N} \right)}{\dfrac{1}{m_A} + \dfrac{1}{m_B}} \tag{7}$$

Tangent Component of the Impulse

The tangent component of the impulse, j_T, can be solved by performing a dot product with the $\hat{T}$ vector on both sides of Equations (5) and (6):

- $\vec{V}_{A2} \cdot \hat{T} = \left(\vec{V}_{A1} + \dfrac{j_N}{m_A} \hat{N} + \dfrac{j_T}{m_A} \hat{T} \right) \cdot \hat{T} = \vec{V}_{A1} \cdot \hat{T} + \dfrac{j_T}{m_A}$

- $\vec{V}_{B2} \cdot \hat{T} = \left(\vec{V}_{B1} - \dfrac{j_N}{m_B} \hat{N} - \dfrac{j_T}{m_B} \hat{T} \right) \cdot \hat{T} = \vec{V}_{B1} \cdot \hat{T} - \dfrac{j_T}{m_B}$

Following the similar steps as in the case for the normal component, subtracting the equations, and recognizing $\left(\vec{V}_{A2} - \vec{V}_{B2} \right)$ is $\vec{V}_{AB2}$ and $\left(\vec{V}_{A1} - \vec{V}_{B1} \right)$ is $\vec{V}_{AB1}$ derive the following equation:

- $\vec{V}_{AB2} \cdot \hat{T} = \vec{V}_{AB1} \cdot \hat{T} + j_T \left(\dfrac{1}{m_A} + \dfrac{1}{m_B} \right)$

Now, substituting Equation (2) for the left-hand side leaves the following:

- $f \left(\vec{V}_{AB1} \cdot \hat{T} \right) = \vec{V}_{AB1} \cdot \hat{T} + j_T \left(\dfrac{1}{m_A} + \dfrac{1}{m_B} \right)$

Finally, collecting terms and solving for j_T or the impulse in the tangent direction result in the following:

- $j_T = \dfrac{(f-1)\left(\vec{V}_{AB1} \cdot \hat{T} \right)}{\dfrac{1}{m_A} + \dfrac{1}{m_B}}$ **(8)**

The Collision Resolution Project

This project will guide you through resolving a collision by calculating the impulse and updating the velocities of the colliding objects. You can see an example of this project running in Figure 9-27. The source code for this project is defined in `chapter9/9.7.collision_resolution`.

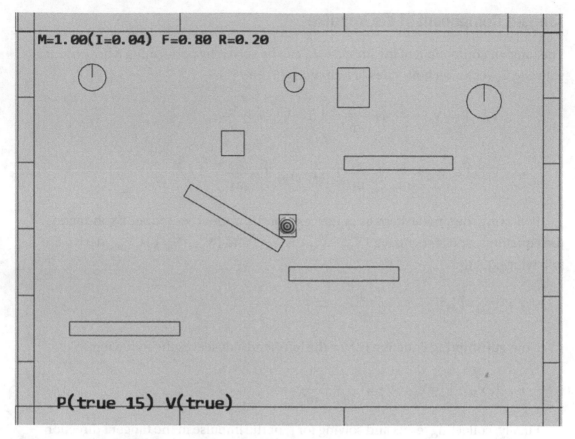

Figure 9-27. *Running the Collision Resolution project*

The controls of the project are identical to the previous project with additional controls for restitution and friction coefficients:

- **Behavior controls**:
  - **P key**: Toggles penetration resolution for all objects
  - **V key**: Toggles motion of all objects
  - **H key**: Injects random velocity to all objects
  - **G key**: Randomly creates a new rigid circle or rectangle
- **Draw controls**:
  - **C key**: Toggles the drawing of all `CollisionInfo`
  - **T key**: Toggles textures on all objects

- **R key**: Toggles the drawing of `RigidShape`

- **B key**: Toggles the drawing of the bound on each `RigidShape`

- **Object controls**:

  - **Left-/right-arrow key**: Sequences through and selects an object.

  - **WASD keys**: Move the selected object.

  - **Z/X key**: Rotates the selected object.

  - **Y/U key**: Increases/decreases `RigidShape` size of the selected object; this does not change the size of the corresponding `Renderable` object.

  - **Up-/down-arrow key + M/N/F**: Increase/decrease the mass/restitution/friction of the selected object.

The goals of the project are as follows:

- To understand the details of the Impulse Method

- To implement the Impulse Method in resolving collisions

Updating the Physics Component

To properly support collision resolution, you only need to focus on the physics component and modify the `physics.js` file in the `src/engine/components` folder:

1. Edit `physics.js` and define the `resolveCollision()` function to resolve the collision between `RigidShape` objects, a and b, with collision information recorded in the `collisionInfo` object:

```
function resolveCollision(b, a, collisionInfo) {
    let n = collisionInfo.getNormal();

    // Step A: Compute relative velocity
    let va = a.getVelocity();
    let vb = b.getVelocity();
    let relativeVelocity = [0, 0];
    vec2.subtract(relativeVelocity, va, vb);
```

```
// Step B: Determine relative velocity in normal direction
let rVelocityInNormal = vec2.dot(relativeVelocity, n);

// if objects moving apart ignore
if (rVelocityInNormal > 0) {
    return;
}

// Step C: Compute collision tangent direction
let tangent = [0, 0];
vec2.scale(tangent, n, rVelocityInNormal);
vec2.subtract(tangent, tangent, relativeVelocity);
vec2.normalize(tangent, tangent);
// Relative velocity in tangent direction
let rVelocityInTangent = vec2.dot(relativeVelocity, tangent);

// Step D: Determine the effective coefficients
let newRestituion = (a.getRestitution() + b.getRestitution()) * 0.5;
let newFriction = 1 - ((a.getFriction() + b.getFriction()) * 0.5);

// Step E: Impulse in the normal and tangent directions
let jN = -(1 + newRestituion) * rVelocityInNormal;
jN = jN / (a.getInvMass() + b.getInvMass());

let jT = (newFriction - 1) * rVelocityInTangent;
jT = jT / (a.getInvMass() + b.getInvMass());

// Step F: Update velocity in both normal and tangent directions
vec2.scaleAndAdd(va, va, n, (jN * a.getInvMass()));
vec2.scaleAndAdd(va, va, tangent, (jT * a.getInvMass()));

vec2.scaleAndAdd(vb, vb, n, -(jN * b.getInvMass()));
vec2.scaleAndAdd(vb, vb, tangent, -(jT * b.getInvMass()));
}
```

The listed code follows the solution derivation closely:

a. **Steps A and B**: Compute the relative velocity and its normal component. When this normal component is positive, it signifies that two objects are moving away from each other and thus collision resolution is not necessary.

b. **Step C**: Computes the collision tangent direction and the tangent component of the relative velocity.

c. **Step D**: Uses the averages of the coefficients for impulse derivation. Notice the subtraction by one when computing the `newFriction` for maintaining consistency with Equation (2).

d. **Step E**: Follows the listed Equations (7) and (8) to compute the normal and tangent components of the impulse.

e. **Step F**: Solves for the resulting velocities by following Equations (5) and (6).

2. Edit `collideShape()` to invoke the `resolveCollision()` function when a collision is detected and position corrected:

```
function collideShape(s1, s2, infoSet = null) {
    let hasCollision = false;
    if ((s1 !== s2) &&
        ((s1.getInvMass() !== 0) || (s2.getInvMass() !== 0))) {
        if (s1.boundTest(s2)) {
            hasCollision = s1.collisionTest(s2, mCInfo);
            if (hasCollision) {
                ... identical to previous code ...

                positionalCorrection(s1, s2, mCInfo);
                resolveCollision(s1, s2, mCInfo);

    ... identical to previous code ...
};
```

Updating MyGame for Testing Collision Resolution

The modifications to the MyGame class are trivial, mainly to toggle both motion and positional correction to be active by default. Additionally, initial random rotations of the created RigidShape objects are disabled because at this point, collision response does not support rotation. As always, you can refer to the source code files in the src/my_game folder for implementation details.

Observations

You should test your implementation in three ways. First, ensure that moving shapes collide and behave naturally. Second, try changing the physical properties of the objects. Third, observe the collision resolution between shapes that are in motion and shapes that are stationary with infinite mass (the surrounding walls and stationary platforms). Remember that only linear velocities are considered and rotations will not result from collisions.

Now, run the project and notice that the shapes fall gradually to the platforms and floor with their motions coming to a halt after slight rebounds. This is a clear indication that the base case for Euler Integration, collision detection, positional correction, and resolution all are operating as expected. Press the H key to excite all shapes and the C key to display the collision information. Notice the wandering shapes and the walls/platforms interact properly with soft bounces and no apparent interpenetrations.

Use the left/right arrow to select an object and adjust its restitution/friction coefficients with the N/F and up-/down-arrow keys. For example, adjust the restitution to 1 and friction to 0. Now inject velocity with the H key. Notice how the object seems extra bouncy and, with a friction coefficient of 0, seems to skid along platforms/floors. You can try different coefficient settings and observe corresponding bounciness and slipperiness.

The stability of the system can be tested by increasing the number of shapes in the scene with the G key. The relaxation loop count of 15 continuously and incrementally pushes interpenetrating shapes apart during each iteration. For example, you can toggle off movement and positional corrections with the V and P keys and create multiple, for example, 10 to 20, overlapping shapes. Now toggle on motion and positional corrections and observe a properly functioning system.

In the next project, you will improve the resolution solution to consider angular velocity changes as a result of collisions.

Angular Components of Collision Responses

Now that you have a concrete understanding and have successfully implemented the Impulse Method for collision responses with linear velocities, it is time to integrate the support for the more general case of rotations. Before discussing the details, it is helpful to relate the correspondences of Newtonian linear mechanics to that of rotational mechanics. That is, linear displacement corresponds to rotation, velocity to angular velocity, force to torque, and mass to rotational inertia or angular mass. Rotational inertia determines the torque required for a desired angular acceleration about a rotational axis.

The following discussion focuses on integrating rotation in the Impulse Method formulation and does not attempt to present a review on Newtonian mechanics for rotation. Conveniently, integrating proper rotation into the Impulse Method does not involve the derivation of any new algorithm. All that is required is the formulation of impulse responses with proper consideration of rotational attributes.

Collisions with Rotation Consideration

The key to integrating rotation into the Impulse Method formulation is recognizing the fact that the linear velocity you have been working with, for example, velocity $\vec{V}_{A1}$ of object A, is actually the velocity of the shape at its center location. In the absence of rotation, this velocity is constant throughout the object and can be applied to any position. However, as illustrated in Figure 9-28, when the movement of an object includes angular velocity, $\vec{\omega}_{A1}$, its linear velocity at a position P, $\vec{V}_{AP1}$, is actually a function of the relative position between the point and the center of rotation of the shape or the positional vector $\vec{R}_{AP}$.

- $\vec{V}_{AP1} = \vec{V}_{A1} + \left(\vec{\omega}_{A1} \times \vec{R}_{AP} \right)$

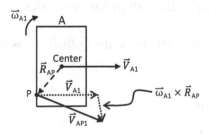

Figure 9-28. *Linear velocity at a position in the presence of rotation*

Note   Angular velocity is a vector that is perpendicular to the linear velocity. In this case, as linear velocity is defined on the X/Y plane, $\vec{\omega}$ is a vector in the z direction. Recall from discussions in the "Introduction" section of this chapter, the very first assumption made was that rigid shape objects are continuous geometries with uniformly distributed mass where the center of mass is located at the center of the geometric shape. This center of mass is the location of the axis of rotation. For simplicity, in your implementation, $\vec{\omega}$ will be stored as a simple scalar representing the z-component magnitude of the vector.

Figure 9-29 illustrates an object B with linear and angular velocities of $\vec{V}_{B1}$ and $\vec{\omega}_{B1}$ colliding with object A at position P. By now, you know that the linear velocities at point P before the collision for the two objects are as follows:

- $$\vec{V}_{AP1} = \vec{V}_{A1} + \left(\vec{\omega}_{A1} \times \vec{R}_{AP}\right) \qquad (9)$$

- $$\vec{V}_{BP1} = \vec{V}_{B1} + \left(\vec{\omega}_{B1} \times \vec{R}_{BP}\right) \qquad (10)$$

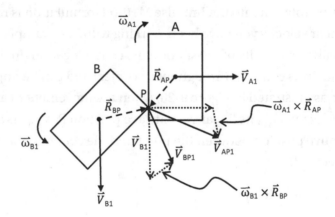

Figure 9-29. *Colliding shapes with angular velocities*

After the collision, the linear velocity at the collision position can be expressed as follows:

- $$\vec{V}_{AP2} = \vec{V}_{A2} + \left(\vec{\omega}_{A2} \times \vec{R}_{AP}\right) \qquad (11)$$

- $$\vec{V}_{BP2} = \vec{V}_{B2} + \left(\vec{\omega}_{B2} \times \vec{R}_{BP}\right) \qquad (12)$$

where $\vec{V}_{A2}$ and $\vec{\omega}_{A2}$, and $\vec{V}_{B2}$ and $\vec{\omega}_{B2}$ are the linear and angular velocities for objects A and B after the collision, and the derivation of a solution for these quantities is precisely the goal of this section.

Relative Velocity with Rotation

Recall from the previous section that the definitions of relative velocity from before and after a collision between objects A and B are defined as follows:

- $\vec{V}_{AB1} = \vec{V}_{A1} - \vec{V}_{B1}$

- $\vec{V}_{AB2} = \vec{V}_{A2} - \vec{V}_{B2}$

These velocities are analyzed based on components in the collision normal and tangent directions in Equations (1) and (2) and are relisted for convenience in the following:

- $\vec{V}_{AB2} \cdot \hat{N} = -e\left(\vec{V}_{AB1} \cdot \hat{N}\right)$ (1)

- $\vec{V}_{AB2} \cdot \hat{T} = f\left(\vec{V}_{AB1} \cdot \hat{T}\right)$ (2)

These equations are derived without considering rotation and the formulation assumes that the velocity is constant over the entire shape. In order to support rotation, these equations must be generalized and solved at the point of collision, P.

- $\vec{V}_{ABP2} \cdot \hat{N} = -e\left(\vec{V}_{ABP1} \cdot \hat{N}\right)$ (13)

- $\vec{V}_{ABP2} \cdot \hat{T} = f\left(\vec{V}_{ABP1} \cdot \hat{T}\right)$ (14)

In this case, $\vec{V}_{ABP1}$ and $\vec{V}_{ABP2}$ are relative velocities at collision position P from before and after the collision. It is still true that these vectors are defined by the difference in velocities for objects A and B from before, $\vec{V}_{AP1}$ and $\vec{V}_{BP1}$, and after, $\vec{V}_{AP2}$ and $\vec{V}_{BP2}$, the collision at the collision position P on each object.

- $\vec{V}_{ABP1} = \vec{V}_{AP1} - \vec{V}_{BP1}$ (15)

- $\vec{V}_{ABP2} = \vec{V}_{AP2} - \vec{V}_{BP2}$ (16)

You are now ready to generalize the Impulse Method to support rotation and to derive a solution to approximate the linear and angular velocities: $\vec{V}_{A2}$, $\vec{V}_{B2}$, $\vec{\omega}_{A2}$, and $\vec{\omega}_{B2}$.

Impulse Method with Rotation

Continue with the Impulse Method discussion from the prevision section, that after the collision between objects A and B, the Impulse Method describes the changes in their linear velocities by an impulse, $\vec{J}$, scaled by the inverse of their corresponding masses, m_A and m_B. This change in linear velocities is descripted in Equations (3) and (4), relisted as follows:

- $$\vec{V}_{A2} = \vec{V}_{A1} + \frac{\vec{J}}{m_A} \tag{3}$$

- $$\vec{V}_{B2} = \vec{V}_{B1} - \frac{\vec{J}}{m_B} \tag{4}$$

In general, rotations are intrinsic results of collisions and the same impulse must properly describe the change in angular velocity from before and after a collision. Remember that inertial, or rotational inertial, is the rotational mass. In a manner similar to linear velocity and mass, it is also the case that the change in angular velocity in a collision is inversely related to the rotational inertia. As illustrated in Figure 9-29, for objects A and B with rotational inertia of I_A and I_B, after a collision, the angular velocities, $\vec{\omega}_{A2}$ and $\vec{\omega}_{B2}$, can be described as follows, where $\vec{R}_{AP}$ and $\vec{R}_{BP}$ are the positional vectors of each object:

- $$\vec{\omega}_{A2} = \vec{\omega}_{A1} + \left(\vec{R}_{AP} \times \frac{\vec{J}}{I_A} \right) \tag{17}$$

- $$\vec{\omega}_{B2} = \vec{\omega}_{B1} - \left(\vec{R}_{BP} \times \frac{\vec{J}}{I_B} \right) \tag{18}$$

Recall from the previous section that it is convenient to express the impulse as a linear combination of components in the collision normal and tangent directions, $\hat{N}$ and $\hat{T}$, or as shown:

- $$\vec{J} = j_N \hat{N} + j_T \hat{T}$$

Substituting this expression into Equation (17) results in the following:

- $$\vec{\omega}_{A2} = \vec{\omega}_{A1} + \left(\vec{R}_{AP} \times \frac{j_N \hat{N} + j_T \hat{T}}{I_A} \right) = \vec{\omega}_{A1} + \frac{j_N}{I_A} \left(\vec{R}_{AP} \times \hat{N} \right) + \frac{j_T}{I_A} \left(\vec{R}_{AP} \times \hat{T} \right)$$

In this way, Equations (17) and (18) can be expanded to describe the change in angular velocities caused by the normal and tangent components of the impulse as follows:

- $$\vec{\omega}_{A2} = \vec{\omega}_{A1} + \frac{j_N}{I_A}\left(\vec{R}_{AP} \times \hat{N}\right) + \frac{j_T}{I_A}\left(\vec{R}_{AP} \times \hat{T}\right) \qquad\qquad (19)$$

- $$\vec{\omega}_{B2} = \vec{\omega}_{B1} - \frac{j_N}{I_B}\left(\vec{R}_{BP} \times \hat{N}\right) - \frac{j_T}{I_B}\left(\vec{R}_{BP} \times \hat{T}\right) \qquad\qquad (20)$$

The corresponding equations describing linear velocity changes, Equations (5) and (6), are relisted in the following:

- $$\vec{V}_{A2} = \vec{V}_{A1} + \frac{j_N}{m_A}\hat{N} + \frac{j_T}{m_A}\hat{T} \qquad\qquad\qquad\qquad (5)$$

- $$\vec{V}_{B2} = \vec{V}_{B1} - \frac{j_N}{m_B}\hat{N} - \frac{j_T}{m_B}\hat{T} \qquad\qquad\qquad\qquad (6)$$

You can now substitute Equations (5) and (19) into Equation (11) and Equations (6) and (20) into Equation (12):

- $$\vec{V}_{AP2} = \left(\vec{V}_{A1} + \frac{j_N}{m_A}\hat{N} + \frac{j_T}{m_A}\hat{T}\right) + \left(\vec{\omega}_{A1} + \frac{j_N}{I_A}\left(\vec{R}_{AP} \times \hat{N}\right) + \frac{j_T}{I_A}\left(\vec{R}_{AP} \times \hat{T}\right)\right) \times \vec{R}_{AP} \quad (21)$$

- $$\vec{V}_{BP2} = \left(\vec{V}_{B1} - \frac{j_N}{m_B}\hat{N} - \frac{j}{m_B}\hat{T}\right) + \left(\vec{\omega}_{B1} - \frac{j_N}{I_B}\left(\vec{R}_{BP} \times \hat{N}\right) - \frac{j_T}{I_B}\left(\vec{R}_{BP} \times \hat{T}\right)\right) \times \vec{R}_{BP} \quad (22)$$

It is important to reiterate that the changes to both linear and angular velocities are described by the same impulse, $\vec{J}$. In other words, the normal and tangent impulse components j_N and j_T in Equations (21) and (22) are the same quantities, and these two are the only unknowns in these equations where the rest of the terms are values either defined by the user or can be computed based on the geometric shapes. That is, the quantities $\vec{V}_{A1}$, $\vec{V}_{B1}$, m_A, m_B, $\vec{\omega}_{A1}$, $\vec{\omega}_{B1}$, I_A, and I_B, are defined by the user and $\hat{N}$, $\hat{T}$, $\vec{R}_{AP}$, and $\vec{R}_{BP}$ can be computed. You are now ready to derive the solutions for j_N and j_T.

Note   In the following derivation, it is important to remember the definition of triple scalar product identity; this identity states that given vectors, $\vec{D}$, $\vec{E}$, and, $\vec{F}$, the following is always true:

$$\left(\vec{D} \times \vec{E}\right) \cdot \vec{F} \equiv \vec{D} \cdot \left(\vec{E} \times \vec{F}\right)$$

Normal Components of the Impulse

The normal component of the impulse, j_N, can be approximated by assuming that the contribution from the angular velocity tangent component is minimal and can be ignored and isolating the normal components from Equations (21) and (22). For clarity, you will work with one equation at a time and begin with Equation (21) for object A.

Now, ignore the tangent component of the angular velocity and perform a dot product with the $\hat{N}$ vector on both sides of Equation (21) to isolate the normal components:

- $$\vec{V}_{AP2} \cdot \hat{N} = \left\{ \left(\vec{V}_{A1} + \frac{j_N}{m_A}\hat{N} + \frac{j_T}{m_A}\hat{T} \right) + \left(\vec{\omega}_{A1} + \frac{j_N}{I_A}\left(\vec{R}_{AP} \times \hat{N}\right) \right) \times \vec{R}_{AP} \right\} \cdot \hat{N}$$

Carry out the dot products on the right-hand side, recognizing $\hat{N}$ is a unit vector and is perpendicular to $\hat{T}$, and let $\vec{D} = \vec{R}_{AP} \times \hat{N}$; then, this equation can be rewritten as follows:

- $$\vec{V}_{AP2} \cdot \hat{N} = \left(\vec{V}_{A1} \cdot \hat{N}\right) + \frac{j_N}{m_A} + \left(\vec{\omega}_{A1} \times \vec{R}_{AP}\right) \cdot \hat{N} + \frac{j_N}{I_A}\left(\vec{D} \times \vec{R}_{AP}\right) \cdot \hat{N} \qquad \textbf{(23)}$$

The vector operations of the rightmost term in Equation (23) can be simplified by applying the triple scalar product identity and remembering that $\vec{D} = \vec{R}_{AP} \times \hat{N}$:

- $$\left(\vec{D} \times \vec{R}_{AP}\right) \cdot \hat{N} = \vec{D} \cdot \left(\vec{R}_{AP} \times \hat{N}\right) = \left(\vec{R}_{AP} \times \hat{N}\right) \cdot \left(\vec{R}_{AP} \times \hat{N}\right) = \left\|\vec{R}_{AP} \times \hat{N}\right\|^2$$

With this manipulation and collection of the terms with a dot product, Equation (23) becomes the following:

- $$\vec{V}_{AP2} \cdot \hat{N} = \left(\vec{V}_{A1} + \left(\vec{\omega}_{A1} \times \vec{R}_{AP}\right)\right) \cdot \hat{N} + \frac{j_N}{m_A} + \frac{j_N}{I_A}\left\|\vec{R}_{AP} \times \hat{N}\right\|^2$$

From Equation (9), on the right-hand side, the term with the dot product is simply $\vec{V}_{AP1}$:

- $$\vec{V}_{AP2} \cdot \hat{N} = \vec{V}_{AP1} \cdot \hat{N} + \frac{j_N}{m_A} + \frac{j_N}{I_A}\left\|\vec{R}_{AP} \times \hat{N}\right\|^2 \qquad \textbf{(24)}$$

Equation (22) can be processed through an identical algebraic manipulation steps by ignoring the tangent component of the angular velocity and performing a dot product with the $\hat{N}$ vector on both sides of the equation; the following can be derived:

- $$\vec{V}_{BP2} \cdot \hat{N} = \vec{V}_{BP1} \cdot \hat{N} - \frac{j_N}{m_B} - \frac{j_N}{I_B}\left\|\vec{R}_{BP} \times \hat{N}\right\|^2 \qquad \textbf{(25)}$$

Subtracting Equation (25) from (24) results in the following:

- $$\left(\vec{V}_{AP2} - \vec{V}_{BP2}\right)\cdot\hat{N} = \left(\vec{V}_{AP1} - \vec{V}_{BP1}\right)\cdot\hat{N} + j_N\left(\frac{1}{m_A} + \frac{1}{m_b} + \frac{\left\|\vec{R}_{AP}\times\hat{N}\right\|^2}{I_A} + \frac{\left\|\vec{R}_{BP}\times\hat{N}\right\|^2}{I_B}\right)$$

Substituting Equation (16) followed by (13) on the left-hand side and Equation (15) on the right-hand side, you get the following:

- $$-e\left(\vec{V}_{ABP1}\cdot\hat{N}\right) = \vec{V}_{ABP1}\cdot\hat{N} + j_N\left(\frac{1}{m_A} + \frac{1}{m_b} + \frac{\left\|\vec{R}_{AP}\times\hat{N}\right\|^2}{I_A} + \frac{\left\|\vec{R}_{BP}\times\hat{N}\right\|^2}{I_B}\right)$$

Lastly, collect terms and solve for j_N:

- $$j_N = \frac{-(1+e)\left(\vec{V}_{ABP1}\cdot\hat{N}\right)}{\dfrac{1}{m_A} + \dfrac{1}{m_B} + \dfrac{\left\|\vec{R}_{AP}\times\hat{N}\right\|^2}{I_A} + \dfrac{\left\|\vec{R}_{BP}\times\hat{N}\right\|^2}{I_B}}$$

(26)

Tangent Component of the Impulse

The tangent component of the impulse, j_T, can be approximated by assuming that the contribution from the angular velocity normal component is minimal and can be ignored and isolating the tangent components from Equations (21) and (22) by performing a dot product with the $\hat{T}$ vector to both sides of the equations:

- $$\vec{V}_{AP2}\cdot\hat{T} = \left\{\left(\vec{V}_{A1} + \frac{j_N}{m_A}\hat{N} + \frac{j_T}{m_A}\hat{T}\right) + \left(\vec{\omega}_{A1} + \frac{j_T}{I_A}\left(\vec{R}_{AP}\times\hat{T}\right)\right)\times\vec{R}_{AP}\right\}\cdot\hat{T}$$

- $$\vec{V}_{BP2}\cdot\hat{T} = \left\{\left(\vec{V}_{B1} - \frac{j_N}{m_B}\hat{N} - \frac{j_T}{m_B}\hat{T}\right) + \left(\vec{\omega}_{B1} - \frac{j_T}{I_B}\left(\vec{R}_{BP}\times\hat{T}\right)\right)\times\vec{R}_{BP}\right\}\cdot\hat{T}$$

Now follow the exact algebraic manipulation steps as when working with the normal component, the impulse in the tangent direction, j_T, can be derived and expressed as follows:

- $$j_T = \frac{(f-1)\left(\vec{V}_{AB1}\cdot\hat{T}\right)}{\dfrac{1}{m_A} + \dfrac{1}{m_B} + \dfrac{\left\|\vec{R}_{AP}\times\hat{T}\right\|^2}{I_A} + \dfrac{\left\|\vec{R}_{BP}\times\hat{T}\right\|^2}{I_B}}$$

(27)

The Collision Angular Resolution Project

This project will guide you through the implementation of general collision impulse response that supports rotation. You can see an example of this project running in Figure 9-30. The source code to this project is defined in chapter9/9.8.collision_angular_resolution.

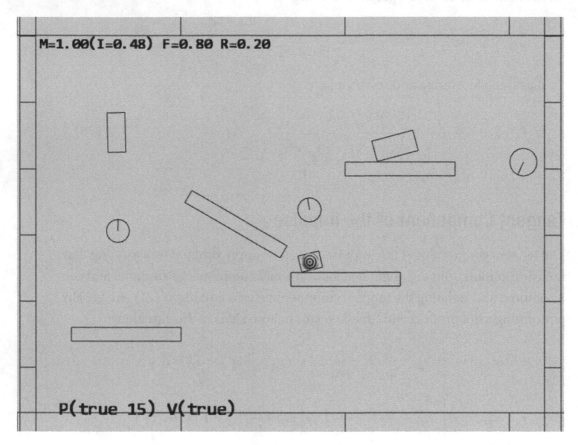

Figure 9-30. *Running the Collision Angular Resolution project*

The controls of the project are identical to the previous project:

- **Behavior controls**:

  - **P key**: Toggles penetration resolution for all objects

  - **V key**: Toggles motion of all objects

- **H key**: Injects random velocity to all objects

- **G key**: Randomly creates a new rigid circle or rectangle

- **Draw controls**:

  - **C key**: Toggles the drawing of all `CollisionInfo`

  - **T key**: Toggles textures on all objects

  - **R key**: Toggles the drawing of `RigidShape`

  - **B key**: Toggles the drawing of the bound on each `RigidShape`

- **Object controls**:

  - **Left-/right-arrow key**: Sequences through and selects an object.

  - **WASD keys**: Move the selected object.

  - **Z/X key**: Rotates the selected object.

  - **Y/U key**: Increases/decreases `RigidShape` size of the selected object; this does not change the size of the corresponding `Renderable` object.

  - **Up-/down-arrow key + M/N/F**: Increase/decrease the mass/restitution/friction of the selected object.

The goals of the project are as follows:

- To understand the details of angular impulse

- To integrate rotation into your collision resolution

- To complete the physics component

Note   The cross product between a linear velocity on the x-y plane, $\vec{V} = (x,y,0)$, and an angular velocity along the z axis, $\vec{\omega} = (0,0,z)$, $\vec{V} \times \vec{\omega} = (-yz, xz, 0)$, is a vector on the x-y plane.

Updating the Physics Component

To properly integrate angular impulse, you only need to replace the `resolveCollision()` function in the `physics.js` file of the `src/engine/components` folder. While the implementation closely follows the algebraic derivation steps, it is rather long and involved. To facilitate understanding and for clarity, the following details the implementation in steps:

```
function resolveCollision(b, a, collisionInfo) {
    let n = collisionInfo.getNormal();

    // Step A: Compute relative velocity
    ... implementation to follow ...

    // Step B: Determine relative velocity in normal direction
    ... implementation to follow ...

    // Step C: Compute collision tangent direction
    ... implementation to follow ...

    // Step D: Determine the effective coefficients
    ... implementation to follow ...

    // Step E: Impulse in the normal and tangent directions
    ... implementation to follow ...

    // Step F: Update velocity in both normal and tangent directions
    ... implementation to follow ...
}
```

1. **Step A**: Compute relative velocity. As highlighted in Figure 9-29 and Equations (9) and (10), in the presence of angular velocity, it is important to determine the collision position (Step A1) and compute linear velocities $\vec{V}_{AP1}$ and $\vec{V}_{BP1}$ at the collision position (Step A2).

```
// Step A: Compute relative velocity
let va = a.getVelocity();
let vb = b.getVelocity();
```

```
// Step A1: Compute the intersection position p
// the direction of collisionInfo is always from b to a
// but the Mass is inverse, so start scale with a and end scale with b
let invSum = 1 / (b.getInvMass() + a.getInvMass());
let start = [0, 0], end = [0, 0], p = [0, 0];
vec2.scale(start, collisionInfo.getStart(), a.getInvMass() * invSum);
vec2.scale(end, collisionInfo.getEnd(), b.getInvMass() * invSum);
vec2.add(p, start, end);

// Step A2: Compute relative velocity with rotation components
//      Vectors from center to P
//      r is vector from center of object to collision point
let rBP = [0, 0], rAP = [0, 0];
vec2.subtract(rAP, p, a.getCenter());
vec2.subtract(rBP, p, b.getCenter());

// newV = V + mAngularVelocity cross R
let vAP1 = [-1 * a.getAngularVelocity() * rAP[1],
            a.getAngularVelocity() * rAP[0]];
vec2.add(vAP1, vAP1, va);

let vBP1 = [-1 * b.getAngularVelocity() * rBP[1],
            b.getAngularVelocity() * rBP[0]];
vec2.add(vBP1, vBP1, vb);

let relativeVelocity = [0, 0];
vec2.subtract(relativeVelocity, vAP1, vBP1);
```

2. **Step B**: Determine relative velocity in the normal direction. A positive normal direction component signifies that the objects are moving apart and the collision is resolved.

```
// Step B: Determine relative velocity in normal direction
let rVelocityInNormal = vec2.dot(relativeVelocity, n);

// if objects moving apart ignore
if (rVelocityInNormal > 0) {
    return;
}
```

3. **Step C**: Compute the collision tangent direction and the tangent
   direction component of the relative velocity.

```
// Step C: Compute collision tangent direction
let tangent = [0, 0];
vec2.scale(tangent, n, rVelocityInNormal);
vec2.subtract(tangent, tangent, relativeVelocity);
vec2.normalize(tangent, tangent);
// Relative velocity in tangent direction
let rVelocityInTangent = vec2.dot(relativeVelocity, tangent);
```

4. **Step D**: Determine the effective coefficients by using the average
   of the colliding objects. As in the previous project, for consistency,
   friction coefficient is one minus the values form the RigidShape
   objects.

```
// Step D: Determine the effective coefficients
let newRestituion = (a.getRestitution() + b.getRestitution()) * 0.5;
let newFriction = 1 - ((a.getFriction() + b.getFriction()) * 0.5);
```

5. **Step E**: Impulse in the normal and tangent directions, these are
   computed by following Equations (26) and (27) exactly.

```
// Step E: Impulse in the normal and tangent directions
// R cross N
let rBPcrossN = rBP[0] * n[1] - rBP[1] * n[0]; // rBP cross n
let rAPcrossN = rAP[0] * n[1] - rAP[1] * n[0]; // rAP cross n
// Calc impulse scalar, formula of jN
// can be found in http://www.myphysicslab.com/collision.html
let jN = -(1 + newRestituion) * rVelocityInNormal;
jN = jN / (b.getInvMass() + a.getInvMass() +
            rBPcrossN * rBPcrossN * b.getInertia() +
            rAPcrossN * rAPcrossN * a.getInertia());

let rBPcrossT = rBP[0] * tangent[1] - rBP[1] * tangent[0];
let rAPcrossT = rAP[0] * tangent[1] - rAP[1] * tangent[0];
let jT = (newFriction - 1) * rVelocityInTangent;
```

```
jT = jT / (b.getInvMass() + a.getInvMass() +
          rBPcrossT * rBPcrossT * b.getInertia() +
          rAPcrossT * rAPcrossT * a.getInertia());
```

6. **Step F**: Update linear and angular velocities. These updates follow
   Equations (5), (6), (19), and (20) exactly.

```
// Update linear and angular velocities
vec2.scaleAndAdd(va, va, n, (jN * a.getInvMass()));
vec2.scaleAndAdd(va, va, tangent, (jT * a.getInvMass()));
setAngularVelocityDelta((rAPcrossN * jN * a.getInertia() +
                        rAPcrossT * jT * a.getInertia()));

vec2.scaleAndAdd(vb, vb, n, -(jN * b.getInvMass()));
vec2.scaleAndAdd(vb, vb, tangent, -(jT * b.getInvMass()));
b.setAngularVelocityDelta(-(rBPcrossN * jN * b.getInertia() +
                        rBPcrossT * jT * b.getInertia()));
```

Observations

Run the project to test your implementation. The shapes that you insert into the scene
now rotate, collide, and respond in fashions that are similar to the real world. A circle
shape rolls around when other shapes collide with them, while a rectangle shape should
rotate naturally upon collision. The interpenetration between shapes should not be
visible under normal circumstances. However, two situations can still cause observable
interpenetrations: first, a small relaxation iteration, or second, your CPU is struggling
with the number of shapes. In the first case, you can try increasing the relaxation
iteration to prevent any interpenetration.

With the rotational support, you can now examine the effects of mass differences
in collisions. With their abilities to roll, collisions between circles are the most
straightforward to observe. Wait for all objects to be stationary and use the arrow key to
select one of the created circles; type the M key with up arrow to increase its mass to a
large value, for example, 20. Now select another object and use the WASD key to move
and drop the selected object on the high-mass circle. Notice that the high-mass circle
does not have much movement in response to the collision. For example, chances are a
collision does not even cause the high-mass circle to roll. Now, type the H key to inject
random velocities to all objects and observe the collisions. Notice that the collisions

with the high-mass circle are almost like collisions with stationary walls/platforms. The inversed mass and rotational inertia modeled by the Impulse Method is capable of successfully capturing the collision effects of objects with different masses.

Now your 2D physics engine implementation is completed. You can continue testing by creating additional shapes to observe when your CPU begins to struggle with keeping up real-time performance.

Summary

This chapter has guided you through understanding the foundation behind a working physics engine. The complicated physical interactions of objects in the real world are greatly simplified by focusing only on rigid body interactions or rigid shape simulations. The simulation process assumes that objects are continuous geometries with uniformly distributed mass where their shapes do not change during collisions. The computationally costly simulation is performed only on a selected subset of objects that are approximated by simple circles and rectangles.

A step-by-step derivation of the relevant formulae for the simulations is followed by a detailed guide to the building of a functioning system. You have learned to extract collision information between shapes, formulate and compute shape collisions based on the Separating Axis Theorem, approximate Newtonian motion integrals with the Symplectic Euler Integration, resolve interpenetrations of colliding objects based on numerically stable gradual relaxations, and derive and implement collision resolution based on the Impulse Method.

Now that you have completed your physics engine, you can carefully examine the system and identify potentials for optimization and further abstractions. Many improvements to the physics engine are still possible. This is especially true from the perspective of supporting game developers with the newly defined and powerful functionality. For example, most physics engines also support straightforward collision detections without any responses. This is an important missing functionality from your physics component. While your engine is capable of simulating collisions results as is, the engine does not support responding to the simple, and computationally much lower cost, question of if objects have collided. As mentioned, this can be an excellent exercise.

Though simple and missing some convenient interface functions, your physics component is functionally complete and capable of simulating rigid shape interactions with visually pleasant and realistic results. Your system supports intuitive parameters including object mass, acceleration, velocity, restitution, and friction that can be related to behaviors of objects in the real world. Though computationally demanding, your system is capable of supporting a nontrivial number of rigid shape interactions. This is especially the case if the game genre only required one or a small set, for example, the hero and friendly characters, interacting with the rest of the objects, for example, the props, platforms, and enemies.

Game Design Considerations

The puzzle level in the examples to this point has focused entirely on creating an understandable and consistent logical challenge; we've avoided burdening the exercise with any kind of visual design, narrative, or fictional setting (design elements traditionally associated with enhancing player presence) to ensure we're thinking only about the rules of play without introducing distractions. However, as you create core game mechanics, it's important to understand how certain elements of gameplay can contribute directly to presence; the logical rules and requirements of core game mechanics often have a limited effect on presence until they're paired with an interaction model, sound and visual design, and a setting. As discussed in Chapter 8, lighting is an example of a presence-enhancing visual design element that can also be used directly as a core game mechanic, and introducing physics to game world objects is similarly a presence-enhancing technique that's perhaps even more often directly connected to gameplay.

Our experience in the real world is governed by physics, so it stands to reason that introducing similar behaviors in a game might be expected to enhance presence. An example of object physics enhancing presence but not necessarily contributing to the game mechanic could be destructible environments that have no direct impact on gameplay: in a first-person shooter, for example, if the player shoots at crates and other game objects that respond by realistically exploding on impact, or if they throw a ball in the game world that bounces in a reasonable approximation of how a ball would bounce in the physical world, these are examples of physics being used purely to enhance presence but not necessarily contributing to gameplay. If a player is engaging with a game like *Angry Birds*, however, and launches one of the birds from their slingshot into the game space and they need to time the shot based on the physics-modeled parabolic arc the bird follows upon launch (as shown in Figure 9-31), this is an example of physics being used as both a core element of gameplay while also enhancing presence. In fact, any game that involves jumping a character or other game objects in an environment with simulated gravity is an example of physics contributing to both presence and the core mechanic, thus many platformer games utilize physics as both a core mechanic and a presence-enhancing design element.

Figure 9-31. *Rovio's Angry Birds requires players to launch projectiles from a slingshot in a virtual world that models gravity, mass, momentum, and object collision detection. The game physics are a fundamental component of the game mechanic and enhance the sense of presence by assigning physical world traits to virtual objects*

The projects in Chapter 9 introduce you to the powerful ability of physics to bring players into the game world. Instead of simply moving the hero character like a screen cursor, the player can now experience simulated inertia, momentum, and gravity requiring the same kind of predictive assessments around aiming, timing, and forward trajectory that would exist when manipulating objects in the physical world, and game objects are now capable of colliding in a manner familiar to our physical world experience. Even though specific values might take a detour from the real world in a simulated game space (e.g., lower or higher gravity, more or less inertia, and the like), as long as the relationships are consistent and reasonably analogous to our physical experience, presence will typically increase when these effects are added to game objects. Imagine, for example, a game level where the hero character was required to push all the robots into a specific area within a specified time limit while avoiding being hit by projectiles. Imagine the same level without physics and it would of course be a very different experience.

We left the level design in Chapter 8 with an interesting two-stage mechanic focused almost exclusively on abstract logical rules and hadn't yet incorporated elements that would add presence to the experience and bring players into the game world. Recall the current state of the level in Figure 9-32.

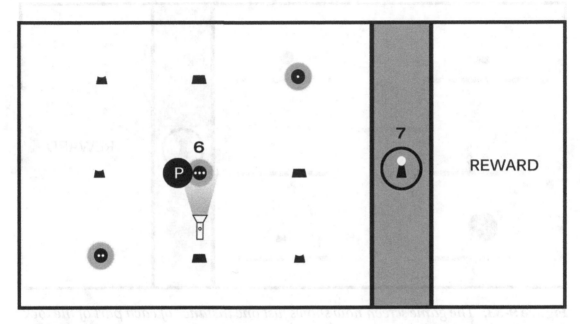

Figure 9-32. *The level as it currently stands includes a two-step puzzle first requiring players to move a flashlight and reveal hidden symbols; the player must then activate the shapes in the correct sequence to unlock the barrier and claim the reward*

There is, of course, some sense of presence conveyed by the current level design: the barrier preventing players from accessing the reward is "impenetrable" and represented by a virtual wall, and the flashlight object is "shining" a virtual light beam that reveals hidden clues in the manner perhaps that a UV light in the real world might reveal special ink. Presence is frankly weak at this stage of development, however, as we have yet to place the game experience in a setting and the intentionally generic shapes don't provide much to help a player build their own internal narrative. Our current prototype uses a flashlight-like game object to reveal hidden symbols, but it's now possible to decouple the game mechanic's logical rules from the current implementation and describe the core game mechanic as "the player must explore the environment to find tools required to assemble a sequence in the correct order."

For the next iteration of our game, let's revisit the interaction model and evolve it from purely a logic puzzle to something a bit more active that makes use of object physics. Figure 9-33 changes the game screen to include a jumping component.

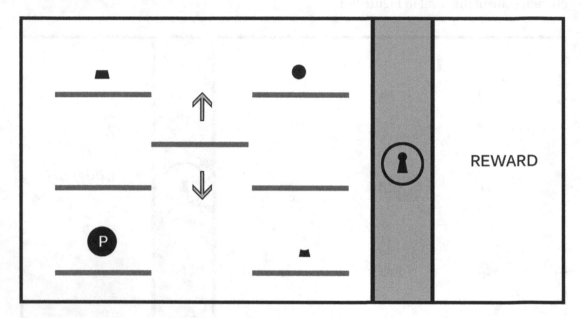

Figure 9-33. *The game screen now shows just one instance of each part of the lock (top, middle, bottom), and the hero character moves in the manner of a traditional jumping 2D platformer. The six platforms on the left and right are stationary, and the middle platform moves up and down, allowing the player to ascend to higher levels. (This image assumes the player is able to "jump" the hero character between platforms on the same level but cannot reach higher levels without using the moving platform.)*

We're now evolving gameplay to include a dexterity challenge—in this case, timing the jumps—yet it retains the same logical rules from the earlier iteration: the shapes must be activated in the correct order to unlock the barrier blocking the reward. Imagine the player experiences this screen for the first time; they'll begin exploring the screen to learn the rules of engagement for the level, including the interaction model (the keys and/or mouse buttons used to move and jump the hero character), whether missing a jump results in a penalty (e.g., the loss of a "life" if the hero character misses a jump and falls off the game screen), and what it means to "activate" a shape and begin the sequence to unlock the barrier.

The game now has the beginning of an interesting (although still basic) platformer puzzle, but we've also now simplified the solution compared to our earlier iteration and the platformer jumping component isn't especially challenging as shown in Figure 9-33. Recall how adding the flashlight in Chapter 8 increased the logical challenge of the original mechanic by adding a second kind of challenge requiring players to identify and use an object in the environment as a tool; we can add a similar second challenge to the platformer component, as shown in Figure 9-34.

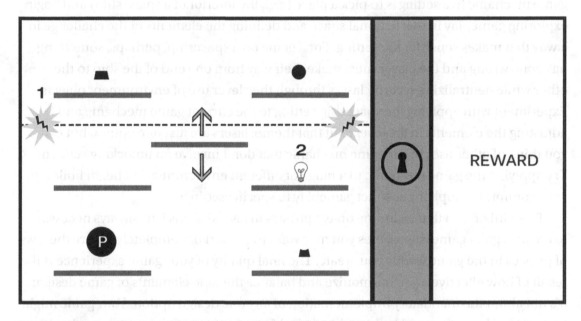

Figure 9-34. *The introduction of a force field blocking access to the upper platforms (#1) can significantly increase the challenge of the platformer component. In this design, the player must activate the switch (represented with a lightbulb in #2) to disable the force field and reach the first and third shapes*

The introduction of a force field opens a variety of interesting possibilities to increase the challenge. The player must time the jump from the moving platform to the switch before hitting the force field, and the shapes must be activated in order (requiring the player to first activate top right, then the bottom right, and then the top left). Imagine a time limit is placed on the deactivation when the switch is flipped and that the puzzle will reset if all shapes aren't activated before the force field is reengaged.

We've now taken an elemental mechanic based on a logical sequence and adapted it to support an action platformer experience. At this stage of development, the mechanic is becoming more interesting and beginning to feel more like a playable level, but it's still lacking setting and context; this is a good opportunity to explore the kind of story we might want to tell with this game. Are we interested in a sci-fi adventure, perhaps a survival horror experience, or maybe a series of puzzle levels with no connected narrative? The setting will not only help inform the visual identity of the game but can also guide decisions on the kinds of challenges we create for players (e.g., are "enemies" in the game working against the player, will the gameplay continue focusing on solving logic puzzles, or perhaps both?). A good exercise to practice connecting a game mechanic to a setting is to pick a place (e.g., the interior of a space ship) and begin exploring gameplay in that fictional space and defining the elements of the challenge in a way that makes sense for the setting. For a game on a spaceship, perhaps, something has gone wrong and the player must make their way from one end of the ship to the other while neutralizing security lasers through the clever use of environment objects. Experiment with applying the spaceship setting to the current game mechanic and adjusting the elements in the level to fit that theme: lasers are just one option, but can you think of other uses of our game mechanic that don't involve an unlocking sequence? Try applying the game mechanic to a range of different environments to begin building your comfort for applying abstract gameplay to specific settings.

Remember also that including object physics in level designs isn't always necessary to create a great game; sometimes you may want to subvert or completely ignore the laws of physics in the game worlds you create. The final quality of your game experience is the result of how effectively you harmonize and balance the nine elements of game design; it's not about the mandatory implementation of any one design option. Your game might be completely abstract and involve shapes and forms shifting in space in a way that has no bearing on the physical world, but your use of color, audio, and narrative might still combine to create an experience with a strong presence for players. However, if you find yourself with a game environment that seeks to convey a sense of physicality by making use of objects that people will associate with things found in the physical world, it's worth exploring how object physics might enhance the experience.

CHAPTER 10

Creating Effects with Particle Systems

After completing this chapter, you will be able to

- Understand the fundamentals of a particle, a particle emitter, and a particle system

- Appreciate that many interesting physical effects can be modeled based on a collection of dedicated particles

- Approximate the basic behavior of a particle such that the rendition of a collection of these particles resemble a simple explosion-like effect

- Implement a straightforward particle system that is integrated with the `RigidShape` system of the physics component

Introduction

So far in your game engine, it is assumed that the game world can be described by a collection of geometries where all objects are `Renderable` instances with texture, or animated sprite, and potentially illuminated by light sources. This game engine is powerful and capable of describing a significant portion of objects in the real world. However, it is also true that it can be challenging for your game engine to describe many everyday encounters, for example, sparks, fire, explosions, dirt, dust, etc. Many of these observations are transient effects resulting from matters changing physical states or a collection of very small-size entities reacting to physical disturbances. Collectively, these observations are often referred to as special effects and in general do not lend themselves well to being represented by fixed-shape geometries with textures.

© Kelvin Sung, Jebediah Pavleas, Matthew Munson, and Jason Pace 2022
K. Sung et al., *Build Your Own 2D Game Engine and Create Great Web Games*,
https://doi.org/10.1007/978-1-4842-7377-7_10

Particle systems describe special effects by emitting a collection of particles with properties that may include position, size, color, lifetime, and strategically selected texture maps. These particles are defined with specific behaviors where once emitted, their properties are updated to simulate a physical effect. For example, a fire particle may be emitted to move in an upward direction with reddish color. As time progresses, the particle may decrease in size, slow the upward motion, change its color toward yellow, and eventually disappear after certain number of updates. With strategically designed update functions, the rendition of a collection of such particles can resemble a fire burning.

In this chapter, you will study, design, and create a simple and flexible particle system that includes the basic functionality required to achieve common effects, such as explosions and magical spell effects. Additionally, you will implement a particle shader to properly integrate your particles within your scenes. The particles will collide and interact accordingly with the RigidShape objects. You will also discover the need for and define particle emitters to generate particles over a period of time such as a campfire or torch.

The main goal of this chapter is to understand the fundamentals of a particle system: attributes and behaviors of simple particles, details of a particle emitter, and the integration with the rest of the game engine. This chapter does not lead you to create any specific types of special effects. This is analogous to learning an illumination model in Chapter 8 without the details of creating any lighting effects. The manipulation of light source parameters and material properties to create engaging lighting conditions and the modeling of particle behaviors that resemble specific physical effects are the responsibilities of the game developers. The basic responsibility of the game engine is to define sufficient fundamental functionality to ensure that the game developers can accomplish their job.

Particles and Particle Systems

A particle is a textured position without dimensions. This description may seem contradictory because you have learned that a texture is an image and images are always defined by a width and height and will definitely occupy an area. The important clarification is that the game engine logic processes a particle as a position with no area, while the drawing system displays the particle as a texture with proper dimensions. In this way, even though an actual displayed area is shown, the width and height dimensions of the texture are ignored by the underlying logic.

In addition to a position, a particle also has properties such as size (for scaling the texture), color (for tinting the texture), and life span. Similar to a typical game object, each particle is defined with behaviors that modify its properties during each update. It is the responsibility of this update function to ensure that the rendition of a collection of particles resembles a familiar physical effect. A particle system is the entity that controls the spawning, updating, and removal of each individual particle. In your game engine, particle systems will be defined as a separate component, just like the physics component.

In the following project, you will first learn about the support required for drawing a particle object. After that, you will examine the details of how to create an actual particle object and define its behaviors. A particle is a new type of object for your game engine and requires the support of the entire drawing system, including custom GLSL shaders, default sharable shader instance, and a new Renderable pair.

The Particles Project

This project demonstrates how to implement a particle system to simulate explosion or spell-like effects. You can see an example of this project running in Figure 10-1. The source code of this project is located in the chapter10/10.1.particles folder.

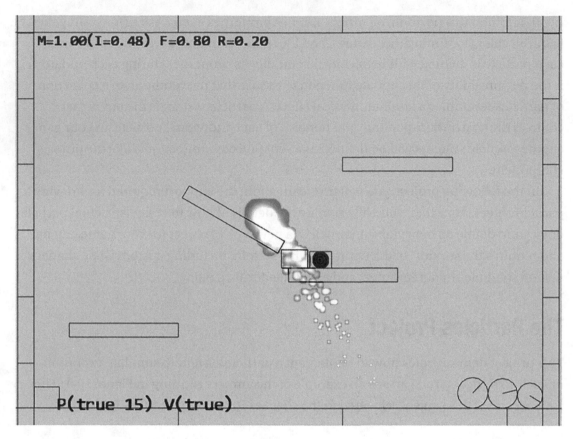

Figure 10-1. *Running the Particles project*

This project is a continuation from the previous chapter and supports all of the rigid shape and collision controls. For brevity, the details of those controls will not be restated in this chapter. The particle system–specific controls of the project are as follows:

- **Q key**: To spawn particles at the current mouse position

- **E key**: To toggle the drawing of particle bounds

The goals of the project are as follows:

- To understand the details of how to draw a particle and define its behavior

- To implement a simple particle system

You can find the following external resources in the `assets` folder: the `fonts` folder that contains the default system fonts, the particles folder that contains `particle.png`, the default particle texture, and the same four texture images from previous projects.

- `minion_sprite.png` defines the sprite elements for the hero and the minions.

- `platform.png` defines the platforms, floor, and ceiling tiles.

- `wall.png` defines the walls.

- `target.png` identifies the currently selected object.

Supporting Drawing of a Particle

Particles are textured positions with no area. However, as discussed in the introduction, your engine will draw each particle as a textured rectangle. For this reason, you can simply reuse the existing texture vertex shader `texture_vs.glsl`.

Creating GLSL Particle Fragment Shader

When it comes to the actual computation of each pixel color, a new GLSL fragment shader, `particle_fs.glsl`, must be created to ignore the global ambient terms. Physical effects such as fires and explosions do not participate in illumination computations.

1. Under the `src/glsl_shaders` folder, create a new file and name it `particle_fs.glsl`.

2. Similar to the texture fragment shader defined in `texture_fs.glsl`, you need to declare `uPixelColor` and `vTexCoord` to receive these values from the game engine and define the `uSampler` to sample the texture:

```
precision mediump float;
// sets the precision for floating point computation

// The object that fetches data from texture.
// Must be set outside the shader.
uniform sampler2D uSampler;
```

```
// Color of pixel
uniform vec4 uPixelColor;

// "varying" signifies that the texture coordinate will be
// interpolated and thus varies.
varying vec2 vTexCoord;
```

3. Now implement the main function to accumulate colors without considering global ambient effect. This serves as one approach for computing the colors of the particles. This function can be modified to support different kinds of particle effects.

```
void main(void)  {
    // texel color look up based on interpolated UV value in vTexCoord
    vec4 c = texture2D(uSampler, vec2(vTexCoord.s, vTexCoord.t));

    vec3 r = vec3(c) * c.a * vec3(uPixelColor);
    vec4 result = vec4(r, uPixelColor.a);

    gl_FragColor = result;
}
```

Defining a Default ParticleShader Instance

You can now define a default particle shader instance to be shared. Recall from working with other types of shaders in the previous chapters that shaders are created once and shared engine wide in the shader_resoruces.js file in the src/engine/core folder.

1. Begin by editing the shader_resources.js file in the src/engine/core folder to define the constant, variable, and accessing function for the default particle shader:

```
// Particle Shader
let kParticleFS = "src/glsl_shaders/particle_fs.glsl";
let mParticleShader = null;
function getParticleShader() { return mParticleShader }
```

2. In the init() function, make sure to load the newly defined
   particle_fs GLSL fragment shader:

```
function init() {
    let loadPromise = new Promise(
        async function(resolve) {
            await Promise.all([

                ... identical to previous code ...

                text.load(kShadowReceiverFS),
                text.load(kParticleFS)
            ]);
            resolve();
        }).then(
            function resolve() { createShaders(); }
        );
    map.pushPromise(loadPromise);
}
```

3. With the new GLSL fragment shader, particle_fs, properly
   loaded, you can instantiate a new particle shader when the
   createShaders() function is called:

```
function createShaders() {

    ... identical to previous code ...

    mShadowReceiverShader = new SpriteShader(kTextureVS,
                                             kShadowReceiverFS);
    mParticleShader = new TextureShader(kTextureVS, kParticleFS);
}
```

4. In the `cleanUp()` function, remember to perform the proper cleanup and unload operations:

```
function cleanUp() {

    ... identical to previous code ...

    mShadowCasterShader.cleanUp();
    mParticleShader.cleanUp();

    ... identical to previous code ...

    text.unload(kShadowReceiverFS);
    text.unload(kParticleFS);
}
```

5. Lastly, do not forget to export the newly defined function:

```
export {init, cleanUp,
        getConstColorShader, getTextureShader,
        getSpriteShader, getLineShader,
        getLightShader, getIllumShader,
        getShadowReceiverShader, getShadowCasterShader,
        getParticleShader}
```

Creating the ParticleRenderable Object

With the default particle shader class defined to interface to the GLSL `particle_fs` shader, you can now create a new `Renderable` object type to support the drawing of particles. Fortunately, the detailed behaviors of a particle, or a textured position, are identical to that of a `TextureRenderable` with the exception of the different shader. As such, the definition of the `ParticleRenderable` object is trivial.

In the `src/engine/renderables` folder, create the `particle_renderable.js` file; import from `defaultShaders` for accessing the particle shader and from `TextureRenderable` for the base class. Define the `ParticleRenderable` to be a subclass of `TextureRenderable`, and set the proper default shader in the constructor. Remember to export the class.

```
import * as defaultShaders from "../core/shader_resources.js";
import TextureRenderable from "./texture_renderable.js";

class ParticleRenderable extends TextureRenderable {
    constructor(myTexture) {
        super(myTexture);
        this._setShader(defaultShaders.getParticleShader());
    }
}
export default ParticleRenderable;
```

Loading the Default Particle Texture

For convenience when drawing, the game engine will preload the default particle texture, particle.png, located in the assets/particles folder. This operation can be integrated as part of the defaultResources initialization process.

1. Edit default_resources.js in the src/engine/resources folder, add an import from texture.js to access the texture loading functionality, and define a constant string for the location of the particle texture map and an accessor for this string:

```
import * as font from "./font.js";
import * as texture from "../resources/texture.js";
import * as map from "../core/resource_map.js";

// Default particle texture
let kDefaultPSTexture = "assets/particles/particle.png";

function getDefaultPSTexture() { return kDefaultPSTexture; }
```

2. In the init() function, call the texture.load() function to load the default particle texture map:

```
function init() {
    let loadPromise = new Promise(
        async function (resolve) {
            await Promise.all([
```

```
                font.load(kDefaultFont),
                texture.load(kDefaultPSTexture)
            ]);
            resolve();
        })
    ... identical to previous code ...
}
```

3. In the `cleanUp()` function, make sure to unload the default
    texture:

```
function cleanUp() {
    font.unload(kDefaultFont);
    texture.unload(kDefaultPSTexture);
}
```

4. Finally, remember to export the accessor:

```
export {
    ... identical to previous code ...

    getDefaultFontName, getDefaultPSTexture,

    ... identical to previous code ...
}
```

With this integration, the default particle texture file will be loaded into the
resource_map during system initialization. This default texture map can be readily
accessed with the returned value from the getDefaultPSTexture() function.

Defining the Engine Particle Component

With the drawing infrastructure defined, you can now define the engine component to
manage the behavior of the particle system. For now, the only functionality required is to
include a default system acceleration for all particles.

In the `src/engine/components` folder, create the `particle_system.js` file, and define the variable, getter, and setter functions for the default particle system acceleration. Remember to export the newly defined functionality.

```
let mSystemAcceleration = [30, -50.0];

function getSystemAcceleration() {
    return vec2.clone(mSystemAcceleration); }
function setSystemAcceleration(x, y) {
    mSystemAcceleration[0] = x;
    mSystemAcceleration[1] = y;
}

export {getSystemAcceleration, setSystemAcceleration}
```

Before continuing, make sure to update the engine access file, `index.js`, to allow game developer access to the newly defined functionality.

Defining the Particle and Particle Game Classes

You are now ready to define the actual particle, its default behaviors, and the class for a collection of particles.

Creating a Particle

Particles are lightweight game objects with simple properties wrapping around `ParticleRenderable` for drawing. To properly support motion, particles also implement movement approximation with the Symplectic Euler Integration.

1. Begin by creating the `particles` subfolder in the `src/engine` folder. This folder will contain particle-specific implementation files.

2. In the `src/engine/particles` folder, create `particle.js`, and define the constructor to include variables for position, velocity, acceleration, drag, and drawing parameters for debugging:

```
import * as loop from "../core/loop.js";
import * as particleSystem from "../components/particle_system.js";
import ParticleRenderable from "../renderables/particle_renderable.js";
import * as debugDraw from "../core/debug_draw.js";
```

```
let kSizeFactor = 0.2;

class Particle {
    constructor(texture, x, y, life) {
        this.mRenderComponent = new ParticleRenderable(texture);
        this.setPosition(x, y);

        // position control
        this.mVelocity = vec2.fromValues(0, 0);
        this.mAcceleration = particleSystem.getSystemAcceleration();
        this.mDrag = 0.95;

        // Color control
        this.mDeltaColor = [0, 0, 0, 0];

        // Size control
        this.mSizeDelta = 0;

        // Life control
        this.mCyclesToLive = life;
    }

    ... implementation to follow ...

}

export default Particle;
```

3. Define the draw() function to draw the particle as a
   TextureRenderable and a drawMarker() debug function to draw
   an X marker at the position of the particle:

```
draw(aCamera) {
    this.mRenderComponent.draw(aCamera);
}

drawMarker(aCamera) {
    let size = this.getSize();
    debugDraw.drawCrossMarker(aCamera, this.getPosition(),
                        size[0] * kSizeFactor, [0, 1, 0, 1]);
}
```

4. You can now implement the update() function to compute the position of the particle based on Symplectic Euler Integration, where the scaling with the mDrag variable simulates drags on the particles. Notice that this function also performs incremental changes to the other parameters including color and size. The mCyclesToLive variable informs the particle system when it is appropriate to remove this particle.

```
update() {
    this.mCyclesToLive--;

    let dt = loop.getUpdateIntervalInSeconds();

    // Symplectic Euler
    //    v += a * dt
    //    x += v * dt
    let p = this.getPosition();
    vec2.scaleAndAdd(this.mVelocity,
                     this.mVelocity, this.mAcceleration, dt);
    vec2.scale(this.mVelocity, this.mVelocity, this.mDrag);
    vec2.scaleAndAdd(p, p, this.mVelocity, dt);

    // update color
    let c = this.mRenderComponent.getColor();
    vec4.add(c, c, this.mDeltaColor);

    // update size
    let xf = this.mRenderComponent.getXform();
    let s = xf.getWidth() * this.mSizeDelta;
    xf.setSize(s, s);
}
```

5. Define simple get and set accessors. These functions are straightforward and are not listed here.

Creating the ParticleSet

To work with a collection of particles, you can now create the ParticleSet to support convenient looping over sets of Particle. For lightweight purposes, the Particle class does not subclass from the more complex GameObject; however, as JavaScript is an untyped language, it is still possible for ParticleSet to subclass from and refine GameObjectSet to take advantage of the existing set-specific functionality.

1. In the src/engine/particles folder, create particle_set.js, and define ParticleSet to be a subclass of GameObjectSet:

```
import * as glSys from "../core/gl.js";
import GameObjectSet from "../game_objects/game_object_set.js";

class ParticleSet extends GameObjectSet {
    constructor() {
        super();
    }

    ... implementation to follow ...

}

export default ParticleSet;
```

2. Override the draw() function of GameObjectSet to ensure particles are drawn with additive blending:

Note   Recall from Chapter 5 that the default gl.blendFunc() setting implements transparency by blending according to the alpha channel values. This is referred to as alpha blending. In this case, the gl.blendFunc() setting simply accumulates colors without considering the alpha channel. This is referred to as additive blending. Additive blending often results in oversaturation of pixel colors, that is, RGB components with values of greater than the maximum displayable value of 1.0. The oversaturation of pixel color is often desirable when simulating intense brightness of fire and explosions.

```
draw(aCamera) {
    let gl = glSys.get();
    gl.blendFunc(gl.ONE, gl.ONE);   // for additive blending!
    super.draw(aCamera);
    gl.blendFunc(gl.SRC_ALPHA, gl.ONE_MINUS_SRC_ALPHA);
                                    // restore alpha blending
}

drawMarkers(aCamera) {
    let i;
    for (i = 0; i < this.mSet.length; i++) {
        this.mSet[i].drawMarker(aCamera);
    }
}
```

3. Override the update() function to ensure expired particles are removed:

```
update() {
    super.update();
    // Cleanup Particles
    let i, obj;
    for (i = 0; i < this.size(); i++) {
        obj = this.getObjectAt(i);
        if (obj.hasExpired()) {
            this.removeFromSet(obj);
        }
    }
}
```

Lastly, remember to update the engine access file, index.js, to forward the newly defined functionality to the client.

Testing the Particle System

The test should verify two main goals. First, the implemented particle system is capable of generating visually pleasant effects. Second, the particles are handled correctly by being properly created, destroyed, and behaving as expected. The test case is based mainly on the previous project with a new _createParticle() function that is called when the Q key is pressed. The _createParticle() function implemented in the my_game_main.js file creates particles with pseudo-random behaviors as listed in the following:

```
function _createParticle(atX, atY) {
    let life = 30 + Math.random() * 200;
    let p = new engine.Particle(
            engine.defaultResources.getDefaultPSTexture(),
            atX, atY, life);
    p.setColor([1, 0, 0, 1]);

    // size of the particle
    let r = 5.5 + Math.random() * 0.5;
    p.setSize(r, r);

    // final color
    let fr = 3.5 + Math.random();
    let fg = 0.4 + 0.1 * Math.random();
    let fb = 0.3 + 0.1 * Math.random();
    p.setFinalColor([fr, fg, fb, 0.6]);

    // velocity on the particle
    let fx = 10 - 20 * Math.random();
    let fy = 10 * Math.random();
    p.setVelocity(fx, fy);

    // size delta
    p.setSizeDelta(0.98);

    return p;
}
```

There are two important observations to be made on the _createParticle() function. First, the random() function is used many times to configure each created Particle. Particle systems utilize large numbers of similar particles with slight differences to build and convey the desired visual effect. It is important to avoid any patterns by using randomness. Second, there are many seemingly arbitrary numbers used in the configuration, such as setting the life of the particle to be between 30

654

and 230 or setting the final red component to a number between 3.5 and 4.5. This is unfortunately the nature of working with particle systems. There is often quite a bit of ad hoc experimentation. Commercial game engines typically alleviate this difficulty by releasing a collection of preset values for their particle systems. In this way, game designers can fine-tune specific desired effects by adjusting the provided presets.

Observations

Run the project and press the Q key to observe the generated particles. It appears as though there is combustion occurring underneath the mouse pointer. Hold the Q key and move the mouse pointer around slowly to observe the combustion as though there is an engine generating flames beneath the mouse. Type the E key to toggle the drawing of individual particle positions. Now you can observe a green X marking the position of each of the generated particles.

If you move the mouse pointer rapidly, you can observe individual pink circles with green X centers changing color while dropping toward the floor. Although all particles are created by the _createParticle() function and share the similar behaviors of falling toward the floor while changing color, every particle appears slightly different and does not exhibit any behavior patterns. You can now clearly observe the importance of integrating randomness in the created particles.

There are limitless variations to how you can modify the _createParticle() function. For example, you can change the explosion-like effect to steam or smoke simply by changing the initial and final color to different shades of gray and transparencies. Additionally, you can modify the default particle texture by inverting the color to create black smoke effects. You could also modify the size change delta to be greater than 1 to increase the size of the particles over time. There are literally no limits to how particles can be created. The particle system you have implemented allows the game developer to create particles with customized behaviors that are most suitable to the game that they are building.

Lastly, notice that the generated particles do not interact with the RigidShape objects and appears as though the particles are drawn over the rest of the objects in the game scene. This issue will be examined and resolved in the next project.

Particle Collisions

An approach to integrate particles into a game scene is for the particles to follow the implied rules of the scene and interact with the non-particle objects accordingly. The ability to detect collisions is the foundation for interactions between objects. For this reason, it is sometimes important to support particle collisions with the other, non-particle game objects.

Since particles are defined only by their positions with no dimensions, the actual collision computations can be relatively straightforward. However, there are typically a large number of particles; as such, the number of collisions to be performed can also be numerous. As a compromise and optimization in computational costs, particles collisions can be based on RigidShape instead of the actual Renderable objects. This is similar to the case of the physics component where the actual simulation is based on simple rigid shapes in approximating the potentially geometrically complicated Renderable objects.

The Particle Collisions Project

This project demonstrates how to implement a particle collision system that is capable of resolving collisions between particles and the existing RigidShape objects. You can see an example of this project running in Figure 10-2. The source code of this project is located in the chapter10/10.2.particle_collisions folder.

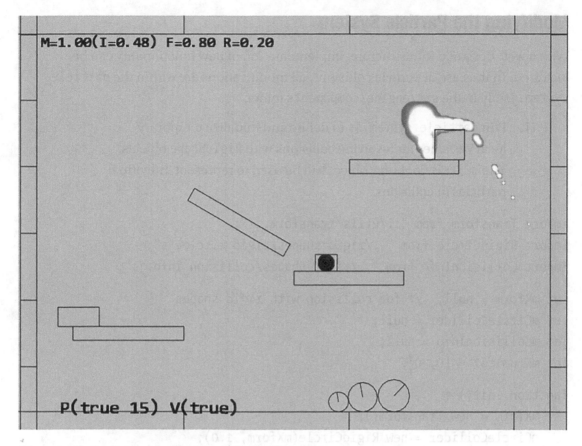

Figure 10-2. Running the Particle Collisions project

The controls of the project are identical to the previous project and support all of the rigid shape and collision controls. The controls that are specific to the particle system are as follows:

- **Q key**: To spawn particles at the current mouse position

- **E key**: To toggle the drawing of particle bounds

- **1 key**: To toggle `Particle/RigidShape` collisions

The goals of the project are as follows:

- To understand and resolve collisions between individual particle positions and `RigidShape` objects

- To build a particle engine component that supports interaction with `RigidShape`

Modifying the Particle System

With a well-designed infrastructure, implementation of new functionality can be localized. In the case of particle collisions, all modifications are within the particle_ system.js file in the src/engine/components folder.

1. Edit particle_system.js to define and initialize temporary local variables for resolving collisions with RigidShape objects. The mCircleCollider object will be used to represent individual particles in collisions.

```
import Transform from "../utils/transform.js";
import RigidCircle from "../rigid_shapes/rigid_circle.js";
import CollisionInfo from "../rigid_shapes/collision_info.js";

let mXform = null;  // for collision with rigid shapes
let mCircleCollider = null;
let mCollisionInfo = null;
let mFrom1to2 = [0, 0];

function init() {
    mXform = new Transform();
    mCircleCollider = new RigidCircle(mXform, 1.0);
    mCollisionInfo = new CollisionInfo();
}
```

2. Define the resolveCirclePos() function to resolve the collision between a RigidCircle and a position by pushing the position outside of the circle shape:

```
function resolveCirclePos(circShape, particle) {
    let collision = false;
    let pos = particle.getPosition();
    let cPos = circShape.getCenter();
    vec2.subtract(mFrom1to2, pos, cPos);
    let dist = vec2.length(mFrom1to2);
    if (dist < circShape.getRadius()) {
        vec2.scale(mFrom1to2, mFrom1to2, 1/dist);
        vec2.scaleAndAdd(pos, cPos, mFrom1to2, circShape.getRadius());
```

```
        collision = true;
    }
    return collision;
}
```

3. Define the resolveRectPos() function to resolve the collision
    between a RigidRectangle and a position by wrapping the
    mCircleCollider local variable around the position and invoking
    the RigidCircle to RigidRectangle collision function. When
    interpenetration is detected, the position is pushed outside of the
    rectangle shape according to the computed mCollisionInfo.

```
function resolveRectPos(rectShape, particle) {
    let collision = false;
    let s = particle.getSize();
    let p = particle.getPosition();
    mXform.setSize(s[0], s[1]); // referred by mCircleCollision
    mXform.setPosition(p[0], p[1]);
    if (mCircleCollider.boundTest(rectShape)) {
        if (rectShape.collisionTest(mCircleCollider, mCollisionInfo)) {
            // make sure info is always from rect towards particle
            vec2.subtract(mFrom1to2,
                mCircleCollider.getCenter(), rectShape.getCenter());
            if (vec2.dot(mFrom1to2, mCollisionInfo.getNormal()) < 0)
                mCircleCollider.adjustPositionBy(
                mCollisionInfo.getNormal(), -mCollisionInfo.getDepth());
            else
                mCircleCollider.adjustPositionBy(
                mCollisionInfo.getNormal(), mCollisionInfo.getDepth());
            p = mXform.getPosition();
            particle.setPosition(p[0], p[1]);
            collision = true;
        }
    }
    return collision;
}
```

4. Implement resolveRigidShapeCollision() and
   resolveRigidShapeSetCollision() to allow convenient
   invocation by client game developers. These functions resolve
   collisions between a single or a set of RigidShape objects and a
   ParticleSet object.

```
// obj: a GameObject (with potential mRigidBody)
// pSet: set of particles (ParticleSet)
function resolveRigidShapeCollision(obj, pSet) {
    let i, j;
    let collision = false;

    let rigidShape = obj.getRigidBody();
    for (j = 0; j < pSet.size(); j++) {
        if (rigidShape.getType() == "RigidRectangle")
            collision = resolveRectPos(rigidShape, pSet.getObjectAt(j));
        else if (rigidShape.getType() == "RigidCircle")
            collision = resolveCirclePos(rigidShape,pSet.getObjectAt(j));
    }

    return collision;
}

// objSet: set of GameObjects (with potential mRigidBody)
// pSet: set of particles (ParticleSet)
function resolveRigidShapeSetCollision(objSet, pSet) {
    let i, j;
    let collision = false;
    if ((objSet.size === 0) || (pSet.size === 0))
        return false;
    for (i=0; i<objSet.size(); i++) {
        let rigidShape = objSet.getObjectAt(i).getRigidBody();
        for (j = 0; j<pSet.size(); j++) {
            if (rigidShape.getType() == "RigidRectangle")
                collision = resolveRectPos(rigidShape,
                                    pSet.getObjectAt(j)) || collision;
            else if (rigidShape.getType() == "RigidCircle")
```

```
                collision = resolveCirclePos(rigidShape,
                                pSet.getObjectAt(j)) || collision;
        }
    }
    return collision;
}
```

5. Lastly, remember to export the newly defined functions:

```
export {init,
        getSystemAcceleration, setSystemAcceleration,
        resolveRigidShapeCollision, resolveRigidShapeSetCollision}
```

Initializing the Particle System

The temporary variables defined in particle_system.js must be initialized before the game loop begins. Edit loop.js, import from particle_system.js, and call the init() function after asynchronous loading is completed in the start() function.

... identical to previous code ...

```
import * as debugDraw from "./debug_draw.js";
import * as particleSystem from "../components/particle_system.js";
```

... identical to previous code ...

```
async function start(scene) {

    ... identical to previous code ...

    // Wait for any async requests before game-load
    await map.waitOnPromises();

    // system init that can only occur after all resources are loaded
    particleSystem.init();

    ... identical to previous code ...
}
```

Testing the Particle System

The modifications required for the MyGame class are straightforward. A new variable must be defined to support the toggling of collision resolution, and the update() function defined in my_game_main.js is modified as follows:

```
update() {

    ... identical to previous code ...

    if (engine.input.isKeyClicked(engine.input.keys.One))
            this.mPSCollision = !this.mPSCollision;
    if (this.mPSCollision) {
        engine.particleSystem.resolveRigidShapeSetCollision(
                                this.mAllObjs, this.mParticles);
        engine.particleSystem.resolveRigidShapeSetCollision(
                                this.mPlatforms, this.mParticles);
    }

    ... identical to previous code ...
}
```

Observations

As in previous projects, you can run the project and create particles with the Q and E keys. However, notice that the generated particles do not overlap with any of the objects. You can even try moving your mouse pointer to within the bounds of one of the RigidShape objects and then type the Q key. Notice that in all cases, the particles are generated outside of the shapes.

You can try typing the 1 key to toggle collisions with the rigid shapes. Note that with collisions enabled, the particles somewhat resemble the amber particles from a fire or an explosion where they bounce off the surfaces of RigidShape objects in the scene. When collision is toggled off, as you have observed from the previous project, the particles appear to be burning or exploding in front of the other objects. In this way, collision is simply another parameter for controlling the integration of the particle system with the rest of the game engine.

You may find it troublesome to continue to press the Q key to generate particles. In the next project, you will learn about generation of particles over a fixed period of time.

Particle Emitters

With your current particle system implementation, you can create particles at a specific point and time. These particles can move and change based on their properties. However, particles can be created only when there is an explicit state change such as a key click. This becomes restricting when it is desirable to persist the generation of particles after the state change, such as an explosion or firework that persists for a short while after the creation of a new `RigidShape` object. A particle emitter addresses this issue by defining the functionality of generating particles over a time period.

The Particle Emitters Project

This project demonstrates how to implement a particle emitter for your particle system to support particle emission over time. You can see an example of this project running in Figure 10-3. The source code of this project is located in the `chapter10/10.3.particle_emitters` folder.

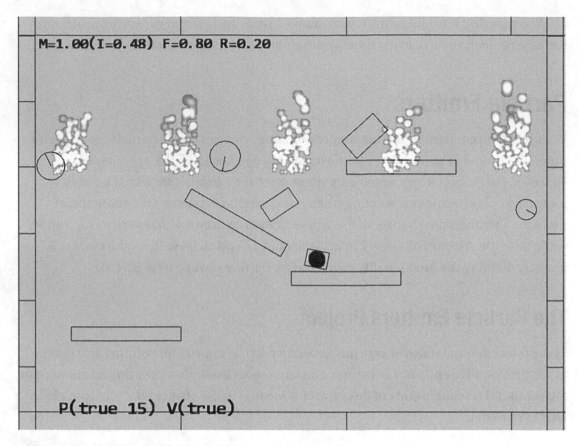

Figure 10-3. *Running the Particle Emitters project*

The controls of the project are identical to the previous project and support all of the rigid shape and collision controls. The particle system–specific controls of the project are as follows:

- **Q key**: To spawn particles at the current mouse position

- **E key**: To toggle the drawing of particle bounds

- **1 key**: To toggle Particle/RigidShape collisions

The goals of the project are as follows:

- To understand the need for particle emitters

- To experience implementing particle emitters

Defining the ParticleEmitter Class

You have observed and experienced the importance of avoiding patterns when working with particles. In this case, as the ParticleEmitter object generates new particles over time, once again, it is important to inject *randomness* to avoid any appearance of a pattern.

1. In the src/engine/particles folder, create particle_emitter.js; define the ParticleEmitter class with a constructor that receives the location, number, and how to emit new particles. Note that the mParticleCreator variable expects a callback function. When required, this function will be invoked to create a particle.

```
let kMinToEmit = 5; // Smallest number of particle emitted per cycle

class ParticleEmitter {
    constructor(px, py, num, createrFunc) {
        // Emitter position
        this.mEmitPosition = [px, py];

        // Number of particles left to be emitted
        this.mNumRemains = num;

        // Function to create particles (user defined)
        this.mParticleCreator = createrFunc;
    }

    ... implementation to follow ...
}

export default ParticleEmitter;
```

2. Define a function to return the current status of the emitter. When there are no more particles to emit, the emitters should be removed.

```
expired() { return (this.mNumRemains <= 0); }
```

3. Create a function to actually create or emit particles. Take note of the randomness in the number of particles that are actually emitted and the invocation of the mParticleCreator() callback function. With this design, it is unlikely to encounter patterns in the number of particles that are created over time. In addition, the emitter defines only the mechanisms of how, when, and where particles will be emitted and does not define the characteristics of the created particles. The function pointed to by mParticleCreator is responsible for defining the actual behavior of each particle.

```javascript
emitParticles(pSet) {
    let numToEmit = 0;
    if (this.mNumRemains < this.kMinToEmit) {
        // If only a few are left, emits all of them
        numToEmit = this.mNumRemains;
    } else {
        // Otherwise, emits about 20% of what's left
        numToEmit = Math.trunc(Math.random() * 0.2 * this.mNumRemains);
    }
    // Left for future emitting.
    this.mNumRemains -= numToEmit;
    let i, p;
    for (i = 0; i < numToEmit; i++) {
        p = this.mParticleCreator(
                        this.mEmitPosition[0], this.mEmitPosition[1]);
        pSet.addToSet(p);
    }
}
```

Lastly, remember to update the engine access file, index.js, to allow game developer access to the ParticleEmitter class.

Modifying the Particle Set

The defined `ParticleEmitter` class needs to be integrated into `ParticleSet` to manage the emitted particles:

1. Edit `particle_set.js` in the src/engine/particles folder, and define a new variable for maintaining emitters:

```
constructor() {
    super();
    this.mEmitterSet = [];
}
```

2. Define a function for instantiating a new emitter. Take note of the `func` parameter. This is the callback function that is responsible for the actual creation of individual `Particle` objects.

```
addEmitterAt(x, y, n, func) {
    let e = new ParticleEmitter(x, y, n, func);
    this.mEmitterSet.push(e);
}
```

3. Modify the update function to loop through the emitter set to generate new particles and to remove expired emitters:

```
update() {
    super.update();
    // Cleanup Particles
    let i, obj;
    for (i = 0; i < this.size(); i++) {
        obj = this.getObjectAt(i);
        if (obj.hasExpired()) {
            this.removeFromSet(obj);
        }
    }
```

```
    // Emit new particles
    for (i = 0; i < this.mEmitterSet.length; i++) {
        let e = this.mEmitterSet[i];
        e.emitParticles(this);
        if (e.expired()) {  // delete the emitter when done
            this.mEmitterSet.splice(i, 1);
        }
    }
}
```

Testing the Particle Emitter

This is a straightforward test of the correct functioning of the ParticleEmitter object.
The MyGame class update() function is modified to create a new ParticleEmitter at
the position of the RigidShape object when the G or H key is pressed. In this way, it will
appear as though an explosion has occurred when a new RigidShape object is created or
when RigidShape objects are assigned new velocities.

In both cases, the _createParticle() function discussed in the first project of this
chapter is passed as the argument for the createrFunc callback function parameter in
the ParticleEmitter constructor.

Observations

Run the project and observe the initial firework-like explosions at the locations where
the initial RigidShape objects are created. Type the G key to observe the accompanied
explosion in the general vicinity of the newly created RigidShape object. Alternatively,
you can type the H key to apply velocities to all the shapes and observe explosion-like
effects next to each RigidShape object. For a very rough sense of what this particle
system may look like in a game, you can try enabling texturing (with the T key), disabling
RigidShape drawing (with the R key), and typing the H key to apply velocities. Observe
that it appears as though the Renderable objects are being blasted by the explosions.

Notice how each explosion persists for a short while before disappearing gradually.
Compare this effect with the one resulting from a short tapping of the Q key, and observe
that without a dedicated particle emitter, the explosion seems to have fizzled before it
begins.

Similar to particles, emitters can also have drastically different characteristics for simulating different physical effects. For example, the emitter you have implemented is driven by the number of particles to create. This behavior can be easily modified to use time as the driving factor, for example, emitting an approximated number of particles over a given time period. Other potential applications of emitters can include, but are not limited to

- Allowing the position of the emitter to change over time, for example, attaching the emitter to the end of a rocket

- Allowing emitter to affect the properties of the created particles, for example, changing the acceleration or velocity of all created particles to simulate wind effects

Based on the simple and yet flexible particle system you have implemented, you can now experiment with all these ideas in a straightforward manner.

Summary

There are three simple takeaways from this chapter. First, you have learned that particles, positions with an appropriate texture and no dimensions, can be useful in describing interesting physical effects. Second, the capability to collide and interact with other objects assists with the integration and placement of particles in game scenes. Lastly, in order to achieve the appearance of familiar physical effects, the emitting of particles should persist over some period of time.

You have developed a simple and yet flexible particle system to support the consistent management of individual particles and their emitters. Your system is simple because it consists of a single component, defined in `particle_system.js`, with only three simple supporting classes defined in the `src/engine/particles` folder. The system is flexible because of the callback mechanism for the actual creation of particles where the game developers are free to define and generate particles with any arbitrary behaviors.

The particle system you have built serves to demonstrate the fundamentals. To increase the sophistication of particle behaviors, you can subclass from the simple `Particle` class, define additional parameters, and amend the `update()` function accordingly. To support additional physical effects, you can consider modifying or subclassing from the `ParticleEmitter` class and emit particles according to your desired formulations.

Game Design Considerations

As discussed in Chapter 9, presence in games isn't exclusively achieved by recreating our physical world experience in game environments; while introducing real-world physics is often an effective way to bring players into virtual worlds, there are many other design choices that can be quite effective at pulling players into the game, either in partnership with object physics or on their own. For example, imagine a game with a 2D comic book visual style that displays a "BOOM!" text-based image whenever something explodes; objects don't show the word "BOOM!" when they explode in the physical world, of course, but the stylized and familiar use of "BOOM!" in the context of a comic book visual aesthetic as shown in Figure 10-4 can be quite effective on its own as a way to connect players with what's happening in the game world.

Figure 10-4. *Visual techniques like those shown in this graphic are often used in graphic novels to represent various fast-moving or high-impact actions like explosions, punches, crashes, and the like; similar visual techniques have also been used quite effectively in film and video games*

Particle effects can also be used either in realistic ways that mimic how we'd expect them to behave in the real world or in more creative ways that have no connection to real-world physics. Try using what you've learned from the examples in this chapter and experiment with particles in your current game prototype as we left it in Chapter 9: can you think of some uses for particles in the current level that might support and reinforce the presence of existing game elements (e.g., sparks flying if the player character touches the force field)? What about introducing particle effects that might not directly relate to gameplay but enhance and add interest to the game setting?

CHAPTER 11

Supporting Camera Background

After completing this chapter, you will be able to

- Implement background tiling with any image in any given camera WC bounds

- Understand parallax and simulate motion parallax with parallax scrolling

- Appreciate the need for layering objects in 2D games and support layered drawing

Introduction

By this point, your game engine is capable of illuminating 2D images to generate highlights and shadows and simulating basic physical behaviors. To conclude the engine development for this book, this chapter focuses on the general support for creating the game world environment with background tiling and parallax as well as relieving the game programmers from having to manage draw order.

Background images or objects are included to decorate the game world to further engage the players. This often requires the image being vast in scale with subtle visual complexities. For example, in a side-scrolling game, the background must always be present, and simple motion parallax can create the sense of depth and further capture the players' interests.

Tiling, in the context of computer graphics and video games, refers to the duplication of an image or pattern along the x and y directions. In video games, images used for tiling are usually strategically constructed to ensure content continuation across

© Kelvin Sung, Jebediah Pavleas, Matthew Munson, and Jason Pace 2022
K. Sung et al., *Build Your Own 2D Game Engine and Create Great Web Games*,
https://doi.org/10.1007/978-1-4842-7377-7_11

the duplicating boundaries. Figure 11-1 shows an example of a strategically drawn background image tiled three times in the x direction and two times in the y direction. Notice the perfect continuation across the duplicating boundaries. Proper tiling conveys a sense of complexity in a boundless game world by creating only a single image.

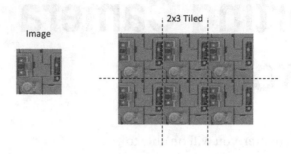

Figure 11-1. *Tiling of a strategically drawn background image*

Parallax is the apparent displacements of objects when they are viewed from different positions. Figure 11-2 shows an example of the parallax of a shaded circle. When viewed from the middle eye position, the center shaded circle appears to be covering the center rectangular block. However, this same shaded circle appears to be covering the top rectangular block when viewed from the bottom eye position. Motion parallax is the observation that when one is in motion, nearby objects appear to move quicker than those in the distance. This is a fundamental visual cue that informs depth perception. In 2D games, the simulation of motion parallax is a straightforward approach to introduce depth complexity to further captivate the players.

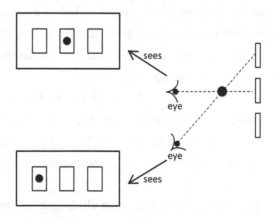

Figure 11-2. *Parallax: objects appearing at different positions when observed from different viewpoints*

This chapter presents a general algorithm for tiling the camera WC bounds and describes an abstraction for hiding the details of parallax scrolling. With the increase in visual complexity of the background, this chapter discusses the importance of and creates a layer manager to alleviate game programmers from the details of draw ordering.

Tiling of the Background

When tiling the background in a 2D game, it is important to recognize that only the tiles that cover the camera WC bounds need to be drawn. This is illustrated in Figure 11-3. In this example, the background object to be tiled is defined at the WC origin with its own width and height. However, in this case, the camera WC bounds do not intersect with the defined background object. Figure 11-3 shows that the background object needs to be tiled six times to cover the camera WC bounds. Notice that since it is not visible through the camera, the player-defined background object at the origin does not need to be drawn.

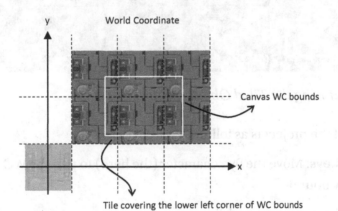

Figure 11-3. *Generating tiled background for camera WC bounds*

There are many ways to compute the required tiling for a given background object and the camera WC bounds. A simple approach is to determine the tile position that covers the lower-left corner of the WC bound and tile in the positive x and y directions.

The Tiled Objects Project

This project demonstrates how to implement simple background tiling. You can see an example of this project running in Figure 11-4. The source code to this project is defined in the chapter11/11.1.tiled_objects folder.

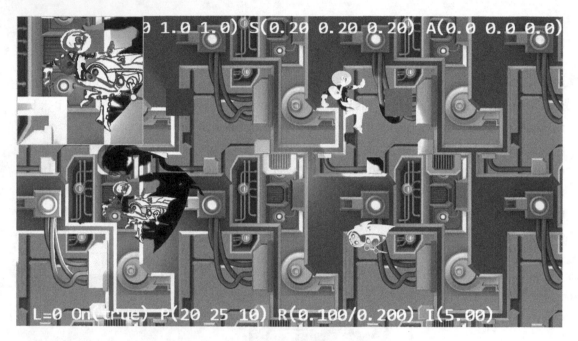

Figure 11-4. *Running the Tiled Objects project*

The control of the project is as follows:

- **WASD keys**: Move the Dye character (the hero) to pan the WC window bounds

The goals of the project are as follows:

- To experience working with multiple layers of background

- To implement the tiling of background objects for camera WC window bounds

You can find the following external resources in the assets folder. The fonts folder contains the default system fonts and six texture images: minion_sprite.png, minion_sprite_normal.png, bg.png, bg_normal.png, bg_layer.png, and bg_layer_normal.png.

The Hero and Minion objects are represented by sprite elements in the minion_sprite.png image, and bg.png and bg_layer.png are two layers of background images. The corresponding _normal files are the normal maps.

Define TiledGameObject

Recall that a GameObject abstracts the basic behavior of an object in the game where its appearance is determined by the Renderable object that it references. A TiledGameObject is a GameObject that is capable of tiling the referenced Renderable object to cover the WC bounds of a given Camera object.

1. Create a new file in the src/engine/game_objects folder and name it tiled_game_object.js. Add the following code to construct the object. The mShouldTile variable provides the option to stop the tiling process.

```
class TiledGameObject extends GameObject {
    constructor(renderableObj) {
        super(renderableObj);
        this.mShouldTile = true; // can switch this off if desired
    }
… implementation to follow …
export default TiledGameObject;
```

2. Define the getter and setter functions for mShouldTile:

```
setIsTiled(t) { this.mShouldTile = t; }
shouldTile() { return this.mShouldTile; }
```

3. Define the function to tile and draw the Renderable object to cover the WC bounds of the aCamera object:

```
_drawTile(aCamera) {
    // Step A: Compute the positions and dimensions of tiling object.
    let xf = this.getXform();
    let w = xf.getWidth();
    let h = xf.getHeight();
    let pos = xf.getPosition();
    let left = pos[0] - (w / 2);
```

```
    let right = left + w;
    let top = pos[1] + (h / 2);
    let bottom = top - h;

    // Step B: Get WC positions and dimensions of the drawing camera.
    let wcPos = aCamera.getWCCenter();
    let wcLeft = wcPos[0] - (aCamera.getWCWidth() / 2);
    let wcRight = wcLeft + aCamera.getWCWidth();
    let wcBottom = wcPos[1] - (aCamera.getWCHeight() / 2);
    let wcTop = wcBottom + aCamera.getWCHeight();

    // Step C: Determine offset to camera window's lower left corner.
    let dx = 0, dy = 0; // offset to the lower left corner
    // left/right boundary?
    if (right < wcLeft) { // left of WC left
        dx = Math.ceil((wcLeft - right) / w) * w;
    } else {
        if (left > wcLeft) { // not touching the left side
            dx = -Math.ceil((left - wcLeft) / w) * w;
        }
    }
    // top/bottom boundary
    if (top < wcBottom) { // Lower than the WC bottom
        dy = Math.ceil((wcBottom - top) / h) * h;
    } else {
        if (bottom > wcBottom) {  // not touching the bottom
            dy = -Math.ceil((bottom - wcBottom) / h) * h;
        }
    }

    // Step D: Save the original position of the tiling object.
    let sX = pos[0];
    let sY = pos[1];

    // Step E: Offset tiling object and update related position variables
    xf.incXPosBy(dx);
    xf.incYPosBy(dy);
```

```
right = pos[0] + (w / 2);
top = pos[1] + (h / 2);

// Step F: Determine number of times to tile in x and y directions.
let nx = 1, ny = 1; // times to draw in the x and y directions
nx = Math.ceil((wcRight - right) / w);
ny = Math.ceil((wcTop - top) / h);

// Step G: Loop through each location to draw a tile
let cx = nx;
let xPos = pos[0];
while (ny >= 0) {
    cx = nx;
    pos[0] = xPos;
    while (cx >= 0) {
        this.mRenderComponent.draw(aCamera);
        xf.incXPosBy(w);
        --cx;
    }
    xf.incYPosBy(h);
    --ny;
}

// Step H: Reset the tiling object to its original position.
pos[0] = sX;
pos[1] = sY;
}
```

The _drawTile() function computes and repositions the Renderable object to cover the lower-left corner of the camera WC bounds and tiles the object in the positive x and y directions. Note the following:

    a.   Steps A and B compute the position and dimension of the tiling object and the camera WC bounds.

    b.   Step C computes the dx and dy offsets that will translate the Renderable object with bounds that cover the lower-left corner of the aCamera WC bounds. The calls to the

Math.ceil() function ensure that the computed dx and dy are integer multiples of the Renderable width and height. This is important to ensure there are no overlaps or gaps during tiling.

c. Step D saves the original position of the Renderable object before offsetting and drawing it. Step E offsets the Renderable object to cover the lower-left corner of the camera WC bounds.

d. Step F computes the number of repeats required, and step G tiles the Renderable object in the positive x and y directions until the results cover the entire camera WC bounds. The calls to the Math.ceil() function ensure that the computed nx and ny, the number of times to tile in the x and y directions, are integers.

e. Step H resets the position of the tiled object to the original location.

4. Override the draw() function to call the _drawTile() function when tiling is enabled:

```
draw(aCamera) {
    if (this.isVisible() && (this.mDrawRenderable)) {
        if (this.shouldTile()) {
            // find out where we should be drawing
            this._drawTile(aCamera);
        } else {
            this.mRenderComponent.draw(aCamera);
        }
    }
}
```

Lastly, remember to update the engine access file, index.js, to forward the newly defined functionality to the client.

Modify MyGame to Test Tiled Objects

MyGame should test for the correctness of object tiling. To test multiple layers of tiling, two separate instances of TiledGameObject and Camera are created. The two TiledGameObject instances are located at different distances from the cameras (z depth) and are illuminated by different combinations of light sources. The added second camera focused on one of the Hero objects.

Only the creation of the TiledGameObject instance is of interest. This is because once created, a TiledGameObject instance can be handled in the same manner as a GameObject instance. For this reason, only the init() function of the MyGame class is examined in detail.

```
init() {
    // Step A: set up the cameras
    this.mCamera = new engine.Camera(
        vec2.fromValues(50, 37.5), // position of the camera
        100,                       // width of camera
        [0, 0, 1280, 720]          // viewport (X, Y, width, height)
    );
    this.mCamera.setBackgroundColor([0.8, 0.8, 0.8, 1]);
    // sets the background to gray

    this.mHeroCam = new engine.Camera(
        vec2.fromValues(20, 30.5), // position of the camera
        14,                        // width of camera
        [0, 420, 300, 300],        // viewport (X, Y, width, height)
        2
    );
    this.mHeroCam.setBackgroundColor([0.5, 0.5, 0.9, 1]);

    // Step B: the lights
    this._initializeLights();   // defined in MyGame_Lights.js

    // Step C: the far Background
    let bgR = new engine.IllumRenderable(this.kBg, this.kBgNormal);
    bgR.setElementPixelPositions(0, 1024, 0, 1024);
    bgR.getXform().setSize(30, 30);
    bgR.getXform().setPosition(0, 0);
```

```
        bgR.getMaterial().setSpecular([0.2, 0.1, 0.1, 1]);
        bgR.getMaterial().setShininess(50);
        bgR.getXform().setZPos(-5);
        bgR.addLight(this.mGlobalLightSet.getLightAt(1));
                                    // only the directional light
        this.mBg = new engine.TiledGameObject(bgR);

        // Step D: the closer Background
        let i;
        let bgR1 = new engine.IllumRenderable(
                                this.kBgLayer, this.kBgLayerNormal);
        bgR1.getXform().setSize(30, 30);
        bgR1.getXform().setPosition(0, 0);
        bgR1.getXform().setZPos(-2);
        for (i = 0; i < 4; i++) {
            bgR1.addLight(this.mGlobalLightSet.getLightAt(i)); // all lights
        }
        bgR1.getMaterial().setSpecular([0.2, 0.2, 0.5, 1]);
        bgR1.getMaterial().setShininess(10);
        this.mBgL1 = new engine.TiledGameObject(bgR1);

        ... identical to previous code ...
}
```

In the listed code, the two cameras are first created in step A, followed by the creation and initialization of all the light sources in the _initializeLights() function. Step C defines bgR as a TiledGameObject with an IllumRenderable that is being illuminated by one light source. Step D defines the second TiledGameObject based on another IllumRenderable that is being illuminated by four light sources. Since the mShouldTile variable of the TileGameObject class defaults to true, both of the tile objects will tile the camera that they are drawing to.

Observations

You can now run the project and move the Hero object with the WASD keys. As expected, the two layers of tiled backgrounds are clearly visible. You can switch off the illumination to the farther background by selecting and turning off light source 1 (type the 1 key followed by the H key). Move the Hero object to pan the cameras to verify that the tiling and the background movement behaviors are correct in both of the cameras.

An interesting observation is that while the two layers of backgrounds are located at different distances from the camera, when the camera pans, the two background images scroll synchronously. If not for the differences in light source illumination, it would appear as though the background is actually a single image. This example illustrates the importance of simulating motion parallax.

Simulating Motion Parallax with Parallax Scrolling

Parallax scrolling simulates motion parallax by defining and scrolling objects at different speeds to convey the sense that these objects are located at different distances from the camera. Figure 11-5 illustrates this idea with a top view showing the conceptual distances of objects from the camera. Since this is a bird's-eye view, the width of the camera WC bounds is shown as a horizontal line at the bottom. The Hero object is the closest to the camera in front of two layers of backgrounds, Layer1 and Layer2. For typical 2D games, the vast majority of objects in the game will be located at this default distance from the camera. The background objects are located farther from the camera, behind the default distance. The distance perception can be conveyed by strategic drawings on the background objects (e.g., grass fields for Layer1 and distant mountains for Layer2) accompanied with appropriate scroll speeds. Take note that positions P_1 and P_2 on background objects Layer1 and Layer2 are directly behind the Hero object.

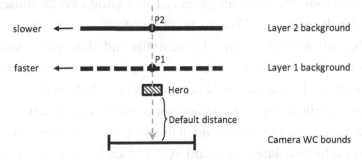

Figure 11-5. *Top view of a scene with two background objects at different distances*

Figure 11-6 shows the results of leftward parallax scrolling with a stationary camera. With Layer1 scrolling at a faster speed than Layer2, position P_1 has a greater displacement than P_2 from their original positions. A continuous scrolling will move Layer1 faster than Layer2 and properly convey the sense that it is closer than Layer2. In parallax scrolling, objects that are closer to the camera always have a greater scroll speed than objects that are farther.

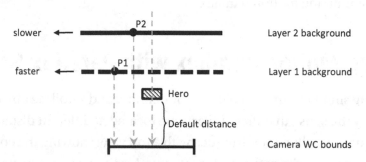

Figure 11-6. *Top view of parallax scrolling with stationary camera*

In the case when the camera is in motion, relative speeds of objects must be considered when implementing parallax scrolling. Figure 11-7 illustrates, with a top view, the situation of a moving camera with stationary objects. In this example, the camera WC bounds have moved rightward by d units. Since the movement is in the camera, all stationary objects in the camera view will appear to have been displaced by the inverse of the camera movement. For example, the stationary Hero object is displaced from the center leftward to the left edge of the new WC bounds. To properly simulate motion parallax, the two backgrounds, Layer1 and Layer2, must be displaced by different relative distances. In this case, relative distances must be computed such that farther objects will appear to move slower. At the end of the camera movement, in the new WC bounds, the Hero object that is closest to the camera will appear to have been displaced leftward by d units, the Layer1 object by 0.75d, and the Layer2 object by 0.25d. In this way, the displacements of the objects reflect their relative distances from the camera. To achieve this, the translation of the Hero object is zero, and the Layer1 and Layer2 objects must be translated rightward by 0.25d and 0.75d, respectively. Notice that the backgrounds are translated rightward by amounts that are less than that of the camera movement, and as a result, the backgrounds are actually moving leftward. For example, although the Layer1 object is translated rightward by 0.25d, when viewed from the camera that has been moved rightward by d, the resulting relative movement is such that the Layer1 object has been displaced leftward by 0.75d.

682

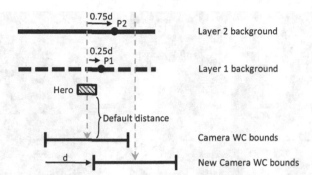

Figure 11-7. *Top view of parallax scrolling with the camera in motion*

It is important to note that in the described approach to implement parallax scrolling for a moving camera, stationary background objects are displaced. There are two limitations to this approach. First, the object locations are changed for the purpose of conveying visual cues and do not reflect any specific game state logic. This can create challenging conflicts if the game logic requires the precise control of the movements of the background objects. Fortunately, background objects are usually designed to serve the purposes of decorating the environment and engaging the players. Background objects typically do not participate in the actual gameplay logic. The second limitation is that the stationary background objects are actually in motion and will appear so when viewed from cameras other than the one causing the motion parallax. When views from multiple cameras are necessary in the presence of motion parallax, it is important to carefully coordinate them to avoid player confusion.

The Parallax Objects Project

This project demonstrates parallax scrolling. You can see an example of this project running in Figure 11-8. The source code to this project is defined in the `chapter11/11.2.parallax_objects` folder.

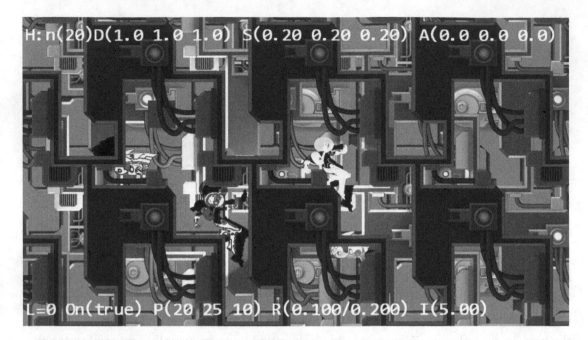

Figure 11-8. *Running the Parallax Objects project*

The controls of the project are as follows:

- **P key**: Toggles the drawing of a second camera that is not in motion to highlight background object movements in simulating parallax scrolling

- **WASD keys**: Move the Dye character (the hero) to pan the WC window bounds

The goals of the project are as follows:

- To understand and appreciate motion parallax

- To simulate motion parallax with parallax scrolling

Define ParallaxGameObject to Implement Parallax Scrolling

Parallax scrolling involves the continuous scrolling of objects, and TiledGameObject provides a convenient platform for never-ending scrolling. For this reason, ParallaxGameObject is defined as a subclass of TiledGameObject.

1. Create `parallax_game_object.js` in the `src/engine/game_objects` folder, and add the following code to construct the object:

```
import TiledGameObject from "./tiled_game_object.js";

class ParallaxGameObject extends TiledGameObject {
    constructor(renderableObj, scale, aCamera) {
        super(renderableObj);
        this.mRefCamera = aCamera;
        this.mCameraWCCenterRef =
                                vec2.clone(this.mRefCamera.getWCCenter());
        this.mParallaxScale = 1;
        this.setParallaxScale(scale);
    }
    ... implementation to follow ...
}
export default ParallaxGameObject;
```

The ParallaxGameObject object maintains mRefCamera, a reference to aCamera and mCameraWCCenterRef, the current WC bounds center. These values are used to compute relative movements based on the motion of the referenced camera to support parallax scrolling. The scale parameter is a positive value. A scale value of 1 represents that the object is located at the default distance, and values of less than 1 convey that the object is in front of the default distance. A scale of greater than 1 represents objects that are behind the default distance. The larger the scale value, the farther the object is from the camera.

2. Define the getter and setter functions for mParallaxScale. Notice the clamping of negative values; this variable must be positive.

```
getParallaxScale() { return this.mParallaxScale; }
setParallaxScale(s) {
    this.mParallaxScale = s;
    if (s <= 0) {
        this.mParallaxScale = 1;
    }
}
```

685

3. Override the `update()` function to implement parallax scrolling:

```
update() {
    // simple default behavior
    this._refPosUpdate(); // check to see if the camera has moved
    super.update();
}
```

The `_refPosUpdate()` function is the one that computes a relative displacement based on the reference camera's WC center position.

4. Define the `_refPosUpdate()` function:

```
_refPosUpdate() {
    // now check for reference movement
    let deltaT = vec2.fromValues(0, 0);
    vec2.sub(deltaT,
            this.mCameraWCCenterRef, this.mRefCamera.getWCCenter());
    this.setWCTranslationBy(deltaT);

    // update WC center ref position
    vec2.sub(this.mCameraWCCenterRef, this.mCameraWCCenterRef, deltaT);
}
```

The `deltaT` variable records the movement of the camera and `setWCTranslationBy()` moves the object to simulate parallax scrolling.

5. Define the function to translate the object to implement parallax scrolling. The negative `delta` is designed to move the object in the same direction as that of the camera. Notice the variable `f` is 1 minus the inverse of `mParallaxScale`.

```
setWCTranslationBy(delta) {
    let f = (1 - (1/this.mParallaxScale));
    this.getXform().incXPosBy(-delta[0] * f);
    this.getXform().incYPosBy(-delta[1] * f);
}
```

When mParallaxScale is less than 1, the inverse is greater than 1 and f becomes a negative number. In this case, when the camera moves, the object will move in the opposite direction and thus create the sensation that the object is in front of the default distance.

Conversely, when mParallaxScale is greater than 1, its inverse will be less than 1 and result in a positive f with a value of less than 1. In this case, the object will be moving in the same direction as the camera, only slower. A larger mParallaxScale would correspond to f value being closer to 1, and the movement of the object will be closer to that of the camera, or the object will appear to be at a further distance from the camera.

Lastly, remember to update the engine access file, index.js, to forward the newly defined functionality to the client.

Testing ParallaxGameObject in MyGame

The testing of ParallaxGameObject involves testing for the correctness of parallax scrolling while the camera is in motion with objects in front of and behind the default distance, all while observing the ParallaxGameObject from a separate stationary camera. The source code of the MyGame level is largely similar to that from the previous project, and the details are not listed. The relevant part of the init() function is listed for the purpose of illustrating how to create the ParallaxGameObject instances.

```
init() {
    // Step A: set up the cameras
    this.mCamera = new engine.Camera(
        vec2.fromValues(50, 37.5), // position of the camera
        100,                       // width of camera
        [0, 0, 1280, 720]          // viewport (orgX, orgY, width, height)
    );
    this.mCamera.setBackgroundColor([0.8, 0.8, 0.8, 1]);
    // sets the background to gray

    this.mParallaxCam = new engine.Camera(
        vec2.fromValues(40, 30), // position of the camera
        45,                      // width of camera
        [0, 420, 600, 300],      // viewport (orgX, orgY, width, height)
        2
    );
    this.mParallaxCam.setBackgroundColor([0.5, 0.5, 0.9, 1]);
```

```javascript
// Step B: the lights
this._initializeLights();   // defined in MyGame_Lights.js

// Step C: the far Background
let bgR = new engine.IllumRenderable(this.kBg, this.kBgNormal);
bgR.setElementPixelPositions(0, 1024, 0, 1024);
bgR.getXform().setSize(30, 30);
bgR.getXform().setPosition(0, 0);
bgR.getMaterial().setSpecular([0.2, 0.1, 0.1, 1]);
bgR.getMaterial().setShininess(50);
bgR.getXform().setZPos(-5);

// only the directional light
bgR.addLight(this.mGlobalLightSet.getLightAt(1));
this.mBg = new engine.ParallaxGameObject(bgR, 5, this.mCamera);

// Step D: the closer Background
let i;
let bgR1 = new engine.IllumRenderable(
                                this.kBgLayer, this.kBgLayerNormal);
bgR1.getXform().setSize(25, 25);
bgR1.getXform().setPosition(0, -15);
bgR1.getXform().setZPos(0);
// the directional light
bgR1.addLight(this.mGlobalLightSet.getLightAt(1));
// the hero spotlight light
bgR1.addLight(this.mGlobalLightSet.getLightAt(2));
// the hero spotlight light
bgR1.addLight(this.mGlobalLightSet.getLightAt(3));
bgR1.getMaterial().setSpecular([0.2, 0.2, 0.5, 1]);
bgR1.getMaterial().setShininess(10);
this.mBgL1 = new engine.ParallaxGameObject(bgR1, 3, this.mCamera);

// Step E: the front layer
let f = new engine.TextureRenderable(this.kBgLayer);
f.getXform().setSize(50, 50);
```

```
        f.getXform().setPosition(-3, 2);
        this.mFront = new engine.ParallaxGameObject(f, 0.9, this.mCamera);

        ... identical to previous code ...
}
```

The mBg object is created as a ParallaxGameObject with a scale of 5, mBgL1 with a scale of 3, and mFront with a scale of 0.9. Recall that scale is the second parameter of the ParallaxGameObject constructor. This parameter signifies the object distance from the camera, with values greater than 1 being farther from and values less than 1 being closer to the default distance. In this case, mBg is the furthest away from the camera while mBgL1 is closer. Regardless, both are still behind the default distance. The mFront object is the closest to the camera and in front of the default distance or in front of the Hero object.

Observations

You can now run the project and observe the darker foreground layer partially blocking the Hero and Minion objects. You can move the Hero object to pan the camera and observe the two background layers scrolling at different speeds. The mBg object is farther away and thus scrolls slower than the mBgL1 object. You will also notice the front-layer parallax scrolls at a faster speed than all other objects, and as a result, panning the camera reveals different parts of the stationary Minion objects.

Press the P key to enable the drawing of the second camera. Notice that when the Hero is stationary, the view in this camera is as expected, not moving. Now, if you move the Hero object to pan the main camera, note the foreground and background objects in the second camera view are also moving and exhibit motion parallax even though the second camera is not moving! As game designers, it is important to ensure this side effect does not confuse the player.

Layer Management

Although the engine you are developing is for 2D games, you have worked with a few situations where depth ordering and drawing orders are important. For example, the shadow receiver must always be defined behind the shadow casters, and as discussed in the previous example, foreground and background parallax objects must be carefully defined and drawn in the order of their depth ordering. It is convenient for the game engine to provide a utility manager to help game programmers manage and work with the depth layering. A typical 2D game can have the following layers, in the order of the distance from the camera, from nearest to furthest:

- **Heads-up display (HUD) layer**: Typically, closest to the camera displaying essential user interface information

- **Foreground or front layer**: The layer in front of the game objects for decorative or partial occlusion of the game objects

- **Actor layer**: The default distance layer in Figure 11-5, where all game objects reside

- **Shadow receiver layer**: The layer behind the actor layer to receive potential shadows

- **Background layer**: The decorative background

Each layer will reference all objects defined for that layer, and these objects will be drawn in the order they were inserted into the layer, with the last inserted drawn last and covering objects before it. This section presents the Layer engine component to support the described five layers to relieve game programmers from the details of managing updates and drawings the objects. Note that the number of layers a game engine should support is determined by the kinds of games that the engine is designed to build. The five layers presented are logical and convenient for simple games. You may choose to expand the number of layers in your own game engine.

The Layer Manager Project

This project demonstrates how to develop a utility component to assist game programmers with the management of layers in games. You can see an example of this project running in Figure 11-9. The source code to this project is defined in the chapter11/11.3.layer_manager folder.

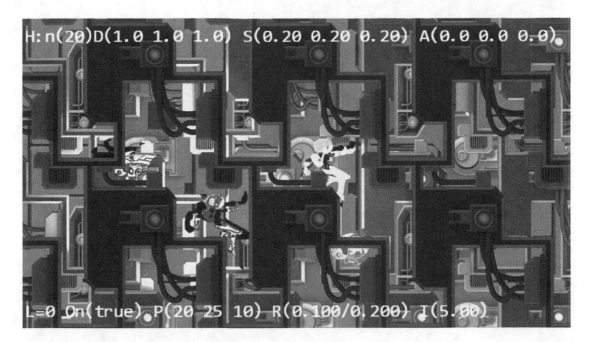

Figure 11-9. *Running the Layer Manager project*

The controls of the project are identical to the previous project:

- **P key**: Toggles the drawing of a second camera that is not in motion to highlight background object movements in simulating parallax scrolling

- **WASD keys**: Move the Dye character (the hero) to pan the WC window bounds

The goals of the project are as follows:

- To appreciate the importance of layering in 2D games

- To develop a layer manager engine component

Layer Management in the Engine

Follow the pattern of defining an engine component, for example, similar to that of physics and particle systems:

1. Create a new file in the `src/engine/components` folder and name it `layer.js`. This file will implement the `Layer` engine component.

2. Define enumerators for the layers:

```
const eBackground = 0;
const eShadowReceiver = 1;
const eActors = 2;
const eFront = 3;
const eHUD = 4;
```

3. Define appropriate constants and instance variables to keep
    track of the layers. The mAllLayers variable is an array of
    GameObjectSet instances representing each of the five layers.

```
let kNumLayers = 5;
let mAllLayers = [];
```

4. Define an init() function to create the array of GameObjectSet
    instances:

```
function init() {
    mAllLayers[eBackground] = new GameObjectSet();
    mAllLayers[eShadowReceiver] = new GameObjectSet();
    mAllLayers[eActors] = new GameObjectSet();
    mAllLayers[eFront] = new GameObjectSet();
    mAllLayers[eHUD] = new GameObjectSet();
}
```

5. Define a cleanUp() function to reset the mAllLayer array:

```
function cleanUp() {
    init();
}
```

6. Define functions to add to, remove from, and query the layers.
    Note the addAsShadowCaster() function assumes that the shadow
    receiver objects are already inserted into the eShadowReceiver
    layer and adds the casting object to all receivers in the layer.

```
function addToLayer(layerEnum, obj) {
    mAllLayers[layerEnum].addToSet(obj); }
function removeFromLayer(layerEnum, obj) {
    mAllLayers[layerEnum].removeFromSet(obj); }
function layerSize(layerEnum) { return mAllLayers[layerEnum].size(); }

function addAsShadowCaster(obj) {
    let i;
    for (i = 0; i < mAllLayers[eShadowReceiver].size(); i++) {
        mAllLayers[eShadowReceiver].getObjectAt(i).addShadowCaster(obj);
    }
}
```

7. Define functions to draw a specific layer or all the layers, from the furthest to the nearest to the camera:

```
function drawLayer(layerEnum, aCamera) {
    mAllLayers[layerEnum].draw(aCamera); }
function drawAllLayers(aCamera) {
    let i;
    for (i = 0; i < kNumLayers; i++) {
        mAllLayers[i].draw(aCamera);
    }
}
```

8. Define a function to move a specific object such that it will be drawn last (on top):

```
function moveToLayerFront(layerEnum, obj) {
    mAllLayers[layerEnum].moveToLast(obj);
}
```

9. Define functions to update a specific layer or all the layers:

```
function updateLayer(layerEnum) { mAllLayers[layerEnum].update(); }
function updateAllLayers() {
    let i;
```

```
    for (i = 0; i < kNumLayers; i++) {
        mAllLayers[i].update();
    }
}
```

10.   Remember to export all the defined functionality:

```
export {
    // array indices
    eBackground, eShadowReceiver, eActors, eFront, eHUD,

    // init and cleanup
    init, cleanUp,

    // draw/update
    drawLayer, drawAllLayers,
    updateLayer, updateAllLayers,

    // layer-specific support
    addToLayer, addAsShadowCaster,
    removeFromLayer, moveToLayerFront,
    layerSize
}
```

Lastly, remember to update the engine access file, index.js, to forward the newly defined functionality to the client.

Modify Engine Components and Objects

You must modify the rest of the game engine slightly to integrate the new Layer component.

Enhance the GameObjectSet Functionality

Add the following function to support moving an object to the end of a set array:

```
moveToLast(obj) {
    this.removeFromSet(obj);
    this.addToSet(obj);
}
```

Initialize Layer in index.js

In addition to import/export the Layer component, modify the engine init() and cleanUp() functions in index.js to initialize and clean up the component:

```
... identical to previous code ...
function init(htmlCanvasID) {
    glSys.init(htmlCanvasID);
    vertexBuffer.init();
    input.init(htmlCanvasID);
    audio.init();
    shaderResources.init();
    defaultResources.init();
    layer.init();
}

function cleanUp() {
    layer.cleanUp();
    loop.cleanUp();
    shaderResources.cleanUp();
    defaultResources.cleanUp();
    audio.cleanUp();
    input.cleanUp();
    vertexBuffer.cleanUp();
    glSys.cleanUp();
}
```

Define the Update Functions for Layer Membership

Define update functions for objects that may appear as members in Layer: Renderable and ShadowReceiver.

Modify MyGame to Work with the Layer Component

The MyGame level implements the same functionality as in the previous project. The only difference is the delegation of layer management to the Layer component. The following description focuses only on function calls relevant to layer management.

1. Modify the `unload()` function to clean up the Layer:

```
unload() {
    engine.layer.cleanUp();

    engine.texture.unload(this.kMinionSprite);
    engine.texture.unload(this.kBg);
    engine.texture.unload(this.kBgNormal);
    engine.texture.unload(this.kBgLayer);
    engine.texture.unload(this.kBgLayerNormal);
    engine.texture.unload(this.kMinionSpriteNormal);
}
```

2. Modify the `init()` function to add the game objects to the
    corresponding layers in the Layer component:

```
init() {
    ... identical to previous code ...

    // add to layer managers ...
    engine.layer.addToLayer(engine.layer.eBackground, this.mBg);
    engine.layer.addToLayer(engine.layer.eShadowReceiver,
                                            this.mBgShadow1);

    engine.layer.addToLayer(engine.layer.eActors, this.mIllumMinion);
    engine.layer.addToLayer(engine.layer.eActors, this.mLgtMinion);
    engine.layer.addToLayer(engine.layer.eActors, this.mIllumHero);
    engine.layer.addToLayer(engine.layer.eActors, this.mLgtHero);

    engine.layer.addToLayer(engine.layer.eFront, this.mBlock1);
    engine.layer.addToLayer(engine.layer.eFront, this.mBlock2);
    engine.layer.addToLayer(engine.layer.eFront, this.mFront);

    engine.layer.addToLayer(engine.layer.eHUD, this.mMsg);
    engine.layer.addToLayer(engine.layer.eHUD, this.mMatMsg);
}
```

3. Modify the draw() function to rely on the Layer component for the actual drawings:

```
draw() {
    engine.clearCanvas([0.9, 0.9, 0.9, 1.0]); // clear to light gray

    this.mCamera.setViewAndCameraMatrix();
    engine.layer.drawAllLayers(this.mCamera);

    if (this.mShowParallaxCam) {
        this.mParallaxCam.setViewAndCameraMatrix();
        engine.layer.drawAllLayers(this.mParallaxCam);
    }
}
```

4. Modify the update() function to rely on the Layer component for the actual update of all game objects:

```
update() {
    this.mCamera.update();  // to ensure proper interpolated movement
    this.mParallaxCam.update();

    engine.layer.updateAllLayers();

    ... identical to previous code ...
}
```

Observations

You can now run the project and observe the same output and interactions as the previous project. The important observation for this project is in the implementation. By inserting game objects to the proper layers of the Layer component during init(), the draw() and update() functions of a game level can be much cleaner. The simpler and cleaner update() function is of special importance. Instead of being crowded with mundane game object update() function calls, this function can now focus on implementing the game logic and controlling the interactions between game objects.

Summary

This chapter explained the need for tiling and introduced the `TileGameObject` to implement a simple algorithm that tiles and covers a given camera WC bound. The basics of parallax and approaches to simulate motion parallax with parallax scrolling were introduced. Motion parallax with stationary and moving cameras were examined, and solutions were derived and implemented. You learned that computing movements relative to the camera motions to displace background objects results in visually pleasing motion parallax but may cause player confusion when viewed from different cameras. With shadow computations introduced earlier and now parallax scrolling, game programmers must dedicate code and attention to coordinate the drawing order of different types of objects. To facilitate the programmability of the game engine, the `Layer` engine component is presented as a utility tool to relieve game programmers from managing the drawing of the layers.

The game engine proposed by this book is now complete. It can draw objects with texture maps, sprite animations, and even support illumination from various light sources. The engine defines proper abstractions for simple behaviors, implements mechanisms to approximate and accurately compute collisions, and simulates physical behaviors. Views from multiple cameras can be conveniently displayed over the same game screens with manipulation functionality that is smoothly interpolated. Keyboard/mouse input is supported, and now background objects can scroll without bounds with motion parallax simulated.

The important next step, to properly test your engine, is to go through a simple game design process and implement a game based on your newly completed game engine.

Game Design Considerations

In previous sections, you've explored how developing one simple game mechanic from the ground-up can lead in many directions and be applied to a variety of game types. Creative teams in game design studios frequently debate which elements of game design take the lead in the creative process: writers often believe story comes first, while many designers believe that story and everything else must be secondary to gameplay. There's no right or wrong answer, of course; the creative process is a chaotic system and every team and studio is unique. Some creative directors want to tell a particular story and will search for mechanics and genres that are best suited to supporting specific narratives, while others are gameplay purists and completely devoted to a culture of "gameplay first, next, and last." The decision often comes down to understanding your audience; if you're creating competitive multiplayer first-person shooter experience, for example, consumers will have specific expectations for many of the core elements of play, and it's usually a smart move to ensure that gameplay drives the design. If you're creating an adventure game designed to tell a story and provide players with new experiences and unexpected twists, however, story and setting might lead the way.

Many game designers (including seasoned veterans as well as those new to the discipline) begin new projects by designing experiences that are relatively minor variations on existing well-understood mechanics; while there are sound reasons for this approach (as in the case of AAA studios developing content for particularly demanding audiences or a desire to work with mechanics that have proven to be successful across many titles), it tends to significantly limit exploration into new territory and is one reason why many gamers complain about creative stagnation and a lack of gameplay diversity between games within the same genre. Many professional game designers grew up enjoying certain kinds of games and dreamed about creating new experiences based on the mechanics we know and love, and several decades of that culture has focused much of the industry around a comparatively few numbers of similar mechanics and conventions. That said, a rapidly growing independent and small studio community has boldly begun throwing long-standing genre convention to the wind in recent years and easily accessible distribution platforms like mobile app stores and Valve's Steam have opened opportunities for a wide range of new game mechanics and experiences to flourish.

If you continue exploring game design, you'll realize there are relatively few completely unique core mechanics but endless opportunities for innovating as you build those elemental interactions into more complex causal chains and add unique flavor and texture through elegant integration with the other elements of game design. Some of the most groundbreaking and successful games were created through exercises very much like the mechanic exploration you've done in these "*Game Design Considerations*" sections; Valve's Portal, for example, is based on the same kind of "escape the room" sandbox you have been exploring and is designed around a similarly simple base mechanic. What made Portal such a breakthrough hit? While many things need to come together to create a hit game, Portal benefitted from a design team that started building the experience from the most basic mechanic and smartly increased complexity as they became increasingly fluent in its unique structure and characteristics, instead of starting at the 10,000-foot level with a codified genre and a predetermined set of design rules.

Of course, nobody talks about Portal without also mentioning the rogue artificial intelligence character GLaDOS and her Aperture Laboratories playground: setting, narrative, and audiovisual design are as important to the Portal experience as the portal-launching game mechanic, and it's hard to separate the gameplay from the narrative given how skillfully intertwined they are. The projects in this chapter provide a good opportunity to begin similarly situating the game mechanic from the *"Game Design Considerations"* sections in a unique setting and context: you've probably noticed many of the projects throughout this book are building toward a sci-fi visual theme, with a spacesuit-wearing hero character, a variety of flying robots, and now in Chapter 11 the introduction of parallax environments. While you're not building a game with the same degree of environment and interaction complexity as Portal, that doesn't mean you don't have the same opportunity to develop a highly engaging game setting, context, and cast of characters.

The first thing you should notice about the *Tiled Objects* project is the dramatic impact on environment experience and scale compared to earlier projects. The factors enhancing presence in this project are the three independently moving layers (hero character, moving wall, and stationary wall) and the seamless tiling of the two background layers. Compare the *Tiled Objects* project to the *Shadow Shaders* project from Chapter 8, and notice the difference in presence when the environment is broken into multiple layers that appear to move in an analogous (if not physically accurate) way to how you experience movement in the physical world. The sense of presence is further strengthened when you add multiple background layers of parallax movement in the *Parallax Objects* project; as you move through the physical world, the environment appears to move at different speeds, with closer objects seeming to pass by quickly while objects toward the horizon appear to move slowly. Parallax environment objects simulate this effect, adding considerable depth and interest to game environments. The *Layer Manager* project pulls things together and begins to show the potential for a game setting to immediately engage the imaginations of players. With just a few techniques, you're able to create the impression of a massive environment that might be the interior of an ancient alien machine, the outside of a large spacecraft, or anything else you might care to create. Try using different kinds of image assets with this technique: exterior landscapes, underwater locations, abstract shapes, and the like would all be interesting to explore. You'll often find inspiration for game settings by experimenting with just a few basic elements, as you did in Chapter 11.

Pairing environment design (both audio and visual) with interaction design (and occasionally the inclusion of haptic feedback-like controller vibrations) is an approach you can use to create and enhance presence, and the relationship that environments and interactions have with the game mechanic contributes the majority of what players experience in games. Environment design and narrative context create the game setting, and as previously mentioned, the most successful and memorable games achieve an excellent harmony between game setting and player experience. At this point, the game mechanic from the *"Game Design Considerations"* section in Chapter 9 has been intentionally devoid of any game setting context, and you've only briefly considered the interaction design, leaving you free to explore any setting that captures your interest. In Chapter 12, you'll further evolve the sci-fi setting and image assets used in the main chapter projects with the unlocking mechanic from the *"Game Design Considerations"* section to create a fairly advanced 2D platformer game-level prototype.

CHAPTER 12

Building a Sample Game: From Design to Completion

The projects included in the main sections of Chapters 1 to 11 began with simple shapes and slowly introduced characters and environments to illustrate the concepts of each chapter; those projects focused on individual behaviors and techniques (such as collision detection, object physics, lighting, and the like) but lacked the kind of structured challenges necessary to deliver a full gameplay experience. The projects in the *"Design Considerations"* sections demonstrate how to introduce the types of logical rules and challenges required to turn basic behaviors into well-formed game mechanics. This chapter now changes the focus to emphasize the design process from an early concept through a functional prototype, bringing together and extending the work done in earlier projects by using some characters and environments from prior chapters along with the basic idea for the unlocking platform game from the *"Design Considerations"* section of Chapter 11. As with earlier chapters, the design framework utilized here begins with a simple and flexible starting template and adds complexity incrementally and intentionally to allow the game to grow in a controlled manner.

The design exercises have until now avoided consideration of most of the nine elements of game design described in the *"How Do You Make a Great Video Game?"* section of Chapter 1 and instead focused on crafting the basic game mechanic in order to clearly define and refine the core characteristics of the game itself. The design approach used in this book is a ground-up framework that emphasizes first working with an isolated game mechanic prior to the consideration of the game's genre or setting; when you begin incorporating a setting and building out levels that include additional design elements on top of the core mechanic, the gameplay will grow and evolve in

© Kelvin Sung, Jebediah Pavleas, Matthew Munson, and Jason Pace 2022
K. Sung et al., *Build Your Own 2D Game Engine and Create Great Web Games*,
https://doi.org/10.1007/978-1-4842-7377-7_12

unique directions as you grow the game world. There are endless potential variations for a game's mechanic and the associated gameplay loops you design. You'll be surprised by how differently the same foundational elements of gameplay develop and evolve based on the kind of creative choices you make.

Part 1: Refining the Concept

By this point you should have the beginnings of a concept using a 2D jumping and puzzle-solving mechanic that revolves around unlocking a barrier and to reach a reward. Recall Figure 12-1 as the final screen layout and design from Chapter 11.

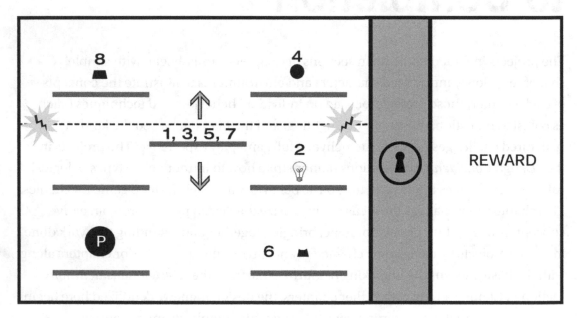

Figure 12-1. *The 2D implementation from Chapter 11*

This design already has a multistage solution requiring the player to both demonstrate timing-based agility and puzzle-solving logic. In the current design, the player controls the hero character (perhaps by using the A and D keys to move left and right and using the spacebar to jump). The player can jump between horizontal platforms on the same level but can't reach platforms above without using the middle "elevator" platform that rises and falls. A horizontal "energy field" will zap the player if they touch it, causing the game to reset. The explicit steps to completing the level are as follows:

1. The player must jump the hero character (the circle with the letter *p* in the center of Figure 12-1) on the moving elevator platform (#1 in Figure 12-1) and jump off to the middle platform of the right column before touching the energy field.

2. The player activates the off switch for the energy field by colliding the hero character with it (#2, represented by the lightbulb icon in Figure 12-1).

3. When the energy field is switched off, the player rides the elevator platform to the top (#3) and jumps the hero to the top platform in the right column.

4. The player collides the hero with the small circle that represents the top third of the lock icon (#4), activating the corresponding part of the lock icon and making it glow.

5. The player jumps the hero back on the elevator platform (#5) and then jumps the hero to the bottom platform in the right column.

6. The player collides the hero with the shape corresponding to the middle section of the lock icon (#6), activating the corresponding part of the lock icon and making it glow. Two-thirds of the lock icon now glows, signaling progress.

7. The player jumps the hero on the elevator platform once again (#7) and then jumps the hero to the top platform in the left column.

8. The player collides the hero with the shape corresponding to the bottom section of the lock icon (#8), activating the final section of the icon and unlocking the barrier.

Writing out this sequence (or *game flow diagram*) may seem unnecessary given the mock-up screens you've created. It's important, however, for designers to understand everything the player must do in exact order and detail to ensure you're able to tune, balance, and evolve the gameplay without becoming mired in complexity or losing sight of how the player makes their way through the level. It's clear from diagramming the previous game flow, for example, that the elevator platform is the centerpiece of this level and is required to complete every action; this is great information to have available in a schematic representation and game flow description because it provides an opportunity to intelligently refine the gameplay logic in a way that allows you to visualize the effect of each change on the overall flow of the level.

You could continue building out the mechanic to make the level more interesting and challenging (e.g., you might include a timer on the energy field's off switch requiring players to collide with all the lock parts within a limited amount of time). However, at this stage of concept development, it's often helpful to take a step back from gameplay and begin considering game setting and genre, using those elements to help inform how the game mechanic evolves from here.

Recall from Chapter 11 that the projects ended with a set of concept explorations supporting a sci-fi setting. Figure 12-2 shows a futuristic industrial environment design, a hero character wearing a space suit, and what appear to be flying robots.

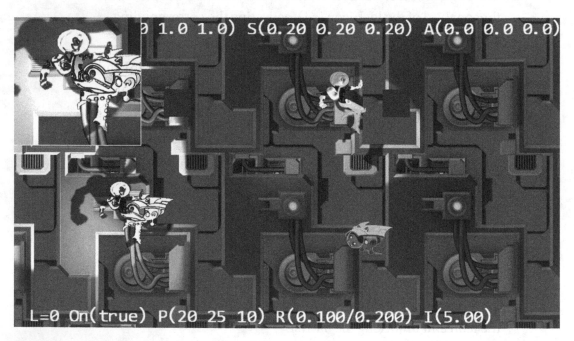

Figure 12-2. *Concepts from Chapter 11*

Note there isn't anything specific about the game mechanic you've been creating that would necessarily lead you in a sci-fi direction; game mechanics are abstract interactive structures and can typically integrate with any kind of setting or visual style.

In this case, the authors chose a setting that takes place on a spaceship, so this chapter will use that motif as the setting for the game prototype. As you proceed through the design process, consider exploring alternate settings: how might the game mechanic from Chapter 11 be adapted to a jungle setting, a contemporary urban location, a medieval fantasy world, or an underwater metropolis?

Part 2: Integrating a Setting

Now is a good time to begin assigning some basic fictional background to evolve and extend the game mechanic in unique ways that enhance the setting you choose (don't worry if this is unclear at the moment; the mechanism will become more apparent as you proceed with the level design). Imagine, for example, that the hero character is a member of the crew on a large spaceship and that she must complete a number of objectives to save the ship from exploding. Again, there is nothing about the current state of the game mechanic driving this narrative; the design task at this stage includes brainstorming some fictional context that propels the player through the game and captures their imagination. Using the few concept art assets already created/provided, the hero could just as easily be participating in a race, looking for something that was lost, exploring an abandoned alien vessel, or any of a million other possibilities.

Contextual Images Bring the Setting to Life

Now that you've described a basic narrative and fictional wrapper that reads something like "Players must complete a series of platformer puzzle levels to save their spaceship before it explodes," swap just a few of the shapes from the previous early prototype with some of the included concept elements. Figure 12-3 introduces a humanoid hero character, platforms that feel a bit more like spaceship components, and a barrier wall with a locked door to replace the abstract lock from the mechanic design.

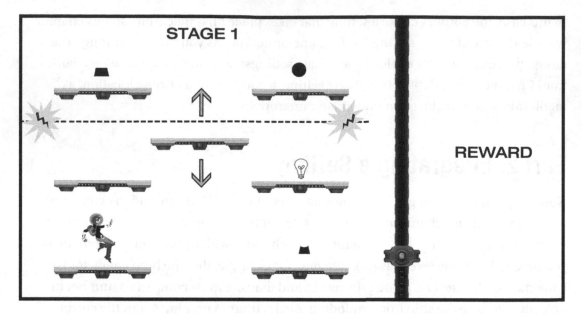

Figure 12-3. *The introduction of several visual design elements supporting the game setting and evolving narrative*

Although you've made only a few minor substitutions and don't yet have the visual elements anchored in an environment, Figure 12-3 conveys quite a bit more fictional context and contributes significantly more to presence than the abstract shapes of Figure 12-1. The hero character now suggests a scale that will naturally be contextualized as players benchmark relative sizes against the human figure, which brings the relative size of the entire game environment into focus for players. The implementation of object physics for the hero character as described in Chapter 10 also becomes an important component of play: simulated gravity, momentum, and the like connect players viscerally to the hero character as they move them through the game world. By implementing the design as described in Figure 12-3, you've already accomplished some impressive cognitive feats that support presence simply by adding a few visual elements and some object physics.

Defining the Playable Space

At this point in the design process, you've sufficiently described the game's core mechanic and setting to begin expanding the single screen into a full-level concept. It's not critical at this stage to have a final visual style defined, but including some concept art will help guide how the level grows. (Figure 12-3 provides a good visual representation for the amount of gameplay that will take place on a single screen given the scale of objects.) This is also a good stage to "block in" the elements from Figure 12-3 in a working prototype to begin getting a sense for how movement feels (e.g., the speed the hero character runs, the height the hero can jump, and so on), the scale of objects in the environment, the zoom level of the camera, and the like. There's no need to include interactions and behaviors such as the lock components or the energy field at this stage because you haven't yet designed how the level will play. For now you're experimenting with basic hero character movement, object placement, and collision. The next set of tasks includes laying out the full level and tuning all the interactions.

The current state of the design in Figure 12-3 still needs some work to provide sufficient challenge. While all the elements of a well-formed level are in place, the current difficulty is trivial, and most players will likely be able to complete the level quickly. There is, however, a strong foundation to begin extending the jumping and sequencing mechanic; to begin, you might extend the horizontal game space to include a more playable area and provide additional room for the character to maneuver, as shown in Figure 12-4.

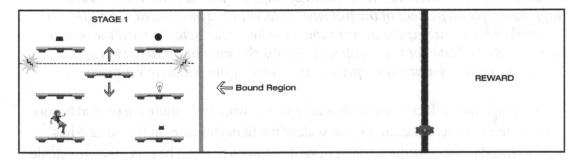

Figure 12-4. *The level design grows to include an additional playable area*

Recall from the Simple Camera Manipulations project in Chapter 7 that you can "push" the game screen forward by moving the character close to the edge of the bound region, which allows you to design a level that extends far beyond the dimensions of a single static screen. You might choose to keep this level contained to the original game screen size, of course, and increase the complexity of the timing-based agility and logical sequence challenges (and indeed it's a good design exercise to challenge yourself to work within space constraints), but for the purposes of this design a horizontal scrolling presentation adds interest and challenge.

Adding Layout to the Playable Space

It's now time to begin laying out the level to make good use of the additional horizontal space. There's no need to change the basic gameplay at this point; you'll simply expand the current level design to fit the new dimensions of the game screen. Figure 12-5 includes some additional platforms placed with no particular methodology other than ensuring players can successfully reach each platform.

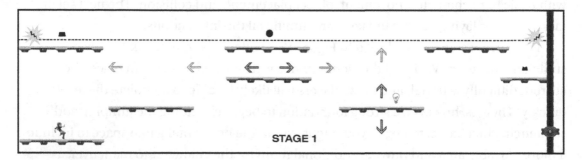

Figure 12-5. *Expands the layout to use the additional screen real estate, the diagram represents the entire length of stage 1 with the player able to see approximately 50 percent of the full level at any time. The camera scrolls the screen forward or backward as the player moves the hero character toward the screen bound regions. Note: for the moving platforms shown, darker arrows represent direction, and lighter arrows represent the range of the platform's movement*

Now that the level has some additional space to work with, there are several factors to evaluate and tune. For example, the scale of the hero character in Figure 12-5 has been reduced to increase the number of vertical jumps that can be executed on a single screen. Note that at this point you also have the opportunity to include additional vertical gameplay in the design if desired, implementing the same mechanism used to move the camera up and down that you used to move it left and right; many 2D platformer games allow players to move through the game world both horizontally and vertically. This level prototype will limit movement to the x plane (left and right) for simplicity although you can easily extend the level design to include vertical play in future iterations and/or subsequent levels.

As you're placing platforms in the level, you will again want to minimize design complexity while blocking out the game flow. Figure 12-5 adds one additional design element: a platform that moves left to right. Try to list the detailed sequence required to activate the three lock sections in Figure 12-5 using the same numbering methodology shown in Figure 12-1. When you're finished mapping out the sequence, compare it with Figure 12-6.

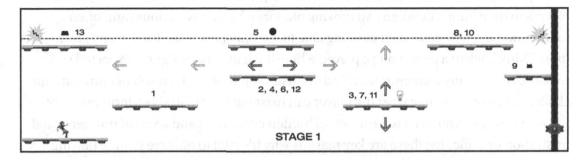

Figure 12-6. *The most efficient sequence to unlock the barrier*

Did your sequence match Figure 12-6, or did you have extra steps? There are many potential paths players can take to complete this level, and it's likely that no two players will take the same route (the only requirement from the mechanic design is that the lock sections be activated in order from top to bottom).

Tuning the Challenge and Adding Fun

In this stage of the design is when the puzzle-making process really begins to open up; Figure 12-6 shows the potential to create highly engaging gameplay with only the few basic elements you've been working with. The authors use the previous template and similar variations in brainstorming sessions for many kinds of games—introducing one or two novel elements to a well-understood mechanic and exploring the impact new additions have on gameplay—and the results often open exciting new directions. As an example, you might introduce platforms that appear and disappear, platforms that rotate after a switch is activated, a moving energy field, teleporting stations, and so on. The list of ways you can build out this mechanic is of course limitless, but there is enough definition with the current template that adding a single new element is fairly easy to experiment with and test, even on paper.

There are two factors with the newly expanded level design that increase the challenge. First, the addition of the horizontally moving platform requires players to time the jump to the "elevator" platform more precisely (if they jump while the platform is ascending, there is little time to deactivate the energy field before it zaps them).

The second factor is less immediately evident but equally challenging: only a portion of the level is visible at any time, so the player is not able to easily create a mental model of the entire level sequence, like they can when the entire layout is visible on a single screen. It's important for designers to understand both explicit challenges (such as requiring players to time jumps between two moving platforms) and less obvious (and often unintentional) challenges such as being able to see only part of the level at any given time. Think back to a game you've played where it felt like the designers expected you remember too many elements; that kind of frustration is often the result of unintentional challenges overburdening what the player can reasonably hold in short-term memory.

As a designer you need to be aware of hidden challenges and areas of unintentional frustration or difficulty; these are key reasons why it's vital to observe people playing your game as early and often as possible. As a general rule, any time you're 100 percent certain you've designed something that makes perfect sense, at least half the people who play your game will tell you exactly the opposite. Although a detailed discussion of the benefits of user testing is outside the scope of this book, you should plan to observe people playing your game from the earliest proof of concept all the way to final release. There is no substitute for the insights you'll gain from watching different people play what you've designed.

The level as described in previous figures currently assumes the hero character can rest only on platforms; although there's no design plan for what happens if the character misses a jump and falls to the bottom of the screen, players might reasonably imagine that it would result in a loss condition and trigger a game reset. If you added a "floor" to the level, player strategy would noticeably change; in addition to removing a significant risk, players would be able to access the elevator platform directly, as shown in Figure 12-7.

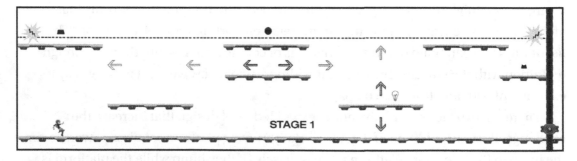

Figure 12-7. *The addition of a "floor" to the game world significantly changes the level challenge*

Further Tuning: Introducing Enemies

You're now experimenting with variations on the level layout to evolve it along with the setting and looking for ways to increase player engagement while also upping the challenge (if desired). Prior to adding a floor, the level had two risks: failing to land on a platform and triggering a loss condition, and colliding with the energy field and triggering a loss condition. The addition of the floor removes the falling risk and potentially decreases the challenge of the level, but you might decide that the floor encourages players to more freely explore, experiment, and pay closer attention to the environment. You're also now becoming increasingly conversant with the gameplay and flow for this mechanic and layout, so let's introduce a new element: attacking enemies (we can't let those robot designs from previous chapters go to waste)! Figure 12-8 introduces two basic enemy robot types: one that fires a projectile and one that simply patrols.

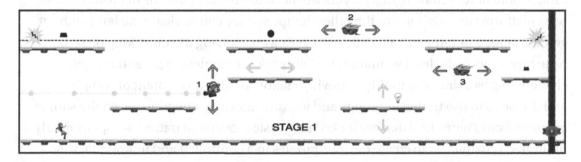

Figure 12-8. *Two new object types are introduced to the level: a shooting robot (#1) that moves vertically and fires at a constant rate and a patrolling robot (#2) that moves back and forth in a specific range*

You've now reached a turning point in the design of this level, where the setting is starting to exert a significant influence on the evolution of the mechanic and game loop. The core of the mechanic hasn't changed from Chapter 11, and this level is still fundamentally about activating sections of a lock in the proper sequence to remove a barrier, but the moving platforms and attacking enemies are additional obstacles and are strongly influenced by the particular setting you've chosen.

Of course, you certainly could have added the attacking enemy behavior while still working with abstract shapes and pure mechanics. It's worth noting, however, that the more complex and multistaged a mechanic becomes, the more the setting will need to conform to the implementation; this is why transitioning from purely abstract mechanic design to laying out a level (or part of a level) in the context of a particular setting when the mechanic is still fairly elemental is helpful. Designers typically want the game mechanic to feel deeply integrated with the game setting, so it's beneficial to allow both to develop in tandem. Finding that sweet spot can be challenging: sometimes the mechanic leads the design, but as the setting evolves, it often will move into the driver's seat. Bring in the setting too soon and you lose focus on refining pure gameplay; bring in the setting too late and game world may feel like an afterthought or something that's bolted on.

General Considerations

Returning to the current design as represented in Figure 12-8, you now have all the elements required to create a truly engaging sequence situated in an emerging setting. You can also fairly easily tune the movement and placement of individual units to make things more or less challenging. Players will need to observe patterns of movement for both platforms and enemies to time their jumps so they can navigate the level without getting zapped or rammed, all while discovering and solving the unlocking puzzle. Note how quickly the level went from trivially easy to complete to potentially quite challenging: working with multiple moving platforms adds an element of complexity, and the need to use timing for jumps and to avoid attacking enemies—even the simple enemies from Figure 12-8 that are locked into basic movement patterns—opens nearly unlimited possibilities to create devious puzzles in a controlled and intentional way.

If you haven't already, now is a good time to prototype your level design (including interactions) in code to validate gameplay. For this early-level prototype, it's only important that major behaviors (running, jumping, projectile firing, moving platforms, object activations, and the like) and steps required to complete the level (puzzle sequences) are properly implemented. Some designers insist at this stage that players who have never encountered the level before should be able to play through the entire experience and fully understand what they need to do with little or no assistance, while others are willing to provide direction and fill in gaps around missing onscreen UI and incomplete puzzle sequences. It's common practice to playtest and validate major sections of gameplay at this stage and provide playtesters with additional guidance to compensate for incomplete UI or unimplemented parts of a sequence. As a general rule, the less you need to rely on over-the-shoulder guidance for players at this stage, the better your insights into the overall design will be. The amount of the early-level prototype you'll implement at this stage also depends on the size and complexity of your design. Large and highly complex levels may be implemented and tested in several (or many) pieces before the entire level can be played through at once, but even in the case of large and complex levels, the goal is to have the full experience playable as early as possible.

Note   If you've been exploring the working prototype included with this book, you'll discover some minor variations between the design concepts in this chapter and the playable level (the energy field was not included in the working prototype, e.g.). Consider exploring alternate design implementations with the included assets; exploration and improvisation are key elements of the creative-level design process. How many extensions of the current mechanic can you create?

Part 3: Integrating Additional Design Elements

The prototype you've been building in this chapter would serve as an effective proof of concept for a full game at its current level of development, but it's still missing many elements typically required for a complete game experience (including visual detail and animations, sounds, scoring systems, win conditions, menus and user interface [UI] elements, and the like). In game parlance, the prototype level is now at the blockout-plus stage (*blockout* is a term used to describe a prototype that includes layout and functional gameplay but lacks other design elements; the inclusion of some additional concept art is the "plus" here). It's now a good time to begin exploring audio, scoring systems, menu and onscreen UI, and the like. If this prototype were in production at a game studio, a small group might take the current level to a final production level of polish and completeness while another team worked to design and prototype additional levels. A single level or a part of a level that's taken to final production is referred to as a *vertical slice*, meaning that one small section of the game includes everything that will ship with the final product. Creating a vertical slice is helpful to focus the team on what the final experience will look, feel, and sound like and can be used to validate the creative direction with playtesters.

Visual Design

Although you've begun integrating some visual design assets that align with the setting and narrative, the game typically will have few (if any) final production assets at this time and any animations will be either rough or not yet implemented (the same is true for game audio). While it's good practice to have gameplay evolve in parallel with the game setting, studios don't want to burn time and resources creating production assets until the team is confident that the level design is locked and they know what objects are needed and where they'll be placed.

You should now have a fairly well-described layout and sequence for your level design (if you've been experimenting with a different layout compared to what's shown in the examples, make sure you have a complete game flow described as in Figures 12-1 and 12-6.) At this point in the project, you can confidently begin "rezzing in" production assets (*rezzing in* is a term used by game studios to mean increasing the resolution— in this case, the visual polish and overall production quality of the level—over time). Rezzing-in is typically a multistage process that begins when the major elements of the level design are locked, and it can continue for most of the active production schedule. There are often hundreds (or thousands) of individual assets, animations, icons, and the like that will typically need to be adjusted multiple times based on the difference between how they appear outside the game build and inside the game build. Elements that appear to harmonize well in isolation and in mockups often appear quite differently after being integrated into the game.

The process of rezzing-in assets can be tedious and frustrating (there always seems to be an order of magnitude more assets than you think there will be). It can also be challenging to make things look as awesome in the game as they do in an artist's mockups. However, it's typically a satisfying experience when it all start to come together: something magical happens to a level design as it transitions from blockout to polished production level, and there will usually be one build where a few key visual assets have come in that make the team remark "Wow, now this feels like our game!" For AAA 3D games, these "wow" moments frequently happen as high-resolution textures are added to 3D models and as complex animations, lighting, and shadows bring the world to life; for the current prototype level, adding a parallaxing background and some localized lighting effects should really make the spaceship setting pop.

The working prototype included with this book represents a build of the final game that would typically be midway between blockout and production polish. The hero character includes several animation states (idle, run, jump), localized lighting on the hero and robots adds visual interest and drama, the level features a two-layer parallaxing background with normal maps that respond to the lighting, and major game behaviors are in place. You can build upon this prototype and continue to polish the game or modify it how you see fit.

Game Audio

Many new game designers (and even some veteran designers) make the mistake of treating audio as less important than the visual design, but as every gamer knows, bad audio in some cases can mean the difference between a game you love and a game you stop playing after a short time. As with visual design, audio often contributes directly to the game mechanic (e.g., countdown timers, warning sirens, positional audio that signals enemy location), and background scores enhance drama and emotion in the same way that directors use musical scores to support the action on film). However, audio in mobile games is often considered optional because many players mute the sound on their mobile devices. Well-designed audio, however, can have a dramatic impact on presence even for mobile games. In addition to sounds corresponding to game objects (walking sounds for characters who walk, shooting sounds for enemies who fire, popping sounds for things that pop, and the like), contextual audio attached to in-game actions is an important feedback mechanism for players. Menu selections, activating in-game switches, and the like should all be evaluated for potential audio support. As a general rule, if an in-game object responds to player interaction, it should be evaluated for contextual audio.

Audio designers work with level designers to create a comprehensive review of game objects and events that require sounds, and as the visuals rezz in, the associated sounds will typically follow. Game sounds often lag behind visual design because audio designers want to see what they're creating sounds for; it's difficult to create a "robot walking" sound, for example, if you can't see what the robot looks like or how it moves. In much the same way that designers want to tightly integrate the game setting and mechanic, audio engineers want to ensure that the visual and audio design work well together.

Interaction Model

The current prototype uses a common interaction model: A and D keys on the keyboard move the character right and left, and the spacebar is used to jump. Object activations in the world happen simply by colliding the hero character with the object, and the design complexity is fairly low for those interactions. Imagine, however, that as you continue building out the mechanic (perhaps in later levels), you include the ability for the character to launch projectiles and collect game objects to store in inventory. As the range of possible interactions in the game expands, complexity can increase dramatically and unintentional challenges (as mentioned previously) can begin to accumulate, which can lead to bad player frustration (as opposed to "good" player frustration, which as discussed earlier results from intentionally designed challenges).

It's also important to be aware of the challenges encountered when adapting interaction models between different platforms. Interactions designed initially for mouse and keyboard often face considerable difficulty when moving to a game console or touch-based mobile device. Mice and keyboard interaction schemes allow for extreme precision and speed of movement compared to the imprecise thumb sticks of game controllers, and although touch interactions can be precise, mobile screens tend to be significantly smaller and obscured by fingers covering the play area. The industry took many years and iterations to adapt the first-person-shooter (FPS) genre from using mice and keyboards to game consoles, and FPS conventions for touch devices remain highly variable more than a decade after the first mobile FPS experiences launched (driven in part by the differences in processing capabilities and screen sizes of the many phones and tablets on the market). If you plan to deliver a game across platforms, make sure you consider the unique requirements of each as you're developing the game.

Game Systems and Meta-game

The current prototype has few systems to balance and does not yet incorporate a meta-game, but imagine adding elements that require balancing such as variable-length timers for object activations or the energy field. If you're unsure what this means, consider the following scenario: the hero character has two potential ways to deactivate the energy field, and each option is a trade-off. The first option perhaps deactivates the energy field permanently but spawns more enemy robots and considerably increases the difficulty in reaching the target object, while the second option does not spawn additional robots but only deactivates the energy field for a short time, requiring players to choose the most efficient path and execute nearly perfect timing. To balance effectively between the two options, you need to understand the design and degree of challenge associated with each system (unlimited vs. limited time). Similarly, if you added hit points to the hero character and made the firing robot create x amount of damage while the charging minion creates y amount of damage per hit, you'd want to understand the relative trade-offs between paths to objectives, perhaps making some paths less dangerous but more complex to navigate, while others might be faster to navigate but more dangerous.

As with most other aspects of the current design, there are many directions you could choose to pursue in the development of a meta-game; what might you provide to players for additional positive reinforcement or overarching context as they played through a full game created in the style of the prototype level? As one example, imagine that players must collect a certain number of objects to access the final area and prevent the ship from exploding. Perhaps each level has one object that required players to solve a puzzle of some kind before they could access it, and only after collecting the object would they then be able to solve the door-unlocking component of the level. Alternatively, perhaps each level has an object players can access to unlock cinematics and learn more about what happened on the ship for it to reach such a dire state. Or perhaps players are able to disable enemy robots in some way and collect points, with a goal to collect as many points as possible by the end of the game. Perhaps you'll choose to forego traditional win and loss conditions entirely. Games don't always focus on explicit win and loss conditions as a core component of the meta-game, and for a growing number of contemporary titles, especially indie games, it's more about the journey than the competitive experience (or the competitive element becomes optional). Perhaps you can find a way to incorporate both a competitive aspect (e.g., score the most points or complete each level in the shortest time) and meta-game elements that focus more on enhancing play.

A final note on systems and meta-game: player education (frequently achieved by in-game tutorials) is often an important component of these processes. Designers become intimately acquainted with how the mechanics they design function and how the controls work, and it's easy (and common) to lose awareness of how the game will appear to someone who encounters it for the first time. Early and frequent playtests help provide information about how much explanation players will require in order to understand what they need to do, but most games require some level of tutorial support to help teach the rules of the game world. Tutorial design techniques are outside the scope of this book, but it's often most effective to teach players the logical rules and interactions of the game as they play through an introductory level or levels. It's also more effective to show players what you want them to do rather than making them read long blocks of text (research shows that many players never access optional tutorials and will dismiss tutorials with excessive text without reading them; one or two very short sentences per tutorial event are a reasonable target). If you were creating an in-level tutorial system for your prototype, how would you implement it? What do you think players would reasonably discover on their own vs. what you might need to surface for them in a tutorial experience?

User Interface (UI) Design

Game UI design is important not just from a functionality perspective (in-game menus, tutorials, and contextually important information such as health, score, and the like) but also as a contributor to the overall setting and visual design of the experience. Game UI is a core component of visual game design that's frequently overlooked by new designers and can mean the difference between a game people love and a game nobody plays. Think back to games you've played that make use of complex inventory systems or that have many levels of menus you must navigate through before you can access common functions or items; can you recall games where you were frequently required to navigate through multiple sublevels to complete often-used tasks? Or perhaps games that required you to remember elaborate button combinations to access common game objects?

Elegant and logical UI is critical to player comprehension, but UI that's integrated into the game world also supports the game setting and narrative. Using the current prototype and proposed systems design as reference, how would you visually represent game UI in a way that supported the setting and aesthetic? If you haven't spent time evaluating UI before (and even if you have), revisit several games with sci-fi settings and pay particular attention to how they integrate UI elements visually in the game screen. Figure 12-9 shows the weapon customization UI from Visceral Games' *Dead Space 3*: note how the interface design is completely embedded within the game setting, represented as an information screen on the fictional ship.

Figure 12-9. *Most UI elements in Visceral Games' Dead Space 3 are represented completely within the game setting and fiction, with menus appearing as holographic projections invoked by the hero character or on objects in the game world (image copyright Electronic Arts)*

Many games choose to house their UI elements in reserved areas of the game screen (typically around the outer edges) that don't directly interact with the game world; however, integrating the visual aesthetic with the game setting is another way to contribute directly to the presence of the game. Imagine the current sci-fi prototype example with a fantasy-themed UI and menu system, using the kind of medieval aesthetic design and calligraphic fonts used for a game like Bioware's *Dragon Age*, for example; the resulting mismatch would be jarring and likely to pull players out of the game setting. User interface design is a complex discipline that can be challenging to master; you'll be well served, however, by spending focused time to ensure intuitive, usable, and aesthetically appropriate UI integration into the game worlds you create.

Game Narrative

At this stage, you've added just a basic narrative wrapper to the prototype example: a hero character must complete a number of objectives to prevent their spaceship from exploding. At the moment, you haven't explicitly shared this narrative with players at all, and they have no way of knowing the environment is on a spaceship or what the objective might be other than perhaps eventually unlocking the door at the far right of the screen. Designers have a number of options for exposing the game narrative to players; you might create an introductory cinematic or animated sequence that introduces players to the hero character, their ship, and the crisis, perhaps choosing something simple like a pop-up window at the start of the level with brief introduction text that provides players with the required information. Alternatively, you might not provide any information about what's happening when the game starts but instead choose to slowly reveal the dire situation of the ship and the objectives over time as the player proceeds through the game world. You could even choose to keep any narrative elements implied, allowing players to overlay their own interpretation. As with many other aspects of game design, there's no single way to introduce players to a narrative and no universal guidance for how much (or how little) narrative might be required for a satisfying experience.

Narrative can also be used by designers to influence the way levels are evolved and built out even if those elements are never exposed to players. In the case of this prototype, it's helpful as the designer to visualize the threat of an exploding ship to propel the hero character through a series of challenges with a sense of urgency; players however might experience a well-constructed side-scrolling action platformer only with a series of devilishly clever levels. You might create additional fiction around robots that have been infected with a virus, causing them to turn against the hero as a reason for their attack behavior (as just one example). By creating a narrative framework for the action to unfold within, you're able to make informed decisions about ways to extend the mechanic that feel nicely integrated into the setting even if you don't share all the background with players.

Of course, some game experiences have virtually no explicit narrative elements either exposed to players or not and are simply implementations of novel mechanics. Games like Zynga's *Words with Friends* and Gabriele Cirulli's hyper-casual *2048* are examples of game experiences purely based on a mechanic with no narrative wrapper.

If you continue developing this prototype, how much narrative would you choose to include, and how much would you want to expose to players to make the game come alive?

Bonus Content: Adding a Second Stage to the Level

If you've completed playing through stage 1 of the included prototype, you'll enter a second room with a large moving unit; this is a sandbox with a set of assets for you to explore. The prototype implementation includes just some basic behaviors to spark your imagination: a large, animated level boss unit hovers in the chamber and produces a new kind of enemy robot that seeks out the hero character, spawning a new unit every few seconds.

Figure 12-10 shows a layout in the style you've been using to prototype basic mechanics.

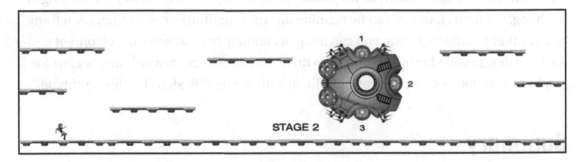

Figure 12-10. *A possible second stage the hero character can enter after unlocking the door in stage 1. This concept includes a large "boss" unit with three nodes; one objective for this stage might be to disable each of the nodes to shut the boss down*

It's a bit of a shortcut to begin the mechanic exploration with the diagram in Figure 12-10, but because you've already identified the setting and a number of visual elements, it can be helpful to continue developing new stages with some of the visual assets already in place. The diagram includes the same kind of platforms used in stage 1, but what if, for example, this area had no gravity and the hero character was able to fly freely? Compare this area with stage 1, and think about how you might slightly alter the experience to mix things up a bit without fundamentally changing the game; you've ideally become fairly fluent with the sequencing mechanic from stage 1, and the experience in stage 2 can be a greater or lesser evolution of that mechanic.

If you choose to include the hero-seeking flying robot units, the game flow diagram will become more complex than the model used in stage 1 because of the unpredictable movement of the new robot types. You may also want to consider a mechanism for the hero character to eliminate the robot units (perhaps even working the removal of robot units into the mechanic for disabling the nodes on the boss). If you find your designs becoming difficult to describe as part of an explicit and repeatable game flow, it may signal that you're working with more complex systems and may need to evaluate them in a playable prototype before you can effectively balance their integration with other components of the level. Of course, you can also reuse conventions and units from stage 1; you might choose to combine patrolling robots with hero-seeking robots and an energy field, for example, creating a challenging web of potential risks for the player to navigate as they work to disable the boss nodes.

You might also decide that the main objective for the level is to *enable* the boss nodes in order to unlock the next stage or level of the game. You can extend the narrative in any direction you like, so units can be helpful or harmful, objectives can involve disabling or enabling, the hero character can be running toward something or away from something, or any other possible scenario you can imagine. Remember, narrative development and the level design will play on each other to drive the experience forward, so stay alert for inspiration as you become increasingly fluent with the level designs for this prototype.

Summary

Game design is unique among the creative arts in the ways it requires players to become active partners in the experience, which can change dramatically depending on who the player is. Although some games share quite a bit in common with cinema (especially as story-driven games have become more popular), there's always an unpredictable element when the player controls the on-screen action to a greater or lesser extent. Unlike movies and books, video games are interactive experiences that demand constant two-way engagement with players, and poorly designed mechanics or levels with unclear rules can block players from enjoying the experience you've created.

The design methodology presented in this book focuses first on teaching you the letters of the design alphabet (basic interactions), leading into the creation of words (game mechanics and gameplay), followed by sentences (levels); we hope you'll take the next step and begin writing the next great novel (full-game experiences in existing or entirely new genres). The "escape the room" design template featured here can be used to quickly prototype a wide range of mechanics for many kinds of game experiences, from the included 2D side-scroller to isometric games to first-person experiences and more. Remember, game mechanics are fundamentally well-formed abstract puzzles that can be adapted as needed. If you find yourself having difficulty brainstorming new mechanics in the beginning, borrow some simple existing mechanics from common casual games ("match 3" variants are a great source for inspiration) and start there, adding one or two simple variations as you go. As with any creative discipline, the more you practice the basics the more fluent you'll become with the process, and after you've gained some experience with simple mechanics and systems you'll likely be surprised by the number of interesting variations you can quickly create. Some of those variations might just contribute to the next breakthrough title.

This book demonstrates the relationship between the technical and experiential aspects of game design. Designers, developers, artists, and audio engineers must work in close partnership to deliver the best experiences, taking issues such as performance/responsiveness, user inputs, system stability, and the like into consideration throughout production. The game engine you've developed in this book is well-matched for the type of game described in this chapter (and many others). You should now be ready to explore your own game designs with a strong technical foundation to build upon and a global understanding of how the nine elements of game design work together to create experiences that players love.

Index

Printed in the United States
by Baker & Taylor Publisher Services

Printed in the United States
by Baker & Taylor Publisher Services